THE ROLE AND STRUCTURE
OF THE CITY
IN THE GEOGRAPHY
OF WESTERN CIVILIZATION

Harper & Row Series in Geography

Donald W. Meinig, Advisor

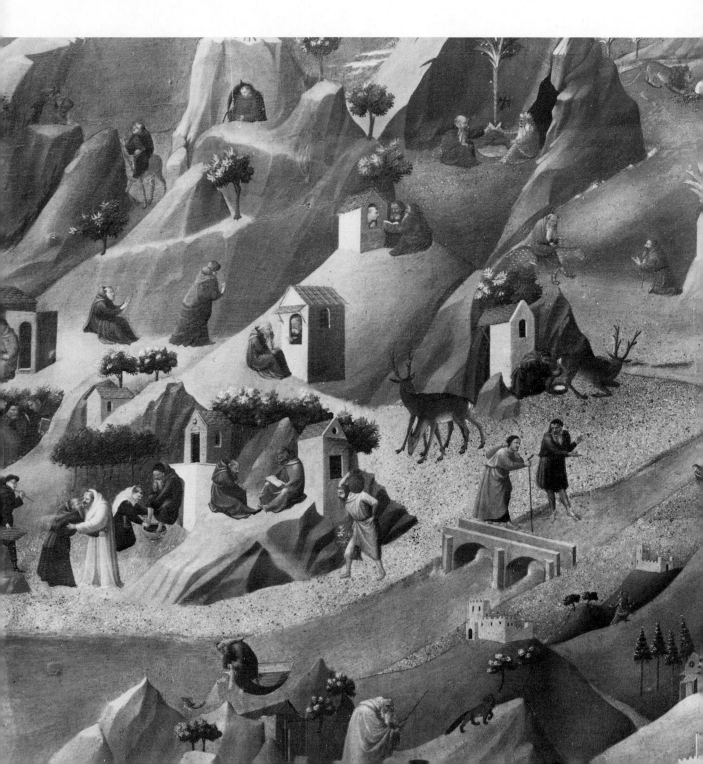

THIS SCENE OF MAN

THE ROLE AND STRUCTURE
OF THE CITY
IN THE GEOGRAPHY
OF WESTERN CIVILIZATION

James E. Vance, Jr.

Harper's College Press

A Department of Harper & Row, Publishers   New York · Hagerstown · San Francisco · London

Library of Congress Cataloging in Publication Data

Vance, James E
  This scene of man.

  (Harper & Row series in geography)
  1. Cities and towns—History. 2. Cities and towns—
Growth—History. 3. Urban economics. 4. Urbanization—
History. I. Title. II. Title. Geography of western
civilization.
HT111.V29   301.36'3'09   77-852
ISBN 0-06-167407-9

Produced by Ken Burke and Associates, Palo Alto

Text and Cover Designer: Christy Butterfield
Copyeditor: Gail Larrick
Makeup: Douglas Luna
Line Illustrator: Carlos Perez
Photo Research: Audrey Ross
Composition: Typesetting Services of California
Printing and Binding: Halliday Lithograph

For Jean and Tiffany, who helped me to see the pattern in this "mighty maze" by encouragement in times of doubt and query in those of unwarranted certainty; and for Zeb, whose example of fortitude was to me as invaluable as his company.

PREFACE

Urbanization has been such a central aspect of western civilization that the forces affecting cities are nearly as diverse as those shaping culture itself. To attempt to survey all that has been written about the western city would be as foolish as it is impossible; there is a certain intellectual isostasy at work which means that as most fact is piled up some will disappear below the base plane and the heights of understanding will not necessarily be greatly increased. In writing this book I have neither sought to provide a survey of western cities nor a simple geography of their location. Instead my purpose has been to search out two aspects of western urbanization: the evolution of the role and purpose of the cities in western society and the processes used by that society to create and transform the physical fabric of those cities. These two concerns are the elements in a study of urban morphogenesis wherein the actual process may explain the shaping of the city, but a rational observer seeks to understand the forces creating the process itself.

Urban morphogenesis, though ever expressed in city form, is best seen as a set of processes in times of fundamental transformation of that morphology. For the western city we may begin the story with the initiation of urbanization of a complex sort, rather than the narrow purpose found in the oldest religious and administrative towns, which came when economic activity gained a full role in the support of cities. Archaic Greece around the beginning of the first millennium B.C. experienced this increasing complexity in individual settlements as well as the formation of the first "system of cities" wherein it was possible to perceive the existence of general rather than idiographic processes. Since that time periods of initiation or transformation have occurred with a certain inexorability: the Roman City succeeded on the Greek; the barbarians' attempt to embrace the late imperial Roman cities fatally disrupted their support, bringing a break in urban evolution; the return of an economic purpose around the beginning of the second millennium of our era shaped the medieval city, which had several expressions, the most interesting of which was for Americans the bastidal new towns of the thirteenth and fourteenth centuries; the subsequent economic "revolutions," the commercial one of the sixteenth century and the industrial one of the nineteenth century, transformed the medieval town into the modern city. Through all of this transformation certain processes persisted, but their nature and impact were periodically readjusted as the role that cities were asked to play changed.

A wide variety of literature must lie behind a book of this sort, so wide in fact that it is impracticable to present a bibliography of contributive works. And a list of works cited can be handled efficiently in the footnotes, which are fully indexed. In order that this book might lead students into a further investigation of the work cited, I have tried to do two things. In those cases where I felt that the work had a literary as well as an informational contribution to make—as in Pirenne's analysis of the medieval city or Engels' description of Manchester in the early industrial era—I have quoted extensively in the hope of engaging the reader's attention enough to cause a further reading of the work. And I have sought where possible to use specific references still in print, and preferably available in paperback editions. In this way I believe individuals and colleges could gain easy access to these supporting volumes.

Because this book represents a summation of my temporary conclusions on urban morphogenesis after some twenty-five years of thinking, teaching, and writing, I have had to cite my own work extensively. I do not view my words as either definitive or conclusive: rather the problem is that urban morphogenesis has been little pursued by others up to now and my words in a number of instances must stand not merely as the initial statements but still as the only statements. My greatest hope is that this book will sufficiently stimulate others to look into the matter of urban morphogenesis, particularly as an evolutionary question, that any later revisions that I may make to this volume will be far less self-citing.

Any product of a long period of work owes a great deal to others, most notably to students and colleagues.

In this I have been extremely fortunate in having been able to work with doctoral students of quick intelligence and questioning minds for a score of years. All of these deserve thanks and some should be singled out for acknowledgment of contributions they may not be aware of having made. In particular I owe an indefinite but real debt to Roger Barnett of the University of the Pacific, Charles S. Sargent of Arizona State University, Elizabeth Kates Burns of the University of Utah, Christopher Winters, Willard Tim Chow of the University of Hawaii, William Code of the University of Western Ontario, Kenneth Jordan of Prairie View A. and M. University, and Martyn Bowden of Clark University. Among my colleagues several stand out for their long and patient assistance in sorting out my ideas through the logic and directness of their thoughts. To John B. Jackson of Harvard University and Berkeley I owe so many intellectual debts that they cannot be specified; to Peter Haggett I must send thanks for a combined stimulation and most necessary questioning of my thoughts over a period which began when we were equally much younger than now; to Yola Verhasselt of the Vrije Universiteit, Brussels, go thanks for making Belgian cities intelligible to me; to Raymond Murphy I wish to express a great appreciation for starting me along the path that led, with many shifts in course, to this book, much as it would never have been his objective setting out in the same pursuit of cities. In the course of the preparation of the manuscript I have found Donald Meinig's criticisms correctly stern and truly welcome, and his encouragement appreciated.

Several authors and their publishers have been very generous in allowing me to quote extensively from their work. I particularly wish to thank the following: Duke University Press for permission to quote almost in its entirety Zelia Nuttal's translation of the town-planning portions of the Spanish Laws of the Indies; Harvard University Press for the quotation of the town-planning provisions of Morris Hicky Morgan's translation of Vitruvius; Alfred A. Knopf, Inc., for the use of descriptive passages from Iris Origo's *The Mer-*

chant of Prato; Harcourt Brace Jovanovich, Inc., for the right to quote Henri Pirenne's *Economic and Social History of Medieval Europe*; Oxford University Press for the use of material from Carl Bridenbaugh's *Vexed and Troubled Englishmen, 1590–1642*; and Stanford University Press for the use of descriptive passages from Henderson and Chaloner's translation of Friedrich Engels, *The Condition of the Working Class in England*. For use of illustrative material I am particularly grateful to John Rogers Flather of Lowell; to the Lowell Historical Society; to Margaret Philbrick of Sheffield, Massachusetts; to the Waltham Public Library, Waltham; Professor H. J. Dyos, Leicester; and the firm of Ray Delvert, Villeneuve-sur-Lot, France. Finally, I wish to express appreciation for the kindness and assistance of several research libraries over a period of nearly ten years, specifically the Public Record Office, London; the Birmingham Reference Library; the Wellesley College Library; Miss Marion Henderson and the Clark University Library; the Environmental Design Library and the Library Photo Service, Berkeley.

In the preparation of this manuscript there are those whose careful efforts would remain unknown if I were not to acknowledge them here. To Miss Agnes Lincoln of the geography department in Berkeley go my great thanks for her help in organizing, and to a considerable degree executing, the typing of the manuscript. In that work Linda Yemoto and Natalia Vonnegut were invaluable. To Gail Larrick I wish to express particular thanks for her exemplary editorial assistance, and for her patience when faced by my sometimes ancient practices. Ken Burke was unfailing in his wisdom as to the production of a book that both pleases the eye and avoids the ponderous quality of a manuscript. For a number of years Raleigh Wilson of Harper's maintained his faith in this work along with an open mind as to what constitutes a textbook. To all of these I wish to express my sincere thanks while shielding them from any responsibility for blots on the page, which are always put there by the writer.

James E. Vance, Jr.

ACKNOWLEDGMENTS

The following materials quoted extensively in the text are reproduced by permission. Acknowledgment is made:

To The Bodley Head for permission to use various extracts from *The Great Fire of London in 1666*, by Walter George Bell.

To Praeger Publishers, Inc., for permission to use materials from *New Towns of the Middle Ages: Town Plantation in England, Wales, and Gascony*, by Maurice Beresford.

To the Institute of British Geographers for permission to quote from *Alnwick, Northumberland: A Study in Town Plan Analysis*, by M. R. G. Conzen.

To H. J. Dyos and the Leicester University Press for permission to quote passages and reproduce illustrations from *Victorian Suburb: A Study of the Growth of Camberwell*.

To the heirs of the author and the Princeton University Press for selections from Henri Pirenne, *Medieval Cities: Their Origins and the Revival of Trade*, translated from the French by Frank D. Halsey (copyright 1925, 1952 by Princeton University Press; Princeton Paperback, 1969) pp. 3–212. Reprinted by permission of Princeton University Press.

To the M.I.T. Press for permission to quote from *London: The Unique City* by Steen Eiler Rasmussen.

To the author and the Princeton University Press for selections from John W. Reps, *The Making of Urban America: A History of City Planning in the United States* (copyright © 1965 by Princeton University Press), pp. 93–177. Reprinted by permission of Princeton University Press.

To Georges Borchardt, Inc., for permission to quote from *Georgian London*, by John Summerson.

The author wishes to express particular thanks to the following for their kind permission to use copyright material in their possession:

To Harper & Row, Inc., for permission to quote from P. Boissonade, *Life and Work in Medieval Europe: The Evolution of Medieval Economy from the Fifth to the Fifteenth Century*.

To the Oxford University Press for permission to quote from *Vexed and Troubled Englishmen, 1590–1642*, by Carl Bridenbaugh.

To the Stanford University Press for permission to quote extensively from *The Condition of the Working Class in England*, by Friedrich Engels, translated and edited by W. O. Henderson and W. H. Chaloner (Stanford: Stanford University Press, 1958), and for the use of the associated diagrammatic map of Manchester.

To the Harvard University Press for permission to quote the passages of Vitruvius dealing with the laying out of towns that bear such a resemblance to those in the Laws of the Indies, those passages contained in Morris Hicky Morgan's translation, *Vitruvius: The Ten Books on Architecture*, copyright 1914 by the Harvard University Press.

To the Duke University Press for permission to quote almost in their entirety the Laws of the Indies dealing with town layout as published in "Royal Ordinances Concerning the Laying Out of New Towns," *Hispanic-American Historical Review*, Vol. 5, pp. 249–254. Copyright by Duke University Press.

To Alfred A. Knopf, Inc., for the use of material in *The Merchant of Prato: Francesco di Marco Datini*, by Iris Origo, copyright 1957 by Iris Origo.

To Harcourt Brace Jovanovich, Inc., and Routledge & Kegan Paul, Ltd., for permission to quote from *Economic and Social History of Medieval Europe*, by Henri Pirenne.

Art and Photo Credits

Cover map   Historic Urban Plans, Ithaca, New York

i   Uffizi Gallery

xx   French Embassy, Press and Information Division

2   Eureka, California, Chamber of Commerce

5   From Rasmussen, Steen Eiler, *Towns and Buildings*, The University Press of Liverpool, 1951. Reprinted by permission.

14   Grant Heilman

18   Ray Delvert

25   Greater Boston Convention & Tourist Bureau

27   Chicago Historical Society

30   Ray Delvert

38   University of California Library Service

41   American School of Classical Studies, Athens

44   From von Grekan, Armin, *Milet*, Verlag Walter de Gruyter, Berlin, 1935.

48   From Roland, Martin, *L'Urbanisme das la Grèce Antique*, Paris, 1956, A. and J. Picard.

53   From Brizio, E. Marzabotto, 1928.

54   Alinari

58   American Academy, Rome

60   American Academy, Rome

60   right, Alinari

62   American Academy, Rome

64   American Academy, Rome

66   Gabinetto Fotografico Nacional

68   American Academy, Rome

71   Alinari

74   Photographie Giraudon

77   German Information Center

78   Rheinisches Bildarchiv

83   German Information Center

88   Ray Delvert

90   German Information Center
93   French Government Tourist Office
95   Ray Delvert
98   Ray Delvert
99   Photographie Giraudon
104   Rijksmuseum, Amsterdam
109, 115   Photographie Giraudon
119   German Information Center
127   Ray Delvert
130   Consulate General of Belgium
131   Alinari
134   Paul Popper, Ltd.
135   Alinari
137   Foto Grossi
139   Alinari
142   Scala
144   French Government Tourist Office
145   Alinari
148   Paul Popper, Ltd.
151   German Information Center
152, 154   French Government Tourist Office
159   Foto Daniel
163   German Information Center
165   The British Library
166, 169   Ray Delvert
173   Courtesy of Sabena Airlines
186, 187, 189, 195, 196   Ray Delvert
200   Darek Balmer, City of Bristol Photo
206–07   Library of Congress
210   Bancroft Library, University of California
214–15   The British Museum
219   Dienst der Publicke Werken, Amsterdam
221   Historical Pictures Service
225   City of Bristol
229   Scala
232   The British Library
237   Photographie Giraudon
240   The British Museum
247   Ministry of Cultural Affairs of Québec
254   New York Public Library
256   New York Historical Society
259   Cornell University Libraries
263   Maryland Hall of Records
265   Library of Congress
268   Cincinnati Historical Society
269   Courtesy of Dr. van den Brent, Institut Belge
271, 275   From Aiken, *The Country Round Manchester*

279   Science Museum, London
283, 285, 288, 292, 296   From Aiken, *The Country Round Manchester*
301   Manchester Public Libraries, Central Library, Manchester
304   From Engels, Friedrich, *The Conditions of the Working Class in England*, Stanford University Press, 1968. Reprinted by permission.
307   From Aiken, *The Country Round Manchester*
310   Institut Belge
314, 315   From Dyos, H. J., *Victorian Suburb, Leicester, England*, Leicester University Press, 1966. Reprinted by permission.
318   Courtesy of Sabena Airlines
320   Institut Belge
321   Commissariat General au Tourisme de Belgique, photo by DeMeyer
327   Museum of the City of New York
330   Slater Mill Museum
333   Courtesy of Waltham Public Library
336   Courtesy of Lowell Museum
338   From Proceedings of the Lowell Semicentennial Celebration
340, 345   Courtesy of Lowell Museum
349   Chicago Historical Society
350   Courtesy of John Rogers Flather
363   Ray Delvert
367, 370   Chicago Historical Society
375   Courtesy of Margaret Philbrick
378, 380   From Edmond Texier, *Le Tableau du Paris*, 1854
381   Collection Sirot
384   Chicago Historical Society
388   Ford Museum Archives
391   From Edmond Texier, *Le Tableau du Paris*, 1854
394   Chicago Historical Society
397   Professor James Vance
398   R. L. Copeland
400   Community Service Society of New York
402   Audrey Ross, Berkeley
405   From Dyos, H. J., *Victorian Suburb, Leicester, England*, Leicester University Press, 1966. Reprinted by permission.
408   Aerofilms
409   California Department of Transportation
412   R. L. Copeland
413   Professor James Vance
418   R. L. Copeland
419   Ray Delvert

CONTENTS

THE ROLE AND STRUCTURE
OF THE CITY
IN THE GEOGRAPHY
OF WESTERN CIVILIZATION

INTRODUCTION: A PROPER STUDY OF MANKIND

Awake my St. John! leave all meaner things
  to low ambition, and the pride of kings.
Let us, since life can little more supply
  than just to look about us and to die,
Expatiate free o'er all this scene of man;
  A mighty maze! but not without a plan.

Alexander Pope
An Essay on Man
1 Epistle i, l. I

When the eighteenth-century poet Alexander Pope made his famous comment that "The proper study of mankind is man," he reflected a thousand years of bias in western society against the close study of the physical expression of life, of society and economy as a polite concern. The bias continues to exist. In social science in general, and in more recent years in geography as well, "the proper study of mankind" has almost exclusively been "man." Little attention has been given to the physical universe, even to those features of it created by man himself. One important result has been a peculiar absence of interest in and concern for the city, the physical entity that is the main home of western man. The purpose of this book is to speak about the city in physical terms and to argue that it too is part of the proper study of man.

Our concern will be with the physical form and structure of the city, its *morphology*. We shall extend morphology to include not only form and structure but also the actual physical expression of that form, and the manner, by chance or by consistent practice, in which the various physical components are related to each other in a system of *form interaction*. As an example, we may note the frequent approximation of the church and the market square within medieval cities. This relationship points to a formal interaction between the church and the square, as well as a functional tie between the two—the role of the medieval church in maintaining the "just price" of goods sold in the market stalls. Today we still find new churches fronting on the square built according to this traditional urban morphology long after the administration of a just price has passed from the church to the state, and in many cases long after the market stalls on the square have had much retail significance. Thus formal interactions may be quite distinct from functional ones. We will seek understanding through a consideration of past practice and process and the physical evidence which remains its main relict.

Winston Churchill asserted that we shape our houses but then they shape us. Without interpreting that view to imply a rigid simplistic environmental determinism, we shall argue that they do indeed shape us more than most social scientists and normative economic and social geographers would allow. To a very great extent, geographers in recent decades seem to have rejected a rigid environmental determinism only to have become dominated by behavioral explanations of economic and social process. Arising from a long craving for some sort of normative process, some modern expression of the law of symmetry, to explain the indigestible wealth of fact, this emphasis has become so strong as to result in a near abandonment of any real concern for the study of morphology and the delineation of its physical processes. The philosophical position is essentially that human beings shape their universe, that the patterns of social institutions reveal consistencies, that an understanding of the processes within those institutions—society, economic system, national psychology, and the like—is sufficient to explain that universe. The fundamental insufficiency of a theoretical construct focusing only on institutional norms is the presupposition that those norms and processes can work without physical resistances from the past. But the condition of an unstructured beginning, a *tabula rasa*, is unusual indeed in human history and pretending otherwise presents more than a little hazard.

The William Carson House in Eureka, California (1884–1886), was shaped by a lumber baron, but we may wonder if, in the end, it did not shape him.

Our purpose is to steer a sound course between a too-simple belief in physical determinism and an equally too-simple belief in a normative geography of institutional process. By its approach to the study of the origin and evolution of the morphology of cities, this book does seek to fill a particular void. It organizes the truths of morphology in such a way as to show the pattern throughout history and the interaction of the processes of morphological evolution with those of other institutional processes.

Covering a range of history from ancient Greece to the present, this book must make use of data which have not been systematically collected and deal with some rarely considered processes. Morphological geography is not a practice, nor does a canon of morphological process exist. A single author, however deep his concern and long his effort, cannot overcome all the neglect of the past. At best he can hope to pioneer in a new field before any further time is lost.

Learning and Teaching in City Form

The mortality of man contrasts sharply with the immortality of cities. We must distinguish between the way that human beings transfer their learning to other generations and the way that transfer of experience and accomplishment is made through cities. Throughout human history until nearly the advent of European settlement in the New World, most men's ideas disappeared at their death. Although they lived in a literate culture, most men were illiterate. In any event, manuscript writing was so narrowly available that the probability of loss of the ideas with the passage of time was very high indeed. To take a specifically germane case, we have left to us only one work of Roman origin that gives in any detail the thinking of those great city builders, or their conceptions and designs for the urban places that were both the instrument of Roman imperialism and the centers of their culture. We must depend on Vitruvius, author of *The Ten Books on Architecture* written in the time of Augustus, for all the literary knowledge that we have of this most important of urban epochs, for which only a modest amount of epigraphic evidence can be taken from inscriptions and other durable writings that have survived the erosion

of time. Trajan's column in Rome might be considered yet another "written" record with its scenes of bridge building and other construction activities. Even so, the record is meager; yet we know far more about Roman cities than we do about some far more recent constructions. How have we learned so much on an essentially unrecorded subject? We know about Rome and her cities because we have looked at, observed, and analyzed those places in their physical remains.

In the study of cities the immortality of the places is a boon to us, if we will let it be. Because social and historical work has so commonly been limited by Pope's dictum as to proper study, the tendency has been to look upon times as unrecorded when no literary record is extant. The physical remains of the past tend to be viewed only as works of "art," and thus as a concern of aesthetics. Certainly Greek kraters are art, but they are also most revealing documents telling us of daily life, though often caricatured as a contemporary Walter Mitty would have perceived it. Given a larger physical creation, such as the apartmented houses of Ostia Antica, we can learn a great deal that is unfiltered by literary or artistic selection.

The record is incomplete—few records are not—so we must develop some system for filling the gaps by logical inference and extension; such a system is suggested in Chapter 1. Not only must we learn from a relatively uncommon system of teaching, reading the evidence of urban activity from the forms that are created to serve it, but also we must drop the dogma that cities can be understood and studied only in terms of human institutions. Man's physical works are more enduring than many of his social and economic processes, so we must accept that the physical inheritance from the past belongs in any analysis fully as much as do contemporary institutional practices.

Class and the City

The particular approach normally taken toward physical evidence, rather than literary records in scholarship, has ruled that tangible things must be "high art," "masterpieces," or at the very least "polite" rather than "vernacular" creations. The tattered papers of the commonfolk may have come to be prized by historians—though they seldom were a century ago—but the physical possessions and housing of the common man are only now gaining the interest they deserve in a democratic society. The elitist bias of history in general, and of architectural history in particular, has meant that far less attention has been given to the physical accommodation, daily life, and sincere thoughts of the average family than has been lavished on the sometimes vacuous observations of the well-to-do. We find studies of European cities that leave us with no inkling of how most people lived, nor any understanding of the social and economic context that explains the only too real historical background of Marxist thought.

The purpose of this book is not philistinism, the rejection of the deliberately beautiful and intellectual, but we must remember that gold is an uncommon element and that life in the palace or the monastery were unusual occupations even in the Middle Ages. In cities, notably, a vital existence derived at least initially and dominantly from production and trade. The situation could not have been otherwise because most of the beauty subsequently introduced into human life and much of the general intellectual advance came as a charge on the merchants' and master craftsmen's enlarging purses. In simple truth far more cathedrals were paid for by the everyday world than by the royal patrons. Even if we seek to understand high art and architecture and the intellectual climate of a time, we must pay more attention than we have previously to the total system that produced the more specialized product.

In the case of cities, the functioning system was so closely woven that even the golden threads rubbed against the stronger but less shiny ones of more commonplace flax, and the pattern was at least as much made up of the one as the other. Taking the Greek cities as a case in point, the *agora*, the functioning heart of the towns, can be understood in its form and functions only when placed within the groundmass of rather modest individual housing. The simple truth is that public open space usually reflects the degree of sufficiency of private livingspace, as the parklessness of current suburbs demonstrates.

Perhaps a more valid reason for studying the everyday life of the city, and the vernacular buildings and layout of the place, has been the increasingly democratic nature of scholarship in the past several decades. If we were to take Pope's dictum totally to heart, then the man who is statistically most proper to study is likely to be socially improper. Everyman is a better democratic exemplification than is a prince or a pope. We need not reject absolutely the notion that great men on occasion reshape history to point out that few great men have arisen. The march of history has generally been led by fairly ordinary persons operating more effectively for change among the masses than the aristocracy.

Certainly ours is a time of little men, so we need no further explanation of our concentration on their peers in the past. Much useful information may be secured on the subject of social geography and the tie it has to the physical form of the city through a survey of Everyman's city in western civilization. Many different physical forms have evolved in the past, so as American cities face a most uncertain immediate future, a better knowledge of urban morphogenesis lends help to prediction and planning. Seeking to elucidate a set of morphological processes at work in cities over a long timespan is thus of quite practical importance.

Morphogenesis and Planning

Chapter 1 sets out to detail some of the ways in which we may look at cities in any era with the idea of understanding the processes at work in shaping their physical build. Although these processes are continuous, their impact will be much greater in their early course than later on in time when the freedom to operate on a *tabula rasa* is lost. In establishing the layout of the streets in a town, a once-and-forever quality attaches to the initial division of empty or agricultural land. The areal base on which a city rests may be subsequently redivided, but for it to have any considerable amount of latitude we must secure, either by intervening catastrophe or massive artificial recreation of the empty slate through "redevelopment," a reinstatement of free choice as a factor in division. In most cases the layout of streets and the parcelling of land cannot be fundamentally changed even if the buildings that originally stood as street frontages on the lots have long since disappeared. We know this in the case of Roman cities where the classical buildings may have mainly disappeared but the street plan persists, as it does in Chester in England and Turin in Italy. Thus, a complete system of morphogenesis, or origin of shape and form, operates as the town is first built up, but morphogenesis is only partial in succeeding times.

The notion of morphogenesis should be drawn in sharp distinction to that of planning: sometimes planning is involved in the shaping of the city but at all times the act of creating morphology must occur. One of the most interesting aspects of morphogenesis is that it is most commonly an expression of institutional attitudes and practices by which a society shapes the forms to its needs. Thus, social, political, religious, cul-

The growth of Turin from
Roman times clearly dem-
onstrates the complexity
of morphogenetic processes.

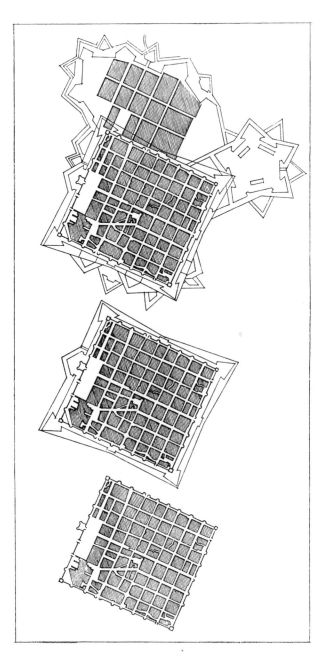

tural, and economic practices are at work, and these processes normally stem from society at large rather than the ideas of a small elite. For that narrower conception we must look to planning, which can be a totally arbitrary act, as it was when Richelieu laid out his patronymic town. Admittedly planning may be democratically based, though exceedingly rarely, so we may nearly equate the notion of development of a place by its citizens with the broader idea of morphogenesis, and of planning with a conferred preconception of the eventual nature of the place, which is seldom determined by consensus.

The literature is full of studies of planned towns. Having been preconceived, self-consciously designed, some record of how and why it was done is usually preserved. A bibliography of those histories of city plans would be massive whereas one on morphogenesis of the whole town would be thin indeed. Already too many volumes have been published on the history of planned cities to be cited. But little has been written about morphogenesis. The work of Professor M. R. G. Conzen in the northeast of England shines forth most prominently as an exception to that dearth. Other examples of this modest literature will be cited in their appropriate place in this book. Because little has been written about morphogenesis, even the word itself is unfamiliar, and its distinction from planning is unclear in most minds. Simply stated, that distinction lies between the creation of a city, or a substantial part of a city, by preconceived design and authoritative control over its development, and a more encompassing practice wherein, *whatever the process involved*, we are concerned with the shaping of the city. Because in the past attention has been so narrowly focused on planning, the emphasis of this book will be on functional morphogenesis, where the need for pioneering is clearer and the joys of discovery are greater.

Morphogenesis in the Western World

This book is not a survey of world cities but will sketch the rudiments of a system of perceiving and analyzing cities as physical entities. Thus, it is restricted to a study of urbanization in the western world—of Europe and the North America of the United States and Canada. To cover all western cities in any work of this scale is impossible even restricting the consideration to Europe and North America. They are too numerous to treat in detail and too diverse to summarize completely by generalization. Yet their shared features may be presented. Since Europe and North America represent the most consistently urban areas of the modern world, and certainly are the fountainhead of most of the ideas and processes of urbanization today, we shall seek to comprehend this area of half a billion people.

The selection of evidence is strongly subjective. Great weight is placed during the Classical Era on Greece and Rome, in medieval times on Italy, Germany, France, and England, and in industrial times on England, Belgium, France, and the United States. This selection reflects the author's "experience" of surviving morphological evidence—more physical relics than is normally the case in scholarship—a dependence necessitated by a repetition of the conditions faced by geographers in the nineteenth century when, because others had not preceded them, they had first to observe before they could analyze.

The exclusions from this book fall in two classes: those places within the western world not discussed because better, more significant, and clearer examples may be cited, and those great cities outside the west left unmentioned because of the physical limits of this work. Scandinavian cities, for example, had little existence until fairly recently; even within the Industrial Era, they have been more parochial than precedent-setting. The great role of Scandinavian towns in the planning literature grows from two concerns largely absent in this book: the concern for the preconceived and authoritarianly planned city, and the notion of socialist rectitude, even race-pride, that some attach to things Nordic. The total disregard for cities outside western civilization in no sense implies that these cities are tangential turnings away from the main development of morphogenetic process. Instead, the problem is that of possibility and competence. The work of Paul Wheatley and others has begun to establish structure and process in Asian cities, but the morphogenetic analysis seems best left to those who have observed and who understand such places.

Changes in Morphogenesis

The study of process always poses a real problem: how can a continuous force be captured for observation and analysis? We may have to start with rather scant, or gross, phenomena, leading to the statement of basic process relationships, and hope as more information is made available to refine those statements of process relationship. We must draw a contrast between the workings of physical science and those of urban morphology. In physical science a fairly small number of absolute, or nearly so, properties can be used to explain physical and chemical phenomena. Such is not the case in matters of men, whose systems are multiple and far more historically relative. Because culture is a conditional equilibrium, or even a periodic chaos, different systems are at work at different times. As we shall see, the reason the Romans set up their cities the way they did was quite different from the reason our grandfathers shaped the post-Civil War city, and we shape the complex place in which we live. Man reshapes the "laws" of social and economic behavior in different eras of history in a way that nature does not.

But are there any eternal verities in the matter of cities? Certainly some biological and psychological qualities of human beings persist: the simple scale of the human body gives a certain quality to people's homes; even though we must stoop to enter a Roman house, we need not crawl to do so. So much attention has been given to the biological and psychological conditions that they will be considered only as they bear upon the other eternal verity of the city, the physical form. That form persists for one of several reasons. The first would be the simple fact that the properties of the physical world are basically unchanging; stones are stable entities save under unfortunate and unusually destructive forces. The raw materials available for the making of cities changed little from the time of Pericles, who died in 429 B.C., to that of President Grant, who died in A.D. 1885. Thus, the plasma of cities has been transformed more often in the last century than in all previous urban history. City form—morphology—tends to change less rapidly than many human institutions because it is nongenerational, lacking the definite life-span of the human organism. Although few seventeenth-century buildings remain in America, and fairly few even in most Old World areas, their death was slow, overlapping the new construction that normally followed precedent in material and design to a degree sufficient to perpetuate the basic elements of form. The housing-tract structure of today is close in form to the houses of colonial America, though the religion or sexual mores of the two times differ greatly.

The structure and form of the city is to a very appreciable degree innate rather than conferred by immediate circumstance. In the long run changes occur, but they come in historical rather than topical timespan, and the process of adjustment is one of evolution, not of revolution. Thus, human culture is a conservative force at work in the morphogenesis of cities. Political and economic institutions may change but such rapid transformations do not, in any automatic way, remake cities. A good test of this notion is found in eastern Europe. There, most human institutions have been rather radically transformed since 1945, yet Sofia, Warsaw, Budapest, and Prague would be basically familiar to the resurrected resident of the pre-socialist 1930's. In truth, Marxist economics, education, social organization, and opposition to formal religion are in practice but, as I have noted elsewhere, no clear Marxist land-assignment system exists and only rather a peculiar reversion to the most capitalist of times in early modern Chicago colors the architecture.[1]

The Time Sequence

Given the staged quality of urban history, we may treat the long range of time covered in this book in three fundamental eras, with times of cultural and morphological transition standing dominant between them. We could begin with the earliest glimmering of urbanization, with the origin of cities. The intellectual problem we face is that of explaining a total change in human institutions and practices, if we assume that the origin of man was evolutionary rather than instantaneous. How did the human species become social in the peculiar way that it is, and how did it turn from what seems certain wandering and dispersed settlement to fixed and urban living? Because this problem is so clearly one of theories of culture, it will be left to other works. An extensive anthropological and geographical literature specifically focuses on the origin of cities, so we may leave the specification of the evidence

[1]James E. Vance, Jr., "Land Assignment in the Precapitalist, Capitalist, and Postcapitalist City," Economic Geography, Vol. 47 (1971), pp. 101–120.

and its intellectual explanation to those immersed in the concern. We may simply take as given the existence of cities and begin our story with two reasonable conditions. The first is that urban history is essentially continuous from that time to the present; the second is that the culture with which we concern ourselves, that of the west, is the containing geographical milieu.

Any considerable body of evidence that can be brought to bear on the question of the morphogenesis of the western city commences with the Greek city-states as they began to develop in the earlier part of the first millennium before Christ. Although great changes took place as those settlements grew and were transformed over a period of nearly fifteen hundred years, and fundamental differences arose between Greek and Roman towns, a basic consistency in cities of the Classical Era until they were atrophied by the barbarian invasions of the west allows us to treat them as a unified intellectual study. All the boundaries are not neat. In the eastern reaches of the Roman Empire, the death of the classical world was a lingering one, and we may with considerable justice call it total only when the Turks captured Constantinople in 1453. By then in the west a whole successor era, that of the Middle Ages, had passed and we may think of 1453 as, in a symbolic fashion, the beginning of modern times. In that year the French finally pushed the English out of the area of French speech (save for a few more years in the curiosity that became the Channel Islands and Calais). This change encouraged the development of political, economic, and social policies that may be summed up under the name of mercantilism, and which led directly to the creation of the Industrial Era, in which we remain to this day.

Essentially, the greater clarity of conditions in the west commends the use of that area as the field in which we seek the intellectual understanding of the evolution of our modern city. The Byzantine Empire that succeeded Rome in the east so clearly became a place of obscurity and backward-turning to the westerner that its title has been used as an adjective for those qualities. And when the end came, urban development had little continuity until, in the nineteenth century, western urbanization was implanted in Constantinople. In the meantime, the eviction of the Turks and other Asian invaders from the borders of Europe had meant the revolutionary substitution of the evolved western European city into an area that had simply carried forward the classical city in its most exhausted form. The cities of Russia were Baltic in origin, those of the Levant heavily French, and those of the Balkans reflective of the cities of the "liberators" who came to dominate them.

In the west the atrophy of the classical city was sharper in form and more narrow in time. Within several hundred years the direction of evolution was reversed and the Roman institutions were first disintegrated and then replaced. Form was borrowed from the Roman past—the then universal church in a most significant decision placed its capital in Rome, not Jerusalem. In the west no essentially continuous practice of urban life and process of urbanization existed; thus the "Dark Ages" stand as a striking period of urban transformation. When, around the end of the first Christian millennium, city filling began again in the west, it was for a purpose and in a social structure vastly different from that of the Roman cities whose physical cells it often occupied. The replacement element was as different from the Roman as is the silica from the carbon in a petrified log: dominion and tribute were the practices of Rome, whereas trade and craftsmanship were those of the true medieval city. Yet the continuity of cities was maintained in more than an oratorical sense; many of the public components of the physical structure of the medieval city were borrowed fairly directly from Rome, the Christian basilica being the case in point. The Middle Ages were a time of urbanization as vital and puissant as had been that of senatorial Rome and distinctly medieval forms and structures soon developed within cities. The most commonly known was that of the Gothic church, whose form and functions would have been both unnecessary and misunderstood among the people of the classical Mediterranean. And in the layout of the town a surpassingly important contrast was introduced: the city's form sprang from its subjugation to the needs of its citizens rather than its gods, as had been the case in Rome.

The discontinuity at the end of the Middle Ages was more biological than functional. The onset of catastrophic plagues in the fourteenth century simply forced a grim effort to hold what ground had already been won in social and economic development. For two centuries the cities became tempering vessels in which durability of purpose was tested and, when present, strengthened. The weak and irresolute sought refuge in the countryside, to flood back into the city only with the onset of the modern era that came into existence when the nation-states emerged as successors to the weakened political power of the cities.

An interregnum occurred in the power of the city. When the nation-state came to stand as the successor to the powerful cities of the Middle Ages in most of western Europe, the city was systematically reduced in power and the countryside was elevated, as a conscious policy of the newly strengthened monarchies. The locus of political domination swung clearly to the landed aristocracy in the centralized states—in England, France, and Spain. Only in a land of cities such as Holland were the worst excesses of rural domination avoided to maintain some democratic balance in government. Thus the discontinuity between the medieval city and that of the Industrial Era was at first a biological attack and then a shifting of the political balance in such a way that the city was for several centuries held in gelded deterioration of its former power. Only when the city produced a new and again vital purpose, as the instrument of the national economic policies, did it regain the powerful role it had held when economy of any wide interest was mainly restricted to the medieval city.

The city stands in western civilization as the major expression of a continuous urban tradition. Starting in the middle of the sixteenth century, cities resumed a critical importance in social and economic institutions, only to be delayed in the full enjoyment of political institutions in many places, most notably in Britain, until the nineteenth century. Perhaps most importantly the city became the instrument of the European domination of the world and for the creation, for the first time, of what came close to being a world economy. The New Lands of the world were planted with European migrants, first in trading towns and then in the spreading rural settlement that ultimately, save in South Africa, destroyed any appreciable survival of the indigenous culture.

Cities represented the first points of attachment of the New Lands to western civilization. They were the places to which the planted settlers first came, and the centers out of which settlement spread to tap the resources of those generally thinly populated areas. And as the economies of the planted regions grew, they expanded in integration with the economies of the homeland. Where the area to be dominated economically was more densely settled, the practice may not have been that of seizing political sovereignty in a total sense; many areas were left as colonies and protectorates. But the instrument of attachment remained the "colonial city" planted by the "colonial power," as was the case with Britain at Bombay, Singapore, and, in a different sense, Hong Kong. When the colonial overlordship ended, the planted form of western urbanism remained and became the model for city development, even when it was locally originated and encouraged. In these ways the city form that emerged with the quickening of industrial activity first in England and the Low Countries, spreading subsequently to France and the United States and ultimately to all of the western countries, came to be spread far more widely in the world than the specific culture which produced it.

The City of Man

The social consequences of this urbanization have been vast, as, in a less obvious sense, have been the political changes in which the urban population has played a major role. The normal heath of mankind now is the city. The study of the city in western civilization is the study of the main elements of world urbanization today.

We may employ the population data of the United Nations as the best, though still a terribly rough, approximation of the conditions today. To begin with the most grating of problems such data present, it is difficult indeed to believe that Bulgaria, Ireland, Mongolia, or Norway is considerably more "urban" than are Belgium and West Germany. It is even questionable that Sweden and New Zealand are more urban than the United Kingdom or the United States. Urban qualities are least pronounced at the bottom of the range of city sizes, so countries wherein the largest city is smaller than Indianapolis (as is the case with Sweden and Stockholm) or Jackson, Mississippi (as with Auckland and New Zealand), are clearly not possessed with the same quality of urbanization as the old great industrial nations. Thus problems arise in comparing data of contrasting origin. The only way to deal with the problem is to be less than totally committed to the data. We must say, for instance, that in Belgium persons engaged in city economic activities have a strong tendency to maintain homes in the nearby countryside, a practice only somewhat less common in West Germany. And in both those countries the agriculture is so profitable as to engage far more hands than in many areas of few and small cities, such as Mongolia. That the proportion of the population engaged in ag-

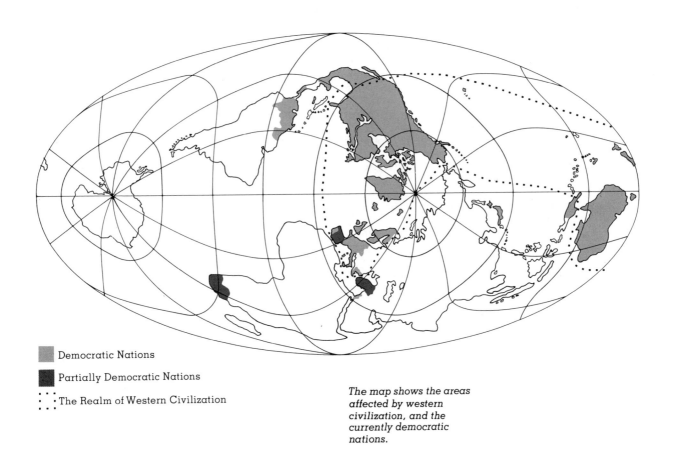

■ Democratic Nations

■ Partially Democratic Nations

⋮ The Realm of Western Civilization

The map shows the areas affected by western civilization, and the currently democratic nations.

riculture helps to determine the appeal of the countryside is also clear in India, Indonesia, China, and much of Asia, where large cities are dotted about an incredibly densely populated agricultural landscape. Most Chileans live in cities because, in fair measure, few Chileans could be supported by the national agriculture, whereas only one out of five Indians can live in cities or the level of starvation would be even higher. Mexico is so urban because it stands a demographic disaster with a population wholly out of reasonable control or restraint. Without going into the mechanics, we may say that the stages of economic and urban development are so intricately interwoven that we can read from the level of urbanization certain conclusions as to economic, social, and, in instances, political conditions.

Turning to the data themselves, as shown in Table 1, we should not overlook the fact that six of the ten countries with the highest proportion of urbanized population are "New Lands" shaped by the mercantile conquest by northwestern Europe of lands which had remained outside their knowledge even at the end of the Middle Ages. Six of the eight other countries in the first fifteen by rank in urbanization were initiators of that northwest European trading conquest of much of the world outside, leaving only Japan and Luxembourg, which was a personal possession of the Dutch royal family in the years of colonization and thus somewhat involved in the mercantile conquest, to be accounted for. Japan is out of this natural grouping only in the sense that she was in Asia and practiced mercantile conquest only in Asia. Not before dropping below two-thirds of the population living in urban areas do we find any national representatives who were not intricately tied in with the mercantile revolution of northwestern Europe and its overseas client areas (with Japan again the geographical but not functional exception). Those countries one-half to two-thirds urban are European but not participants in the mercantile revolution until later on in this history (Greece, the Soviet Union, and Austria, with Lebanon being a mercantile land but outside Europe); major New World mestizo nations (Cuba, Mexico, Brazil, and Peru); or countries held in political bondage until well into the nineteenth century (Iraq, Bulgaria, Poland, Ireland, and Finland). Switzerland fits no common explanation.

The economic basis of a high level of urbanization seems unassailable on this evidence, even if the precise working of that dependency is not simple or certain. The separate components of explanation that reflect back on the great mercantile florescence that northwest Europe enjoyed at the beginning of the Industrial Era, and which she shared with a number of overseas dependencies starting with the independence of the United States in 1783, suggest that in that conduct of long-distance trade lies much explanation central to the present facts of world urbanization. We shall repeatedly return to the notion of a mercantile basis for settlement location and size.

The political content of high levels of urbanization is commonly overlooked. Fifteen of the twenty countries with the highest level of urbanization are true democracies in a world not overly inhabited by such forms of government. Of the other five, three are committed to a radical form of socialism. Among the next twenty countries (ranked twenty-one to forty) only seven are democracies, though that is a better showing than among the next twenty, of which only four maintain democratic governments. Whatever the causative factor may be, the significant fact is that of the twenty most urban countries, 75 per cent have democratic governments; of the next twenty only 30 per cent do, while for the next twenty, with their smaller urban proportion, only 15 per cent are democratic. Thus the world's more urban lands are those wherein popular government is most common and most secure. We shall see that this condition was associated as well with the reemergence of cities in the Middle Ages.

The social structure of cities has commonly contrasted with that of the rural areas that surrounded them. In the Classical Era, as we shall see, the city was the dominating focus of power and learning to the point that the English language has inherited from those places the term for learning and the restraint of base cravings and passions. When people were urbanized in the classical world, they were civilized as well. Now we divide those qualities, believing that rural people with refinement and learning equal to that found among the city folk may be equally as "civilized."

Cities Make Men Free

Among the Greeks the first modification of the fierce, semi-biological loyalties of the rural clan was shaped when representatives of those primal groupings of people came together in cities. Through the process of *synoecism*, or the joining together of a number of formerly rural and localized clans in the founding of a city, a more varied and tolerant society was shaped. Two forms of government—democracy and socialism—grew directly from city life. Democracy was

Table 1 The Proportion of Urbanization in Major Countries

Rank	Country	Population Urban under Local Definition (%)	Rank	Country	Population Urban under Local Definition (%)
1	Australia	85.56	32	South Africa	47.93
2	Israel	84.35	33	Panama	47.83
3	Sweden	81.40	34	Hungary	47.55
4	New Zealand	81.35	35	Iceland	46.48
5	Denmark	79.93	36	Mongolia	46.40
	(England and Wales)	(78.25)	37	Norway	44.86
6	Netherlands	77.71	38	Syria	43.30
7	United Kingdom	76.91	39	Egypt	42.88
8	Canada	76.09	40	Cyprus	42.40
9	Chile	75.97	41	Iran	41.90
10	Venezuela	75.72	42	Korea	41.17
11	East Germany	73.78	43	Romania	41.15
12	United States	73.48	44	Belgium	40.16
13	Japan	72.17	45	Dominican Republic	39.76
	(Scotland)	(70.85)	46	El Salvador	39.43
14	France	69.99	47	Ecuador	39.15
15	Luxembourg	68.40	48	Yugoslavia	38.56
16	Greece	64.84	49	West Germany	38.43
17	Cuba	60.47	50	Turkey	37.55
18	Mexico	60.27	51	Jamaica	37.08
19	Iraq	60.21	52	Paraguay	35.71
20	Lebanon	60.11	53	Morocco	35.18
21	Soviet Union	58.32	54	Albania	33.46
22	Bahamas	59.74	55	Gabon	32.00
	(Puerto Rico)	(56.48)	56	Philippines	31.74
23	Brazil	55.90	57	Zambia	30.38
24	Bulgaria	55.18	58	Guyana	29.53
	(No. Ireland)	(55.11)	59	Ghana	29.00
25	Switzerland	54.59	Selected:	W. Malaysia	28.72
26	Peru	53.97		Sri Lanka	22.36
27	Poland	52.89		India	20.17
28	Ireland	52.23		Tanzania	19.42
29	Austria	51.86		Indonesia	17.42
30	Finland	50.93		Pakistan	13.12
31	Nicaragua	48.61		Uganda	7.67

devised while the tolerance of strangers, innovation, and change was greatly increased over the levels characteristic of the rural clan era. A city could comprehend a polyglot and an ethnically diverse population and shape social institutions to deal with it. As many anthropologists and sociologists have shown, in matters of social structure cities became places of change whereas the countryside remained a bastion of the conservative defense of the existing order. The pariah tended to be hounded in rural areas while he might be taken up in the city, or at least left in peace.

Since classical times the city has ever been the refuge for the disbeliever and the innovator. When medieval society and economy in the countryside became rigid, as it did when feudalism was dominant there, the need arose for a refuge of freedom and a field where original thought would be smiled upon. The escape to the city was sought by many who came, in the end, to reshape the world. Because Germany was perhaps the most feudal of lands, keeping some of the practices on the law books until Napoléon abolished them along with their creaking Holy Roman Empire in 1808, we still cite the medieval aphorism *Stadtluft macht frei*—cities make men free. In the Middle Ages the city stood as a small enclave of individualized life in a vast land of traditional privileges. The institutions that came to control the city, the gilds, were the product of direct effort and expended labor and had as their purpose the sheltering of a working membership against as many misfortunes as man might forfend. As political autonomy was gained by city corporations, control of the city tended to fall into the hands of the collected gilds. In the end the chartered privileges came to vest not in the hands of workers, which the gild members had originally been, but in the control of the administrators of the gilds of latter days, who often knew little of the actual work. At that point urban society tended to be as rigid and stratified as that of the countryside, and as lacking in economic vitality.

The resistance to change, even in cities, which came at the close of the Middle Ages meant that some new economic and social force was needed to continue the evolution. It came in the opening of the world beyond western Europe to the activities of her citizens. The great Mercantile Revolution of the sixteenth, seventeenth, and eighteenth centuries so transformed the scale of demand for goods that the medieval practice of craftsmanship, with its institution of the gild, failed to cope. So long as the gilds could control the course of city life, experimentation with massive manufacture had to be extra-urban. In the meantime the cities were being increasingly more dominated by merchants rather than craftsmen until, in the eighteenth century, most of the gild privileges were sufficiently reduced to permit the return to the city of large-scale, post-gild manufacturing.

At that juncture, existing social institutions were no longer effective for the increasingly large number of workers who were encouraged into the city either by the rural depopulation of "enclosure" of common lands or the prospect of money wages in factories. Early industrial society was, for the workers, a society of great nakedness to misfortune and mistreatment. The gilds had been abolished or corrupted, and urban government was dominated by the only power that lay within the town, that of the merchant class. The social welfare institutions of the state had been shaped to aid all the poor, who at the time were more rural than urban. These institutions worked modestly in the countryside but hardly at all in the city. For more than a century the city became a place of great economic vitality but great social disorganization and privation. Out of that trial came the second of the two fundamental forms of government engendered by city life, that of "socialism," the acceptance of the view that society had rights along with individuals and that social objectives stood above economic ones. We should not forget that it was in cities in the industrial districts of Britain, the United States, and northwestern Europe that socialism was nurtured and came (by the end of the First World War) to be a coherent system of government, economy, and society.

This brief summary of the evolution of urban institutions supports the division into stages of what was a fundamentally continuous city development from classical Greece to the present day. Three great eras emerge: the Classical Era and its cities, which were the focus of civilization, the temple of the gods, and the basis of the state; the Middle Ages and its cities, which were the refuge of freedom and individuality in a constrained economic and social world; and the world of mass institutions—economic, political, and social—which we tend to summarize as the Industrial Era, with its need to shape new forms and structures and quite different governments and societies.

The Organization Employed in This Book

The relative neglect that attaches to the physical form and structure of cities makes it necessary to present some ways of looking at that intellectual concern. In the first chapter we take up the way in which we may begin to present and understand the morphogenesis of cities in western civilization. We will delineate some of the more essential characteristics of physical build and present proposals as to how the evidence that emerges might be read.

With tools in hand, we may practically turn to the great features of the evolution of the form of western cities. The second chapter concerns the cities of the Classical Era of the Mediterranean which were shaped to gain the attention and support of the gods and to provide the instrument for political domination and conquest of the world beyond the homeland. The natures of the city of trade, as developed by the Greeks, and the city of conquest and tribute, as brought to a high art in the hands of the Romans, are shown and the physical contrasts between the two forms are established.

Because of the surpassing importance of medieval experience in urban practices and forms even down to the present day, it is desirable to look in greater detail at the second of the great urban eras. This undertaking is encouraged by the far greater survival of actual physical evidence from medieval than classical times, as well as the more complete written material that has come down to us from that more recent past. In the third chapter, the decline of Rome and the long night of urbanization that had to pass before the light returned with the medieval city is discussed. Greatest attention is given to the role that these towns played as refuges for freedom and workshops for change. In the fourth chapter, the city of the Middle Ages is considered, with its greater development and more confident use. The medieval city as a home of contemporary liberalism is sketched with particular attention given to the actual build of the places.

The transition of the medieval to the industrial city depended to a great degree on the creation of a physical form and a social milieu that could be accepting of change. Limitations on use, design, and personal participation had to be reduced and an easily reproducible morphology and set of urban institutions devised. In the newly created towns of the Middle Ages, the *bastides*, experimentation critical to the mercantile occupation of the lands outside of western Europe was carried out. Thus, in a study of bastides in the fifth chapter we see the origin of the vast urban explosion of western civilization into that part of the world that lay beyond its reach until the time of "discovery."

While the mercantile nations were using the city as the instrument for plantation and conquest, the less vital European states were turning inward and using the city not to glorify the gods, as had the Romans, but to glorify the newly dignified rulers. The city of the Renaissance and baroque periods on the continent of Europe became a thing of elitist preconception, divorced from functions other than ostentation, and developed in almost wholly architectural terms. The sixth chapter deals briefly with these places, the merchants' towns and the prince's capitals. The short discussion of the latter is justified first by the excess attention they have received in the literature on urban development and, second, by the little significance this type of morphology has had in subsequent urban history, other than in the hands of authoritarian builders.

The great surge of urbanism that has come under the impact of mercantile and industrial expansion since the sixteenth century cannot be considered so generally as is the city during the Classical Era or the Middle Ages. In the seventh chapter the mercantile city of the sixteenth, seventeenth, and eighteenth centuries is analyzed, both for itself and as the direct ancestor of present cities. The change from a dynamism almost entirely mercantile to one based as well on manufacturing is covered. In the eighth chapter, the sketching of the fundamental physical form of present cities is begun. With the impact of vast scale growth in the late nineteenth century the industrial city changed in its social, political, and economic institutions while developing a morphology which remains with us. This chapter covers the city in western civilization since the middle of the last century.

We are not concerned with the future beyond setting a conceptual base for its contemplation. Thus, the last chapter seeks more to summarize and clarify the view of the past than to delineate the prospect of the future. Nonetheless no work of this scope can stop without brief notice of what the truths discerned mean in terms of mankind's urban expectations.

We seek to establish in this book a form of questioning, observation, ordering, and analysis with a quite concrete purpose, proposing an integrated set of processes that explain the shaping of cities, today and throughout time.

1. THE PRACTICE OF URBAN MORPHOGENESIS

An initial interest in the physical nature of cities grew from the observations of the unknown, and their recording and presentation in written form to the western world, that was the work of geographers up to the time of the First World War. Then the profession turned from this concern with space within the city to the question of where cities were found in space. For geographers the years between the two world wars were taken up with the pursuit of an assumed regional regularity. The educated professions assumed that geographers, if they no longer explored the unknown as they had done in Victorian times, sought to order knowledge into useful geographical packages called *regions*. Thus the historian, economist, or planner could hold up against his array of data a template of area, from which he could read all sorts of spatial associations to the data that really concerned him. Geographers strove to oblige until it became clear that no natural, general regions existed, but only very rough divisions that must be defined by selected, specific criteria.

At that point geographers philosophically denied the existence of general regions as earlier they had denied geographical determinism. They began to search for institutional process within a particular branch of human activity and its geographical pattern. Until recently their main concern has been with the distribution of economic activities and conditions. Not surprisingly, the common concern of urban geographers was why cities were located where they were and what work was accomplished in those specific locations. In essence, their study became that of the location of cities in space.

The most widely touted theory within geography, that of central-place activities, was proposed in 1933 by the German economic geographer Walter Christaller. In the forty years since then, the search for central-place hierarchies of cities has been as intense as the search for composite regions was when Christaller wrote. The results have been similar; in some places central-place hierarchies can be discerned but in many more they cannot. Because geographers are honest if not always imaginative, they have sought hard for an understanding of the distribution of cities in the hope that Christaller can be modified in such a way as to accord a better "fit" with reality. In that search they have mainly disregarded the matter of what happens in the space within the cities they are seeking to place in a broader spatial context.

Space within Cities

We seek an understanding of cities and the role they play in the scene of man by looking within them to see how people have used them and what physical demands have been made on them, and by asking what this tells us about the location of these, the largest intimately integrated institutions and the greatest of human physical artifacts. An equally significant question can be answered only from within: what is the structure of the city even after its location has been explained in broader terms?

Other academic disciplines have been concerned with questions internal to the city but none has a responsibility for the physical build of the place. Historians have recently increased their attention to cities, and a new urban history is emerging which seeks to understand the nature of the proletarian citizen as well as the civic leader. Sociologists have always been most concerned with city people because in urban environments social institutions are most readily observed and compared and the social processes are most clearly perceived in research. Economists have always made an important, but largely unglamorous, study of land economics, to which in recent years have been added subfields—welfare and consumer economics—that are heavily urban in their interests. But none of these other studies concerns itself with the physical form of the city.

Architectural history and the practice of city planning, with attention to its history, might be thought to look at form. However, a kindly scrutiny of those fields shows that, much as they are concerned with the physical features of the city, they are not concerned with settlements, either as a totality or in an organic, evolutionary way. Architectural history has mainly concerned itself with "high architecture," as expressed in great buildings built by practicing architects and normally quite deliberately expressive of the concerns of a small, highly self-conscious elite. Thus from that most admirable discipline we have gained a much better understanding of the impact of educated taste and architectural technology than of actual city form. The history of city planning, as opposed to the professional practice of city planning, has been almost exclusively concerned with preconceived design in towns, and most heavily with the utopian or ideal cities, most of which never were transferred from paper onto the ground.

We are fundamentally concerned with space *within* cities. From the work of others we now have views as to "social space" within the city, the land economics of urban activities, and the design concept of space in art, architecture, and preconceived planning. Their undertakings are not insignificant or invalid, but in our terms they are insufficient to encompass the total morphology of the city. Expressed another way, a reality of space exists within cities just as do the realities of social interaction and economic activity. If one concentrates on society, then social institutions and social space suffice to provide the substance of understanding. But if one looks at space as a reality, as a force operating independently of institutions, and as a medium for people to use in expressing many institutionally derived objectives, then a great interest and real need arises to look at space *tout à fait*. It might be argued that space is always dependent upon people and their society or economy, that it is constantly relative to those institutions and is thereby subservient to their processes. The evidence does not support such a position. Economics presents the strongly held principle of "distance decay" in social questions; one of the fundamental explanations of the operation of innovation and the diffusion of ideas is the contagion theory, which holds that ideas and practices will diffuse if peoples are in contact but will fail to do so if empty space intervenes.

We shall look at space for its own sake, and specifically its expression in cities, which we call *urban morphology*. To do that, we need tools, so we shall explore the concepts of urban morphogenesis that might be used in that task.

The Concept of Normative Structure

In geography, the interest has been in the location of cities and other social and economic phenomena in broad-scale space, and an earnest effort has been made to determine a normative geographical structure for those activities. Christaller's proposal of a central-place hierarchical arrangement of towns was such an undertaking, as have been proposals of "market potential," "population potential," and even "rank-size rule" ordering of towns in space. The basic assumption in all of this work is that *natural order* awaits discovery. Because the human mind, and even more the computer, can deal effectively only with a very modest set

of causes, the practice has been to assign causation to one or two major forces leaving most of the others to most secondary consideration. Christaller argued three basic points: (1) the natural, universal distribution of population was dispersed in the countryside; (2) to gain goods and services beyond their shared capacity to produce them, people must physically converge on towns where centralized goods and services were to be had; and (3) such physical convergence is greatly influenced by the growing burden of increasing distance, to the point that eventually new central-places will be set up in some sort of hierarchical relation to all other central-places in order to be nearer to the most distant customers of the original place. The assumption behind his theory is that the understanding of this interrelated set of processes furnishes us with the perception and explanation of a natural order of city siting and use.

Later, we will examine both the assumptions and the reality of this theory, but now let us use it as an example of the way assumptions of normative process have been employed to seek order and understanding in a factually complex world. We may argue that no innate quality of normality forbids its expression *within* as well as outside cities. Thus, we may seek to state such process theories in urban morphogenesis, as well as in the much more widely sought theories of regional relationship.

In seeking an understanding of normative structure within cities, two real problems arise, those of excessive particularization and excessive aggregation. An instance of the first is found when considering the residential unit—the house in most of human history and the apartment of late. The housing unit may be defined as the basic physical unit or cell of urban morphology, as has been done by general historians and by those concerned with architecture in particular. The main difficulty comes when we try to determine how typical their description of a particular building is for all the buildings of the city. We have tended to gain an exaggerated view of past housing conditions by a heavy reliance on the writing of a small literate elite. In the same way, those outside the United States gained a most elevated view of the physical possessions of ordinary Americans during the Depression of the 1930's when their view of housing was based on the American movies so widely seen in that era. But historical records are not socially or economically balanced. The rich and powerful are far more likely to survive in records than are the relatively poor and powerless mass of the population. The worst examples of a time have a way of becoming the prime examples of history. If we look at any one building as the example of a time, we must try to see how well it represents the norm we seek.

The problem of aggregation shows up in the tendency to take some reasonable norm and make of it reality. Three examples—one from the Classical Era, another from the late Middle Ages, and the third from modern America—give us the clearest view of the difficulty. In many textbooks of planning and architecture three illustrations will be reproduced that have become so widely presented as to be taken as representative truth. The first shows a Roman military camp, the *castrum*, either as a theoretical construction or in some actual occurrence. Normally a careful selection has been made from among the hundreds of *castra* that were built so the "example" will most simply, and *perfectly*, reproduce the theory as expounded by masters of Roman centuriation. Thus, the prime example becomes the norm. This practice also shows up when an author wishes to talk about the fascinating towns, or bastides, that were founded in the Middle Ages. The practice is to reproduce the ground-plan of Monpazier in the Agenais of southwestern France to represent the bastides. Again the perfection of the plan rather than the representative quality of Monpazier settles the

choice. Finally, textbooks usually show some plan for a grid-pattern town in the American Middle West and leave in our minds the notion that all is symmetry, order, proportion, and uniformity there.

The difficulty in each of these examples is that the medium gives an erroneous message. Most Roman cities were laid out according to principles (the nature of which we shall consider in the next chapter). Subsequently the medieval bastides did have principles at work during their construction that made them towns of rather democratic proportion in land-assignment. And the Middle Western town was orderly only on the first map filed in the country courthouse. But great physical variety existed even within this general conceptual agreement.

When we look at these towns on the ground we find, for example, that the Roman *castrum* pattern for a settlement was a religious and military conception far more than it was the actual plan for development. Places of Roman origin share certain qualities but

their common elements come from an adherence to principles rather than to a rigid plan. A city is an organism which evolves as all organisms do, in response to genetic signals—concepts of what a city should do and how it should interact in its parts—such as those which make all men and women basically "alike" but infinitely different. In a world of three billion people, no two are really identical. In the same way, city building responds to "genetic" signals but never produces an identical product. Thus, to take Monpazier as what *the bastide* was when it was built is no service to truth. I have on occasion wished that Monpazier would disappear into separated pieces in a hundred museums so that no one would ever again think of it as whole, the substance of an aggregate reality.

If our interest is in hypothesized normative process or abstract form for its own sake, the use of the ideal is of some value. If we seek to understand something less neat and far less abstract, we should eschew the ideal and look at the human world with the wondrous variety the quality of humanness implies. We can thus work inductively from the detail to a state of generalization of process. We take account of variety *to begin with*, rather than argue that a simple normative process has, *by corruption*, produced the vast variety of the world. In the deductive approach, which envisages normative processes shaping cities, all variation stands either as an *a priori* result of some presumptive relationship or as static introduced by the imperfect rationality of mankind. In the inductive approach, the generalization is always *a posteriori*, first taking into account the conditions found in cities and then dealing

in a rational balancing with the seemingly contradictory conditions, ultimately arriving at an inductive generalization (or statement of process) that is fundamentally inclusive of diversity.

Idiograph and Induction

The effort to synthesize the numerous studies made of individual cities is far from new. Within the field of geography, the tendency has been toward the study of the concrete and the hitherto unknown or undescribed. Each part has been assumed to be a component of a more universally interesting whole. With few exceptions, the part has turned out to be an idiograph, complete in itself and of specific meaning only to the precise subject of the study. Thus newer city monographs have collected on shelves as did the classical regional monographs of the French school during the Third Republic: as an impressive collection of scholarship but hardly the skeleton of a broader truth.

The failure of local, idiographic studies to advance broad understanding rather than local knowledge encouraged a complete shift in the viewpoint on cities. Instead of building up from the parts, it was argued that understanding would come from soaring above

Monpazier (opposite) in the Aquitaine of southwestern France is the most regular of bastides and the most often cited, yet even it is not as regular as its formal plan would suggest.

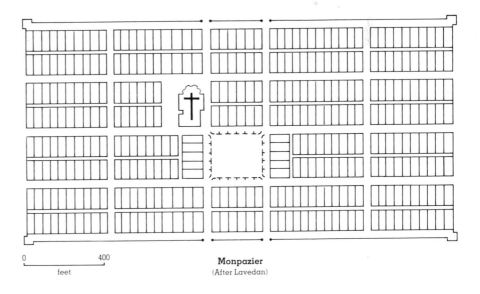

0   400
feet

Monpazier
(After Lavedan)

and projecting downward on local reality a natural order that had been arrived at *a priori* and from which explanation of the local pattern could be gained deductively. Not only did this elevated viewpoint hold out hope for a success that had not come with idiographic collections but it was much more economical and less confusing. No longer were facts of equal importance; only those related to the deductive system need be considered. If from them a plausible fit with the theory could be established, then the other facts were not equal facts, but rather lesser realities that could be disregarded as not contributing any percentage of cause to the pattern proven from above.

But by deductive reasoning we know little about the processes shaping cities. We have found that by soaring above, we can see only certain things. The censuses of various nations have for many scholars become the view of the ground and those things not collected by enumerators are not part of the picture. Unfortunately for our present interests, census enumerators have never turned any attention on the subject of urban morphology.

But even if the census sufficed, which it certainly does not, we have a much more fundamental reason for eschewing the soaring deduction: its use depends upon standardization of data and procedure. In those terms local studies have little use; historical facts, whose survival is greatly adventitious, have almost none. To attempt to shape an understanding of urban morphology over the long life of the western city, we must deal with diverse materials and sources seemingly too unstandard to be handled by most deductive systems. Thus, it is useful to propose an inductive approach to the considerable body of facts derived from locally based and formally unrelated studies.

situation was the assumed wider interconnections of the city and its surrounding area. This analytical device held a truth of a somewhat overly simple sort. Cities do have a fundament, which today tends to be rather too much belittled in our overfocus on social and economic institutions. San Francisco gains much of its character from its most eccentric site, as do New York City and Montréal. And who would argue that the etiolate image of Indianapolis is not in large part an outgrowth of its two-dimensional site? Thus, truth in siting is too often disregarded today.

Situation, the other component of the classic dichotomy of city location, has fitted somewhat better into the highly statistical study of modern cities, for implied in it is the notion of economic location, which the census data measure better than geographical location. Yet even in this regard, much needs be dealt with as a local matter. Looking again at San Francisco, New York City, and Montréal, we find the situations of the three are in one way similar: each is at the estuarine outlet of a major river system, and each was the entrepôt settlement from which a great valley—the Central Valley of California, the Hudson, and the St. Lawrence—was tied in with a larger economic world. This *original situation* can be considered fundamental to the founding of the town. Coming up to the present, the pattern is not shared. Montréal still has its initial situation in large measure but New York is far less influenced by its river system and San Francisco little indeed. In fact the port function of San Francisco is a pale shadow of what it was when the place was founded. We need, then, to study cities and their situation, so that we may deal with either persisting original conditions or their virtual destruction and replacement. This inductive study is essential, and national standardization on the present is a camouflage of truth.

Site and Situation

Not all local fact is grist for a larger mill; some items are simply unique. Even so, the response of the whole local system to that unusual fact may be in itself a great help in discerning how the more widely shared elements of morphogenesis work, particularly with regard to the physical site of the city. While the focus of urban studies lay on the local, the great tendency was to simplify the notion of location into a supposed dichotomy of site and situation; *site* was the physical nature of the ground on which the city was built, and

Stages of Truth

Because morphology can be immortal, though it often is not, we must take account of the past even to understand the narrowly defined present. To hold that the past is precept and continuous is a truism. Nevertheless, these patent truths force upon us the resolution of several methodological problems. If the precept of the present is continuous, how then can we most validly study it? The problem arises because of the discontinuous record we inherit and because, even if we could

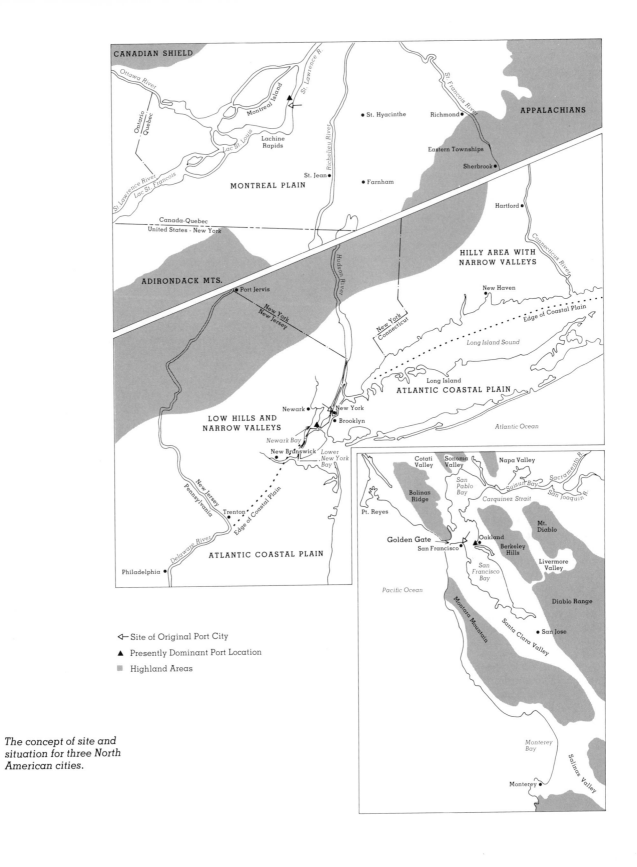

CANADIAN SHIELD

Ottawa River

Ontario
Quebec

St. Lawrence R.

Montreal Island

Lachine
Rapids

Lac St. Louis

St. Lawrence River
Lac St. Francois

St. Hyacinthe

Richmond

APPALACHIANS

St. Francois River

Eastern Townships

Sherbrook

Richelieu River

St. Jean

Farnham

MONTREAL PLAIN

Hartford

Canada-Quebec
United States - New York

ADIRONDACK MTS.

Port Jervis

New York
New Jersey

Hudson River

New York
Connecticut

HILLY AREA WITH
NARROW VALLEYS

Connecticut River

New Haven

Edge of Coastal Plain

Long Island Sound

Long Island

ATLANTIC COASTAL PLAIN

Newark

New York

Brooklyn

LOW HILLS AND
NARROW VALLEYS

Newark Bay

Atlantic Ocean

New Brunswick

Lower
New York
Bay

New Jersey
Pennsylvania

Trenton

Edge of Coastal Plain

Delaware River

ATLANTIC COASTAL PLAIN

Philadelphia

Cotati
Valley

Sonoma
Valley

Napa Valley

Sacramento R.

San Pablo
Bay

Suisun Bay

San Joaquin R.

Bolinas
Ridge

Carquinez Strait

Pt. Reyes

Mt.
Diablo

Golden Gate

Oakland

San Francisco

Berkeley
Hills

Livermore
Valley

San
Francisco
Bay

Pacific Ocean

Diablo Range

Montara Mountain

Santa Clara Valley

San Jose

Monterey
Bay

Salinas Valley

Monterey

←— Site of Original Port City

▲ Presently Dominant Port Location

▨ Highland Areas

*The concept of site and
situation for three North
American cities.*

follow the development of cities continuously over a three-thousand-year period, the effort would overtax our abilities. We need an economy of effort and of attention, as well as a system that allows us to cantilever across gorges of unrecorded evidence.

Attention to the *stage of morphogenesis* becomes both a convenient and a necessary tool. If we know that a city was founded at a particular time (a fact more likely to survive the destruction of record than some others), and we know the form of town that existed at that time, we are in a position to draw certain inferences as to the philosophy and motivation of the founders. If we find a shared philosophy, as we do in the bastides of the Middle Ages or the towns of the nineteenth-century Middle West, we can establish certain processes that were at work. We can then reason from that establishment to a general morphogenetic process, with its associated physical build of city in response to determinate conditions. What we talk about is *stage* rather than *time;* the bastides were built mainly from the middle of the twelfth to the middle of the fourteenth century, whereas the Middle Western towns came largely in the nineteenth, but each was an initial stage.

Time does have an impact. Certainly the rapidity with which a carpet of new towns spread across the Middle West was much greater than the slower progress of the bastidors across the devastated areas of Europe in the Middle Ages. And the easier flow of information in the last century as opposed to eight hundred years ago meant that the pattern in America was more consistent. But we should not become deterministic on the matter of the diffusion of information and ideas, for much of the greater consistency in America was the result of a rapid spread under a single political control, as opposed to the great political fragmentation of medieval Europe.

To point up precisely what is meant by *stage,* we may define by exclusion. Stage is not chronological time, it is morphological time. In the initial stage, we may make two assumptions: (1) the form of the town will tend most clearly and simply to reflect the purpose for which the settlement was established, and (2) the most obvious expression of the practices will then be used in town building. This will be true whether we consider the Greek *polis* or the English New Town of the post-war years. And as the town comes to undertake several different functions, the evidence becomes more mixed. For example, Bath in England was originally laid out by the Romans as a watering place, a literal bath, so it had a fairly obvious conformity to the special needs of that purpose. In the intervening two millenia Bath has been used for many purposes—abbey of the Middle Ages, local market town, show-ring of Society in Restoration time, and home of the Admiralty in war-

time, just to mention a few. Each of these activities has left its mark, some more than others. The Romans gave that particular cast to the place that is always allowed to the founder; the eighteenth-century peacocks of Beau Nash built so extravagantly that their tracks are still clearly in evidence; the Admiralty during the Second World War made less of a splash, perhaps because it was so far from its accustomed habitat.

From the successive transformations of Bath, and any other city that has lived very long, clear stages in use are obvious, but such clear relics of that use do not remain. We know fairly well what the Romans did at Bath from the way they built, and we know what the empty Society of the eighteenth century did there because their buildings and street layouts remain until today. But the reuse made of the Roman buildings throughout the Middle Ages and the reoccupation of the buildings of regal Bath between the eighteenth century and today are not so clearly shown on the ground. Thus, for evidence on those scores we turn to places with clearer relics from which we may gain a much better understanding of shifts in urban processes. From those other examples we may project into a city such as Bath, where the evidence may be obscure, some understanding of what was happening at a particular time. Such a procedure has pitfalls and we must make certain assumptions as to the universality of particular conditions, but when we have fragmentary contemporaneous evidence from the place or observations from a succeeding time that seem to confirm our view of what was going on during the evidentiary gap, our risk in assumptions is reasonable.

We should be clear in our minds that an early, or even initial, stage can be a very durable attribute of morphology. Street plans are laid down on the ground to survive truly incredible destruction and adversity. Turin and Chester have pedestrians following literally in the footsteps of the Romans, even though the buildings of Turin reflect mainly the grand designs of Piedmontese kings and of Mussolini, and those of Chester the smaller perceptions of the medieval English and the modern alderman. In the same way buildings are among our more plastic creations, surviving changes in geography and style that transform Diocletian's palace at Split into slums and the mews of Victorian coachmen into the flats of Bentley-driving gentry in today's London.

Function and Form in Morphogenesis

The architectural revolution of the International Style, signalling the birth of a "modern architecture," represented itself (with the overdramatization so much a part of cultural warfare) as an utter break with the past. To press that point, dicta of all sorts were made up and adopted as the creed for a new religion. The one that most concerns us is the dictum "form follows function." Such a dictum could have seemed new or radical only in a nation so besotted with romanticism as was Germany in the nineteenth century. When we look at the house in classical Athens, the buildings in the medieval bastides, or the farmhouses of eighteenth- and early nineteenth-century New England, the pretentiousness of the Bauhaus and its theorists is most evident. Yet we must accept that their conditioning has been effective, leaving many intelligent people with the view that the Baltic culture just after the First World War first discovered that a building is beautiful by being appropriate to its function. We must put the lie to this anti-historical nonsense; quite demonstrably, in vast periods of human history, building has been predicated entirely on fulfilling a particular function in terms of the best technology then available. Perhaps the house of the medieval town had less light than one in Dessau in the 1920's, but not by design. So long as timber or masonry construction had to be used and glass was very costly and poor, little else in lighting could be accomplished, however much one wished for better conditions. We know that the wish was for light: far more work was carried on out-of-doors and the working days were of variable length (as were the working hours) according to the season and the length of daylight. Structural necessity, not lack of awareness of the functional needs, led to most of the characteristic forms of the medieval city. In fact most medieval solutions were far more truly functional than have been those of Baltic design, given the technology available to their use. Even in the nineteenth century, the Boston and Salem rockers of Massachusetts were far more comfortable than any chair designed by Mies or his Scandinavian disciples; according to their dictum, the rockers must be more beautiful than their own chairs.

Throughout most of urban experience in western civilization, distinction must be made between the validity of the "form follows function" doctrine in the earliest stage of an area within a city and its bearing upon subsequent reuses of that same area. The question is not one of the age of the city but rather the stage of the area within the city because most cities grow by accretion of parts. A city such as Paris has quarters which derive part of their form from the acts of the Romans and others from the doctrines of Le Corbusier, a range of thought with vast differences of philosophy and aesthetics and a range of time of two thousand years. In normal circumstance the oldest creations lie at the center and the newest at the edge, yet in some cases the pattern is reversed—as in Paris with Baron Haussmann's rebuilding in the nineteenth century, or in Boston with Edward Logue's destruction and reconstruction of much of the Federalist town in the years since the Second World War. Then we must use morphological staging as our measure rather than time of first urbanization.

Function has always been a difficult thing to understand, and most builders have dealt more successfully with forms than with the purposes of their constructions. Thus reading function from form is a hazardous occupation, perhaps particularly so in the works of the greatest architects, who tend to be those with both the freest hand and the most dogmatic viewpoint. The extravagant buildings of the Renaissance were no more functional than the glass-box office buildings constructed today in the blazing sun of Dallas. In each case the internal use of the building is subjugated to the pompous image produced by its exterior, and neither is ideal for the conduct of productive work. In contrast, similar features may represent sharply differing adaptations of form to function. For a man today, the low doorways of our ancestors, and their scaled-down furniture, are constraining, but no more so than the buildings and the furniture of a dainty Frank Lloyd Wright who built dogmatically small after men had grown taller. Given those conflicting relationships of form and function, we must be very careful how we read from one to the other. And we must watch for the transformation of older buildings. The cutting of windows in medieval buildings as they were transformed in the seventeenth and eighteenth century for handloom textile production tells us much about changing urban function as does the cutting of a New Road or a Commercial Road through surviving medieval cities such as London.

Morphological Adaptation

One of the more common structural processes is that of adaptation of city forms from one stage to another and from one form-and-functional relationship to another. We shall see repeated instances of such transformations. The *agora* in the Greek town became a religious place transformed to a multitude of other uses from school room to political hustings. The *basilica* began as a place of public and private business among the Romans but came after Rome was Christianized to be the holiest of religious places. And the public building-forms of an autocratic Rome served both as the model for a most democratic Washington when Arthur Brown, Jr., was seeking the proper symbol for his Federal Triangle, and as the birthplace of the United Nations when that institution was founded in Brown's Roman Opera House in San Francisco in 1945.

Who can truly believe that form follows function so much as adaptation follows change? And even in more modern, or at least unself-conscious building, the practice remains. America is blossoming with transformed mills in New England, markets in Omaha, railroad stations in Savannah and Spokane. Their architects follow the lead of Lawrence Halprin and William Wurster who revamped a disused chocolate factory in San Francisco. But even Ghirardelli Square was not the first such reuse in recent America. A New York specialty store developed its first branch in Boston in the 1950's in the only-recently-abandoned building of the Museum of Natural History, which itself was a successor tenant to a land-grant college that in a declining agricultural state had become the Massachusetts Institute of Technology. How wonderfully flexible the urban fabric is! Once we reject the canon of modern architecture which decrees generational shift and destruction with change, we find that instead of this rather rootless nature for cities we have a real continuity with support in human cravings. Such continuity refuses to suffer the oversimplification of modern design into a "law" that form follows function.

Critics often look upon the adaptation of buildings from the past, and parts of towns that survive as entities, as a dull-witted escape into nostalgia or romanticism. Their argument is that innovation rather than adaptation is the measure of art—to be a rootless pioneer is to have the greatest freedom. We see a certain wisdom in what they say when we compare the showy "modernistic" qualities of Toronto's rather effeminate City Hall with Boston's innovative, rather brutish but powerful contemporary civic headquarters. But the truth is that at no period in urban history has a city been simply a matter of contemporary practices, and thus free of either the past or the future. The Washington of the early nineteenth century reflected little of the past but left great holes for the future, as is the case with Brasilia today. And in Rome, London, or Boston the past is everywhere. Almost without question Boston's City Hall is so impressive because it is framed by Faneuil Hall from the eighteenth century and the Quincy Market and the Sear's Crescent from the nineteenth. Its framing on the north by the new Kennedy Government Center adds no luster to the concepts of modern architecture, and no argument for destruction of the buildings of the past.

Preconception and Organic Growth

Pioneering has always captured our imaginations. It is not strange that the process of city-making is commonly brought to mind as the act of one great builder, be he a Roman consul planting Mediolanum, Milan's roots, or L'Enfant envisioning Washington. Yet such total preconception of a city is fortunately rare—fortunate because few men have done the job well, and rare because such overall plans have required a degree of power and control uncommon in history. What then are the alternatives? We find in broad terms that cities fall into two classes. The *preconceived city* is laid out by an emperor, bishop, or other authority possessed of the power to start a settlement from scratch, still believing strongly that his work is that of city founding, and thus needful of an elaborate and inclusive plan. The *organic city* includes those settlements established at a geographical point but left to evolve in physical pattern as functions and fates determine.

The creation of a single building or even of a pre-planned city is fairly easy to comprehend, but to see all of the processes that go into the creation and evolution of a city without a plan is difficult. We know from observation that most places grow by these organic processes, so they must exist and their nature needs to be better understood.

The concept of form follows function works fairly well in dealing with the initial stage in the shaping of the organic city, but where do we go from there? Physi-

Boston's new city hall, built in the 1960's (Kallman, McKennell, and Knowles architects), broke cleanly away from the historical structures typical of the nineteenth century and the dull purity of absolute forms of more recent decades.

cal adaptation comes about when the functional demands outreach the tolerance of the form to deal with that change. This insufficiency comes in two ways:

space may be insufficient to deal with the new demands, or needs may arise which cannot be met in any way by existing structures. If we take as an example the Industrial Revolution of the textile industry in the eighteenth century, we find both insufficiencies: the original hand production of textiles, starting with the spinning of yarn, had been a domestic activity and was easily carried on in the home. But to improve the standard of quality and, incidentally, to speed up the production, exercise of greater supervision over the weavers, in particular, became desirable. They were collected together but no longer could the cottage contain them; instead "factories" were built where the hand operations could be carried on under the direct supervision of factors. Thus, a scalar change without any transformation of actual function carried on within the structure brought a new form of building.

Later in the Industrial Revolution the need for yarn to feed the looms of greater productivity brought on the need for the other kind of structural change, that in fundamental form. As first machines and then waterpower were put to use in spinning yarn, locational and formal change became necessary. The water mill, with its riverside setting and vertical compaction, permitted the mechanical transfer of the rotative power of the mill wheel to machines nearby. At that juncture suddenly the siting of the factory became significant. Initially the site had simply been a spot where a potential factor could effectively bring together a potential workforce of the scale and ability he needed. With the coming of mechanical power, the location of the availability of that power determined the site of the factory.

This analysis may serve to introduce the notion of the *adaptive process* in urban morphology. Through it we may learn a great deal from a Janus-like analysis wherein we build a bridge of probable relationship between the two stages of city form. Commonly, evidence remains both as to the earlier as well as the subsequent form of the city; what is missing is the transition process. By contrasting the two forms, we may often establish what new demands are cared for in the new form. Thus we can make deductions as to that change of function in the city, which frequently goes unrecorded in historical records.

Connectivity in the City

Whereas states tend toward revolution and radical transformation, cities tend toward tenacious endurance and evolution.

The most notable absence in the study of city forms has been the notion of evolution, a grievous omission when we are dealing with entities that are, under most circumstances, nearly the most long-lived of all human physical creations. While any idea of a greater Greece is patent imagining today, the cities of *magna Grecia* remain; the Greek Patriarch lives in Istanbul as a tolerated and exotic Christian in a Muslim city whose mosques copy the architecture of early Christendom if they do not use those ancient buildings themselves. The nation-state, which seems so powerful and fundamental today, is a late and transitory successor to the en-

during city. The notion of eternal Rome rings true, but who would believe an enduring Italy? In little over a hundred years of "national" existence, the fundamental form of the Italian government has seen revolutionary change several times, as well as almost endless instability and tinkering. But Rome endures and evolves as do Istanbul (Constantinople), New York (New Amsterdam), Bombay, Singapore, and a number of other great cities for which the founding state has shriveled or disappeared.

Time bears far less on the city than it does on individuals, political systems or states. Napoléon captured most of Europe and swept away the Holy Roman Empire, an institution which had endured for thirteen centuries, yet he did not fundamentally change any city, even Paris. But he cocked a snook at Christendom and history when he destroyed the Roman church's greatest political creation (begun when the pope crowned Charlemagne emperor in the year 800) and the line of dynastic legitimacy for a millenium of history. After Waterloo no attempt was made to undo the emperor's work of demolishing such European institutions, but had he destroyed a city, such indifference would have been rather improbable. Witness the rebuilding of Washington after the British burned it, the medieval rebuilding of Milan after its savaging by the Holy Roman emperor, and the rebuilding of London, Rotterdam, Warsaw, and a number of German cities since 1945.

Within urban evolution are basic processes, several of which we have already discussed:

(1) Stages in urban experience are related to the functional life of the town more than to the chronological time of history.

(2) Although stages change with the passage of time, physical traits of the city tend to persist, once established, and no city ever absolutely denies its past.

(3) What change in cities are particularly the functions undertaken and carried on at various stages in the course of urban evolution.

(4) With those changes in function comes a need to adapt the physical form of the town, so the process of adaptation is a notable feature of cities and one that tends to set the city apart from the nation-state.

(5) Adaptation works not only on the physical structure of cities but also endless compromise is made between form and function, to the point that the process is more one of mutual transformation than a free rein for function over form. In this fundamental persistence of mutual adaptation, we find the basis for urban evolution and continuity.

(6) Throughout history the city has proven particularly susceptible to enlargement, and catastrophe is the main interruption in the course of scalar growth, as in the fall of the Roman state or the plagues of the

Middle Ages. Otherwise the city has grown even when states are contracting (as they have recently been, with the notable exceptions of the surviving imperialist powers—the Soviet Union, India, and China—each of which has grown significantly since 1945).

(7) That tendency toward continuing growth has made morphological and functional dynamism a notable feature of cities. In cities we find particularly active experimentation with physical forms—planning and design of buildings—and social and economic systems—capitalism in the Middle Ages and socialism in the nineteenth century.

(8) Dynamism has been expressed through the operation of two related processes, that of congregation of forms and activities and that of segregation between forms and activities.

(9) This physical growth and increasing complexity of structure within the city has made necessary an ever-enlarging concern with the connectivity among the various congregations of buildings and activities.

(10) The evolutionary nature of the city attaches not merely to forms and functions but also to the third of the major components of urban physical structure: connectivity.

On this tripod—*form, function,* and *connection* among forms or functions—we must base our analytical procedures, and within it we must shape our methodology.

Some periods are dominated by the creation of new forms, functions, or connections, and in some periods maintenance of existing patterns seems dominant. Because of the fundamental interaction among these three aspects of physical structure, change in one is likely to induce rather marked change in the others. Sometimes the form changes, as in the case of steel-cage construction which, after its introduction in Chicago in the 1880's and '90's, worked a major transformation in functions. From its use came in considerable measure the apartment house, the large department store, and the office building; in connection with its use arose the need for subways and elevated railways, and the division between commercial and residential parts of the city with the need for mass transit. At other times a major transformation in functions leads directly to great changes in building form and city layout (multistory construction to tap mechanical power during the Industrial Revolution, single-story construction to make use of the automated technology with the introduction of computers and the mechanical handling of goods). Connection is also effected (the single-story plant must be located toward the edge of the city to gain adequate space at a reasonable cost, which requires the substitution of automotive transport of goods and people for the former movement by public and common carriers). And the

The Home Insurance Building (1884–1885), by William Le Baron Jenney, was the first skyscraper in that it had a skeleton of iron and steel and merely a skin of brick and stone. The top two floors were added in 1891, something possible with iron construction.

introduction of a new technology of movement, such as came with the internal combustion engine, radically shifts the conditional balance that existed before its utilization in both form and function.

Periods of Adaptation

The cities we are concerned with have a collective history of more than two thousand years; we may look at them only at rather infrequent moments during their evolution to modern times. The search of the urban scene is most rewarding in times of *morphological adaptation*, which tend to come when the main action of political or economic change is focused on cities. By concentrating our attention on periods of adaptation, we may begin to establish the dynamics of urban form.

The Greek City-State

Cities existed before the time of the Greeks but "[t]he Greeks do not appear to have been inspired initially either to develop cities or to devise for them a new form of urban government by any direct impulse from the older civilizations of the Middle and Near East."[1] Earlier cities—those in the Indus and Nile valleys and in Mesopotamia—had been the creations of absolute monarchs, though perhaps Sidon and Tyre had been the earliest beginnings of *the city of man* as opposed to the palace of the king extended; at best they were transitional forms. Only in the archaic period in Greece, beginning around 900 B.C., was the city of man formed. Then, in contrast to earlier "urban" places, a morphology which could hope to be continuous throughout subsequent history without reference to dynastic whim or succession was shaped by structural processes, as distinct from royal fiat. "During the seventh and sixth centuries, therefore, the Greeks through their own talent and in response to particular local circumstances evolved the city-state."[2] This era becomes our first period of adaptation, truly one of initiation when a fundamentally rural and pastoral land was first urbanized.

The city-states grew in size and expanded in numbers by new colonizations until the Persian Wars, which ended in 479 B.C. In those wars many cities were destroyed so a new era of urbanization began when peace returned. From 479 (or perhaps 404 B.C. with the close of the Peloponnesian War) until the capture of Greece by Philip of Macedon (338 B.C.), the Classical Age of the Hellenes witnessed the adaptation of the

earlier organically evolving city into a more preconceived, planned place. The rebuilding after the Persian destruction made that morphological transformation both possible and likely in a culture gripped by a new rationalism.

The Etruscan-Roman City

The next period of adaptation that concerns us was fairly contemporaneous with the reconstruction of cities under Greek rationalism, though it operated in a quite different geographical situation. In Italy, beginning around the year 800 B.C., a group of pastoral aristocrats, the Etrusci to the Romans, began to establish "cities," of which at least twelve were built. These places seem to have been established to serve, perhaps mostly as religious centers, the surrounding countryside, as evidenced by the absence of popular participation in government and the heavy dependence upon slavery in nearby agriculture. These Etruscan towns were the first indigenous congregated settlements in Italy, and the direct ancestors of the Roman city. In establishing their towns the Etruscans observed elaborate religious practices and, in turn, made of them *the city as a temple;* the process of initiation, the process of land-assignment, and the physical form of the city were greatly influenced.

Disintegration and Decline in Roman Urbanism

The course of Roman urbanization is detailed in the next chapter. That halcyon period closed as surely as it began, as a consequence of the fortunes of the state. The Romans, using the Etruscan practices and forms, had projected urbanization over the whole western world, using cities to exact tribute and taxes from a subject realm. But Rome both as a state and as a system of cities began to shrink rapidly once military power was no longer sufficient to perpetuate that tribute. In the fifth and sixth centuries of our era, Rome as a vital state disintegrated, leaving many parts denuded of urban populations, though not of the physical relics of a great system of cities. Those remains passed into oblivion more slowly, by the removal of a bit each year through the agency of weathering and human quarrying.

Two sections of the once-continuous Roman Empire maintained some functioning urbanization for many centuries—Byzantium centering on Constantinople in the east, and Septimania preserving the urban culture of the west in Provence and Languedoc in southern France. Byzantium withered slowly, finally disappearing with the conquest of Constantinople by

[1]*Mason Hammond*, The City in the Ancient World, *Cambridge: Harvard Studies in Urban History, 1972, p. 152.*
[2]Ibid., *p. 174.*

the Turks in 1453. Septimania was lost in the evil Albigensian Crusade of Pope Innocent III and Philip-Augustus of France begun in 1207. But Byzantium and Septimania can be given only minor notice in a book with as long a story as this. Each played a crucial supporting role in this scene of man, and must be considered, but neither was the ultimate hero. He came unexpectedly as the scion of the semi-barbaric west where the urbanity of Rome survived just enough that it might, in the hands of a vigorous society, restore cities to their essential place in human life.

The Merchants' Town and Medieval Urbanization

The same crusading spirit which was so corrupted by Innocent III did enter importantly into the return of cities to the west. Even before the expeditions to the Holy Land, the rise of distant trading had begun in Italy, Germany, Flanders, France, and England; the Crusades, however, demonstrated beyond doubt the tie between economic overlordship and political expansion. The Venetians and citizens of other Italian city republics had played a critical role in financing and outfitting the expeditions, and they gained in return what we today would term "trading concessions" in the Levant.

The brawn of the expeditions was provided most notably by the Normans of western France and England. On their return from the Holy Land they brought two invaluable experiences as trophies of the Crusades: a much clearer notion of the ultimate riches to be gained from expanding the trade of a duchy or a kingdom, and a considerable technical knowledge of the arts of castellation and urban fortification. Those trophies, combined with the general mercantile inclinations at home, soon produced the great merchants' towns of Europe beyond the Alps, which within the course of several centuries came to equal those of Italy and ultimately totally eclipsed them. The shadow was cast on Italy by the better developed role for the common man in the communes of Flanders and Germany and in the tendency toward open-minded appraisal of thought and condition more true of Europe beyond the Alps. The collegial form of civic government was the institution most responsible for the advance of the west. But the concentration of interest in western cities on the matter of commerce and the avoidance of the cruel political factionalism internal to the Italian city led the way to the ultimate supremacy of the city of northwestern Europe from medieval times until the beginning of this century.

The Adaptation to Collegiality in the Bastide

The great periods of adaptation mentioned to this point are widely known and accepted. The same cannot be said for the next transformation of which we take note—the founding in the High Middle Ages of the new settlements that have come to be known collectively as *bastides*. The word derives from the great development of these places in Languedoc and Aquitaine in southern France, the same Septimania that the Albigensian Crusade sought so viciously to destroy. In so doing they created such an urban wasteland that new beginnings could be made. The adaptation was to a nondynastic and nonecclesiastical role for settlements, particularly one rather separated from the geographical servitude and social deficiency comprehended by the then-current rural system of feudalism. The bastides were not fully nonfeudal; feudal landholders set them up, but the new settlements were without the serfdom, geographical bondage, homage, and fealty characteristic of the feudal society. In these towns where collegiality ruled, the purpose was so strongly that of economic development of waste lands that the distinction to the earlier town founding in the Middle Ages was most marked. The bastide was a philosophical as well as a morphological ancestor of the American city.

The bastide building was a classic instance of adaptation of the functions of the town to a new purpose— the occupation of underdeveloped regions by a free pioneering population, something not too frequently undertaken since the time of the Greek colonists. Between 1150 and 1350 more than a thousand bastides were established. An examination of their location, layout, and social and political organization provides us with a useful insight into what cities might look like when democratic institutions came to rule more widely in western civilization.

The Absolutist's City; The Renaissance

The faint beginnings of the popular city in the bastide failed to accomplish much of a hold on western urbanization for centuries. Instead the age was one of political and religious absolutism. A Byzantine visitor to Innocent III's Rome noted that he was "the successor not of Peter but of Constantine." The desire to recapture the "grandeur" of Rome in a great Renaissance swept over a Europe of kings by divine right and popes by apostolic succession. Whoever the god, the morphological contrivance to his glory tended to have shared characteristics, most notably disregard for functions other than grand display and procession. These are functions, whatever we may think about their justice, so the Renaissance city was functional in these terms. Fortu-

Fourcès (Lot et Garonne)
was laid out as a bastide,
but in a circular form.
It is doubtful that it
has grown much during the
last seven hundred years
or changed its form rad-
ically. Note the arcades
ringing the squares.

nately the popular city began to gain ground over that of the autocrat, so the Renaissance as a model for us today is of most limited interest.

The Emergence of the Mercantile City

The age of mercantilism commenced only in odd ways, as most ages begin, but by the sixteenth century it was a coherent and articulated system which could guide the politics of a state. For the practice of mercantilism, cities were a critical feature. From them the ships set sail for distant ports with goods to sell and returns to be collected. To them from the surrounding countryside came the flow of staples to sustain such a distant trade, and within them tended to grow up the crafts that transformed either the national staple or the imported one into goods that moved ultimately either landward or seaward in the search for customers. A true circularity was found between the mercantile economic philosophy and the urban settlement form. Cities needed trade to grow, and trade needed cities to have goods to handle.

With mercantilism came a potent force for the establishment of cities in distant lands, notably in North America. The first American cities were mercantile places, set out under the operation of a mercantile system of urbanization. They were highly receptive to a socially and economically liberal form, such as that pioneered in the bastides first laid out in France in 1144 but more widespread in the thirteenth and fourteenth centuries. Thus, the mercantile expansion elevated the economic purpose of the city to the summit and brought to America the society, economy, and, to a considerable degree, religion of the bastide.

The Industrial City

The evolved form of the mercantile system was a fundamental base on which rose the great surge of industrialization that swept western civilization during the eighteenth and nineteenth centuries. The expansion of the demand for goods was a necessary precondition for the growth in production of those goods. Furthermore, the mercantile city played a role in encouraging an Industrial Revolution, by providing the necessary risk capital for nascent industry, the business practices and systems of organization that would allow distant and future dealings to take place and, in many cases, the simple plots of ground and workforces for early attempts at organized manufacture.

The early development of industrial cities came in England and Belgium for quite predictable reasons. England and Belgium had great amounts of coal, a long history of textile manufacture, and a generally numerous rural population whose labor was not fully engaged. Britain had areas of wool production in most counties and Belgium had in the episcopal County of Liège. England was the premier mercantile nation and therefore the most likely to sell large amounts of goods. She was the first nation to mine coal in vast amounts but, as a land of large landowners and rural tenancy, had potentially many surplus people resident in the countryside. Hers was unlike the situation where a traditional peasantry had vested rights in the small plots they tilled, as in France. When industrialization came, it took courses which influenced urbanization in sharply differing ways. In Britain the quick turn to coal for powering machines went along with the landlessness of the rural working class to encourage industrialization within existing cities, and the cities' consequent growth to great size during the early years of the Industrial Revolution. In America, where waterpower remained the force for mechanization for fifty years after industrialization came and where the rural population in New England tended to be underemployed but landowning, factories were set up in the country bringing urban growth to the site and creating new cities in the nineteenth century. Few cities in England began as industrial places—not Birmingham, Manchester, Nottingham, or Cardiff, which just grew into such towns. In the United States many cities that began as factory towns changed over the years into more broadly based urban centers.

We will consider the industrial city under each of these adaptive processes—enlargement of the existing settlement in Britain and initiative of new urbanization in America. In each case the three aspects of the physical city—form, function, and connection—as well as the human systems at work there—the journey-to-work, the provision of housing apart from ties of employment, and the expanding role of the nuclear family—are considered.

The Modern City

The commonly used term "postindustrial city" contains such a misapprehension of the past that we will not use it. It suggests several partially or completely wrong assumptions: (1) that in a clearly defined period of the "industrial city," industry has been the main cause of urbanization, (2) that there was a clearly defined "preindustrial time" with demonstrably "preindustrial cities," and (3) that the post-Second World War trend toward the substitution of high energy consumption for high labor input will persist. The basis for the term is particularly Gideon Sjoberg's title *The Preindustrial City*, which in a world of assumed symmetry seems to many to require a "postindustrial time."[3] Sjoberg tells us that "[o]ur principal hypothesis is that in their structure, or form, preindustrial cities—whether in medieval Europe, traditional China, India, or elsewhere—resemble one another closely and in turn differ markedly from modern industrial-urban centers." Sjoberg means by "form," "numerous patterns in the realms of ecology, class, and the family, as well as in their economic, political, religious, and educational structures, arrangements that diverge sharply from their counterparts in mature industrial society." If the word "form" is used in its more normal sense of the physical characteristics of cities, then the resemblances are too slight between the medieval and the Roman city to justify such lumping together. And even in many institutional characteristics—such as the national economic system—a rather fundamental difference is apparent between the preindustrial Roman city, the preindustrial medieval German town, and the equally preindustrial English port of the seventeenth century.

Many objections may be raised to Sjoberg's work; for instance, his dichotomy of human experience into a "feudal" time and an "industrial-urban" society is too gross. The Middle Ages were far from entirely feudal and more recent centuries even more so. And much of the industrialization in the past and even now is not so

[3]*Gideon Sjoberg*, The Preindustrial City: Past and Present, *Glencoe, Ill.: The Free Press, 1960. The quotation is from pp. 4-6.*

very urban.[4] If Sjoberg's "preindustrial city" was not really preindustrial, then the modern city doubtless cannot be labeled "postindustrial." It is simply modern in the sense that it is the city of our own experience.

To date the beginning of the modern city is difficult. As I wish to look in detail at the modern city of the United States, I have adopted the close of the Civil War, basically a hundred years ago, as the beginning of modern urbanization. At the close of the war, the United States had nearly overtaken Britain as the premier industrial nation, was incontestably the greatest agricultural producer, and incidentally was a military power with which Europe had to contend. When after Appomattox we frowned southward, the Emperor Napoléon the Third quickly withdrew to Europe, leaving the unfortunate Maximilian to a usurper's justice before a firing squad in 1867. And when we expressed our just indignation at the unneutral support of the rebel cause by the English ruling classes the response was a rapid setting up of a quasi-independent government for Canada, shed of the more obvious features of British imperialism, under the British North America Act, also of 1867. If the United States could without firing a shot face down the two imperial giants of the world, little question remains that this immediately post-Civil War period was the beginning of the American century of urban dominance, and the beginning of the modern city, for our purposes.

[4]This is not the place to pursue a full critique of Sjoberg's work, and I am not the man for the job. John Langton in a recent article has compared Sjoberg's and my own ideas on the "preindustrial city" and though finding us both wanting, still decides "Vance's stress upon the importance of economic power and relationships as ecological determinants within the city undoubtedly gets nearer to the truth of the matter than Sjoberg's feudal social order, in which the dominance of an elite group was derived from non-economic and extra-urban sources." John Langton, "Residential Patterns in Pre-industrial Cities: Some Case Studies from Seventeenth Century Britain," Institute of British Geographers, Transactions No. 65, July, 1975, pp. 1-27. The note is to page 22.

Periods of Initiation and Adaptation

The times of initiation of urban development must of necessity be infrequent. When the archaic Greeks began city building early in the first millennium before Christ, they could do so in a situation of considerable freedom, a situation that did not come again in history. Instead times arose of only relative freedom: at the onset of town formation soon after the year A.D. 1000 when the medieval city was shaped rather in opposition to the land in which it must stand; again in the twelfth century when a number of wastelands of Europe (those in southern France, in Germany east of the Elbe, and somewhat later in the areas of Spain recaptured from the Moors) were the scene of active town founding in the form of bastides; and most strikingly in the North American New World where, after 1600, more towns were formed within the course of three centuries than had ever been true in such a short period of time. Because we can learn most about urban morphogenesis by observing the process of urban initiation, we will concentrate on these particular scenes of what was a continuous urban experience.

Contrasted to the times of real urban initiation were times of adaptation to changing demands on cities, or responses to more limited catastrophes visiting particular cities. Times of significant adaptation, of great concern in a study of urban morphogenesis, include the Persian Wars that destroyed so many Greek towns just after 500 B.C.; the conquest of Greece by Rome, and the supercession of Greek practices by those of the more directly religious Romans; the shift from the more narrowly bounded medieval to the more commercially extensive mercantile city; and the onset of industrialization at the turn of the nineteenth century.

Finally, we may define times of urban decline or stagnation: the course of urban history following on the decline of Rome; the demographic crisis in urban history as a consequence of the plagues of the late Middle Ages; and the more narrowly regionalized experiences of Italy and Germany in the seventeenth, eighteenth, and early nineteenth centuries. In a search for process such times hold only minor interest.

The General Processes of Urban Morphogenesis

Before looking at actual evidence of how cities are shaped and transformed over time, we may usefully ask what the general processes of urban morphogenesis are.

Land-Assignment

The first dynamic of city form applies as readily to the adapted city as it does to the newly initiated one. In each case some basis must be established for the assignment of land within the city to its several possible uses. If we deal with the initial stage of urban development, no great problem arises in resolving land-assignment, with few if any competitors for the often single function that brings a town into being. Once the town grows and evolves, however, problems of land-assignment are likely to be knotty. It is far from automatically the case that the first use in time has the primary choice in internal space. Quite possibly, that first use may be shunted aside in favor of a later but more economically aggressive function.[5] For this reason the process of land-assignment is essentially the first dynamic at work in the city. It operates in two ways, serving during the period of initiation as the major determinant of the design of the place and during a period of transformation as the major determinant of the processes of adaptation.

Connection

The second process to bear upon the morphogenesis of cities is that of connection. Once a settlement grows beyond the level of a village or a small town, the matter of connection must be taken into account for its own innate qualities. These qualities have two expressions: internalized and inter-functional connections. Ties exist between such functional areas as come into exis-

tence within the city; there are even connections internal to such a functional cluster of activity, which John Rannells called *linkages* (in a study establishing the various expressions of connective relationships).[6] Thus, we may adopt his term to refer to internalized connections.

For the ties external to the functioning cluster we may easily adopt the common descriptive English term, the *journeys*, which fall into several obvious classes—journeys-to-work, to shop, to sell goods, to attend to social needs, and a number of others. These connections are inter-functional.

Quite a bit has been written about these journeys, most commonly about those to work or to shop. Heightened concern for social welfare in cities has recently turned the attention of geographers to such questions as the "delivery of medical service," access to employment, and the availability of cultural institutions. Although these many different journeys are strong shaping forces in the physical build of cities, apparently only my writing on the journey-to-work has dealt specifically with the morphogenetic contribution of repeating movements internal to the city.[7] The medium of transportation can be shown to play a critical role in determining the form of the city shaped by the journey-to-work (see the "Labor-shed" article), a statement that must be construed in both physical and financial terms. Thus, the impact of transportation innovation will be differentiated by class of income and type of employment.

The connection between workplace and residence throughout human history before the early nineteenth century, and before *the generalization of housing*, required few journeys-to-work. But with the development of massive factories employing hundreds or thousands, this journey rose to great importance, and its dynamic impact on city form was great indeed.

[5]*For a presentation of the major questions with respect to land-assignment and the practices that have grown up under different economic systems, see James E. Vance, Jr., "Land Assignment Practices in the Precapitalist, Capitalist, and Postcapitalist City," Economic Geography, Vol. 47 (1971), pp. 101-120.*

[6]*John Rannells, The Core of the City, Publications for the Institute for Urban Land Use and Housing Studies, Columbia University, New York: Columbia University Press, 1956.*
[7]*My elucidation of morphogenetic processes related to the internal journeys is contained in three articles: "Labor-shed, Employment Field, and Dynamic Analysis in Urban Geography," Economic Geography, Vol. 36 (1960), pp. 189-220; "Housing the Worker: The Employment Linkage as a Force in Urban Structure," Economic Geography, Vol. 42 (1966), pp. 294-325; and "Housing the Worker: Determinative and Contingent Ties in Nineteenth Century Birmingham," Economic Geography, Vol. 45 (1967), pp. 95-127.*

Initiation and Transformation through Adaptation

Constantly in attendance to these processes are those already mentioned—initiation of form and its transformation—which need no further elaboration in this simple catalogue of forces at work in cities.

Capital Accumulation and Transfer

The next process to be considered is that of capital accumulation and investment—transfer—for the construction of the physical forms of the city. In the simplest terms, we must be aware that at the stage of initiation little resource (of labor or capital) will be available for the creation of large buildings or vast built-up areas. The exception to this rule shows its validity: when a city is created from outside in response to the desires of economic or political interests elsewhere, the general truth that the beginnings of urbanization are likely to be small and tentative, and organic in form in all likelihood, is not always applicable. The Romans could build elaborate towns on the Dalmatian coast through transfer payments from elsewhere, just as Washington and Brasilia were built. But if a town were to grow on its own, it must do so by accumulation of resources to support that increased size. In part, the repeated reconstruction of towns results from a sort of economic ratchet, which makes do with existing physical provision until the resources are available for enlargement, modernization, and a greater show of prosperity and probity. This ratchet had already become a part of the dynamics of cities in Greek times when it was expected that successful leaders would endow Athens with new monuments, to celebrate themselves and to gain the approval that was Athens' to give.

In the Renaissance the ratchet was so fast-moving that cities could hardly stand the strain. Popes and princes had to assert their power and culture by rebuilding, not so much to improve the functioning of the city as to magnify its grandeur. The popes did have fountains built in Rome, but many more closer to the needs of the people could have been built if the worldly glorification of the papal reputation had been pushed farther into the background.

In modern America, the hand of business has turned the ratchet, leading to the construction of office buildings of great boasting and inhuman sheltering. The glass-curtain-walled structure in a hot sunny climate cannot be seen as functional, but rather as showing the corporation administration to be *au fait* with style, if not with the desirable conditions of labor. When energy becomes more costly, as assuredly it will, the folly of much of modern skyscraper architecture will be emphasized, and a new ratchet for reconstruction will take hold.

Speculation

Even before the seventeenth century, speculation on land in cities had begun, but by then two necessary preconditions had come into being: (1) the creation of a system of capitalism needed if individuals were to engage in this activity and profit from the sale of land, and (2) the understanding, rough as it might be, of the patterning and transformation of the physical structure of cities, which was required if investors were to anticipate change in use value, and profit from it speculatively.

A process had transpired in medieval times which we might justly term "proto-speculation." Individuals and institutions, particularly church foundations, had commonly let out for an annual rent lands and buildings in their possession. Kings and great ecclesiastics who held lands commonly joined in *paréage* with bastidors seeking to found a town and gain, again in parity with the settlers, a greater profit on the success of the place than they would have gained from the simple agricultural, or even pastoral, use of their lands. In any event, they earned their *cens* (quitrent) from the settlers in a fashion far more stable than was true of their portion of the manorial production. But under *paréages*, capital (in the sense of land) was tied up for long periods of time. True speculative profits were not so readily obtained as under later practices of fully developed capitalism. Nonetheless, the act of bastide formation was an excellent training ground for the later practices of capital formation.

Planning and the Market

Planning has been a process at work in cities from the very earliest times. When cities were the creation of the king's whim, they were most assuredly as planned as were facets of New York City built to the whim of Robert Moses. To a very considerable degree, any preconceived town pattern is an act of planning; it always contains assumptions as to the desirable gross form of the place, its probable size and function, and a number of other culturally derived "goods." Only since the development of the capitalist city in the sixteenth century has planning become a separate concern, one viewed by its proponents as a white-hatted defense of the interests of society against the black-hatted interests of capitalism and speculation. The critical point is that the capitalist city was the city of the individual, dominant in a way that the medieval and earlier towns were not. Then, the gild or the monarch, or both, were both in control of city development and presumably so vested with authority because they held the common good paramount. With the introduction of capitalism, no such presumption of the care for the common good could be made. An urban dualism was introduced: development, speculation, and individual desire were seen as the work of a god of darkness; restraint, public action, and authoritarian control were seen as the work of enlightenment. In this dualism the rub comes in the creation of city forms. Under absolutist governments there was usually established a view of appropriate culture and design, as well as proper purposes and undertakings. The rich could be allowed to move to London by royal exception, but not the poor. In imperial Rome, in the Paris of Napoléon III, and in the London of Victoria, taste was arbitrary, but all-powerful, as the Albert Memorial so sadly confirms.

For all the castigation of "private" development as the work of a god of darkness, it did possess a mechanism of popular control and adjustment lacking under either royal fiat or much of latter-day planning. The *mechanism of the market* determined the form and extent of development and periodically adjusted those qualities to the shifting demands of the people. The main trouble with the market until recently has been that it reflected the interests of only a part of the populace: a large part in the United States because of the higher standard of living and the lesser role of established privilege, but a much smaller part in Britain. In this contrast is to be found much of the difference between the two nations in appraisal of the efficacy of the market and, in turn, of the need for planning.

In a very specific way, planning and the market mechanism are necessary components of a single overall process shaping urban form. As the market is reduced in contribution, planning must be increased; if one is in complete control, serious deficiencies in morphogenesis result. The experience with the industrial city of the nineteenth century, which we will see through Engels' eyes, confirmed how insufficient was total capitalist, market, control; experience in eastern Europe with the total municipalization of land and total control of development by planning has shown how equally rigid and disregardful of the individual an anti-market system can be.

Segregation, Congregation, and Junction

The activities that grow up in cities show a strong tendency to come together in limited areas of specialization drawn into a congregation by the internalizing linkages among them. Whether it be the use of shared sources of materials, the selling to a common body of customers, the practice of a specific religion, or the speaking of a particular language, the institutional practice shapes the *process of congregation*, which is internally induced and highly responsive to matters of scale. A few persons doing a particular thing normally congregate, but not in an obvious congregation. When numbers are increased to the point they present an areally extensive pattern, then a geographical congregation is to be seen.

In contrast to a congregation is a similarly extensive grouping of ostensibly similar individuals induced by external forces. Instead of being *drawn* together they are *forced* together by segregation. The *process of segregation* is more widely attributed than is justified by facts. To show the difference between congregation and segregation, we may examine the case of orthodox Jewish settlement in American cities. One of the provisions of orthodox Judaism is that the members of a congregation may not drive between sundown on Friday and sundown on Saturday. Thus attendance at a synagogue, which is essential to the practice of the cult, must be on foot. Clearly a very strong force is at work among orthodox Jews to live near the synagogue. At times allegations have been made that Jews are discriminated against, and segregated in housing. To the extent they seek to maintain such a congregation as I have described, this assertion is invalid. On the other hand, those American blacks who are of vastly varying religious attachment, often of quite diverse birthplaces, and frequently of different education and income levels, who similarly "live together" in a black district, are obvious victims of segregation unless they live there through personal choice, shunning the socially upward and geographically extensive mobility of the American suburb. Finally, in American cities the blacks are mostly segregated, whereas the Jews, Italians, Poles, Germans, and Swedes are largely congregated.

The operation of congregation and segregation reaches beyond the housing of particular social groups into the assignment of land to commercial, industrial, and institutional activities. Recently we have seen a strong tendency for medical facilities to congregate just as medieval teaching functions congregated into student quarters such as the Left Bank in Paris, which was already a student quarter with extraterritorial administration during the Middle Ages. In the commercial aspects of city life, congregation works mainly along institutional lines. In the classical city, the government often set up specific quarters for tradesmen and required their congregation there, particularly if they were foreigners complying with extraterritorial laws and social practices. In later centuries the institutional basis changed: commonly, the need to grant a charter of rights to a collegial body, a synthetic person or corporation, required congregation. The gild and the occupation congregation were the result. In this way the corporation could supervise and in turn be easily supervised.

Junction is a subprocess which seeks neither to collect together by internal desire nor to exclude through

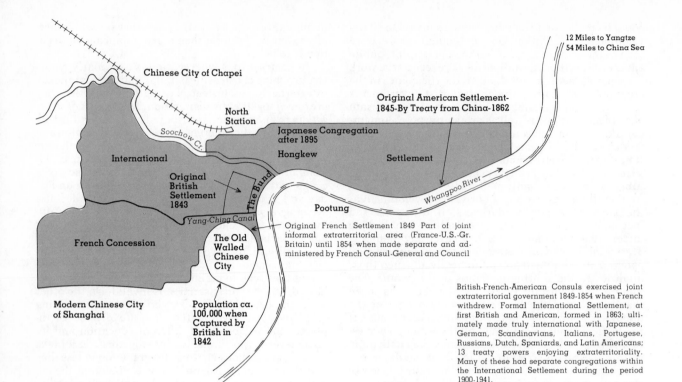

Chinese City of Chapei

North Station

Original American Settlement-
1845-By Treaty from China-1862

12 Miles to Yangtze
54 Miles to China Sea

Soochow Cr.

Japanese Congregation
after 1895

International

Hongkew

Settlement

Original
British
Settlement
1843

The Bund

Whangpoo River

Yang-Ching Canal

Pootung

The Old
Walled
Chinese
City

Original French Settlement 1849 Part of joint
informal extraterritorial area (France-U.S.-Gr.
Britain) until 1854 when made separate and administered by French Consul-General and Council

French Concession

Modern Chinese City
of Shanghai

Population ca.
100,000 when
Captured by
British in
1842

British-French-American Consuls exercised joint
extraterritorial government 1849-1854 when French
withdrew. Formal International Settlement, at
first British and American, formed in 1863; ultimately made truly international with Japanese,
German, Scandinavians, Italians, Portugese,
Russians, Dutch, Spaniards, and Latin Americans;
13 treaty powers enjoying extraterritoriality.
Many of these had separate congregations within
the International Settlement during the period
1900-1941.

*Pre-war Shanghai was a
city of congregations, in
this case clearly de-
fined by treaty provisions
between China and the
Treaty Powers.*

external pressure. Its purpose is simply to keep things together for mutual benefit. In junction all institutions divided are in basic agreement as to the wisdom of the process. It is meant to apply specifically to the matter of providing connectivity among various congregations, if you will, to afford a pattern of use and form common to all congregations.

The street is a concrete example of forms introduced by the *process of junction* to gain universal interconnection. Commonly within the medieval city, quarters were so self-contained as to be forbidden and largely unknown to outsiders. These areas are often called "residential mazes" with the idea that they were deliberately made so arcane that the outsider could not pass easily about the quarter. In a sense this practice would be a negative process, one of disjunction. In a rather striking example of the conflict between congregational concerns and those of junction, we may observe that the present argument as to freeway building

within American cities resolves itself in these terms. Many city congregations view the freeway as an intrusion on their "rights" to the unrestricted use of "their land," yet they expect when they wish to go elsewhere to have junction—freeways—that get them there with expedition and ease. San Francisco began this disjunctive movement in the early 1960's when it refused more urban freeways, yet the flood of San Franciscans heading for resorts on weekends makes necessary driving in the surrounding areas dangerous and unpleasant. More recently in the city of Berkeley, where local social congregation in neighborhood "turfs" is carried to an extreme, a street-closing program has been undertaken which fundamentally returns a modern city to the conditions of the medieval Italian city-republic with its clan quarters forbidden to outsiders.

Morphogenesis as Synthesis

Although these processes have been dealt with individually, obviously they work in conjunction to shape the city. This overall effect of processes is what I have called urban morphogenesis—the creation and subsequent transformation of city form. Morphogenesis, like most processes, operates more radically at some times than others, with intervening periods of conditional equilibrium. The medieval city could persist so long as the occupational household combined the residence and work place of most employed hands. But with the onset of the Industrial Revolution this correspondence was no longer true; the journey-to-work was introduced, and the conditional equilibrium of the city was so disrupted that a new era of massive morphogenetic change was induced, leading in the end to a new form of the city with residential separation and strong class congregation. Other disruptions of equilibrium can be introduced by new productive processes (the suburban factory or warehouse), new transportation (the automobile suburb and outlying shopping center), or new social conditions (the flood of rural poor into central cities). Social and morphogenetic processes interact constantly and intimately but social process does not subsume all of the explanation of city form. We must look at morphogenesis itself to find a full answer to how the city got its shape.

In the end all is change, though it may come at differing rates. When we ask how the city got its shape we may think back to Kipling's elephant's child who was "full of 'satiable curiosity, and that means asked ever so many questions'" during "High and Far-Off Times." For us the first of those times is perhaps more Far-Off than High. We must turn next to archaic Greece to observe the first usable example of the interacting forces and processes that create urban morphogenesis. So we must now set off "a little warm, but not at all astonished" to seek an answer to the way the city got its shape. In so doing we must try to share with Kipling's Mariner the practice of "infinite-resource-and-sagacity."[8]

[8]*Rudyard Kipling, "The Elephant's Child,"* Just So Stories, *New York: Doubleday Page & Company, 1917. The second quotation is from "How the Whale Got His Throat."*

2.   THE GODS LOOK DOWN: THE CLASSICAL CITY

For several millennia before our scientific age, not much thought was given to why cities existed, or why they stood where they did. They were thought to be part of the organized world given to man by gods or God, who decided upon their form and placement. Even in the more recent Christian era, though the divine generosity was less formal, people continued to thank God for His providence and to seek His support in a preservationist instinct. These thoughts represented faith, not scientific curiosity; so long as they persisted little concern was given to the actual origin of cities, the provenance of their morphology, or their placement in the world's space. Acts of God were not necessarily intelligible to men so, in essence, why ask about them? The worm of curiosity so condemned in Genesis peeped out again only in the last century when the post-Darwinian students looked at the origin of man, and those interested in cities began in similar fashion to question the neatly divine origin of those places.

Although Darwinian thought may have made a shambles of Eden and other divine contributions, such as monarchies, paradoxically, the evidence strengthened that gods really did create the earlier cities—not in reality, but certainly as humans conceived the truth. Paul Wheatley and others have looked at the origins of early cities[1] but without considering the morphological process at work in them, which we shall now summarize.

The Classical City of Divine Architecture

The signal feature of pre-Christian urban history was the belief that the gods played a central role in both foundation and organization. Almost all towns were felt to be protected and occupied either by individual gods or gods in pantheon, but not all towns were physically structured in accordance with assumed divine logic. In times of slow growth, there was a much stronger force toward locally-based and determined structure with practical considerations paramount, or *organic growth*, than toward the application of a divine architecture. *Preconceived growth* is town planning and

For its full unfolding two conditions are needed. The age must be one in which, whether through growth or through movements of population, towns are being freely founded or freely enlarged, and almost as a matter of course attention is drawn to methods of arranging and laying out such towns. And secondly, the builders of these towns must have wit enough to care for the well-being of common men and the due arrangement of ordinary dwellings.[2]

The real problem to our coldly rational eye was to sustain a plan. Slow expansion allowed for forgetfulness or changed concepts, whereas an initially complete layout of the city, or its rebuilding after a catastrophe, permitted the single integrated concept to be applied.

The most ancient world held relatively few states large enough to require a number of cities, so even preconceived plans applied to a single city or a small system of cities. As states expanded geographically, the strong urge was toward replication of design, notably so in states of reasonably central administration. Two conditions had to be met: (1) the city must have rational expectations of survival and prosperity—not always the case in a time when destruction by a conqueror could be so complete that a place eluded efforts to rediscover its nature or occasionally its specific location, and (2) the central authority had to desire to create an urban orthodoxy that would help to maintain the widespread state. Consistent views have always tended to produce similar morphologies.

In seeking a standard solution to the physical form of cities, city founders could most probably turn to the gods for justification, if not for guidance. The main public expression of urban life was religious and some argue that cities first came into existence for religious purposes. The temple anchored the city at the close of a history of nomadic wandering about the land without fixed abode. Around that temple, residence was spread; in the wake of residence came the trading and handworking activities that ultimately supported the city. The main public buildings of the Greek city were temples of one sort or another. This narrow inheritance made the American attempt in 1783 to use the Greek Republics as a model for the restoration of republican government so peculiar in architectural terms. Temples make dark and drafty houses and bad places of assembly. Yet the Greeks seem to have had no other building that anyone would find worthy of emulation in a cold or wet climate. The Greek theater was even less appropriate to American climatic conditions than the temple, and the acropolis, a fortified hilltop, was

[1]*Paul Wheatley*, The Pivot of the Four Quarters: A Preliminary Enquiry into the Origins and Character of the Ancient Chinese City, *Chicago: Aldine Publishing Co., 1971.*

[2]*F. Haverfield*, Ancient Town-Planning, *Oxford: The Clarendon Press, 1913, p. 11.*

*The Hephaisteion, ca. 449–
444 B.C.*

not needed.[3] Seeking to copy Greek buildings, we could find only the temple.

Any generalization about the internal structure of Greek cities is difficult because only fragmentary evidence survives, and because the "city-state" political organization worked somewhat against the shaping of a *standard* city. Arthur Evans[4] tells us that Knossos in Crete possessed a three-element structure with (1) a labyrinth at the center, serving as the palace of the

king-priest by housing his retainers and the various ceremonial courtyards, reception rooms, and storehouses of a powerful ruler. (2) Around the palace were ranged a series of free-standing "burgher" houses occupied by the leading townsmen, separated from one another by narrow lanes that were little more than drains. The palace and townhouses were so continuous that a close-packed town was created. (3) Farther from the religious-political heart of the city was a broader band of lowly abodes, built of rubble, seemingly leaning on each other in groups of two- and three-story buildings that formed a *street-block* delimited by narrow lanes.

Several important facts emerge from this description. As early as ca. 1560 B.C., class stratification of the town was demonstrated by both geographical and architectural distinction. Whatever the class of dwelling, the building, either free-standing or as a street-block, possessed a fundamental *locational identity*. The lines of access to the houses, lanes, alleys, and narrow ways—which can hardly be called streets—

[3]*For a discussion of the impact of Greek and Roman thought and urban morphology on nineteenth-century America, see James E. Vance, Jr., "The Classical Revival and Urban-Rural Conflict in Nineteenth Century North America,"* The Canadian Review of American Studies, *Vol. IV, No. 2 (Fall, 1973), pp. 149-168.*
[4]*Arthur Evans,* The Palace of Minos, *London: Macmillan Co., 1921-1936.*

followed upon the placing of buildings instead of the building site coming into existence from the street-plan, as today. A certain modular quality to houses is suggested; note the very clear distinction between the burghers' and the laborers' dwellings, but the absence of distinction among the derivative streets.

If we advance the notion that most cities have some sort of *normative component*, the house at the base and the quarter or district at the summit, then the size of the normative component is an observable and ready measure of the degree of "planning" or preconception to be found in the place. To add a single house is probably the most basic manner of growth for a town, requiring, in the simplest instances, only the decision of the builder and owner. To add a district or a virtually incremental city is the most elaborate form, and needs either a vast centralized power or a broad agreement among citizens. In any event, the ultimate design and size of the town must be perceived. Using this proposed scalar measure of the normative component we may say that the simplest or most dubious places add only buildings, with those increments serving to recount for us the unrecorded contemporary thoughts on the likelihood of the city's growth. Cities basically expand *organically*, with a house added when the need is felt and, in all probability, in a rather unstructured fashion. Growth merely takes place at the edge—the most central site still open for development. When wider knowledge of the probable future of the city or a grand design for its enhancement is available, the increments are likely to come in a more structured fashion and over a geographical area not necessarily limited to the physical edge of the city. If a massive quarter is conceived of, the houses can with reason be built over the entire area of the addition.

The Role of the Colony and Plantation

The division between organic and preconceived growth appears most clear when we consider the early instances of full-town planning, which came when population pressures forced an exodus from a prior place, most likely built along organic lines. When a city in the Hellenistic world reached a size that created a demand for food equal to that produced in the area that could supply the city, a self-evident pressure arose for some relief mechanism. Long-distance trade ties might have been established, with goods flowing in from a greater area, or the now too-great population could have been spread over a larger producing area. Both solutions were used in classical times, with the Greeks inclining toward migration and the Romans toward trade. Paradoxically, the political difference between the two states was greater than the morphological contrast in the cities they produced. Out of trade and tribute expansion, as well as other motives, came the Roman Empire and its pattern of urbanization. Out of the migration of people to some distance from the mother city came the confederations of Greek city-states.[5]

Roman provincial cities were truly colonial settlements in the modern sense; a large group of inhabitants, normally of indigenous origin, were held in political domination by outside conquerors. The layout of both city types was almost exclusively preconceived. If we reflect on the necessary prerequisites for such planning, we realize that some notion of the ultimate size and function of the place was required, as well as both the authority and precept to create and execute an overall design. Whether a Greek plantation city or a Roman colonial city was to be built, its founders had these requisites. Other ancient societies as well possessed them, particularly when the religious nature of the place was clear. As distant in space and society as were ancient China and pre-Columbian Yucatan, each produced preconceived towns, seemingly because each viewed the town as a critical part of religion. But our search is for the emergence of the city in a western society only quite recently become knowledgeable about either ancient China or the Mayan settlements. Similarity may have existed among the classical, Chinese, and Mayan notions of urban conception but we may reasonably view these as separate, independent origins rather than as any diffusion of a single creation. Thus, we may leave to others a concern for the nonwestern creations.

[5]*Unfortunately the term* colony *seems now to connote the control of an indigenous population by a ruling group introduced from outside. When the endless debates on "colonialism" take place in the United Nations, we hear as much confused terminology as piteous self-excuse. The Greek colonies were for the most part made up of Greeks or slaves they captured elsewhere; in the same way, the thirteen American Colonies were settlements of Englishmen. The Providence Plantations at the head of Narrangansett Bay provide us with an alternative term. It originally meant planting of men and women at some distance from their homeland, precisely the situation we deal with in classical times so, seeking to avoid the imprecise, polemic, and derogatory qualities of the term colonial today, let us call the creations of human migrations "plantation cities."*

The Role of Catastrophe

Faced with need to create a town, settlers or conquerors must have been forced to improve on experience. It is hard to imagine that any leader faced with the problem of laying out a town would merely build his abode, leaving all else to chance. Athens might have grown in that way but it was unlikely that fully supported Athenian plantations would. We do know that for a time plantations were rather inchoate in morphology, possessing the temple and the meeting place—the *agora*—but beyond that conforming to the socially structured but unplanned qualities of Knossos described above. Once the planting of settlements became common, rationality seems to have entered. The first recorded instance is slightly different from the simple plantation but it serves to bring out a second historical process in the shaping of cities, that of a physical catastrophe and its aftermath.

In 494 B.C. the Persians sacked and destroyed Miletus, the greatest of the Ionian plantations in Asia Minor. For fifteen years the city, or more exactly its remnants, was held by the conquerors, but after its liberation in 479 or 466 B.C., it was rebuilt on a preconceived, regular pattern. Again the necessary prior conditions were met; Miletus had been the greatest of Greek mercantile cities before 500 B.C., dominating the Black Sea trade and establishing some fifty trading entrepôts on the Hellespont, Propontis, and the Black Sea. Although the city never recovered that status after the Persian Sack, its rebuilders could reasonably impute to it a future deserving a true urban morphology. Yet in distinction to its earlier slow advance to supremacy in a mercantile settlement system, Miletus was now born both anew and nearly full-grown. Both the site and the probable scale of the new Miletus were determined; only the layout of the town seems to have been at issue.

The Modular Division of Land

Our records are almost nonexistent, though Aristotle confirms their truth when he tells that "Hippodamus, the son of Euryphon, a native of Miletus, [was] the same who invented the art of planning cities, and who also laid out the Piraeus [the port of Athens]."[6] The invention he made was not certainly unknown before his time but his role seems to have been to first bring it into a body of morphological practice, formalized and probably stated as a principle of town formation in an era of active town plantation, and to push its adoption. In Aristotle's words, Hippodamus was "a strange man, whose fondness of distinction led him into a general eccentricity of life . . . ." From the hands of this eccentric came the rectilinear street-grid, which has been endlessly criticized by recent generations of planners for being both too mundane and too monotonous, a strange fate indeed for Hippodamus's ideas.

The street-grid is fundamentally a land-division practice and is not necessarily conceived of as a particular circulation system. It does afford routes to get about the town; any public way will do that. But little evidence suggests that the grid was advanced for that purpose. Again Aristotle furnishes us the clue, in an instance where almost no others are to be had, when he tells us, "The city of Hippodamus [Miletus] was composed of 10,000 citizens divided into three parts—one of artisans, one of husbandmen, and a third of armed defenders of the state. He also divided the land into three parts, one sacred, one public, the third private: the first was set apart to maintain the customary worship of the gods, the second was to support the warriors, the third was the property of the husbandmen." The grid facilitated the creation, *de novo*, of a land-use and occupational separation when the design size was fairly apparent. Although laid out on the grid, Miletus contained empty street-blocks well into Roman times, and the streets of the grid so disregarded terrain as to make it obvious that their function was cadastral more than circulatory. Haverfield holds that the introduction of the grid came when

> In the Macedonian period the individual cities came to be parts of a larger whole, items in a dominant state, subjects of military monarchies. The use of public buildings, the splendour of public festivals in individual cities, declined. Instead, the claims of the individual citizen, neglected too much by the City-states, but noted by the

[6]*Aristotle,* Politics, *II,V (Jowett's Translation).*

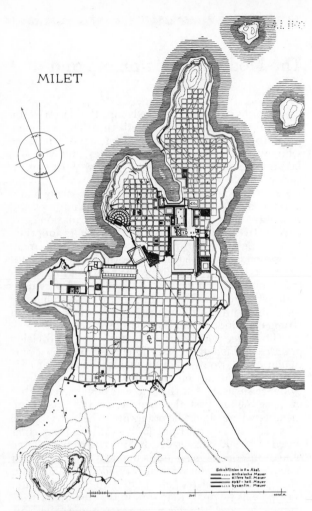

MILET

Map of Miletus as laid
out by Hippodamus, ca.
450 B.C. From von
Gerkan, Milet.

Difficult as it is to assert a simple causative tie between the grid-pattern town and the existence of responsible citizenry, some sort of interaction seems likely. Once the ordinary citizen—a member of the burghal class, the bourgeoisie, a body of freemen, or even the proletariat—enters into consideration in laying out the town, a quite natural force seeks the creation of a basically *modular division of land.* Looking again to Knossos, we may recall the *evolved division of land,* starting with, and centering on, the king-priest's palace, surrounded by the residential area for his retainers, and filled in at the edge by a band of mean housing casually thrown together by what we would call the working-class. Knossos' structure can hardly have been planned; at best, we can say that it must have emerged in response to what today we would think of as a land-rent principle—that is, the group with the better ability to pay for space is located closer to the city center or political seat than that with the lesser ability. Probably no actual "rent" or tax was paid but great differentials must have existed in the authority of the command of different classes for the use of specific sites. Clearly, strong class division must have existed from the beginning and militated against a cadastral regularity, though it seems quite logically not to have repressed a certain consistency in building-type within the specific class area.

An odd element of support for this notion of the classlessness of the grid pattern comes from ancient Athens in the laudatory comment of Demosthenes:

The great men of old built splendid edifices for the use of the State, and set up noble works of art which later ages can never match. But in private life they were severe and simple, and the dwelling of an Aristides or a Miltiades was no more sumptuous than that of an ordinary Athenian citizen.[8]

We must assume that class distinctions existed, but their puritanical repression seems to have produced a rather uniform, if distinctly mean, city. Athens seems to epitomize the city of organic growth, as inchoate as Knossos but not class-divided by reason of the self-denial of ostentation it honored. Public display was its glory; when we think of Athens our vision is of the Acropolis and its temples—its public buildings, if you will—not of its houses. As noted before when Federalist America sought to mold itself after Athens, it was forced to live in clapboard temples because no one wished to live in the Athenian house.

newer philosophy, found consideration even in town-planning. A more definite, more symmetrical, often more rigidly "chess-board" pattern was introduced for the towns which now began to be founded in many countries round and east of the Aegean. Ornamental edifices and broad streets were still indeed included, but in the house-blocks round them due space and place were left for the dwellings of common men. For a while the Greeks turned their minds to those details of daily life which in their greater age they had somewhat ignored.[7]

[7]*Haverfield, op. cit., pp. 16-17.*

[8]*Demosthenes, "Third Olynthiac," Oration, 25.*

Miletus: The System in the City

Reflection upon the creation of Miletus by Hippodamus brings forth one fact as central to the morphogenesis of cities as the more clearly perceived matter of regularity and the grid: the role of total conception alongside preconception. Perhaps Hippodamus's greatest contribution was in seeing the city as a total system and providing for the complexity of elements it needed. His three parts, though a bit crankish to our thinking, still represent the assertion of an integration of reality to include all the elements of an actual system. Even after several centuries, not all the street-blocks enclosed by the grid of streets were occupied. At first this fact might suggest that the conception and the need were greatly out of phase, but it could as well suggest that, in a conception of a total system, room must be left for growth and evolution. We can draw an analogy to the periodic table of elements. That table was devised before all the elements occupying places within it were known, and some still elude our search, but the overall system is perceived and erected because the basic relationships are understood. In the same way, Hippodamus understood, however oddly, the system of the city, and devised a physical form in which it could grow. The great contribution of such a context of appraisal is that it creates a form sufficiently adaptable to handle growth and change over a very long time. Instead of castigating the preconceived town, with its modular components, as dull-witted, unaesthetic, and somehow speaking of a lower use of man's intellect, we might better view it as one of the great inventions of the human mind. It raised proportion, adaptability, and a certain equality to the central place in the constitution of cities. We may then question the assumption, so common in European aesthetic thinking, that such a rare creation was mechanical and uninspired.

Greece: The System among the Cities

Is there a system among cities that has equally valid dynamics? Haverfield suggests that the Greek mind assumed that cities existed within a broader system than that internal to their borders. Without question, the central-place theory of Walter Christaller and his disciples furnishes such a broad system (see Chapter 3), but the existence of a larger systemic relationship among cities does not by itself prove Christaller to have been correct in detail, merely in broad purpose. When discussing the Mercantile Era of the sixteenth century (Chapter 6), I will suggest a different system among cities that fits better with geographical reality than does Christaller's rather medieval notion. And that mercantile system among cities would provide a far more convincing explanation of the geographical extent and the alignments of trade flow among the Greek city-states than could central-place theory. Finally these towns came into existence largely as part of a trading network, were successful or faltering with respect to those long-distance flows, and stagnated, and in many cases actually vanished, when the network of trade broke down.

Hippodamus's conception of the system within the city thus shaped the most universal expression of the morphology of towns; the conception, by the late medieval merchants of France and England, of the system among cities shaped the modern economic world as we know it. Details have in each case remained to be filled in, as in the periodic table, but the grand design was one of the mind—be it Hippodamus's or the great Renaissance architects' in the fifteenth century.

The Common Morphological Elements

We have no checklist of common elements in Greek cities. Nevertheless, certain consistencies may be cited to convey a general picture, even if it does not accurately portray any single place.

Every place, however chaotic or ephemeral, must have a ground plan, as even the medieval fair had a pattern for the duration of its meeting. The two versions of the ground plan were the evolved organic layout and the modular preconceived design. Common sense tells us that the organic was the earlier of the two. The older Greek cities appear to have had a point of location—often a rocky hill guarded by cliffs—on which the religious and defensive structures of the place were set. An *acropolis* may ultimately have been endowed with sacred significance but its precise location seems surely to have been a result more of geomorphology than of hagiography. Once its site was determined, the acropolis fostered the town, furnishing the religious justification for the place and protecting its inhabitants in case of attack. When the gods smiled upon it and the walls preserved it, a town could grow, soon clothing the hillslopes with other public buildings and housing.

To serve the acropolis itself what may well have been the first type of urban open space was shaped. We might term it a *circulation area*, implying a moderately equal proportion between length and breadth. The typical pattern would be a series of public buildings scattered about an area, as in Athens' Acropolis, or ranged around one, as became more typical of the wall of buildings enclosing the Greek *agora* in the planted cities.

The residential areas would logically cluster around the point of location for the city. At first they might exist in some form of *cellular accretion*, with the house being the unit of growth, located as close to the outermost existing house as building techniques and the most primitive form of circulation would permit. In essence intersitial space would be private, or at least excessively parochial, and certainly spatially minimal. Narrow paths between buildings would suffice and their direction could be determined by the needs of the immediately adjacent residents. The result was the *residential maze* we read of in the sociological literature, which is often endowed with, if not actually overweighted by, all sorts of psychological and defensive justification. The ancients themselves seem to have perceived the defensive qualities of the maze. Aristotle tells us the narrow and tortuous streets of Athens were an enigma deceiving to strangers and a labyrinth dangerous to enemies.[9] No doubt the maze produced these effects, but were they the reason the city grew in such a way? Cellular accretion would produce such effects even among most outward-looking people living in total peace with the world.

The problem with the residential maze is that, as a complete ring around the acropolis, it would serve effectively to immure the place against external contact. Thus, we may easily explain the next contrast we perceive, that between the paths of the maze and the preexisting pattern of roads that must have been present at the time the would-be inhabitants selected their point of location. These roads would have given access to the fields that fed the city, to battle sites, and to the sea that was Greece's national highway. As housing clustered about the acropolis, it would tend to group into mazes whose extent would be determined by the width of a sector interstitial between two roads to the outside and as deep as the peripheral growth of the city required.

The roads to the outside would quite easily allow greater visual depth than the paths of the maze, so we should not be surprised that newly endowed public buildings would be built where a road afforded a distant prospect of the structures. The wish to endow the city with a new building would be joined with the desire to make such a building impressive to the beholder, an objective impossible within the residential maze. Self-conscious architecture withers without public adulation so only the vernacular form can live in the crowded area of organic growth. For that reason the Greek cities, even when basically organic in their growth, appear to have evolved at least a limited use of preconception in the location of public buildings and the opening of vistas along which to admire them. It is a short step, intellectually, from such a limited use of forethought in morphology to its common practice. The need to use even rather short stretches of straight street to gain a perspective of a building was made necessary when we appreciate that in Athens, outside the *agora*, the only open space was an area of 20 by 40 meters in front of the principal fountain.[10]

Once the concept of the straight street as an adjunct of monumental public architecture had been established, several amplifications were possible. The street might be made straight over a greater distance, permitting an even more impressive view, or it might be made wider, to gain a similar end. Given the relatively undeveloped state of Greek engineering, only the second course was of much importance. Greek building depended almost wholly on post-and-lintel construction, which limited the clear span that could be accomplished and placed a rather low height limit on building. These building strictures seem to be the reasons for widening the street along which a prospect was to be gained. We learn again from Aristotle that Hip-

[9]*Pierre Lavedan*, Histoire de l'Urbanisme: Antiquité-Moyen Age, *Vol. 1, Paris: Henri Laurens, 1926, pp. 114-115.*

[10]Loc. cit.

podamus first urged both wide and straight streets. We can only infer that he may have been among the first to realize that to view public buildings properly it was more important that the street be wide than that it be excessively straight.

Hippodamus is generally credited with inventing the grid-pattern or at the least the orthogonal town, much as that claim is unfounded. What he did do was to institutionalize it as the way a proper city should be laid down. It is doubtful that his streets would today be thought very wide, but for their time they seemed so. In the absence of accounts as to why he surveyed as he did we can only guess that it was to permit the distant prospect and to gain modular land-division rather than to encourage an improvement in the exterior architecture of private dwellings. There can be little doubt that no real desire could be felt for the embellishment of the private house when its exterior could be seen from no more than 5 to 10 feet away. Thus we have little reason to question the plainness of the exterior walls of buildings in the housing maze, though we know their interior courts were often quite elaborately decorated. We may more easily imagine the extreme narrowness of these alleyways in the ancient Greek cities when we note Plutarch's observation that in those places the custom was to knock on the inside of a door before opening it (in the normal fashion outward) to avoid striking and injuring passersby. Consequently the Greeks had a word for knocking from the inside as well as the outside.[11] When the straight, widened street was introduced the revelation of the exterior of the house must have been even more startling than had been the exposure of the public buildings. From this we might expect a great flowering of domestic architecture, yet the evidence from Greek times is not very clear.

We must take note of the paucity of record that has come down to us with respect to everyday building in this first time period we have considered. We can reconstruct the groundplan of a number of Greek houses since excavation of ruins normally tells us where both the internal and exterior walls of the house were to be found. Seldom do we learn much about the superstructure. To use what little evidence we have, we must first set the frame in which the urban morphology evolved.

Internal Structure of the Greek City

The Greeks were in our lexicon an ancient people; thus they viewed the establishment of a city as a religious act. Augeries were employed, orientation to celestial bodies was common, and the nexus of the city always remained in its temples. The Greek temple was not a meeting place, but a building dedicated to a god in the hope of gaining protection, into which individuals entered to pay the god homage. If the populace or a selection from its numbers were to meet, that coming together normally took place outdoors. For that purpose the Greeks created a public open space, called the *agora*, which was first merely circulating space with buildings spread about it, as exemplified by Athens' "Agora of the Potters."[12] Apparently the role of the *agora* did not change as the years passed, but its shape became stylized; fairly clear evidence suggests that Hippodamus was the first to give regular form to the open space. His was a regular design for the *agora* to be laid out in the reconstruction of Priene, when that city of Asia Minor was moved away from the floodplain of the Meander River in the fourth century B.C. As far as we can tell Hippodamus advanced this notion of regularity more for religious and metaphysical reasons than for practicality. He was a Milesian, and in Miletus Thales and Pythagoras had introduced the primitive Egyptian geometry to the Greek world, and vastly improved upon it. Hippodamus worshipped order and possessed a mystical view of numbers, to the extent that he found three social groups in Greek society, three districts for their residence in the city, and even three divisions of law. In his hands it was quite to be expected that the formless circulating space of the early *agora* should be transformed into the rectilinear, ultimately enclosed, space of the *agora* as it was built in new plantation cities laid out during the two centuries before Christ.

Initially the *agora* was an area with symbolic buildings surrounded by potential meeting places but in Hippodamus's hands a ternary system was applied. The *agora* became a sheltering portico for the merchants in distant trade, a political forum with the creation of the Bouleuterion, and a marketplace for the sale

---

[11]*Plutarch*, Pyrrhus, *34, quoted in Lavedan*, op. cit., *p. 115.*

[12]*See Lavedan's discussion of the shape of the agora*, op. cit., *Vol. I, pp. 169-176.*

of all sorts of perishable goods.[13] And it was given an ordered outline. His subsequent design for the south *agora* of Miletus was that of public square so architectural in its details as to have been at home in the rational design of the Renaissance, nearly two millennia later. Surrounding these squares that were coming even in themselves to stand as monuments, with their porticoes of columns often several ranks deep, were cubicles which seem to have been intended as shops for artisans and merchants. As the squares were repeated in the design of a single city, it seems to have become true that one or several would take on the commercial functions leaving others to religious and political uses. Even within a single *agora*, specialization of activity would lead to clusters in parts of the vast open courtyard. On the west side of Priene's *agora* the sellers of food gathered; in the courtyard itself were numerous, ultimately a clutter of, monuments; and on the north side lay the offices of the magistrates.[14] In a real sense the *agora* was a primordial central business district, locationally unspecialized in its early days but ultimately possessed of distinct functional parts, sufficiently adjacent to each other to permit a single visit to accomplish several goals.

At first, in the stage when the *agora* was merely a place for buildings; those structures appear to have been specialized enclosures for religious or governmental purposes without the capacity to shelter crowds that such activities might today imply. Popular assemblies were held in the circulating space around the temples and rooms of the magistrates. As the central area evolved, two growth processes took hold. The first led to specialization of a building to the particular process it served, and the second to some vertical differentiation within the building. These *segregating processes* seem to have existed in cities from their inception, and in ancient Greece we can begin to trace their consequences.

The formal organization of the *agora* area, dating from the fourth century B.C., merely established a conscious design to care for the segregation that was taking place. Perhaps the first separation came when what have been called the "theatrical" activities of urban life came to be cared for in an open amphitheater in a form we still term a Greek theater. These theatrical undertakings were not merely drama as we know it but included all manner of public spectacles and activities which could be observed by large crowds; by *thea* the

Greeks meant "the act of seeing." Thus formal observation of a locationally fixed activity by a large group required a specialized building with an amphitheater shape.

The *agora* evolved into a formal area mainly in the use of its open space. The establishment of a theater was one separation; another was the creation of arcades. The Greeks termed them porticoes because they did not know how to build the arches that make a true arcade, but we may use that later term as more suggestive to us of the ground plan and enclosure of the place, if less correct as to its method of roof-spanning. These arcades were in truth specialization of open space, and intended for the ternary functions that Hippodamus observed in his analysis of the activities carried on in the *agora*. For religious activities, a long, perhaps more enclosed, portico was shaped, to which the name *stoa* was given. In these *stoa*, one of the walls parallel with the long axis was commonly solid while the other was colonnaded. Not all *stoa* were for religious purposes but when a covered spot for quiet meditation was sought, it normally became *stoa*like in form.

The second of the ternary functions, commerce, was apparently provided for in two ways. In some *agora*,

Plan of Athenian Agora.
From R. Martin:
L'Urbanisme dans la
Grece Antique.

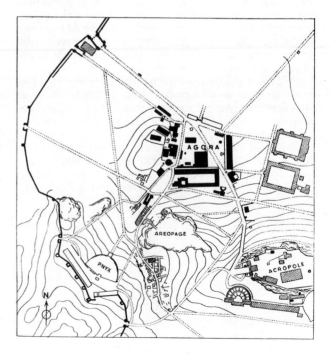

[13]Ibid., p. 171. Lavedan says, "The perishable food market had special provision, notably tables for the sale of fish, some pipes for washing, water in abundance, and cool cellars underground."
[14]Anthony Kriesis, Greek Town Building, *Athens: The National Technical University of Athens, 1965, pp. 75-86.*

trading took place in an open corner of the space; in others, a covered colonnade came into use. This portico produced a "public market" open on all sides but in which the wares were sheltered more from the ever-present Aegean sun than from its erratic rainfall. Such open porticoes of the merchants must have suffered from security problems, tolerable when the merchant came to the market for a single day but ever more onerous as he became a perpetual seller on that site. Although no records tell us why the change came, we may infer that the appearance of enclosed shops ranged along the sides of such a colonnade, leaving at least one side open, served to allow the merchant to be "in the market" without having to remove his wares each day at nightfall. From the fourth century B.C. onward, this alignment of shops has been a characteristic feature of marketplaces, and seemingly its evolutionary history had to be repeated in the Middle Ages and again in more recent times.

How much locational specialization was there in the *agora* market and in other areas of shops? The evidence exists that ultimately the *agora* became too small to contain all the merchants' premises. Athens, in addition to the potters' *agora* already mentioned, had quarters for marble workers (observed by archeologists through the vast accumulation of marble chips), armorers, and other craftsmen, as well as sellers of wine, oil, and other commodities brought into the city. We cannot establish a detailed picture of the commercial geography of Athens or other classical cities but we can reasonably accept the idea that one did exist. The segregation was horizontal, into the quarters already mentioned; it seems also to have been vertical to a small degree. Foundations remain that suggest the existence of upper-story storage of goods, as well as "living over the shop." We know there were two-story porticoes and we can only hazard that some might have been similar in layout to the multistory shop arcades of the nineteenth-century American city. The geographical anchor of all this internal structuring of commerical areas was an *agora*. Traders first congregated there; from there, they came to occupy more differentiated craft and traders' districts.

Not only was the *agora* the anchor of the commercial geography but also it served to fix the pattern of housing, which grew either organically or in a preconceived pattern around it. Both history and logic tell us that the first residential development came in the mazes of rather plain houses reached by narrow alleyways, and in a city of true antiquity such as Athens this pattern persisted even well after the time of Hippodamus. Housing-blocks are not clearly discernible in these cities, despite the fact that the Greek house became rather consistent in its room components, focusing on the courtyard of an inward-looking house. Un-

fortunately, our knowledge comes from more lustrous houses of the wealthy. The vernacular house of the urban masses remains in shadow.

For the rich, the house was a succession of often stately rooms, starting behind the plain facade with a columned *peristyle* and succeeding to the *megaron*, a vast classical equivalent of the Victorian drawing room. Like it, this room was often divided into two parts by door piers which afforded a wide-open connection when desired. Beyond, or sometimes before the megaron, lay the courtyard, off which were placed a lavatory, bedrooms, and entrances to a cellar or upper story, if these existed. The cellars may have been religious—related to the cult of the underworld more than the storage of amphora. We know little of possible upper floors because their evidence has been totally carried away by time. What emerged for the wealthy is a low house pierced by courtyards to let in light, walled against the outer world, and probably including ostentatious rooms for social purposes and mean quarters for slaves and retainers. We are interested less in the variation and elaboration of these houses, for they must have been numerically exceptional, than in their *enclosure*, their *low height*, and their *individuality*. They might be assembled slowly and in an evolving pattern, as in the older cities, or they might be grouped into street-blocks after the fourth-century urban revolution, but they remained cloistered, flat, and personal.

Today we wish to know how the masses lived, but the answers are sparse. Their houses were probably equally as enclosed and low as those of the aristocratic citizens, but perhaps less individual. Priene, for example, had some four hundred dwelling houses and an inferred population of around four thousand, yielding an average per-dwelling population that was unlikely to have been approached by the family of the poor.[15] As well there must have been decay of the house fabric on a major scale, as in Pergamon the Astynomi were enjoined to enforce housing repair upon owners and to fine them if necessary as a compulsion.[16] The poor probably lived in one- or two-room "houses" having party walls shared with adjacent "houses," small provision for sanitation, little specialization of rooms, and probably even less concern for the public impressions of the house. They had no room for entertaining, certainly little decoration, and probably no formal architecture. These buildings were built of rubble and perhaps easily prey to collapse; the surviving laws repeatedly call for the repair of houses. They were without water and sewerage provision, and almost certainly they classed as the most basic accommodation that could be envisaged. Because of their rickety qual-

[15]*Haverfield*, op. cit., *p. 43*.
[16]Ibid., *p. 54*.

ity it seems unlikely that they were multistoried. They did shelter the poor population, but more against the sun than the rains. The ancient commentators began a clamor against the mild Mediterranean winter that can only be understood in the context of badly designed and poorly constructed housing, either in the time of Pericles or of the Grand Tour of the eighteenth century. In classical times when regular planning was introduced calls were made for the east-west alignment of the important streets, with narrow crossing streets and an emphasis on the south-facing facade of the block.[17] These plans turned the backs of the houses to the cold north wind in wintertime and allowed the sun to flood the street. In a very early awareness of public hygiene, it was argued that the prevailing westerly winds would also clear the air in the compact housing quarters as they swept along the wider streets extending parallel to an east-west axis. Some Greek theoreticians even advocated houses taller on the south frontage, to gather winter heat, with low northern sides to protect against the bora blowing in winter from the north, and possessed of deep eaves to give protection in the summer from high rays of the implacable sun.

The cramped site of many Greek cities, on cliffed spots gaining natural protection or on narrow colluvial slopes between such rocky hills and the sea, meant that the suburb as we know it was missing. In a few instances Greek colonies already scattered around an estuary or on an extensive plain might grow together to form a polynucleated city. Yet this joining of formerly separate villages tended to leave them as discrete units, each possessing an *agora* and the other physical attributes of a city. The explanation of such continuing identity may lie in the traditional balance to be maintained between the supporting countryside and the city which produced it, particularly in the planted cities. So commonly does the history of a city show it to be a planted settlement with its hinterland growing about it in a seemingly indivisible symbiosis that we may question whether a higher level of association ever seemed fitting. We do know that despite the paucity of surviving evidence, the main segregation of groups within Greek cities shows up not so much racially or by class as by geographical origin. Attica, before Pericles called its residents into Athens (431 B.C.), consisted of *demes*—large villages strangely anticipatory of the New England town in location, function, and government—whose residents on arrival in Athens seem to have continued their geographical loyalties. As other peoples came to live in Athens or the Piraeus they settled in quarters grouped by place of origin. With such associations strong in the Greek mind, we may fairly say that Hellenic urban geography revealed little

of an hierarchical quality. Instead the process of collecting people periodically into the city—*synoecism*—forged an intimate tie between city and countryside.

When we ask what the limits were of classical Greek cities, notably Athens, we must begin to appreciate the evolutionary quality of the towns that ultimately gained ascendancy. Athens began as a fortification of the Acropolis within which all of the urban functions were clustered. Slowly the hilltop became the sanctuary of the gods and the citadel of the government, with housing pushed outward down the slopes of the hill. We know that these residential areas must have been enclosed by a wall, and that the focus of the commercial life of the city came to rest in the *agora* in a hollow between the Acropolis and another hill, the Pnyx. Probably in the sixth century B.C., we may reasonably assume that the *process of land-use separation* was already at work. The original area that was the whole town, the Acropolis in this case, had been transformed into a specialized area by the external clustering of those activities that could gain through migration. This shift was itself a process, as observable in archaic Athens as in twentieth-century New York, that led within a city district to *functional simplification*, wherein one use gains ascendancy and the others formerly intermixed with it depart to an area which they, in turn, may dominate.

The wall would continue to be pushed outward as this spread of the urban fabric took place. This constant juxtaposition of forces—growth pressing against circumvallation—would tend toward rachet-like expansion. As pressure built up within a particular wall, crowding would increase, leading in turn to a leap over the wall into what were unprotected sites. Those exposed sites would eventually call for a new wall for their protection and the city would reach a temporary adjustment of the forces of growth and circumvallation, only to start the rachet movement again if expansion continued.

Let us look specifically at Athens. In 480 B.C. the Persians invaded Greece, captured Athens, and destroyed both the buildings on the Acropolis and in the city. We may be convinced of an organic growth process in the morphology of cities but we cannot exclude extinction from it. But unlike a single organism, a city can survive as a vital force either by the flight of a component of its population, which returns to begin again, or by the transplanting of a new vital force from outside. In Athens' case the indigenous vital force continued the city's history. Themistocles led the Athenians back into the cycle of organic growth, which was an enlightened replication of past history. The first efforts were those of rebuilding the city's walls but ex-

[17]*See Lavedan, op. cit., Vol. I, pp. 142-146.*

perience survived and the functional simplification undertaken before the onslaught of the Persians was introduced at the beginning of the reconstruction of that city we now think of as Classical Athens.

The reconstruction of Athens took place in the century in which Hippodamus proposed the application of preconception to city structure. In fact, the port of the city, the Piraeus, was rebuilt on his plan, and ultimately connected by the "Long Walls" to Athens itself. As the city recovered its fabric, a pattern emerged that combined organic with designed growth. The *agora* was more regular than previously, and certainly much more massive, having several instances of a two-story *stoa* of shops, but it was not rectangular as in the truly new towns. The housing, what little we know of it, was improved and probably better served by streets, yet in no way did it match the beauty and order of the public buildings and public areas of the city. Only when the Romans came, initially in the second century B.C., does the domestic architecture seem to have received much attention.

In the second century A.D. Hadrian endowed Athens with many monuments, not least among them Hadrianopolis, a newly walled area of villas, gardens, and baths on generous sites. By the Roman period Athens had become rather an urban museum, repeatedly the recipient of benefactions from kings and magnates beyond its boundaries but exercising no function beyond the perpetuation of increasingly more archaic morphological solutions. The Greek city was the model for antiquity and Hellenic architecture was its paradigm until the Romans faced the problem of designing and constructing a thousand towns and of engineering buildings on a scale previously unimagined. The ironic *finis* to the Greek urban epoch came in 15 B.C. when the Roman magnate Vipsanius Aggripa presented Athens with an *odeum,* to seat a thousand persons, built along the lines of Greek architecture with a roof-span of some twenty-five meters. But the enclosure collapsed and had to be reduced to two halls seating only five hundred.

Rome Creates an Urban Geography of the West

The busy disorder in the private parts of the city and the perpetuation within the walls of loyalties and associations stemming from the village origins of the people have given the Greek city an oriental cast in the eyes of most western observers. And the city-state that formed the ultimate unit of Hellenic life and politics was obviously an expression of the joint forces of sensate satisfaction and social intimacy which westerners have envisaged as more strongly motivating the peoples of the Levant than those of the more primitive and puritanical west. Hyperbole and individuality were to become keys to Greek character while democracy emerged as the expression of her political ideals. As Aristotle saw the city-state, "It comes into existence for the sake of mere life, but exists for the sake of the good life."[18] The goals were highly personal and immediate, a fact clearly reflected in the Greek attitudes toward city morphology. The house was a family affair located within a residential maze, a situation quite logical to a self-concerned parochial people. Religion was personalized, without a class of priests. Government was conducted, in the ideal, by an approximation of universal manhood suffrage and, in practice, by at least aristocratic representation. Education was at the hands of tutors. The glory of the city-state was in the quality of life there obtainable. One wonders, in fact, how self-denying Sparta was; perhaps only the contrast gave her reputation to her. In any event the city-states tended to adopt individual and locally justified morphologies eschewing any consistency that might permit us to designate "The Greek City." The only consistency was introduced by the Milesian Hippodamus, reared in the birthplace of formal geometry and in the intellectual climate of rationalism, or even numerical mysticism, when he advanced the notion of the regular, grid-pattern town and the ternary division of functions within the city. Other Greek cities adopted this viewpoint toward morphology not out of any feeling of Hellenic solidarity but seemingly from a reverence toward rational thought and a craving for a domesticated and locally identified religion.

The long course of western urban experience has shown only occasional agreement with these ideals and

[18]Politics, *1252b 29, quoted in Cecil Bowra*, The Greek Experience, *New York: The New American Library, 1957, p. 77.*

practices so we must ask what interrupted the propagation of the Greek model of urban life. Certainly no more urbane design could have been found; never since classical Greece has the city been more completely the center of life, the ideal community, and the humanistic institution it then was. Utopians, beginning with Plato and Aristotle, "regarded the city-state as the logical end of social development and framed their conceptions of ideal societies on it."[19]

The propagation failed in the hands of the Romans, ironically the intended perpetuators of the Greek urban tradition. Their experience is a warning to us that simple replication of morphological components does not necessarily produce identical cities. The Romans followed the plans but changed the purpose, and the use came in the end to dominate.

The Romans in the beginning shaped a city-state much along the lines of those in the Hellenic east or in the planted Greek towns in southern Italy and Sicily. In Latium the symbiosis between countryside and city was similar to that in Attica. Leading citizens tended also to be leading landowners and farmers, on the model of Cincinnatus, so we may accurately look upon the early years of Rome as shaped by the Greek model of life. But the people living within the city-state of Rome were fundamentally different in outlook from the Atticans; whether the mythic mating of lupine bandits and the stolen Sabine women is an adequate explanation of the contrast can be argued. Clearly, however, the Romans took the basic Greek city form and turned it into an instrument of political and economic organization not inherited from Aegean society. Perhaps the seeds were there; the Greeks had used the city-state in their planted places, making it the missile of economic expansion and the institution of cultural identity. The Black Sea towns were Greek in thought, speech, and general culture even if their ties to Miletus were weaker than those the Romans later developed with their diaspora. The distant planted-towns, a number of which were in southern Italy, traded with Greece and lived in her culture, but were distinct in their fundamental identity and independence. They were equals to Athens, Sparta, or Miletus even if they might look toward them for intellectual guidance and markets for their goods.

What the Romans made of the city was an instrument of political and economic control. The Greek planters had been peers going to plant a new and equal Greece; the Roman colonists were delegates of the Roman state—be it republic or empire—going to occupy a point of control in the provinces. The Greek planted town was located for its local economic potential, whereas the Roman colony—and it was truly a

colony in the modern sense of shaping a colonial society—was placed within an elaborate system focussed on Rome and reaching outward to the borders, the *limes*, of the empire. When the system failed, as it did much later, the delegate-city failed in a way that Greece's planted cities never did; they persisted down to the Turkish invasion and then changed their stripes rather than abandon their existence.

Perhaps the contrast between the Greek and Roman cities can be accounted for by some complex behavioral theory of history, but our search remains focussed on the way the internal structure of cities in the west evolved. We will turn away from the contrast of the two leading classical cultures and look transitionally at one of the ancient world's lesser cultures, that of the Etruscans.

Catching the Attention of the Gods

In the words of Pierre Lavedan, "The Etruscan cities occupy a critical position in the history of urbanization . . . [because] All the structure (*l'amenagement*) of the Roman city was derived from them and, by Rome, that influenced was passed on to many people."[20] The contribution of the Etruscans was a ritual to be used in the setting up of cities to focus the attention, and thereby presumably the protection, of the gods on that particular place. Further, given a ritual of location and orientation, it would follow that the shape of the city would be predetermined. With a linear base and a specific size, probability would call forth the grid-pattern town, as apparently it did. Only when ritual is standardized for a fairly large group of people can it be looked upon as a shaping force for cities; otherwise it is only an idiographic explanation of the outline of a particular place. In Greece so long as no metaphysical quality attached to the laying out of towns, only the temples and *agora* were the common feature of cities, but, when the Hippodamian proposal was advanced, Greek cities became patterned, admittedly formed in

[19]Loc. cit.

[20]*Lavedan, op. cit., Vol. I, p. 98. Some recent writers disagree with Lavedan, finding Etruscan cities not so regular as he supposed and arguing instead that Roman towns were more shaped by the Greek than the Etruscan precedent. Thus, the view is advanced that the plowing of the sacred furrow was more a religious than a morphological control with the orthogonal shape coming from Greece rather than the structuring within the* pomerium.

response to rationalism rather than ritual of a simply religious sort. But among the Etruscans, the *libri rituales* governed their conduct in the founding of cities, the placing of gates, and the prosecution of daily life.

The city was seemingly the basic governmental unit with a League of Twelve Cities, comprised of a group whose membership list has not survived, standing as Etruria. When the Etruscans expanded, sometime before the sixth century B.C., from their hearth in present-day Tuscany both north to the shaded slopes of the Appenines and south into Latium and Campania, they shaped a "state" composed of two such duodecimal leagues. From their obscured origins through a considerable domination of a younger Rome by the Etruscan Tarquin kings down to the battle of the Vedemonian Lake (309 B.C.), Etruria was independent, wealthy, civilized, and emulated by the Romans. So, as Lavedan suggests, we must seek in her history the foundation of western urbanization as a morphological system.

The foundation of the Etruscan city followed a precise course, only the initial element of which is unknown to us. We cannot determine on what basis they chose the precise locations of the places, but evidence suggests that a combination of defensive position and productive tributary area would account for most choices. Certainly the Etruscans were not simple farmers shaping central-places in their midst; they dominated the Tyrrhenian Sea, controlled Corsica, and carried on an extensive long-distance trade which must have made them more wealthy than Rome almost until the advent of the Christian Era, as we have material evidence they were.

Once the site was chosen, the Etruscan ritual intervened and recourse was taken to consult the *auspices*, the tools of augurs. Auguries did not locate cities, but they might lead to the rejection of a proposed site. If those auspices favored the site, then they created a *mundus*, by dividing the place from the undifferentiated mass of land about it. The *mundus* came to be symbolized by a collection of monuments and temples, often located in the inner *pomerium*. To define a *mundus* an enclosing furrow must be plowed with a bronze share drawn by a white ox and a white cow harnessed together. At the proposed location of gates in the city

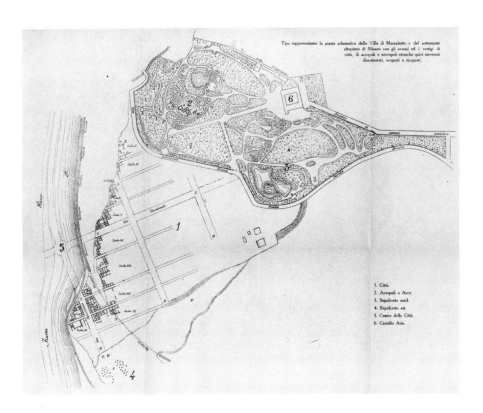

Map of Marzabotto, the Etruscan town.

The Etruscan Gateway of
Perugia furnishes evi-
dence of the size and
importance of cities in
the Etruscan league.
The loggia at the top
of the left buttress is
not part of the original.

wall, the share must be lifted to leave a connection to the outer world. The sod cut by the plow must be thrown inward, apparently as a symbolic beginning of the wall that ultimately would defend the city. That defense had ritualistic expression in the *pomerium*, which for the Etruscans was a band of ground on both sides of the wall left clear of obstruction. Such an enfilading band, shorn of its mystical qualities, remained common in European cities until the late

nineteenth century. It existed simply so attackers could be shot at along the length of the wall as well as before and behind it. For the Etruscans it was undoubtedly both a practical necessity and a symbol of the edge of the realm of the god's support, the *mundus*. The Romans lost much of the practical need for walls when they conquered their known world but they continued the practice of building light walls for their religious virtues. With the Roman acceptance of Christianity by Constantine in the fourth century A.D., those virtues seemed to disappear, but rather soon the practical need for circumvallation returned, to persist until long-range guns finally made walls obsolete in the late nineteenth century.

The world within the sacred furrow seems to have had no regular shape, posing a problem if we seek to derive any consistent pattern for cities. Some authors have tended to discount the Etruscans as the originators of the regular Roman town because the furrow did vary but Lavedan supplies a most plausible explanation. He argues that, though the furrow was irregular in shape, it was bordered on the inside by the band of open land, the *pomerium*, which could serve as a transition to a regular street pattern. But how do we account for the creation of a regular grid in an irregularly enclosed area?

The explanation lies in a second operation that attended the layout of the town, that of giving it its *orientation*. Urban creation required a baseline upon which division would be based, and it took no exaggeration of practice or mysticism to propose the rising sun in the *east* as the basis for orientation. Projecting a line thence to the point of the setting sun created such a baseline.

Before looking at how this base produced the full cadastral structure of the city, let us compare the Greek and the Etruscan city, with their contrasting solutions to the same problem at very much the same time in history. The Greeks created the domain of the gods in the acropolis; the Etruscans defined the gods' domain as the full area within the *pomerium*, though religious activities came to be centered in the collection of monuments and temples in the *mundus*. For the Greeks the city grew around the temple (acropolis) whereas for the Etruscans the temple was merely a specialized corner of the god's domain. In Greece the city spread around a sacred point by organic growth processes, whereas the Etruscan city was preconceived, with a fixed area and structure from the beginning. The Greek city was ever an "open system" in which only the morphology of the small initial core was determined in the beginning. The Etruscan city was largely a closed system at the start with most morphological processes already fixed. Thus, the nature of the religious precinct in the city may be most important just for this determination of the way the city will grow. Even a partial adoption of the religious *mundus* of the Etruscans involved the Romans in dividing up an area in the beginning rather than building it up as needed, as among the Hellenes.

The *Cardo* and *Decumanus*, and What Followed

The east-west line already mentioned may not have been precisely oriented—"east" depends upon the day of the year involved—but still it was the basal coordinate. The *Gromatici*, based considerably on Etruscan practice, describes the *decumanus* as a line connecting east and west *ab oriente ad occasum*.[21] From the *decumanus* was projected perpendicularly a line that was basically north-south, called the *cardo*. That line furnished the other axis necessary to define a system of regular divisions of land, which was surveyed by sighting on the sun with a *groma*. As early as the laying out of Marzabotto in the fifth century B.C. we see the Etruscans shaping a rectilinear town, exactly as one would expect with a coordinate system extending from a *cardo* and *decumanus* intersection at a right angle. In primitive Marzabotto, located fifteen miles south of Bologna, the street-blocks formed are not identical with one another but they are regularly rectangular. No doubt the surveying practices inherited by the Romans from the neighboring Etruscans were those of grid-pattern towns. Our problem is not how to account for the regular Roman provincial cities but rather how to explain the irregularity of Rome itself.

By common agreement Rome is believed to have grown by synoecism, with a village on the Palatine hill serving as the core. The neighboring hills are by tradition thought to have been the site of villages, housing other ethnic groups, which came to join the Palatine in founding a city. The groups involved were probably not very different in level of urbanity from the early residents of Attica who combined a rural with an urban residence, returning to the countryside at times of harvest, during the hot months, and when food was scarce. Legend has it that Romulus and Remus were suckled by the wolf (though not because of famine) and grew to manhood on the site of Rome. There Romulus adopted the Etruscan rite in laying out Rome. The legend accounts for Romulus killing his twin brother during that rite because Remus ridiculed its character. History accepts at least the general truth of this legend and fills it out with details of the joining of the villages, though somewhat questioning the assumptions of great ethnic diversity. Yet the relationship of the Tarquin kings to

[21]*Frontin*, Gromatici, *I, pp. 15 and 27, quoted in Lavedan*, op. cit., *p. 102.*

the Etruscans can be shown and little question remains that the early Romans adopted the Etruscan *land-division practices.*

The legend tells us that Romulus plowed a furrow with an ox and a cow to define Rome, and Plutarch held that that furrow was circular in outline. The streets and buildings within the *pomerium* on the Palatine hill probably had no very regular layout, but when the Palatine joined with its neighbors to form Rome, some order was introduced; a great sewer, the *Cloaca Maxima,* was built through an intervening valley to drain it, providing a site for the great central meeting place, the *Forum Romanum.* The fundamental expression of this synoecism was that creation of the *Forum,* which came to be the Greek *agora* writ large, a place where men met and political and commercial life centered. To provide access to the *Forum* the cliffed sides of the original hills were cut down and regraded to make possible the building of streets up the sides of the hills, a process continued into our times. The *Forum* became as well a point of beginning for a *cardo* and a *decumanus,* leading, in turn, to a somewhat irregular rectangular street system. In Rome not all was preconceived; the original villages had grown organically, so the pattern could not be simple. Much of the wealth and effort of imperial Rome was turned toward making the city appear more preconceived than it really was, laying out the later *Fora* of the Emperors, *Forum Julium, Forum Augustum, Forum Pacis, Forum Nerva,* and *Forum Trajiani.*

Tradition has it that a settlement of shepherds from the Alban hills founded Rome but they seem to have given up their external loyalties before doing so. The internal organization of the Eternal City was locally determined and evolved, organically, over time, coming to be characterized by a markedly social-class pattern of residence. Originally a functional separation seems to have existed between the religious city, *Roma Quadrata,* surrounded on the Palatine hill by a *pomerium,* and some sort of military camp with a wall. As the city evolved, Pierre Grimal tells, "Before long we could perceive city quarters in the course of formation: the patricians automatically inhabited the Palatine Hill or the heights of the Quirinal; the lesser people crowded together [*entassé*] in the narrow valley of the Suburre, between the Viminal and the Oppius; and the plebians in particular lived on the Aventine, whose eccentric location long left it thinly populated." This teeming city did share its markets. "In the depression between the Capitol and the Palatine two streets, the *Vicus Jugarius* and the *Vicus Tuscus,* were lined with stalls and workshops where the artisans worked." Along the banks of the Tiber where goods could be landed easily, and drovers camped, were a cattle market (*Forum Boarium)* and a vegetable market (*Forum Holitorium).* Thus, as Rome evolved it began to combine the class-specific residential districts with the general shopping districts that we find in large cities today.[22]

Rome seems to have proven intractable in this search for order and grandeur largely because of its excessive vitality in a republic and empire that focussed prosperity and regard so heavily on the capital. The greatest honor open to the provincial worthy was his citizenship in Rome, which should clarify for us the distinction that existed between the metropolis and all other places. As a consequence, two morphological patterns seem to have arisen: that growing at Rome, and that planted elsewhere. Population size accounts for much of the contrast; Rome probably had a population of at least one million and possibly as much as a million and two-thirds under the empire.[23] The physical history of Rome must also be considered; the city emerged and grew by the interplay of such diverse forces as to make a consistently grained morphology most unlikely. Rome might more easily decree the pattern of *Mediolanum* (Milan), whose size and purpose were rationally assigned in the Romanization of Cisalpine Gaul, than Rome could gain enough ground on the almost continual growth crisis within the capital itself to hope for more than alleviation of the most urgent problems found there. Efforts were made to give Rome the trappings of a properly ordered urban design but they won little against the yeasty organic growth of the place.

---

[22]*Pierre Grimal,* Les Villes Romaines, *Collection Que Sais-Je?, number 657, Paris: Presses Universitaires de France, 1971, p. 40. The* pomerium *of the original Palatine city,* Roma Quadrata, *lay along the foot of the artificially steepened slope of the Palatine to an angle point at the* Ara Maxima *in the* Forum Boarium *(the cattle market mentioned which must have lain just outside the original Roman walls), the* Ara Consi *in the* Circus Maximus, *the* Curia Veteres *(near the Arch of Constantine), and the* Sacellum Larum *(as the north angle). Pliny tells us there were three gates: the* Scalae Caci *on a roadway built sloping upward toward the heights of the Palatine, the* Porta Romanula, *and the* Porta Mugonia, *with some relics remaining of the last two. The first expansion of the* Roma Quadrata *came when the Esquiline and Caelian hills were joined with the Palatine and the intervening valleys were drained and used for the* Forum Romanum. *Later another six or seven hills and the valleys among them were joined into a great city and surrounded by a wall built by the Emperor Aurelian.*

[23]*Jérôme Carcopino,* Daily Life in Ancient Rome, *New York: Bantam Books, 1971 (Yale edition 1940), p. 24.*

The Exceptional Model

Our search for the general features of city form cannot truly comprehend Rome yet it cannot overlook it. The city was so much the giant of the ancient world that not until modern times did other cities reach the population it held at the time of the empire, and not until it became Mussolini's capital did Rome again reach that figure. The greatest problem we face is in dealing consistently with the layout of streets and the scale of Roman buildings. The streets were mean and disorderly whereas the buildings were impressive and disorderly.

Once Rome's synoecism took place, an attempt was made to confer upon the city the *cardo* and *decumanus* and give it the three gates which an Etruscan city was thought to require. These streets show up more by their compass-orientation than by their width or grandeur. The *decumanus* was represented by the *Via Sacra* and the *cardo* by a way from the *Porta Janualis* to the city wall in the *Porta Romanula*. Each of these streets left the *Forum* by a gate, the *Janualis* opening to the north, the *Janus Imus* to the east along the *decumanus*, and the *Janus Medius* to the south along the reverse projection of the cardo.[24] Apart from these accomplishments the effort at order was largely unsuccessful outside the *Forum*, whose reorganization will be discussed later. Still the only two streets in imperial Rome that had any width were the *Via Sacra* leading north out of the *Forum* and the *Via Nova* flanking it and leading east.[25]

In Rome herself at that point we can forget the standard practices of the *limitatio*, the division of the city into blocks, which was accomplished by Roman surveying (*centuriatio*), because the Eternal City lacked a standardized pattern. As Carcopino noted, the city's streets reflected their rural antecedents, which had been tracks for men moving on foot, termed *itinera*; cart paths permitting only one vehicle, the *actus*; and the road on which vehicles could pass, the *via*. In the city were passages usable only by pedestrians, the *angiportus*; alleyways some ten feet wide so as to allow projecting balconies on adjacent buildings, called *semitae*; and the *viae* which with a width of fifteen to twenty-five feet were direct descendants of the rural *viae*. Rome was a vast warren of *angiporti* and *semitae* for the most part, incredible as that may seem for what even today would be a large city. The crush of pedestrians was so great that Julius Caesar decreed that no wheeled vehicles might circulate in the city before dusk or after dawn in the hope that the mean circulation system might continue to serve, even if badly. And the nighttime din of carts overladen (because of their small size) with goods, with wooden axles badly greased, and walled in by tall buildings was evidently frightful indeed.

The *specialization of streets* arose in Rome completely within a system of organic growth, save for the two *viae*, and apparently in response to the desire to minimize the amount of land taken away from buildings. It might be argued that in organic growth a *conservation principle* leads to the provision of no more than the minimum circulation space. If an alleyway (*semita*) will suffice, do not build a *via*. This conservation principle can be traced down nearly to the present, and stands in opposition to the *standardization principle* found under planning and the city of preconception. In the second instance the fear always assails the planner that his vision may be clouded, that the street will ultimately need to carry more traffic; thus, it must be built large enough in the beginning. Unfortunately to build large enough for all futures is hard and it is easy to build too large for many presents and futures.

In Roman cities outside of the capital the street system was both rectilinear and more regular, under the aegis of the *limitatio*, standing commonly with square blocks but occasionally with rectangular ones. The practice of centuriation produced the regularity which worked in the following fashion. First in time came the location of the *decumanus maximus*, the primary east-west baseline. Whether it was struck to be oriented to some celestial event or just to be a rational baseline is argued by classical scholars, but no doubt it existed and on it were erected the other elements of centuriation. First among these was the cutting of the *decumanus maximus* by a perpendicular, the *cardo maximus*, usually at an intersection which by intention would be the heart of the putative city, that is its *forum*. Parallel to the *decumanus maximus* would be laid out a set of *decumani* to form divisions within the four initial quarters of the rectilinear city—the *decumanus maximus*, as an east-west line, divided the city between a *regio sinestra* and a *regio dextrata* whereas the *cardo maximus*, on a north-south line, separated a *regio antica* from a *regio postica*.[26] In theory the *decumanus maximus* should be about forty feet wide but the *cardo maximus* only twenty feet, and the lesser streets laid out parallel to the two coordinates were even narrower. But this template of streets served most effectively to separate out street-blocks normally both regular in size and rectilinear in shape. The general name for these

---

[24]*Lavedan, op. cit., p. 108.*
[25]*Carcopino, op. cit., p. 51.*

[26]*Lavedan, op. cit., p. 179.*

was *insulae*, for they were islands of a sort. Unfortunately the term was also used to designate what we might call an apartment house, for the very good reason that those buildings tended to occupy a whole *insula*, thus taking the name of the lot for the structure on it. To add to that confusion, not all apartment-house *insulae* did occupy a full block so the tally of such buildings, taken several times over the centuries, is not a census of blocks but of structures. And as such it is not a census of apartments either; at least most scholars do not think it is.

This orderly arrangement of space was fairly typical of provincial towns but not of Rome, which continued to expand massively, changing its full complement of monuments to the occasion. When the imperial *fora* began to be laid out by Julius Caesar around 54 B.C., land was so costly in Rome that Julius had to pay a hundred million *sesterces* for a cramped site for his *Forum Julium*.[27] Over and over again land in the imperial city changed its use, to suit dynastic whim, to care for a growing population, to provide entertainment for an increasingly worrisome proletariat, or because of the repeated fires. Much as Nero wished after his famous conflagration to improve the layout of Rome, he was almost wholly unsuccessful. The city was too vast and yet too crowded, a yeasty mix of forces, to permit the imposition of an overall order *ex post facto*. Instead glorious public buildings were constructed, seemingly flung onto the ground where a hole or a cheap lot could be found. The various ceremonial clusters, notably the *forum maximus* that had served as the first center of Rome after synoecism, gained a site by dint of filling and draining a marsh that had collected in the depression among the hills. The imperial *fora* that succeeded it, seemed, in turn, to take the place of the organized street plan found in other Roman cities. The *fora* exhibited design, symmetry, and display, and held the clustering of most of the civic offices, functions, and provision of shops for certain specialized occupations. Similarly the *circus maximus* and the *Amphitheatrum Flavium (Colosseum)* opened up an otherwise jumbled and packed city.

The tendency is to look upon the public display of imperial Rome as a decadence of self-congratulation by successive emperors, yet it might be viewed as well as a device to create urban open space in the only way that it might effectively be done in a city where an increasingly factious group of plebs made fundamental change almost impossible. Already in 44 B.C. Caesar was undertaking to distribute free grain (probably wheat) to a population of 150,000 and as the empire continued this group of potentially riotous persons expanded greatly.[28] As the emperors often used the plebs to a political purpose they had little chance to remake the city to their incidental or ultimate discomfort. Nero after the great fire of A.D. 64 managed to reform what we would term the building code but he failed to replan the city's layout because to do that would have stretched the fabric of society to the rending point.

The Forum Julium.

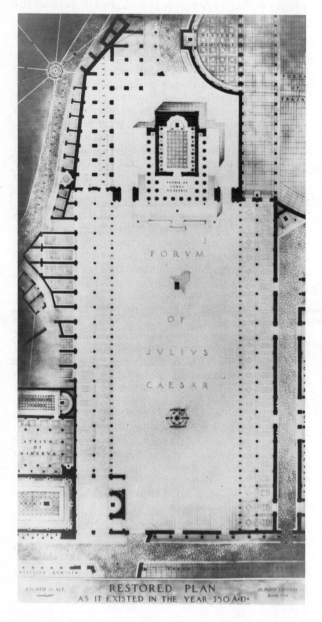

EIGHTH SCALE

RESTORED PLAN
AS IT EXISTED IN THE YEAR 350 A·D·

OLINDO GROSSI
ROME 1934

[27]"Rome," Encyclopaedia Britannica, *11th Edition, 1910, Vol. 23, p. 601.*
[28]*Carcopino*, op. cit., *p. 20.*

Rome and the City House

We know that Athens and other Greek cities grew apace in the Hellenic period but little has survived of their domestic architecture, either in writings or in archaeological remains. Athens itself had shrunk to a city of 5,000 people when liberated from the Turks in 1833 so the lesser buildings had been little used and badly preserved. These were probably largely constructed of rubble masonry with a poor or absent mortar bond so over at least a millennium of declining use they largely disintegrated. The stones of Athens remained, but as a heap they tell us little.

Rome and her empire instead furnish us a wealth of detail. Because some cities continued to be used, the buildings were kept up or incorporated in other structures (as in the church of St. John and St. Paul on the Caelian hill); other towns might be virtually abandoned without a major relict population (as in northern Gaul or in Rome's port of Ostia). The Romans were so very much more skilled as builders as truly "to build for the ages." Starting in the second century B.C., concrete infilling was used as the core of walls and cement mortar in places. Both materials were strong and remained as a cast of the idea the architect had in mind, unlike the situation experienced when the stone blocks of Athens fell into a heap. The Romans may not have invented the city but doubtless they developed the fundamental module of most subsequent cities, the apartmented house.

The bucolic country ancestors of the Romans probably lived in timber huts of post-and-lintel construction roofed and walled by mats of reed or withies. Like most rural habitations these would be expanded by adding another unit of similar form until a new module—the courtyard enclosed by single-story rooms—was shaped. In masonry construction this became the basal Roman house built with two courtyards, the *atrium* and the *peristyle*, inward-looking, with blank walls to the street, and light and ventilation provided by the opening of the court. In Pompeii rich and poor lived in these atrium houses, though the poor had a single room opening off a court rather than the whole building. Because Pompeii was the best preserved Roman town, and the first to be studied when archaeology was begun as a serious study in the nineteenth century, the notion grew up that the courtyard house was the Roman norm, a notion which appealed to our grandparents because it showed the continuity of history from the Greek to the Roman house.

Unfortunately Pompeii was far from typical, in much the way that Newport (Rhode Island) or Carmel (California) would afford future excavators an odd vision of contemporary American housing.

As small settlements, Roman cities might be composed of such atrium houses but once growth became brisk these houses would tend quickly to yield to larger multistory structures, just as the brownstone has yielded to the tall apartment house in Manhattan or Chicago's North Side. Certainly only the very well-to-do could preserve a flat house in the face of vastly increasing land prices such as those already experienced in Rome by the time of the late republic. At first, the courtyard house was transformed by the addition of casual extenders—penthouses built on parts of its roof to add an attic or a bedroom or two, infillings of the courtyards, or possibly cellars dug in the relatively soft tuff of Rome. The courtyard house was initially conterminous with its lot, leaving no peripheral open space for subsequent enlargement. The sort of casual extension possible under such conditions was rather small; to add penthouses would soon cut off the light in the atrium as well as disrupt the collection of rainwater in the *compluvium* of the roof for storage in the *impluvium* in the court itself. And despite all the aqueducts that survive as the glory of Rome, those conduits more often led to public fountains than to domestic faucets, or their ancient equivalent, so the system of roof collection was important. Added to the pressure of increased land rents was the real possibility of destruction by fire of the older buildings, which were built somewhat more of timber and used tuff as a stone, one that did not stand up to fire.

The conditions in the city of Rome encouraged innovation which led in two directions. For the wealthy a larger house requiring less land had to be devised whereas for the ordinary people some less land-consuming house must be found. Initially the mass of people had crowded into older buildings that had experienced rather piecemeal transformation—families occupying parts of previously individual houses and casual extensions to the structure itself—but subsequently new forms were shaped. The wealthy began to occupy multistory buildings, still inward-looking with rooms opening on several levels around a courtyard. Thus was devised the house of the magnate, which in succeeding centuries changed little other than coming to be called a *palazzo* by the people of the Middle Ages. The Romans termed this a *domus*, a somewhat wry antecedent for our generic term for everyday life. When, in the fourth century A.D. the Romans collected statistics on the parts of the city summed into the *Regionaries*, 1,782 *domus* were found. Thus the *domus* was hardly the standard type of dwelling in a city of certainly a million souls, particularly since a *domus* was a single-family residence, though that family in all likelihood had numerous retainers and slaves.

These were "city mansions," to give them a closely approximate modern name; "palace" is a bit grand for the class, though not for individual examples. Originally they stood as building units, but as land rents rose, even the rich felt the pinch and, to borrow Lucius Beebe's phrase, only the "Big Spenders" continued to occupy independent houses. At that point the analogy with the medieval *palazzo* becomes precise, though not signalled by a distinction in Latin; the *domus* could be either a freestanding palace or a rich apartment located almost invariably on the first floor of a larger building. Much as these apartments were part of an apartment building otherwise listed, the *domus* was tallied in the *Regionaries* as such, meaning that of the eighteen hundred such dwellings only some were true palaces, though the proportion cannot be determined.

The more common abode was furnished in these massive buildings which must by some measure have been the building module of the Roman city, the *insulae*. We may assume that these structures were from four to six stories high, as Augustus decreed that *insulae* could be no more than 70 feet in height (Nero reduced it to 60 feet), which would allow at most five or six stories as we count them.[29] Such a uniform height is a joint result of housing pressure and civil restraint. Rome was greatly crowded, which increased its land rents, though the crowding itself is a sufficient explanation for housing pressure. Yet it could not be allowed to grow too tall, so the Augustan and Neronian limits were set. It appears that the Insula of Felicula next to the Pantheon stood much taller, how tall we do not know, causing both wonder and condemnation.[30] In general the height limit was established because the buildings were dangerous, because of both fire and structural failure. Accounts have it that it was a daily occurrence for *insulae* to collapse, killing occupants and pedestrians alike. Though built of masonry, these structures were both thin-walled and wooden-floored;

Typical Roman atrium house, 4th–3rd century B.C.

Reconstruction of large apartmented building in Ostia shows the shops found on the first floor, with their mezzanines and three floors of cenaculae above.

[29]*Russell Meiggs*, Roman Ostia, *Oxford: Oxford University Press, 1960, p. 236.*
[30]*Carcopino, op. cit., p. 29.*

they burned rapidly and failed spectacularly, leaving the poorest tenants in the attics no escape from being roasted alive. The emperor's hope was that escape down four flights of stairs might be possible when a greater run would not. Like many imperial expectations this seems to have been somewhat chimerical but like many imperial decrees it persisted despite that fact.

The apartmented *insula* seems to have had a fairly consistent structure, though it varied widely in design. It was normally a rectangular building with relatively smooth sides rising perhaps four to six stories in height, with a sloping roof, though some appear to have had merely a terrace on top. The body of the building commonly held an opening—sometimes little more than the nineteenth-century "airwell," but in the better buildings a true courtyard surrounded by balconies that gave access to the separate apartments, termed *cenacula*. Perhaps the most distinguishing feature of the *insula* was that it opened by windows and balconies to the outside of the building, unlike the atrium house and, to a lesser degree, the self-contained *domus*. The *insulae* had rows of fairly large windows facing outward on the city streets as well as windows and doorways opening onto the interior galleries. In this way the thickness of the building could be increased without abandoning the natural light, which was all that Rome had save for poor and smokey oil lamps. Glass seems to have been uncommon so windows were closed either by solid shutters or by selonite, a crystalline form of gypsum, which gave some light, though less than was needed.[31] These apartments had no effective heating; at least no chimneys or other flues survive and the possibility of an open brazier burning charcoal, the rural and palatial form of heating in central Italy, seems small.

Much as we are taught that the Romans solved the problems of public sanitation, some question remains as to their effectiveness. No doubt exists that the Romans were the first to devise an adequate system for bringing water into the city; after all, they were the first to make daring and effective use of the arch—a prime requisite in any system where the distribution of water depended upon straight gravity flow. The aqueducts were true monuments, named for the emperor or magnate who built them as a gift to the city. When they reached the city they did continue on to particular quarters in what we would term "distributaries," but for most people the flow stopped at a public tap or conduit. The public fountain, in classical times and until very recently, was not merely an element of Roman display; it was the public tap as well. A modest number of *insulae* seem to have had water connections but because of the open, gravity flow of the water, these could not normally be led to the upper stories. Such conditions created a fairly inverse relationship between height in the building and social quality of the occupants. Let it be recalled that the *domus* of the wealthy tended to occupy the ground floor of these apartmented buildings. In the attics, the poor found shelter, but neither water nor sewage in most cases.

Jérôme Carcopino has given us a detailed analysis of the municipal services of Rome. He concludes that, as with water, the city was well served by the main sewage system—so well that as we all know the main sewer, *Cloaca Maximus*, is in use up to the present.[32] What the Romans did superbly was to build vast engineering works; they did not provide for the universal use of those services. In Rome it seems that the upper stories were perhaps most commonly not provided with sewage collection, though in Ostia drain pipes seem somewhat more common[33] with privies provided on most floors. In Rome massive public latrines have been excavated, which served both their obvious purpose and that of social gathering, as attested by their decoration and lack of interior privacy.

Later-day delicacy toward corporal needs seems largely absent in Roman cities where urinals might stand exposed at the entrance to impressive public buildings and brothels could operate freely "after the ninth hour."[34] At the same time in decoration and furnishing the Romans carried delicacy almost to the extreme; their houses had little furniture but rather collections of small *objets d'art* which served to show the wealth of the owner and which were displayed ostentatiously on a pole stand that must class as the original for the Victorian "whatnot." Similarly, in public buildings detailing could be carried to great extremes of lavishness suggesting an aesthetic sensitivity strangely paired with the "blood sports" in the Colosseum. Perhaps violent contrast was one of the more significant features of their lives. Thus it is not surprising to find the Romans displaying the first really modern approach to housing urban masses and, in their engineering, the initial awareness of what a large city needs in municipal services. But alongside their dwellings and aqueducts, we find the continual collapse of *insulae*, nightsoil flung from top stories into the narrow streets, and dirt and bugs in *cenacula* whose windows opened onto squares with ploshing fountains.

[31]Meiggs, op. cit., p. 239. Meiggs apparently incorrectly identifies it as "selinite" but neither Merriam-Webster nor the Oxford English Dictionary identifies such a substance.

[32]Carcopino, op. cit., pp. 43-50.
[33]Meiggs, op. cit., p. 240.
[34]Carcopino, op. cit., p. 289.

Without question the *insulae* became the pattern of Rome as time passed. In the fourth century A.D., 46,602 *insulae* were recorded but we do not know into how many further parts, the *cenacula*, these buildings were split. Certainly we are dealing with a total of apartments that must have numbered in the hundreds of thousands. To contain this number even within the walls of the imperial city required teeming quarters of tall buildings separated from each other only by narrow access streets, *vici*, which seem to have become the main open space outside of the spectacular *fora* and buildings at the center. It has been argued that the passion for ostentatious public buildings was so great, and so well backstayed by money from senators and emperors, that part of the city's crowding came from displacement of people for these great architectural and planning works. We do know that Rome experienced a continual rebuilding process under which land rents continued to rise, leading in turn to reconstruction of existing buildings to make them more capacious to house a growing mass of people. The economic returns seem to have been high for the landowner, and possibly his lessee, the occupant of the ground-floor *domus*, who in turn might let out the upper stories to increasingly large numbers of tenants. The rents were often high: "We know in Caesar's day Caelius paid for his annual rent . . . 30,000 sesterces ($1,200.00)."[35]

import of ready-made articles was, however, exceptional. A very large proportion of the goods that were sold in the shops were made on the premises. A terracotta relief from a tomb in the Isola Sacra cemetery shows a shopkeeper with a wide range of tools for sale: on the same relief a craftsman is shown making tools. This is a fair illustration of typical Roman practice, for production and distribution were normally in the same hands."[36] And apparently most streets were lined with these shops, suggesting a classical origin for the geographically integrated daily activity pattern of common people.

Meiggs provides us a general picture of these shops-with-residences:

> The commonest form of shop resembles the Pompeiian type and can still be seen in many Italian towns today (1960). On the street is a large room in which the goods are stacked and sold; behind it there is a smaller room which can be used for production or for extra accommodation. In the corner a wooden staircase leads up to a small mezzanine floor where the family live. The shop front during the day is completely open; at night wooden shutters are run across. Some shops have no back room and were perhaps confined to retail trade; others have a back room as large as the shop, suggesting larger-scale production. Not all shops have living quarters above them.[37]

Commerce in the Roman City

So few detailed records survive that we cannot answer two fascinating questions about the Roman city: (1) in what way did this primitive land-rent system work to sort out activities in space, and (2) what was the functional geography of these cities? Some broad facts do, however, survive and they help us to reconstruct the land-use pattern as it existed in the time of the empire.

We may safely conclude that the ground floors of the *insulae* tended increasingly to be occupied by shops; numerous surviving wall footings in Timgad and elsewhere show the door openings of such shops ranged in long ranks along the frontage of more important streets. In some cases, these shops seem to have been both workplace and residence, as evidenced by such survivals as the lofts or mezzanines of Roman Ostia. These were the premises of producers more than traders. Despite its lesser stature as a town, in Ostia, "The

A reconstruction of an Ostian apartment structure: the rear facade of the "Insula dei Dipiuti."

[35]Ibid., p. 30.

[36]*Meiggs*, op. cit., p. 271.
[37]Ibid., pp. 272-273.

The shops were commonly in ranked frontages along the streets but "occasionally they are grouped together in independent architectural units," or bazaars. When Trajan constructed his vastly monumental *forum* in Rome at the opening of the second century A.D., it was provided with arcades of many shops apparently clustered to some degree by the type of goods fabricated and sold. To argue that complex distinctions existed between shopping areas may be too bold, though likely at least a two-part division was made between local shopping facilities and those of a more specialized, comparative quality in the arcades surrounding the *fora* of Roman cities.

The Economic Colony

Ostia, the original port for Rome, furnishes us clear evidence of the existence of a long-distance trade carried on by various types of wholesalers, *mercatores*. Their premises can be distinguished from the local shops by their size and the succession of modular spaces logically viewed as storage rooms, as they lack the wide open facade necessary to provide light and observation for selling. The collection of these *horrea* into courtyards was evidently common and their siting shows us whether they were intended for local provisioning or as stages on a longer trading linkage. Those central to a town can be inferred to serve that place but those with a riverbank location seem to have been intended as transfer points; we know that Ostian warehouses supplied riverboats on the Tiber with grain for Rome that had been brought in turn from North Africa or the Crimea in seagoing barges.[38]

As already noted, the continuing growth of the city's population made grain a crucial commodity and one with great political significance. In attempting to unseat existing dynasties of dictators and emperors, pretenders often sought to use the scarcity of grain for the populace to raise a mob. With the practice of free distribution of breadstuffs to an urban proletariat, numbering ultimately in the hundreds of thousands, the supply line for this politically motivated benefaction became a central concern of the Roman emperor. In part the conquests of distant lands, notably Egypt, were motivated by the desire to increase the supply of grain for the city of Rome. But to make use of that greater provision, a system of long-distance trade had to be worked out and the physical facilities for its conduct constructed. We can examine briefly the effect of the imperial trade of Rome on the urban structure of the capital.

Ostia had been the initial port of Rome located, as its name tells us, at the mouth of the Tiber. Even this outlying port was not the initial provisioning point for the city; while the environs of Rome, Latium, fed the city, grain could be collected there and dispatched to granaries in the city. From those granaries the populace secured wheat for their bread. But with the success of wars against other tribes in Italy and against the Carthaginians, a class of magnates arose in Rome for whom increases in wealth were related most closely to what we would term "land speculation." The economic aristocracy began buying lots in Rome and, as the Latin peasants tended to abandon the land in response to the seemingly greater attraction of the burgeoning city, farming land outside the city.[39] As the magnates took over the Roman countryside they found it more profitable, and we suspect more attractive visually, to transform a grain-producing area into a grazing area. The result was a decline in the local provision of grain and an increase in the demand projected to distant producing areas. At that juncture Ostia was transformed from a naval port to an integral part of the economic geography of the city of Rome. This period seems to have witnessed the beginning of the urbane use of the countryside that came when the city wealth and culture were projected outward to transform Latium.

As Gaul and Egypt began sending grain as a tithe to Rome, Ostia became Rome's first developed port, after having been her first planted colony—for naval defense—in the fourth century B.C. Because the imperial city lay some miles inland from the mouth of the Tiber, the river's mouth became a site of economic settlement only when Rome needed a point of attachment to a maritime supply route bringing goods by merchantmen from an initially thalassic empire. The port that emerged was a river-mouth port built with quays on the bank backed by warehouses *(horrea);* access to the sea was impeded by a typical river-mouth bar and river navigation to the landward city was subject to great fluctuations in water level. As the demands on the port increased, alleviation of the impedances became a national concern. To correct the river-mouth bar, the emperor Claudius in A.D. 42 began construction of an artificial harbor at Portus, located several miles north of the mouth of the Tiber. The harbor was presumably protected from the silting problem which ultimately added the problem of shallow water at the quays of Ostia to the constant difficulty of its bar. Yet that solu-

[38]Cf. *Meiggs, pp. 270-298.*

[39]Op. cit., *p. 27.*

The entrance to one of the
great warehouses at Ostia:
the Horrea Epagathiana.

"wholesalers" and foreign traders, or merchants, in most Roman cities. And, as in the case of Rome herself or Ostia, those merchants would tend to locate peripheral to the city rather than central to it, as did the retail traders clustered around the various *fora*. In fact, in Rome a special district outside the city's walls and along the bank of the Tiber became the workplace of the merchants. This *emporium* extended for hundreds of feet along the Tiber (487 meters) and back from it for some distance (90 meters), and was enclosed by a wall and paved.[40] After 193 B.C., goods could be set down there from river boats and held for later distribution to city traders. The next year a specialized lumber dock was added where timbers from up-river or brought from the west coast of Italy or Sardinia could be discharged and held for use in the rapid expansion of the physical build of Rome that came both by intensification of land-use and expansion of the city area. Additional *emporia* have been found by excavation in Ostia and other places, suggesting a clear distinction both in the Roman economy and the Roman mind between wholesale and retail trade. The *emporia* were the workplace of wholesale merchants, whereas the *insulae* and *cenacula* served to house the premises of retail shopkeepers. The *horrea*, storing grain, oil, and other staples, were an even different component of an extensive trading system which tended to be located at the edge of a city or port accessible to a strongly ordered and organized flow of goods from established and specialized sources. Both within the *horrea* and the *emporia* must have been found merchants whose jobs were to anticipate the needs of the city and express those needs in forward orders to distant sources, and men who never directly dealt with the ultimate consumer.

A test of the direct tie between the extensive trading system and the size of the city is furnished by the decline and deterioration of the entrepôts with the shrinking of Rome. Due both to barbarian invasions and the visitation of the plague, the city's population declined in the third century A.D., and that drop was reflected in the fast disintegration of Ostia. With smaller needs the imperial ports to the north of the Tiber could suffice, leaving the original colony to stagnate. Ultimately, with the collapse of the Roman Empire and the shrinking of Rome to a small city with mainly local importance, Ostia died, persisting only as a quarry for local builders. Its mercantile system collapsed and with it the city, which had housed at least 50,000 people in the second century A.D. No longer was it a social and economic reality but despite the destructive forces of nature and man much remained. "If we wish to clothe the bare bones of the (surviving) marble

tion was only good for a time. Then an additional port, Portus Augusti, had to be added to the one begun by Claudius (which was named for Trajan, Portus Traiani). Finally, silt from the Tiber was carried northward in sufficient quantity to agrade the shore so heavily that all three ports now lie some distance inland. Rome in modern times depends instead on Livorno or Naples some distance away.

The Distant Trade of Rome

Although no other part of the empire had such a specialized pattern of places engaged dominantly in long-distance (wholesale) trade, doubtless the extensive and economically integrated nature of the Roman Empire led to the existence of what we would term

[40]Op. cit., p. 30.

plan of Rome with the flesh of buildings a visit to Ostia is an essential complement to a visit to Rome . . . . The streets of Ostia as rebuilt in the second century are the best illustration we can find of the *nova urbs* created by Nero after the great fire (of Rome) of A.D. 64."[41]

Tribalism in Roman Cities: Lyon

The Greek practice of living in basically tribal quarters within the city may have persisted though the evidence is not full enough to say. We do know that as Christianity made inroads in Roman society, it tended to be centered in a particular part of the city where the temple of the Christian cult could be built, taking for its design the covered place of assembly found generally in Roman towns, the basilica. In Cuicul (present-day Djemila near Constantine in Algeria) the Romans built a Christian quarter in a southern suburb focusing on the basilica, baptistry, and bishop's palace.[42] The notion of the functional quarter, when function is defined as a particular public purpose for the existence of the town, seems to have existed in the great center of Roman Gaul, *Lugdunum*, which became the modern city of Lyon. Starting as a Celtic town of small size, *Lugdunum* was transformed just after Caesar's conquests into a proper Roman provincial town by the laying down of a regular grid over those older remnants. A *forum*, some of which survives, provided the center of city life but, because *Lugdunum* quickly became the great trading center of Gaul, it was necessary to shape a merchant's town at the foot of the ramparts on which the original *forum* was built. Continuing growth of trade caused a quarter for wine merchants to be laid out on the island surrounded by the Rhône and the Saône, *Canabae*. Finally a religious quarter arose at *Condate*, north of the island, where the two rivers came together.

One can see that the history of Lugdunum *faithfully reproduces the development of functions performed by the city: Roman outpost at first, she became a crossroads of commerce by road and by river, and soon the spiritual center of a new province. And, each time a new quarter*

came into existence to respond to the needs which created it. Still, nothing a priori *and no preconceived theory there interfered with the free play of geographic laws.*[43]

Yet we may validly question Pierre Grimal's judgment that no preconception was at work, only the force of "geographic laws." The quarters may have grown up according to those laws, but the shape of the city within the quarter and the forthright division of functions among the quarters came in response to a particular concept of how cities should be built and where the various functions should be carried on. The religious precinct of the *Condate* became a place where each town of Gaul came annually to make sacrifices at its own altar, as well as at the altar that was federal to all such towns. Clearly a special design must have existed to guide this development. In the center as well the *forum* was from the beginning a formally designed space and an amphitheater was soon built nearby.

The City Beyond the Walls: Dioecism

From the Roman experience we can first perceive a persistent expression of city life undervalued for nearly two millennia: the existence of a city life outside the city walls. To set the stage, we should recall that in the Greek pattern of urban settlement the force of synoecism was at work seeking to join dispersed rural settlements into an urban entity. A duality of residence emerged; most city dwellers considered their roots to be planted in the countryside they had come from initially. In the summer heat or in times of adversity and famine these city dwellers returned "home;" perhaps even more importantly, the residential structure within the city reflected these origins with quarters occupied by descendants of people who came from fairly definite rural locales. Under this synoecism the city and the country were one, and citizenship could be held by those few who remained continuously in the countryside as much as those who returned there only periodically from a normal residence within the urban walls. The relationship was clearly expressed in the Greek political unit, the city-state, which comprised a

[41]Op. cit., *pp. 13-14.*
[42]*Grimal,* op. cit., *p. 112.*

[43]Ibid., *pp. 116-117.*

The exurban spread of
aristocratic residence
reached its epitome in
Hadrian's villa at Tivoli.

city and the region around it that had the most direct
and continuing synoectic association.

Whether we accept the mythological account of
Rome's founding as historical fact or not it seems reasonable to draw a distinction with Greek experience:
Rome was the hearth and from it Roman power and
culture spread outward to overrun Latium, Etruria,
Italy, and ultimately the western world. There was a
single Rome, and citizenship in the republic and empire implied a man's rights while in Rome more than
his rights when he might be at home in the provinces.
The concept was one of the city as the *fons et origo* of
civilization, power, and culture—exactly the inverse of
the Greek notion. Thus we find the substitution for the
Greek synoecism of a new force that we might, in the
absence of a Greek term, make parallel by calling it
dioecism, the periodic dispersion of initially urban
population into the countryside.

This dispersion differs totally from the Hellenic
example; there danger and crisis depopulated the city,
whereas in the Roman instance adversity drew citizens
within the walls and closed the gates. Only in prosperity and peace was the countryside part of city life, and
the reality of *pax Romana* brought forward the urban
occupation of rustic areas. When that peace declined,
the first signs of change appeared in the disruption and
abandonment of the rural part of this geographically
complex pattern of dual residence.

The fundamental unit of the rustic part of the
Roman duality was the *villa*, a suburban or rural residence of a person of means. The word derives from

vicus, a row of houses in the city, implying both the
urban origin of the settlers and affluence sufficient to
permit them accommodation adequate for a fair retinue of minions. The ultimate in villas was probably
that of the emperor Hadrian at Tivoli near Rome. In a
park setting he shaped a melange of extravagant buildings suiting his indulgent fancy, and supplying us with
a generic term for a more democratic frivolity in our
day—such as Copenhagen's Tivoli Gardens. As wealth
accumulated in the hands of Roman senators and other
aristocrats and among the administrators and proconsuls in the provinces, the villa became a necessary
symbol of middle- and upper-class standing. Perhaps
because even the magnates of Rome could occupy only
fairly cramped sites within its walls, when they went
out to their country villas they sought a sense of open-
ness as expressed in landscaped and organized gardens; the almost inevitable chaos of the crowded city
was left behind and nature was made to conform to
man's mental design in the countryside. The Alban
Hills and the coast south of Ostia both became dotted
with villas, giving evidence that already in the time of
the empire the bucolic landscape and the marine relief
were considered proper contrast to urban life. In the
Alban Hills, however, Rome was nearby and the association was nearly a suburban one but the journey to
the Ostian coast was 20 to 25 kilometers (12 to 15
miles), so the degree of rustication was greater.

Throughout the empire, villas served as evidence of
the attainment of Roman civilization. Ian Richmond
notes of them that their "distribution had an extent
which the world was hardly to see again."[44] Numbers

[44]*Ian Richmond, "Architecture and Engineering," in J. P. V. D.
Halsdon,* Roman Civilization, *Baltimore: Penguin Books, 1969,
p. 138.*

of these villas have been excavated; we know them as large and urbane structures decorated with mosaics, fountains, statuary, and murals, more reflective of the city in the countryside than the other way around. As we noted in discussing Latium, the creation of these country estates worked a transformation of the rural economy and its landscape that cannot be overlooked in any analysis of the physical structure of the city, even though that structure was definitely extramural.

As the Roman civilization was assailed by barbarian invasions, this component of settlement withered first under the chill of violence and disorder. In 455 the Vandals attacked the Ostian coast, and it is likely that the marine relief to city life held less appeal after that. Certainly within a century or so most of the countryside of the decaying empire became unsafe and brutal, a quality it retained throughout the "Dark Ages." City men gave up dioecism as a practice and spent five hundred years seeking the doubtful protection of walled cities increasingly too commodious to be defended by the shrinking urban populations. Ultimately many places shed much of the physical city of the Romans, huddling instead in a corner protected from a decaying ruin as much as from the countryside by new walls enclosing the most defensible fragment of the once-large imperial city. But it should not be lost on us that Roman civilization sought refuge in the city, maintained its existence there, and ultimately blossomed forth from that seedbed.

City and Countryside

The existence of the two processes, synoecism and dioecism, suggests that the relationship between city and country cannot be assumed to repeat forever throughout history. Doubtless people lived in small, probably wandering bands before they became settled and their first settlements would seem rural to us. But once cities came into being, did they similarly evolve from a rural to an urban state in all instances? This question is not an idle one but is fundamental to most of the theoretical proposals about cities, as we shall see when we consider the Middle Ages and the two theories historically rooted then. Both von Thünen's "isolated state" and Christaller's "central-place" revolve at least in part around the question of synoecism versus dioecism, though neither phrased his argument in those terms.

Historically either process seems to find support;

the coming together of rural people to found and use a city while continuing an attachment to the countryside was strongly the Greek way, whereas the dispersion of city dwellers into the adjacent open spaces and their shaping of an urban extension better describes what the Romans did. Interestingly, many of the words we use to compliment the countryside—idyllic, arcadian —we inherit from the Greeks, but when we intend to insult that area we turn to Latin derivatives—rustic, villainous, sylvatic, savage, bucolic, and rural. Only the Latin word "pastoral" conveys any feeling of appreciation for the countryside, and most of the societies derived from Roman culture most directly tend to employ words of rural reference derogatorily— heathen, pagan, yokel, peasant—while viewing urban reference as complimentary in tone—courtly, courteous, urbane, civilized, and citizen.

The contrast between the Greek and the Roman dynamics of settlement ostensibly offered to later times a choice of practice. Presumably cities could grow out of the land, serving as the locale for the exchange of goods among agriculturalists and the site for collection of potential exports and distribution of goods imported from outside the local system. The walls of the cities served to protect these specific economic functions, leaving unsolved the problem of rural security. Protection could be afforded only very close to the town; more distant areas must depend upon local strongpoints, fortified villages or, later, castles. Operating under such a rurally-based system the Greeks shaped first the city-state with an intimate admixture of rural and urban residence and then the planted city as a means of dealing with growing population and expanded political interest. In essence these planted communities repeated the scale of the mother state but, unlike the situation found in the older Greek settlements, the new fields of settlement offered no base for synoecism. Even if an aboriginal population remained, and often it was nearly decimated before the planting, the city founded was not a bringing together of its members. This circumstance was likely to set up a cultural and political contrast between the city and the countryside, with the power and decision to effect the settlement pattern remaining largely within the walls.

We may conclude that synoecism is a practical possibility only in a two-stage settlement history, starting with a rural base of an indigenous population and leading to urbanization only as that rural population reaches a level of productive surplus necessitating the establishment of inter-family exchange. If instead the city becomes the instrument of planting population and political power in a different area, its tie to the countryside must be by dioecism. The existence of a prior settled population does not change the conditions; if they come into the city it will be in a dependent, if not actually enslaved, relationship. The planted city, whether a demographic expansion (as were some of the Greek city-states) or a colonial settlement seeking outright the domination of a native population, spreads its culture and influence outward, whereas an emergent central-place witnesses the inward collection of rural attitudes and institutions. Rome herself was an example of a city which, as it became more powerful, spread out to dominate its environs in Latium. And as the empire based on Latium spread, it used the city as the fundamental instrument of cultural, political, and economic integration of the vast state. If Greece was a case of rural implosion to form a city, Rome was a case of urban explosion to shape an empire.

The truth that planted cities spread outward to dominate the region in which they are sited was the prime tool of Roman conquest. By devising a network of settlements and planting its cities, Rome came to dominate the west politically. And because each of those cities was a germinal point for the outward spread of culture, economy, and political power, the area of the western world came under Roman sway. This point must be understood to comprehend the decline and fall of Rome. If the system had been produced by synoecism, then its destruction would have been slow and mainly biological. Because the system was from the beginning geographically integrated and areally comprehensive, once the core network was disrupted, the collapse was rapid. The populations remained but the basis of urbanization disappeared and the settlement pattern of the western Roman empire rapidly disintegrated into a series of small rural strongpoints, moated keeps and, later, castles, with a battlefield strewn with the dead and decaying bodies of previously most vital cities. In the eastern Roman empire the network continued later in history, and had a stronger base of places that had been originally Greek

Model of imperial Rome, including the Capitol, Forum, and collosseum.

city-states. So in Byzantium the classical city persisted but ultimately died. By looking at that area, we may find the thin thread of continuity between classical and medieval urbanization and we may set a template for judging how much had changed when the Middle Ages brought cities back to the western Roman world.

The City in Byzantium

The Roman Empire had always been cosmopolitan, permitting a large measure of cultural individuality in the various provinces. Rome, strongly self-confident, was so obviously the nexus of civilization that she had little fear of localized heterodoxy. A plural society had always been acknowledged in the relations with the Hellenic east: Greek was the language of the eastern realm and the practices there were heavily dependent upon the older civilization. Customarily, a truly vice-regal official administered the east, so no great rupture with Roman tradition was felt when, in the third century A.D., the emperor Diocletian decreed that henceforth, an eastern as well as a western emperor would rule, and each would have an assistant called caesar.[45] The political system was unworkable but its geographical point had been made: the empire needed two capitals even if it could not function well with two emperors. When Constantine emerged victorious over his last rival, Licinius, in 323, imperial competition disappeared, though a capital for the eastern empire seemed an accepted notion. And in 330 A.D., Constantine chose its site, at the Golden Horn on the Bosphorus, and decreed its construction as the "New Rome which is Constantinople." Within a decade the city rose impressively on its own seven hills, combining a conscious effort to inherit from the art and learning of Hellenistic civilization and from the political and administrative success of Rome. The speech was Latin but the culture was Greek, save in the important exception that "the individualism which was essential to Hellenic culture could not long outlast the passing of the city-state . . . into a world-empire in whose direction the Greek had no part."[46]

The various trials of the western empire increased

so that within little more than a century of Constantinople's founding it became the dominant city of the dying classical world. To follow the details of the relations between Rome and Constantinople would be impossible here; at least formally, ties persisted for many centuries. Before 480, on occasion both eastern and western emperors ruled, and when in 395 the nominally eastern emperor, Theodosius, died, the last instance of a single man's controlling both east and west passed as well. From then until 480 there were two emperors and in that year, when Julius Nepos died, the title of emperor disappeared from the declining western empire. Subsequently the true descendant of imperial Rome lay only in the east.

For clarity this eastern empire can be called the Byzantine; within urban history, it carried on the classical tradition which virtually disappeared from the west. This fact must not be overlooked. It is easy for those of us in western society to think that Rome and the present are separated by a discontinuous urban history, making the classical city little more than a distant curiosity.

The Byzantine city is not so well known as we might wish, yet several of its attributes are clear. Physically the cities fell into two classes: the metropolis and the provincial towns. Runciman holds that Constantinople was a city of at least a million people at its height of power and it shared with an earlier Rome the status of the dominant element in the life and culture of its empire. Public buildings outshone any provincial rival, art and learning clustered there, and life outside the capital was viewed as boorish if not actually brutal. Rustication was a powerful form of punishment classed with blinding or other mutilation. Perhaps even more than in Rome the metropolis dominated because, as the center of eastern Christendom, Constantinople had been able to collect a vast array of those relics that assumed surpassing importance in medieval Christianity. Basing its state on religious orthodoxy within a very complex racial geography, the Byzantine Empire shaped a durable polity that lasted for more than a millennium. Byzantine emperors could have been born in Spain or in Armenia and yet not be disqualified so long as they remained the caesaropopist leader of this theocratic state. As that leader the emperor became a semi-divine, a status that brought forth a particular urban geography clearly revealed in Constantinople.

The metropolitan domination of the city on the Bosphorus was its most striking quality. The size of the place, nearly five miles by four miles within the ultimate walls completed in 439, made this the greatest city in the western world, and one wherein the life of the empire centered more certainly than had the older empire in Rome. The key was the indivisible quality of

[45]*Steven Runciman*, Byzantine Civilization, [*first published 1933*], *Cleveland: World Publishing Company, 1956, pp. 19-20.*
[46]Ibid., *p. 14.*

authority in the Byzantine Empire: the emperor was viewed as a demi-god, a descendant of Christ's forebears, the shepherd of orthodoxy, and the sole political power.

In Constantinople, most of the elements of the Roman city were perpetuated. The *fora* here served severally as the focus of religious life (the *Augustaion* with the church of St. Sophia), of commercial activity (the *Forum* of Constantine), and of more parochial purpose. As the center of eastern Christendom, Constantinople needed a great church, seemingly to replace the crucial focus that Rome had had in the pagan buildings of Trajan's *forum*. That need was met on Christmas Day in 538 with the dedication of the vast church of the Holy Wisdom, Hagia Sophia, which Justinian the Great had had built to replace a smaller one destroyed by the Nika riots of 532. It had a profane rival in the great open Hippodrome used for chariot races, political conflicts, the exalting or insulting of emperors, and the creation of martyrs in the flames at the stake. All these diversions were furnished free to the mob, as was bread for many centuries, emulating the control measures on the masses used by the imperial government of the older Rome.

We know little of the houses of this Constantinople because the Turks so transformed them after 1453; we can judge that they were similar to those in Rome—open courtyard houses for the well-to-do, here built with two stories rather than a single one, and possibly apartmented buildings for the masses, though that is less well known. There seem to have been quarters determined by ethnic origin, a major morphogenetic element in such a polygot city, but nationality was a concept they lacked. The district served perhaps as a reception area for immigrants in a society which valued accomplishment only as success in the metropolis itself; it was not a refuge in a continuously plural society. The first object of the education which the Byzantines so revered was to Hellenize the speech of children. In fact the aesthetes of Constantinople were notorious, displaying a sneering misunderstanding of their language when pronounced with any accent other than their own, and frequently carping at emperors whose rise to the throne brought in vigorous blood but who had adopted only in maturity the Greek culture. The society that resulted was educated but close-minded and the residents of ethnic housing quarters would all have sought as quickly as possible to adopt that intellectual elevation. Byzantine culture seems to have had an indifference to nationality but an intolerance to difference that we can still perceive at work in present-day France. It produces a most distinct social geography of the city.

Perhaps the greatest contrast between the old and the new Rome came in Constantinople's role as a port.

Constantine had selected the site as one of great military importance but also as one where all of the threads of a ramified trading empire could be collected. First the Greek and then the Roman expansion had placed a facade of trading towns on the Black Sea shore, and these became the inheritance of Byzantium on the Bosphorus. As well the increasingly important trade route across Persia from India and the East led to Trebizond on the Black Sea and then to the Golden Horn. This more northerly connection to the East gained importance with the ferment and Muslim frenzy of the Arabs who, after 641 and the invasion of Egypt, placed a barrier across the traditional route to the Orient via Suez. Trade with Syria and Egypt continued but declined from the time when these areas had been important parts of Byzantium. Instead the empire looked more to the north and east and became the great entrepôt of distant Asia in its trade with Europe. At Constantinople silk fiber became the gold of commerce and the emperor monopolized its weaving into fabric.

To maintain this treasury it was necessary to make the city a great *emporium* of waterborne commerce and to tie it by sea-lanes to distant maritime clients. In this way the waterfront of Constantinople became dotted with small artificial basins at which the tiny ships of the time could be tied to the quay-walls. The other cities of the empire came for the most part to be its ports, but were both commercially and politically subservient. Nonetheless the one case of a detached and somewhat rival Byzantine state came when the great eastern port of Trebizond became a separate state in the chaos that resulted from the Latin conquest of Constantinople in 1204 during the Fourth Crusade. The noble Alexius Comnenus escaped Constantinople, going to her client, Trebizond, to set himself up as the Grand Comnenus, the emperor of a detached Byzantine empire which lived for nine years longer than the restored central state itself, that is until 1461 when Trebizond finally fell by betrayal to the Ottoman Turks.

Both in Constantinople and in Trebizond the seeds of the decline of the empire were sown during the Fourth Crusade, that strangely redirected undertaking which was captured by the house of Hohenstaufen and the Venetians and diverted from the recapture of Jerusalem (from the Egyptians) to the destruction of the Greek Byzantium through the western capture of the New Rome that was Constantinople. In 1204 the Germans and the Normans conquered Constantinople and installed the Latin empire of the east for a period of sixty years. That substitution drove the Comnenni to Trebizond, but it also began the final destruction of the eastern empire, which became complete only in 1453 when Constantinople fell to the Ottoman Turks and the last remnant of imperial Rome and its fundamentally urban culture and polity disappeared. But much as the

Crusades fairly directly destroyed the last of the old order, they rather paradoxically brought in the new.

In the next chapter, we will discuss the emergence of the western city from the darkness and neglect that followed on the shrinking of the empire in the west after the year 480. But we may take note of the contribution of the east to that emergence and the role that the Crusades played as an agent of cultural continuity.

The Trading Overlay

At Ostia, old Rome's first port, excavations have revealed a number of *statio*, rooms where occupations were carried on either in manufacture or trade, and among these was a rank of shops for *navicularii* fitting out ships for trade with distant ports.

There were the fitters of Alexandria, for instance, the fitters of Narbonne and Arles in Gaul, those of Cagliari and Porto-Torres in Sardinia. There were those of celebrated and forgotten ports in northern Africa; Carthage, whose mercantile fleet the mosaic artist has stylised; Hippo-Diarrhytus, the modern Bizerta; Curbis, now Courba to the north of the Gulf of Hammamet; Missua, now Sidi Dand, south-west of Cape Bon; Gummi, now Bordj Cedria, at the base of the Gulf of Carthage. . . . Incomplete though this enumeration is, it may seem overdetailed to the reader. But if, instead of merely reading through a list of place-names, you decipher them yourself at Ostia, and yourself step on these naive pictures in which each (trading) corporation tried by a sly touch to define its business and evoke the memory of its distant home, you cannot fail to be seized with admiration before the spacious and impressive reality which these modest tokens represent. . . . But apart from the esplanade which they adorn, their lines embrace all the expanse of land and sea between the Isthmus of Suez and the Pillars of Hercules. And suddenly you see the throngs of people, strangers to each other, born in far distant lands, rowing to meet each other here in answer to the needs of Rome, and you feel that there gravitates for ever round this unforgettable enclosure (in Ostia) not only the mass of goods which Rome appropriated for herself in every corner of the earth but the cortege of docile nations whom she consecrated to her service.[47]

One of the corporation of traders' mosaics still to be found in Ostia Antica.

[47]*Carcopino, op. cit., pp. 175-176.*

The relationship is clearly that of metropolis and client, of the foreign-born trader coming to live under Roman law and countenance to facilitate the flow of goods to the world's greatest consumer. And the spread of the empire to include the entire Mediterranean world served to make this trade internal to the state, though no doubt still aided by migration of North Africans or of Levantines to Ostia and Rome. The critical point for our attention is that in this single system of trade, the *navicularii* resided alongside the local shopkeepers and sold apparently to the same body of customers.

With the decline of the empire in the west, trade there shrank in its geographical extent and for the first millennium of the Christian era Constantinople and the empire of the east tended to maintain this traditional trading system. The city on the Bosphorus had early become a fundamentally coastal state with Byzantine ports spread around the Black Sea, the Aegian, the coast of Levant, the islands of Sicily and Crete, and the extremities of the Italian peninsula and its east coast as far north as Ravenna. And the history of that Byzantine state was that of slow truncation of these distant ties. When in 439 the Vandals established themselves at Carthage, the *mare nostrum* of the Romans was no more; quickly the facade of undefended ports that ringed the Mediterranean had to be walled and garrisoned. At the end of the sixth century the eastern emperor Tiberius abandoned his Italian lands to the Lombards to save the empire of the east. Old Rome became politically detached, coming then under the sway of the Latin pope. In 638 the Arabs captured Jerusalem and in 641 they successfully invaded Egypt, removing most of the eastern coastline of the Mediterranean from Byzantine control and leaving its southern boundary on the Taurus mountains of Anatolia. The eighth century saw the final loss of Italian lands north of Calabria, the ninth the capture of Crete by Arab pirates and the overrunning of Sicily and Calabria by Arabs; although south Italy was recaptured, Sicily remained in Arab hands until liberated by the Normans between 1070 and 1090. And that liberation was accomplished by the two forces emerging in the classical world—the French-Norman barons seeking to carve principalities out of the lands lost by Byzantium to the Muslims, and the Italian city-states which sought to take over the Asiatic trade from the Syrians and the merchants of Constantinople—when the Norman Duke Roger d'Hauteville was aided by the citizens of Pisa.

The decline of the empire of the east was first expressed geographically with this loss of the Levant and Egypt to the Saracens and of Sicily finally to the Normans. Ultimately, however, the loss was even greater;

she lost full sovereignty over the trade that made her wealthy. The "Holy War" of the Crusades became the fundamental instrument of the east's decline as well as that of the west's reemergence as a scene of urban activity. Without going into the religious and political basis of the Crusades, we may note certain events that bore heavily on this shift of the focus of urbanization. Several parties were common to most of the seven recognized Crusades—obviously the ecclesiastical power in the west, the papacy; the French, German, and English feudal nobility who were perhaps as much gripped by the desire for the expansion of the realm open to their feudal system and to their dominion as by a wish to take the Cross; and the merchants of the reviving cities of northern Italy who sought to gain a firmer control over the trade of the east. The ascendancy among these somewhat conflicting groups basically determined what the campaign accomplished and where it led.

The First Crusade at the end of the eleventh century was an Holy War to recapture Palestine, and particularly Jerusalem, from the infidel, and it succeeded in that undertaking. But its success was expressed not in the creation of a sacred state administered by the western pope, but by the shaping of a Franco-Norman kingdom of Jerusalem to which the west introduced feudalism and western trade. Significantly the towns came to be administered directly by a burgher government, and the knights who had won the Holy Land and held its land in feudal tenure from the King of Jerusalem were forbidden to live in the towns. During its life, from 1100 to 1143, the Latin Kingdom of Jerusalem survived by trade. Its southerly extension to the Gulf of Aquaba was determined by a desire to gain access to the Indies via the Red Sea, a geographical proposition which is not foreign to our times.

The main assistance that the Frankish knights had had during this liberation had come from the Italian trading towns. So the merchants from those places began to operate in the Mediterranean ports of the Latin Kingdom in the Levant, where they were even granted special burghal courts to oversee their commercial life. In return for their support the Venetians had asked a freedom from tolls in these ports and one-third of the space in any city they helped conquer. The Pisans and Genoese operated in similar fashion, establishing the notion of special privilege in trade and political extraterritoriality in town. When the Venetians gave further help to Baldwin II in 1128 they gained a Venetian quarter in Jerusalem. While all this was going on the Venetians lost similar privileges they had enjoyed in Constantinople since 1080 so the basis of a later fight was set. "The Venetians, however, maintained their position in Palestine; and their quarters remained, along with those of the Genoese, as privileged commercial franchises in an otherwise feudal state."[48]

The Second and Third Crusades do not concern us as they were not of urban significance, but the Fourth does. Although initially intended as an expedition to recapture Jerusalem, which had been retaken by Saladin in 1187, the Crusade beginning in 1202 became primarily an attack of western commerce upon the empire of the east. To gain Venetian transport and assistance, the crusaders agreed first to retake the Dalmation port of Zara (Zadar) from the King of Hungary and give it back to the great trading republic of the Adriatic. Then the expedition was totally diverted from the Holy Land seeking to capture Constantinople and make of it a Latin empire, and perhaps more lastingly, a western commercial entrepôt. Thus, in 1204 the capture was effected and the eastern empire was opened to western traders.

By this cession the west obtained the basis of an extensive trade, which would lead to a revival of urban life on a large scale in the west, and knowledge of the functioning urban institutions of the east that might be carried home with them. The second point should not be overlooked: much as the Roman empire had brought city life to all the lands from the Irish Sea to the Caspian, its relicts in the west were physical museums of urban life rather than continuing institutions. When the English, Franks, and Germans returned from the Fourth Crusade they brought home vivid experience in the world's greatest city and knowledge of a system of trading towns impossible to obtain in the west. And so long as they controlled Constantinople (until 1260) and tiny remnants of the destroyed Latin Kingdom of Jerusalem (up to the final capture of Acre by the Muslims in 1291), the west possessed a flow of eastern goods that stood in great demand at home.

To understand this appeal, we must appreciate that long-distance trade comes first in luxuries rather than in lowly staples. Only a good of great rarity and irrational appeal can carry the burden of the great transportation costs that attend upon the initiation of long-distance trade. The silks of Constantinople and the jewels and spices of the Indies could be sold profitably in the west. And the rise of demand there was such that a new era of urbanization was inaugurated. We are basically concerned with that flush of creativity in cities and its historical geographical consequences.

The medieval urban revolution of the west, however, did not come without forebears. They were perhaps in significant terms first the individualistic, parochial city-states of Greece, where political institutions were forged but from whom came a rather weak economic organization. The Romans of the Classical Era showed the way for cities to exist as a vast integrated system and first perhaps used the city as the center of culture and political life. The Roman city showed that the notion of the city's growing out of the countryside, so often repeated as fundamental "truth" even down to the present, was at best a special case of truth. Into this progression, the cities of Byzantium fall not so much in an active role, but as conservators of a great urban tradition. For a time they controlled their own urban course. But with the onset of the Crusades a new dynamic was introduced which first allowed the west to refound an urban course and then gave to it the economic basis for its growth and geographical expansion.

It would be as grievous an error to think our urban history in the west to be discontinuous as it is to think our cities the scion of a fully agriculture inheritance. We must be aware of the continuity of urbanization since Athens and Miletus, and be conversant with the shift of urbanization emphasis from Greece, to Rome, and then on to Constantinople. We must be aware of the shift again to the west, particularly to the hearths of a resurgent urbanization in European life in Lombardy and Flanders, which supplied many of the personae of the Crusades. But we must as well be aware of the stagnation and even disappearance of the city in the west during the second half of the first millennium of the Christian Era. If the urban slate was not vacant it was at least very nearly empty when the first outlines of the medieval city in western life were drawn. In abandoning our consideration of the east at this point we do not turn our backs on a continuingly vigorous city life. Athens and Constantinople begin a decline that lasted until the nineteenth century when only the diffusion of clearly western urbanism returned them to the scene of man.

[48]*Ernest Barker, "The Crusades,"* Encyclopaedia Britannica, *11th Edition, 1910, Vol. 7, p. 530.*

3. THE DISINTEGRATION INTO FEUDALISM AND THE DAWN OF FREEDOM

On Christmas morning in the year 800 the Roman pope, Leo III, placed a golden crown on the head of Charles the Great, Charlemagne, as he rose from prayer at services in St. Peter's basilica in Rome. Charles affected surprise; his contemporary biographer, Einhard, tells us that Charlemagne would not have entered the building that morning had he known this event would take place. This tale may have sufficed in the age of romantic chivalry but in our cynical times doubt does intrude. Nevertheless, the act of Charlemagne's crowning serves well to divide the classical from the medieval times. Although Charlemagne was proclaimed emperor and *augustus*, those offices could function only in the west. Yet his sway there finally signalled the end of the orthodox succession from the Caesars and the establishment first of a rival to Byzantium and second of what we have come to call western civilization. We are most concerned with that tradition, for within its diverse components the city we wish to look at arose, and the present-day concept of the city in almost all cultures was founded.

The medieval city, as a physical entity and an economic and social institution, established the basic conditions for the domination of modern history both by the political control of the west and by its form of urbanization. Even now, when that political domination has largely disappeared, the urban power shows little sign of decline. Just as the Roman city lasted for a thousand years after the Roman Empire, so the western city carries on after the end of western suzerainty.

The Survival of the Roman City in the West

We may profit from a few rather summary conclusions about the history of Rome's decline to help us visualize the experience of cities during the four centuries between A.D. 400, when Alaric led his Visigoths southward across the Alps for the first barbarian invasion of Italy, and A.D. 800, when a coequal but separate western Holy Roman Empire was created by Leo III and Charlemagne. Those four centuries held numerous barbarian invasions, attempts to control Italy by Byzantium, betrayals, murders, assassinations, and other evidences of destruction of the political and economic order. The city as the central institution of Roman life suffered early in this anarchy and came to be its most obvious victim.

To understand why, we must consider the role the city played in Roman life. First it was the organic base on which the Roman state grew; largely by replication of that organic unit did Rome take over the Mediterranean and west European world. Just as the republican Romans had spread outward from Rome into Latium, coming to be the political overlords of the countryside in the process of dioecism, so the imperial Romans by dioecism took over their empire, effectively controlling and organizing it through a system of cities.

The Roman Empire was a system of cities interconnected but singly focussed, reaching from Mesopotamia to Hadrian's Wall in northern England, as a political and economic unit, though the fundamental structure was that of a vast area tributary to Rome herself. In the view of the empire, the Eternal City should also be the center of life, culture, political power, and luxury. To fulfill that role, the empire must produce for Rome and, to a lesser degree, for the cities planted by the Roman dioecism in Gaul, or Spain, or Mesopotamia. To support their roles as the provincial expression of the imperial state and civilization, these Roman cities of the empire had to harvest a greater return from their hinterlands than their own efforts had produced. As Robert Latouche has noted of all Roman cities, "They were centres not of production, but of expenditure. They constituted for the Empire sources, not of wealth, but of impoverishment."[1]

In such a political situation the economic system must be heavily centered on the *support* of cities, with every effort made to cause more goods to flow to the center—either Rome herself or her provincial progeny. If the flow of slaves and goods could be maintained, so might the political system, but once the flow decreased, the central city was likely to suffer badly. The denizens of late imperial Rome lacked the patriotism of their republican forebears, showing a tendency to betray the city for material rewards. In Gaul, the chaos of the third century arose when the Alamani and the Franks broke through the Danubian *limes*, the border defenses, leading to a successful Gallic Empire under Postumus that lasted for a decade (259-269). Only the restoration of those border defenses by a strong central authority under the emperor Diocletian destroyed the Gallic separatism and that of the princes of Palmyra in the east. These events foretold the ultimate experience of Rome and her cities.

At the close of the third century the pattern of Roman defense began to change from one based on frontier protection (and within those *limes* the maintenance of the *pax Romana*) which had allowed open cities. Traditionally walled cities had been necessary only toward the edge of the empire, but, as the whole

[1] *Robert Latouche,* The Birth of Western Economy, *New York: Harper and Row, 1966, p. 5.*

Aachen Cathedral was begun
during Charlemagne's reign,
and the octagonal section
to the left was completed
at that time in Roman-
esque style. The Gothic
choir, to the right, was
completed in the early
fifteenth century.

the beginning of a secular demographic decline. Slave trading fell with the extinction of Roman conquests. A fairly virulent onset of plagues and epidemics appears to have flared up in the second century, continuing until the mid-sixth century.[3] With circumvallation went population decline, so little need arose to reconstruct the city cores now surrounded by walls. In fact, the urban history of the late empire and succeeding centuries appears to have been one of contraction. The city became both a refuge and a quarry—even in Rome, where Aurelian's Wall was made up of "ramparts hastily thrown together, the masons using indiscriminately altars, inscriptions, columns, whatever material came to hand."[4] The first wall at Autun in Burgundy, built in the early empire, extended for 5,922 meters, whereas the second, constructed in the late empire, was only 1,300 meters.[5] The city did not die, but without question its survival was largely one of hibernation, though some active summers interrupted the ageing process.

Understanding the rapidity of the contraction of the Roman city depends in part on awareness of the basic support of these places. The view is fairly widespread that the barbarian invasions "destroyed" these cities, leaving us with some notion that the hordes sought to shatter a higher civilization. But the "barbarians" were more foreign than vicious, more desirous of participating in the Roman luxury than of destroying it, and were not at all numerous. They were vigorous and uninhibited, qualities that did not jibe too well with the fragility of Roman civilization in its later stages. The foreigners wanted to be Romanized, and were to a considerable degree, so the destruction of the Roman urban geography was not their intent. The collapse came because the conditions that allowed the barbarians to enter the empire also tended toward the dismemberment of its integrated network of cities.

The truth of this assertion is shown by the restoration of the "Roman Peace" in the fourth century when, under Diocletian and Constantine in particular, the *limes* were restored and the empire was ostensibly reintegrated. But the restoration was illusory. Diocletian never succeeded in making Rome whole. He himself established his capital at Nicomedia (fifty miles east of Istanbul) but subsequently added three capitals in an attempt to control a disintegrating empire. They were at Mediolanum (Milan), Augusta Trevivorum (Trier) and Sirmium (in northeast Yugoslavia). In each he placed a member of the imperial quadrumvirate of two emperors, *augusti*, and two heirs apparent, *caesari*.

imperial structure began to show cracks, even Rome in A.D. 271 had to be walled by the emperor Aurelian. Previously the imperial city and the larger provincial towns of Gaul and Italy had grown unhindered by walls. "Spacious and airy, possessing many fine, handsome public buildings, they were often completed by residential suburbs much favoured by the wealthiest inhabitants, as for instance those of Trinquetaille at Arles and of Sainte-Colombe at Vienne, separated by the Rhône from the main block of town buildings."[2] But the threat that came with the failure of the *limes* caused walls to be thrown up rapidly in the third and fourth centuries, and certainly the "open city" began to shrink and disappear within the walls.

In part this contraction was probably urged on by

[2]Ibid., *p. 7.*

[3]*Robert S. Lopez,* The Commercial Revolution of the Middle Ages, 950-1350, *Englewood Cliffs, N.J.: Prentice-Hall, Inc., 1971, p. 12.*
[4]*Latouche,* op. cit., *p. 7.*
[5]Ibid., *p. 8.*

This system rapidly deteriorated into a factionalism tied to geographical partitioning. Even while the quadrumvirate lasted, the emperor Honorius in 402 shifted the dominant capital to Ravenna from Mediolanum, where it had been for a century. Already Constantine had moved the eastern capital fifty miles westward to the Golden Horn, founding Constantinople in 330. By the end of the fifth century the division between east and west was becoming decisive and after that century there were no emperors of the west. Instead the Gothic invaders established themselves in the Po Basin, raising Mediolanum to a higher political position than Rome, creating the Lombard Kingdom with its crown of iron, and causing the eastern empire to set up a rival capital at Ravenna on the remnants of land they held in Italy. We need not follow all of the peregrinations of the seats of government or the varying fates of Rome under the early Roman popes, but we will note the clear destruction of Rome as the primate city of the empire.

The consequence of this destruction was the parcelling out of the area that had previously been tributary to Rome and the near destruction of the integrated network that focussed trade and administration on the Eternal City. In this dismembered state the provincial cities did not gain at Rome's expense: they all lost, and the "total urbanization" was not so great as it had been.

To understand this absolute decline of city life we must be aware that the city was economically a parasite on the countryside (but we must beware of generalizing this relationship as the one found throughout time between cities and the countryside). The Romans were architects and engineers but they were not merchants who could occupy and use effectively the structures they knew so well how to build. To cite several instances of their failure: the Romans had a superbly integrated system of very expensive military roads extending from Armenia to the lowlands of Scotland, but these roads were too narrow to carry the carts that would have been necessary for effective long-distance trade; the city of Rome was the largest ever built up to its time but it seems to have experienced no economies of scale in the production of goods and to have engaged in no considerable export of manufactures that might have repaid the empire for the vast incoming flow of raw materials and food; and the Romans viewed trade as so lowly an occupation that even the possibly higher economic return from it could not persuade Roman patricians to take it up in place of the less rewarding practice of agricultural capitalism. The basis of Roman wealth remained extractive. Taxes were drawn in ever harsher sums from an empire that was declining in wealth. The Romans captured slaves whose sweated labor would allow the poor manufacturing technology of the times to creak onward for a

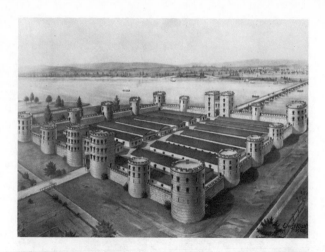

Fort Deutz and the Rhine bridge were built by the Romans to defend the limes *against the unconquered Germanic tribes on the east bank of the Rhine.*

couple of additional centuries. The accumulated wealth of their neighbors was plundered to add capital to the Roman pot, but that wealth was consumed to maintain the decadent grandeur of Rome.

When taxation dried up, when enslavement was reversed allowing the enemies to capture and sell Romans, and when plunder was beyond the reach of the legions, the Roman urban system collapsed, not all at once but with irreversible certainty. In this sequence we find the basis of the *process of contraction* that was the Roman dynamic from around the year 300 to the time of Charlemagne. The failure of the Roman system, its parasitism on the distant countryside, and its critical dependence upon the network of urbanization brought the functional structure down. Let it be emphasized that the barbarians did not do it; they sought with all their might to preserve Rome but they lacked the numbers or the skill to do so, as the Romans lacked the energy or the will. We tend to look upon the Romans as superb city builders, which they were only in the precise sense. They were great engineers, but as breadwinners who could maintain the life of the cities they designed, they were incompetent. Not insignificantly, the political successor of the Roman emperors, the Roman pope, is still denominated the leading engineer—*pontifex maximus.*

Contraction Almost to Extinction

The search for the roots of the modern city in the western world must take place in the "Dark Ages," whose obscurity unquestionably hides a revolution of urban life similar to that of the seventeenth to nineteenth centuries. To borrow a modern term, the Dark Ages are perhaps more a "black box" than a time of collapse of civilization as they once were thought: at the onset of the ninth century the classical Roman city still existed whereas at the close of that period a new form of city emerged. The process of transformation may not be fully chronicled but its outcome is reasonably clear and well-known.

Charlemagne's Holy Roman Empire was ostensibly shaped from a Roman inheritance, but it was markedly different from its predecessor. It contained most of present-day East and West Germany, The Netherlands, Austria, and Czechoslovakia, which had not lain within the older *limes*, whereas it omitted Spain, southern Italy, the Balkans, the Near East, and North Africa, which had. The Holy Roman Empire was basically German rather than Roman. Charlemagne may have been crowned in Rome but he lived, when he was at home, in Aix-la-Chapelle, Aachen, at the juncture of modern Belgium, Holland, and West Germany. Much of the time he was wandering about his empire, pushing its limits outward in warfare, enjoying its pleasures in hunting, or seeking its governance by periodic residence in Frankfurt or some other provincial city. The cities of the Holy Roman Empire either stood as contractions of formerly more extensive classical towns, or were newly founded by the Franks in that part of Charlemagne's empire added by those warriors to what they had taken over from the Romans. In either case the towns were small and weak. Seemingly, the Franks inherited an almost dead institution and they possessed too little personal understanding of its form to rejuvenate it.

The Franks had been barbarians with a history of movement rather than strongly fixed settlement. For many years they were thought to have been practitioners of a primitive collectivism, *Markgenossenschaft*, but that view has been rejected by recent historians who think instead that the Franks ultimately became at best a village people.

The hamlet appears to have been, in many instances, their primitive unit, for though the Germans (Franks) had little liking for town life they seem from early times to have been loath to live in isolation. Families willingly joined together in small settlements (Weiler) consisting of several homesteads detached from each other, wooden huts covered with thatch, or even underground shelters roofed with turf, examples of which can still be seen (among the people of Germanic origin) in Iceland. Huts and shelters were dotted here and there without any preconceived plan and the same lack of order was evident also in the villages, groups of dwellings believed to represent a more recent stage of settlement. To these villages which have no set plan, German scholars have given the name of Haufendorfer ("thrown-together villages").[6]

Around these *Haufendorfer* the land was organized in private holdings cultivated by the residents. The Frankish invaders brought this pattern with them into Gaul when they crossed the *limes*, which extended basically along the Rhine from Lake Constance to the North Sea.

When the Salian Franks gained control of this area in the fourth and fifth centuries, they brought with them a form of settlement different from the one the Romans had developed in Gaul and a contrasting viewpoint on property. The Franks had shaped a society dependent upon small landholding and, in simplest terms, the sanctity of private property. Of the Salian Franks, Latouche concludes, "What a study of the Salic Law does bring out . . . is the strong preference of the Franks for individual ownership. . . . This makes it clear that the Frankish occupation strengthened the small peasant and family holding in those areas in which the Franks settled. . . ."[7]

The Franks introduced to Gaul, and to its border zone with Germany, private smallholdings that contrasted sharply with the landed estates that the Romans had developed there. Those Roman *villae* were the domain of a group of aristocrats, *potentes*, who shunned trade as ungentlemanly and who had come to look upon country living as the proper state of those possessed of power. At the same time the Franks were bringing in the peasant holding for the masses, their leaders were taking over the notion of the *villa* and transforming it into what we now term the medieval manor. In doing so, however, they were introducing a potential conflict with their own followers of lesser status who held strongly the Frankish view of a free peasantry. This view was protected by a Salic Law which came to be recorded, and thus less subject to tampering, when the art of writing was learned from the Romans.

A second conflict grew up in a rather complicated

[6]*From August Meitzen*, Siedelung, *Vol. I, p. 47, in Latouch, op. cit., p. 33. Emphasis supplied.*
[7]*Latouche, op. cit., p. 80.*

way when the Franks invaded this frontier zone just west of the Rhine. As a barbarian group they had lacked any understanding of speculation on capital and lending money at interest, as noted by Tacitus,[8] yet they held to private ownership of property. When they moved into the frontier of Gaul, the migration was in part a peaceful fusing of peoples, so the Franks took over some of the practices of the Romans. One practice often frowned on but engaged in of necessity was trade for profit and the use of capital for interest. Mingling all of these practices, the Franks brought forth a powerful potential for important advances in the world of trade. But as their skills were ripening, Christianity overtook them, and they were confronted with the attitude enunciated by the Fathers of the Church, who looked upon profit and money interest as *turpe lucrum*, sinful gain.

No doubt the realization of the potential to trade was further put off by the romantic chivalry that gripped the Carolingian court. Under chivalry the hauteur of the Roman *potentes* was accepted into medieval society thriving at the manors given to knights of the court. It became one of the elements of faith in the countryside that trade was of questionable morality, in agreement with the Fathers, and of low caste, in line with the thinking of the lords of the manor. Yet the powerful brew compounded of the grain of Frankish private ownership and the yeast of the Roman attitudes toward profit was ageing away in the Frankish kingdoms stretched across northern France, the Low Countries, and Germany while Europe cavorted with Charlemagne and his knights. It did not come into its own until the short-lived Carolingian Empire collapsed resoundingly in the ninth century.

The Processes of Contraction and Parochialization

Historians extensively discuss the reasons for the Dark Ages of urbanization which came in the ninth and tenth centuries. The great Belgium economic historian, Henri Pirenne, argued that the breaking of the Mediterranean trade link, due to the coming of the Muslims, brought on economic stagnation and decline in Europe. That Mediterranean link had for Rome been "the

bulwark of both its political and economic unity."[9] Pirenne held that the barbarian invasions had not led to urban decline, because the "supposed dislike of the barbarians for towns is an admitted fable to which reality has given the lie." On the frontiers barbarians may have pillaged and burned Roman towns but "it is none the less true that the immense majority survived the invasions." Most of the larger cities of that part of Europe held by the Romans are even today those founded by that empire.[10] "It is also well established that these cities were centers of an economic activity which itself was a survival of the preceding [Roman] civilization." All cities were markets for the surrounding countryside, "the winter homes of great landed proprietors of the neighborhood and, if favorably situated, the center of a commerce the more highly developed in proportion to its nearness to the shores of the Mediterranean."[11] This last condition reveals the critical nature of the link across the Mediterranean, broken by the radical transformation of the urban geography of Europe.

The barbarians did not seek to destroy cities; nevertheless they experienced their decline. The change came in an odd way, as trade contracted under the barbarians from the general exchange of bulk commodities—grain, oil, wine, and the like—as under the Romans, to the trading in small quantities of high luxuries. Two processes were at work: contraction of all trade into a much smaller compass than before, and parochialization of the provision of most staples into local production and consumption. This change in trade created two new institutions that became archetypal of the Dark Ages: first, contracted trade, and its hand-over to a group of foreign merchants able to deal internationally in a new multinational and multi-religious western civilization; second, the creation of a new rural economy to care for what were now localized productions and demands—feudalism, with its economic backstay, the manor. The international traders came to be known as "Orientals," which translates today to Jews and Levantines or Syrians. As non-Christians they could trade with Islam more successfully; as international men they could pass through a newly fragmented Europe serving, strangely, as the agents of the papacy, collecting the massive tithes which beggared Europe outside Rome and kept the Roman curia in luxury and hauteur. As papal agents, these Orientals could cross the multitude of frontiers yet remain exempt from the exactions that made trade almost impossible to the Frenchman or the German.

[8]*Tacitus*, Germania, 26, *translated by H. Mattingly, West Drayton (Middlesex): Penguin Books, 1948, p. 122.*

[9]*Henri Pirenne*, Medieval Cities: Their Origins and the Revival of Trade, *Princeton: Princeton University Press, 1925, pp. 1-2.*
[10]*Ibid., p. 11.*
[11]*Ibid., p. 13.*

Thus, they conducted what little distant trading was done, in lines where the price could be vastly inflated to reflect the difficulty encountered. Only luxury items moved any distance.

The parochialization of staple provision shaped the feudal economy, causing a strong push toward *autarky*—local self-sufficiency—so that each area could produce only the most essential of products. Necessity became institutionalized to the extent that manors of petty feudal holdings sought self-sufficiency and rigid control of trade. On the one hand, they were assured a continuing sufficient supply of those things produced locally before feudalism by keeping the items at home; on the other, this rigid control sought to protect infant local activities against periodic disruption through more distant trade. And finally, the absence of much long-distance trade necessitated a system of financial support for the manor or barony through excises on goods locally exchanged. Market tolls, murrage tolls to cover the assumed cost of providing walls for protection, pontage at local bridges, and other tithes, assizes, and excise taxes assured that the protected local economy furnished the feudal lord the support that had come previously from exactions on more distant trade. In the end the desire to defend those local excises was crucial in seeking a clearly defined parochial trading area.

The processes of contraction and parochialization in the Dark Ages had two rather distinct expressions even within the low level of urban development characteristic of the time. The dependence upon the foreign trader led to the need to create areas of tolerance within the small towns where alien religious and social practices would be permitted under the notion of extraterritoriality. Quarters were defined for Syrians or Jews distinct from the rest of the orthodox, Catholic town. As agents of the Roman curia these unbelievers were protected and given great power. In part, a strong rejection of this ultramontane meddling caused the main western nations to evict the Jews in the later Middle Ages, as they did the Jesuits in the nineteenth-century period of anticlericalism.

The parochialization of the staple economy to that of the manor or barony had two effects on cities. First it greatly reduced the need for, and support of, cities. Roman towns shrank in size as well as in numbers as distant trading no longer amounted to more than a periodic peddling of luxury goods by foreign traders. In their place came the local central-places for the feudal economy, little more than marketplaces to which the countrymen came in order to swap with one another the goods produced in the local "natural economy," as it is sometimes called. These central-place villages were the outgrowth of feudalism and were new on the urban scene, literally unknown among the Romans and

little developed wherever the distant-trading economy could be preserved. Thus, Walter Christaller's central-place theory, which we will subsequently examine, was an outgrowth of the two contractive forces of the Dark Ages.

The constraints placed upon the "Oriental merchants" circulating through the Europe of the early Middle Ages reflected their moral ambiguity, which Pirenne cites. "The oriental merchants of the Frankish Empire were virtually engaged in wholesale trade. Their boats, after being discharged on the quays of Marseilles, certainly carried back, on leaving the shore of Provence, not only passengers but return freight." Among the most important of those freights was "human chattels—that is to say slaves."[12] This was a trade of slaves for luxuries; western Europe provided the unfortunates and the Levant the luxuries. Providentially the disruption and chaos of post-Charlemagne Europe substantially cut off the supply of slaves. In their absence, the Syrians and Jews no longer very actively sought to trade. With wholesale trade in the hands of foreigners, town life began to suffer an eclipse. In the fifth century industrial production in Europe was declining and trade was so precarious that export over any distance became nearly impossible. In that situation the occupation of merchant fell "into the hands of Orientals, chiefly Syrians . . . . These men engaged in trade fully alive to the risks it entailed in an unsettled age, and determined to reap enormous profits, drawing upon themselves universal execration in the process." In such a climate of trade it is little wonder that "[i]t was probably at this time that lack of merchants resident in towns which were becoming ever more depopulated gave rise to the practice of entrusting to specially commissioned agents the task of buying articles and provisions unobtainable in the local market."[13]

The process of contraction led oddly to more markets than existed with distant trading. But Pirenne holds, "The great number of markets (*mercatus*), which were to be found in the ninth century, in no way contradicts [the notion of the decline of trade.] They were, as a matter of fact, only small market-places, instituted for the weekly provisioning of the populace by means of retail sale of foodstuffs from the country."[14]

"For an economy of exchange was substituted an economy of consumption. Each demesnes, in place of continuing to deal with the outside, constituted from this time on a little world of its own. It lived by itself and for itself, in the traditional immobility of the patriarchal form of government. The ninth century is the golden age of what we have called the closed domestic

[12]Ibid., *pp. 19-20.*
[13]*Latouche*, op. cit., *pp. 27-28.*
[14]*Pirenne*, op. cit., *pp. 34-35.*

economy and which we might call, with more exactitude, the economy of no markets."[15]

In that economy the central-place was born. Local people traded among themselves and only specially constituted agents—either Oriental peddlers or servants of the monasteries and great manors sent to buy at a distance—had any trading function independent of actual production and consumption. It was a world of no markets, which saw the rise of the chapman, or peddler. It had no true cities, in Pirenne's view. If by *city* is "meant a locality the population of which, instead of living by working the soil, devotes itself to commercial activity, the answer [to whether there were cities in the Dark Ages] will have to be 'No.' The answer will also be in the negative if we understand by 'city' a community endowed with legal personality and possessing laws and institutions peculiar to itself." But if by *city* is meant a place of administration and fortification, then the Dark Ages had nearly as many cities as the later Middle Ages. "That is merely another way of saying that the cities which were then to be found were without two of the fundamental attributes of the cities of the Middle Ages and of modern times—a middle-class population and a communal organization."[16]

Other views of this question have been set forth. Robert Latouche found an eclipse wherein the economic functions largely departed the city while the religious ones remained and probably expanded. The veneration of relics and the maintenance of Catholic sees in former Roman cities played a particularly great role in maintaining a continuity to urbanization in the ninth and tenth centuries.[17]

More recently Robert Lopez has seen a less continuous break in the urbanization process, catching sight of a glimmer of urban restoration in the tenth century which faltered then but became continuous from the eleventh. Significantly he sees in the Byzantine continuation of the Roman Empire and the Muslim Caliphates that came to power in the Near East a lack of vigor fundamental to shaping a new form of urbanization. Rather, he argues, the failure of Charlemagne's attempts to shape an Empire of the West cleared the stage for the new form. "[H]ad the Carolingian Empire endured, Catholic Europe might perhaps have become a centralized, authoritarian, land-rooted monarchy combining Byzantine with Barbarian characteristics. It crumbled before the end of the ninth century, and the budding nations of the West were released to work their way up by trial and error, in an original way."[18]

I would argue the case differently. Much as the city

of the west went into eclipse, it emerged from the Dark Ages *as the basic institution of power and with the only social institutions capable of integrated expansion.* In the western city were pioneered the economic weapons by which conquest and consolidation could be carried out—mercantile support and the founding of taxation on commercial prosperity rather than tribute. Neither the Byzantines nor the Muslims learned these lessons so well, though we must admit that the eastern Emperors and the Caliphs mastered part of the lesson; Constantinople created an imperial monopoly for silk textiles and sought to maintain the royal grandeur on that base.[19] And the Muslims were far ahead of the early Christians in granting honor to the merchant and trader, not alone because the Prophet himself had held that occupation. On the plunder from traders whose course to Mecca Muhammad and his forces intercepted, Islam based its ultimate campaign against that city. By gaining the tribute that had traditionally gone to Mecca, Islam could mount its efforts to convert the world to its view.[20]

The Church Preserves the City

The Roman city became a fossil shell, beginning in the fifth century but most notably at the end of the ninth century in late Carolingian times. What then became of cities? Who could benefit from possession of such a fossil shell? The answer is obvious: the medieval church. Despite the humility and simplicity on which Christianity was founded, the formal church, which viewed itself as the instrument of ecclesiastical continuity, quickly eschewed such gentle poverty. When Constantine was won over to the new faith, he was not gripped by any will to abandon either his power or its physical expression. In the New Rome that was Constantinople, grandeur was decreed. Soon the greatest church in Christendom—the church of the Holy Thought, Hagia Sophia—was built and opened with Constantine's boast, "Oh, Solomon, Thou art Vanquished." Though the eastern and western churches ultimately sepa-

[15]Ibid., p. 46.
[16]Ibid., p. 56.
[17]*Latouche*, op. cit., p. 97.
[18]*Lopez*, op. cit., p. 26.

[19]*See Steven Runciman*, Byzantine Civilization [*first published 1933*], Cleveland: World Publishing Company, 1956, Chapter VII.
[20]*Alfred Guillaume*, Islam, *Harmondsworth (Middlesex): Penguin Books, 1954, pp. 20-54.*

---

rated, neither sought austerity or simplicity of structure. The Roman church deliberately attempted to become the successor to Constantine as much or more than to Peter. In this attempt, the geographical system of cities that the imperial Romans had shaped was most appealing to the powerful clerics.

Not only were the cities themselves useful but also the system of tribute on which they were founded seemed directly applicable to the new religious empire. We have already seen the significance of the collection of tithes from all parts of Roman Christendom; it was important enough to make allies of the curia and the Orientals. While Catholics were told by Ambrose and other Church Fathers that profit itself was dubious, interest on money was sinful, and trade suspect, the

The cathedral in Trier, to the left, was begun as a Roman building before the inhabitants were Christianized, and transformed into a church for the powerful Prince Bishop of Trier.

pope did not inveigh against the traders from the east whose transport of tithes supported the power and pomp of the church.

Because the cities so symbolized established authority, yet stood so useless in early feudal times, the church was probably the only institution giving them much thought. Tours, Lyon, Narbonne, Cologne, Trier, and a number of Roman towns became the seats of powerful bishops, who wielded influence within the church but also served on occasion, or commonly, as lay lords of the cities themselves. The bishops of Trier were among the great magnates of medieval times and, even as late as the beginning of the Industrial Revolution, the Prince Bishop of Liège was a ruler of great significance. The church as the most universal institution of its time maintained considerable trade. Even more, its practices of relic worship and pilgrimage encouraged travel. Several of the bastides which we will consider in Chapter 5 began as way-stations on the great pilgrimage to Santiago de Compostela. Thus, the glimmerings of an economic purpose for towns greater than their rather rustic base of serving as tiny central-places were first seen by the church.

Society Diffuses in the Countryside: Feudalism

At the same time the church came to dominate cities, in the countryside a new order which reflected in part changes begun in Roman times was coming into existence. While the empire was growing, interregional commerce had been "more lively, but dwindled as the entire Roman world became more and more uniform. Differences in latitude, and hence in climate, are not exceedingly great between one Mediterranean region and another; wherever they went, the Romans planted the vegetables and trees which they liked, and shunned both the far North, where grapes would not ripen, and the far South, where olive trees would not grow."[21] And craftsmen in Roman towns learned to reproduce the products of Greece and Italy. The real change came, however, when the Carolingian Empire shifted the basis of power to those rural estates that had evolved from the Roman *villae*. For a while after Charlemagne the integrated imperial state could be maintained but the vote of the knife led to assassination of so many of the Frankish kings that the coherence of the rural aristocracy nearly disappeared. In its place came the concentration of real political power and economic concern on the rural manor operated under a system of feudalism.

The late French historian Marc Bloch remains the most respected scholar of feudalism; we may usefully adopt his definition of that system. The age was an interregnum of great length between the highly centralized organization of the Roman Empire and a return to that integrated state at the hands of the fifteenth- and sixteenth-century French and English monarchs who pioneered the "nation-state." European feudalism was "the outcome of the violent dissolution of older societies," unintelligible outside the context of the Frankish invasions of Gaul at the time of the collapse of the Roman Empire. Those invasions "by forcibly uniting two societies originally at very different stages of development disrupted both of them and brought to the surface a great many modes of thought and social practices of an extremely primitive character." The primitive qualities were shown by "a far-reaching restriction of social intercourse, a circulation of money too sluggish to admit of a salaried officialdom, and a mentality attached to things tangible

and local." But the transitional quality of the custom of the period was clearly shown by the fact that when "these conditions began to change, feudalism began to wane."[22] In this broad context cities shrank until feudalism came into bloom; as it withered, cities grew anew. The system of feudalism and the structure of cities appear historically to be reciprocal.

Most significantly the cause of this period of urban eclipse was the concept of wealth innate to feudalism. Historically the system had grown up to provide fighting men to sovereigns of one sort or another who were engaged in endless bloody bickering. Unlike the Romans these kings and princes had no real source of money after the era of plunder and tribute passed. So in return for the dual grants of "homage" and "fealty," passed upward from their feudal vassals, the sovereign made to them a retributive grant of a "benefice," almost invariably a source of income. In an agricultural economy this practice meant that the sovereign gave to a knight an estate of some sort from which that vassal could hope for economic support. The scale of the estate was normally proportional to the importance of the vassal because the benefice was a substitute for any salary he might expect for his services. Principal feudatories, the major servants of a king—dukes, margraves, and counts in the lay establishment and important bishops and abbots in the ecclesiastical one—could expect large domains, which they in turn divided into smaller benefices for their subfeudatories. This system of support for the monarch and for his principal feudatories required geographical division of the economy because the area a man might dominate was in direct proportion to the scale of his wealth.

We must note the different conditions in Byzantium and their ultimate impact on the emergence of a new form of city. In the east, feudalism was only partial. The one element of genius carried forward from Roman times to the Byzantine Empire was that of administration, both centrally and in distant provinces. This effective control was an aspect of peaceful administration, but not one of defense. The soldiers of Byzantium were forever losing the empire, but when they held it the administrators showed their ability. That ability was built considerably on what we would call a civil service—a professional, paid administrative force. With the concept of pay considered normal and facilitated by continuingly effective taxation which returned money to the imperial treasury, there was no need for the principal feudatories found in the west. The real need was for soldiers to defend the empire. So the Byzantine emperors devised a limited feudalism

[21]*Lopez*, op. cit., p. 7.

[22]*Marc Bloch*, Feudal Society, *Vol. 2 (Social Classes and Political Organization), Chicago: University of Chicago Press, 1954, p. 443.*

which "created tenements charged with military obligations to the State—true fiefs in one sense, but differing from those of the West in that they were peasant fiefs, each consisting of a small farm. Thenceforth it was a paramount concern of the imperial government to protect these 'soldiers' properties', as well as smallholdings in general, against the encroachments of the rich and powerful."[23]

So long as Byzantium could maintain this alliance between a peasantry and the imperial administration, the dual needs of taxation and defense could be met. The Roman form of city could continue. Once the alliance failed, as it did when the soldier peasants fell in debt, a group of magnates interposed itself between the peasant and the emperor. These men furnished the money for taxes and gained control of the peasants as fighting men, using that control to reduce the absolute power of the emperor and the geographical integrity of the empire. A system of petty fiefdoms emerged, the geographical system of trade was disrupted, and the east could no longer maintain the Roman type of city as it had managed to do long after the west. But by then, at the end of the eleventh century, the west itself was emerging from overpowering feudalism into a new era of urbanization. Its organization and form became the model for the world, while Byzantium's city kept being barely revived just before death took hold. The Turks in the fifteenth century breathed a bit more life into the Byzantine form of administration, but by the late nineteenth century that civil service was truly dead, swept away almost without trace in the Balkan Wars at the turn of the century and in the First World War in the Near East.

In the west and in feudal times, the equation of areal dominion and possible wealth is striking.

[T]he feudal system meant the rigorous economic subjection of a host of humble folk to a few powerful men. Having received from earlier ages the Roman villa [which in some respects anticipated the manor] and the German village chiefdom, it extended and consolidated these methods whereby men exploited men, and combined inextricably the right to the revenues from the land with the right to exercise authority; it fashioned from all this the true manor of medieval times. And this it did partly for the benefit of an oligarchy of priests and monks whose task it was to propitiate Heaven, but chiefly for the benefit of an oligarchy of warriors.[24]

[23]Bloch, op. cit., p. 444.
[24]Ibid., p. 443.

Feudalism in Person and in Land

To understand the geographical impact made by the introduction of feudalism, we must note the two institutional expressions of that system: one in the personal relations among men and the other in land-holding practices. Lest objection be raised to discussing men alone, it should be made clear that in the Middle Ages—and particularly in the land greatly shaped by Frankish legal practices, as was the heartland of feudalism found in the Loire valley of France, in Burgundy, and in the Rhine valley with all its tributaries —it was the treatment of men that mattered. Lords dealt with their male vassals, assuming that, in turn, the women and children related to those men were thereby comprehended.

The personal relationship of feudalism was already anticipated by the Romans who had evolved *patrocinium*, not without considerable official opposition because of its tendency to diminish the central power. Under the practice of *patrocinium*, certain men placed themselves in a personally dependent status by asking a patron to accept them as clients in return for various services rendered in a fully contractual relationship. In essence, this system was one of the strong caring for the weak, but the return to the strong tended to increase over the years to the point that their clients became increasingly unfree if not truly enslaved. In Gaul, the Romans had found a similar practice among the Celts they conquered, so *patrocinium* was well established there before the Frankish invasions in the middle of the first Christian millennium. The invaders themselves had a form of personal dependency that still further encouraged the perpetuation of *patrocinium*. As the practice became institutionalized in the Middle Ages, men *commended* themselves, and thereby their families and descendants, to powerful men, seeking social, economic, and military protection in return. This act of commendation was particularly common among the landless who could barely survive economically in that era of low productivity and great disruption of distant trading. Written contracts of commendation were not uncommon, creating a "relationship of protection and support on one side, and of free service on the other." These contracts established the essential features of medieval labor practices in the countryside.

In the matter of land-holding the Romans also supplied the essential ingredient of feudalism. In place of fee-simple tenure—the medieval equivalent of what

The legend on the map reads:

- ····· Limit of Charlemagne's Empire ca. 814
- —·— Limit of Holy Roman Empire Around the Year 1000
- —··— Boundaries of Kingdoms and Independent Duchies Around the Year 1000
- Heartland of Feudalism
- Areas only Partially Feudalized
- Areas Subsequently Feudalized

Scale 1: 13,500,000, one inch = 216 miles. Conic Projection

0 100 200 300 400 500 Kilometers
0 100 200 300 Miles

IRELAND, NON-FEUDAL

FRIESIA, NON-FEUDAL

KINGDOM OF DENMARK

DUCHY OF POLAND

Feudalism Introduced into England by Norman Conquest 1066

HOLY ROMAN EMPIRE

DUCHY OF BOHEMIA

MORAVIA

FRANCE

KINGDOM OF HUNGARY

KINGDOM OF BURGUNDY

Venice

KINGDOM OF CROATIA

PRINCIPALITY OF SERVIA

DUCHY OF GASCONY

KINGDOM OF LEON

KINGDOM OF NAVARRE

Saracenic Pass

States of the Church

Norman after 1080

Limit of Charlemagne's Empire

Saracenic Possessions

Saracenic Possessions

Feudalism Introduced into Southern Italy and Sicily by Norman Conquest 1042-1091

Longitude West of Greenwich   Longitude East of Greenwich

The feudal parts of Europe.

we think of today as unrestricted personal ownership —stood the practice of *precarium*. This name derived from the original prayer made by a potential user of land to the alodial owner of that land as he sought to *use* the land for a particular purpose and under established conditions. The relationship was very similar to our present-day leasehold tenure, though it normally lacked the measure of productive value that rent today implies. Instead, land was *held of* (from) another for use, particularly in return for military or administrative services. In the early stages of feudalism the holder had no recourse against the owner, who might call in his land and terminate for any, or no, reason. Custom later gave some protection to the rights of vassals holding land, commonly assuring tenancy for their lifetime but seldom granting the right of bequeathal. Instead *heriots*, special duties inflicted at the death of the tenant, might be imposed along with refusal of succession.

In a time when money was extremely scarce and the king's purse was frequently empty, feudal tenancy provided a way of establishing military and administrative control over areas somewhat removed from the king's castle. Major feudatories came to hold land of the king which they commonly furnished to subfeudatories as manors or even baronies. Each held of the other in a defined and circumscribed use-relationship comprehended by the practice of *precarium*, "a form of renting land not intended primarily for income" but rather for establishing an administrative and military relationship among men.

The land-holding relationship of *precarium* created the political geography of the Middle Ages, assuring the nearly total domination of political life by the countryside and the feudatories based there. The lords saw anything that diminished their control of land, or the labor force to make that land productive or to defend it, as a threat to the proper functioning of the feudal system. Other lords of manor or barons of baronies might threaten them but the established practice of personal combat handled that threat. The cities that began to grow up around the year 1000 stood as the exogenous force in feudal life. They interrupted the continuity of land-holding and tended to disrupt the autarky of the manor. Worse, the fledgling cities came to disturb the traditional working of the personal relationship of *patrocinium*. Under established custom, with the force of law, serfs who were tied to rural land under contracts of commendation could escape that relationship by going to and remaining uncaptured in a city for a year and a day. Thus arose the medieval saying *Stadtluft macht frei*, city air makes men free.

The Manor: The Anti-City

The manor was truly an economic institution, though it had legal, customary, and social attributes. Its purpose was to maximize sufficiency of local provision by undertaking to grow as many necessary crops as possible, to fashion its own tools, to weave and make its own clothing, and otherwise to create a closed economic system. Did this system come from desire or resignation? Did the manor seek autarky or merely accept it in a world where trade had become very difficult? Without question, the lords of manors appreciated the value of trade; they used most jealously any market privileges they could garner, as well as rights of pontage, murrage, tollage, and other levies on goods moving in trade through their domains.

Much as lords might accept the desirability of increasing the geographical system of trade, geographical and political conditions made enlargement unlikely. As in the Roman Empire, a strong force must have existed under feudalism and within the system of manors leading to the creation of identity. If one seeks self-sufficiency to cut down money flows in a time when money is rare, then one tends to try to do everything that the climate and resources allow. Thus, if one member of the oligarchy produces certain commodities, every member is likely to produce them; there being no other basis both of wealth and power than land, monopoly of its produce and the local market would be most natural. One can then ask how much extra-manorial trade is likely. The manorial market is valuable mainly because the lord can control the economic lives of his vassals, use the satisfaction of their needs to gain wealth (either through market tolls or through purchase or barter of goods produced on the manor, in which he has the landlord's share of interest), and exact the largest possible share from the overall produce of the manor. In essence, the manorial system offered a great incentive for the lord of the manor to deny economic access to his tenants to any but himself. No better system could be devised to damp down tendencies toward urbanization.

The conflict arose between the lord of a potential trade center and his peer in the countryside. Since the return to be earned from the manor and the wealth of the master stood in direct equation, two courses were open to the lord seeking to maximize his economic position: (1) he might seek to produce an item for sale through a possible city market in open trading, thus earning money which he could in return employ to buy goods to compensate his feudal minions for their efforts oriented to this money economy, or (2) he might seek to contain the economic activities of his manor to reduce the outflow of money; that is, he might seek a localized autarky. Clearly neither system would be absolute even in feudal times but one or the other course would probably dominate.

The key to which form of economic endeavor— autarky or specialization for external trading—would take over on the manor lies not in the manor itself *but in the successful survival of a nonmanorial urban market.* This argument contradicts much of the established thinking on the trade-base of urbanization but logic requires the introduction of such a caveat. The central-place theory holds that cities grow out of rurally-based "support" of customers seeking to converge on a town market to secure satisfaction of their physical wants and demands for service. Yet if we examine the feudal economy, which has at least implicitly been assumed to have created this central-place pattern, we find that the process does not work out as the theory assumes. Trade among self-sufficient economic units does not bring towns into being. We may assume that within any geographical region sufficiently interconnected to permit trade in feudal times, uniformity of productive opportunities was sufficient to make inter-manorial trade idle. The productivity of the manor was shaped to create as closed an

The manoir in the French department of Lot et Garonne still shows some of the characteristics of medieval manors that gave it its name. Outbuildings and barns were used for manorial artisans and stores, and the house itself sheltered a large biological and occupational family.

economic system as the local resources would permit. Natural disaster might project the manor into outside purchasing but normally such trade would exist only for those items of desire that could not be produced on the manor. For the most part the local failure would be in luxury items which only the lord or his most intimate retainers would purchase. The basis of trade existed, but on nothing like the scale assumed in central-place theory.

In a geographical situation where cities are interspersed throughout a rural manorial economy, we may reasonably assume trade in basic commodities. Townsmen could not and would not practice the sort of autarky typical of the feudal countryside; for them, trade would be absolutely essential to survival. Much of the accepted thought would have it that towns grow out of the countryside *to care for its demands* rather than that they have a separate and independent existence. Yet we find the separate existence must be the case, for there was no large basis for trade among manors.

Among the Romans the city came from a system independent of the countryside; to the extent it survived, we may assume that feudalism and urbanism are two distinct systems, each with a striking historical base and possibly of simultaneous occurrence. We may question the relative power of the two systems: the Romans and their eastern successors in Byzantium managed to maintain an extensive-urban system whereas, following Marc Bloch's argument, the grafting on of the Germanic notion of localized *chiefdoms* first disrupted and then replaced the Roman system in the west by one we call *feudalism.* This substitution was no doubt slow but could not have been stopped once the concept of the manor was shaped as the basic component of power, protection, and trade. Every withdrawal of land from the Roman extensive-urban system weakened it, but the system could continue so long as any remnant remained of its original purpose —interconnecting distant places and providing an externalized system.

A Germanic Theory of City Formation and Support

In 1933 the German geographer Walter Christaller published what has come to be a classic proposal in which he sought "the causes of towns being large or small, because we believe that there is some ordering principle heretofore unrecognized that concerns their distribution."[25] That ordering process is, in its most fundamental form, a "crystallization of mass around a nucleus" according to a "centralistic principle" which produces a "central organ" that may be either a medieval town or a modern town, a village, or a vast metropolis.

Quoting Robert Gradmann, Christaller states that the *"chief profession* of a town [is] namely, 'to be center of its rural surroundings and mediator of local commerce with the outside world.'"[26] The framework of Christaller's thought is regional and "The chief profession—or characteristic—of a town is to be the center of a region." The only alternative comes in "dispersed places, i.e., all those places which are not centers." Such dispersed places may be "areally bound ones—those settlements the inhabitants of which live on their agricultural activities, which are conditioned by the land area surrounding them." Or they may be "point-bound ones—those settlements the inhabitants of which make their living from resources found at specific locations," such as mining settlements or towns "bound at absolute points (not relative ones as in the case of central-places)—for instance, bridges and fords, border or custom places, and especially harbors." Christaller finds a major exception to this dichotomy between areally bound and point-bound places in those "settlements which are not bound to a central point, an area, or an absolute point. Monastery settlements (but not shrines, which are usually bound by the place of miracle) are examples," as are "settlements of workers who perform work in the home, and *large industrial settlements,* the locations of which are seldom determined according to any economic advantages such as transportation facilities or the labor supply."[27]

We may emphasize the strong areal and rural base that Christaller uses. Constantly he reiterates his notion that towns grow out of the countryside, that the flow of country people to and from the town accounts for its location and functions. He does not accept a long-distance, systemic, base for cities, or the notion that the town may preexist the rural hinterland and, in fact, bring that agricultural development into being. Looking back at the history of the classical city, both Gradmann and Christaller accept the possibility of a Greek-style synoecism but overlook entirely the possibility of the geographically extensive dioecism such as Rome brought into being. In their minds, evolution can come only from the gathering together of small, local, agricultural support in the erection of central-places.

Christaller next defines the method of this collection of small increments of support. He introduces the notion that people seeking to secure a good or service will establish a limit on the distance they are willing to travel to obtain that good. This property of local trade has been rendered in English as the *range of a good;* it is measured in radial distance from a center when that place still serves as the origin of goods or services for the "dispersed population" living outside the town. Related to this property of convergence is the notion that in creating and maintaining that central-place, a minimum total of activity would support a retailer or service worker there. Christaller called this activity the "inner range of a good," because it referred to the minimum radial distance from the center that would be large enough to enclose a population sufficient in number to support one unit of retail trade or service. Because of this marginal quality of the inner range, American geographers have tended to substitute the term "threshold," leaving "range" to designate the maximum travel distance of potential customers. Thus *threshold* refers to the minimum total of support that will bring a retail trade into being, and *range* to a maximum distance people are willing to travel to secure that particular good.

It is assumed that if the population density increases, a threshold population can be secured from a less extensive area. Equally, if the threshold can be tightened up, a considerable economic advantage would fall to the potential customer if he could secure his good by traveling less distance. The Christallerian argument is that alternative central-places would spring up somewhere outside the original town, cutting a new tributary area out of its original hinterland. In this way, the argument holds, successive basic central-places will be carved out of potential-customer regions, and in this process we can find the explanation for a dense distribution of towns across an agricultural region.

The other dynamic quality that Christaller seeks is found in the erection of a superstructure of larger

---

[25]*Walter Christaller,* Central Places in Southern Germany (Die zentralen Orte in Süddeutschland), *translated by Carlisle W. Baskin, Englewood Cliffs, N.J.: Prentice-Hall, Inc., 1966, p. 2.*
[26]*Robert Gradmann, "Schwäbische Städte," in Zeitschrift der Gesellschaft für Erdkunde [1916], p. 427, quoted in Christaller, op. cit., p. 16.*
[27]*Christaller, op. cit., p. 17. Emphasis supplied.*

towns on this basic central-place base. If the range of a commonly sought good is limited, that of a rarely purchased good can be assumed to be much greater. Thus the trading town in which it is purchased may be far more distant from the customer. Related to this quality is the lesser frequency of purchase, which implies that a larger threshold population will be needed to support one establishment providing that particular good or service. Thus the basic central-places will stand in relationship to a smaller number of more specialized places—with higher threshold populations and greater ranges of goods. If this second step is possible, so are further increases in threshold and range, leading to ever smaller numbers of central-places of increasingly higher "order." The result is a hierarchical place pyramid, broad on the bottom to include all the basic trading towns, with the one dominant city of a country at the top.

Failings of Central-Place Theory

Let us examine critically the basic tenets of central-place theory in light of the historical geography of West European urbanism up to the time of the classical-medieval transition.

Although not formally stated, central-place theory has woven within it an assumption rooted deeply in the German attitude toward settlement and cities. The Germanic notion of the local chiefdom was the contribution the Franks brought to their forcible embrace of Roman civilization. Charlemagne, though a great warrior and a quintessential Christian ruler, was a barbarian Frank in his understanding of cities. When he died the Frankish practices inherited from a spacious rural past took bloody effect. His empire was divided, as every schoolchild knows, among his three sons, and Europe has never been the same again. That dynastic history does not concern us, but rather the practice of *viewing land as personal holdings unrelated to a broader geographical system of regional or economic integration.* The Romans would never have split their empire into bits; instead they created four jointly-ruling emperors in an effort to maintain its geographical integrity. But the Germanic Franks did split Charlemagne's empire among his three sons, and their heirs in turn split it much more complexly.

This concept of land as the personal possession of the sovereign or the major feudatory fostered the pe-

culiar economic-geographical pattern of the Middle Ages. Land was used selfishly and defensively, kept apart from its neighbors in the interest of increasing the landowner's return to maximum possession. As powerful families, and the dynasties that followed their founders, married, gave birth to sons, and witnessed the death of the successive generations, the view of land as personal property was enhanced. A powerful duke or count might hold manors in a dozen different areas; his possession was most important in determining the economic practices employed there. Given the commonly discontinuous nature of feudal family holdings, it is not the least surprising that economic separation usually dominated over economic integration.

In this basically Germanic context of settlement, Walter Christaller shaped his theory. A man may write unaware of the parochial quality of the geographical environment in which he operates. The notion that towns grow out of their adjacent countryside would not sound questionable to Christaller, raised in Bavaria where the last vestiges of feudalism had been given up less than a century before his birth. Only in 1808 was the practice of serfdom abolished there. And "[o]n the whole serfdom appears as a characteristic corollary of

Dinkelsbuhl was one of the prosperous walled towns of southern Germany which sprang up and assumed importance under the Heerschildordnung of feudalism and the hierarchichal arrangements of central-place theory.

feudalism. It grew up as a consequence of customary subjection and natural husbandry; it melted away with the coming of the industrial and commercial age."[28] No one would question Christaller's wide knowledge of commerce but we have on the evidence of his own major work the justification for doubting that his system had much applicability to the location of industrial activity. His was a late feudal picture and pertinent as such to the Germany when he wrote. But this picture was a poor design for discussion of the industrial world without a feudal past in which all Americans, and many other people, live.

Central-place theory is a classical expression of the economic design based on excise taxation—the imposition of levies on the transport, import, export, storage, and sale of goods in clearly defined geographical markets. Related to excise levies was the requirement of charters of right to engage in trade, again a way to "tax" entry to and participation in trade. To give a charter value, local monopolies on entry and participation are essential. Thus, by splitting land holdings into manors or defined fiefdoms, lords could gain more repayments for charters than otherwise, a fact that would have encouraged the minute parcelling out of medieval holdings, as history tells us happened. Within the Holy Roman Empire, this minute geographical division was carried to the extreme. In an area of that empire, at Berneck in Bavaria, Walter Christaller was born in 1893 and made the early observations in support of his theory.

After the creation of the notion of the nation-state, other forms of taxation came to substitute for excise levies. Edward IV of England in the mid-fifteenth century was the first king to turn away from land-grabbing as a source of revenue and begin investment as a road to personal wealth. In this he followed on the model of the Renaissance magnates of Italy. But as late as 1785 the Bavarian king, Charles Theodore, had so little attachment to his kingdom that he plotted tiresomely with the Hapsburgs in an attempt to swap that south German realm to Austria in exchange for the Austrian Netherlands and the title of king of Burgundy. It is inconceivable that the French or English king would have so lacked national patriotism in the eighteenth century, but such was the case in still-semi-feudal south Germany, where central-place theory was first worked out.

If we accept the proposal that Walter Christaller was operating in an historical-geographical context that carried feudal notions as near to the present as is to be found anywhere in western civilization, then we can relate his theoretical proposal, central-place theory, to the rural-urban structure of feudal times to some useful effect. Feudalism in its essential form was basically a rural system. What towns *grew out* of feudalism, rather than surviving from earlier times in the inhospitable medium of feudal rural structure, would of necessity be based on agricultural support. Additionally, they would tend to have as their tributary areas (within the composite upper range of their collective goods) that amount of country over which the lord of their domain held sway. Because his wealth was the wealth of his domain, he would try hard to prevent trading beyond his bounds. Thus, in trying to account for the size of tributary areas we are to a reasonable degree accounting for what had been historically the possible domain of the basic subfeudatory. Phrased another way, we are answering the question of how much countryside a baron could defend as his own in a time of political fragmentation and conflict when the desire for increased wealth led almost inexorably to the coveting of another man's domain.

A further component in this shaping of the basic trading place to emerge from the originally rural-agricultural medium of feudalism is to be found in serfdom itself. One of the fundamental concepts of the institution exists when "serfdom is very often conceived as a perpetual adherence to the soil of an estate owned by a lord" on the part of the laborers in those fields so "serfdom became the prevailing condition of the lower orders during the middle ages."[29] The serf possessed a half-freedom, which Paul Vinogradoff saw as an outgrowth of a dual background that brought into a single medieval serving class the descendants of Frankish and Roman slaves (for whom feudalism decreed the loss of half their enslavement) and the descendants of the overrun Roman *coloni* (for whom feudalism meant the loss of half their freedom). A consequence of that half-freedom was particularly the loss of the freedom of movement while keeping, by custom, a fair part of the freedom of person. What resulted was a praedial attachment which decreed that the serf must not leave the immediate confines of the domain to whose soil he stood in "perpetual adherence." Given this loss of the freedom of movement, it is not surprising that rural people went only to the lowest order trading place, normally within the lord's domain, to satisfy their wants. This tradition began as early as the seventh century in Bavaria[30] and lasted there for a thousand years, to within one lifetime of Christaller's birth.

[28]*Paul Vinogradoff, "Serfdom,"* Encyclopaedia Britannica, *11th Ed., 1910.*

[29]Loc. cit.
[30]Ibid., *p. 665.*

The *Heerschildordnung*

Accepting the low order of mobility under feudalism, we still must deal with the superstructure of trading places that Christaller erects on this settlement base. One of the key characteristics of German feudalism may furnish us at least a partial explanation not fully dependent on the normative economic geometry that the author of central-place theory employs. Under German feudalism an ordering of feudatories grew up, called the *Heerschildordnung*, which depended upon an assumption that some gradation of rank related to the size of the holding. The practice was never very neat. "Actually not even in the most regular of feudal countries, like England or Germany, was there any fixed gradation of rank, title or size. A knight might hold directly of the king, a count of a viscount, a bishop of an abbot, or the king himself of one of his own vassals, or even of a vassal's vassal, and in return his vassal's vassal might hold another fief directly of him."[31] Much as the individual organization was disordered, the notion of the geographical order did exist. Baronies were the most basic component, just as the barons were the building blocks of the political system, and came ultimately to be the basic element in the judicial system. Larger in size were the domains of counts and, in increasing scale, those of viscounts, margraves, and dukes. One man might—through conquest, inheritance, or marriage dowry—be a duke and a baron, or hold any other combination of titles, but an integrity to the geographical units remained, sometimes recognized in the bestowal of lesser titles on the heir to the greater title or even on the cadet line of the family.

The existence of a geographical ranking of feudal fiefs meant that a basis for larger trading places always existed even within the closure of the feudal economy. The Holy Roman Empire, a strange conglomerate that left Germany both the largest "state" and the most divided one, encouraged this sort of compartmentalization of land even in an era when the nation-state was elsewhere long established. We should not forget that Germany's first effective customs union, the famous *Zollverein*, dates only from 1834. The free flow of customers and goods could only begin to develop in that area in the hundred years before Christaller formed his theory, whereas it had been possible for up to five hundred years in England and for only a slightly

[31]*George Burton Adams, "Feudalism,"* Encyclopaedia Britannica, *11th Ed., 1910.*

shorter time in France. Areas such as those in Germany and Italy characterized by feudal survivals, where feudalism was given up only in the nineteenth century, could accomplish long-distance trading. But what success they had in overcoming the geographical compartmentalization came not in the rurally-based feudal area but rather in the exceptions to its uniformity found in the nonfeudal free cities. The Venetian *empire da mare* or the Hanseatic League were exceptions, but they were exceptions as well to Christaller's theory; they were not central-places serving as the focus of a region but were instead what he largely disregarded as either "point-bound" places or industrial places with home production.

I wish to propose that Walter Christaller's central-place theory represents a very special case rather than a universal prescription. It is both culturally and geographically relative to the Germanic feudal institution and its realm. And perhaps most importantly, *it is basically a rural rather than an urban system*, depending upon the evolution of an agricultural system and culture into an urban one. But central-place theory does not prove able to explain some considerable number of situations where feudalism was more short-lived (as in England), less complete as a system (as in Byzantium), or actually absent (as in most of the New Lands). Additionally our survey of the transformation of the classical world into the medieval world has shown that cities did persist, admittedly small and weak but still present. To deal with that situation Christaller is inadequate, as he is to handle either Byzantium or the New World. We need not reject central-place theory but rather restrict it to that area where historical geography justifies its application—to the groundmass of feudal land in western civilization. Even there we must maintain the exception of the germinal Roman towns that limped through the Dark Ages, and probably the development of towns in Britain, France, the Low Countries, and Italy after the close of the general feudal era in the thirteenth century. Central-place theory may serve to explain some German urbanism well up to the nineteenth century and some events in western civilization in general between the ninth and thirteenth century, but it should not be viewed as an explanation of urbanization, either universally or throughout time.

What will replace central-place theory? When we consider the mercantile city of the fifteenth through seventeenth centuries, I will propose the mercantile model of settlement in an historical-geographical context. Its contrast with central-place thinking comes in the role to be played by a geographically extensive trading, administrative, and protective system. Already we have seen that such an extensive system existed in Roman times; the germ of its rebirth remained even during the shadowed time when feudalism emerged to dominate western civilization. The nonrurally-based city was that germ. But before we follow its course through the period of rural domination, we shall look at the physical expression of the geographical parochialism of the feudal era.

A World of Parts: Manor and *Bourg*

The geographical partitioning that feudalism brought into being is expressed in three dominant ways: as the baronial unit of administration and justice, as the closed economy of the manor, and as the protective unit of the castle with the attendant settlement. Despite all the elaborate upward ties of homage and fealty represented by the feudal system, effective sovereignty really lay in the barony. The baron possessed almost absolute powers over his serfs and tenants. The manorial economy concerns us directly; its nature helps to explain why the town was not a significant component of feudal settlement. The word used was "town," not "village" or "nucleation." Villages were perhaps the most common form of settlement in Frankish Europe, though Neustria in the west had a greater number of dispersed farm settlements than Austrasia in the east. Villages were a form of rural settlement brought about at least in part by the need for defense at a time when the "Roman Peace" no longer stretched across the land. These clusters of dwellings had nothing directly to do with the execution of urban functions, and the traditional concept of classical geography that the village grows to the town and the town in turn to the city is little supported either by history or logic. Villages remain villages, for the most part, and towns begin as towns. The manorial economy needed villages to carry on its attempt at autarky as well as to gain some physical protection. But manorial autarky ruled out the true urbanism of town life.

This point is made more clearly when we introduce the notion of the military strongpoint, the fortified town, known in French as the *bourg*, in German as the *burg*, and in Erse as the *burgh*. To understand these towns, we may draw some contrast with the manor. The manor was a social and economic organization because it was the basic unit of land ownership. The most common benefice from a major feudatory to his vassal was the bestowal of the occupance of such a unit of agricultural land, presumably large and diverse enough to permit the reasonable expectation of self-sufficiency. To it were attached the basic administrative rights—the manorial court with its additional judicial functions. The only institutionally required outflows from such a manor were those of feudal tribute to the liege lord, often a thin trickle indeed, and the tithe due the church. Even the tithe was often diverted to the local lay lord rather than flowing in the channels of the universal church. In light of these facts the manor can be looked upon as so fundamentally parochial in its economy as to be only the weakest encouragement to urban foundation. The small local stream of tithes might continue the germ of the Roman city, if the church dominated it, but otherwise the manor brought about village rather than town support.

Quite in contrast stood the *bourg:* it gained significance by increases in scale in a way that the manor did not. If a baron sought truly to dominate an area, he would seek to build such a fearsome castle that he could stand immune to conquest, with an homage and fealty that would rest lightly on him. In such immunity lay true power and freedom, as well as possible domination of others if they lacked similar protection.

Laroque Ste. Marguerite (Aveyron) shows, in a small town of the present, the relationship between the bourg and the faubourg in the middle ages.

Feudal Europe is full of examples of political power brought about and backstayed by the possession of a fearsome castle, depending upon nature's gift of an easily defensible site or upon walls of exceptional strength.

In the castle we encounter the most notable morphological contribution of the feudal times. The manor was the *villa* carried forward with relatively little change. The town was so vestigial as to lack any new components other than the Christian churches, and often, as in Syracusa or Rome, even these were renovations of Greek or Roman temples. The basilica, which stood as the great church of early Christendom, was an architectural form taken slavishly from the Romans who had used both the term and the form to describe law courts and other places of public resort. Only in Byzantium was the church given a form all its own, the domed place of assembly fully developed in Hagia Sophia.

To understand the role of the castle and the decline of the independence of the city, we must review a few facts that account for the creation of private fortresses. When Charlemagne's empire began to disintegrate after his death, one of the most significant indications of the geographical collapse came when, in 877, Charles the Bald granted the right of inheritance of titles and regional administration to his lords, thus reducing the geographical authority of the crown. This decline was particularly noticeable in contrast to the authority of his grandfather, Charlemagne, who required his lords to live around him in Aachen "in such a way that, shrewd as he was, through the windows of his private apartment (in his palace), he could see everything they were doing, and all their comings and goings, without their realizing it. In the same way all the houses of the nobles were built high off the ground, so that the retainers of his nobles, the personal servants of those retainers and every other passer-by could be protected from rain or snow, cold or heat, and yet the nobles themselves could not hide from the eyes of the ever-vigilant Charlemagne."[32]

That Charles the Bald could not maintain this surveillance became clear even before he gave hereditary nobility and power to his lords in the last year of his life. Earlier in 864 Charles had ordered the demolition of buildings put up without his authorization. These buildings were fortresses built by nobles whose power was gained originally while they served as royal agents. But with decline in central authority of the Carolingian Empire, "The walls of the old Gallo-Roman cities which had fallen into ruins and sometimes even been completely demolished, were built up again; above all, castles—fortresses in other words—sprang up almost everywhere, and these numerous *castella*, erected more often than not by royal agents, even-

[32]*Notker the Stammerer*, Charlemagne, *an account contained in Lewis Thorpe*, Two Lives of Charlemagne, *Baltimore: Penguin Books, 1969, p. 128. (Notker the Stammerer, who was born ca. 840 and died in 912, was a monk at the Benedictine monastery at St. Gallen in Switzerland.)*

tually became a source of anxiety to Charles the Bald himself . . . ."[33]

The state was doubly perplexed: the new walls and fortresses were constructed to deal with the threat and invasion of brigands and pirates from Scandinavia who sailed up the rivers destroying the Carolingian civilization and exacting tribute, yet the walls gave power and protection to dissidents among the king's nobles. In the end they fostered true geographical feudalism, destroying the effectively extensive state, and became the instrument of the creation of a new form of extensive state when, in the hands of a partially civilized Norman horde, the practice of *personal colonization* was devised.

This practice grew out of the social organization of this second wave of barbarians who attacked the realm of western civilization. Just as the Germanic invasions had changed the Roman Empire, shaping an amalgam of centralized Roman state and Frankish chiefdom domain, the second wave transformed the feudal order of the late Carolingians into the instrument of a new but much more divided colonization. The Greeks had planted settlers to found new city-states largely populated by the demographic overflow of Greece. The Romans had conquered and subjected brutal peoples in a true colonial movement, largely seeking power rather than population outlets, and giving the vanquished the institutions and culture of the centralized Roman state while shaping an integrated and extensive economic, political, and social system. The Franks had invaded and used that extensive system but had not added much to it other than the concepts of homage and fealty to a person rather than the abstract state, thus laying the foundation of feudalism. It remained for the barbarians from the north to take up that concept of fealty and its adjunct, the conferral of a benefice of land, and make of them the instrument of a considerably personalized form of colonization. If it was right and legal that the Holy Roman emperor might give land to a baron for his support, then it was a short step to accepting the proposition that the baron might add to his own support by gaining more land in whatever way he could.

The raiding first practiced by the Norse turned into actual settlement in 911 when the treaty of Saint-Clair-sur-Epte signed between King Charles the Simple of France and Rollo, the leader of the invaders, gave to these Norse men the city of Rouen and certain enclaves on the Channel coast. This occupation came at a turning point in the historical geography of cities, to which the Normans were themselves contributors. Under the first two Charleses, the Frankish cities had

[33]*Latouche, op. cit., p. 219.*

remained essentially undefended by walls; those that existed were inherited from Roman foundations rather than built by the Franks. But when the wild Danes and Swedes—the Norse—began their piratical attacks in the ninth century, Charles the Bald commanded that Le Mans in Maine and Tours in the Touraine be fortified "as a defense *for the people* against the Northmen."[34] Archbishop Fulk of Rheims had his city's walls rebuilt between 884 and 900, as did the bishop of Cambray in the same period, and Bishop Erluin fortified Peronne in 1001 "as a defence against marauders, and a refuge for the husbandmen of the country."[35]

These efforts to build or restore city walls need be understood as an attempt to protect *the people* against invaders in a state where the frontiers had been breached. So long as those lines had remained secure, the Frankish empire had sought to avoid internal fortifications so as to maintain a central authority, as we have seen from Charlemagne's careful watch on his nobles. With the frontiers weak, the city became a secondary refuge.

The first castle is lost in the incompleteness of history. Likely it may have emerged either in the Touraine, Maine, or Anjou. The disintegration of the Frankish empire of the west, first into Neustria, led finally to the creation of a group of important domains possessed by counts—Anjou, Rennes, Nevers, Vendôme, Tours, Vexin, as well as others—who came to covet their neighbors' possessions—always their lands and often their wives and daughters so as to gain those lands. Taking one example, we see Count Fulk Nerra of Anjou, who was born ca. 970, succeeding to his father as count at the age of seventeen and having to repel an attack by the Count of Rennes on Nantes soon thereafter. Little more than a boy, he set about making marriage alliances that eventually brought to his family the countship of Vendôme and Touraine, and by arms he secured the countship of Maine. His heirs came ultimately first to rule as dukes of Normandy and then as kings of England (beginning with Henry II). All of this activity had to be based on the ability to defend lands gained by conquest or inheritance, either of which was likely to be challenged. Fulk Nerra was surnamed "the great builder," apparently because he constructed so many castles. The design for these had evidently been worked out over a number of years. As early as 889, Fulcher, bishop of Nantes (then part of Anjou), built a wooden tower surrounded in all probability by earth-

works. Laon had such a wooden tower—a keep—before 931, as did Amiens (950), Coucy (958), Chalons (963), and Rheims (988). But the first stone keep was built by Fulk Nerra about the year 994 and had the basic elements of the castle—a stone tower and a surrounding wall. The keep became the most powerful component of the early medieval landscape.[36]

Although these castles were not devised by the Normans (in fact, they were built for defense against them), those medieval bullies took up the form most effectively. As usurpers in a foreign land they found themselves in need of personal protection both against the populace they were seeking to dominate as serfs and the remnants of the imperial power they sought to reject. Theirs became a game of overawing the people and snubbing the kings, in which the castle was a major instrument. In 1080, the decree of the council of Lille-

La Sylvestrie, a fortified manor near Villeneuve-sur-Lot in Aquitaine, shows the form and strength of medieval walls.

[34]*From the* Annales Bertinianorum, *quoted in Ella S. Armitage,* The Early Norman Castles of the British Isles, *New York: E. P. Dutton, 1912, p. 65.*

[35]Chron. Camarense et Atrebatorum, *quoted in Armitage,* op. cit., p. 66.

[36]Armitage, op. cit., p. 72.

bonne (an ancient Roman town in Normandy) sought to limit "according to the custom of Normandy" the building of castles with moats deeper than about ten feet, with walls of complex structure, or emplaced on an island or a rock without the "express permission of the suzeraine," that is, the king, a count, or a grand feudatory.[37]

The reasoning behind this decree is clear when we follow the history of the Normans. Rollo and his descendants held at first only a few spots of land granted by the treaty of Saint-Clair-sur-Epte but they used this endowment to gain control of what became Normandy. In doing so they used vassals to administer and defend local areas, or seigneuries. But fealty was weak and of short duration among the Normans both because of their recent barbaric past and because so much of the relationship with the vassals was that of paymaster and mercenary. Only by exercising control over vassals could the counts keep their own realms intact, and largely by subverting the vassals of another could they add to their extent. Thus feudalism had some hierarchical structure from the very beginning, and the history of the institution is one of reducing the power of the lower orders in favor of the primary one. In France and England this upward concentration of power was nearly complete by the end of the medieval period, but in Germany and Italy, the process was completed only in the nineteenth century.

More than any other group, the Normans used the castle to dominate an alien and often hostile population. In France they built castles with the same objective the Roman builders had. One "has only to open his Caesar to see how familiar wooden towers and wooden palisades were to the Romans" in their conquest of Gaul,[38] and we must turn to the Normans to see how the stone tower and its rubble-filled *enciente* became the instrument of a new economic empire. The Norse conquered Normandy for economic advantage; as Normans, they went on subsequently to conquer England for greater gain. In each case they constructed motte castles, keeps surrounded by an embankment or an actual wall, to dominate the conquered land. "M. Viollet le Duc says that the Normans were the first people in Western Europe to build castles not as isolated fortresses, but as part of a scheme of general defence in which the individual castle became subservient to a political idea, which affected the geographical distribution of the fortresses, and even their individual planning and arrangement."[39] That political idea was the conquest of an extensive area and the subjugation of its people to a ruling group of foreign origin determined, at least initially, to maintain cultural distance. When the Norse invaded France, they seem not to have fully understood that idea; they were transient raiders receptive to their subjects' culture. When the Normans expanded from France in 1066 they entered England with the notion of permanent conquest, possessed of a system of colonial occupation made up of the castle and the feudal order. They fully desired to maintain their recently adopted French way of life rather than their more historical native culture, the Anglo-Saxon and Danish institutions of England. They were to become lords and strangers, and the castle was essential to that purpose.

The contrast is well shown when we examine Rollo's settlement in his newly conquered capital, Rouen, and William the Bastard's in his, London. "We are told that Rollo restored the walls and towers of the *cities* of Normandy, and it is clear from the context (of Dudo's contemporary history of the Normans) that the *castra* of Rouen, Fécamp, and Evreux, which are mentioned, are fortified cities not castles. Even the ducal residence at Rouen is spoken of as a *palatium* or an *aula*, not as a castle. . . ."[40] But William, who because of his success was now called the Conqueror, had constructed in London a motte castle, the Tower, which stands still as the most perfect remnant of Norman fortification established to overawe a hostile and restive people.

The rebellion of the nobles of Normandy during his youth had taught him the role of the castle in enhancing or thwarting authority. The first duke of Normandy, Rollo, had divided the lands he conquered among his piratical comrades as inheritable property, and their duty to him remained only in the defense of the dukedom of Normandy against outsiders. Rollo's grandson, Duke Richard sans Peur, introduced the new French feudalism among his peers toward the middle of the tenth century. Until then, they had ruled with the duke in council, but he shaped a system of homage and fealty that replaced allodial (essentially private) property with feudal benefices and submission. A century later those vassals rose against William the Bastard, questioning his right to the duchy because of his rank as no more than the natural son of the earlier duke. William defeated the nobles but they had, in resisting him, for the first time constructed castles in which they might seek independent power.[41] When William, as the Conqueror, set out to implant a foreign hierarchy on England, he strongly attempted to avoid a repetition of this pattern of revolt.

William could hardly avoid building castles in England. The Normans could not have occupied the country without them; the natives rebelled against the oc-

[37]J.-F. Finó, Fortresses de la France Médiévale, *Paris: Éditions Picard, 1967, p. 81.*
[38]*Armitage, op. cit., p. 78.*
[39]*Alfred Harvey,* The Castles and Walled Towns of England, *London: Methuen, 1911, pp. 1-2.*

[40]*Armitage, op. cit., pp. 76-77.*
[41]Loc. cit.

cupiers throughout William's lifetime. He essentially exterminated the native barons and even the more important freemen in putting down the resistance, so the peace he gained was restive and resentful, requiring the Normans to guard themselves constantly. Further, William had, in mounting the Conquest, depended dominantly on mercenary soldiers drawn from Flanders, Catalonia, and Germany, whom he had to pay off with lands in England since he lacked any easy access to money. Those mercenaries could be expected to use conquest themselves, if the opportunity were offered, so William found himself defending the newly stolen crown against many of his "supporters" as well as his "people." The Norman keep of the Tower of London was a structure outside the city of London guarding William's front against the frustrated anger of the English; it also was secure above all other fortifications to guard his rear against the disloyalty of his recent hirelings.

Geographically, too, the castles were not isolated fortresses, but were arranged on a definite scientific plan. Strong castles were placed at almost all the large towns, not so much to provide homes for their lords as to overawe their turbulent inhabitants; Derby alone among county towns probably did not substitute a masonry castle for its early (defensive) mound; many of the lesser towns were similarly threatened or protected; the river valleys, the main channels of traffic, had castles posted at every coign of vantage, the important fords and bridges being especially guarded; on the coast, particularly in the southeast, the part most obnoxious to invasion, all convenient landing-places were similarly protected; other castles kept open the main lines of communication across country, and in dangerous districts each large estate possessed its agrarian castle, which though primarily built for the protection of the tenant [lord] and his dependents, their flocks and their herds, performed its part in the general defence of the neighbourhood. Such castles were particularly numerous on the Scottish border and in the Welsh Marches, where they stretched tentacle-like into the valleys of Wales, and especially along the fat and fertile belt of land between the south Welsh mountains and the sea, reaching to the great fortresses of Pembroke and Haverfordwest, and keeping open the main road to Ireland.[42]

Yet with this truly national system of castles built over a relatively short time and shaped in what we can see to be a fully conceived plan, William sought to avoid furnishing the geographical backing for any partition of effective sovereignty. No counties palatine would arise in the Conqueror's England save under his direct control, and he planned against them by spreading the manors granted to any one lord over the whole king-

dom, making sure none too many of them were in one place.

This defense of central authority by dispersal of private estates created in the higher peerage of England an interest in the royal realm as an entity, and in the maintenance of a national economy missing in much of western Europe. Although an earl might be given defensive responsibility for a county, he was not given the legitimate possession of its wealth and the submission of its barons as would have been the case in France. No palatine dukes were created such as those in Aquitaine or Burgundy, nor powerful counts to match those in Toulouse or Flanders. If the regional nobility presumed toward independence by building unauthorized castles which seemed to question the royal writ, those adultine structures were ordered demolished. The king ruled in the whole of England, and he intended to maintain a country of central authority based on the incontestable and undivided right of conquest.

When William king of England and duke of Normandy attempted to keep his original domain in Normandy together he called upon his vassal, the seigneur of Perche, Robert II of Belleme, to hold the duchy's eastern frontier in Vexin against Philippe I of France. Henry I and II of England continued the building of a defensive line of castles, and Richard the Lionhearted gave it a primary citadel in the Château-Gaillard, perhaps the greatest of the medieval fortresses in France. These castles were built not in relation to a system of internal governance as before but rather to deal with the almost ceaseless warfare of the first Hundred Years War.[43] Geographically this shift was even more fundamental, representing the creation of a physical form, perhaps more appropriately termed a "fortress" than a "castle," whose purpose was to guard a frontier rather than assure royal sway within the kingdom.

The fortress was anticipated in the castles built to guard landing places on the Channel coast, passes in the Alps, and other such gaps in a naturally adequate frontier. Yet this beginning use hardly predicted the ultimate nature of the form which came to stand as totally distinct from the feudal castle as that structure had from the fenced agricultural *villa*. The fortress was an element in independence of sovereignty which pitted one powerful ruler against another, be it the king of England against his French cousin or the independent city in Germany or Italy against the pretentious Holy Roman emperor. The Château-Gaillard of 1196–1198 was merely the initial form of fortress to be followed by many others—Ghent, Gisors, Fréteval, and the Crusader fortress Krak in Syria—as the rulers sought to advance national purposes in an international context. Fortresses guarded the frontier at Château-Gaillard,

[42]*Harvey*, op. cit., p. 3.

[43]*Finó*, op. cit., pp. 117-118.

The Château-Gaillard, the first important siege castle in the west, was built on a pattern brought back by the crusaders from Palestine. This fortress guarded the boundary between English and French possessions on the Seine and was built by Richard-the-Lionhearted.

and greatly strengthened city walls joined together and overlooking the enemy's approach from without. Where external threats were slight, as in England, fortification never progressed much beyond the administrative castle of the Normans, but where fears of invasion remained, the fortified citadel was built on the national frontier or at major interior cities.

The Walls of Paris

As an example of this morphological transformation we may look at Paris, a modest town (called Lutece until the fifth century) occupying two sandy islands in the river Seine. Walls of a sort seem to have surrounded this city of fifteen hectares. When Clovis in the fifth century created a successful Gallo-Roman kingdom he made Paris, as it then came to be called, his capital. On his death the city actually disappeared when disorders caused all the inhabitants to depart for the greater safety of lightly fortified *villae* in the surrounding countryside.[44] In the ninth century the newly created French state resurrected Paris as its capital, which remained without any defenses other than the decrepit Roman walls until the Norse sailed up the Seine in 885. Then the counts of Paris, the Eudes, and her bishop worked feverishly to construct wooden walls and towers, barely managing to resist a siege of a year's duration which the Normans mounted. Only an army of 40,000 men sent by the Holy Roman emperor succeeded in raising that seige and, when these relief troops sought to exact a payment in money for their services, the citizens of Paris revolted, refused allegiance to Charles the Fat, the emperor, and established the French kingdom as a distinct political entity. At its heart lay the newly walled capital city.

After a period of nearly two hundred years of feeble government leading to the detachment of Normandy, Aquitaine, and Burgundy-Arles from Charlemagne's France, the Capetian dynasty began the reintegration of the nation. To accomplish that goal they had to make of their capital a strong citadel. Louis VI began in 1113 to fortify Paris with new walls, really only her second

defended a suzeraine against more powerful neighbors at Ghent, and served as a base for invasion and occupation of a foreign land at Krak and Palermo. The critical difference between castle and fortress came in the scale of possible conflict. The castle had been threatened with possible civil disturbance, but the fortress had to survive the more drawn-out siege within the capability of a sovereign ruler such as the King of France, the Count of Flanders, or the Norman King of Jerusalem.

In an historical geography of cities, this shift of the castle's role to poliorcetic defense from the earlier purpose—a king's attempt to overawe his urban subjects—meant a new morphology. In place of the moated keep at the edge of the town came the citadel

[44]*Ed. Bureau*, Conférence sur les Différentes Enceintes de Paris, sa Topographie et les Fortifications de 1840 (Conférences du Ministère de la Guerre 1869-1870), *Paris: Librairie Militaire de J. Dumaine, pp. 6-8.*

line succeeding to those insular palisades created by patching up the Roman defenses to resist the siege of 885. The right bank of the Seine was invaded by the city and enclosed with the wall, and a citadel was constructed in the Château du Grand-Châtelet. In this structure Paris followed the normal practice of tying together a citadel and the new stronger and higher wall, in this case with crenulations at its top and towers to provide descending and enfilading fire of arrows along its face.[45] The left bank of the Seine had also become the site of settlement as the city grew under the Capetian monarchs but this university quarter was left outside the city's walls—one wonders whether to protect the city from the students or to sacrifice them to the possible envelopers.

Fifty years after Louis VI finished his wall, the city had so expanded that a new enclosure had to be built, "to assure the new conquests [of provinces recovered in Normandy and Burgundy] and to provide protection for the numerous suburbs *(faubourgs)* which had grown up outside the wall of Louis VI . . . ."[46] Between 1190 and 1211, King Philip-Augustus built a wall that for the first time enclosed the whole city and both banks of the Seine and was strong enough to serve as a national bastion. This wall was eight feet thick and had large towers spaced at an interval of twenty to twenty-five *toises* (a *toise* was just under two meters long), in which were located the gates of the city. Unlike the earlier walls, that of Philip-Augustus was "crenulated" throughout its entire length. Tooth-like rises on the top of the wall allowed the archers to obtain protection while they fired through the lower gaps.

Yet even these strengthened walls were a temporary solution in a time of national warfare such as the Hundred Years War. England sought repeatedly to capture the crown of France, at least symbolically, by taking Paris. The capture of the French king in the Battle of Poitiers (1356) caused the Parisians under the leadership of the provost of the gilds, Étienne Marcel, to further strengthen the walls, particularly by digging a deep ditch at their face. Within the city, some internal defense was provided by chains that could be strung across the entrances of streets to strengthen a fence of boards maintained there in readiness. Thus *la barricade* was invented, later to be strengthened by piling up the paving stones that had begun to appear in Parisian streets during the reign of Louis VI.[47]

These barricades of Parisian invention played a

strong role in the internal disorders of the twelfth of May, 1588—"the day of the barricades"—when the Parisian populace rose against the decadent Henri III, again in 1789, and in the Commune of 1871. Under the Normans the castle had frowned down upon an open city to maintain order. When the exigencies of national survival required the walling of the city, the great urban fortress served a dual role—to make a citadel in the city as a unit of defense and to give a refuge and strong point for the monarch in his rule over a restive and not wholly loyal urban populace. But *la barricade* gave to that populace a counter defense which they used to effect in 1588, 1793, 1871 and again in the riots of 1968.

Toward the close of the Hundred Years War, Paris required new citadels and new walls. Étienne Marcel had begun one at the Louvre and Charles V joined with Marcel's successor as Provost of the merchants (mayor) in the construction of another on the other side of the city at La Bastille. These citadels served both to defend the city against the outsiders and to symbolize the royal power with respect to the common people. The Revolution of 1789 effectively destroyed the Bastille, and that of 1848 nearly did the job for the Louvre.

During the commune of 1871, the "fédérés" who rose against the government they feared would be royalist topped the Colonne Vendôme on May first. The column had been cast from captured German cannons in 1810 and topped with a statue of Napoléon I. The painter Courbet was considered the instigator of its destruction and was forced to pay for its restoration in 1875.

[45]*Le Grande-Châtelet came to be abandoned as a citadel when the next line of walls was built but it was transformed like its much later successor, the Bastille, into a grim prison throughout much of medieval time.* Ibid., *p. 13.*

[46]Ibid., *p. 17.*

[47]Ibid., *p. 20.*

The Four Roles of the Medieval City

Even in the Dark Ages, which closed in the aubade of the twelfth century, cities began to evidence the roles they would play in the true light that shone in late medieval times. Four such roles can be observed, each loosely tied to a structure of protection during the full medieval millennium (A.D. 500 to A.D. 1500). This morphological association makes use of the various physical structures we have just been considering.

Subjugate City

The first in time, if not in importance, of these urban roles is rather static: the city might merely be a tolerated survivor of past times—as, for example, the Roman cities of the western empire—and exist as a *subjugate city* under feudalism. Throughout medieval times these cities might exist as captives of a rurally dominated polity, remaining small places more versed in history than in power. Episcopal sees made use of them; they often had a baronial castle nearby from which feudal control was exercised and to which in extreme danger the small population might resort for the ultimate in available protection. The small cities of feudal Europe—of Germany, the Alpine lands, and the Latin Balkans in particular—took on this form. The normal morphological associate of these subjugated places was the thin, low and relatively simple medieval wall enclosing a tiny place which served as a market town for its local agricultural area. Only when some unique commodity which might be traded advantageously at a distance was available in the vicinity would the feudal market town have any appreciable external connections; in the absence of such a commodity the seigneur increased his wealth to the maximum by closing off his estate from the outside world as much as possible and internalizing its economy. His objective was achieved in most cases with a two-part morphology comprised of the thinly walled market town, carrying on only the most basic of economic activities, and his castle, which might lie somewhat removed from the town. His absolute control of the place was such that he need not keep a constant eye on it, and its activities were so marginally attractive that no outside power would covet it greatly. This pattern of closed economic entities was widespread in Thuringia, Swabia and Franconia, Luxembourg, Styria, and parts of the Latin Balkans, where Walter Christaller found the models on which to base his central-place theory.

Imperial Free City

Even in the darkest of times a distinction must be made between the town that stood essentially in servitude to the local baron, as if it were one of his serfs, and one that was fundamentally his equal. Some places always existed that had gained from the king or Holy Roman emperor subfeudatory powers similar to those of barons. These *imperial free cities* were especially common in Germany, where the elaboration of the feudal order was greatest and central authority was at its weakest. Those towns that possessed some unusual attribute, normally long-distance trade, could force from the Holy Roman emperor a treatment similar to that afforded to rural feudatories.

The signal of the change from the decline of Roman urbanism to the rise of its medieval successor came when the city *corporation* was established. The city corporation could give homage and fealty to the king and gain in return powers with respect to the collection and payment of taxes, the exercise of justice, and the conduct of economic activities that formed a benefice. The normal relationship came under a charter specifying duties and privileges, a contract between the sovereign and the city corporation. Like any contract, this charter might be renegotiated, granting more privileges to the corporation or exacting from it more duties (or taxes). Because those corporations had a more favorable experience with amassing wealth than the king had in conserving his receipts, it proved fairly easy for the city corporation to use some short-term exigency of the crown as a bargaining point to gain a greater long-term freedom, just as a powerful major feudatory could trade his military might in a campaign for a larger domain when the battle was won.

In this legal context the imperial free city emerged, not fully independent of the empire but equal in its hierarchy to the most important agents of the crown. In Germany, where an oligarchy elected the Holy Roman emperor, some of the free cities were Electors equal to those of Saxony or the bishop of Trier, for example. Because this freedom, though not complete, was still a very valuable exemption from the constraint and rigidity of feudal life, most free cities were careful to make themselves powerful against their peers, the other major feudatories who might covet their sources of wealth, and against the sovereign, who might wish to recapture some of the powers previously granted to the free cities. To accomplish these two goals the free city had to be well protected with walls. Lübeck and Hamburg were among the most heavily guarded places. Towers and complicated gates guarded against surprise and high, thick walls against successful siege.

The economic power of the free city gave it an important edge over most of its military opponents. Every warrior from the baron to the emperor was usually on the edge of bankruptcy, forbidding the accumulation of materiel of war and food and fodder to mount a successful siege. At this stage in the poliorcetic competition the free city had a distinct advantage that lasted until cannon were widely adopted. So the morphological associate of the imperial free city was the heavy urban wall and the great accumulation of the materiel to resist siege. Unlike the Paris of Philip-Augustus, these cities were not frowned over by citadels built to enforce regal suzerainty, any more than the chateau of a powerful duke was guarded by one of the king. The free city was the peer of such royal agents and had to be treated in the same way.

Independent City

A third role for cities in the Middle Ages evolved where conditions encouraged power and freedom for urban men but worked against an effective feudal hierarchy. The Holy Roman emperors had tried to enforce feudalism in the Po Basin of Italy but they had not succeeded very well. The relative advantage in the production of wealth enjoyed by German cities in the north operated in Italy as well, allowing the emergence of truly *independent cities*. These places were little distinguished from the free cities save for their possession of ultimate sovereignty. To protect themselves from other independent cities and from the cravings of the Holy Roman emperor and his peer-in-covetousness, the pope, the independent cities of northern Italy had to build walls of similar strength to those of Lübeck, and had to store supplies in warehouses as large as those in the Baltic port.

Colonial City

The independent cities of Italy and the imperial free cities of Germany gained, through their freedom from feudalism, an ability to grow economically as the subjugated towns could not. The almost undivided control exercised there by a baron was likely to force the constraint of trade—within what Christaller calls a tributary area—to the local town. As Marc Bloch told us, "Trade, therefore, was not nonexistent, but it was [within the manorial economy] irregular in the extreme. The society of this age was certainly not unacquainted with either buying or selling. But it did not, like our own, live by buying and selling."[48] The feudal order so lacking in dynamism became an instrument of preservation rather than growth. Powerful families might engage in dynastic aggrandizement but the evi-

---

[48]*Bloch*, op. cit., *Vol. 1, p. 67.*

dence from Germany showed the difficulty of shaping the nation-state under feudalism. This assertion is best supported by evidence furnished by the fourth purpose for which cities existed in medieval times, that of supporting the geographical expansion of a political state, an activity fundamentally antipathetic to the purposes of the feudal order. When lands changed hands under feudalism, the economy internal to the addition tended to remain as before, though its riches might flow to a different coffer. But national expansion caused a major reorientation of the economy, commonly a major transformation of the culture of the area, as well as the shift in political control. Thus, new centers—*colonial cities*—were founded to aid in these fundamentally changed relationships. The Norman kings of England and of Sicily and other Mediterranean realms were perhaps the first to devise these colonial cities: they were certainly the masters of the art if not its inventors.

The Colonial City in Europe and the Mediterranean

The Normans played a central role in the Crusades of the twelfth and thirteenth centuries. Going to the Holy Land as soldiers of the cross, many Normans stayed on to found feudal holdings in the Levant, in the islands and peninsulas of southern Greece, in Sicily, and in Calabria and Apulia in southern Italy. In this activity the Normans were following on practices they had learned in their conquest of England. The same warriors were not always involved but in that relatively simple society and time, the word of the English colonial experience must have been widespread among this still relatively small group.

The great authority on the Normans, Edward Augustus Freeman, held that "these two conquests, wrought in the great island of the Ocean and the great island of the Mediterranean [Sicily], were the main works of the Normans after they fully put on the character of a Christian and a French-speaking people. . . ." He notes that a contemporary historian, Geoffrey Malaterra, had long ago set "the Normans before us as a race specially marked by cunning, despising their own [Scandinavian] inheritance in the hope of winning a greater, eager after both gain and dominion, given to imitation of all kinds . . ." and "holding a certain mean between lavishness and greediness. . . ." In England the Normans became Englishmen "because there was an English nation into which they could be absorbed. The Normans in Sicily could hardly be said to become Sicilians, for there was assuredly no Sicilian nation for them to be absorbed into."[49]

What the Normans learned about colonizing in these pre-Crusade endeavors they combined with a knowledge of fortification much advanced by the campaigns to the Holy Land and their admininstration of that area after its conquest. In that operation the Normans had partners drawn from their Italian "bankers"—those from Venice, Genoa, and Pisa who furnished the supplies and ships for the sea-borne Crusades—who learned as well from this early religious-colonial episode. The Normans returned from the Levant as masters of the siege castle, the Italians as masters of the trading port dotted along the shores of a foreign but trade-bound land. The Normans used their knowledge to complete their conquest of England, adding Wales and parts of Ireland to their realm, and to hold the line against French encroachment in Normandy, Anjou, and Aquitaine. The Italians, particularly the Venetians, used their equally specialized knowledge to shape an *empire da mar* spread by a hundred trading harbors along the east shore of the Adriatic, into the Greek islands, and even as a foreign colony across the Golden Horn from Constantinople in Galata. The Norman towns were all-of-a-piece colonial cities. Not surprisingly, then, the French and the English, successors to the Normans, knew best how to shape medieval bastides, built in considerable numbers during the period of the Crusades. They knew, too, how to build the colonial cities of the continents beyond Europe that shaped both the New World of European plantations and the Imperial World of European political conquest.

The City's Emergence in the High Middle Ages

During the second part of the Middle Ages, beginning in the twelfth century with the emancipation of the city from much of the repression of feudalism, the traditional function of urban places as the cradle of change was restored. The result was the birth of a conflict that still persists. The conservative, often hierarchically ordered countryside, where wealth came in tangible and geographically accountable property, came into conflict with the evolving and socially mobile city, where wealth came in transferable capital whose return disappeared unless it was put to work, most effectively in geographically extensive trade. Throughout this period the conservative, hierarchically organized Roman church, medieval Europe's greatest land-owner, made a moral question of a clearly economic argument, attempting to contain or even stamp out the substitution of the city economy for the feudal one, to avoid any questioning of the western Catholic order. This repression ultimately destroyed the universality of that church, though it did not destroy the castigated cities nor the economic, social, and religious liberalism that grew up in them.

---

[49]*Freeman wrote some fifteen volumes on the Normans and an unfinished* History of Sicily, *but his most succinct statement is contained in his article on "Normans" in the 11th Edition of the* Encyclopaedia Britannica, *cited above.*

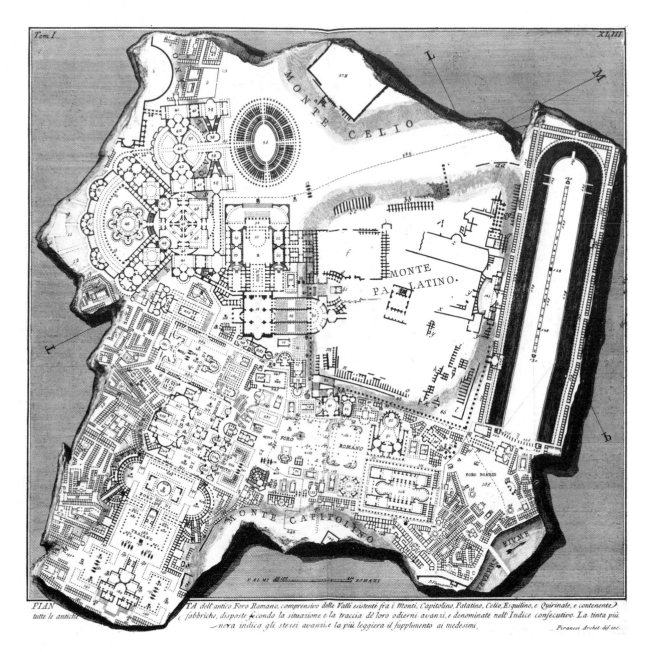

PLAN
tutte le antiche

TA dell'antico Foro Romano, comprensivo delle Valli esistenti fra i Monti, Capitolino, Palatino, Celio, Esquilino, e Quirinale, e contenente
fabbriche, disposte secondo la situazione e la traccia de' loro odierni avanzi, e denominate nell'Indice consecutivo. La tinta più
nera indica gli stessi avanzi, e la più leggiera il supplimento ai medesimi.

Piranesi Archit. del. inc.

The collapse of the Roman
Empire was more a politi-
cal than a morphological
break. Many Roman monu-
ments continued on throughout the Dark Ages, lending
mute testimony to how
radical the geographical
disintegration had been.
The stones of Rome were
only slowly dislodged by
gravity or the quarrying
of medieval builders.
This etching is an 18th-
century reconstruction by
Gianbattista Piranesi.

4. THE EXPRESSION OF LIBERALISM: THE FACE OF THE MEDIEVAL CITY

This painting by Bacchiacca, "Sheltering the Pilgrims" (1540), shows the crossing of the Via della Spada and the Via della Belle Donne in Florence, suggesting the nature of the high north I Italian house in the late Middle Ages.

The fully developed medieval city emerged sometime in the thirteenth century, a time of fundamental reorientation of human activity. It had completely original qualities, both socially and morphologically. Our inheritance of those qualities is great indeed; modern cities draw more from the Middle Ages than from the Classical Era, however much the Founding Fathers of the American Republic wished and thought otherwise. Urban evolution in western civilization has been essentially continuous since that birth of the medieval city.

The most notable feature of the medieval city was its effective separation from the countryside. It was not an "up-to-date" instance of classical synoecism; in the Middle Ages once people left the land they were reluctant to return to submit again to the restriction of geographical and personal freedom. Similarly, the medieval city was not a modernized Roman one; in place of the great military and administrative roles assigned to towns under the empire, urbanization under medieval controls had a strongly economic quality. That quality has remained the most central to urbanization in the eight hundred years of western life since the medieval city was devised.

It is sometimes assumed that the city in the Middle Ages was always the seat of a king or powerful lord or bishop, yet the truly important towns were frequently not. When the Count of Paris, Hugh Capet, became king of France in A.D. 987, he began a split between his interests as local lord and as sovereign that widened over the years, causing the king to depart Paris more and more frequently, to have on occasion to besiege the city to return, and finally to abandon it completely (in the seventeenth century with Louis XIV's permanent move to Versailles). In England conditions were not so different. Westminster became the royal seat, and the kings of England were allowed in London only by special permission. The monarchy became the fountainhead of the traditional, rurally-based *order*, whereas the city was the font of innovation and the urban-based efforts toward transformation and liberalization.

The medieval cities were in other ways functionally separated from the countryside, especially in their economic life, which was their most novel feature when they rose to importance. Like the castles, they might challenge the kings' authority, but unlike those feudal strongholds that had been the summit of morphological ingenuity and creation during the Dark Ages, they did it with a system of support fully outside the medieval order.

As the French historian Boissonade expressed it a half century ago, "Feudal government was designed rather to hamper than to assist commercial activity. Moreover, the public opinion of all classes misun-derstood the role of trade, and continued to look upon the trader as a parasite, a speculator, a usurer, and movable wealth as the fruit of fraud and rapine, but not of labour. Moreover, the conditions of economy on the great domain left only a limited field of action in commerce."[1] Thus, "(d)uring the first two centuries of the feudal age, a movable or money economy, which has its source in commerce, possessed only an infinitesimal importance." In geographical terms "economic life had become, as it were, stationary in this purely agricultural society, enclosed in a rigid framework of the landed aristocracy." In the only markets to function within the feudal order, "a man would trade a horse for a sack of [grain], a piece of cloth for a measure of salt, a pound of pepper for a pair of boots." In truth, "the only markets known were local, held in the gateway of a castle or monastery, or on the outskirts of a neighbouring town. Insecurity, anarchy, the multiplicity of seigneurial monopolies and tolls, the scarcity and difficulty of means of transport, the chaotic diversity of weights and measures and moneys, the scarcity of currency, and the imperfection of instruments of credit were all obstacles to the circulation of merchandise."[2]

If we look at this succinct description of the nature of trade in the feudal centuries (the ninth and tenth) in terms of the argument for and against central-place theory, we find substantial contravention in historical and geographical terms of its basic assumptions: the city's location is determined by a geometry of access from potential customers to a central-place at which they may secure, with the least geographical effort, the satisfaction of their demands for goods and services, and thus cities grow out of the countryside. As Boissonade and virtually all historians of the Middle Ages would have it, (1) the location of the market was due to historical forces of privilege held by a lord, agglomeration of dynastic land-holdings, the natural occurrence of a strongpoint, or the somewhat adventitious bequeathal of lands to the church, rather than any historically discernible normative geography; and (2) this trading in local markets was not geographically free; it converged on the market held by the lord, not always the closest possible market. Virtually no evidence points to a heirarchy—a nesting, as the central-place theorist would have it, of such places. Boissonade's

[1] P. Boissonade, Life and Work in Medieval Europe: The Evolution of Medieval Economy from the Fifth to the Fifteenth Centuries, *translated by Eileen Power (French edition, 1921; English translation, 1927), New York: Harper and Row, 1964, p. 159. Professor Power characterized this work as one of popularization but she thought enough of it to undertake its translation and "popularization" among the English economic historians of whom she was the doyenne.*
[2] Loc. cit.

"natural trade" was parochial or highly periodic, with those goods not found naturally in the vicinity being furnished by itinerant traders, peddlers, distinguished most in a legally sedentary medieval population by their possession of no fixed abode. In law their property was viewed as *waif* (implying goods washed up on shore by an act of God), hardly the status that would be accorded to a denizen of a closed, ordered central-place, or feudal, system.

The Two Classes of Medieval Settlement

We might recognize two basic forms of nucleated settlement in the later Middle Ages. *Natural settlements*, to borrow and reshape the economic historian's phrase, emerged inside a closed political-economic domain, whose extent was due to historical rather than geometrically determinative forces and whose market would be sited because of those same human rather than mechanical forces. *Systemic settlements* were based on long-distance trade but, of necessity, possessed of an independence from the constraining feudal order that produced the more repetitive natural settlements. In essence towns were patterned in two ways, and the two were to a fair degree in conflict, or at least in competition.

The natural settlement of the lord's domain emerged within an area whose size and shape would be determined not by the convergence of customers, but because it would stand a defensible and administratable unit. "Geographical base" was not geographically determined; rather it was geographically described. Its modal size was more likely to come from realities of demography than geography. If a grant were given to support a subfeudatory in reasonable fashion, then the areal scale of that grant would depend upon the productivity of the land, rather than the outer limit of practicable access to the lord's market. True, most individual medieval grants were small enough to permit this access by customers, but it is extremely doubtful that the overlord used this attribute to determine how much land he would grant as a benefice to his feudatory. The common usage of the term "tributary area" for the collecting area of a market is more historically accurate than those who use it might suspect. Due to the modal scale of such domains, they tended to be relatively evenly spaced about the countryside. But because they were based on closed domains and a natural economy, these small places were ranked in a single order without any heirarchical superstructure. What nonlocal trade existed was almost certainly carried on not by distant trading centers but by peddlers bringing wares within the closed-economy area and taking from it, most frequently, goods obtained in barter.

Standing in sharp contrast to this constrained pattern were the systemic settlements, those that participated in a geographically extensive system. The systemic town would of necessity stand outside the local closed economies, and held a status far more independent of feudalism than the local market town. Systemic places might be divided into "feudal towns" and "non-feudal towns" but such a dichotomy would not be historically accurate. Most systemic towns were at least ostensibly still existent within a feudal system; their distinction was that they had managed to break the conservative, order-maintaining quality of that political and social order. Tribute, if it was paid, was likely to be determined by contractual relations, which limited its scale and gained in return some "liberties" and "freedoms" from the endless, stultifying regulations of feudalism. The greater the economic power a city possessed, the larger its body of freedoms was likely to be, because the wielding of that economic power gained for the urban settlement its degree of departure from the rigid traditional feudal order.

Because cities had different degrees of economic power as well as differences in history, they had contrasting freedoms. These distinctions allowed differences in the role that a town might play in an extensive trading system. Some towns were free, as in upper Italy. Others were nearly free, as were the imperial free cities of Germany. Some were still integrated to varying degrees within the feudal order, as in France, south Germany, and the Holy Land, and some were under fairly direct control of the crown, as in England. Given this diversity of status, the probability of classes of towns was strong. This tendency toward differentiation would further be enhanced by the fairly direct relationship between freedom and economic power. Those places already possessed of a high level of freedom would tend to gain thereby a greater access to trade; consequently, they would even further extend their lead over places of lesser freedom.

All of these general truths lead to the realization that *if an hierarchy of towns did develop, it was likely to do so within the systemic settlements rather than within the natural ones.* But within the systemic settlements the differentiation would be more functional than hierarchical because the trade they practiced was proto-wholesaling rather than the retailing. In retailing the customer remains an indivisible unit, having to go in turn to a diversity of geographical locations. In wholesaling, on the other hand, the powerful tendency was toward specialization in trade, with one man serving as the agent to facilitate trade in wool while another facilitated the trade in a different staple, such as fish. The first man might be a resident of Calais, while the second lived in Bristol, leading not to an hierarchy of places so much as to a system of places distinct to each staple of trade. Thus, even in systemic settlement staple-specific systems were more likely than general ones, and a greater ability to maintain an historical lead was enjoyed by an early center independent of any dependence upon "status" within an hierarchy.

To recapitulate, the systemic settlement grew first out of separation from the feudal order which allowed the town to push out trading linkages beyond its own "natural" domain, which in most cases would be very limited in a geographical sense. Exceptions to this rule included the *empire da mar* that Venice shaped which was geographically extensive and clearly a case of the flag following trade. Most peoples, however, substituted a pattern of trading alliance for political control; more common than the Venetian type of empire was the *hanse* of trade, an alliance among fairly independent cities which sought mutual gain through a facilitation of long-distance trade. Unlike the Venetian system, the hanseatic system might be viewed as one of special-purpose association; the basic sovereignty of the city remained unchanged while special arrangements were made with respect to trade. The result was the growth of the notion of extraterritoriality as a fundamental concept operating within the important towns of the medieval trading networks.

Extraterritoriality Fosters Trade

To understand extraterritoriality we must look again at one of the fundamental social concepts of the Middle Ages, that of "settlement," which held that a person possessed a high degree of geographical identification. Under feudalism and commendation, a weaker man made a contractual relationship of homage and fealty to a stronger man who, in return for the services of the man commending himself to him, offered protection and a form of support. Men either were participants

(vassals or lords) in such a contract or they stood totally "foreign" (from the Latin *foris*, outside) to the locale; they resided outside and were probably commended to another lord. One was either part of the specific feudal order, a denizen, or else he was outside it, an alien. As a denizen, he was subject to its exactions. A man might be both lord and vassal; the king of England was for a time the vassal of his French cousin, while he in turn was the lord of his own vassals in England. In each *office* he was either vassal or lord, not both, though he as a *person* might at the same time be both.

The desire of lords to have their vassals in their domain made residency one of the duties of the vassal in serfdom. Only when on the lord's errand could the vassal be legally absent from his realm. This notion of geographical identification of man with place meant that no practice existed to care for the stranger in one's midst. Since he was considered outside the local law, yet within its jurisdiction, he was placed in a most unfavorable position, particularly if he carried with him movable wealth, as did the traveling trader. "His goods, his ships, his person, were exposed to seizure and confiscation by virtue of (local) rights of escheat, waif, or wreck. Upon him fell the revenges and retaliations which the feudal lord considered it was his right to exact from the enemy lord to whom the merchant was subject."[3] Given feudal legal practices, the traveling trader was easily prey to extortionate relations from the denizens; for example, he could not enforce a contract, as he could not be a legal party to a suit in that jurisdiction.

If long-distance trade were to be engaged in, some legal basis must be found for this stranger. The solution came in a notion similar to that of the divisibility of person under the feudal order; as we noted, a king might himself be both lord and vassal. Similarly a trader might be both alien and denizen, in the sense that for trading purposes he was resident, but for other purposes he was foreign. To make this specialized citizenship work, a specific location where men gained the particular local rights they sought was usually necessary.

At first that locale of special privilege was provided in the periodic fair, held under the authority of an important temporal or spiritual lord. Because the church was the one effective international organization, a cer-

[3]Ibid., p. 160. Escheat *is the notion that property within a political jurisdiction reverts to that jurisdiction if no legal inheritor or other recipient of its bestowal exists under the laws of that administration. Clearly the foreigner found in a jurisdiction where he had no legal status could be deprived of his goods as failing to have right to them, not being permitted to possess property in that jurisdiction. If that were too difficult a legal argument, then* waif *might prove an easier basis for confiscation.*

This fourteenth-century illustrated manuscript, *Grandes Chroniques de France,* shows the Lendit Fair at Saint-Denis.

tain logic held to the role of great monasteries and abbeys as the authorities granting privileges to hold a fair. Saint-Omer and Saint-Denis in France serve as examples from an early time, as does Winchester in England. The geographical result of this tendency of fairs to be associated with ecclesiastical foundations was that they also tended to be rural in site, or at least suburban, as were Saint-Denis outside Paris, Bartholomew Fair outside London, and Stourbridge Fair in the fields to the east of Cambridge. In such places it was quite easy to set up a special jurisdiction and a special court for transients' law—the Piepowder court—which gave strangers a legal status during the time of the fair.

The real problem arose in trying to devise a way to grant specialized status to periodic residents of a city, as opposed to those staying briefly on the site of a suburban fair. The problem was solved by establishing special districts within the city which might stand legally extraterritorial to it. Such districts were particularly needed during the early stages of city building when feudalism was declining and the traders were likely to be foreigners in religion as well as politics. Just as the late decades of the Roman Empire witnessed the concentration of trade into the hands of the Orientals, so the early decades of the emergence of medieval trade also saw these true outsiders dominating the activity. Their social and religious practices were beyond legal recognition in the world of medieval orthodoxy (in much the same way that being a gentile in present-day

Israel leads to considerable legal problems, even though one may live there under a state of toleration). Additionally, they were not able to become participants in legal actions for damages, recovery, and other aspects of contract. The practical solution was to be found only in courts of special jurisdiction. If, for example, the Jews were to shift from their almost universal wandering life in western Europe to one of fixed abode in towns, those towns had to think in terms of some level of extraterritoriality for them.

The notion of strangers resident within became generally accepted in the medieval city and institutions were shaped to deal with the problems thus raised. Although they might be disqualified from such things as participation in the freedom of the city restricted to those of full citizenship and orthodox Christian belief, in those matters of trade which brought them to the city, the strangers were likely to have fairly effective freedom and protection. Otherwise, being international persons, they were free to migrate elsewhere, which served as a defense against unreasonable exactions by the citizens and their king. In turn, the cities' defense against the unreasonable exactions of the international traders came from the ever-present ability to evict them from the market and force them to depart from the realm, as was done on several occasions. The beginning of greater orthodoxy in religion and economies led to the expulsion of the Jews from England in 1290; only the return of dissent in theology and liberalization in economies, which came under Cromwell's Commonwealth, allowed their return.[4]

The Shaping of the Ghetto

Much has been made of the creation of the ghetto in Italy during the twelfth century. Unquestionably the church, in the Fourth Lateran Council of 1215, required Jews to wear distinctive clothing and forbade religious argumentation between Jews and Christians, but the Council essentially stamped out religious questioning wherever it arose. In the end the Jews fared far better than the Cathari, those Christian reformers merely attempting to root out the luxury and indulgence of the

[4]*Friedrich Heer,* The Medieval World *[first published in Germany as* Mittelalter *in 1961],* New York: New American Library, *n.d., p. 310. The French case is covered by Heer on p. 82.*

medieval church, who called down on their heads the Albigensian Crusade. During that Crusade the urban fabric of southern France was badly damaged and had to be remade in a new form, as we will see in Chapter 5. Most of the Cathari were slaughtered, as the medieval Jews were not; the pious and puritanical Christians were offered no place of refuge more extensive than fire and the stake. In the ghetto the Jews were offered a true refuge. They had neither to recant, as the Cathari were demanded to do, nor to leave. Their quarters near the Ghetto forge in Venice preserved the medieval Jewish community of the city and gave to most western languages one of the most misrepresented, misunderstood, and misused words.[5]

The statelessness of the Jews made of their extraterritoriality a somewhat different thing from that of the Italians or Germans in London, Paris, and other large medieval cities. The Jews sought to maintain an exotic culture solely on such an extraterritorial base, as they have sought to do until fairly recent years, and this practice produced both misunderstanding and friction. Jews have often been pictured as mistreated because they were merchants, but traders who were denizens needed no special protection. The Jew's office was not what threatened him but rather his insistence on participating in the economic life of the country without accepting the responsibilities imposed by its history and culture. It was easy to dislike and distrust a group who demonstrably recognized only limited loyalty to the city, rejected religious beliefs in a manner that would have led native Christians to the stake, and badly concealed a disdain and contempt for the indigenous social and cultural attitudes. Whether the outsiders were Jews in Venice, Germans in Novgorod, Genoans in Constantinople, English in Madras, or westerners in China early in this century, the principle remained the same. They were strangers in the midst of an homogeneous culture; all too often, the culture did not reject them, but they ostentatiously rejected the culture. So long as they sought to remain apart, they ultimately would be kept apart. In a time of difficulty when a cause for God's wrath must be found, the strangers were logical candidates.

In Novgorod, the German merchants built their own town surrounded by walls (much like those of the castle keeps which shielded the Norman conquerors in the twelfth century) to protect themselves from the ire of the Russian populace. To a lesser degree these enclaves of foreigners were to be found over much of Europe. In Bergen, a bit of the German hanse merchants' quarter, the *Tyskebryggen*, survives, so we can imagine how their brothers lived in their settlements in Bruges, London, Novgorod, and elsewhere. In these specialized quarters, the Germans were permitted to carry on their own way of life, use their business practices, conduct their dealings in German, and maintain their social and religious customs. They were normally subject to their own laws and customs, not those of the host country, and were permitted to engage in trade with natives in a legal context that would be missing elsewhere in the realm.

Thus, extraterritoriality had two forms, cultural and economic. To divide the two was difficult in most cases, as cultural strangers normally sought residence to engage in specific economic activities. The Jews had been money-lenders and to a lesser degree international traders even under the Carolingian Empire; the northern Italians (the Lombards of the Middle Ages), who devised the first effective banking system, were settled throughout western Europe to provide international exchange of money and credit; and the Germans of the *hanse*, seeking to become the late medieval wholesalers in the northern world, established their warehouses—*stahl-* or steelyards—at the edge of many cities. On a more periodic schedule, the Venetians sent northwestward their fleet of galleys each year in the attempt to dominate all the onward connections from their vast emporium of the spice trade. Not until the middle of the sixteenth century did the English feel strong enough to put down this incursion of outside galleys trading at dockside in Southampton and London. Fired by the newly advocated mercantilism, they shifted the mercantile frontier far into the Mediterranean to the new port of Livorno (Leghorn), where they began to conduct the Anglo-Italian exchange. Finally, extraterritoriality grew out of weakness and dependency and was cut off at the base when power was gained by the granting nation.

The Hearths of Medieval Urbanism

Two areas of medieval Europe were particularly significant in the ultimate spread of urbanization: Flanders, and the Po Basin and Tuscany. In each, large and important towns were kept busy and prosperous by manufacture at the hands of skilled artisans and the trade of the goods carried out by quick-witted traders traveling all over Europe. These areas might be called *trade-originating Europe.*

From these hearths, city-filling spread widely to turn small towns into truly great cities. In particular,

[5]Ibid., p. 310.

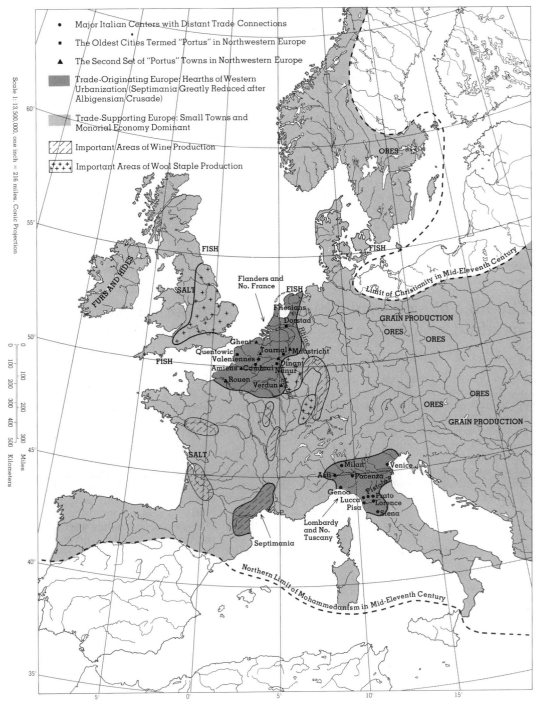

Major Italian Centers with Distant Trade Connections

The Oldest Cities Termed "Portus" in Northwestern Europe

The Second Set of "Portus" Towns in Northwestern Europe

Trade-Originating Europe: Hearths of Western
Urbanization (Septimania Greatly Reduced after
Albigensian Crusade)

Trade-Supporting Europe: Small Towns and
Monorial Economy Dominant

Important Areas of Wine Production

Important Areas of Wool Staple Production

Scale 1: 13,500,000, one inch = 216 miles, Conic Projection

0 100 200 300 400 500 Miles
0 100 200 300 400 500 Kilometers

60°

55°

50°

45°

40°

35°

ORES

FISH

Limit of Christianity in Mid-Eleventh Century

FURS AND HIDES

FISH

SALT

FISH

Flanders and
No. France

FISH

Friesians
Dorstad

GRAIN PRODUCTION

ORES

ORES

Ghent
Quentowic
Valenciennes
Amiens Cambrai Namur
Rouen
Verdun

Tournai Maastricht
Dinant

ORES

ORES

GRAIN PRODUCTION

SALT

Milan
Asti Pacenza
Genoa
Lucca Prato
Pisa Florence
Siena

Venice

Pistoia

Lombardy
and No.
Tuscany

Septimania

Northern Limit of Mohammedanism in Mid-Eleventh Century

5° 0° 5° 10° 15°

Longitude West of Greenwich   Longitude East of Greenwich

*Map of trade originating in
Europe.*

growth came in towns where the staples needed in an industry could be collected from their rural producing areas: Norwich, Colchester, and Boston in the east of England; Bristol in the west, Liège in eastern Belgium, which collected fleeces from the Ardennes, and the Spanish ports that collected them from the vast pastures of Iberia. In contrast to the hearths, these areas where cities were fewer but often of considerable size and importance became *trade-supporting Europe*. This trade-supporting Europe felt much of the initial change of the Industrial Revolution of the eighteenth century. Finally, in a third realm almost outside trade where neither staples nor manufactures were to be found—as in thinly settled parts of distant kingdoms—*feudal Europe* with its antipathy to cities remained for centuries longer.

cities, determined on the basis of terrain and natural lines of access. If cities do grow out of the countryside, then these qualities and the density of rural population in the area furnish the answer to where cities will be located. If one assumes, as the historical evidence strongly indicates, that cities do not grow for the most part out of their countryside, then other elements must be considered to account for the use of only a small number of the potential sites.

The fundamental assumption of the mercantile model is that conditions of long-distance trade have more bearing on the successful development of a potential site than do its immediate environs. The cases of Bristol and Venice may serve to substantiate this position, each having become great in medieval times primarily because of long-distance trade.

The Rise of Medieval Cities in the Twelfth Century

Urban innovation was brought on in the twelfth century by an effective combination of a number of different conditions: population had increased in recent generations; greater civic freedom allowed cities to grow and experiment; a revival of the eastern trade in spices and luxuries came with the Crusades; and the reintroduction of waterpower mills in the west was added to a number of other technological and social changes. Few sizable towns were in existence in Europe in the year 1100, save those in upper Italy, Provence in southern France, and the Byzantine Empire, so the processes of internal development worked on a rather empty slate.

Our first concern in discussing the creation and shaping of cities is clearly the "potential location for cities." The conditions built into a geometric abstraction such as Christaller's model of normative economic structure will answer the question as to the placing of settlements. But when an effort is made to answer the general question of location in a historically responsive manner, something more is needed. I shall work towards a *mercantile model* as a more historically valid explanation of the location of cities than Christaller's neat but ill-fitting structure.

The mercantile model rests on the assumption that a number of geographical locations are possible for

Historical Events, Chartered Rights, Potential Locations

Charters provide us with most of the written evidence we possess of when, where, and how cities were established during the Middle Ages. Unfortunately they seldom tell us why the place was given the distinctive and valuable privileges they enumerated. In seeking an explanation we should realize that "Great lords, however, were quick to see the economic and financial advantages which might accrue to themselves and their territories from the advancement of 'their' towns, and consciously set about their promotion." But this viewpoint was far from universal in medieval Europe. "Pioneers of this policy were the counts of Flanders and the Capetian kings, who took care both to keep for themselves the two most important cities of their kingdom, Paris and Orleans, and to strengthen their power by taking towns in the lands of the great feudatories under their special protection. In the Angevin Empire [within France], the English kings, as Dukes of Normandy and vassals of the French crown, promoted the towns of Rouen, La Rochelle, Bayonne and Bordeaux, in keen competition with their suzerain in Paris."[6] Thus, the potential town gained a certain weight in its struggle with the great lords; it might succeed in convincing him that his prosperity could be enhanced by a

[6]Ibid., *pp. 84-85.*

greater degree of economic, and incidentally personal, freedom for the burgesses of his town. Perhaps more importantly, once the great lords—basically kings, regional dukes, and palatine counts such as those of Toulouse—had envisaged the potential wealth to be gained from serving as the lords of trading towns, they had the geographical raw materials to aid such prosperity. The course of a baron with a localized manor was limited to jealously guarding the local trade by enclosing it within the domainal economy. But being great lords, the kings, dukes, and palatine counts could favor "their" town by giving it privileges denied to others, mainly that of engaging in long-distance trade. We have seen how shrewdly the Capetian kings held Paris and Orleans. The Burgundian, Spanish, and Austrian lords of Flanders were equally shrewd, elevating Brussels at the expense of Mons or Louvain, largely because that city fell in the lands directly held by the Counts of Flanders and their Hapsburg heirs.

Not all towns made it, however hard their lords and commonalty tried. Some never transformed a potential for growth into actual construction, and others faltered after making a serious beginning. "Cities which had been wealthy and flourishing were laid low by more successful rivals, as for instance in Italy: Amalfi, Siena, and dozens of smaller towns failed to hold their own against Venice, Milan, Florence and Genoa. New foundations often turned out to be unsuccessful speculations. *They attracted insufficient trade and traffic*, and after a few generations, as the grass grew again, the town reverted to its former agricultural status, or the port silted up. . . ."[7]

Social Urbanization

Once a city had been founded in a place that possessed the potential for trade, the first process that began to fill its walls might be termed *social urbanization.* That social movement responded to the classical dynamics of migration; the personal serfdom of the countryside and the inability to own property there created a *push-factor* that encouraged men to leave the feudal domain, often by stealth, while the greater hope of personal freedom and prosperity in the city formed a *pull-factor*

[7]*Ibid., p. 70. Emphasis supplied.*

to draw refugees from the country within its walls. This migration was first a physical translocation but its continuing impact was cultural, as settlers from a rural background must necessarily make massive adaptations to city life. Adaptation must have dominated medieval society in the twelfth century in much the same way it dominated American city life in the nineteenth, simply because the urban demographic base had been small and the migration influx had been relatively as great. The impact of urban culture on the simple rural migrant must have been greatest in the "communes" of Flanders and parts of northern France and in the towns of the county of Toulouse in the south where city life was more free and the government of the towns fell more directly in the hands of the citizen burghers.

The rural implosion on the town seems to have focussed on two distinct modes of settlement, as Professor Friedrich Keutgen noted long ago.

There is evidence that in the quondam *Roman towns (in the north) the German newcomers settled much as in a village, i.e. each full member of the community had a certain portion of arable land (some of which might lie within the commodious Roman walls) allotted to him and a share in the common. Their pursuits would at first be mainly agricultural. The* new towns, *on the other hand, general economic conditions having meanwhile begun to undergo a marked change, were founded with intention of establishing centres of trade. Periodical markets, weekly or annual, had preceded them, which already enjoyed the special protection of the king's ban, acts of violence against traders visiting them or on their way towards them being subject to special punishment. The settlers invited (to the New Towns) were merchants* (mercatores personati) *and handicraftsmen. The land now allotted to each member of the community was just large enough for a house and yard, stabling and perhaps a small garden (50 by 100 feet at Freiburg, 60 by 100 feet at Bern). These building plots were given as free property or, more frequently, at a nominal rent* (Wurtzins) *with the right of free disposal, the only obligation being that of building a house.*[8]

Keutgen's picture is basically typical of the medieval German realm: Germany herself, present-day Austria, The Netherlands, Flanders (both Belgian and French), German Switzerland, and Alsace. In contrast stood the world of the Italian urban communes with their more continuing link to Roman urbanization, which resulted in a more "political" component

[8]*Friedrich W. E. Keutgen, "Medieval Commune," Encyclopaedia Britannica, 11th edition, Vol. 6, p. 785. Emphasis supplied.*

in city life and in the control of urban government on the peninsula. Throughout the barbarian invasions of the fifth and sixth centuries, the northern Italian towns had tenuously hung on to their identity and some freedom, though they tended to be dominated by bishops whose yokes had to be thrown off to gain the enhanced freedom that came in the twelfth century. This persistence of Roman foundation, save in Venice which was founded only during the barbarian invasions, maintained a particular relationship of town and country. In upper Italy, and to a lesser degree in Languedoc, which until the Albigensian Crusade of the thirteenth century was more Mediterranean than French, the town dominated the countryside with either the city republican government, as in Italy, or the counts palatine, as in Toulouse and Narbonne, effectively controlling the countryside. In these *city-dominated landscapes,* most nobles with estates in the surrounding countryside (the *contado* in Italy) were expected to maintain city houses and to reside in them for at least part of the year so they might be watched over by the urban authority.[9] The pattern of these cities around the northern shore of the Mediterranean became domination of an area outside their walls until the boundary with the area *tributary* to another city was reached. Thus, there was never the loss of urban experience on the part of all classes of society or the need for a new period of acculturation of country people as was necessary in the Germanic, French, and English lands.

This considerable migration of country-men to the city presented difficulties which necessitated the creation of institutions to acculturate the migrants, or else to contain their rebellion against the new demands of employment found there. Urban Holmes has noted that "there was something in the air of the medieval community such as London which we moderns are apt to forget. This thing was authority. There was unquestionably much mob violence and considerable injustice on all sides practiced everywhere daily. But even the outraged person felt awed by authority, whatever form it took." The potential always existed for changing allegiance but not for lawlessness. "Rebellion in twelfth-century England and France meant attachment to another overlord; it did not mean becoming a law unto oneself, unless the rebel chanced to be placed very high." The city rabble, the *ribauz,* could rise and men-at-arms could waver. But authority—that of the bailiffs over the *ribauz,* and that of the feudal oaths and

villeinage over the men-at-arms—normally kept matters in hand when competent authorities were in control.[10]

These negative forces had to be applied. There were as well positive institutions, whose purpose was to use the productivity and skill of the recently settled city men while constraining too-exuberant outbreaks of personal liberation—the gilds which so widely controlled city life. Their job was made far easier than that of their modern equivalent by the fact that rural landowners had no great wish to lose potential workers, even fairly poor ones. The burden of welfare was not shifted from the country to the city as at present, and little urban unemployment occurred; a certain vigor was found among the migrants to the city, who had often fled the serfdom of the countryside with ingenuity and determination not characteristic of human castoffs.

A sharp distinction arose between the towns north of the Alps and those in the Mediterranean. To the north the towns were new social creations founded strongly on economic purposes, with power held by the more economically important men. In the south the towns were of great antiquity, having been founded by Greeks, Romans, or Etruscans for purposes long since lost, for the most part. These towns had survived into the Middle Ages mainly because of their Roman walls and because they had been taken up by the church as seats for the episcopal government they adopted. Increased political power for the urban families came only when the Guelph-Ghibelline conflict made henchmen and supporters valuable to emperor and pope alike. The domination by a single, coherent, evolutionary body such as the burgesses of northern towns was missing and the Mediterranean towns remained more bound up in social contest than in the advancement of trade. Because these Mediterranean towns were immured for so long during the barbarian invasions, manufacturing rather than trade dominated urban life. The contrast had great historical-geographical significance: craftsmen tended toward parochialism and protectionism, merchants toward worldliness and freedom of exchange. Do not forget that the *hanse* was a league of merchant towns, something unthinkable among craftsmen. Even in trade, the north exercised less parochialism and suspicion, as is demonstrated by the outcome of the decline of the Hanseatic League and the collapse of the Venetian *empire da mar.* When the League disintegrated, it left many great cities— London, Antwerp, Frankfurt, Bremen, Hamburg, and a lesser string about the Baltic and in Russia; when the

9 In Zoë Oldenbourg's *Cities of the Flesh, much of the activity takes place in cities, Toulouse and Narbonne, despite the story's concern for the lives of knights with feudal domains. In those towns the alliance between the free-thinking Cathari merchants, Jews, and the nobility was formed quite in contrast to conditions in most of northern Europe.*

10 *Urban Tigner Holmes, Jr.,* Daily Life in the Twelfth Century, *Madison: University of Wisconsin Press, 1952, pp. 36-38. Paperback edition, 1962.*

Venetian Empire collapsed it left mostly a string of beautiful fossils—Ragusa (Dubrovnik), Trogir, Rhodes, and Corfu among them—but only one real city, Venice.

Only in the invention of banking did Italy show the vigor of the commercial north. But because banking lay so near the edge of medieval ethics, being easily condemned as usury, and because it proved so sensitive an institution when the national economy was being hammered out in the fourteenth and fifteenth centuries, the first act of powerful kings was to evict the Italian bankers. Not having shaped a political empire to match their economic power, the Lombard bankers were forced to return to Italy, adding stagnation in banking to the earlier stagnation of manufacturing and urban factionalism. This illness crippled the Italian city-republics of the late Middle Ages.

Both north and south the city had been the seedbed of religious dissent and striving for freedom. The first strong expression of that dissent came with the emergence of the dualists, the Cathari, who in the twelfth century questioned the luxury and corruption of the Roman church from their centers in several cities in the Po Basin, most importantly Milan, and Narbonne, Beziers, and Toulouse in southern France. The barbaric crusade organized against them by the pope and the king of France destroyed this and most subsequent questioning in the south, so the flower of cities

which had remained in Languedoc since Roman time withered. Subsequently cities continued their dissenting role but mainly north of the Alps where John Wycliffe and John Huss preached within the walls of receptive towns.

Religion and the Medieval City: Cluny and Nonretributive Trade

A fundamental dichotomy has been drawn between the organic and the preconceived city. When we apply that distinction to medieval towns we find that many things had changed since the Classical Era. Thus, when towns began to be founded anew after the Dark Ages, they were at first outside the established order of feudalism, and they became, quite naturally, the locale for experimentation and change. Unlike the experience in Roman Gaul, that in medieval France called forth the individual, atomic qualities of towns. No standard was

Much of the great Cluny Abbey was destroyed during the French Revolution, but until that time it was the largest church in France and one of its more powerful monastic establishments.

applied and no rule had to be followed. Religion had become transmuted. It no longer found physical expression in the city as holy territory, bounded by *pomerium*, and protected from evil spirits by the plowing of the sacred furrow. The individual now protected his salvation through repeating acts of his own, executed within the walls of a special part of the city, the early Christian basilica. No line now divided sacred from profane territory; thus the protected world had no extent and, ultimately, no limit. Necessity required two forms of defense against evil: the sacrament for the soul of the individual, and the wall for the safety of his person against other persons. Two institutions evolved from the one that had been the Roman city—the city corporation for the physical defense of the person and the church for his salvation.

Closer analysis shows that this complicated division has great bearing on the historical geography of cities. We might characterize the Roman settlement as a "temple of the whole" about which altars might be scattered, but which lacked the notion of division between daily and religious life. Citizens did not assemble to worship in a particular place and at a specific time so much as they worshipped individually and motivationally. Temples were small and normally without professional clergy. Religion was more useful as the backstay of the state, the city or the empire, than as the comfort of the individual. As Jérôme Carcopino saw it,

> ...With its indeterminate gods and its colourless myths, mere fables concocted from details suggested by Latin topography or pale reflections of the adventures which had overtaken the Olympians of Greek epic; with its prayers formulated in the style of legal contracts and as dry as the procedure of a lawsuit; and its lack of metaphysical curiosity and indifference to moral values; with the narrow-minded banality of its field of action, limited to the interests of the city and the development of practical politics–Roman religion froze the impulses of faith by its coldness and its prosaic utilitarianism.[11]

In the second century A.D., the brittle dissatisfaction offered by Roman religion opened the way to the introduction of elements from the east. These elements transformed the basis of religion from the state to the individual, and introduced passion, mystery, and personal salvation to central consideration. Christianity ultimately triumphed among these oriental cults and the Roman Catholic church became the expression of religion in the cities of western civilization.

The Roman church faced the paradoxes that must beset all usurpers: how does one succeed to an institution one has previously opposed? Having fought for

religious toleration as the only protection of an incipient cult, Roman Catholicism on gaining power began a slow reversion to the deadening orthodoxy that had gripped Rome and turned toward an aristocratic theocracy similar to that of Nero's time. The Roman church took over the provincial cities of the Augusti as the seats of their own proconsuls, the bishops and archbishops. Later, when they created princely cardinals, they revered them with the Roman term *vir eminentissimus*, as "their eminences." The result was a strangely untidy recall of the imperial past in the religious institutions of the Middle Ages, and a confusing role to be played by the Roman church in the cities that emerged after the Dark Ages. The city and religion were no longer one and the same, yet they were not separate. The adoption of the aristocratic theocracy by the church tended to perpetuate the bias against commerce that had flawed Roman society. The social attitudes of the church were so doctrinaire that the vital sustaining flow of even modest profit was cut off from trading enterprises. And the tendency that merchants had to shake the existing order came to be characteristic of the whole population of the towns merchants founded, calling papal condemnation down on them.

To characterize the cities as anti-clerical and potentially heretical would certainly present a false picture. For the most part the burghers were devout in their catholicism and generous to the church, particularly in its local expression. Gilds were the patrons of particular churches; they built almshouses and hospitals and endowed educational and religious foundations. But the tendency of the medieval Roman church to support what today we would characterize as "reactionary" governments and institutions always placed the merchant community slightly apart from the church and potentially divisionist in its thinking. During the High Middle Ages the church and the merchants maintained western orthodoxy but the seeds of ultimate dissent were present. The successful development of the city, which necessitated first a conflict with feudalism and its natural economy, and ultimately the destruction of that medieval order and its replacement by the state and its national economy, arose when the local commercial community came to have a power greater than the parochial clerical one. The rural society continued its traditional ultramontane slant while cities came to be Gallicist in viewpoint.

To understand the nature of the conflict between burgher and cleric, we must perceive that the Roman church encouraged and demanded the maintenance of an established order, as had feudalism. Possessing too much business initiative was thought to be a misplacement of zeal, which should focus on the church rather than the counting house, and to seek to transform local natural economies into components of larger trading systems gained no grace for the geo-

---

[11]*Jérôme Carcopino*, Daily Life in Ancient Rome, *New Haven: Yale University Press, 1940, pp. 121-122.*

graphical pioneer. The church was so suspicious of profit, so dubious of change, that it wished to maintain surveillance of business; it could do this most by localization.[12] The somewhat oversimplified notion remains that the church sheltered long-distance trade during the Dark Ages, thus showing its regard for that activity.

True, the church did smile on certain aspects of long-distance trade, particularly after the Cluniac revolution of the tenth century. "The abbots of Cluny were as proficient in collecting real and movable estates as in attracting devoted souls. With commerce, however, they were ill at ease; a man of high dignity might perhaps do some buying and selling through a trusted middleman, but would hesitate to expose his name on the market place." In part the objection stemmed from social theory. "In the theoretical structure of feudal society there scarcely was room for a middle class between the exalted religious and lay lords and the lowly but irreplaceable laborers. Paupers were more acceptable than merchants: they would inherit the Kingdom of Heaven and help the almsgiving rich to earn entrance." Although temporizing was well developed along some lines, it failed in commerce. " . . .Every code has its exceptions, but the bias (against commerce) existed in the tenth century as in the age of Augustus, in Germany as in China; it is not entirely dispelled today. It took exceptional men in exceptional circumstances to break the spell and make commerce the most rapidly expanding, if not the largest frontier of the medieval West."[13] Those exceptional men were almost completely absent from the medieval Roman church, as they had been from the late Roman Empire. It remained particularly for the unorthodox, the somewhat heretical, and certainly the Gallican to supply the distinctive qualities that could develop urbanism and commerce, the greatest of medieval frontiers.

The Cluniac monasteries may have supplied the model for the growth of systemic cities, if not the leadership. Starting from a few monasteries centering on Cluny, twelve miles from Mâcon in eastern France, the movement ultimately joined 314 monasteries spread from the Holy Land and Poland to England and Scot-

land. Given that geographical range and administration by a fierce authoritarianism vested in the Abbot of Cluny, it is not surprising that a considerable flow of goods and what was essentially "tribute" moved about the system. To facilitate that flow, the Cluniacs fell back on the use of middlemen, demonstrating that prosperity followed the pushing outward of a trading frontier even in the guise of a severe monasticism, a propensity best implemented by harsh central authority. But the Cluniac trading league was a rather backstairs affair in its moral position within the medieval church, and was too clearly a thinly disguised system of tribute to a foreign cleric (exceeded in power only by the pope in Rome), to remain tolerated with the growth of mercantilism and national consciousness. In the reign of Edward II of England (1327-1377), annual remittances from England to the Abbot of Cluny averaged some two thousand pounds (which might well represent a million dollars today), when the national wealth was small indeed.

The tributary systems of both the Roman Empire and the medieval Roman church lacked any very considerable retributive qualities. When lay partners trade, each gains something, presumably of equal value, in return for his shipments. But under a system of exacted religious tribute, little comes back other than intangibles such as the Roman Peace or the church's grace. When the peace ended, no reason remained to continue the tribute, and when the grace lost its value, men were inclined to embargo the tribute. As the English separatist church gained support, the Cluniac monasteries were "naturalized" (first at Lewes in 1351 and then elsewhere). The tribute was cut off, flowing after the dissolution directly into Henry VIII's treasury. Since monastic "trade" was more accurately exaction, it did little to fill out the proto-cities it may have founded. Cluny, Lewes, and the other monasteries proved remarkably weak bases for continuing urbanism. A visit today to the very fountainhead at Cluny is a journey to a small country town, while Lewes is best known as a railroad junction on the route of the boat-train to Newhaven. Only when flow is retributive will growth take place in both places. The Abbot of Cluny's basilica, built in the twelfth century, was the largest church in Christendom (until the pope's in Rome exceeded it in the sixteenth century) while the cathedrals in England, and Poland for that matter, had to remain small, if more architecturally glorious. But Cluny as a town was stunted. When the French Revolution closed the monastery and razed the basilica, little remained to reflect the power that had focussed medieval Europe's attention on the place.

The organic nature of the medieval city was real while that of the church must be questioned. As laymen began to seek out the frontiers of trade and urbaniza-

[12]For a detailed discussion of the church's notions of just price, profit, and the location of trade in the Middle Ages, see James E. Vance, Jr., The Merchant's World: The Geography of Wholesaling, Englewood Cliffs, N.J.: Prentice-Hall, Inc., 1970, especially Chapter Four, "Growth in the Power of Exchanging." See also John W. Baldwin, "The Medieval Theories of the Just Price," Transactions of American Philosophical Society, new series, vol. 40, pt. 4, 1959.

[13]Robert S. Lopez, The Commercial Revolution of the Middle Ages, 950-1350, Englewood Cliffs, N.J.: Prentice-Hall, Inc., 1971, pp. 59-60.

tion, they pioneered routes of commodity flow and founded or filled towns built on profit. If trade was healthy, the city and its partner places prospered and grew; if not, then towns shrank, even to extinction, in a way not common in the church. The Normans sought to encourage trading towns both in Normandy itself and in England after the Conquest. Their efforts in the homeland were largely frustrated by their loss of long-distance connections in northern France due to the resurgence of the French monarchy. As a consequence their Norman towns for the most part failed, withering into villages, whereas their English places burgeoned.

Organic Growth and Freedom

The burghers' town, with its organic growth shaped by practicality, represented a historical break that began an emancipation of common people that had never previously existed. Cities did not become democratic overnight, though important advances were made in the twelfth and thirteenth centuries (and subsequently lost in the urban contraction of the fourteenth and fifteenth centuries). Instead of instant democracy, this medieval urbanization produced physical form for the city which could become the backstay for a relatively democratic life.

The first contribution of the organic form to the improvement of the lot of the common people came in the creation of *an expansible city*. Within it, changes in function and in overall demand could be more easily comprehended and satisfied. It is a sobering truth, even today, that a constraint of city growth almost inexorably favors the elite at the expense of the common people. Beauty, order, administration, and other goals may be advanced to justify "control," but the actual quality of life for the common people will not necessarily be enhanced. So when burghers devised a process for urban growth that became highly responsive to demand, they probably unconsciously shaped a way of caring for the average resident that was a great advance on the past.

The second contribution of the organic form came in its encouragement of what we would today call *functional architecture* through the shaping of the medieval house. This remarkably adept structure was socially democratic in its inclusiveness, permitting the city of the time to expand its support functions, both in trade

and in manufacture. For a working populace this adaptability to the demands of occupations was a real benefit.

Yet another contribution of the organic growth of cities came in its hospitality to *functional separation* on the ground. If we reason that the clustering of workers in the same trade produces benefits for both workers and society through increase in technical skills, greater likelihood of invention, and more effective structuring of the market, the practical dynamics of the medieval city were finely wrought to accomplish those ends. As new trades emerged, space was made available to them, and as old trades were transformed, their new demands could be met. Since the broader distribution of material benefits was one of the great social advances of the medieval city, economic advance may to a real degree be equated to social advance. The creation of *capital* wealth was at first an emancipation of the common man from slavery to *landed* wealth under feudalism. Capital wealth is less emancipating today, but we do not need to know the present to understand the Middle Ages. We may, however, better understand the present by knowing those times in their turn.

The wonder of the medieval city was its cordiality to new institutions, structures, and groups. This liberal and innovative climate of the city has tended to become hidden behind two situations often misunderstood when presented nakedly, unrelated to their complicated times. The most deceiving of the two is the already mentioned creation of a Jewish housing area in cities of late medieval time. These ghettos are taken as symbols of an urban repression and given a self-centered central importance by some observers. Most people in western civilization were not Jews, were not much in contact with them, and were themselves treated to restrictions different in kind but not in degree. Thus only cultural myopia can explain why the ghetto has been given such a central role in the story of the medieval city.

The other situation masking the basic and initial liberalism of the city in the Middle Ages is the eventual narrowing of urban franchise and participation to a small group of freemen. By the sixteenth and seventeenth centuries, this concentration of power was a major fault in the urban system, not in the medieval city *ab origine*, but in its late and corrupted form. In the beginning the voice in city government was widespread and well listened to, which means, initially, a strong popular input in the shaping of city institutions. The most concrete result was the confraternal or collegial group, with its tendency to occupy a particular segment of the city. In such a social geography, it does not seem quite so negative and repressive that the Jews also should occupy a particular quarter and engage in those activities characteristic of their confraternity.

The final contribution of organic growth in cities is the sensitivity of that process to *regional variation*. Different lands did possess different needs, so regional variation of the city form to a degree not typical of the Greek or Roman cities was not without value. Classical city forms did vary—we know, for instance, that the Roman city in Britain tended to be composed not of blocks of flats found in the Mediterranean *(insulae)* but rather of free-standing single-family houses—but those preconceived city plans had a certain antigeographical rigidity. In the Middle Ages sharp regional variations in city form emerged and we may distinguish merely as examples the northern and the Mediterranean towns, or the Germanic from the English house. This creation was organic, not the aping of aristocratic and metropolitan precepts.

The Point of Origin

Certain general practices attached to urban places in western civilization. Perhaps the most obvious was the reuse of the quiescent if not abandoned Roman towns when a new purpose for cities arose. Throughout Gaul, Cisalpine in the Po Basin and Transalpine in France, Roman towns virtually in ruins awoke to a rattle of new activity, fleetingly in the time of Charlemagne but more permanently during the tenth and eleventh centuries. In Germany, Spain, and England the rebirth was less striking, perhaps as much because the Roman past was less sure and extensive as because of any weakness of the urbanization trend in the Middle Ages.

When trade integration returned in the High Middle Ages, a location the Romans had pioneered might well regain its appeal. The roads built by the Romans could still be used in places; their spatial judgment had normally been astute so their town locations were likely to return to importance with the resurgence of distant trade. Their crumbling town could be refurbished again, or used as a quarry adjacent to a desired site. Few places returned rapidly to their classical magnificence. Boissonade tells us the average size of the rebounding medieval town may have been little above 1,000 to 1,500 souls.[14] These towns cannot have been totally mundane as the Roman amphitheaters, arenas, and other public works must have been gener-

[14]*Boissonade, op. cit., p. 114.*

ally in evidence. Trier on the Moselle had its great Roman gate—the Porta Negra, Arles its arena, Nîmes its temple and arena, and Vienne its Pyramide and the largest theater in Gaul.

Sometimes the Roman inheritance was lacking, either because the Romans had failed to site a town at a spot where one now seemed needed, as at Pavia or Venice, or had failed to conquer the territory and plant any towns, as north of the Danube and east of the Rhine in Germany. Other general practices attached to the siting of towns in those places. In much of France, Germany, and England, the fortified castle became the urban germ. In some places these castles were located where the Romans had had a villa but nothing larger; in others, at sites whose defensibility was so striking as to gain more significance in the chaotic times of feudalism than in the more stable ones of the Roman

Petrusbrunnen in Trier standing in front of the Steipe, the meeting place of bourgeoisie and artisans during the Middle Ages.

Peace. The requirement of the feudal era for many strong-point fortresses provided a much denser net of possible town locations than did the Roman system of fortified towns within their relatively secure provinces. One might argue that feudalism built so many castles that only with difficulty could any town be founded at a distance great enough from a castle as to seem independent of it. Correspondence in geographical location does not always demonstrate causal succession of forms.

However, evidence suggests that the strong-point was the common locating force for the town, other than the Roman settlement, begun in the Middle Ages. Traditionally, the strong-point on its rock is envisaged as the *bourg*, the germ of settlement drawn from the feudal order, charged with the self-defense of the small enclosed domain; nestled below it, the settlement of merchants and workers seeks the protection of the fortress by living in a *faubourg* or *portus*. Such a model of settlement equates lordly protection with town founding, which was often the case, yet often the town and the knight were engaged from the beginning in a conflict that seems ill-represented by the *bourg-faubourg* theory.

A third possible site for a town, apart from a Roman resurrection or a feudal *faubourg*, was the geographically distinguished site as yet unoccupied. These places were relatively few in number. Venice is the most obvious instance—a place, well protected from the barbarian invasions of northern Italy, where in the fifth century a settlement arose. From that beginning grew a town which by 1002 had subjected the whole Adriatic shore to its sway, by 1082 had gained a hundred-year access to free trade in the Byzantine Empire, and in 1204, during the Fourth Crusade, had led the religious warriors first to the Golden Horn to capture Constantinople for Venetian trade. Notable among other sites first occupied in the Middle Ages were those places that first gained trading significance—as resting places on new routes, the sites of fairs, ports on seas only recently opened to trade, or entrepôts in new trading territories. As new foundations, they might exist to all intents outside the system of inherited hierarchy which often subjected the resurrected Roman town to the power of a bishop and the *faubourg* to that of a feudal baron.

Organization of the Site

Towns might be fully or partially organic, or predetermined by some preconception of the ultimate nature that the places should take, which we may call the *cadre* for growth. In resurrected towns, organic control was normally somewhat limited, even to the imposition of a full preconception. Chester, Cologne, Lyon, and Turin were all strongly influenced not only by medieval growth processes but also by those of the Romans, yet to call them Roman towns would be too forceful. The street pattern may have been inherited from the Classical Era but the houses that bordered those streets and the urban institutions that came into prominence were creations of the Middle Ages. Probably no fully preconceived towns *(sensu strictu)* were founded in the Middle Ages but some towns combined organic and designed growth, with the relative weight of the preconception largely a function of the sturdiness of the physical survival from the Classical Era. The medieval mind was not much gripped by classical precept—that view came in the Renaissance and flowered in the nineteenth century—so the burgher of the year 1200 would not self-consciously reproduce the past though he might take its remnants as a useful windfall.

Shaping Processes

The medieval townspeople shaped a physical structure that grew mainly by *adaptive incrementation*. As places that began as fishing ports—Great Yarmouth, Amsterdam, and even Venice—grew to great cities, they had to change both the land-assignment and land-division practices and the actual structures built in the city. Thus, unlike the situation in Roman towns, a constant *evolution of forms* was active to the extent the medieval city reflected a functionalism unknown in the Classical Era. There were no "orders" of building, no inviolate or immutable forms; a town could change in form as much as in function. Thus each increment to town growth serves us as a tangible record of the functions then conducted there, because its form, which tends to be preserved, was functionally determined when first laid out and developed.

The Origin of the Medieval House

Given its functional architecture, the medieval house reveals its origin in its initial purposes—the housing, nearly always, of both workers and their work. Medieval towns were founded (or refounded) mainly to engage in productive activities of either trade or manufacture, in contrast to the Roman towns which were at first basically administrative and military places. Rather than the center of administrative and military power, the medieval city was usually a near pariah within the feudal order that commanded and controlled those activities. Only in the absence of a strong feudalism, as when a bishop controlled a town and its environs, was a town north of the Alps likely to engage in administration over rural areas. Only in Italy, where the city had vanquished the countryside early in the post-Roman period, did cities tend to be the centers of military power and the garrison of large numbers of soldiers. The medieval purpose of towns was heavily economic, and where bishops or urban communes were absent, the alloy of administration and military power was largely absent.

Even if the economic purpose was controlling, how was it expressed on the land? As a broad frame in which to see morphological expression, we may look at M. R. G. Conzen's classic study of Alnwick.

Functionally the geographical character of a town is determined by economic and social significance within some regional context . . . . Morphologically it finds expression in the physiognomy or townscape, which is a combination of town plan, pattern of building forms, and pattern of urban land use . . . . The town plan has attracted attention as a subject where the interests of the geographer and others such as historians, archaeologists and town planners converge . . . . Yet . . . . urban morphology has remained strangely deficient in its depth of treatment, largely through neglect of significant plan detail . . . . Similar criticism applies to other morphological aspects. As a result our geographical comprehension of townscapes is hampered by the lack of a theoretical basis yielding concepts of general application.[15]

[15]*M. R. G. Conzen,* Alnwick, Northumberland: A Study in Town-plan Analysis, *Publication No. 17, The Institute of British Geographers, 1960, p. 3.*

Conzen proposes that we concern ourselves with "three distinct complexes of *plan elements*: (i) *streets* and their arrangement in a *street-system*; (ii) *plots* and their aggregation in *street-blocks*; and (iii) buildings or, more precisely, their *block-plans*."[16] Such a system of analysis allows us to look in detail at the physical build of the city, to discern processes at work and to establish a comparative morphology. We will emphasize the *building* as well, seeking to use it as *a module from which all other aggregations are shaped and whose scale and functions are the most basic considerations in any city.*

In cities, in places where space is at a premium because of the constraint imposed either by circumvallation or by pedestrian access to a focal point, does the house decide the size of the lot, or the plot determine the ultimate outer dimensions of the house? This question can be answered historically; we can learn whether a plot-map came first, fixing divisions on the land to which subsequent building must conform, or whether the lots were made to conform to the normal house of a certain size in the region. Yet such a resolution may be illusory. Perhaps a considerable circularity lends to the process: the space needs of the total urban activities are projected into the practicable walled area, thus largely determining the amount of land available to become resolved into a plot, creating the practical size which best compromises between individual and community needs. Perhaps in some cases the individual building is determinative of the plot; in others the reverse is true. And in the greatest number of instances, the two forces may compromise.

In the Middle Ages certain truths helped to determine the size of houses, and thereby the plot sizes that could be used efficiently. First, a particular type of construction was used within a region. Eclecticism in architecture came with a greater availability of architectural design information and with the easing of the problems of assembling building materials at a particular site. In the Middle Ages information tended to be parochial and materials to be difficult to gather even from the neighborhood. Exceptions to both those generalizations included Caen stone from France used fairly widely by the Normans when they conquered England, and the architectural forms seen in the East employed by men coming back from the Crusades. But those exceptions tended to come mostly in public, monumental, and basically religious buildings for which distinction was sought. The initial house of the burgher was unlikely to be built either of imported stone or in any exotic manner.

The basic component of the burgher's house was wood in the form of structural timbers of some size. Though it is now hard to believe, medieval Europe was

[16]Ibid., p. 5.

more a land of forests than any other landscape, so lumber was relatively plentiful and reasonably cheap (because it came from close by and did not have to carry much cost of transport). Oak seems to have been the favored wood, though beech must have been used, as well as some other hardwoods. Softwoods were scarcer in that band of broadleaf forest native to Europe from England eastward to the Russian plains. Scandinavia was softwood country, but not a land of towns for the most part. In the Mediterranean, wood had become scarce even by medieval times, and stone was cheaper. In the central band from England to Poland, lumber was least expensive.

A certain modular unit for construction applied to hardwoods. A beam of some 16 to 20 feet was the modal product of the greater number of forests. Trees did grow taller than the norm, though to gather them meant careful searching in the forest and, most likely, a longer haul, both of which would make unusual timbers expensive. Modal size was not the single controlling factor; the sag that affects any beam suspended between two upright posts must as well have borne on the question of beam size. Sag is a function of beam cross section as well as span so the answer is hard to resolve at this late date without access to cost and availability figures. For whatever reason, the modular beam seems to have ranged between 16 and 20 feet.

The other modular value of the house comes from the height at which this beam will be supported above the floor. This is not a question of material but rather one of people, for the purpose of the house was to enclose their activities. Again, an average gains control; too-high ceilings would be wasteful, even if a few men and women in the Middle Ages were tall. We may assume then that the height of posts used to hold up the beams would be enough to clear most people's heads but not enough to clear them all. With little furniture in houses and not very much machinery in workshops, the scale of men fixed the height of posts, which ranged on the average between perhaps 6 and 7 feet.

To utilize these two modular values we need to understand the basic structure of the medieval house. Both stone and timber houses would be influenced to some degree by the size of timbers available; even stone buildings normally used a fair amount of wood in flooring and upper stories. The all-timber house of central Europe was a simple derivative of the material available. So long as fair-size trees were to be had, the cost of producing timber components of a house was the cost of felling the tree and shaping it into a beam or post. In a two-variable equation, cost of material (wood) and cost of labor (shaping into a beam or post) were worked out to the least-cost compromise. In general to over-use wood was cheaper than to economize on it and then have to pay large sums for the laborious work of hand sawing it in a pit. Heavy timbers were the basic com-

ponents of construction (just as they were in colonial America where similar conditions obtained), and they tended to be assembled into that very simple structure produced by heavy, relatively rigid and unsagging beams and posts.

This *post-and-lintel* construction produces a building comprised of bays 6 to 8 feet high and 16 to 20 feet wide and deep, with a horizontal plan 16 feet square, and a story height of 7 or 8 feet depending upon the rigidity of the timbers and bracing at the corners, where they commonly were mortised into each other. Given good beams and posts, one modular unit can be built on another to a height of as much as six to eight modules, producing a building 50 or so feet high at the facade. Total height may be considerably greater than that when a steeply pitched roof is added. In post-and-lintel construction the actual wall is merely sheathing to keep out the elements and provide privacy for the occupants. If we were to strip a typical medieval building of its walls, we would be left with a series of beams, lintels, plates, rafters, and flooring. The structure would look very much like the initially-erected steel-cage skyscraper, before windows, mullions, and other sheathing are added, except that the structural components would be shaped from wood and would be possessed of its strengths and weaknesses.

The use of post-and-lintel construction had two important influences on the physiognomy of the city: it gave a basic module on which the shaping of plots could be based (the bay of 16 to 20 feet, or its simple divisions into 4 or 8 feet), and it determined that differentiation among buildings would be largely surficial and flat or, at most, in low relief. The second condition arose because of the constraints of the construction style. Finally, the plastic quality in post-and-lintel structure was found in the infilling of the rectangles delimited by the 16-foot beams, at the floor and ceiling of a story, and the posts at their ends. This infilling was constructed sometimes of withies woven into a hurdle and plastered with clay mud, sometimes with bricks with smaller timbers inserted to give stiffness to the wall (half-timbering), and sometimes with studs on which laths and plaster were fixed.

The flat, often basically smooth surfaces must at first have stood untreated but soon they became the main medium for decoration in the medieval city. In some places, notably in the Alpine lands, the flat plaster surfaces were decorated with mural paintings, often in strong colors. Innsbruck and Augsburg still display such wall paintings. In other places, more commonly it seems in the north of France and in England, the plaster surfaces were scored with true graffiti in regular patterns often produced by a comb, giving them the common English name of "combwork." Elsewhere the infilled surfaces were of brick, as commonly found in the Low Countries and Baltic cities such as Lübeck; the decoration came from placement of the surface bricks to form observable patterns. Medieval architecture, though highly functional, tended toward a certain uniformity of construction technique which meant that the urge for differentiation and expression had to be concentrated in surface detailing. The result was that the medieval town of Europe north of the Alps had the textural uniformity of primitively modular construction but the surficial variety of distinct regional cultures seeking to relieve the innate sameness of the townscape.

To the south the survival of the Roman urbanism in upper Italy, in Provence and Languedoc, in the Aquitanian Basin and Catalonia, and in scattered places all around the Mediterranean meant that the Middle Ages could do no more than transform an existing physique. The eleventh and twelfth centuries brought fewer innovations than scalar changes. The northern Italians—from Lucca, Siena, Pisa, Genoa, Florence, and other city republics—devised the system of banking and record keeping that allowed medieval trade to develop. They gained in return handsome profits that encouraged both growth in the city's population and the enlargement and enrichment of its fabric. To accomplish those ends a new architecture had to be devised, based on Roman practices but possessed of an expansibility needed in the burgeoning economic places of the Middle Ages.

What form did the expansible city structure take? To answer that question we must reflect on the structures those medieval Italians inherited. The Romans, both at home and in their provinces, showed a remarkable affection for the use of brick in building. Certainly in the Mediterranean, where timber was becoming scarce even at the end of the Classical Era, bricks or their natural peer, rubble masonry, were the standard materials for construction. As we know from observing the ruins in Rome today, monumental buildings were at heart brick with no more than a thin veneer of marble to strike the innocent with awe; the brick wall and vault were the mainstay of Mediterranean building. Thus, classical decoration was peculiarly similar to that of the European north in the Middle Ages, except that in classical times the decoration was added to buildings themselves and was more subject to design variation than was that in Rouen or Lübeck in the year 1200.

Brick vault architecture was more versatile than post-and-lintel, a fact we have witnessed in the rather monotonous temple-form buildings shaped by the Greeks using these same horizontal beams and vertical columns. In Greece the buildings were rather uniform in structure but were infinitely varied in proportion and texture. Roman buildings were more varied in basic form, seemingly because the use of masonry of the small module—bricks or rubble or ashlar blocks—

encouraged experimentation. The Romans perfected the use of the arch, the vault, and the dome—masonry constructions that afforded the possiblity of considerable variation—as well as spanning devices that could open up the interior of buildings as had been impossible using the restricted spanning potential of the wooden beam. Larger buildings could be built and greater openings attempted. We know from Ostia in particular that ordinary houses made use of arches on the ground floor to satisfy the conflicting demands of open fronts for shops and weight-bearing sufficient to allow multistory construction. The arch could support a deadload of upper-story walls that would have kept the lintel short and heavy.

The Roman *insula*, with its apartment house of *cenacula*, could rise a number of stories. It depended on a particularly Roman structural form: the weight-bearing wall fashioned from brick, with the lower or wider openings supported by either true semi-circular arches, as on the ground floor, or low-arched courses above windows, as on the upper floors. This apartmented-house was not easily expanded because it depended upon heavy weight-bearing walls of masonry. To build a five- or six-story house, one must plan both the foundations and the lower walls to carry the weight needed to maintain the structural integrity of the building. If the ground-floor openings were too wide, the height of the building could not be increased, other than by filling in those apertures, nor could its height be raised if its lower walls and foundations were too light. The Mediterranean house had an integrity when built that defied change.

The increase in population within the confines of the more constrained walled medieval city of the Mediterranean forced changes that would allow the structure to be expanded. The initial transformation may simply have been to build on top of the older structure, trusting to previous over-building to carry the load. When cracking appeared, narrowing openings might stabilize the strain on the lower structure. But the cost in possible reconstruction would have been considerable. The next logical transformation would have been to lighten the added floors by substituting wood-frame and thin infilling of walls for the ponderous masonry structure that the Romans and their descendants had favored. All around the Mediterranean today we can find these composite buildings—stone on the ground, and possibly the second floor, with wood-frame construction above. They seem to have been a response to the needs for higher buildings when growth came within the confined space of the walled city. Whether the building was one of antiquity transformed or one built *de novo* in the Middle Ages doesn't matter; the workings of even a primitive system of land rent would make the new and the transformed conform in general terms.

Other expansive architectural devices seem to have emerged from the pressure of people. The arcade allowed the house to encroach on the street space while at the same time furnishing the covered passageway so much enjoyed by the imperial Romans. We can scarcely distinguish the arcades built to satisfy the desires of a Mediterranean people for protection from the sun in the stifling summer and from the sharp warm rains in the sodden winter, and those colonnades built to expand the area of the structure by encroaching on the street-space. The effect was the same. Even in Ostia upper stories were allowed to project outward on a corbel, gaining greater area while leaving the street free of obstruction. Whether by overhang or by arcade, houses gained capacity at the expense of the street, but only at the time of initial construction. For subsequent expansion, other forms were needed. Projections were built from the surface of the structure as oriels, penthouses, or even *hautpas* in the arcades at their front. Given the durability of the masonry structures, it was fairly simple to attach these light, timber additions to give a bit of space here and there. The result was the very diverse Mediterranean house, transformed over many centuries and in many ways, and certainly unlikely in its more advanced stage to reflect, in any clear way, either its initial or most subsequent functions. The Mediterranean house tells us more of its history than of its use.

The Mediterranean houses in general show somewhat greater consistency than do those north of the Alps, though in detail they are more varied. To cite a few instances: the Italian house varies around a basic norm of stone construction and relatively square structure showing differences in height between the south of Italy, where it is usually two, or at most three stories, and the north where it is taller, reaching normally to three or four stories. The house in northern Portugal and Galicia in Spain is again stone-built but combines a structure not very different from post-and-lintel framing, though it uses granite uprights and spanning pieces, with a more rectangular shape to produce a tall, open-facaded house transitional between the Mediterranean and transalpine Europe. And in southern and central Spain the basic stone house becomes "introverted," turning an almost blank wall to the street while opening out around an interior courtyard. As in all such diversities, combinations add further to the variety; Cadiz in southwestern Spain has tall, courtyard houses while in Taranto in southern Italy the stone houses are tall, narrow, almost overhanging, with definite elongation away from the street.

Initiation and Continuing Practice

Searching for an analytical frame in which to deal with the morphogenesis of the medieval city, we arrive logically at a fundamental distinction between the initial, experimental, organically adjustable acts of people and those that usually come later in town growth, commonly made uniform by the constraints within a conscious tradition. When the medieval city was in the process of invention, perhaps in the eleventh and twelfth centuries, house form was still unfixed, depending upon the availability of materials at the least cost and upon the construction technology available to the builders. Further, the purpose for which a building was constructed would rule on its form. The act of initiating building was strongly controlled by organic forces, as we have used that term, and provides us with the most direct and unobscured surviving evidence of cause and purpose, save in the odd circumstance where epigraphic evidence was created and has endured. Ideally, we should seek this *initiation of form* to understand cause.

Since the freedom to shape a new urban form was much greater north of the Alps than in the classical world, we witness two different processes at work during the same period of history, which reveals two methodological truths. First, a nonhistorically-based process model is likely to fail us grievously in actual application to the analysis of a large area, even at one time. Second, an understanding even today of so simple a thing as the basic architecture of a house may be rather unintelligible without an understanding of history. For example, today most German construction depends heavily upon the use of concrete yet the architecture of much of the urban scene belies that fact. Only by realizing that medieval Germany was a land of plentiful wood and a firm understanding of wooden construction can we explain the present-day use Germans make of a plastic masonry, trying hard to render it as wooden construction. In contrast we might note that the Romans built in brick, forming a building technology that did not need to change greatly when concrete was substituted.

Turning again to the contrast between initiation of urban structure and rejuvenation of past structures, the layout of the urban plot is informative. We may reason that the shape and size of the city plot, what today we call a "lot," reflects the thinking at the time it was divided from a larger whole of unused or else agricultural land. Once the plot is separated and sold or leased, it possesses an integrity that is difficult to change. Certainly it may be further divided with somewhat greater ease than it may be rejoined with adjacent plots. To divide may be the act of one man involved with a single plot, but assembling parcels affects at least two parcels and often several owners. In the Middle Ages (before urban land assumed a strong role in capital accumulation) the economic constraints to assembly might have been less, but because land was less interesting as a commodity susceptible to incremental gain, inducing owners to sell might have been more difficult. By the sixteenth century, when land had become a standard commodity open to speculation, the resistance to assembly was great. Once divided into plots, urban land takes on a particular grain that is perhaps the most enduring physical aspect of the city.

The Shape of Lots

Although we cannot answer categorically the question of whether the nature of house construction determined the scale of the lot, seemingly the modules of construction tended to determine the frontal dimension. How deep in proportion to the frontage did lots tend to be? This question is not trivial, for the medieval house and lot of our stereotypical notion seem less common than we supposed.

To explain the misinterpretation of geographical fact we must consider traditional exposition of topographic history. That common description holds that in laying out the medieval city, the objective was to furnish each citizen, or burgher, with frontage on the important street where he might carry on those economic activities which supported his family and his associated workers. In this view the street-frontage was the critical commodity, and the size of the lot was an outgrowth of family and household needs. Implicit is the thesis that the city grows out of the countryside, with the burgher representing a transitional form of half-farmer, half-craftsman raising much of his own provender in conjunction with the pursuit of his trade. Thus, the lot would need be rather large, to allow the family to maintain a cow, chickens, perhaps a pig, and to plant fruit trees and a kitchen garden. Given the high value attaching to street frontage, such a large lot could be provided only by shaping the *burgage plots* as long and narrow, extending to a considerable depth from the street frontage. In his classic study of Alnwick, Conzen describes a situation conforming almost exactly to this model. In that town of citizens half-farmer, the

economic activity which made the townsman a burgher was carried on at the *plot head* next to the street. The assembly of plots presents a characteristic pattern.

The individual burgages generally form rather long narrow strip-plots *laid roughly at right-angles to the street-line and parallel to each other. They tend to be oblongs but are often locally deformed in adaptation to site conditions. A characteristically informal, lamellate layout results and when it is duplicated on either side of the same street . . . (W)hat has just been described is so typical of the medieval main streets, or the widened "street-market" variants found in most of our market towns, that this plan-unit may well be termed the* High Street *layout.[17]*

Within the overall pattern of High Street layout the plots were used for several functions.

The greater intrinsic value of the actual frontage normally imparts a tadpole structure to each plot. The plot head *at the front contains the* plot dominant *or main building, housing the essential part of the land use of the plot, together with its yard. The* plot tail, *generally the larger part in the case of burgages, is occupied by the "garth" or garden and often accommodates subsidiary buildings or* plot accessories. *The burgages commonly have no front-gardens, i.e., the* street-line *and the actual or geographical* building-line . . . coincide. . . . *Plot dominants occupy the full frontage and so form* rows *or* serried lines of diverse buildings along the sides of the street, *which represents one form of* closed building development *common to the kernels of historic towns.[18]*

Conzen finds that a rather standardized pattern results despite the diversity of architectural style. Arguing that medieval architecture in England was based on the 16- to 20-foot "bays," he finds Alnwick's module was usually one rod wide, either 16 feet as at present or 18 feet as in some places during the Middle Ages. Given the small size of his town, and the assumed lesser pressure on the land,

The evidence indicates then that in Alnwick 28-32 feet was the original standard of burgage frontage, a measurement not infrequently found in medieval towns. The smallest (frontage) measurements recorded in Alnwick, 14 feet and 16 feet, are the halves of the two prominent units. They represent the common lower limit of "bay" widths in earlier construction. A standard frontage of 28-32 feet therefore seems to imply that a row house occupying the head of a standard burgage normally formed a building unit of two structural bays. That traditional building methods were in use in Alnwick for a long time, probably right up to the early Georgian period, may be inferred from

[17]Conzen, op. cit., p. 28. Alnwick is pronounced an´-ik.
[18]Ibid., pp. 31-32.

Tate's statement that during the fourteenth, fifteenth and sixteenth centuries the houses of Alnwick were generally low and small single-storey thatched buildings. The prevailing house depth of 18-20 feet . . . indicates the traditional block-plan of the smaller "eaves house," i.e. a small row house fronting the street with its eaves instead of its gable.[19]

Conzen pictures a small quasi-rural town, perhaps as much the home of rural people as of town artisans. That the plot-head building was larger along its street frontage than in its depth, that it was a single story, that it was laid out in simple "cruck" construction,[20] and that its thickness was only that of a single bay, or room, indicates that the Alnwick house was not a truly urban structure.

This last point supplies us an insight as to the role of evolution in shaping the medieval plot. Doubtless in street-villages (string towns or *Strassendorfer*) the general origin and development envisaged by Conzen for Alnwick would be characteristic: the "High Street" would come first, with little anticipation of shaping an urban warp and woof of parallel and intersecting streets. The dominant High Street would make the intersecting streets more significant than any streets that might be laid out parallel to it. Under such conditions, a strong morphological force would work against a great deepening of the lots, since the side-street frontages would be used slightly, and use of the rear end of the plot would hardly be common. The backs of the High Street lots would be so far removed from the flow of customers as to be disregarded but the lots on the near end of the side streets might be quite close to that flow, requiring only a minor turning out from the main stream of commerce.

But this morphology of semi-urbanism is based both on limited economic dependence on city activities and on conscious doubts as to the growth of a town. The low intensity of land-use that Conzen cites supports that view.

Roof orientation tells us a good deal about morphogenesis. Looking at Alnwick, laid out in rows of single-story houses joined at the gable-ends, we can see that the builders of those houses had little actual or anticipated use for the attics, particularly as storage or work space. By butting one gable against the next, they cut off a main access to light, save in the end houses, and eliminated the simplest form of raising and lower-

[19]Ibid., pp. 33-34.
[20]Cruck construction was based on the most primitive technology, which called for using timbers taken from curved trees to form a pointed arch joined at the ridgepole, on which a gambrel roof would be borne. Normally the crucks would perform the function both of the posts and of the roof-beams. Such construction would be practicable only for single-story or story-and-a-half buildings and those of little width.

ing goods from an upper story. The pulley-beam and attic door were ruled out, unless a large and inefficient dormer was built to carry the attic floor forward to the front of the building. In a city, neither single-story nor cottage architecture would have been practical. Instead the tendency was to build a second floor, turning its gable to the street. We know, for example, that despite the traditional Anglo-Saxon practice of single-story construction, two-story buildings had become common in English towns by the tenth and eleventh centuries.[21] And we can reason that turning the gable-end to the street is more utilitarian on a narrow lot, giving full windows in the attics as well as affording access to them by pulley-beam and doorway.

Controls of Linearity: "Radiocentric" and Elongated Towns

Though actual observation put in question the "High Street model," good reasons exist in morphological theory for a second look. When we assume that a city will be surrounded by a wall, as was normally the case in western Europe outside of England, we must ask what restraint on "free form" circumvallation would introduce. The most logical and observable of those restrictions would be an excessive linearity of city outline. Since the shortest line enclosing a unit area is that of a circle, none can doubt that in the Middle Ages, other things being equal, city men would attempt to surround their towns with basically circular walls. The examples are legion, though Montluçon in France just north of the Massif Centrale is perhaps the most graphic.

At Montluçon, a hill on the right bank of the river Cher was occupied by a fortified chateau around which the town grew in proper *faubourg* fashion. As Lavedan expressed it, "The agglomeration formed in this way displays a perfectly circular shape with two concentric walls, one around the chateau and the other delineating an exterior contour. A number of radiating streets tie the two elements together. The regularity of the ensemble is interrupted only by the cutting off of a third annular ring which remains incomplete."[22] He also notes the similarity of medieval Bristol and Aachen

[21]Encyclopaedia Britannica, 11th edition. vol. 4, p. 593.
[22]Pierre Lavedan, Histoire de l'Urbanisme: Antiquité-Moyen Age, Paris: Henri Laurens, 1926, Vol. I, p. 259.

Gourdon in Lot et Garonne is a striking example of the "radio-concentrique" town.

(Aix-la-Chapelle) whose circular outlines are nearly as striking, though they are lost to us today.

Certainly not all medieval towns were so clearly circular and concentric in their layout, but unquestionably the pull was strong toward building a wall as short in length as the local conditions would permit: reasoning and field observation lend abundant support to that truth. In such a situation the problem is not to explain the circular, but rather to account for the linear with its increased demands for walls and the population to man them adequately. In the instance of Alnwick we face no problem; it was an open town defended only by its castle, a situation common in England but not elsewhere until the nineteenth century. The Continent had elongated walled towns—Bern is perhaps the clearest example, with its single Grande Rue along the long axis of an entrenched meander, or Gubbio in the Umbrian hill country of northern Italy. Any examination of town plans confirms that the elongated pattern was exceptional, and the basically circular one more normal. In fact, in his classic study of the layout of towns, Pierre Lavedan found the circular so often the norm that he contrasted the classical towns with the medieval mainly in terms of circular focus. "The essential fact of medieval urbanism is the establishment of towns in which all the lines converge toward the center and in which the outline is generally circular: it is that which contemporary theorists term *'le système radio-concentrique.'* "[23]

Lavedan notes that the radial-concentric town "is not found in all countries of Europe with the same frequency. Some, such as Italy, remain more profoundly

[23]Ibid., p. 250.

impregnated with the tradition of Roman urbanism, which is radically opposed to this layout. Others, such as England, find it repugnant, perhaps by *'tempérament ethnique.'* But in France, Germany, and the Slavic countries numerous examples are to be found."[24] Exception must be taken to his analysis of the absence of radial-concentric towns in England, but there seems little gainsaying the explanation of their infrequency in Italy. The Roman inheritance was both concrete and cultural. Many places were Roman towns merely remodeled into medieval places; others were built by peoples steeped in the notion that regular layout was the urban design. In England, however, the notion of *tempérament ethnique* seems utterly extraneous, more a possibility than an explanation. Britain was much less characterized by walled towns than by castle towns where defense was afforded by a moat and a strong keep in which the population might seek refuge, and from which a punitive expedition might ultimately be launched. Where walls did exist, as at Bristol, Newcastle, York, and Norwich, their outline was fairly circular, though only in Bristol did the streets within the wall have any really concentric quality. Thus Lavedan's observation of fact is correct but his analysis of cause seems less convincing. It might more plausibly be argued that the impact of walls, even where present, was not so great in the insular kingdom as on the Continent.

Walls were a civic burden in at least two ways: they were expensive to construct and maintain, taking civic resources that might more productively be used on other undertakings, and they were of little practical use unless well-manned. Thus, constant vigilance was required to make walls work. In England the early centralization of the state and the transformation of conflict to internal dynastic competition meant that the castle remained a reality when civic walls were used largely to maintain law and order within the town. As protection against theft and riot and the intrusion of outside traders, the wall must have remained a light construction, easily extended and virtually unmanned.

City Walls and Their Effects

The role of the wall in creating an orderly, at least partially preconceived pattern of streets was well understood by early urban morphologists. In *The Castles and*

[24]Loc. cit. *The term* tempérament ethnique *seems best left in the original, as it does not seem plausible in English.*

Walled Towns of England published in 1911, Alfred Harvey said, "As a general rule the walled towns were much more regular in planning of their streets than those towns which were always open; this is more especially the case in those which received their mural girdle early, and particularly in towns of Roman foundations. It is not so generally noticeable in the case of cities which grew up as open towns, and were only enclosed at a later date. Thus Norwich, which began as a cluster of houses round the castle and monastery, and was walled in after a lapse of 200 years, is as wildly irregular in its planning as such [open] towns as Birmingham or Leeds."[25]

Harvey noted a tendency for English towns to be unwalled until the Norman Conquest when those Continental overlords brought in circumvallation as a general practice. Even so, the "walls of English towns seldom or never compared in dignity or strength [or constraint, we might add] with similar fortifications on the continent, but they proved themselves sufficient to offer a very respectable defence to such attack as they were liable to meet with."[26] And the walls built by the Normans and Edwards soon lost much of their significance as either town protectors or bridles on its growth. Seemingly this morphological experience made the English town foreign to the model or radial-concentric urbanization more than did the English *tempérament ethnique*. And thus the English town with its High Street layout is no more than a special case in urban morphogenesis.

On the Continent where towns were contained within their stronger walls, less proclivity was shown toward open, moderately occupied lots. Harvey notes that as time went on the gardens disappeared from the English walled town; Europe had relatively few gardens to begin with, and they disappeared early except where circumstance left the wall "overfit" to the town. This excess of circumvallation was present in some Roman towns that never in medieval times filled up the walls built in classical times: Rome herself was the most striking example, being overfit until well into the nineteenth century. In other instances the demographic scourge of the medieval plagues was such that the town rattled around in its earlier walls until population recovered during the Mercantile and Industrial Revolutions. These situations where spatial pressure was absent were far from frequent or normal; instead, on the Continent, the city wall tended to encourage a shortage of building land at most times, relieved only occasionally through the periodic extension of the walls to take in new open land that might serve to reduce the pressure.

[25]Alfred Harvey, *The Castles and Walled Towns of England,* London: Methuen & Co., 1911, pp. 200-201.
[26]Ibid., p. 193.

The Land-Occupation Module Shapes a True Street-Fabric

The land-occupation module introduced a three-dimensional quality into space within the walls. Its simplest expression came in a system devised to make use of the area away from both the initially occupied streets and the main streets that emerged from commercial activity. Some effort was made to even up the use of streets for economic activity. The crossing streets in the urban fabric would gain strength relative to the warp of original occupation. To create this more even use, the elongated burgage plot gave way to lots of lesser depth, affording more direct access from building sites to open streets. Plots with a moderate depth required planning for use of the back of the lot, and were distinct from those of excessive depth (as in the High Street model), where any real use of the back space required a secondary street or alley to reach what would be a rather long string of buildings. When we discuss the impact on cities of the Industrial Revolution, we shall see that the layout of British and Continental towns differed considerably because the High Street layout so common in Britain was uncommon in Europe itself. In Britain the "court" gave access to intensified housing deep in these lots, whereas on the Continent the Industrial Revolution led not to building backward on the lot, but to the upward building of high workers' tenements. Even during the Middle Ages the contrast led to the creation of two norms of building layout: the *courtyard house* in the compact, intensively occupied towns, and the *alley house* where the lots were served by access in one direction alone.

Whether the courtyard house shaped the street-blocks it occupied or the blocks created the courtyard house is not clear. We do know that, with space at a premium, the street-blocks tended to become more equidimensional and thereby more likely to be assembled in a regular or approximately regular pattern. What Harvey termed the "wildly irregular pattern" is a result of land-use which focusses heavily on a single street-frontage of a block. With such linear incrementation along radiating, often rural, roads the eccentricities of terrain and history come to dominate, overpowering the forces normally at work to make the most intense use of urban land, which tend toward compaction and regularity.

The compact block and the compact lot furnished the greatest usable street-frontage. This fact seems to account for the basic consistency of street-blocks in medieval times. Few medieval towns were built on a grid save those with Roman roots and those new towns of the era, the bastides. But surprisingly many medieval towns show not "wild irregularity" but neat consistency of block size and a reasonably equidimensional quality in their plots. They show a *street-fabric* rather than a High Street pattern. Streets are reasonably interwoven roughly parallel to one of two axes meeting at approximate right angles. This pattern is not a set, preconceived plan with true rectangular blocks, fully parallel streets, and a clearly determined grid pattern, but a remarkably *consistent division of land* (land-occupation module) both into modular blocks and modular plots. The dynamics seem undeniably those of organic growth rather than of planning, but given the constraints in growth of the wall surrounding the area and the shortage and valuable quality of enclosed land, the forces at work seem to have produced a normative, if not a rigid, pattern. In this context the High Street model that Conzen discerned in England stands as no more than a special case valid for towns where circumvallation was a weak constraint or absent.

The control in this constrained growth may most fundamentally have been the value conferred on land by its scarcity, but the actual shaping of the blocks and lots was geared to the exactions of terrain and the functional needs of the medieval economic place. It is hard to generalize the effect of terrain when each town had a distinctive site. Nevertheless, terrain and distance worked as reciprocals. In setting up a marketplace quarter or an occupational district, trade-offs would be made between horizontal extension and vertical development (including the use of both rising or falling ground and superpositional stories). If short horizontal extension would include the desired space, and was available, then the use of steeply rising or falling ground would be avoided. But as land pressure increased, an internal constraint must have been interposed by adjacent occupation districts which would not themselves yield to encroachment, forcing instead the use of steep side streets. Such unused outlets would be less likely to remain on a flat site, so the same force of growth there would lead immediately to superpositional expansion.

Even in organically growing cities, where the plan evolves as the demand for additional space arises, so long as the town remains walled and space enclosed in those fortifications maintains a reasonable level of scarcity, a *consistent* and *structured* ground plan will tend to evolve. Street-blocks will not be identical or rectangular but will tend to be proportionate. Block dimensions will normally be reasonably equivalent, with any ratio above one-to-two (length to width) coming not from the operation of economic and social forces but from the extremes of site terrain. Within the basically proportional blocks, lots of similar dimen-

sional balance would be laid out and occupied. Because those plots would avoid excessive depth or narrowness of frontage in relation to depth, they would demand either a single building occupying the whole plot or a courtyard building, built possibly in stages, furnishing interior access by way of a covered passage beneath the facade building.

Downward Division and Upward Assembly

The totality of the classical city was established from the beginning, though it might be added to in later years by similar large-scale increments. Thus, the finer aspects of urban morphology were conferred by *downward division*. In the medieval city those finer aspects came in the beginning and tended to produce a city by the *upward assembly* of the modular parts. In the classical city the monuments and deliberately impressive streets were established within a previously-thought-out whole where the vista was important and where location within the city of these morphological features assumed considerable significance. But in the medieval city, the intimate individuality of each town assailed the visitor, and the internalized qualities of buildings and space gained the greatest significance. The Middle Ages were the time of the cloister, the courtyard, and the market square. In the great cathedrals of the time, even those marvelously light and architectonic Gothic structures, the interior counted. The outside was often hidden by a close crowding of city houses, with only the west front of the buildings treated to exterior adornment. A few cathedrals stood on open ground with full exterior sculpturally treated, but they were the exception.

The Marketplace

The widespread textural consistency in the street-fabric that characterized these medieval cities was interrupted in one important way, by the street market. Some commentators on the medieval town feel its retail-trading origin can be read clearly from the cen-

The Grand' Place in Brussels
preserves the shape of the
medieval "burgage plots"
even in facade houses
built in more recent
centuries.

verbal contest; or they were in a building, as Venice's fishmarket still remains. Beyond these street markets were numerous specializations of the street because of width or by intended use. One of the more striking examples of street adjustment to specialized need is found in the old city of Syracusa in Sicily.

The Syracusa of Greek foundation seems the last place to find the complexity of organic growth represented by the specialized street. But the fabric of the place was destroyed in the earthquake of 1693; when the town reconstructed, it expressed in the naming and layout of individual streets the diversity of functions that had come to be carried on in the street of a town in a warm, dry climate. In the Middle Ages it is doubtful that the streets would have been physically so differentiated; thus the seventeenth-century reconstruction probably preserves distinctions more of function than of design. In Syracusa, we find *piazzi*, wide open spaces intended for symbolic and social purposes; the *piazza maggiore* of the Renaissance Italian city; *fora* carried over from the Roman use of a Greek town; a wide *corso* for strolling; *viae* for normal circulation; *viali* to afford access within the old tightly built quarter of the town; a *lungomare* along the shore where boats could unload; and the other market layouts specific to a particular need.

Evidence supports the notion that markets may initially have been held in ordinary streets with the somewhat variable street lines common in the Middle Ages. Choosing a wide stretch of street in which to display goods brought in for the day, traders at first departed with the waning of the daylight. But those engaged in full-time commerce would seek to store their goods nearby; in that way, the houses fronting on the market street would gain value. Given the rise in significance of a street, or more particularly its frontage, it would be a short step to the creation of a market quarter in which retail trade would be clustered.

Departing from the Roman practice of providing a building—the early basilicas—for the conduct of trade heavily controlled by the state, medieval town authorities yielded control and provision for selling to the merchants and the impact of organic processes. When the town was small a single wider street or a field at the edge of the tiny town would suffice. But with the economic success of the town, the marketplace became incorporated into the fabric of the settlement as housing grew to surround it. The existence of that marketplace as a focus of urban interest separate from the church is demonstrated by the great number of cathedrals that are not built on the square, or that lie even today at the edge of the city. Bourges and Chartres in France and Salisbury and most other English cathedrals show this peripheral location. Only in Italy, where the Renaissance *piazza major* came to be built, is the big church usually on the main square. In Flan-

tral location of the street market and its use as the site for the important civic buildings, even the dominating church or cathedral. Such an argument tends to hide truth in circularity: the marketplace would be the site for large ostentatious buildings for the obvious visual endowments of the place. The cathedral in particular was often not on the marketplace and is today so placed as much by nineteenth-century "restoration" and razing as by original siting. Town halls were normally on the square, but those monuments of civic boasting were almost universally built long after the city was founded, and thus tended to be placed on an open space where ostentation gained the highest reward. Brussels' *Grand' Place* contains her strutted pride from the late Middle Ages, the fifteenth-century city hall, but her thirteenth-century cathedral is elsewhere.

The specialization of streets was not limited to a division between market and common way. A good-sized town had many markets: markets for perishable produce, grain for baking or feed for domestic animals, hay and, near the coast, fish. Sometimes these markets were square-like widenings of the street, such as in London's fishmarket in Billingsgate, with its notorious ders and Germany the center of affairs and the locale of the church are clearly separated.

The Separation of Functions

The classical city exhibited two types of functional separation: social classes were separated from one another, and most types of economic activity were apart from residence. This separation was horizontal within the city, and was a matter of institutional forces. The Romans sought to care for industry and trade in established places with special physical provision. Only in the smallest shops were workplace and res-idence combined. And among the imposing buildings, private as well as public, careful separation of the mundane from the exalted was maintained.

In considering conditions of land-use separation in the Middle Ages we must distinguish between the two basic urban realms of western civilization: in the Mediterranean world *social division* seems to have remained an important component of urban morphogenesis, whereas in the lands across the Alps economic forces were largely controlling urban structure. The south had considerable social segregation, but to the north *functional segregation* was the controlling force. To add another contrast, the Mediterranean city, particularly as expressed in northern Italy, was a place of discrete and very definite social quarters, whereas the northern city, particularly as its developed in the lands around the North Sea, was a place of well-perceived occupational quarters. *This contrast led in the south to a city of factions and in the north to one of*

The Piazza del Campo in Siena is a striking example of the piazza in an Italian medieval city, a meeting place of the populace for sports, meetings, and on occasion, conflicts.

gilds. The tower palace became the architectural expression of the Mediterranean urban power structure; the differently-towered gildhall became the focal building in the north.

We cannot summarize internal separation simply for the Middle Ages, and perhaps its simplicity in the Classical Era comes mainly from the paucity of information on which we must build our analysis. We will look first at the medieval city of the Mediterranean, more transitional in form than the northern city and, in real terms, the first expression of the modern city.

The Mediterranean city of the Middle Ages inherited most of its ground plan from classical times. The grid of streets of relatively equal importance, the fairly equidimensional street-blocks, the squarish houses of stone construction, and the tendency to a single civic forum—the *piazza major* of medieval Italy—can all be traced directly to Roman practice. But a ground plan does not automatically control all aspects of the functional organization of the town, and the medieval Italian city developed important modifications of the Roman social and political organization of urban space. Perhaps the most striking modification came in the introduction of *factional society,* growing out of the conflict between the loyalty to one overlord or another.

Along with this almost classical urge to faction, immortalized in *Romeo and Juliet,* went a further disruptive force which might be termed the *urbanization of feudalism.* In Italy as elsewhere, the feudal order was based mainly on the division of the countryside among barons demanding fealty from their villeins. But the survivals of Roman cities were powerful enough both to encroach through territorial political expansion on the countryside and, ultimately, to force the nobles to take up city residence so they might be watched and kept in some sort of subservience to the city authority. But taking up residence in towns did not end the nobles' search for henchmen, and many candidates stood ready for the job. Fritz Rörig clearly portrays the role of factionalism in shaping medieval Europe, contrasting Germany and Italy.

It is a fact of profound significance that both these countries which provided an immediate stage for the universal policies of the Emperor—Germany and Italy—differed in the formation of their national state and ended in extreme political disunion and internal strife. But in the territorial formation of states on the old imperial soil in Italy the towns had a far more important role to play than they did in Germany. In Germany the political future belonged to the emergent states bearing the stamp of territorial feudalism. The formation of territories by the imperial towns did not produce zones of power of any significant size, even in their greatest manifestations, as for example the territory of Nuremberg; and the country towns, until the fifteenth century, were only able to assert their independence when the circumstances were favorable. Not so in Italy. Here the towns did not develop, as in Germany, within the power system of the countryside, but grew at the expense of feudal power areas until finally city-state bordered on city-state. The rural nobility was forced into the municipal sphere of interests. But in the process the leading classes of the individual towns–with the sole exception of Venice–lost their internal solidarity. In all the larger towns families of different political outlook–even the old opposition of Guelphs and Ghibellines was still going strong–regarded each other with hate or mistrust; at the same time the lower classes, organized into guilds, were striving for political power.[27]

Little wonder that the faction became the social unit, because it was at first the more critical political unit, shaping a town of quarters ready for riot and infinitely suspicious of others equally enclosed by the city wall. The Palio, the famous horse race in Siena, is a Renaissance replacement of the often-more-serious-than-recreational games and combats held during the Middle Ages in the city's great square, the Campo. Then the three main parts of the city—Terziere di Città, Terziere di San Martino, and Terziere di Camollia—participated in such activities as *le Pugna* (the punching) which had to be abolished in 1324 when it proved intractable to being restricted to simple sportsmanship.[28]

City of Factions

What then is the morphology of a city of factions? Its beginning lay in a fact observed by the eleventh century chroniclers of Milan who realized that citizens of that powerful but representative town "when they lack external adversaries . . .turn their hatred against each other."[29] The need was for a city form that might afford protection for groups, against the threat posed by their neighborly enemies, when all lived within the enclosing city wall. It was not possible in times of peace to surround the faction with walls and an empty glacis in which the evil intentions of a neighborly enemy might be perceived and dealt with forcefully. The city had to continue as a governmental and economic entity, usu-

[27]*Fritz Rörig,* The Medieval Town, *Berkeley: The University of California Press, 1967, p. 56.*
[28]*Aldo Lusini and Sandro Chierichetti,* Siena, *Siena: Stefano Venturini, 1961, pp. 31-37.*
[29]*Quoted in Daniel Waley,* The Italian City-Republics, *New York: McGraw-Hill Book Co., 1969, p. 164.*

ally as a commune in Italy, which required daily association. Yet each political or social faction in the place had to live and operate from an internal strongpoint in which it could gather to defend its factional interest and from which it could sally in an attack on those outside the faction.

The state of bristling accommodation which obtained in the Italian towns made them clusters of self-seeking minorities only occasionally, and then only in response to great external danger, able to join in a majority action. Though the medieval city communes of Italy are often viewed as great cohesive bodies possessed of liberty and a common will to resist the enslavement of rural feudalism or urban capitalism, they were none of that in collective action and all of that in individual thinking. The city residence of knights, first invested with nobility for their power in the countryside, brought within the walls all the personal animosities and practices of revenge typical of the half-civilization of the Italian feudal order. Equally, the striving of merchants for wealth and power domesticated within the city class conflict between them and the nobles, on the one hand, and the mass of workers on the other.

The factional geography was comprised of two morphological components: the tower and the quarter for henchmen. The tower determined location; once built, it tended to be surrounded by the residences of the supporters of the faction—the henchmen. The towers were both defensive and, to quote a contemporary contract, might "be necessary for doing harm to their enemy or enemies."[30] Most cities in upper Italy bristled with towers; in 1160 the Jewish traveler Benjamin of Tudela described Pisa as "a very great city, with about 10,000 turreted houses for battles at times of strife."[31] Attempts were made to limit that strife by controlling the height of towers, but most agreements seem to have been an invitation to even further conflict. Daniel Waley sees these structures as an outgrowth of the close social and political ties between countryside and city, with the city's victory in forcing the rural nobility to reside within her walls standing as pyrrhic indeed.

But this vertical quasi-military domestic architecture demands rather more explanation. It represents the import into the city of a form of watch-tower which was very common in the countryside. Moreover, the institution which made the tower a necessity was itself familiar in rural areas: this was the blood feud or vendetta, a tradition both of violence in settling (and prolonging) private disputes and of unwillingness to settle such matters in the courts. Essentially the purpose of the tower was defensive; its owner's home was his castle, to which he could retreat

if under attack and where he might hope to conduct a prolonged defense. It became conventional for those who could afford it to inhabit a "house tower". Many did so because they had inherited one from ancestors and this was the accepted form of residential architecture, rather than because an aristocratic way of life dictated an unending series of vendettas for all. It has been suggested that the high cost of land within the cities encouraged vertical building: there is probably some truth in this, but most cities normally had unused building space and in the main the towers should be seen as the product of fear, fashion and a taste for display, rather than an economic necessity. Some towers were set very close to each other, as may still be seen for example, at San Gimignano and Bologna. In these circumstances fighting from tower to tower, as described by Benjamin Tudela, may have taken place and some advantage could be derived from building higher than one's neighbour, but normally ostentation must have been the main motive for building very high.[32]

The component of ostentation in the building of towers came to be an integral element in Italian urban morphology, gaining ascendency as the military requirements declined. Such ostentation in the Mediterranean was more than skin deep, more than detailing on the facade and painted murals; ostentation was first having a taller tower and ultimately a larger and more pompous palace.

The most fundamental factions allied families of similar political view, usually in an effort to dominate the city government partly by their own power and partly by borrowing the power of the Roman pope and his henchmen—the Guelphs—or the German emperor and his supporters—the Ghibellines. Such accumulations of power were made most effective by massing residence in a particular part of the city, isolating a particular quarter to the use of that group. In this creation of factional districts we find a peculiar urban manifestation of the very rural notion of *territorial conflict*.

The establishment of the family compound as one of the modules of urban structure, probably first in a tower house and later in a *palazzo* of Renaissance design, demonstrates the socially stratified nature of the urban morphogenesis in Italy. For magnates, this compound, somewhat consistent in form but variable in capacity, was the clay from which a city was to be shaped. The number of members of powerful families and the nearly feudal retainers who surrounded them determined the commodiousness of the form. We might assume great luxury and vast personal space in a tower house, but those that survive suggest more that a large group of people were forced to live together. Thus, when physical protection declined somewhat as a critical need, the tower was redesigned to become a bit

[30]Ibid., *p. 175.*
[31]Itinerary of Benjamin of Tudela, *p. 5, quoted in* loc. cit.

[32]Ibid., *pp. 176-177.*

The Asinelli and Garisenda towers in Bologna are distinctive for their height and the fact that they lean badly, but they may serve as examples of the tower houses so favored in the Middle Ages.

more livable and somewhat more opulent, yet retained its frowning sense of menace to those who might wish to do harm to the family and its supporters. At that stage the Renaissance palace was born, preserving the large modular size of the family compound with its residence for numerous retainers but becoming more gracious in its apartments and more carefully conceived as an architectural creation. The *palazzi* of Florence clearly demonstrate this transformation, combining a rather formidable grace with the reminder of ancient and arbitrary power present in the tall tower. (Such personal palaces strangely gained great popularity in North America at the beginning of the twentieth century for use as city halls and railroad stations. The almost anarchic history of the form and the disdain for democracy possessed by its developers was completely overlooked, creating for the historically minded observer a totally garbled symbolism.)

The family compound could scarcely serve those residents of the city whose presence depended upon urban activities distinct from the implosion on the city of an older rural nobility. The parvenu nobles whose status grew out of urban-based commerical activities might copy the tower-house and massive *palazzo* but the small men—the workers in shops, the petty traders, and the laborers—gained nothing from such a morphological solution. The governing *popolani* in most cities began the shaping of a class solidarity when

they made it a serious, even capital, crime for a common man to submit himself anew as vassal to a magnate. Thus, a form of housing had to be devised that was not rooted in the urbanization of the feudal order. That form evolved in a most natural way, by the reflective return of the urban masses to the precedent that lay at their feet, the ground-plan inherited from the Romans. The street-block of relatively equal dimensions, its division into more-or-less square plots, and the fairly equivalent use of all street frontages persisted from classical times as established concepts, if not as very vigorous practices. No doubt the essential continuity of urban history in upper Italy assured this return; even crumbling buildings still persist in occupying and identifying an ancient system of land-division. Any return of vitality to the town will rejuvenate the relicts, producing a clearer reflection of the ancient pattern.

The diversity of the second of the two housing modules that grew up in the medieval city of the Mediterranean was the effect of different post-Roman experiences on a formerly rather consistent fabric. As a result, the house remained a quite variable raw material for even further evolution in the urban revival of the eleventh, twelfth, and thirteenth centuries. Unquestionably a family relationship remained; the Mediterranean cities were more like each other than they were like the cities of the north. But unlike the cities of the north, those of the Mediterranean did not represent a rather new, functionally-derived structure. Instead they represented, first, a rather rigid preconception of what a city should be, impressed on many different landscapes by the imperial Romans; second, a thousand years of quite contrasting conditions in Spain as opposed to Italy and in turn as compared to Provence and Languedoc; and third, a considerable differential in the impact of the late medieval urban revival—with upper Italy and southern France standing at the center and Spain, Portugal, and southern Italy seeming urban backwaters by comparison. This differential in historical transformation came to be expressed in the Mediterranean towns when growth returned. Responses to the new demands for an encompassing and expanding city could hardly fail to be distinct in the various regions.

The solid base for similarity existed in the Roman town-plan as it actually survived or was reproduced in neighboring new towns. The diversity came in what was built to fill the persisting land-use modules. The intensity of need was the fundamental determinant of the newer building: where the force of urbanization was weak, low houses occupying the squarish plots sufficed; where the city was burgeoning, essentially straining the form it inherited, the squarish plot remained, but the building set on it was higher and more likely to intensify the use of land. To supply actual examples: the house in Iberian cities tended to be squat and rather open, though still basically a square. It tended to enclose a courtyard, or patio, introducing open space to the city fabric. This low, square building with its enclosed open space might be considered an inheritance from the centuries of Moorish control in Granada, Sevilla, and other southern cities, but less so in the towns of northern Portugal and in Cantabria, where a similar squatiness, square-building, and courtyard enclosure exists. Evidence supports the notion that whatever the history of Moorish occupation, intensity of demand finally determined the height of the house. That evidence is furnished by the Gothic quarter of Barcelona largely shaped in the High Middle Ages.

Houses in Italy

In upper Italy the city house for the common people was taller than that on the fringes of Iberia, southern Spain, and the Balkans. Seemingly the ground floor was taken up with the shops of both artisans and merchants, while the upper stories housed workers and masters. One common characteristic of these tall Mediterranean houses was their use of arches to support the heavy weight of the masonry walls of upper stories while affording an increasing opening of the wall at its base. Perhaps to make up for the constraints imposed on merchants and craftsmen in the factious Italian city, the public market and market-hall gained greater importance, not for wholesale trade, as in the impressive cloth markets of Ypres, Bruges, and Krakow, but for the daily trading in consumer goods, as in the food market-halls at Orvieto and Venice. The two somewhat conflicting needs of an especially secure house and an open selling place could be met by the tightly shuttered Mediterranean house for residence and the market-hall for selling.

Little documentary evidence survives to help us reconstruct the full pattern of life in the northern Italian city during the Middle Ages—the way the ordinary people lived and how they were housed. It would be valuable to know with more certainty the role played by occupation and employment in providing workers' housing. Were most ordinary men housed in buildings owned and provided by their employers, or did a generalized rental market make shelter available to workers? As the Italian cities were the largest in the western world, we might logically anticipate that rental housing-provision would appear first there. We do know of the widespread practice of "putting-out"

yarn for weaving into textiles, with merchants serving as the organizers. In addition, we know that the system of "truck," wherein these factors of production issued script or credits for the purchase of food and staples, rather than money, was already developed in northern Italy.[33] Members of the working class were clearly becoming more impoverished as a result of the competition with the capitalist magnates over the rewards to the various elements of production. Looms were increasingly mortgaged, suggesting that it is highly unlikely that many weavers would have been able to pay for their housing.[34] Housing must have been provided by the factors organizing production by "putting-out," or the rental market in houses must have been sizable. But the details are missing.

Gubbio in Umbria preserves a number of medieval houses that show the affinity between the Roman city house and that of the true Middle Ages, the more equidimensional plots, the rough stone construction with use of arches on the first floor, and the gently sloping roofs. Note the tower house in the background.

[33]*Rörig*, op. cit., *pp. 84-89.*
[34]Ibid., *p. 85.*

Little evidence remains as to the nature of housing for the common man but certain logical assumptions help us to fill the gaps. Once a rental market for housing is established, constant pressures urge reduction in the size of individual units. If capital is cheap, then new competitive housing might be provided; if it is dear, then the only way to keep it in housing is to increase the return on a particular investment. Usually such an effort not only reduces the size of units available to workers and their families but often leads to sharp increases in rent, even for the diminished units. Another way to increase the return on capital is to diminish the actual investment by allowing the deterioration of the property. All of these influences came into play when the rental market for housing replaced the provision of shelter by masters of a craft, as during the High Middle Ages. As that era waned, the quality of housing declined in most cities; we must conclude that the tenements of the working class in the Italian cities probably became smaller, more crowded, and more expensive, further worsening the condition of that class.

One of the most common responses as people crowded into the medieval cities was the enlargement of structures by adding on all sorts of often rather jerry-built extensions. Houses were pushed backward to fill the entire burgage plot; extensions encroached on the street in the form of bay windows and shed-like lean-tos, or more commonly as overhanging extensions of upper stories sometimes, as in the "covered streets" in Cahors and Perigeux, as a full bridge across the street.[35] Such crowding was normally unpleasant but proved in the long run to be even dangerous.

Housing Pressure and the Plague

Beginning in the eleventh century, housing pressure built up but was repeatedly relieved by inadvertent but positively draconian reductions in urban population. These were brought about by "massacres provoked by the great wars which were then bleeding Christendom white," by the ravaging of the countryside by bands of brigands, and by "excesses of religious fanaticism" such as the brutal Albigensian Crusade we shall note in the next chapter. Famines were frequent, sweeping Austria in 1343 and France in 1351, 1359, and 1418. "The last carried off over 100,000 persons in Paris,

[35]Lavedan, op. cit., p. 409.

where groups of twenty or thirty poor wretches at a time died of starvation on the dung-heaps, and where wolves came to devour the corpses." Earthquakes destroyed other areas, such as Villach in Carinthia, and the sea battered a number of towns on the slowly subsiding coast of Holland. "But worst of all were the ravages of epidemic maladies, leprosy, and typhus, which raged among the masses, who were already weak from want and wretchedness."[36]

Given the epidemic quality of these diseases and the deteriorated state of much of the housing, doubtless the ravages were most severe in cities. In a generally grim situation, the Black Death of 1348 to 1350 savaged Europe to such a degree that her population did not recover for several centuries. Estimates hold that central Italy lost two-thirds of its population, while between one- and two-thirds of the population died in the Po Basin, northern Spain, France, England, and the Low Countries. "The towns were attacked with special severity. Venice lost two-thirds of its population; Bologna, four-fifths; Florence, 80,000 to 100,000 souls; Majorca, 30,000; Narbonne, 30,000; Paris, over 50,000; Strassburg and Bâle, 14,000 each; Vienna, 40,000. . . . As far as can be calculated [the Black Death over a period of repeating epidemics between 1350 and 1450] cost from twenty-four to twenty-five million human lives."[37]

Just as the pressures on urban accommodation in the medieval cities became generally very strong, the repeating visitations of the Black Death transformed the problem from one of too many people seeking too few accommodations to that of too few people effectively to carry on the economic life of the city, or any other productive enterprise for that matter. We might first reason that with such population decimation, labor would become scarce and thus more adequately rewarded. But such was not always the case as the established order sought to defend itself against this operation of free-market forces. The almost immediate response in England to the decimations of the Black Death was the adoption of the "First Statute of Laborers" in 1351, seeking to set the wages that workers might receive and requiring that able-bodied persons accept a job if offered. The power of land, wealth, and position all continued so strong that, at least in broad terms, the *status quo* could be made to prevail despite changing conditions.[38] What could not be done was to restore by natural increase the half or more of the average city's population that had perished in the great

[36]*Boissonade*, op. cit., p. 284.
[37]Ibid., p. 285.
[38]*Edward P. Cheyney*, An Introduction to the Industrial and Social History of England, *New York: The Macmillan Company, 1908, p. 107.*

plague. Some relief came through the increase in the mobility of rural people consequent to the severe disruption of the manorial economy which brought recruits to the city. Unfortunately the urban economy was not thriving enough in these times to absorb as many as might otherwise have come, so the majority of cities knew a long period of stagnation.

Stagnation during the years after the middle of the fourteenth century simply meant that no effective form of worker housing was devised in the Mediterranean towns during the Middle Ages. The Roman *cenacula* continued to be used with perhaps more decline in quality than improvement in design. Crowding and filth crept farther into the city fabric, and the extravagant architecture of Renaissance palaces, churches, and public buildings merely accentuated the growth of disequality in the Mediterranean city. This worsening condition was aided by the decline in quality of government and the narrowing of the franchise from the times of the healthy city-republican communes.

The Merchant Shifts from Commerce to Manufacture

A detailed reconstruction of the life of a merchant born in Prato just outside Florence and first active at Avignon in Provence is made possible by the survival of detailed account books, records, and correspondence. The life of Francesco di Marco Datini (1335-1410) has been widely studied because of this wealth of record, and from it we can learn quite a bit about the growth of the late medieval trading and manufacturing town and the role played by the gilds.[39]

Datini was rather poor and an orphan, so his rise to wealth and power serves well to show the basis of trade

This wooden model of Siena in the fourteenth century is based on Ambrogia Lorenzetti: The City of Good Government (c. 1337–1340) and suggests the nature of housing at that time, particularly the tower structures.

The Middle Ages in the Mediterranean led the magnates into the Renaissance, but led the poor into a further retrogression. We are left great buildings by architectural giants but a vernacular building as well, that was, if possible, meaner and less satisfactory than the one left by the previous era. Thus we may justly view the Middle Ages in the south as an era that began with true southern radiance but ended with most of the practical advances in the qualities of everyday life in the city occurring elsewhere. The pomp and display of a corrupt and selfish church and aristocracy came alight with the Renaissance but for true urban development this was, for all its brilliance, an artificial illumination of the real city.

as the maker of capitalists, and capitalism. Setting forth from Prato at the age of fifteen, in 1350, he went to Avignon to seek his fortune. The pope was then ensconced in that great trading town, where the south and the north met and exchanged goods. He was surrounded by a court of cardinals and other satraps who joined their monarch, despite his rustication on the lower Rhône, in a passion for the luxurious goods from Italy and the East. When Datini arrived, Clement VI "was still upon the papal throne, and his court was the most brilliant in Europe," so a number of artisans had collected within the walls of this crowded and squalid town. In a situation common elsewhere in France, but

[39]*The best summary of Datini's life is contained in the biography by Iris Origo,* The Merchant of Prato, *New York: Alfred A. Knopf, 1957.*

no doubt exaggerated in Avignon by the presence of the fugitive papal court, a large proportion of the artisans and merchants were Italian.

Even more numerous than the artisans were the Italian merchants and tradesmen. They monopolized the luxury trade and (with a few Jews) the banking tables. They dealt in wheat, wood, cheese, and vegetables; they imported horses, cloth, armour, and spices; they were taverners and middlemen, and they lived in a tight little community of some six hundred families (in a city of about 30,000 inhabitants) under the jurisdiction of their own consuls, forming their own confraternities, and keeping their own feast days.[40]

Datini seems to have accumulated a tiny capital which he used promptly and to great effect to engage in the importation of luxurious cloth and armor for sale to the court and the numerous soldiers of fortune who collected in that vital city. Without following Datini's course in Avignon we may note its general success, to the extent that he returned to Italy a rich man in 1383.

Though Avignon had many artisans catering to the needs of the papal court, it was not in the true sense a manufacturing town. It seems not to have produced the exportable surplus that would have given it a role in provisioning other places. But Prato and Florence were at the time of Datini's return among the larger manufacturing towns in Europe. Along with Bruges, Ghent, and the other larger towns of Flanders, Florence dominated the market for fine textiles. Along with Milan, Bologna, Venice, and other larger towns of Tuscany and the Po Basin, Florence demonstrated that industry could become a major support for ubanization. Datini's course upon his return was to enlarge the nature of his merchant functions, establishing trading warehouses first in Florence's natural port, Pisa, and then in her alternative one (used in times of conflict with the city near the mouth of the Arno) in Genoa. To extend his reach to Catalonia, as much to secure wool staple as to engage in pure trade, Datini opened a warehouse in Barcelona, and others in Palma on Majorca, Ibiza, and San Mateo in Catalonia. The last three were primarily to gain fairly certain access to the wool coming both from Spain (San Mateo) and from North Africa (Palma). All of this provision was necessary because on his return the merchant of Prato became important in the wool textile industry.

Europe in its primitive state had to be clothed either in skins or cloths made of its native fibers, which were for the most part either flax or animal hair, specifically wool. Every part of the continent had some rough cloth of its own manufacture so the textile trade as it evolved was specifically the distribution by merchants of cloths of unusually fine manufacture. At first

the finest cloths were the woolens woven in Friesland, shipped by merchants in the Low Countries. Then Flanders took over as the manufacturer of the highest quality textiles; in the early Middle Ages, trade flowed from those marshlands to the rest of Europe. In this trade we must distinguish between the movement of the staple of manufacture, wool, and of its product, the cloths. At first the Flemish meadows had supported enough sheep, but when the trade outdistanced the local growth, the staple had to be imported from elsewhere, particularly England which produced the finest quality of wool available in medieval Europe.

Manufacturing and the First Urban Revolution

These well-understood facts explain the relative roles of trade and manufacturing in the support of city growth in the Middle Ages. Without question, the large-scale urbanization of the Middle Ages came from manufacture as much as, and perhaps more so, than from trade. Since trade led to manufacture and fabrication to selling, it is hard to establish whether a city (such as Bruges in Flanders) grew at a particular time for one reason or the other. But unquestionably the large urban places were also the large manufacturing places, and certainly where large clusters of towns occurred within a relatively limited area, the contribution of manufacture was clear. The two hearths of urbanization in the Middle Ages—Flanders and the Po Basin—were well filled out by the towns of artisans at work in their shops. When trade flourished, as at Venice, it tended to bring in its wake a growth of workers' towns which contributed the cargoes taken to the Levant or to northern Europe.

In Florence, we have a lucid explanation of the interaction of local and long-distance trade, and of trade as a whole and manufacture. In Datini, we have a personal record detailing the shifts that the individual capitalist made from one activity to the other.

Florence was of Roman origin, as were most towns in Italy, but assumed little importance until late in the Middle Ages. "Until the end of the twelfth century, Pisa surpassed her inland neighbor in size, population, and wealth."[41] This dominance can be related fairly di-

[40]*Ibid., p. 9.*

[41]*Gene A. Brucker,* Renaissance Florence, *New York: John Wiley & Sons, 1969, p. 52.*

A medieval panorama of Florence from a detail in the 1342 fresco "La Madonna della Misericordia." This suggests the large number of tall houses to be found in a truly important city engaged in long-distance trade, such as Florence was in Datini's time.

When the Guelphs were victorious within the city, Florence came to be the leader of the papal faction in northern Italy. She was rewarded handsomely by an appreciative Curia who appointed her to collect and forward to Rome the tribute exacted by the papacy from the docile medieval world.

Papal approval allowed Florence to take over the banking functions pioneered in nearby Siena as the merchants in the city on the Arno used their position to monopolize banking and trade in Europe north of the Alps. The tie between trade and banking was direct; gold and credit, transferable over great distances, were required to dominate so far from the banks of the Arno. "In Bruges, London, and Paris, in the Mediterranean ports of Barcelona, Marseille, and Tunis, in the Levantine marts, Florentine merchants bought and sold, invested, exchanged coins, and sent home profits from their varied activities." Because of the long-standing mistreatment of Naples by her papal overlords, the "kingdom of Naples was most intensively exploited by these entrepreneurs" who were the chosen bankers and agents of the Curia. "Florentine companies possessed a monopoly of the region's grain trade; their personnel collected taxes and rose high in the bureaucracy. The Angevin kingdom was to Florence by the early fourteenth century what India was for England 500 years later."[42]

The Florentine merchants gained both wealth and experience in their role as bankers to the Vatican. As traders in London, Bruges, and Avignon they learned much about the English staple, the Flemish manufacture, and the Provencal trade. In this context we find Florence transforming herself from a town of bankers and traders to one important in manufacture as well. "International merchants and bankers contributed significantly to Florentine prosperity, but their activity was not the main factor in the city's economic growth and the quadrupling of her population during the thirteenth century. The miracle was wrought by the woolen cloth industry."[43] Thus, as early as the High Middle Ages, the truth central to urban growth in the nineteenth century—that factories fill out towns more completely than do shops—was already observable.

Entering late into cloth manufacture, Florence could profit at the expense of Flanders. At first the Italians imported cloths and perfected them through finishing, but ultimately all stages of manufacture came to flourish along the Arno. Prato in Datini's youth had already become important in the fulling of woolen cloth; other towns around Florence had assumed importance in other processing. But perhaps most important in her rise to supremacy in woolen manufacture was Florence's enjoyment of an outlet for the sale of

rectly to the office Pisa performed during the earlier Middle Ages when she competed with Genoa, Venice, and Barcelona in carving out a maritime empire in the Mediterranean. In these competitive efforts the various religious crusades of the eleventh and twelfth centuries supplied the arc of high voltage that projected the previously fairly local trading power across the greater distances of the open Mediterranean. Once contact had been established, the flow of goods was discontinuous, but served nevertheless as a source for the increasing wealth in those merchant ports. In the meantime Florence was a small city located fifty miles from the coast, engaged in the pernicious sport of the Italian Middle Ages, intraurban warfare. Eventually the Guelphs prevailed and the Ghibellines were evicted from the town, their *palazzi* torn down to provide the open space that became the Piazza della Signoria.

That victory of the forces of the Roman pope began the growth of the great medieval commune; it opened the way for projecting the modest power of Florentine trading impulse over much greater distances. Having missed out on the accumulation of charge that burst forth during the Crusades, Florence had to gain its outward projection literally under the skirts of the clerics, as the tax-collectors of Latin Christendom.

[42]Ibid., pp. 53-54.
[43]Ibid., p. 54.

goods. "In their struggle for supremacy, Florentine manufacturers were aided by good fortune. The Flemish cloth industry was declining in the late thirteenth century, just as Florence's own production was expanding. Moreover, the city's mercantile network contributed to the growth of the cloth industry by supplying capital, by arranging for the purchase of high-quality wool in England and Spain, and by efficient and aggressive marketing of finished cloth."[44]

Into this milieu Datini returned from Avignon; he made great use of it by establishing collecting points for staple in the West Country of England and in Spain, and by becoming a manufacturer of great importance in Prato. In Florence and elsewhere in the woolen trade such a rearward integration from factory to staple-buying was common, but required both access to money and the ability to conduct business over great distances and long periods of time. The Italians, with their banking and the development of the new practice of bookkeeping, were initially the best at establishing these ties of agency and long-distance trade, and Datini merely serves as an example drawn from many.

Even in the thirteenth century to talk about urbanization without account of industry was unwise, and to view the main determinant of city location and growth as the conflux of rural customers on a market-town was distinctly an extraction rather than a distillation of truth. If we reject the validity even in the Middle Ages of central-place theory it is because we believe of too much abstract thinking as did Grover Cleveland, "It is a condition which confronts us,—not a theory."

The city that grew fat on the banks of the Arno became powerful in size as well as in connections. An estimate undertaken in 1338 ranked Florence as Europe's fifth city, exceeded only by Paris, Venice, Milan, and Naples.[45] Its physical form furnishes a picture of the elements and composition—houses, blocks, and overall plan—that made up the Mediterranean city at the end of its most active and significant period.

Florence began the twelfth century relatively small, some two hundred acres surrounded by a wall, and grew directly with the recession of feudalism and the advance of commerce. Society had always questioned the relations between city and country: power was in the hands of a patriciate which shunned commerce and industry within the city and gained its wealth from the fields while living in the city. When the Roman Empire fell, the contest largely disappeared with the decline of cities, but when they grew again, beginning around the year A.D. 1000, conflict returned. In Italy it took on a peculiar cast, urbanizing rural feuding by forcing

noble families to live in the cities. In the end cities became residual legatees, gaining ultimate control of their rural estates. In this way they came to be comprised of several geographical expressions.

The city in the absolute sense was that area within its walls, whether the initial two hundred acres of Florence or its subsequent enlargement to some fifteen hundred acres. The boundary represented by the wall was puissant beyond the simple ability to repel attackers: citizenship might well be vested only within the wall; collection of murrage tolls was founded on the notion of value rendered by affording access to the privileges that lay within; and those within were exempt from feudal and imperial exactions that most likely existed outside. Beyond the walls was a band, in Italy the *contado*, a "rural area surrounding the city, which formerly had been under the jurisdiction of the feudal power and later came under the commune's control. Florence's *contado* extended from Empoli and Prato in the west to beyond the Arno and Sieve rivers in the east."[46] Even farther away was the *distretto*, a zone gained by the city through its own subjugatory efforts rather than by succession to feudal rights, as in the *contado*.

The substantial import of this evolution comes from what it tells us about city-country relations. South of the Alps the Roman Empire declined more through the disintegration of imperial ties than because of the total destruction of Roman institutions, notably cities. The resulting jealously independent towns and estates—the urban commune and the rural *latifundium*—often united in an alliance against another commune and its associated *latifundia*. This political alliance of *citta-contado-distretto* produced a two-edged sword in the matter of economic development. It assured a fairly extensive tributary area for a city, which meant these cities could grow early in the history of urban revival after the Dark Ages. But in contrast to the situation north of the Alps, where feudal rural organization conflicted early and heavily with the nascent cities, in Languedoc, Provence, upper and parts of southern Italy, cities possessed some independence of action. Thus it was difficult in the Mediterranean lands, where an extensive city-system was typical, to expand beyond the early city-system. In the north, on the other hand, once the feudal economic order was broken, vast growth for commerce and industry, under the political-economic philosophy of national mercantilism, was assured. The city-system ruled long in Toulouse, Narbonne, Beziers, Avignon, Milan, Florence, and the cities of the Exarchate, as well as in many other towns of the Mediterranean. It brought early city

[44]Loc. cit.
[45]*The estimate of Giovanni Villani, quoted in Brucker, op. cit.,* p. 51.

[46]Ibid., *p. 4.*

power but ultimately stultified the further growth that made Europe north of the Alps the leader after about the year 1600, when the Commercial Revolution of the sixteenth century had tipped the scale against the *citta-contado-distretto* system.

One is forced into a rather puritanical conclusion in this contrast between the Mediterranean and the north. Because the cities had to struggle so hard to come into renewed existence and to rise in power against the highly elaborated and powerful feudal system, their institutions and practices gained particular strength. City air did make men free, as the medieval German saying *Stadtluft macht frie* declared. In doing so, it shaped a society, and ultimately a set of economic practices and religious beliefs, internally consistent and generally opposed to the factional, repressive, and lowly-productive society of the countryside. Finally, neither the Commercial Revolution nor the Industrial Revolution took place in the seat of economic power in the High Middle Ages. Already in the late Middle Ages, the greatest advances toward responsible government were occurring where rural-urban conflict seemed most strident. The city communes in central and northern France, in the Low Countries, and in parts of Germany, as well as the more powerful of the city corporations growing up in England, were creating civic institutions to care for the economic and social interests of the average person. They were also extending the franchise in city elections far beyond the narrow patriciate that literally "governed" the Mediterranean town, commonly tyrannizing the less powerful and the poor.

Florence as an Example of a Mediterranean City

Not only in urban-rural relations but also in morphology a sharp contrast can be drawn between the physical form of the Mediterranean city and that north of the Alps. We have viewed the differences in platting and street layout. But let us look in detail at Florence, which serves as an archetype of the south at least symbolically, if not in all details.

Since the general outlines of the southern house and the factional quarter have been established, we can easily understand the specific qualities of the city on the Arno. A difficulty faces us from the very beginning because although adequate "evidence from documents and buildings survives to describe the aristocratic mode of living in Renaissance Florence, (the) information on lower-class housing is scantier and more fragmentary. The dwellings inhabited by the urban poor were primitive and unsubstantial; they have not survived the ravages of time."[47]

Gene Brucker turned to tax records which offered some glimpse of how the working class lived. "Most artisans and laborers lived in small houses of two or three stories (one room per story) or single-room cottages . . . .Tax records contain a few references to buildings in which rooms or stories were rented out to several individuals or families, but the apartment house was a rare phenomenon in fifteenth-century Florence."[48] But the notion of reducing the quality of residence for speculative gain in rent, if not of property value itself, had seemingly entered the minds of men like Datini who had capitals to invest. One Alessandro Borromei, a wealthy Pisan émigré with large real estate holdings in Florence, was reported in 1427 to have bought the palace of the noble Amieri family. "He converted this structure into a multiple-unit tenement, renting shops on the ground floor to merchants and artisans, and single rooms in the upper stories as living quarters."[49] Clearly fifteenth-century Florence must have been entering a stage when the prototypes for worker housing were beginning to shift from the country cottage to the townsman's house, necessarily transforming its interior arrangement. We witness this shift all over western Europe; the scale of city activity increased as the reach of the resident traders was pushed outward and the calls they placed on indigenous manufacture were enlarged. The technology of cottage industry continued but, when located in the city, the physical provision to shelter it changed.

The role of the factional quarter persisted, though its expression seemed to hide its origins. As Brucker notes, the distinctive feature of Renaissance Florence was the heterogeneity, in social and economic terms, of neighborhoods and quarters. The rich had no quarter of their own, as had been true in Imperial Rome, and there were no districts solely occupied by the poor. Cottages and *palazzi* were intermixed, as were woolen factories and retail shops, churches and religious foundations. As in Roman times, shops occupied the ground floor of sometimes palatial buildings and the rich merchant and shoemaker might live side-by-side. Brucker tells us that this great mixing of classes and occupations resulted from Florence's method of growth (organic in our terms) and a social practice wherein each

[47]Ibid., *p. 22.*
[48]Loc. cit.
[49]Ibid., *p. 23.*

important family was associated with a particular neighborhood. There the founder of the family had first resided and subsequent generations had remained clustered for protection in a city of factionalism. Even after 1400, when the threat was much less, there was still great social pressure to remain in the "family neighborhood" to enhance the political role of one of the main elements of the urban patriciate.[50]

Only in a city ruled by authoritarian patriarchs and divided by factionalism would such a social geography be shaped; we do not see this pattern north of the Alps. Its persistence to the south even into modern times may help to explain the differences in the location of higher income in lands of northern European colonization and lands of Mediterranean settlement. Throughout Latin America, the rich and powerful seem to favor central-city residence to a degree unknown in North America above the Rio Grande. Possibly the role of social and political leadership enjoyed by the powerful patriciates in Mediterranean cities may in some way be thus expressed in overseas areas.

We have given sufficient notice to the tower-house and its cluster, but we should look briefly at the compound of the merchant and the street of the manufacturing *fattor*. Datini's time and experience give us a picture of the trader's compound.

The centre of their life, as for every merchant in foreign trading settlements, was their own fondaco—*the group of buildings which was at once shop and office, warehouse and dwelling. If at home (at Florence), in Calimala or Por S. Maria, a* fondaco *was often merely a merchant's counting-house and shop (above which, perhaps, he lived), in settlements abroad it still kept much of the character of the Arab* funduk *from which it took its name. Originally built, no doubt, to shelter merchants and their wares from the assaults of wild desert tribes, these fondachi still had something of the aspect of fortified castles. In their great inner courtyards the long trains of pack-animals were watered and stabled, the slaves assembled for inspection and sale, and the bales of merchandise unpacked and stored, while the buildings served as offices, warehouses, and dwellings. Here under the jurisdiction of their own consul . . .the merchants could safely transact their business according to their own laws, and pray to their own God. Here . . .they tried to teach their Moorish slaves the rudiments of Tuscan cooking.*[51]

This picture of the *fondaco* does not distinguish quite so clearly as we might wish the trading compound of the native from that of the foreigner. Each would tend to

have a cluster of buildings surrounding a courtyard in which goods were loaded, unloaded, sorted, and inspected. If located in a foreign land, its gate and walls might be sturdier and the functions of the consul and accompanying chaplain were introduced. In such a situation the merchant would be a foreigner to the culture and the polity, tolerated for the time being but not fully admitted to its life because of his insistence upon maintaining ties to an alien state, culture, and possibly religion. Just as the Jew might live in a ghetto to maintain his identity, the foreign merchant must live and operate in an enclosure with a similar degree of extraterritoriality. Among Mediterraneans this enclosure was the *fondaco;* for Germans it remained a *stahlyard,*

The Palazzo Riccardi Medici in Florence is still suggestive of the secure home of the leader of a political faction in an Italian city. No longer a simple tower, it still remained a frowningly powerful structure.

[50]Ibid., *p. 23. Emphasis supplied.*
[51]*Origo, op. cit., p. 120.*

which the English corrupted into "the steelyard," as at London. The domestic trader still favored the cluster of buildings about a courtyard since pilferage and theft were ever-present problems.

For a picture of the establishment of a wealthy and powerful merchant we may turn to a striking survival, the palace of the great French merchant Jacques Coeur, in Bourges in Berry. Probably the most splendid building built by a commoner in France during the Middle Ages, this magnificent palace still combined the counting-house with the chateau. A great doorway opens from the street into a courtyard where goods as well as noble guests were received and dispatched. Stair-towers led from an arcaded ground floor, where goods could be stored and trade and inspection carried out in rainy weather, to the upper floors. A second level was given over to elegant rooms for Coeur and his family; the attics were used for storage and the counters at which less bulky goods were traded. Jacques Coeur need not defend himself against a foreign populace or as yet against a suspicious monarch—he was the king's treasurer until his fall from favor in 1451. Yet he felt it necessary to have an enclosure in which to trade and his attics for storage were remarkably proof against pilferage not only by being at the top of his palace, but further, because the building was erected atop the walls of the Gallo-Roman city of *Avaricum*.

The Rise of Industrial Quarters

Much as Florence was a great combination of hundreds of family neighborhoods, such as the cluster of the Albizzi along the Borgo degli Albizzi or the palaces of the Peruzzi around the Piazza dei Peruzzi, there was some concentration of workers in particular trades in certain streets. These suggest the partial existence of occupational quarters so typical of cities north of the Alps. Even more they herald the initial stages of the creation of true industrial quarters in cities.[52] In Florence, Brucker tells us that cloth manufactories were widely spread, but some of the most demanding and mechanized of the stages of the production were beginning to show concentration. Dyeing, washing, and soap-making clustered on the banks of the Arno. In

other trades such as arms-making, forges were concentrated, and in certain pariah industries it was decreed that they must locate at the edge of the city.[53]

Areas of Customer Access and the Rise of Land-Rent

Among the merchants who sought to deal directly with the public, perhaps for only a part of their total sales but still for a component of sufficient worth to influence the choice of premises to be occupied, location was based not on *occupational association* but upon *customer access*. "Rents for both houses and shops were naturally higher in the center, and they tended to diminish as one moved toward the periphery. Commanding very high prices were shops located near the Piazza della Signoria (Palazzo Vecchio) and the Piazza del Doumo (cathedral), or along the street connecting these squares."[54] Brucker shows that a retail clothing shop near the center rented for 118 florins per year in 1427 and a barber shop on the Piazza della Signoria went for 27 florins. Houses near the center rented for about 25 florins annually but at the edge such houses could be had normally for less than 10 florins annual rent. As might therefore be anticipated the poorer workmen—cloth workers, servants, and casual laborers—lived at the city's edge. In those areas with the most badly paid workers—wool carders, beaters, and combers—the rents for truly slum dwellings were one or two florins a year.[55]

Already in the fifteenth century, provision of housing for workers was strongly based on rent and rent-paying ability. Some instances of the self-contained establishments, where master and workmen occupied the same quarters, were quite ample in scale. In Datini's great house at nearby Prato we find such an example. "It will be observed that, though there were many servants (in Datini's house), there were no servants' rooms—the explanation being that they slept wherever was most convenient—in the kitchen, on the

[52]*Brucker, op. cit., p. 23.*

[53]Ibid., *p. 24.*
[54]Loc. cit.
[55]Loc. cit.

landing, or on truckle beds in the room of their master and mistress."[56] Normally some one or several of the employees in the counting-house also slept there. The independent worker, at least in the sense that no one cared much for his wealth, health, or soul, was cast out into the rental market for housing, to fare badly for the most part. No doubt to a considerable degree the uncertainty of the market for rental housing caused its provision to be halting and inadequate and its pricing often to be unreasonable in terms of current wage levels.

The Nature of Medieval Housing

Appraising the qualities of medieval housing is in some ways difficult. The Middle Ages were a time very different in ways and goods from our own. People had not become accustomed either to privacy or to many possessions. The fact that Datini's servants slept all about him demonstrates how little architectural elegance

The courtyard of the Palais de Jacques Coeur in Bourges is essentially that of a fondaco made elegant to impress the boyhood acquaintances.

had to do with physical separation; elegance was for ostentation and display, not for retreat and privacy. One of the great contributions of the Tuscans to medieval architecture was the *loggia*, originally either an open but covered space between the house and the street, or else a covered gallery wide open to the street but raised to the top story of the building to gain more air during the stifling heat of the Italian summer. In both forms entertainment was "staged" to be observed by the common people in response to the strange notion, which long persisted, that for the poor to watch the feasting and extravagance of the wealthy was a most welcome treat.[57]

The inventories of furnishings that have come down to us from medieval times suggest an austerity within the rooms. As Iris Origo notes of Datini's inventory, "The list of furniture, as in most houses of the time, is to our eyes rather meagre. . . . By far the most important piece of furniture was the bed. In Francesco's [Datini] and Margherita's room it was 6 *braccia* wide (about 4 yards), with a low footboard all around it which fulfilled the double purpose of bench and chest." Heavy bedcovers and feather comforters appear to have been used. "Thus, in bed, at least Francesco and Margherita—even though they probably slept naked—cannot have suffered from the cold!" In addition, the room held coffers and chests, in which the wife's dowry was stored, as well as "a *cappelinaio*, or hatstand, a cupboard, a single chair, and, finally, both in this room and in the best guest-room, a *desco da parto dipinto*, or painted 'tray for childbirth.' Such trays [were] so called because they were often presented to women after childbirth. . . ."

This set of appointments may sound lavish for a bedroom, but the bedroom was the main room of the house, where much of the time at home was spent and where visitors were entertained. The title "gentleman of the king's bedchamber" was in no sense symbolic when it originated, for it was there that gentlemen-in-waiting waited upon the king, as ladies-in-waiting attended the queen in her chamber.

Elsewhere, the Florentine mansion held mainly armoires and chests, a few wooden chairs, a table or two, some benches, and other beds. The "main hall seems to have been furnished very barely, and chiefly with tables: one large dining-table eight *braccia* long (5½ yards), one long walnut trestle-table, and two small round tables. There were also two reed chairs and one bench and five pine poles for hanging up the washing; in the loggia a wooden press, a pail, and some jugs and glasses. Datini's office, too, had a small bed in it and the rest of its furniture was a big trestle-table with a little stool, a long bench (no doubt for clients and

---

[56]*Origo*, op. cit., *p. 248.*

[57]*For a discussion of the* loggia, *see Origo*, op. cit., *p. 247.*

peasants), three cassapanche, and two shields with Francesco's crest." Even the guest room in which Datini entertained Louis II of Anjou had merely a double and a single bed, and some chests.[58]

This detail of the furnishing of one merchant's house should make clear to us that household belonging were few even among the wealthy, though they may have entertained extravagantly. "Perhaps the most sparsely furnished rooms were the kitchens. The downstairs kitchen contained only a dining-table, a *madia* (the flour-chest which is still to be found in every Tuscan kitchen), a wooden sink, a safe for dried meat, and the usual truckle-bed: the upstairs kitchen, only two wooden tables and a chest." Cooking utensils were massive and simple for the most part. The *haute cuisine* of the European aristocrat lay several centuries away and across the Alps. Italian cooking then, as now, depended mainly on freshness of ingredients and amplitude of quantity to gain what distinction it might. Stoves were primitive, often merely a brazier burning away in the middle of the room, which helps explain the evolution of a quickly prepared cuisine with little dependence upon long cooking. The French had the oven and the Italians the medieval equivalent of a "one-burner." The persistence of culture cannot be questioned when we look at the grip of these cooking practices even today, when the stove has come belatedly to Italy.

If the simplicity of the rich man's house has been established, we need not doubt that the working class lived sparely indeed. Evidence suggests that the poor family had only a single room where they lived, slept, cooked, and ate. Little evidence of their furniture survives but doubtless it was meager; probably a simple pallet, or if they were skilled, the luxury of a bed, some bed-clothing, a table, maybe a bench, a chest, and a brazier. So long as the concept of privacy was limited, the goods that a family possessed would hardly require more than a single room for their housing.

In a situation such as that in Prato—the "Italian Manchester"—or Florence, the invasion of the household by various processes of manufacture must have been widely felt. We know that certain quarters were occupied by specific trades and certain streets by particular operations. "Even today Prato has a *Via dei Lanaiuoli* (wool merchants), *dei Cimatori* (wool clippers), *dei Tintori* (dyers), and close beside them (as was always the case wherever ready money was likely to be required) the *Via dei Guidei.*"[59]

The domestication of industry is strongly suggested

The Piazza della Signoria in Florence in the sixteenth century had become a Renaissance piazza major used for all sorts of civic activities. Here the hanging and subsequent burning of the Catholic reformer Savanarola, who first angered the pope and ultimately the Florentines, took place.

[58]*Origo*, op. cit., *pp. 250-263.*

[59]Op. cit., *p. 36. Prato is characterized as the "Manchester Toscano" in Piero Bargellini,* Florence, *Paris: Presses Universitaires de France, 1964, p. 279.*

by the absence, for the most part, either of surviving factory premises or records thereof. We know of the merchant's courtyard and of some of the mechanized workshops of the Middle Ages, such as the fulling mills in Prato and around Bristol. But we know little of the actual premises in which other operations were carried out, suggesting that those activities were undertaken in the house or apartment where the worker lived. We shall examine the physical structure of the worker's quarter in Chapter 7, but let us note its arrival on the stage of urban morphogenesis. For the most part there was no geography either of commercial establishments or of factories. In a few cases, such as that of the Piazza dei Peruzzi in Florence, a grouping of merchants from a single family may have created a "commercial quarter;" the grouping of processors needing a single localized resource, such as the water provided by the canals dug across Prato's "meadow" or through medieval Augsburg, may have led to an "industrial district." For the most part the medieval Mediterranean city was broken down into family quarters in which all of the multiferous activities of the age were carried on. The physical structure of the city grew, not out of economic functions, but rather from the social geography of the time and place.

The Medieval Structure in Cities North of the Alps

The fascination of the Middle Ages is greatest when we turn north of the Alps. In the youthful cities in the north and west of Europe, the rootstock of the Roman city was still vigorous enough to allow the successful grafting of vital and functional morphologies characteristic of the economic creations of the medieval commerce. The Romans had built cities all the way from the Welsh and Scottish marches to the Rhine and Danube. Something of that heritage had survived into the eleventh and twelfth centuries even after five hundred years of quarrying by Frankish and Anglo-Saxon farmers living nearby. The quality of the site, in particular, remained, leading fairly promptly to the resurrection of city growth once the long-distance connections were renewed with the end of the Dark Ages. The frequently wooden buildings of Roman urbanization in these distant reaches of the Empire had been swept away but the street-grid and other elements of the urban support structure often survived. And in a few places Roman monuments remained, battered but not demolished— the gates of Autun and the great Porta Negra of Trier, the amphitheaters at St. Albans, Moudon, and Autun. Finally the site of the Roman settlement and the often considerable remains of the Roman road system stood as the significant bequest of the empire.

Whatever the form of the modular plots found in the medieval cities of the north, the buildings placed on them grew out of a fairly consistent need and a basic technology common to most of the lands in the north and west of Europe. The need was to house a population directly engaged in commercial and craftsmen's activities, who were in many instances the political and social leaders of the town. This combination of economic activity and political control distinguished the north from the Mediterranean. Although in the north conflict might arise between the burghers and their lord, as for example between the leading men of Ghent and the Counts of Flanders, there was no herd of petty nobility steeped in notions of feudal vassalage, which disintegrated the society in the typical Italian town.

In the north the city powers in conflict or cooperation with the suzerain did not lead to endless blood-feuding and retaliation, as in Italy, but to one of two normal relationships. If the burghers were powerful in comparison to the overlord, the urban commune emerged, as in Flanders during the High Middle Ages; on the other hand, when the suzerain came to dominate, as did the Spanish overlords in later centuries, a cruel and despotic repression of civic liberties took place. But there was not the malady of internal conflict that became the wasting disease of the Mediterranean city. When the evil of Austrian and Spanish control was overthrown, the north still had a firm basis for civic cooperation and development that did not exist in Italy at the end of the Middle Ages.

In considerable measure the eclipse of the Italian city as the urban leader in Europe stemmed from this contrast between its internalized conflict and the conflict with a basically outside force found in the north. The contrast was like one between a pain coming from external pressures which, when relieved, leaves the body able to recover its health and an internal cancer which saps the body's basic vitality. As we shall see, the efforts of the despotic popes could "beautify" Rome in the sixteenth and seventeenth centuries but their highly undemocratic practices left it a pathetic shell of a city until Pius IX, Pio Nono, was deprived of control in 1870.

The absence of unremitting internal political conflict did not mean that all was harmonious in the north. Competition was active, with occasional outright conflict, but it generally stemmed from efforts by various groups to gain similar objectives, though with different apportionments of the ultimate benefit. Workers and masters argued over wages and powers, and various gilds sought to monopolize particular activities to the exclusion of others. Contest was not missing, but dogma; basic agreements existed as to the needs for civic liberties and common efforts were made to expand the economic sphere of the city. Just as the conflict between city and suzerain was fundamentally an externalized fight, so the objective of the northern city tended to be scoring off against another city rather than one's closest neighbor. Some cities lost their external support, and thus shrank as economic organisms, but the towns that prevailed grew rapidly. The urban glory of Europe moved north of the Alps by the close of the late Middle Ages. The architectural grandeur of the Renaissance cities in the south confuses the truth. These fast became the glittering facades of nearly empty purpose surrounding a decadent aristocracy of feudalism and the church with a pomp it did not earn and could not maintain. When the vital forces of the Enlightenment, economic liberalism, and increasing personal liberty emerged in the seventeenth and eighteenth centuries, the rot behind the facades of Rome, Naples, Milan, and Florence began to show through.

Competition and Its Restraint Shape the Northern City: The Gild

Just as the factional conflict of the Mediterranean city helped to shape its urban morphology, the occupational competition in the north helped to determine the shape of the city there. To understand the role of occupation, we must look at the institutions that came to represent collective economic interests. Evidence suggests that early in the course of urbanization of the north the city's economic life was conducted on a rather individual basis. Some men, and occasionally women, proved better merchants or craftsmen than others; that is, they were more economically successful, not necessarily more skillful workmen. The medieval notions of profit, just price, and excessive ambition in the material world were greatly challenged by too obvious an individual success. A church, utterly dependent upon a traditional order for survival in the face of obvious corruption, was strongly urged to

a course of resisting change, institutionalizing balance and order, and rejecting the notion of individual decision in matters of ethics, freedom, and conscience. Demonstrably, *collegiality* was far to be preferred to individuality, save in the instances of divine ordination thought to be the foundation of the decrees of monarchs, temporal and spiritual.

To maintain order and balance became the central purpose of medieval economic institutions, though breaks in the smooth flow of that tradition did take place and were often the events of which history takes the greatest notice. Still in seeking to understand the normal development of northern cities and their morphogenesis we must be concerned with the institutions as generally conceived.

Fritz Rörig visualized the origin of the gild, which became the institution of order and control, as first rooted in the conflict between the workers in newly established towns and the ecclesiastical authorities and lay overlords who tended to dominate those places. Conflict had been present even when the town's residents were mostly independent workers at a craft. When the long-distance traders settled in the proto-towns the situation of conflict was enhanced because they brought their own law with them, the law merchant that they had developed on long "trading journeys which at the time were still conducted in the cooperative manner of a caravan. Nor did the traders who settled in the new towns wish to abandon this spirit" when they settled down. "The guilds were an inevitable consequence. This was where they met together [and] where they celebrated their festivals, which occasions were liable to be rather more sumptuous than the spirit of ecclesiastical decorum considered appropriate." Gilds combined men of common economic and social interest and formed a strong force against the bishops' efforts to force more production from reluctant workers through the powerful threat of excommunication. The gild was "an organization in which the small man in the town—the artisans and small shopkeepers—saw a remedy for his complaints against the bishop and his officials."[60]

Boissonade finds a different origin for the grouping of small men for fraternal purposes in these "secret associations, brotherhoods, gilds, *stellungen*, prohibited by the authorities, wherein were organized seditious movements, and those peasant revolts which broke out on all sides in Italy, Gaul, Fresia (Holland), Flanders, Saxony, at irregular intervals during the eighth and ninth centuries." Those original uprisings of "bands of serfs and their womenfolk, who were more cruel even than the men, attacked seignorial domains,

[60]*Rörig, op. cit., pp. 19-20.*

pillaged, burned, tortured, massacred without discernment or pity until a cruel repression brought them back for a while to obedience."[61] The return to "obedience" came with the acceptance of an established order repressive of human freedom and the concerns of the common man and was, as a consequence, restive indeed. The reestablishment of that order strengthened the loss of geographical freedom that became serfdom, tying the more common folk to the lands they tilled and making escape from the countryside the only possible emancipation. Because the church was the largest landowner of medieval times, it made common cause with the powerful nobles in enforcing this geographical bondage, adding the weapon even more awful in medieval times, denial of indulgence and solace to serfs who broke their enforced contract to remain in the country.

Henri Pirenne looked for the basis of urban liberty in the functional contrast between urban and rural institutions. "In no civilization is city life evolved independently of commerce and industry." Pirenne goes on to argue specifically of the medieval city, "At no era in history is there so marked a contrast as that which their social and economic organization presented to the social and economic organization of the country." And the contrast was greatest in human qualities: "Never before had there existed, it seems, a class of men so specifically and strictly urban as was the medieval bourgeoisie."[62] In Greek city-states, synoecism tied the country and town together from a rural beginning; in Roman times, the tie was as strong but knotted in a reverse direction. But in the Middle Ages the country and the town were in constant confrontation with one another.

That opposition was probably of little worry to the rural magnates—barons and great ecclesiastics—until "[t]he organization of commerce in the Middle Ages . . . obliged the peripatetic . . . 'merchant venturers' . . . to settle at fixed points." That obligation came because "[i]n the interval between their trips and especially during the bad season which made the sea, the rivers and the roads impassable, they necessarily had to gather in certain places in the region."[63] With this powerful economic group possessed of good organization and a virile will resident periodically in towns, those places took a firmer stand against the repressive policies of baron and churchmen. We have tended to inherit a most partisan view of this period, as Pirenne explains, because what records and accounts survive

were prepared by churchmen who presented their view of the time and their obsession with the religious purpose. "They could not neglect the recital of the wars and political conflicts which reacted on the Church, but there was no reason for them to have taken pains to note the beginnings of city life, for which they were lacking in comprehension no less than sympathy. . . . As for first-hand sources—that is to say, written and compiled by townsmen—there are none in existence earlier than the end of the twelfth century. . . . [Then a few] maps and records supplement this poverty to a certain extent."[64] In light of this poverty of sources, Pirenne calls for a recourse "to inference and hypothesis in this study of origins." Accepting that *modus operandi*, in the study of morphogenesis the existence of maps assumes greater importance to us and the survival of some physical pattern within the city can serve as an invaluable crutch to steady inference and to serve as the tool to focus hypothesis.

Which of possible sites for towns will be taken up and developed? Central-place theory supplies an answer, but history shows it unresponsive save in the most dominantly feudal of areas. As Pirenne points out, rich areas "in the agricultural and desminial civilization of the Middle Ages [places such as Stavelot and

These houses in the Grand' Place of Brussels present elaborate facades that bespeak the prosperity and power of the gilds, whose houses these are (restored after the French bombardment of 1695).

[61]*Boissonade*, op. cit., *p. 101.*

[62]*Henri Pirenne,* Medieval Cities: Their Origin and the Revival of Trade, *Princeton: Princeton University Press, 1925, pp. 135 and 136-137.*

[63]Ibid., *pp. 139-140.*

[64]Ibid., *pp. 145-146.*

Malmedy] . . . were notable for their wealth and influence. But situated too far from the great highways of communication, they were not affected by the economic revival nor, so to speak fecondated thereby. In the midst of the flowering which it inspired, they remained sterile, like seed fallen upon stony ground. *None of them rose above the rank of mere half-rural market-towns."* Clearly two systems of settlement existed in the Middle Ages; one we might call "central-place" in deference to Christaller and the other "mercantile" to reflect both purpose and origin. One explanation, one model, cannot serve for both these systems of settlement location and support. As Pirenne noted, these central-places (as we have called them) "had on the whole only an auxiliary function. Adapted to a social order very different from that which witnessed the birth of cities, they could not have been able to give birth to the latter by their own forces. [Cities] were, so to speak, the crystallization points of commercial activity. It did not arise from them—it came to them from without (in long-distance trade)."[65]

Looking at the economic institutions within the cities that were growing on distant trade, Pirenne notes in a different study, *Economic and Social History of Medieval Europe*, "It is a familiar fact that the clergy were a foreign element in the medieval town, their privileges excluded them from sharing in those of the city." In this status they were allied to the great rural landowners, and with them it was true that "Amidst the commercial and industrial population [of the city] their economic role was simply that of consumers." Noting the residence of nobles in Italian towns, and their involvement in trading and merchant navigation in some of them, he contrasts the lands north of the Alps. "In Northern Europe, on the other hand, almost all the nobles left the [Roman] towns to settle in their castles in the country [and they were not forced by the towns to return as in Italy]. It is only in exceptional circumstances that a knightly family is to be found, here and there, isolated and, as it were, astray in the midst of bourgeois society. It was not until the end of the Middle Ages that the aristocracy, by that time less quarrelsome and more eager for comfort, began to build themselves luxurious town houses."[66] For the rural aristocracy, those town houses were to remain a secondary residence occupied only periodically during a "social season" shaped by their peers in the countryside, not by the bourgeoisie.

Thus, in the northern city the ground was left clear, uncluttered by inherited power, for the shaping of the

first truly urban society, of which we have the great good fortune to be the heirs. When the formerly wandering merchants settled on the ground, they could begin to organize social, political, economic, and even religious institutions to meet the needs of the two supporting activities of a town—commerce and industry. Though industry was less widespread than commerce, it tended to follow in the path of commerce for supply of the trading goods on which it relied. The first urban institution tended, therefore, to be the gild merchant which had existed even while the merchant venturers were peripatetic and came to be domesticated when they took up city residence.

The functions of the gild were several: to assure the quality of production or the ethics of trade; to serve as a representative element in the creation of a collegial form of city government; to care for the social and personal security needs of its members; to limit the entrance to trade in the guise of assuring the mastery thereof by the applicant; and, less consciously, to shape an organization whose power would be sufficient to defend the rights of merchants, craftsmen, and the city against the repression by the established order of aristocracy and church. For each, an "aversion to trade was unconquerable."

[65]Ibid., *pp. 151-152. Emphasis supplied.*
[66]Henri Pirenne, Economic and Social History of Medieval Europe [*original edition in French, 1933*], *New York: Harcourt, Brace and Company, 1937, pp. 168-169.*

The Portus: The Place Where the Merchants' Town Began

The wandering merchants often settled first at the gates of the town, the *portus*, which initially was a small specialized settlement set up in timid fashion at the foot of a *bourg* or at the gate of a tiny walled village. These may have been the most common form for the settlement of merchants but we cannot be sure. Preexisting towns included those of ecclesiastical and palatine origin as well as fortified villages.

Details are lacking concerning the gradual peopling of towns. It is not known how the first traders, who came to locate there, settled in the midst of the preexisting population. The towns, whose precincts frequently included empty spaces occupied by fields and gardens, must have furnished them at the start with a place which soon became too restricted. It is certain that in many of them, from the tenth century on, they were forced to locate outside the walls. At Verdun they built a fortified enclosure (negotiatorum claustrum), *joined to the city by two bridges. At Ratisbonne the "city of merchants" (urbs mercatorum) arose beside the episcopal city, and the same thing is to be seen at Strasbourg and elsewhere.*[67]

Thus, the general practice, either in the classical model of the castle *(bourg)* and its merchants' camp below the walls *(faubourg)* or in the *urbs mercatorum* outside the bishop's town, was that of a separate, self-contained area in which the merchant practiced his art.

Such a place was called, in medieval terms, a *portus.*

Between a portus *and a market or a fair the distinction is very clear. While the latter were periodic meeting places of buyers and sellers, the former was a permanent place of trade, a center of uninterrupted traffic. After the seventh century Dinant, Huy, Valenciennes and Cambrai were places with a* portus, *and in consequence transfer points. The economic slump of the eighth century and the Norseman invasions naturally ruined their business. It was not until the tenth century that the old* porti *took on new life or new ones were established, as at Bruges, Ghent, Ypres, St. Omer, and elsewhere. At the same date there appears in Anglo-Saxon texts the word "port," employed as a synonym for the Latin words* urbs *and* civitas, *and even at the present day the term "port" is commonly met with in the names of cities of every land of English speech.*[68]

The *portus* became the first place where mercantile government could be envisaged and a law distinct in its practices worked out. In the market town itself, the regulations were those of baronial or clerical overlord aimed at restricting sharp trading practices, gaining a proper assize of goods, and a tax return for the privilege of the market. This form was essentially domestic law of a particular sort. For the fair something else was needed as the merchants found operation impossible in a context which viewed them as aliens. The special code for the fair, *pied poudre* or *piepowder law,* was created and restricted to its geographical locale. Under it, alien and denizen were equal, but only within the fair confines, for interests directly associated with it, and for its term.

The *portus* when it grew up was both continuous in occupation and geographically determinate, to the extent it had to seek its own law to survive socially and economically. Market regulations applied to retail trade alone, piepowder law to the special temporal and geographical conditions of the fair, and feudal law to a serfdom unable to move or to engage in the realities of trade. As Pirenne saw it, "The bourgeois themselves were far from taking up a revolutionary attitude towards this society. They took for granted the authority of the territorial princes, the privileges of the nobility and, above all, those of the Church. . . .They merely desired a place in the sun, and their demands were confined to their most indispensible needs." Those needs attached to the residents of a particular area so, given the strongly territorial quality of medieval law, special laws could be adopted to gratify needs.

Of the latter, the most indispensible was personal liberty; without liberty, that is to say, without the power to come and go, to do business, to sell goods, a power not enjoyed by serfdom, trade would be impossible. Thus they claimed it, simply for the advantages it conferred, and nothing was further from the mind of the bourgeoisie than any idea of freedom as a natural right; in their eyes it was merely a useful one. Besides, many of them possessed it de facto; they were immigrants, who had come from too far off for their lord to be traced and who, since their serfdom could not be presumed, necessarily passed for free, although born of unfree parents. But the fact had to be transformed into a right. It was essential that the villiens, who came to settle in the town to seek a new livelihood, should feel safe and should not have to fear being taken back by force from the manors from which they had escaped. They must be delivered from labour services and from all the hated dues by which the servile population was burdened, such as the obligation to marry only a woman of their own class and to leave to the lord part of their inheritance. Willy-nilly, in the course of the twelfth century these claims, backed up as they often were by dangerous revolts, had to be granted.[69]

To understand the growth of towns we must keep clearly in mind the attachment of liberty to place; to understand the growth of capitalism we must keep in mind as well the extinction of the duty of heriot which had until the late Middle Ages diminished the individual's possession on death.

The geographical concept of the merchant's *portus* furnished the legal basis for the peopling of cities through the transformation of serfs into cityfolk. "Freedom became the legal status of the bourgeoisie, so much so that it was no longer a personal privilege only, but a *territorial* one, inherent in urban soil just as serfdom was in manorial soil. In order to obtain it, it was enough to have resided for a year and a day within the walls of the town. City air makes man free, says the German proverb."[70] Admittedly the lord could recapture his errant serf if he caught him within the year, but the natural antipathy between burgesses and barons made the search of even a nearby city difficult, and of a distant one impossible. We cannot measure the impact this feudal law had in setting up migration over a fair distance; we can logically assume that it encouraged it.

[67]*Pirenne,* Medieval Cities, op. cit., *pp. 146-147.*
[68]Ibid., *p. 149.*

[69]Ibid., *p. 50.*
[70]Ibid., *p. 51. Emphasis supplied.*

In this view of late medieval houses from Nürnberg the Dürer-Haus stands at the center with its steeply pitched roof with dormers and the sort of window that could be used with a pulley to raise goods to the attic for storage. To the right is the Pilatus-Haus.

With a legal mechanism making rural implosion on the city possible, the growth of the town was assured if economic demand materialized, as we know it did particularly in the twelfth century. "Thus the medieval town was essentially the home of the burgesses; it existed only for them and because of them. It was in their own interest, and in their own interest alone, that they created its institutions and organized its economy."[71] The institution most universally adopted

[71]Ibid., *p. 169.*

was the confraternity of workers in a particular trade. Since these gilds were not everywhere the same, no concise picture of them will apply in all aspects to any particular city, or in any specific aspect to all cities. Yet we must examine the gild to understand the internal physical and social structure of the town in the Middle Ages.

The Occupation Quarter in Europe North of the Alps

The discontinuity of urban institutions in Europe north of the Alps led to a sharply contrasting social foundation for cities there as opposed to the Mediterranean. The gild took the place of the political faction, and the *occupation quarter* replaced the factional district. These gilds, preexisting the city residence of merchants, became the basis for the collegial government of towns when these powerful and energetic men came to settle there. The expressions of the gild—its hall, and the shops and houses of its members—met the eye of the visitor in the north, rather than the tower houses and the restive collection of people centering on them typical of Italy. In many places the gilds assumed the support of particular parish churches so religion in turn took on this occupational division, to such an extent that the medieval city of the north became a physical collection of occupation quarters and a political college of gild representatives.

The gild fitted particularly well in the ordering of medieval society. Individuals were seldom thought of outside their class, and overlords and monarchs desired to deal with corporate entities rather than individuals. The tendency toward syndicalist combination was further strengthened by the nature of medieval taxation; excises on sales, transactions, and other activities might with some assurance be anticipated and commuted into an annual value. Thus, if a king found himself short of money (a regal fault to this very day), he might anticipate taxes ultimately due him by trading important privileges to a gild, or the collection of gilds that formed the town, in return for early "payment" of the expected return from the excise. Given their power and increasing wealth, the gilds often managed to commute many small payments into one large one, buying for the future freedom not yet enjoyed by that group. So the fondness that governments have ever had for dealing with a corporation (in lower levels) joined with the search for increasing social, economic, and even religious freedom by the townspeople to strike a bargain unapproachable in the faction-divided city of the south.

The gildhall became the locus of the basic component of the collegial organization and the repository of its charter. Charters were of such a value in holding the monarch to his past bargains, as the Massachusetts Puritans learned five hundred years later, that they must be guarded with great care and displayed with equal pride. The gildhall was the center of the life of men in trade because trade was at the core of their existence. As the economic community in a town gained control over its own activities, the gild came to represent the basic unit of government. It controlled access to the status of freeman by requiring mastery of a trade and admission to the "mystery"; it sent representatives to serve on a board of aldermen who ran the town. In controlling a trade, the gild was a mechanism for both quality and maintenance and economic balance. To be admitted to a gild, a boy had first to be apprenticed to a working master (except in some minor exceptions). Although apprenticeships could vary, they were normally for seven years, during which the apprentice lived in the household of the master under a legal contract, an indenture. Special conditions might be made—the boy might be provided with a feather bed or given a certain endowment on completion—but he could neither reside elsewhere nor work for another, save on forfeit of a considerable sum. Often the apprentice had no blood relatives in the town so he also needed protection; the master also wished to protect both his considerable fee, in a number of cases, and the labor of the apprentice.

Those workmen trained in the mystery of a trade but not admitted to the gild as freemen and masters were called journeymen. They engaged to work for another, but not under an indenture, as did the apprentices. In the absence of an active rental market for housing in the medieval cities, journeymen often had to be sheltered at night as well as during the day. They came to form the third component of the *occupational household*, which was both the social unit of medieval life in cities of the north and the structure that formed their morphological module.

The Functional Development of the Northern House

We may now understand how the basic building structure of the medieval town of the north came into being. The construction of the time, as we have noted, was made up of bays shaped by posts and lintels of relatively small dead weight. Depending upon the in-filling, this structure could be remarkably light in relation to the

The great spire of Strasbourg Cathedral was the tallest in medieval Europe, towering above houses that were themselves often five or six stories in height. These roofs were of flat tiles and often broken by dormers.

space it enclosed, so relatively great heights could be attained. We cannot determine the tallest timber structure from the Middle Ages but certainly it must have been of seven, eight, or even nine stories. Such heights would have been tall for private buildings even a hundred years ago, so due respect must be paid the medieval timber builders. Height alone did not faze these carpenters and masons, as their church towers show. Salisbury rose to 404 feet, Strasbourg to 466 feet, and Cologne and Ulm were designed to 515 feet and 528 feet respectively, though they remained uncompleted until the nineteenth century. We may reason that medieval builders did carry timber construction to the limit of their technology, or at least to the extent necessary to provide the space required by the sometimes large occupational households of the time.

The result was the tall, narrow house normally elongated away from the street and buttressed by its neighbors. The use to be made of the house was reflected in its structure. The master, his family, and his apprentices and journeymen formed not merely an economic but a social unit. Thus, the medieval burgher's house must needs contain (1) production space, if he was a craftsman, (2) selling space, whether he was a merchant or a craftsman, (3) storage space for the staple of his production or the goods of his sale, (4) housing for him and his biological family, and (5) housing for an apprentice or two, and quite possibly for a journeyman, and even his biological family. To contain such an occupational household a large building was needed, which has misled some into thinking that the quarters of the medieval merchant were quite spacious. In fact even a quite prosperous merchant had few physical possessions and little privacy or space. He and his family probably occupied only one or two rooms, sharing a single bed in many cases and using only a few chairs and benches, a simple table, and some armoires and storage cupboards. People at ease tended, as did monarchs as we have noted, to recline in bed, both for its comfort and for the warmth its covering afforded in the bone-chilling winters of northern Europe. What heat there was came from fireplaces, which also served as the cooking place of the simple and unrefined food of the time.

So simple was the design of houses that merchants of substance had little more than a "hall"—a large room which served most of their needs. "Their hall took up the full height of their house from floor to rafters, and in the two-storied back portion of the house, they used the ground floor room as a store (storage room), and the upper floor, which had to be reached by outside stone or wooden stairs, as the solar or private room in which members of the family slept. Kitchen, brewhouse, and dairy were banished into separate outhouses as a pre-caution against fire."[72] These were outstanding merchants though "not rich enough to build on a baronial scale, but they aped the aristocracy as sedulously as they could."

In England, internal peace and the minor constraint of town walls meant that houses tended to be lower and more elongated on the ground than on than on the Continent, where greater danger from external attack required the walls to be maintained until the nineteenth century; houses thus tended to be made high to contain the large occupational household. But in both places, *most of the functional separation of the city took place within the house.*

The typical pattern gave over the first floor to selling, by merchant or craftsman; the front of the house normally opened through fairly wide, shuttered windows and doors to the street. Goods were displayed for sale; the craftsman might also use this area as a workshop. If he needed more space for manufacture, that might be secured on the second floor, or even at the top of the houses, where the improved daylighting made weaving or other fine handworkings more practicable. Since this society worked from dawn to dusk, its workdays were longer in summer than in winter, and in those places where light was best.

Generally, the second story was used to house the master and his family and their simple possessions. Apprentices and journeymen occupied a third or even possibly a fourth story. The attics stored staple away from the destruction of dampness and rats, and whatever food the occupational household might lay up for winter or times of shortage. Thus, the high pitched roofs of the medieval houses had a distinctly functional quality, affording a large amount of dry, covered space for such storage in an economic situation where transport was commonly interrupted and consistently unreliable. To reach these attics, doors were let into the gable, if these overlooked the street, or dormers closed by doors were let into the gable roof and extended to reach the front wall of the house. Pulleys, though apparently not blocks, were used to raise heavy bundles directly from the street to these openings. Given the impedance of movement in vehicles along the bad roads of the Middle Ages, it was much more efficient to handle goods vertically with a pulley than horizontally in a cart.

[72]*J. J. Bagley,* Life in Medieval England, *New York: G. P. Putnam's Sons, 1960, pp. 60-61.*

The sixteenth-century
Kammerzell House in
Strasbourg was six
stories, two under the
roof where the pulley
beam for raising goods
for storage can be
clearly seen.

Morphological Differences Within the City

Though the primary division of land-use within the medieval city came in the vertical separation of functions, specialized buildings and land-uses existed on the ground as well. Commonly these specialized uses—including the castle, the church, abbey, monastery, gildhall, later on the city hall, and quite commonly the covered market-hall—lay within a great areal mass of modular buildings given over to the sheltering of occupational households. What was the original morphological feature around which these occupation houses and quarters were ranged? In the *bourg-faubourg* model of medieval city origin, the castle clearly served as the grain around which the concretion of the city grew, though as Lavedan noted, "It is not always very easy to designate precisely the element of attraction, in particular to choose between the church, the castle, and the square, when they are found united at the same place. In all these cases one finds a square and one can maintain that there was no other origin for the *'radio-concentrique'* plan of the city."[73] This *radio-concentrique* town has a fairly simple but definite morphogenesis, beginning with the point of urban initiation—be it church, castle, or trader's mart—and growing outward along roads originally converging on that point. Because the area within a particular radius increases geometrically with movement away from a point, a conservative force works to limit the outward extension of the town and encourage a compact form.

This circular form of the medieval town has commonly been asserted to be the result of circumvallation. But, in fact, we often find considerable areas of open land within walls, as well as cities of circular form which were never walled, or ineffectively so. The geometrical increase in spatial increments to the city with outward growth, as much as anything, shapes a circular form for the city. Extension comes in a web of radiating roads converging upon a small central point. Growth is not by preconception, though it may be by periodic incrementation, with annular rings brought into possible use but not fully built upon for many years. This case would exist particularly with the periodic enlargement of the city area contained within walls, but it is also true in American cities where walls

[73]*Pierre Lavedan*, Histoire de l'Urbanisme: Antiquité-Moyen Age [Vol. I], Paris: Henri Laurens, 1926, p. 261.

were almost unknown. Finally, the conservation of radial effort within a city decrees circular outline regardless of any possible circumvallation.

Let us assume the clustering of common specialized institutions at the convergence of the roads leading to a potential town site; merchants would be likely to settle near those institutions in their *portus* (or *faubourg*, if a castle dominates the cluster). To serve those coming in from outside to buy their wares, the merchants would find it advantageous to be at the edge of the small settlement, though not too far to the side if access by all the converging roads is desired. Thus, as the city grows, the quarter selling at retail would tend to cluster and remain near the convergence of the external routes, favoring none over another. In wholesale trade the customers would be fewer and more likely to be professional peddlers and chapmen aimed toward a trading partner well known to them rather than to the general public. Thus, warehouses could be toward the edge of the city on one side—as they were at St. Denis, Winchester, Stourbridge, and Lübeck. We should therefore distinguish the marketplace from the fairground as we do the market from the fair as institutions.

The marketplace was originally an open space, not necessarily given over only to selling. The medieval town square had a number of other purposes. It might be a *place d'arms* where the burghal militia gathered in times of danger to be dispatched along radial streets to the part of the wall in greatest danger.[74] Or it might be the site of civic procession and pageant, when illumination was afforded almost entirely by the sun. Or it might be a buffer between the *bourg* and the *faubourg*. Only as the town's population grew and occupational specialization became possible would the retail market really be needed. Initially the burgher raised much of his own food; his time was not fully occupied by the exercise of his trade, and he lived in a town where space for gardening and pasturage of animals was not yet scarce. But with urban growth we may logically reason that his specialized skill came into increasing demand, as did the urban land that served as his garden plot, and thus increased in value. This conjunction of demands would tend to make the purchase rather than the production of food a common practice.

Given a potential market for the sale of food and other simple daily needs that might earlier have been met by household efforts, retail trade could be established. But in the beginning it would be somewhat experimental and, in all likelihood, periodic. In the Middle Ages:

The diet of the masses was mainly vegetarian and frugal, two meals being usual. There is a medieval saying that

angels need to feed but once a day, mankind twice, and beasts thrice or more. The impression we have of colossal meals washed down with great quantities of wine, mead, and beer derives from occasions in the lives of royalty and aristocracy which chroniclers have recorded for special reasons. Such feastings were the exception, even for the rich. The many feast-days of the calendar were counterbalanced by even more fast-days, when the morning and evening meals were limited by strict rules.

Except that they feasted more frequently, many of the richer classes shared the diet of the artisans and townspeople, which consisted of some kind of soup in the morning and of porridge or soup, fish and vegetables in the evening. Apart from bread and cakes, cereals in the form of pastry were still a luxury because of the cost of fats. Meals of fish—fresh, dried, or salted—were much more frequent than nowadays, for meat was still expensive and was taken hardly more than once a week. Water and milk were drunk, as were beer and wine by those who could afford them. The choice was largely regional; thus beer was more common in the northern districts of Germany, wine in the south.

Medieval cities took great pains to obtain regular and cheap food supplies for their artisans. The rise of agriculture and husbandry in Flanders was a leading factor in the independence of the Flemish towns and their successful resistance to the encroachment of royal power.[75]

Under these circumstances we could hardly expect a very elaborate physical provision for retail trade.

Instead the most primitive provision was made to do. The open space in the town, for whatever purpose established, was occupied one day a week, or perhaps two, by carts brought in from the surrounding countryside, from which the farmers would sell their fresh vegetables, a bit of meat, or other local agriculture produce. Barrows might contain fresh fish from local rivers or the nearby coast, or salted and dried fish sent in barrels.

The almost universal practice in western Europe was the strict control of these markets by both church and state. State controls arose because the markets occupied public space and exercised a privilege for which the lord wished recompense. The church was concerned with severe limitation of profit and control of weights and measures. Because the public space had other uses, the privilege of occupying was commonly granted for one or, at most, two days. In a few sizeable places, such as medieval Cambridge, a "perpetual market" was granted which might be open on all workdays, while Sunday was not yet the day of pause in human industry it became at the hands of religious reformers in the sixteenth and seventeenth centuries.

[74]Ibid., p. 261.

[75]Charles Singer, et al., A History of Technology, *Oxford: Oxford University Press, 1950, Vol. II, p. 123.*

These first patterns of retailing found in the medieval city may be seen to be of the most elemental provision. Throughout history the unhoused, periodic, and commodity-specialized trader has served as the pioneer, as much in medieval French or German towns as in towns of the nonwestern world, or in Berkeley as the street hawkers in today's youth culture. When either demand or supply is problematic, street hawking in towns or peddling through the countryside becomes the standard practice.

As support for retail trade became assured, and as the essentially market-gardening production of food was shaped around the cities of Flanders, the Rhine valley, and northern and eastern France, local selling could take on a more settled abode, both in towns, as opposed to the hawker's circuit and, within the settlement in the marketplace. At first, the retailers were likely to substitute a modest covered stall in the open square for the barrow or wagon that previously sufficed. As trade grew, the chance increased for the transformation of the single-day market to one of longer term, requiring, if carried to full-time selling, the separation of the market functions of the square from its other civic and religious uses. Thus, we find that as cities grow they tend to have several open spaces, one or two of which become institutionalized as markets—often called the "old" and the "new" markets—while other spaces become true public squares free of the impediments of trade. With such segregation, the marketplace itself can begin to be filled with light, flimsy, but unmovable structures.

A frequent argument has been that increasing trade at this point further encouraged the urge to permanency, causing the retailers to move indoors into shops on the first floor of the houses surrounding the marketplace. Doubtless partial historical and geographical truth stands behind this view, but it is too simplistic to represent accurately all of the processes at work. The fundamental fault of such a model is that it ignores the fact that from the very beginning there were, in fact, three kinds of trade: (1) selling local goods to the local populace, which was likely to be a fairly small-scale activity, probably conducted by the principals involved; (2) selling imported goods to that same populace, an even smaller activity in most cases and thus not usually a sufficient support for an entrepreneur; and (3) the selling of local or imported goods to customers located at some distance from the town, the scale of that activity depending upon the extent of the territory dominated by the town in that trade.

We have so far been concerned only with the first of these types of trade. When the peasant came to town to sell his domestic surplus, "he supplied a tiny market, usually held periodically, where he sold perhaps three eggs, a chicken, several pounds of wool, and sometimes even a little cloth woven in the household."[76] The supply of goods was small, and we may reason that such a provision could serve only a relatively modest demand focussed on that place. The temporary barrow in the public square would serve both participants well. But as the population grew, the need arose to assure a larger and a more predictable supply of goods. To do so would require the exercise of forethought and the geographical search for goods, activities likely to be undertaken only by professional traders. Their livelihood came not from production—as did that of the peasant with his three eggs, one chicken, bag of wool, and cloth—but from an exercise of the agency of trade.[77] However, these professional merchants would have little interest in trading only in the small local surplus or in selling only to what might be a modest local market. If the city were large, local custom would suffice, or if the locally-produced surplus were massive, then the traders might be content with its sale, though obviously such a sale would have to be to a larger market than that furnished by the customers flocking to the town's marketplace. Thus the professional trader would of necessity (and personal interest) seek to expand his field of endeavor beyond the parochial interests of the town itself, becoming in the process what the medieval chroniclers term a "merchant"—a long-distance, basically wholesale trader. In these accounts, "sellers" served the local market and "merchants" encountered a geographical search in their efforts to obtain a source or sale.

Large-scale trading, then, fell largely into the hands of merchants, and they were most often confronted with the problem of storing large quantities of goods. A considerable part of their activity was taken up with anticipating further demands and placing orders, often in distant places, so as to have goods on hand ultimately to meet those demands. In such an activity the storehouse became a needed structure in the city. We may recall that in the Roman Empire, the anticipation of demand and its fulfillment fell to the lot of the state, which maintained *emporia* at Ostia or on the banks of the Tiber in Rome itself. In the Middle Ages neither the demand nor the concentration of agency of trade was such that these vast buildings might be constructed, filled, and emptied by sale. But a beginning of a return to forethought and search in trade was made and the merchant became the leading commercial figure of the medieval town by using such talents.

[76]Georges Lefranc, Histoire du Commerce, *Paris: Presses Universitaires de France, 1965 [Que Sais-Je?, No. 55], p. 27.*
[77]*For a detailed discussion of the role of the agency of trade in the support of towns, see James E. Vance, Jr.,* The Merchant's World: The Geography of Wholesaling, *Englewood Cliffs, N.J.: Prentice-Hall, Inc., 1970.*

In that role as leader, the merchant tended to occupy a particular physical position as well as a social and political one. His house must needs be relatively easy for strangers to locate, and accessible for goods coming into or being dispatched from the town. Finally, the scale of the premises must be great enough to permit the storage necessary to support his considerable selling activity. Given these needs, the merchant tended to locate his house on one of the squares or river banks within the town, often that in which the market was held. From this fact arises the confusion as to morphogenesis within the market. Because the merchant's house might look out upon the marketplace, it is easy to assume that it essentially grew out of that institution. Yet when we examine the evolution of the functional role and physical provision for merchants, we see it had only a partial relation to the marketplace itself. Doubtless merchants would sell the goods they dealt in to local people, but few merchants would have possessed the power they did were they totally dependent, or perhaps even fundamentally dependent, upon the local trade. Functional efficiency of a different sort, and ostentation within a wider world, brought the merchant burgher's house to the square. The fact that he traded with his neighbors in a ground-floor counting-house or shop should not be allowed to confuse our understanding of his activities.

The test of this reasoning comes in those places where the merchants' houses lie at some distance from the marketplace, as they do in Venice, Augsburg, Antwerp, and a number of other superlatively important *emporia* of the Middle Ages.

When the scale of local demand rose the merchant became interested in supplying its needs. The specialization of labor, so much the foundation of development theory in economic thought, could also take place. In a town with a demonstrated market for a particular class of goods, the artisan could take up residence; in fact, the trade itself might there be begun with the slow evolution of the skill and technology that came ultimately to attach to the "mystery." In the shaping of the physical structure of the city this meant that with increase in urban size, and market, the occupations could begin to emerge as coherent local activities where the union of practitioners into gilds might take place. We have already seen that the nature and functions of the gild made clustered residence desirable. Thus, just as the gild merchant tended to cluster around squares where large, obvious, and ostentatious buildings could be built, the other gilds shaped their own quarters.

A tie existed between these two evolutions. With the existence of a strong gild in a particular type of manufacture, we might expect a considerable as well as a highly competent production of goods. Fairly probably, such a production might overreach the demands of the town itself, leaving a surplus for possible export. In that case the members of the gild merchant would be the men most versed in *geographical search*—as much for markets as for sources of goods. They would have the associations with traders elsewhere, as well as the geographical knowledge of possible markets, to aid the craftsmen of the gild in selling their products at a distance. Such a symbiosis is the product of an urban life and production, not of the agricultural hinterland which might have grown up around the town to supply its needs.

If we carry all of this evolution of the city functions and forms to a logical conclusion, we end with a town divided among trades—both in long-distance selling and in craft manufacture—whose interests encourage clustering in the urban space. From this end comes the *occupation district* as the second-level modular unit in the morphology of the medieval city, where the first-level module was the house-shop structure with vertical segregation leaving the first floor to be used in a nearly identical way throughout the quarter. In the city of the Middle Ages, we find a different kind of segregation, into occupation quarters. Still the first floor would remain in commercial usage even if in differing trades.

The Quarter of Tolerance

The main exception to this broad picture of two related modules is the district of extraterritoriality or ethnic identity. We have seen that the traders coming in from outside were often permitted, sometimes required, to live and work in a defined quarter where they might be subject to their own laws and practices rather than those of the denizens. Similarly, certain minorities with different culture, religion, and ethnicity might be tolerated within an orthodox native body when confined to a distinct, definable, and delimited quarter where their heterodoxy might exist without infecting the natives. No clear exception is made to the general model of dual separation represented in these two types of "outsiders" living within the city. Normally, the tolerated outsiders were engaged mainly in one or a small range of trades. The Jews and Italians were money-lenders, bankers and, in earlier times, long-distance merchants. The Germans of the Hanse took over these trades in the late Middle Ages. The main justification in the medieval mind for the toleration of outsiders, disbelievers, and those of external loyalty was that they performed a service to the natives that warranted toleration. of qualities automatically suspect, feared, and even reviled. Once the functional role disappeared, no justification remained for permitting heterodoxy.

We should avoid the pitfall to understanding represented by applying present-day dogma to past acts and events. No German, Italian, or Jew possessed a whit more basic tolerance than did the Frenchman or Englishman who held him to living in his "quarter of tolerance." Need could make foreigners living within the city far more adaptable than the natives, but that fact does not represent a fundamental philosophical difference. The diaries of Lombards resident in the north, the assiduous defense of Hebrew practices of law and customs by Jews living in medieval Europe, and the creation of German compounds in cities around the Baltic by and for *hanse* traders all speak to the same dogged attachment to particular external views and practices despite free residence in the country. Those living in "quarters of tolerance" were not slaves so their frequent cries of enslavement ring rather hollow; normally they were slaves to their own property, refusing to yield it as a price to leave the country, rather than being actually held personally in bond. We must appreciate the medieval view that national strength and wealth came only by striving to hold as much specie

and staple within the country as humanly possible. This view may be economically unsound, as Adam Smith showed, but his writing was five hundred years in the future.

The quarter of tolerance was the morphological expression of the needs of a particular kind of long-distance traders. These traders were foreigners living for a time within the society of a country, tolerated as other foreigners would not have been for the critical needs of that distance trade to the national economy. The *quid pro quo* was fairly obvious in the case of the Italians and the Germans, though, as the Middle Ages advanced, the balance between the benefits came more into question. But for the Jews the situation was far more obscure; they had no homeland whence they came and to which they returned on retirement from trade. Additionally, they had no national staple sought in other lands, unless it was gold, and that commodity was of particular sensitivity in medieval times as much for its scarcity as for its symbolic role in national wealth. So in a number of cities the quarter of tolerance of the Jews had to be larger than that for the Lombards or the *hanse* because it became a "homeland" in miniature.

Today it is hard to see the problem, because tolerance is considered a right of the individual or the group: in no sense was it such in the Middle Ages. As a result, to permit such a quarter to exist meant both to delimit it geographically and to constrain its residents to particular occupations. This second consequence arose from the equation in the medieval mind of the ideas of residence and occupation. You could not have workmen in a particular trade wandering about the city with no effective supervision, and through the absence of a gild, no provision of social welfare. Jews could join gilds, but only very selected ones, those that could undertake to deal with their highly ambiguous status. The Germans and the Italians had little reason to join gilds; their trading organizations were as powerful as the local gilds and fully as able to care for the trade and its practitioners.

From House to Quarter to City

A medieval house in
Ypres (Ieper), Belgium,
is more characteristic
of the housing of work-
ers in textile towns
where light was needed
and the crowding was not
so extreme.

The modular components of the medieval town build
up to a single entity—the city, as we know it. Yet the
forces which actually shaped it cannot be fully revealed
to us. They were unremarked at the time of operation,
and no medieval town of sufficient size has come down
to us enough unchanged to permit our "reading of
the rocks." If we are to answer questions about process, we must rely on a fair component of conjecture.
Fortunately, we are not without a script, even if a modest one. In 1603 the English topographer John Stow
published his *Survey of London*, to which he appended
a relic from the twelfth century, *Libellum de situ et
nobilitate Londini*, in which William Fitzstephen set
out to present the London of that time.[78] Fitzstephen's
description is the oldest detailed account of a city that
remains in western European literature. From exam-
ining it we may sense, if not read directly, certain morphological forces at work.

Fitzstephen begins by noting the glories of London,
citing its "abundant wealth" and "extensive commerce." The implication comes through that these result from its situation on the Thames. In essence we
have the merchants' town, a fact made more evident
when he notes farther on that the king's palace lies
"situated in a populous suburb, at a distance of two
miles from the city." Thus, two points of initiation
occur in what became a great city even in the twelfth
century, and the notion of the *bourg*, with its *faubourg*
hovering in its shelter, is far from the universal situation that some historians would have it.

The sense that the city is for merchants is enhanced
by Fitzstephen's comment: "Adjoining to the houses on
all sides lie the gardens of those citizens that dwell in
the suburbs, which are well furnished with trees,
spacious and beautiful." From other evidence we know
that these houses were commonly occupied by powerful noblemen and bishops who must needs be resident
near the court but wished not to be under the control of
the merchants' town with its collegial government by
gildsmen. Thus the settlement really had three components: the merchants' town, the king's court, and the
residential area for the country magnates, of the sword
or the mitre, who maintained an astute spatial independence from either of the other powers.

In that suburban area were mills "whose clack is

---

[78]*John Stow*, The Survey of London, *London: Everyman's Library Edition [1912], reprinted 1960, pp. 501-509.*

very pleasing to the ear" (suggesting those powered by water, as windmills were thought to screech), the tillage of crops yielding "Ceres' plenteous sheaf," and "an immense forest, in which are densely wooded thickets, the coverts of game, stags, fallow-deer, boars, and wild bulls." The image comes through of a countryside reduced to the control of the city rather than one exercising domination over the settlement, as Christaller would have it. And the suburb, a band of residential land-use related directly to the city, can be seen even in the twelfth century, which should put the lie to the notion that the automobile began the spreading out of the housing fabric of cities. That fundamental process was seemingly an outgrowth of rural security: once security could reasonably be assured, those with economic independence from city toil could and sometimes did seek to live outside the bustle and constraint of the town.

Within the town, "The artizans of the several crafts, the vendors of the various commodities, and the labourers of every kind, have each their separate station, which they take every morning." There were as well "wine-shops which are kept in ships and cellars, (and) a public eating-house." In the Middle Ages, wine was drunk fresh from the harvest and pressing, so the first ships to arrive from Gascony would be most sought after to replace the fast-declining vintage of the previous year. On Fridays at a horse fair outside the gate at "Smooth Field," agricultural implements and beasts were also sold.

In the twelfth century we already can see the notion of periodic residence at work in the case of the process of *class assembly*. For the elite of society and power— the nobility and the bishops—rural residence of necessity enforced isolation. That select group gained their power through administration of rural territory: the bishop had his see and the baron his manor, the earl his county, and the duke his principality. But in seeking to consort with his peers, each was required to remain in the city. For that reason, "Moreover, almost all the bishops, abbots, and great men of England, are in a manner, citizens and freemen of London; as they have magnificent houses there, to which they resort, spending large sums of money, whenever they are summoned thither to councils and assemblies by the king or their metropolitan [the archbishop, originally resident in London, was subsequently removed in titular residence to Canterbury, though maintaining a London palace at Lambeth at least as early as Fitzstephen's time] or are compelled to go there by their own business."

Class assembly became a strong force in shaping cities, adding to their fabric buildings of a magnificence unmatched in medieval times in the buildings of merchants. Class assembly, like the city residence

of Italian nobles, in the end proved highly inimical to the political and social health of cities. The presence of the aristocracy tended to corrupt the original collegial government by burghers, with its reasonable representation of the social and economic mass of the city, into one of privilege and selfishness. The rotting of the English boroughs came not merely through loss of population, as the term is usually used, but was influenced by the increasing limitation of the franchise to a small group, as the most powerful city men joined with the leaders of the gentry seeking periodic residence in the city.

Fitzstephen concludes his account in the frequent English fashion by expatiating at immoderate length on the sports of London and the citizens' use of the fields around for jousting, wrestling, stone-throwing, and a full range of other purposeless heavings. The presence of dramatic presentations in the twelfth century foretold Britain's magnificent obsession with drama, but also suggested the tendency for a national culture to depend upon a center from which such reasonably popular activities could be spread outward. Formal education, as at Cambridge and Oxford, could be isolated into the countryside, but not such popular education as the morality plays of the Middle Ages. London had drama at least eight hundred years before it gained a university, which came only first in a most timid way, and then not before 1826.

The Medieval Land Market

Evidence concerning the value given to land in various sections of the medieval city is scant indeed, yet seemingly differences occurred from place to place. The enclosure of land by the wall may not alone have made urban land scarce; the legal availability of land may have tended as well to create a scarcity value. Feudal landowners hoarded land; many of them were so struck with terror as they approached death that bequests to the church, in craven search of salvation, were very common. By the late Middle Ages the church was a powerful, sometimes almost monopolistic landowner, to the extent that those seeking land within the city may have had difficulty obtaining it, particularly by freehold occupation. As the most certain source of wealth and security, land was more endowing than speculative.

In her classic study of the merchant class in

medieval London, Sylvia Thrupp shows that, "One of a merchant's chief motives in acquiring real property and rents was to provide for the future of his wife and children in event of his early death. As has been shown [from a study of marriage contracts], many purchases were made under the pressure of marriage settlements; another urgent incentive was the desire to leave a source of income out of which chantry priests could be hired to sing for the family souls. *Under favorable conditions the returns were probably not much below average trading profits.*"[79] These land-investment purposes were not likely to encourage dangerous practices of speculation, particularly as more and more land fell into the hands of the church—one of whose firmly held beliefs was that undue profit, *turpe lucrum*, was the work of the god of darkness.

Merely because the land market was likely less fluid and volatile than it was to become in the seventeenth century, we should not discount its influences. No doubt in the earlier years of medieval urbanization a high degree of parity held between ownership of land and buildings and practical use thereof, but as time passed reasons for ownership divorced from occupational use increased. We have already seen the rise of class assembly; we must now look at it from an economic viewpoint. In doing so, we find perhaps the first evidence to support the notion that the countryside determined the size and significance of cities. But the grave question remains whether the existence of the city forced upon those living in the country some periodic assembly of the aristocratic classes in the city.

Professor Thrupp furnishes us a valuable picture of how very great indeed were the ties between the merchants of London and the manors, but the ties were those of ownership from the center rather than complete domination by the barons and bishops. It was a two-way street—the "great men" of England's countryside did collect in London for part of the year, but ever more commonly the powerful merchants began to buy manors in the rural areas to furnish themselves with food, peace and quiet, and ultimately the trappings of gentility.

Professor Thrupp believed that about 15 per cent of the London merchants owned country land in the beginning of the fifteenth century and, including town holdings, "The number of citizen households that were backed by landed property, then, must have been between 900 and 1,000" in a total merchant class numbering no more than 3,400 households.[80] "The merchant who was both successful and socially ambitious might by the time of his death have a third to half of his fortune or more in the form of lands."[81] A considerable part of this property was probably acquired as a result of the foreclosure of mortgages merchants had taken in security for loans made to previous owners. Perhaps more by this means than by outright speculative increases in land values were fortunes from land collected.

Perhaps fully as strong a force in projecting the city merchant's interests in land outward was his desire to shift his role from prosperous tradesman to prideful gentleman. Since lands with feudal history equated gentility with service to the king, particularly with raising men-at-arms in time of war and administering justice and charity in time of peace, one could far more easily become a gentleman outside the city than within. The wealthy merchant could live as a gentleman in the country while earning the support of that unproductive life by labor on some days in the city.

It may be granted, at least, that the possession of a country house could set a city merchant on the way to changing his class status. If, as many of the wealthier men are known to have done, he then assumed the social role of a gentleman in his county, serving on public commissions, acquiring private hunting rights, modernizing his manor house, making arrangements to marry his daughters into gentle families, and preparing at least one of his sons for one of the careers that were associated with gentility, the degree of change was certainly significant. In so far as can be judged from office-holding and marriage into older families, assimilation to the landed gentry was still further advanced in the second generation after such a move, and in the counties more distant from London there might be a severance of all formal ties with citizen life.[82]

In such fashion, class assembly in the countryside worked to draw out of the city those wealthy citizens who saw their future in gentle rather than productive roles. But like the country magnates coming to the city for periodic residence, the wealthy merchants tended very much to cluster together in the pastoral environment around the city. "Two of the citizens' favorite counties, where their purchases of land were most frequent, were Middlesex and Surrey."[83] These areas then became the "Home Counties" of urban gentry, much as Bloomsbury and Mayfair became "The City" in later centuries for rural gentry resident for a time in the city.

---

[79]*Sylvia L. Thrupp.* The Merchant Class of Medieval London, *Ann Arbor: University of Michigan Press, 1948 [paperback 1962], p. 122.*
[80]Ibid., *p. 125.*

[81]Ibid., *p. 127.*
[82]Ibid., *p. 280.*
[83]Ibid., *p. 284.*

Processes of Assemblage in the Medieval City

The Middle Ages were a time of slow, almost cellular, shaping of the town. Its parts were brought together in no conscious design, save possibly one determined by the demands of fortification. But this time was not one of elaborate, often theoretical, defensive structures; they came with the use of gunpowder and the creation of the structurally theoretical world of the Renaissance. We may however cite a few of the forces dominant in medieval city growth.

The first process serving to shape the medieval city we might justly call *concretion*—the deposition from a fluid state of a body of different composition that lies within and surrounded by a groundmass of contrasting form and function.[84] The groundmass was the feudal countryside, and the fluid that collected and concreted in its midst was trade, wandering and periodic at first, but ultimately settled and of characteristic physical presence. This concretion of long-distance trade was the nucleus for the main medieval cities. In a study wherein he set out to find a central-place system for the Middle Ages, Josiah Cox Russell found instead that the great and lesser entrepôts of distant trade and the connections among them comprised the skeleton of medieval urbanization.[85]

So long as the medieval city was being produced by concretion of fluid elements from outside, its size would be enlarged directly by accretion, the slow and simple growth of a single form. We must distinguish concretion, the collection from outside inward, from *accretion*, the physical expansion of the city by adding layers to its form. Cities have always grown most fun-

damentally by accretion, simply because when new needs expand the necessary size of the city, the easiest place to increase its physical extent is around its edge, where "redevelopment" is of countryside rather than of existing city. The city form accretes on land taken from the country. So long as a single concretion of activity is taking place, the accretions may not differ in structure from the earlier germ. But, if several different kinds of fluid are concreted inward, we are likely to get knobs or bands of differing composition, still in physical association but not in simple chemical bond. The same process has been at work in the city: we know that so long as merchants built their town *tout simple*, the place might grow but would be unlikely to separate into distinct physical entities. Individuals might shift from one place in the city to another, but the physical form they would occupy would remain unchanged and highly consistent in form. With several concretions from the outside, the chances of necessary physical distinctions would rise rapidly. Just as bands occur in modules within rock, physical knobs—multiple nucleations—occur within the city. We have seen how class assembly for the "season" within the city ultimately created distinct residential quarters for the magnates coming to consort with their peers. Equally, the merchants of the town seeking to rise above simple citizenship left for the clearly exurban "Home Counties," where they hoped through the dusting by a different geography to gain gentility.

Obviously congregation is a social process but its direct physical expression occurs in socially specialized areas. To take one case, the extraterritorial quarters of medieval cities—the Hanseatic steelyards or the Jewish ghetto—emerged not because their residents were doing things very different from the natives, but because they had contrasting social and legal practices in the pursuit of what might be a common occupation. The result is a *social separation* largely divorced from the previous economically functional separation found in the city. So long as cities existed as rather parochial places, little need arose for social separation; once they became diverse in activity and in both class and ethnic social status, such separation was needed.

The third fundamental process at work in the medieval city was *physical separation*, based either on the function to be carried out—which led to the occupation quarters so typical of the time—or on the social class and caste to which the residents adhered—which led to aristocratic suburbs, merchants' manor belts, Jewish ghettos, and Hanseatic steelyards, as the case might be. These various separations came, with the passage of time, to take on distinctive physical forms to match their increasing social and functional separation. And once those physical forms had been de-

---

[84]*This geological term seems particularly appropriate as an expression of what was going on in medieval cities. Merriam-Webster defines it as "a mass of mineral matter found generally in rock of a composition different from its own and produced by deposition from aqueous solution in the rock." These concretions stand rather like the medieval merchants' town, filling a space carved out of the groundmass—the feudal economy of the countryside—but filled with a different substance, city form, brought by the slow accumulation of that material from a fluid state.*

[85]*Josiah Cox Russell*, Medieval Regions and Their Cities, *Bloomington: Indiana University Press, 1972. For a critical analysis of Russell's study, see my review in the* Journal of Urban History, *Vol. I (1975), pp. 484-488.*

Bamberg shows the more
equidimensional plots
of the south German
towns and the tendency
for much larger units
of housing than were
to be found in the Low
Countries or England.

veloped along specialized lines, they themselves
tended to reinforce the process of separation.

We may distinguish two forms of separation: the
active choice to divide, and externally enforced division. *Congregation* implies deliberate coming together;
segregation connotes forced division, leading in turn to
a clustering that may be voluntary only after the acceptance of a *fait accompli*. Medieval cities usually had

directly outside their walls shanty settlements where
all manner of rejected civic activities lodged, even if
very badly. Some activities were merely noxious, such
as slaughtering; others were illegal, though tolerated.
Still others were legal under specific circumstances, as
in the case of fairs with their own commercial law administered by a piepowder court.

The medieval city held a large array of geographically specific law and practice, resulting in the
intimate use of areas to partake in one legal practice, or
instead to avoid it. Ecclesiastical foundations might
well seek to reside outside the city so as more fully to
control their property and practices; thus we find a
range of activities that were voluntarily or necessarily
extramural. Legal accommodation was given to this
idea in that some structures and areas within cities
could be given a conferred extramural quality—as in

Ely Cathedral or the embassies of foreign states—without being outside the city. In England today, county buildings may lie on a city's High Street but in law reside outside its bounds.

Paris in the Middle Ages faced a significant application of this concern for extramural status in its university quarter on the Left Bank. The problem arose from the fact that students came from all over Europe to study there and wished to return home on completion of their labors. Thus, while in Paris, they found themselves in a legal quandary produced by medieval ideas as to the three classes who belonged to a city; citizens, who had been born there or formally accepted to citizenship; "foreigners," who were merely subjects of the king born elsewhere and not given local citizenship; and aliens. Medieval practice assumed that only citizens could reside for any time in the city—often inns had to lie outside the gates to avoid the question whether the wayfarer was residing overnight in the town. So the vast group of "foreigners" and aliens flocking to a university posed a legal problem to the medieval mind. Paris got around it by restricting the university to the Left Bank, giving a special law there that permitted the outsiders to remain without legal contest. In Britain this problem did not arise; the universities were outside London, and were more expressly ecclesiastical foundations which normally possessed this quality of legal extramurality to shelter strangers.

These relations have the full complexity that medieval legal practice could summon up; a geography of law existed unlike anything that has followed. The ghetto was part of a vast array of such quarters and districts. The rule of law in the Middle Ages was indeed a powerful force in shaping cities.

Finally, we need mention the process of *reconstruction*, which we have already seen in the special application of the accretion of rural land into the city. Reconstruction occurred within the city, but not so much in the manner we know today. Our level of rebuilding is very much tied to the operation of land economics; in the Middle Ages functional change rather than shifting values created most reconstruction. A merchant might need more space, or his interests might evolve from some level of production to a concentration on trade alone. In response to those shifts, he would seek to gain more appropriate accommodation, most likely where his property stood. As a result, we find the medieval house a marvelously evolving structure given to all sorts of physical additions and adjustments. The haute-pas, the penthouse, the ell, and a dozen other additions were sufficiently common as to have specific names. Because medieval structures were transformed rather than replaced, few indeed stand as built. Inference from physical evidence is thus difficult, but it suggests that

reconstruction was a factor in the conservation of overall patterns in the city (and by the way in the employment of materials); even though a city grew in size and importance, it might be expected to reflect conditions from earlier times.

The medieval city had great rigidities of institutions and laws but remarkable flexibility in the use of its physical structure. Only when the institutions became creakingly conservative did the structure become rather frozen. And as the late medieval city found a new form, for a time a new society allowed the medieval man to jump over the walls and begin his journey to the modern era.

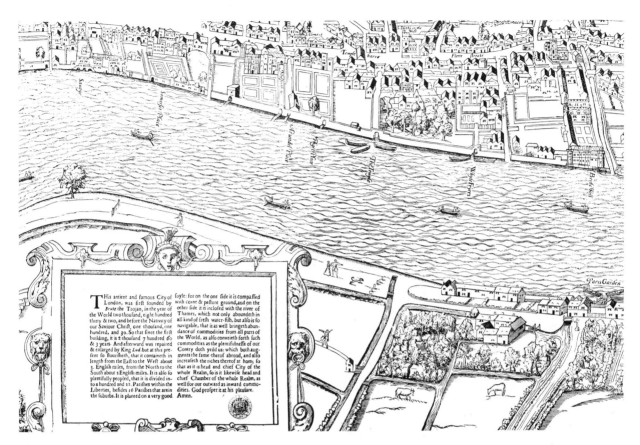

Ralph Agas' map of London (ca. 1560–1570) shows the large houses that lined the Thames, often with gardens, along the Strand west of the gate of the City at Temple-barre.

5.   A TOWN FOR EVERYMAN: THE LATE MEDIEVAL BASTIDE

The ease with which we can collect a vivid and encompassing view of the medieval city speaks strongly to its vitality and active role in the life of the times. Many democratic traditions cited today in support of civil liberty and economic justice began in those times. Similarly, the contribution of towns to the material prosperity of citizens, both lowly and exalted, first then became apparent. Social structures based on ethnic identification and residential division (by cultural attachment) gained greater sway in the complex trading towns of the late Middle Ages than had been possible in the less far-ranging commercial towns earlier in that era. The half millennium that has intervened since the close of the Middle Ages may have shown a secular decline in universal ethnic identification. But recent trends toward greater social complexity—"cultural pluralism"—reversed the course and made medieval experience of more direct relevance to our understanding of cities today. A particularly sharp contrast between the medieval town and the current one is the vastly enhanced role of economic class in modern cities.

Two periods of morphogenetic experimentation and transformation come clearly into focus as times in which to seek explanation and understanding of the emergence of economic class as a force in the shaping of cities. The first period came when men could begin to conceive of the city as a physical and functional entity, subject to a preconception of design that differed greatly from the slow organic evolution that had occurred during the Middle Ages. From this conscious design came the *bastide*. The other period centers on the radical transformation of the scale of *economic activity* in cities, which grew into the Industrial Revolution of the seventeenth, eighteenth, and nineteenth centuries. During this period, the space within cities was so radically expanded that the question of distance as a factor internal to the city gained economic significance, with land-rent emerging as the mechanism for measurement of "value" and the assignment of location. The outcome was the modern metropolis.

Even in the organic towns of the High Middle Ages, economic distinction was made among people, but without the locational association and interclass separation that have existed for the last several centuries. The rich merchant lived above his counting house and the prosperous craftsman above his workroom. But as some men gained great wealth they also began to grab great political power. Possession of that power seems to have made them desire physical demonstration of their distinction. Unlike the Pearly King and Queen, the medieval magnate could not wear his wealth incontestably blazoned on his coat; he sought to show it in the build of his house. That search for morphological distinction allied the powerful merchant politician with the bishops and noblemen who lived in the town in increasing numbers as the fourteenth and fifteenth centuries advanced. This alliance elevated design of houses and housing quarters to the central concern of the elite and, as a result, of the increasingly less democratic city governments. The city of the Renaissance was shaped and became the habitat of princes possessed, by the late fifteenth century, of absolute power.

While the Renaissance city was being shaped to the desires of the leisured group possessed of great and arbitrary authority, wastelands of one sort or another had grown up in odd crannies of Europe. These had arisen from the religious conflicts, the Hundred Years War between France and England, and the great folk battles between Spaniard and Saracen, German and Slav, and the Balkan peoples and the Turks. A set of new settlements had been established first to reoccupy these wastelands but even more to make them flower economically. These bastides became the closest thing the Middle Ages produced to a classless society, and served as a laboratory for social, economic, and religious innovation that was to bring forth many institutions and attitudes. They shaped the beginnings of the modern world, and the tradition of relatively egalitarian economic settlements that became the basis for the urban structuring of the European plantations overseas, most notably in North America. Before considering the nature of the bastide we must see how class division came generally to medieval cities.

The Rise of the Class-bound City

The lever the townsman used to raise himself and his family above the level of the mass was his pile of capital. It bought him a country house with the potential for social elevation; it could also mean that his sons might inherit position without the hard labor of learning a trade and gaining admission to the status of freeman. A "gentleman" might always be given civic freedom without mastery of a trade. Unlike the feudal lord of the manor, whose path of power was the traditional deference given his family by the serfs with backs bent in his service (his exalted status was birthright knowledge to all men living in his neighborhood), the city merchant often needed obtrusive assertion by visible and understandable physical symbols. The city house, first perhaps only a roomy example of the modular form in most towns, soon became a mansion reflective of growing capital. To show the facade of the house became of critical importance, as that was the only part the masses would ever be invited to observe. In the fifteenth century, with the concern for the external appearance of the house, prominent, observable sites for the location of private houses became important for the first time since the fall of Rome.

The early organic growth of medieval towns made the creation of impressive building sites extremely difficult. Few had any clear view of what the ultimate form of the city would be. Only as city experience informed as to the way they would grow and the processes involved was it practical to think about city design to accomplish specific aesthetic, architectural, and social ends. By the thirteenth century the form had become organized, if not really standardized, and a town could be thought about as an entity. Once a reason arose to perceive future forms and uses, as it did when men sought to build impressive structures, the process to accomplish that goal was now understood.

The Palais de Jacques Coeur in Bourges was the grandest house of a commoner in medieval France, one bought through wealth gained as a merchant. The courtyard served his commercial needs and the great attics of the building stored the goods he sold at counters there.

The Example of Jacques Coeur

We may look in detail at the medieval treasurer to the king of France, Jacques Coeur, and his palace to see how the craving for display arose, and how it was satisfied. Starting as a bright young man at Bourges in central France, sometime around 1418, Jacques became an entrepreneur in the full sense of the word. "It was to hard work, patience, and attention to detail that Jacques Coeur owed the fortune which seemed to his contemporaries all the more fabulous because its sources were afar and it was made by calling upon original techniques." The ingenuity required of the merchant is attested to by his multifarious undertakings, clearly attended by a success that made the French of his time liken a great reward to making one *"riche comme Jacques Coeur."*

Those vast riches came from many places. "Given responsibility for striking of royal coinage, Jacques Coeur, already a merchant, became at the same time the supplier to the King and the Court, and as well their official purchasing agent." We begin to see the role of capital: "At the same time seller and buyer, he became lender, and above all lender capable of long-term credits." Such a patience with capital was required by the realm in which he operated. "His business was located not only in France at Paris, Bourges, Lyon,

Montpellier, Marseille, but as well in Bruges [Belgium], Florence, Barcelona, and even at Beirut, Alexandria, and Damascus. He built a fleet, developed traffic in all directions, even from the West to the East. He bought afar the gold which he paid for with silver bullion from his mines in France and doubled in each strike the value of his stake."[1] But it must have been in his home town that the great merchant had to set about demonstrating his rise.

In 1443 Coeur had bought the ground necessary for the building of a great city house, a true *palais*, on the ramparts of the Gallo-Roman city which Bourges succeeded. The district had served for over three centuries to house the more noble buildings of the town: the cathedral, one of the greatest of France; the archepiscopal palace, only just come to be occupied by a new archbishop, Jacques' son, Jean; and the Palais of the Duc de Berry, one of the most intellectual of France's great lords. "It was not merely a vast city palace, closely akin to the palaces of patrician families in Italy,

[1]Jean Faviere, Le Palais de Jacques Coeur, *Bourges: Desquand, 1972, n.p.*

which he had wished to be possessed of; he had hoped to do better still and to join a comfortable residence, endowed with commodious apartments and rich reception rooms, to some premises well adapted to the needs of his business." Coeur thus mingled the practical concerns of the self-made magnate with the social striving of the *noveau riche*, and in proportions of his interest only larger in totality (rather than different in kind) from those that have commonly divided the attention of the successful bourgeoisie over the centuries. His location had to be close to that of the social peers he sought to court; at the same time, it had to have "premises well adapted to the needs of his business."

Because the *palais* still stands, restored more or less to its initial form, it provides a useful insight into desires of the successful merchant seeking to carry on his trade in the late Middle Ages. "The general plan announced this to be a city mansion [*hôtel*] of the classical age: the mansion at the back of a courtyard elongated at each side by low wings which closed upon an entrance pavilion."[2] Great mansions in French towns followed this courtyard pattern as long as they were being built. Much of the ground floor space in the entrance pavilion and the wings was opened through arched bays to the courtyard, furnishing covered sites susceptible, it seems, to use for storing wagons and carts and for the conduct of trade. The upper stories contained large, richly decorated apartments, seemingly furnished sparsely when built, as well as a storage place in the attics to which the local producers could bring their agricultural products for sale. Little "adaptation" of this great high attic to the efficient conduct of trade seems to have occurred despite its counter and measuring containers. Producers had to carry sacks on their backs up the long winding stairs, and Couer's servants had to bring them down again when staples were sent onward to Paris or the East. No evidence survives of a pulley that might have been used to raise and lower goods more efficiently, as in the high-houses of Amsterdam.

Everywhere in the Palais de Jacques Coeur, decoration recalls its builder's trade as the base of his wealth: tropical trees—oranges, date palms, and others whose species is not so easily determined, but clearly foreign to medieval France—ships, and other commodities to be found in the trade with the Levant are there, in the carvings of cornices, firebacks, and window enclosures, as well as in the mural decorations still surviving in some rooms. Unquestionably, Jacques presented the provenance of his fortune for the world to see. The whole sense of the *palais* even today is one of pride in commercial accomplishment. We can read as well the pains that the merchant took to make that prideful

[2]Ibid., *n.p.*

boast directly before his youthful friends and acquaintances; his palace was not in Paris or Orléans in the full gaze of the court, but rather in Bourges, where those providing the social stock from which he sprang could see it without looking far. The literature is full of analyses of the ostentatious buildings constructed by these unself-consciously vain merchants; it says little of the vanity in geography that compelled these magnates to choose very specific places in which to place their "Boasts." For some it might be Paris or London or, much later, Fifth Avenue, but for many, it must needs be the home town. Because increasing numbers of men wished to assert their success, each large town had to set aside a quarter for Boasts, just as the eighteenth century gentleman's park had its vale for a Folly.

Coeur and his son Jean illustrate the two aspects of boasting—the father, the self-made man, built his palace to glorify the individual; the son held his pompous office before the eyes of the commonalty to strike awe and gain deference. Palaces such as Jacques Coeur's were to become rather common structures in cities in the succeeding five hundred years, but when it was built the only model he might consider was the building occupied by his son as an archbishop. The church had increasingly glorified individual men; thus the practice of making a physical assertion of status was well established when Jacques bought his ground. His purchase spread assertive architecture to the rich. With the Mercantile Revolution just beginning, far more rich men existed than princes, dukes, and elevated prelates; thus the spread of *morphological assertion of status* led ultimately to a far more powerful element in urban morphogenesis.

We should not leave Jacques in simple arrogant pride, for his fate was different. When the king's mistress died suddenly in 1450, Jacques' fortunes began to turn. Eighteen months later Agnes Sorel, a woman who owed Jacques money, and an Italian courtier accused him of having poisoned her. Now the whole thing appears to have been a simple frame-up, abetted by the envy and covetousness of the king and court. Coeur was convicted and sentenced to jail. His properties were confiscated and divided among Charles VII and his favorites. As the wealthiest private citizen France had ever produced, Coeur was ripe for plunder in a time when an individual had little defense from a grasping monarchy and a voracious church. Jacques in 1455 succeeded in escaping from his jail in Poitiers, fleeing first to semi-independent Provence, and then to the security of Rome where the pope welcomed him. Coeur was appointed captain of the fleet, being dispatched to relieve Rhodes from the increasing pressure of the Turks after their capture of Constantinople two years before. While underway, Jacques was suddenly stricken and died at the island of Chios in the Aegean.

Our concern for Jacques Coeur is not merely because he built a palace that survives as one of the most useful pieces of morphological evidence about economic activity in the Middle Ages. His history also represents the apotheosis of an era nearing its close. Coeur lived at a time when the merchants of France and England were just beginning to break out of the systemic constraints imposed at the time of the Crusades, when the Italian trading cities—Genoa, Pisa, Venice, Amalfi, and Florence—gained control of the trade with the East. On that base the Italians shaped a particular type of city, perhaps best exemplified by Venice, run by the merchants who, in due course, assumed for themselves both a tyranny of the city's people and the ennoblement of their own families.

People in the Middle Ages seem not to have understood the necessary tie between some modicum of democratic liberty and the continued economic development of the state. Under the oligarchies that arose in the Italian trading cities, the progressive impoverishment of the state was too easily overlooked in the face of increasing enrichment of the family. The death of Venetian independence came only in 1797, at the hands of the French, but the weakness that led to that fate began five hundred years before when the patrician oligarchy was completed. From then on, Venice lacked any effective popular participation in the government. Personal and family greed gained a control that led easily to endless wars, the late-in-the-day adoption of feudalism as a method of economic-geographical organization of the lands that the republic had previously won through her "support" of the Crusades, and the imposition of a rigid monopoly for her merchants in the Levantine trade. The factionalism within Venice was so extreme that only the ceaseless conflict with the other republics and duchies of Italy matched its evil. Selfishness was the way of life, leaving the state often the loser and the common people invariably the victim. The notion of the commune, then growing in Europe north of the Alps, which produced some civic compassion and the search for shared advance, was missing.

Not surprisingly, these late medieval merchants were selfish and small-minded men, grasping wealth and power for themselves and their families. Feudalism had engendered a fairly selfish view of geography as well as power; one sought to gain domains to increase one's wealth and to perpetuate that possession within one's family. Neither civic nor national goals led the lords of towns and the monarchs of countries to fight for distant lands, but grasping family greed. When the heirs to the first Angevin count began their conquests by marriage and by warfare, they came to rule over a vast area, serving at one time or another as kings of Jerusalem, England, Aragon, Sicily, Naples, and even Hungary. But little of their rule went to the credit and betterment of the town of Angers, and certainly none to the interests of France. The seemingly endless wars of succession were mainly great explosions of family avarice which stretched the fabric of western civilization nearly to the breaking point. Is it much wonder that merchants tended to view their role as entirely one of advancing the family fortunes?

In this context Jacques Coeur seems a transitional figure. His search for wealth ranked well with his near neighbors, the Counts of Anjou, causing him to be treated with the mixture of deference and envy that those rulers called down upon themselves. Coeur's fall was largely due to his having more power than the system would allow to a private individual. But before his imprisonment, he expressed that power in the way of his peers—through socially assertive building which shows a megalomania equal to the demands of his position. Throughout his palace, his heart-shaped arms are emblazoned in carving and painting to the point it is the family that stands out. Jacques was in that way the summation of his times.

Yet he also seems the harbinger of a new era in which scientific trading practices were introduced, order was given to the conduct of long-distance trade, and the national economy was beginning to emerge. As keeper of the king's mint, Coeur had to reorganize a much debased coinage; he seems to have accomplished the task with skill. He was France's first modern businessman and one of Europe's great merchants. But he lacked the application to more selfless interests than those typical of his time. The notion of raising the lot of mankind as a whole was slowly emerging, finally breaking the obsessive hold of the Germanic clan system which had flooded over Europe at the collapse of the Roman empire. The urban commune had been shaped in northern Europe to begin that reform, in the towns alone; the countryside was still too committed to feudalism, the social disease brought by the barbarians. Only when the national economy began to take form in France and England, forcing the rapid dissolution of the narrow domainal economies, could much change occur in the countryside.

If Jacques Coeur had taken up the interests of the commune and the development of the mercantile economy, we would know him better than we do because he would have been the initiator of the modern world. But he was too involved in the end of the medieval era to assume the role, so he remains a relatively obscure but nonetheless fascinating figure.

Other men and other forces were left to hammer out the transition between the early economic order in which the town and country were contending adversaries and the modern one where they are clearly integrated. We may best begin analysis of that complex transition by contemplating the emergence of civic parity and reasonable urban democracy. In that development, the *bastide* of the High Middle Ages fills the important gap between the tolerated town located within a mass of feudalism and the encouraged town in the midst of the national economy.

The Urban Commune:
A Step on the Way

The real nature of things is succinctly expressed in Henri Pirenne's statement, "Democracy in the Middle Ages, as in modern times, got its start under the guidance of a select few who foisted their programme upon the confused aspirations of the people."[3] As he shows, the drive for a civic responsibility similar to that already granted in the burgeoning Italian city republics took first hold in the episcopal cities north of the Alps. In those bishops' towns in upper Italy and the northwest of Europe, a level of concern for the populace existed that might be lacking in the feudal countryside.

But the more the bishops were conscious of their duties, the more also they had to defend their government against the demands of their subjects and endeavor to keep them under an authoritative, patriarchal regimen. The confusion of spiritual power and temporal power in their hands, moreover, caused every concession to seem to them to be a peril to the Church. It must not be forgotten that their functions obliged them to reside permanently in their cities and that they feared, with good reason, the difficulties which would be caused them by the autonomy of the burghers in whose midst they lived. Finally, it has already been seen that the Church had little sympathy with trade. This unsympathetic attitude must naturally have made the Church deaf to the wishes of the merchants and of the people who were grouped behind them, have prevented an understanding of their wants, and given a false impression of their real power. Out of this came misunderstandings, clashes, and soon an open hostility which, after the beginning of the eleventh century, was to end in the inevitable.[4]

Success attended the attacks on episcopal tempo-

ral power first in upper Italy where a number of towns gained political control by the local populace. "Towards the end of the eleventh century there emerged, with royal (or imperial) sanction the institution known as the consulate, at Lucca and Pisa in 1081, at Milan in 1094, at Genoa in 1099; during the first thirty years of the twelfth century it appeared at Bergamo, Bologna, Modena and Verona, and in 1138 at Florence. This was a specific indication of the growing political maturity of the communes, whose municipal government was becoming all the time richer, more varied and more independent."[5]

Contemporaneous with these events in Italy were the faltering steps toward municipal autonomy in the North "in the region of Flanders and the North of France. There is nothing surprising in this, since that country, like Lombardy, had been the scene of vigorous commercial activity." And almost everywhere, the merchant group provided the "select few who foisted their programme upon the confused aspirations of the people." Pirenne tells of the events in Cambrai, in Flanders, as the first instance of such blows for municipal liberty; his account effectively summarizes the morphological and social conditions attending this effort.

During the eleventh century the prosperity of this city was well advanced. At the foot of the original town clustered a commercial suburb, which had been surrounded in 1070 by a wall. The population of this suburb endured with scant patience the authority of the bishop and his castellan. It prepared in secret for revolt when, in 1077, Bishop Gerard II had to absent himself to go receive in Germany the investiture at the hands of the Emperor. He was hardly en route before, under the direction of the richest merchants of the town, the people arose, took possession of the gates and proclaimed a commune. The poor, the artisans, and the weavers, in particular, launched themselves still more passionately into the fray when a reformer-priest . . . denounced to them the bishop as a simoniac and inspired in the depths of their hearts the mysticism which, at the same era, was arousing the Lombard Patarenes. As in Italy, religious fervor lent its strength to the political demands and the commune was sworn in the midst of general enthusiasm.[6]

The interjection of a puritanical religious element in this movement should not be missed. Both in Flanders and in Lombardy the drive for civic liberty was joined to one for reform in the Roman church, which took the form in a number of places of adherence to the Bogomil

[3]Henri Pirenne, Medieval Cities: Their Origins and the Revival of Trade, *Princeton: Princeton University Press, 1925, p. 179.*
[4]Ibid., *pp. 179-180.*

[5]*Friedrich Heer*, The Medieval World: Europe 1100-1350, *New York: New American Library, 1962, p. 76.*
[6]Pirenne, op. cit., *pp. 184-185. Simony was the buying and selling of church offices.*

or dualist theology. The Paterenes (dwellers in the rag-pickers' quarter) were initially a party seeking to end the practice of priestly marriage but ultimately became one of the factions in the dualist Cathari whose brutal extinction was gained in the Albigensian Crusade two centuries later. Thus, from the very beginning of the fight for the urban commune, an undercurrent of religious dissent and purification existed. As we shall see, even the destruction of the Cathari and many of their towns did not dissuade their successors in the new towns, the bastides, built on the ashes of the Albigensian Crusade, from seeking anew to reform the church that had such a long history of enmity both to democratic liberty and economic liberalism.

Though the Cambrai commune was temporarily suppressed by their bishop when he returned in haste, in the end most of the towns that sought to create an urban commune prevailed. Pirenne points out that the monarchy, particularly Louis VI in France, took up the cause of the commune and began, perhaps vaguely at first, but ultimately with clarity of perception, to understand the fact that the city was more the friend of the national state than were either the great feudal lords or the ecclesiastical magnates. The lords were little concerned other than for their families, while the clerics could not distinguish between the willing devotion they easily received in matters of faith and the grudging obedience to simple force they secured in their role as rulers. As Pirenne saw it, "The clear interest of the Monarchy was to support the adversaries of feudalism . . . .The entry of the burghers upon the political scene had as a consequence the weakening of the contractual principle of the Feudal State to the advantage of the principle of the authority of the Monarchial State. It was impossible that royalty should not take count of this and seize every chance to show its good will to the communes which, without intending to do so, labored so usefully for it."[7]

The medieval town is essentially unintelligible outside the context of trade, a form of commercial activity quite wide-ranging when compared with the domainal economy of the feudal state. Both the great vassals and the great clerics had secured their power by dismembering a national monarchial state, be it the Roman Empire or Charlemagne's, and they could not be expected to favor its resurrection. "On the other hand all the incentives which inspired the bishop to oppose the burghers carried no weight with the princes. They professed no hostility in regard to trade; on the contrary they were experiencing its good effects."[8] At first the princes might shy away from too broad an extension of the principle of commercial freedom to extend to the full realm or even well beyond its limits. But later experience, as well as evolving economic understanding, encouraged the rulers to grant increasingly broad rights and freedoms to towns, and finally to give them incentives to push the trading frontier well beyond the national sovereignty. In that latter campaign, Jacques Coeur served France so well. Unfortunately he did so at a time when the individual still had no security if he rose to such heights as to encourage the king's envy. When the courtiers could encourage that, even the most powerful merchant was likely to fall.

Cities, however, held reasonable security of person,

Antwerp was the greatest entrepôt of trade north of the Alps, a fact reflected in her great public buildings and solid bourgeois houses.

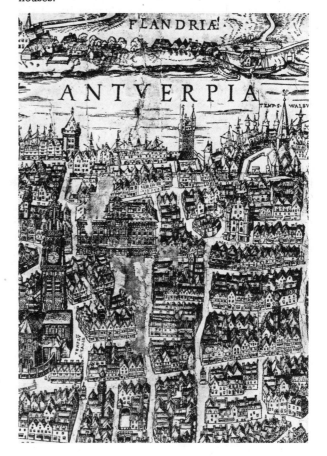

[7]Ibid., *pp. 186-187.*
[8]Ibid., *p. 189.*

of land, of goods, and of equitable judicial procedures, up to a point. To defend those rights the city had a distinct territoriality, separated from the different laws and practices of the countryside, a set of punishments visited on those living within its boundaries if they broke its rather severe restraints, and a system of taxation to pay for the building of strong walls to defend it against outsiders. As Pirenne has said, "[T]he city of the Middle Ages was simultaneously a legal district and a commune." The legal administration was in the hands of the magistrates whereas the general administration was in the hands of a council, each group drawn from the citizenry by majority will.

The medieval city that emerged with a communal government was a fully developed system to provide for economic and social health and security for its citizens. Pirenne has likened its completeness and originality as a system to that developed for the building of the great Gothic cathedrals: "'[L]et each man help the other like a brother,' says a Flemish charter of the twelfth century, and these words were actually a reality ... This was because, in reality, each individual life depended directly upon the collective life of the municipal association. The commune of the Middle Ages had, in fact, all the essential attributes which the state exercises today." Unfortunately the parallel with the state was so strong that the town shared most of its weaknesses. "To the ardor of local patriotism corresponded its exclusivism. From the very fact that each city constituted a State, cities saw in one another only rivals and enemies. They could not rise above the sphere of their own interests."[9]

The system that was worked out so thoroughly and so successfully within the city walls disappeared at the gates. Only in the later Middle Ages did people begin to have some hazy idea of the city as part of a larger interdependency, which might equally profit its corporators as had the medieval commune. For such a larger system to function, an economic system had to come into being fully emancipated from the narrow regionalism, the gross greed, and the central trading-town ideas of the earlier communes.

The civic spirit which animated them was singularly egotistic. They jealously reserved to themselves the liberties they enjoyed within their walls. The peasants who dwelt round about them did not seem to them to be compatriots at all. They thought only of profitably exploiting them. With all their might they stood on guard to prevent the peasants from freeing themselves from the industrial system of which the cities had a monopoly. The task of provisioning these cities was likewise imposed upon the peasants, who were subjected to a tyrannical protectorate whenever it was possible to do so, as in Tuscany, for

[9]Ibid., pp. 218-219.

example, where Florence subjected to its yoke all the surrounding countryside. [In sum] the city of the Middle Ages, as it existed in the twelfth century, was a commercial and industrial commune living in the shelter of a fortified enceinte and enjoying a law, an administration and a jurisprudence of exception which made of it a collective, privileged personality.[10]

That personality might on occasion produce a superb example and halcyon times, but only with some increased understanding of the interdependence of individual cities was advance very general. Before such broadened understanding came, glory often died with its time and the relative abilities of individuals and generations tended to create compensating decline, due to conflict, to match growth, due to victory. The Italian communes showed how short the truly communal existence might be by turning to tyranny and oligarchy by the fourteenth and fifteenth centuries.

The institution of the city was raised to an advanced form, perhaps more coherent than today, during the High Middle Ages, but not until the very end of that era was the congress of those institutions worked out. The bastide plays an unusual and certainly relatively unappreciated role in that developing urban congress, in those parts of Europe where communal retrogression had been avoided.

Bourgs, Faubourgs, and Bastides

To set a contrast to the model of urban morphogenesis that Henri Pirenne brought to our attention in his *Medieval Cities* of 1926, we may best recall it to mind. In studying the emergence of the commune in Flanders, Pirenne tells us, "All these cities show, first, the characteristic feature of having been organized around a central burg which was, so to speak, their nucleus. At the foot of this burg was grouped a *portus*, or 'new burg,' populated by merchants to whose numbers were soon added artisans, either free or serf, and where, after the eleventh century, the textile industry came to be concentrated. Over the burg as over the *portus* extended the authority of the castellan."[11] From this description, this model is commonly referred to as that of the *bourg and faubourg*, using the French form to create a more felicitous pairing.

[10]Ibid., pp. 219-220.
[11]Ibid., p. 191.

Fundamental to the *bourg-faubourg* model is the notion of prior authority and, as the legal form and social practices of the commune evolved, a certain element of class conflict. Gerard II was not an isolated tyrant and the tension between the local lord and the town populace was a commonplace of the era. In the *bourg* both the morphology of the place and the legal standing of the townsmen partook of several somewhat conflicting systems. To cite one example: when the merchants first took up residence in the *portus*, they undoubtedly did so at the legal sufferance of the lord of the *bourg*, if not in outright commendation to him, which made them liable for labor and military service to that lord. The land they held in possession was under a form of leasehold, which preserved to the landlord considerable power to affect the lives of the merchants.

But as the merchants gained economic power, they tended as well to secure more personal freedom. "With freedom of person there went on equal footing, in the city, the freedom of land. In a merchant community, land, in fact, could not remain immobile and be kept out of commerce by unwieldy and diverse laws that prevented its free conveyance and kept it from serving as a means of credit and acquiring capital value." In explaining the reason for this shift in the view of land and the strong effort that merchants made to transform its legal status when held by them, Henri Pirenne saw evolution of rights to property as certain. "This was the more inevitable in that land, within the city, changed its nature—it became ground for building. It was rapidly covered with houses, crowded one against the other, and increased in value in proportion as they multiplied. Thus it automatically came about that the owner of a house acquired in the course of time the ownership, or at least the possession, of the soil upon which it was built."

At that point the continuing conflict with the ancient landlord was likely to be resolved in a final, legal form. "Everywhere the old desmesnial land was transformed into 'censal estate,' or 'censal allodium.' City hold thus became free hold." In contrast, in the countryside, occupation and utilization of land was likely to be by feudal or at best leasehold tenure until the nineteenth century.[12]

Though most conflicts between the past system, the feudal order, and the newly shaped mercantile order tended ultimately to be resolved in favor of the latter in cities, the discord also tended to create a rather narrow-minded defensiveness among burghers. This attitude was reflected in the quite unlovable practices they adopted toward other men, in the countryside around the city and in other towns. Past grudges and present contest do not make men generous to those of

[12]Ibid., *p. 202.*

different status living nearby or even to those living far away in the same status. Only when a slate clean of such discord could be found might we hope for some larger system of human interaction.

Extension came through one of two systems: the first—the counter model—was a very restricted form of interaction focussing mainly on the economic component of human activity; the second—the bastide model—was later in time and encompassed a more complete range of human endeavor.

The Counter Model of Narrow Freedom

The *hanse* had only a very partial role in the economic activity within the city, but was an institution that tended to continue the discordant organization of the town's life. Specifically, a *hanse* was a gild or trading association within a single town; the term has come to refer to the league worked out among such organizations in a string of towns in Europe north of the Alps. Thus the Hanseatic League was a definite organization, which sought *in a very limited fashion* to overcome the constraint on long-distance trade imposed by the defensive, parochial concerns of townsmen seeking earnestly to gain internal freedom within their own particular commune. A fierce competitive effort was involved but not a nationalistic one, as we understand that term. We tend to think of the Hanseatic League as a Germanic enslavement of other less aggressive peoples. The Germans were haughty and arbitrary merchants, seeking to gain concessions without giving them, but in the west they were not seeking political domination.

A similar situation existed with respect to the operations of the Mediterranean merchants in the area north of the Alps, and we subsume the activities of the Venetians and other Italians and their trading expeditions under the rubric of the counter model.

This model implies the creation of a *limited purpose-specialized activity linkage among otherwise independent cities.* The organization would tend to offer profit to all participants (though less than a fair share, it would seem, to staple producers); only in a small way did it represent a national undertaking. The form is rather similar to the "multinational corporation" of the present day; like it, the league tended to be reviled by contemporaries not for its "nationalism" but for its "soulless pursuit of profit."

The morphogenetic expression of the counter model was the extraterritorial quarter within the city, or at its edge. These *kontors*, or steelyards, as they were called in London, stood somewhat with respect to the native city as the *portus* had with respect to the *bourg*. The steelyard and *faubourg* were both outside the existing local legal and taxing system, operating under special, permissive regulations allowed by the suzerain who believed his losses by the exception were more than made up by his gains from the economic activity it encouraged. Just as the *faubourg* sought to institutionalize its communal privileges, so the steelyard attempted to fix its monopoly of distant trade. But history was against the establishment of such privileges. The experience with the creation of trading communes had suggested to the crown that more was to be gained by limiting the conduct of trade to the king's subjects, securing from them payments for the privilege, than was to be secured from granting its conduct to those who could, like the great vassals, stand somewhat independent of the sovereign. After a couple of centuries the evidence was clear; the king understood that what he needed was a *national system of trade* quite distinct from the one the merchants in a single city might shape, and fully equal to that organized by foreign competitors such as the Hanseatic League or the Venetians with their trading galleys.

The conditions that made the German and Italian trading ventures powerful from the thirteenth through the sixteenth centuries began to wane around 1550. Soon after 1500 the new Portuguese trading route to the East around Africa provided competition for the Venetians. The French and English economies were strengthening and becoming national, rather than broken into the efforts of a few competing ports. After four hundred years of subservience to foreign traders, France and England emerged as the great commercial powers of Europe, pushing the mercantile frontier away from their own ports and to the ports of north Germany and Italy, even forcing the creation at Livorno of an English trading entrepôt in Italy. To accomplish this turn-about, a new national economy was necessary, as well as the extension of trade across the Atlantic and to the East. New trading practices had to be shaped and new forms of settlement employed. A domestic network of trade had to be worked out, for which the bastide was a highly important innovation.

The Planted Town in Europe: Colonization at Home

Traditionally, history is divided into European and "colonial" phases and stages, yet I wish to suggest that before colonization spread across the broad western ocean, it already existed within Europe. It was particularly tied to the attempt to expand local economies into national economies, both by substituting national initiative for local and by creating a form of colonial settlement, the bastide, which might be used to develop the wastelands or less-than-fully-developed regions of the kingdom. No wonder that the most active of the European bastidors, those shaping these settlements, were a couple of centuries later the great colonizers of the New World. Although the Germans and the Spaniards did build many bastides, they did so for political conquest rather than economic development. Throughout the most active times of overseas colonization, they lacked the national economy at home to make the most of the form as an economic development device. In the end the Spaniards in the New World shaped not a true bastide but instead a Roman *castrum*, an armed camp to exact tribute from a subject people.

The Bastide

The instrument of colonial settlement may have been fairly clear in the sixteenth century when the call to the New Lands was voiced, but that settlement form—the bastide—had evolved over a period of nearly five hundred years. During that same epoch, the "counters" of the Germans and Italians were to have their greatest spread and be most effective in repressing full-fledged economic development in northwestern Europe. The very term *bastide* recalls a set of specific circumstances that brought the new town into existence and gave it the particular qualities that would be of such importance in settling the New Lands of the New World.

No doubt the notion of a planned, preconceived town was not what brought about the founding of new settlements but rather the great need that existed for towns in an area deficient of them. The townless waste might be small—part of a forest, a bogland only currently being cleared, or an estate as yet not fully developed. It might, on the other hand, be vast by the standards of the time, such as the area devastated by the savage Albigensian Crusade of the thirteenth century. In either case, the actual, planted town would be much the same but in the vaster areas, the systemic ties among towns might be quite different, since they were products of the times rather than inheritances of

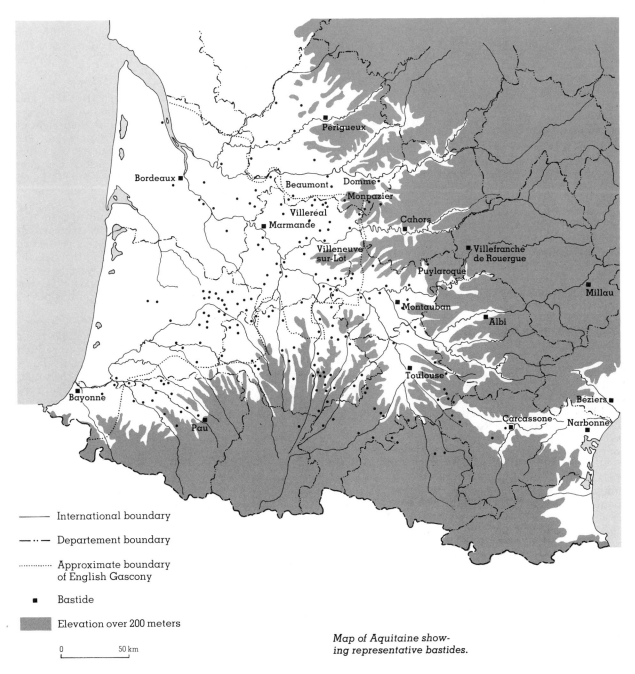

International boundary

Departement boundary

Approximate boundary of English Gascony

■ Bastide

Elevation over 200 meters

0   50 km

Map of Aquitaine showing representative bastides.

cloudy provenance. Thus it serves our purposes better to look at the situation in southwestern France where geographical scope existed both for many new towns and for a reasonably extensive network of economic interaction among them. As an experiment for New World settlement, this was the best Europe had to offer.

The field for town founding was clearest in Gascony, Guienne, Perigord, and Languedoc in southern France. Under the Roman Empire, and its successors in the Gallo-Roman Empire, urbanism was particularly strongly developed in southern France—in Provence, Languedoc, and Aquitania of today, in the Po Basin of Italy, and in Flanders. In the lands of the Counts of Toulouse, urbanism seemed to have its Gallic flowering, both in the sense of the number and importance of towns and in the existence of an urbane culture. There, too, in harness with the towns of the Po Basin, religious dissent was most open. The towns of the south were the home of merchants, both Christian and Jew, who were particularly enlightened for their time and perhaps the precursors of a later humanism. The southern countryside possessed a nobility strongly inclined toward a movement to purify the church and to adopt a dualist theology. Dualism argued that God is both good and evil, and that the earthly realm belongs to the evil God; thus physical death would release the soul from life in a world of evil into a world of good. No better device had existed to encourage physical bravery and theological tenacity, conditions that made the dualists (the Cathari or Albigensians of this area; the Patarenes in Milan), tenacious and effective critics of the established church. They were as well among the first "universalists," holding that all men would be saved, a position which would have shattered the power of the medieval Roman church. The escape from the imprisonment of the captive soul housed in a body in an evil world made the Cathari joyous in death, quite in contrast to adherents of the Roman church, whose deathbed fear of possible perdition often shattered their courage.

Starting in 1207 the pope, Innocent III, and the curia exerted an increasingly severe pressure on the independent-minded Albigenses, a group who saw themselves basically divested of the Roman priesthood, standing in permanent opposition to the license, corruption, and venality of the Roman church. Local bishops who seemed too weakly opposed to the Cathari were soon stripped of their authority, and Rome sent in bitter monkish zealots—Dominicans in particular—who increased the pressures: using first the sermon, then the ban, followed in turn by excommunication, imprisonment, and ultimately the stake. But the Albigenses held firm and, at last, after ten years, Innocent III struck with a most unchristian venom. He called upon the French king, Louis VIII, to invade and destroy the Albigeois, Béziers, and the Toulousain. In that he

was successful, though Louis died on his return to the north. Now the Midi that had till then been at best a nominal fief of France, with essential independence for its lords and a much higher development of urban life, was firmly attached to the French kingdom, and its firmer attachment was in the interests of the crown and the realm.

Soon after the vicious capture of the south, the French crown fell vacant, under the operation of the Salic law which ruled that Charles IV's closest male relative, Edward III of England, was unable to succeed him when the senior male line became extinct. Instead the succession passed to a cadet branch, the Valois, and the Plantagenets of England began the Hundred Years War, seeking what they believed to be their rightful succession to the French crown. The events of those 116 years were devastating. The most constant pressure between the two contestants was felt on their common frontier in southwestern France, between the Guienne controlled by the kings of England and centering on Bordeaux, and the Limousin and Perigord of the kings of France. In the smaller Perigord and Agenais districts, a wilderness (which had in part been created at the time of the Albigensian Crusade) separated the two forces. Within that largely vacant area, they sought during the grim years of intermittent warfare to use new towns both for the production of rents for the constantly depleting royal exchequer and as strong-points in a seemingly interminable war.

The other instances of medieval town-building on a large scale—in Germany east of the Elbe, on the coasts of Wales, in southern Spain and elsewhere—were often cases of planting a victorious population on the lands recently conquered, in many cases to assure the subjugation of the rural population. In southern France the situation was more directly that of town-founding for less aggressive purposes, even despite the dynastic conflict between the king of France and the king of England. The history of the Hundred Years War lacks the nationalistic content that we have come to think an essential ingredient of any conflict; it was a conflict concerned mainly with the more directly acquisitive aspects of dynastic possession. In that milieu the new town, the bastide, became an essential element in the drawn-out battles for possession.

The most commonly understood derivative of the word "bastide" today is *bastille*, which was once widely used in northern France to designate a fortress. T. F. Tout in *Medieval Town Planning*, certainly the seminal work on bastides in English, drew the comparison between the bastille and the bastide and left the suggestion that the defensive quality of these places gave them their name.[13] Yet in looking at them we find that

[13]*T. F. Tout*, Medieval Town Planning: A Lecture, *London: The University Press, 1917.*

sometimes the bastide was unwalled, suggesting that a distinction must be drawn between the use of the new foundations as a defensive place, a strong-point, and their use to plant settlement and to utilize economically deserted lands.

The key to the question of whether these were defensive places, with normal fortification, or simply towns that might or might not be walled is to be found in the relations between the town and the populace of the surrounding countryside. Where a hostile subjugated population was held in rural serfdom (as in German conquest east of the Elbe) or in continuing resistance but at bay in marchlands (as in the investing of Wales by the English kings, particularly Edward I, of the twelfth and thirteenth centuries), the bastide would of necessity have to be defensive in every instance.

Maurice Beresford tells us Wales had only one *burh*, town borough, before the Normans came in the role of kings and barons of England—Clwydmouth, presently Rhuddlan. The other eighty-six medieval boroughs in Wales were of English foundation. Of those, eighty-four were preconceived planted towns falling generally under the rubric of bastides, as we use the term. The tie between town founding and defense of an overlord population is well shown in what Beresford terms "The classic statement of the tie between castle and town," in George Owen's *Pembrokeshire*:

And the saied lordes att their first coming to those lordships by conquest, espyenge out the fertile partes in ech countrye, builded their castles for thmselves and townes for their owne soldiers and countryemen which came with them to remayne neere about them as their guarde, and to allwayes ready to keep under such of the countrye inhabitantes as wold offere to rebell . . .and by this meanes all the townes and castles in most part of Wales . . . were first built. [14]

In the German east a series of defensive villages, *Rundlings*, was devised to allow the new settlement of a Teutonic population in a land captured from Slavs and certainly not "given up" by its original owners. In such a situation defense became part of daily life leaving the survival of the invaders dependent upon their protective organization and building.

The situation in the south of France, within the realms of both the French and the English kings, was rather in contrast. The populations had different suzerains, but ethnic contrast was absent between the townsmen and the country population. Even the English plantations were inhabited by francophonic vassals of the English king, not by his anglophonic dependents. The new place became an instrument of dynastic competition, not of new conquest and subjection; thus, not all towns need be fortified, mainly those adjacent to the frontiers that were often of rather long standing during the 116 years of the Hundred Years War. That frontier ran most consistently in the Agenais and Perigord, with the English to the west and south and the French to the east and north.

In his recent monumental study of these bastidal places, Maurice Beresford derives the term more precisely than did Tout two generations ago. "The Gascon word *bastide* was the usual term for the planted town in south-western France, and in its Latin form *bastida* occurs in almost every foundation charter . . . .The word bastide derived originally from the southern form of the verb meaning 'to build', the same word which in modern French has become *bâtir*." [15] These towns were quintessentially conceived of as a complete unit and then laid down on the ground in that fashion. Although Beresford applies the English term "new towns" to these places, I have rejected it as parochial and meaningless in American English. In the United States "new towns" have been built in every generation on a scale such that town founding is considered a continuing process. And the places in southwestern France founded before and during the Hundred Years War are so distinctive as to deserve the use of the name that those living when they were established gave them.

The bastide was not an unquestionably urban form. Many of these towns remained the tiny plantations in rural settings which they began. They warrant extended discussion because they were newly created in the thirteenth and fourteenth centuries as integrated units, and often survive fairly much as they were originally laid out. All these factors permit us to use the bastide as a surviving morphological record from which we may infer some of the forces that came to account for the structure of medieval and Renaissance cities. The very success of a city has, in most cases, meant that its morphological record has been written over by later changes, leaving us with little on which to base our judgment of what determined the original form. And it is a rare good fortune that the bastide as a form emerged at that stage in history when the organic city of the earlier medieval times was giving way to the much more thought-out Renaissance creation.

Unfortunately most that has up to this time been written about these "planned" cities of the Renaissance has focused almost exclusively on grand plans done by architects and princes for the creation of high-art buildings, leaving us with a geography of monuments in a desert of misunderstanding of the real town where they stood. By learning about the form of the bastide, not usually very crowded with monuments,

[14] *Quoted in Maurice Beresford,* New Towns of the Middle Ages, *New York: Frederick A. Praeger, 1967, pp. 527-528.*

[15] Ibid., *pp. 8-9.*

we may help to make the urban desert visible, with plants that have always been present, shadowed by contemporary failure to record their nature and forgotten after the historical destruction of what records of commonplace buildings may have existed.

A real difference exists between preconception and rigid planning. To visualize the overall purpose and structure of a town requires a prior idea of what the town will do and what physical provisions will be needed to carry out that purpose. There may be no actual design of the buildings or even necessarily of the street-grid, just a general conception of how large the place will be and what it will do. In contrast, rigid planning determines the aesthetic qualities of the place—its visual image—and requires a detailed design that must be adhered to over a long period of time. The simple, preconceived town will have some *planned components*—the church and the marketplace—but other *evolved components* will be determined by the course of events in the town as it grows and matures. In the planned town, all growth is likely to be ruled by planned components.

Since the Renaissance, the arguments of ardent proponents of the planned town have usually been highly intellectualized and commonly rather authoritarian. Cardinal Richelieu had a town laid out on his estate that is frighteningly orderly and "visual," leaving one with the view that people must have had to become stereotypes to be allowed to live there. Versailles, Karlsruhe, Nancy, København, and the Rome of Sixtus V all partook of this visual regimentation of mankind to satisfy the ego of authority. Välingby outside Stockholm accomplishes the same result in recent time, with a bloodless bureaucracy substituted for the absolute monarch of the seventeenth century.

The Economic Role of the Bastide

The bastide has been dealt with almost exclusively as a rigid, geometric creation in the literature of urban design and city-form. Given an interest in design rather than morphogenesis, such a misrepresentation is likely to take place; in most instances, the eye sees what it seeks and architectural and urban historians have sought the regularity, the self-conscious design. If we turn the quest to the forces at work in shaping the city rather than the acts of individual designers, richer evidence confronts us than a crisply correct Monpazier or Aigues Mortes; we see instead towns of human quality, only vaguely correct, and, in fact, quite adapted to the accident in nature and human thought.

The fundamental dynamic of these places was preconception, not regularity. Most founders (and a number of their names and purposes are well recorded in Beresford's study) wanted to build a town *de novo* and rather quickly. We cannot reconstruct their thoughts, yet logic suggests that they did not first-off say: "It shall be foursquare, meticulously ordered, and of pleasing overall design!" We must be skeptical that the plan shape of the place was thought very important. Maps were little known, and isometric or perspective drawings virtually unknown; the human eye would not be able to see the town as a totality save in a few exceptional sites which might be viewed both at a distance and from above. Villefranche de Rouergue might have been so seen, but certainly neither Monpazier nor Aigues Mortes on its dead-flat plain was so conceived. Thus, regularity must have been the result of forces other than self-conscious design, at least in the beginning. As experience with bastides became more rich, we might expect the individuals invested with the job of establishing the town to think in terms of overall design. Even then, the use of certain fundamental dynamics of design rather than copies of existing plans seems to have created regularity.

The establishment of a bastide was a determined act supported by a lord, either temporal or ecclesiastical, into whose purse the quitrent, *cens* in French, would fall. Normally possession of land determined both who the founder would be and where his town would be placed. If the king held lands in his own name, he was likely to seek their development by placing a new town upon them. If he wished to found such a new town in a particular place, he commonly sought by thinly veiled confiscation or by exchange to gain possession of the title to the site he wanted. Commonly, "joint-ventures" were undertaken through the institution of *paréage* between king and vassal or bishop and petty nobility. Among the lesser lords and the magnates of the Roman church possession of a domain was determinative. The numerous inheritances by the church from penitents were often rather geographically scattered, so we find bishops and other ecclesiastical leaders developing bastides in places well away from their sees. The bishop of Winchester in southern England created bastides in six different places, only four of which were within the rather wide limits of his own county.[16] The town-founding efforts of temporal lords were often equally wide-ranging as their possessions were commonly made up of inheri-

[16]Ibid, *p. 441.*

tances and dowries gained in a very direct effort to expand the family holdings.

Once a landowner had decided to found a town, he would most likely consider geographical location, with two questions in mind: Where was there a deserted or under-used tract of land within his domains? And where within that general tract was there a precise site conducive to the building of a town which might return the largest total *cens* to its lord? As we shall see, these questions have initially entered the minds of land speculators throughout the ages. To a very considerable degree, the bastide founders of the Middle Ages were among the forefathers of the speculator who has done so much to shape the urban geography of the Industrial Age.

The tract within a broad domain that the landowner would choose to develop by the building of a new town was likely to lie at the frontier of existing settlement, if such a margin existed. In general, to the north of the Alps the lighter soils were among those first cleared for agriculture so the bastides were set up on the heavier lands, particularly in copses and woodlands. Even within existing farmland, potential might remain for a planted settlement. "The planted towns were particularly likely to increase the demand for food, since many of them had no agricultural land beyond their walls. The land immediately surrounding them already belonged to the fields or commons of an older settlement and the burgesses [of the bastide] could claim no part of them." This new place detached from agricultural pursuits was far less common in Gascony and the Perigord than in England; in those provinces, the unsettled sections were far more extensive, and organically evolving towns were absent from wide areas, having failed to develop or having been destroyed in the Albigensian Crusade or the Hundred Years War. In England, however, the "organic towns, being promoted villages, already had their fields and were not so dependent on food grown elsewhere."[17] Thus, the landowner who planted a new town might well add to the market for the produce of his existing estates.

Beresford summarizes graphically the role of the new town in increasing the wealth of the great landlords whose grip on the countryside was so selfish but yet so strong.

Yet there was an important difference between the increase in a lord's income that came from the sale of more demesne produce and an increase that came from the successful plantation of yet another town. In order to obtain any extra demesne produce, the lord (or his stewards) had to jerk into faster action the whole apparatus of villein services (for in the period of greatest urban expansion,

[17]Ibid., p. 75.

after 1150, production by conscripted villein labour was normal in the manors of the English lowlands). When village populations were small it had been possible to increase the demesne (and its product) by taking in assarted land, but as the thirteenth century progressed, the ploughs came nearer and nearer to the margins of cultivation and England began to look like a fair field over-full of folk. Attempts to wrench a greater product from the soil came up against the dumb resistance of the peasantry and the harsh fact of diminishing marginal returns. Compared with these wrestling matches, how effortless it must have seemed to be able to increase one's income by using seigneurial authority to say, "Let there be a town."[18]

In Gascony the picture was different and more interesting. The margins of settlement had not been reached and the bastidors were true pioneers in a forested land. The English examples leave us with the sour taste of grubbing for profit in a milieu of repression of basic human liberties whereas the French cases show a much more palatable social situation, matching the clean pleasantness of the wines whose grapes were grown on the newly cleared fields. The forceful extension of a mercantile frontier was leading to the planting of bastides in the Perigord and Agenais; that situation cannot help but suggest a strong parallel with later and more distant extensions of such mercantile frontiers.

Bastides and Staple Production

Given the fundamentally economic motive for the creation of bastides, we need not amplify the discussion of the functions initial and fundamental to their support. We know from records of the anxious desire that early settlers include a goodly number of merchants as well as the necessary craftsmen; special inducements were offered such men to settle in a bastide. To make these towns prosperous, and thus most rewarding to the landowner creating them, the merchants would best engage in distant trade rather than the sort of local retailing that took place among denizens in the marketplace. Distant trading was made possible only by creating a local agriculture productive of "trade goods," those staples that would stand the heavy cost of transportation in the Middle Ages. In that interest, we find bastides tending to be located on the major rivers of southwestern France—or at least to be only a short

[18]Ibid., pp. 75-76.

distance from their banks, possibly served by another bastidal port located directly on the bank, as Villeneuve-sur-Lot, one of the important bastidal creations. But something must be transported, so crops and products were chosen in reference to distant markets. Thus, the greatest distinction in the bastidal settlement and its economy would be between the farmer producing only for local consumption—food, wool, and wood—and his brother producing staples for export from the locality. It was not, as might be assumed on the evidence of the earlier split between mercantile town and feudal countryside, the divide of the city walls.

The tying together of bastide and countryside seems to have had great social importance. We know that most settlers in the town also owned two kinds of land outside its walls (or confines, if walls were absent). They held what might be called "allotment gardens," in a *bari* just outside the walls, where vegetables and herbs for home consumption could be grown. Farther away, many, though not all, townsmen had true agricultural holdings where they could grow crops in sufficient volume to produce a surplus for export out of the community. Grain growing (wheat and barley) and grazing were almost universal undertakings. But in the Aquitainian Basin of southwestern France, grapes were grown for wine production. That production of wine makes this area useful in the study of medieval distant trading. The English, who held the main part of that area, were so unfortunate as to live north of the line where drinkable wine might be grown. Thus, they had to import wine from their French possessions, and it moved in strikingly large quantities for the Middle Ages. All the conditions were present for the shaping of a system of trading towns, back-stayed by staple-producing agriculture, such as became the design for the world that Europe developed overseas after the onset of the Commercial Revolution.

This system of trading towns was settled by a large body of what were essentially yeoman farmers, *censitaires*, who paid a quitrent annually to the lord. They were otherwise free to pursue their own course without feudal duties or the geographical restrictions associated with feudalism. The destructive class of divisions which still plague Britain were largely missing, and a new society could be formed to match the new morphology of these towns. In that relatively liberal milieu, many economic, social, and religious advances could be attempted and perfected. From this overall concept of the town, a model for later use in the New World was fashioned.

Blandishing Settlers

Because these new towns lay away from existing cities and outside the established feudal order, they had to recruit settlers; to do so required the creation of pull factors that would encourage a basically conservative, even timorous, people to pick up stakes and move into the danger of the unknown. To gain that level of adventurousness the initiating landowners had to offer truly novel advantages, the more important of which were the chance to make a real economic advance and the opportunity to gain personal and social freedom not previously available. In a way the Turnerian thesis of the impact of the frontier in national life applies to the thirteenth-century bastides as it did to the trans-Appalachian settlements in nineteenth-century America. Thus most charters, and the other evidence that survives from the time, indicate a greater level of freedom for the residents of the bastides than was common elsewhere. Taxes were often remitted for a time after settlement, settlers were normally made free men (absolved of any prior feudal duties) on taking up residence in the new town, and certain rights of local self-government were granted. And, as in Flemish communes in their earlier years, the tenure of land in bastides was considerably more free than that of peasant farmers in the countryside.

A Practical Place of Real Equality

In searching out the morphogenetic processes that shaped the bastide, we shall first consider how the economic purpose and the social equality of the places were expressed concretely in urban forms. For such a complex economic creation to work, it had to come into full operation as quickly as possible. A single basically self-sufficient agricultural estate could operate independent of those around it. But a town such as the bastide with its occupational specialization could not stand so easily, if only one of a very small number of families was occupied with a particular activity. No doubt the failure rate (which was moderately great among these new towns, if Beresford's research is as complete as it seems) tells us that where the critical number and mix of settlers was not to be found, the town withered almost on initial sprouting.

To develop a town as quickly as possible, yet with the necessary initial complement of people and activities, required at least some broad conception of the town's layout on the ground. One hesitates to use the term "plan" because it suggests determination of the look of the place—that the aesthetic image and ordered and balanced fundament were the objects the founders had in mind. No doubt, with the range of bastide initiators, some founders may have envisioned such a self-conscious "design," but in most cases likely all they sought was rapid and relatively complete development. They formed a concept of what a town *de novo* would contain and how, with the least impediment to "normal" growth, that end could be accomplished. Thus the regularity among bastides comes probably not so much from an effort at design as from an effort to remove conditions impeding growth. These impediments might be introduced by large or inconveniently located private land-holdings, by interruptions in street patterns making local circulation difficult or inefficient, or by the absence of certain fundamental functional components of a town—its market, its church, its occupation quarters—requiring subsequent spatial additions or serious replatting of the town. Let us use *"pattern"* to indicate the ground layout of the town to avoid suggesting that someone prior to its establishment drew a formal "plan."

The most probable pattern was the regular grid of streets. Such a pattern avoided many resistances to rapid, orderly growth by providing a continuous, integrated, and fairly fine-grained circulation network within the town. Quite in contrast to the organic layout of the earlier medieval town, the grid pattern of streets would show less tendency toward distinction; it had no High Street and, in turn, fewer narrow cul-de-sacs. Further, pedestrians might follow alternative courses to pass from the edge to the center of the town, offering potential shopkeepers a greater number of reasonable sites for their shops than the organic place had. No doubt some sorting out of these pedestrian flows took place, as not all streets could lead from gates in the wall to the central marketplace. The level of distinction, however, would have been less ruthless than in the older organic towns with their few streets radiating from the marketplace to the gates.

Another virtue of the grid-pattern in a new but preconceived town would be its assurance of reasonably proportionate plots for building. In the older towns, the High Streets, with often rather unimportant streets leading out of them, had made the lot rather

like the tourmaline crystal, red with the fire of activity at one end and often a lustrous but quiet green on the other end. The economic consequence of what Conzen termed the "High Street layout" was a sharp division in the utility of urban land, leaving open to question whether such a pattern was really very efficient or productive. Any rational economic appraisal of the utility of land within a wall might have suggested to an intelligent initiator, and they were often both bright and shrewd, that a rectangular lot of fairly equal dimensions would be the most productive way to use a scarce land resource. Such a reasonably equidimensional lot would make more likely the use of all or the better part of the plot for activities directly associated with city functions, leaving to allotments or gardens outside the walls the raising of kitchen produce. The grid pattern itself would as well make for relatively better and more consistent circulation within the walls or confines of the town.

We need not prove that the knowledge of the street-grid had survived from Roman times; we may logically infer that the form would have been reinvented if the need were felt. The high development of cities in Gallia Narbonensis, one of seventeen provinces into which the Roman Empire was divided, is well recorded; we know of the existence there of Nimes, Narbonne, Béziers, and Toulouse. Languedoc "was rich and flourishing, crowded with great and densely populated towns . . . it prospered under Roman rule as perhaps no other part of the empire did" [James T. Shotwell]. The cities were not only large and prospering but cosmopolitan as well; the council of Narbonne in A.D. 589 noted the residence of five races—Visigoths, Romans, and Jews in large numbers, and Greeks and Syrians less numerous in the population. Soon the Arabs became a force in Septimania (the land of the seven cities: Agde, Béziers, Carcassonne, Elne, Lodève, Maguelonne, and Narbonne), adding their urban tradition to those already present. The resulting culture was the most urban to be found in the west, rich in poetry and drama, courtly in the extreme. If any area across the Alps managed to preserve the Roman civilization with its urban and urbane practices, it was Septimania, and Aquitaine farther to the west. Doubtless Roman city-designing practices would have been fully appreciated in such an area until the culture was shattered in the Albigensian Crusade. Appalling as that campaign of ecclesiastical sadism was, fortunately it was not complete. Despite the best efforts of the inquisitors, some educated and worldly men were left to carry forward the traditions of a higher culture—among them, the look of imperial Roman towns. But having abandoned the religion of ancient Rome, which used the city as temple in a particular design to serve that

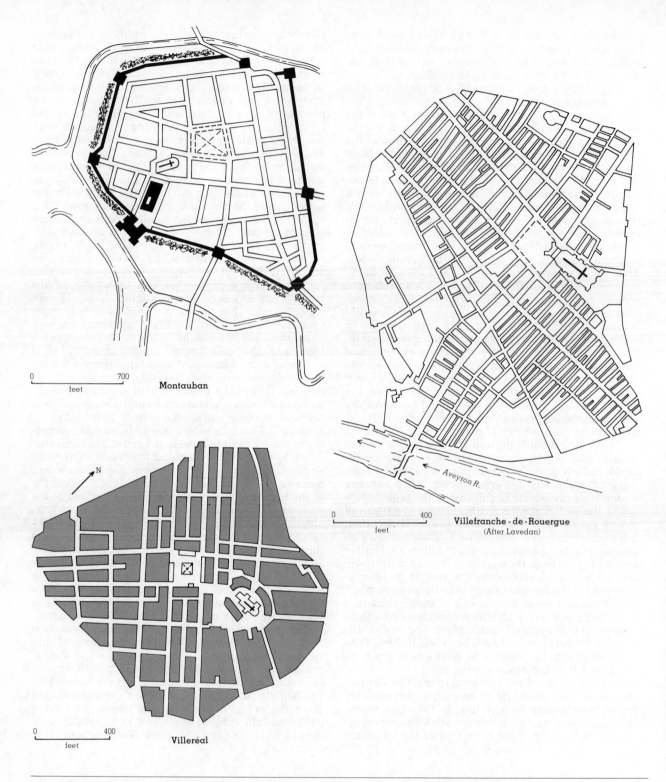

Montauban

0 _____ 700
feet

Villefranche-de-Rouergue
(After Lavedan)

0 _____ 400
feet

Aveyron R.

N

Villeréal

0 _____ 400
feet

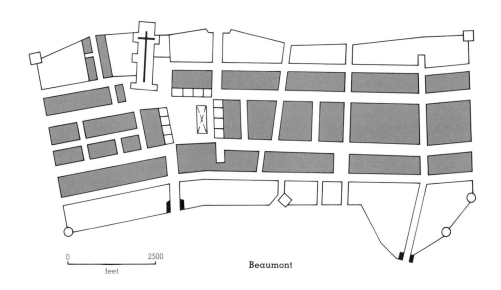

Beaumont

0   2500
feet

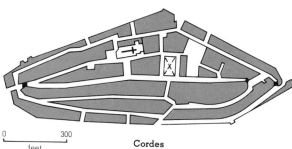

Cordes

0   300
feet

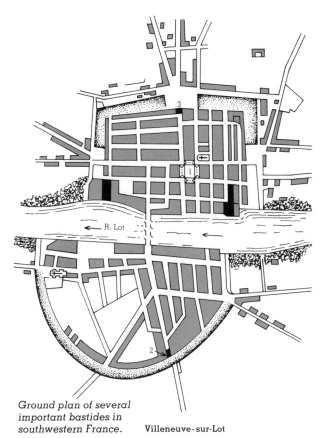

← R. Lot

Ground plan of several important bastides in southwestern France.

Villeneuve-sur-Lot

purpose, the survivors in Septimania would likely have recalled the efficiencies of the orderly Roman system without seeking to restore the rigid, orthodox application that the primitive religion of Latium carried with it.

The bastides reveal an almost infinite variation in actual pattern; yet most have elements of a *system of thought* that can be analyzed as a whole. They are orderly and seemingly logical, possessed of a functionally effective interconnectivity of streets that avoids the maze-like quality so characteristic of the Middle Ages. (This pattern suggests to some observers that the medieval man sought exactly that confusion of the outsider when he so involuted his alleys and streets.) In addition to interconnectivity, the bastides show a rectilinearity of plots. This form suggests that the house intended for these building sites was viewed as possessing a fairly consistent module and an architecture which had the efficiency of the relatively equidimensional box, whatever that shape lacked in grandeur and visual impressiveness.

Villaneuve-sur-Lot was an important bastide founded in 1253 by Alphonse de Poitiers. The rectangular layout of the town, with its square of arcades, is easily seen on the north bank of the Lot where it served as an anchor for a string of such fortified towns in the Guyenne.

Gothic Architecture and the Bastide

Invention in building, and by extension in city layout, was central to the thought of the Middle Ages, the era that saw the invention of the classical form of the bastide, first made use of in Montauban in 1144, and of Gothic architecture. No precise date may be given for the creation of the Gothic system.

Both conceptual and geographical ties exist between the new architecture of the Middle Ages and the new towns of the time. The conceptual tie centers in the replacement of an excessive concern for form, the organizing principle of the Roman town pattern and of Romanesque architecture, by a much more fluid and adaptable concern for function, which became the organizing principle for both Gothic architecture and the bastide. Each was highly ordered and proportional, certainly more so than the more rigidly defined but somewhat chaotically executed systems that preceded them. That order and proportion was not given by dicta laid down by a particular religious and social hierarchy, but was an establishment of proportion and organization brought on by the willing adoption of an extensive, highly integrative system. This system sought to relate the various parts of the operating mechanism not by static ordinal decree but in a dynamism gained from a complex interrelated system of flows and forces. The cathedrals in Normandy and the bastides in the Perigord were spare, neat, and complete, and thus of surpassing beauty in many cases, but they were not in the least doctrinaire. No two were identical and none sought to force the compartmentalized view of space characterizing both the *bourg-faubourg*, because of its initially unfree situation, and the Romanesque church, because of its complete differentiation between the wall and the roof in structural and visual terms.

How then did the Gothic architecture and the new town with its social and economic liberalism relate to one another? Which Gothic church came first is still debatable, not because we are unaware of the first fairly complete structure built under the system, but because a number of earlier experiments were made with the system's fundamental element, the pointed arch. Pointed arches were used in the Byzantine and Saracen buildings before they appeared in the Gothic, but with that later system, the construction of more lightly supported vaults and arches became possible. With the rebuilding of the west front of the royal abbey at St. Denis on the outskirts of Paris between 1132 and 1140, we have the first large project in the style.

Even at the beginning the Gothic system engendered controversies between the ascetic Cistercians, who seemingly opposed any grandeur, and the more recently emerging orders, who looked upon the Gothic as an expression of a more humanist element. The Abbot Suger of St. Denis was such a humanist operating still within a more sacerdotal society; he brought forth a new type of building geared to the needs of the time and unpredicated on long tradition. But his society and region still opposed either free enquiry and effort or greater personal freedom and responsibility. The Gothic church of the north of France reflected this essential conflict. Many physical qualities of its new form suggested dynamism and the interaction of the elements of a system. Yet the finished product was used by a religious group of increasingly dogmatic and authoritarian cast of mind, the scholastics, for whom the rediscovery of classical scholarship had merely lent yet another element of authoritarianism to go with the apostolically asserted one of the pope. John Harvey has supplied the key explaining how the illiberal patron came to use a basically liberal architecture; he shows us that most of the great Gothic cathedrals were built by lay architects merely in the employ of the church magnates.[19]

But in the south of France the Ile conditions differed from those in the royal realm of the Ile de France and its nearby counties. In the south in the twelfth century, suzerainty of the king of France was still weak and the control by the local counts, notably he of Toulouse, was consequently strong. The result was a greater humanism, since the tradition of urbanization, culture, and religious questioning was more firmly established. The Cathari with all their strong views were not dogmatic and authoritarian; in particular, they favored preaching to the members of the sect. The church was as a consequence a place for the assembly of members and preaching by their teachers.

Elements of class did arise among the citizens of the Midi, but equality was greater there than in the more feudal and less urban north. The lesser isolation in the south of France of the clerics, particularly the teaching friars who were to become more common, meant that the churches were not parcelled out into class-oriented segments which hid the practice of religion almost fully from the view of the people, as the older Romanesque buildings had and as new Gothic churches in the north continued to do. What Alexander Neckam could revile in the north as "the superfluous and vain inventions in buildings" became in the south

a means toward a more intelligent populace and a greater sense of civic participation. Hardly in the south could Neckam have cried, "O vanity," as he did when visiting the Paris that was just constructing Notre Dame. In the Midi "hall-churches" were designed for a community.

So it is that another most important influence was brought to bear on the design of churches. Besides the general desire for unity of spatial composition, there was now a particular demand of the friars for open churches in which sermons could be preached to large congregations. The idea of the church as a preaching space was the practical outcome of humanized, almost vulgarized religion.[20]

Monflanquin was a hilltop bastide with a fortified church (in the middle of the eastern edge of the old town), a fully arcaded town square, and the normal îlots despite its circular outline determined by the steep slopes of the hill. It was founded by Alphonse de Poitiers in the thirteenth century.

[19]*John Harvey*, The Gothic World, 1100-1600, *New York: Harper & Row [Colophon Books], 1967, p. 8.*

[20]Ibid., *p. 84.*

In no small way, this transformed role of the priests came from the challenge of the Cathari.

While one symptom of the Gothic age was the increasing influence of the lay craftsmen, on the other hand the Church itself was being penetrated by a different kind of humanism, giving rise to the orders of Friars. The great movement of the Albigenses was essentially a reawakening of the Mediterranean pagan culture, a revolt against the dead hand of Romanesque sacerdotalism . . . .And though this great culture perished, it succeeded all the same in effecting a radical change in the outlook of its persecutors.[21]

Thus the Gothic hall-church of the southwest came to express the final extinction of the tradition, begun among the Romans and Greeks for western civilization, that the elect and powerful of the temporal and ecclesiastical institutions were the agents for all in the matter of religion. The hall-church at last witnessed the shift from the church as shrine to the church as place of thinking participation in religion. The Cathari had shown that the common man did have both intelligence and sincere faith, rather than simple craven obedience, and could participate in social institutions. Unfortunately the intellectual recognition of man was not complete, and the preaching friars themselves became rigid and authoritarian as time passed. Still, the institution of participatory religion was at hand, most strongly planted in southern soil, and the pattern taken in the towns built to repair the countryside that the Albigensian Crusade had ravaged came as well to reflect the new role for the common man.

Interaccessibility and Popular Provision

The emergence of the average citizen to a position of concern, which was represented in the building of the Gothic cathedral, appeared as well in the shaping of the bastide. We may question whether democracy, either as an operating system of government or as a humanist viewpoint on social justice, was consciously understood or sought at that time. But the practices made necessary to gain settlers for the bastides, with the speed needed for their economic survival and prosper-

ity, led to such an ultimate outcome. Whether the cause was philosophical or practical matters not; the outcome was remarkably similar. Henri Pirenne said, "Democracy in the Middle Ages, as in modern times, got its start under the guidance of the select few who foisted their programme upon the confused aspiration of the people."[22] The "few" must have been those needed to initiate the settlement of the new bastidal creation. Since it seems most bastidors were townsmen led to migrate elsewhere, they must have required inducements to move from an existing town. The carrot held before them was an economic and social liberalism denied them in the older towns. Through moving they could hope for more freedom, greater control of their property, and some relief from the class- and church-ridden qualities of an increasingly conservative medieval urban society. The design of freedom appears in the physical build of the bastides.

The grid-pattern of streets was the beginning of such a more equal treatment. This layout of the town was not rigidly rectilinear (though many bastides were), but rather an expression of the desire for interconnectivity and proportion. Puylaroque in Bas Quercy and Domme in Perigord in southwestern France are examples of bastides without rigid plans; their locations on the top of steep hills seem to have dictated the use of subparallel streets; even, in the case of Puylaroque, streets radiating somewhat from a center near the impressive fortified church. The use of straight streets and the division of the land into rather consistent plots shows up in these grid-patterns. These qualities are more indicative of the bastide than is the checkerboard so often thought the key. If anything supports the argument that these were not preconceived *designs* but rather preconceived towns, it is this consistent interconnectivity and proportion in the face of a fair range of specific patterns on the ground.

The street-pattern of the bastide can be thought of as logically consistent and initially complete, sufficient for the laying out and development of an economically viable place with a considerable diversity of activity. In these proprietorial creations, the layout of the streets determined the ultimate grain of the town, not, as in the organic towns of earlier centuries, the nature of the individual holding, the burgage plot in many cases. The whole town was not an abstract creation of some designer's mind. Instead, the creation of an orderly framework furnished interaccessibility among the lots and proportion, within which the long-standing organic processes could be allowed to work.

The way these processes worked emerged in the buildings that came to fill in the spaces bounded by the streets of the bastide's pattern, whether the typical grid

[21]Loc. cit.

[22]*Pirenne, op. cit., pp. 184-185.*

or a more specific layout for a particular terrain. We cannot describe the infilling for all bastides. Beresford lists 184 undoubted bastides in England, around 8 for Wales, about 125 for Gascony, and omits any lists for Languedoc.[23] In addition, he does not mention a number of bastides even in southwestern France—for example, Puylaroque, Villefranche de Rouergue, and Sauveterre de Rouergue. When the bastides

Sauveterre de Guyenne was chartered in 1283 by Edward I of England to be built in his Aquitainian possessions and given six fairs a year. The paréage contract was between three lords, includ- ing the abbot of Blaismont, and the local settlers, who laid out the typical orthogonal plan but with the outline of a cross.

created in Languedoc, the most obvious of which is Aigues Mortes, are added,[24] we must deal with as many as three hundred in southern France alone. Adding the Savoyard examples and those in the German marches across the Elbe, as well as those of Britain, there must have been at least a thousand such creations in the later Middle Ages merely in the lands of western and central Europe. The bastides of southern Spain built by Their Most Catholic Majesties on lands recaptured from the Moors swell an already sufficiently impressive total. No catalogue of these new creations of the late Middle Ages exists, but we cannot doubt their real importance in any study of urban morphogenesis.

[23]*These lists refer to his gazeteers of England, Wales, and Gas-cony given in Beresford, op. cit.*

[24]*Charles Higounet in his article "La Frange Orientale des Bas-tides," in* Annales du Midi, *Vol. 61, 1949, shows just over fifty on a map of Languedoc and its immediate borders in the Vivarois, Rouergue, and Toulousain.*

The New Bastidor's Plot

If the burgage plot was the basic module of the organic medieval city, the bastidor's plot was the *basic component* of the laid-out town—*but not its module.* Instead, the street-blocks served in the later town to establish the pattern, though the plots had a proportionate quality. The plots seem to have been conceived of as the space necessary to an individual or family economic unit for the conduct of the activity that would support it, and at the same time not waste space within the bastide. Since trade and artisan manufacture were the two activities for which the towns were established, though walled bastides might stand as strong-points on the frontier of the realm in times of warfare, the marketplace and the craftsmen's streets must be given most fundamental attention. The bastide plan in its archetypal form was the physical expression of such attention. Always located near the center of the grid-layout was a *market square,* one of the modular street-blocks left free of buildings and used for the sale of agricultural produce. Typically, this marketplace was apportioned periodically into sites for small barrows and stands on which farmers sold produce. At night and when the market was closed, the square would be swept clean of commercial activity to become a place of social contact among town residents. This nonpermanent quality of the market barrow, and its clustering in the square, tells us much about the specific role of the activity carried on there. This market was essential to the sustaining of the town, but was not the reason the town existed. In most places the barrows occupied the square not every weekday but only at certain specified times. Such a periodic effort seems hardly to have been the reason for the founding of a new town.

Around the square the more fundamental activities of the town—those affairs which kept the citizens busy every day save Sunday—began to show up. Immediately adjacent to the square in the bastides of southern France, and sometimes in Savoy, Switzerland, and other Germanic lands, the houses tended to reflect the selling and buying function carried on there through the construction of a covered arcade in which activities could continue even in wet weather. Sometimes even in the square itself stood such a shelter, now usually termed a *market hall,* in which certain activities that must transpire, whatever the weather, could continue. In Villereal in Perigord, such a structure stands in the center of the square, though there are some arcades at the side of the open space. Certainly market halls were not limited to bastides, but they seem to have been common there; unfortunately most have disappeared in the last couple of centuries, because of their wooden construction.

The real trading life of the towns was located in the arcades at the side. The more important merchants normally resided in the houses fronting on the square. In those towns where an arcade, called in the bastides a *cornière,* had been built, those traders seem to have spread their wares brought from distant places under the shelter they afforded. These *cornières* seem to have been rather consistently possessed of arched openings, both toward the front, giving onto the square, and to each side, leading to the *cornières* of adjacent houses to create a continuous arcade along the sides of the square. To call these features "arcades" may be imprecise, as they were probably not actually arched over, save at the openings in the house walls. Under the house itself, the ceiling of the *cornière* was usually flat, carried by wooden rafters, and closed by floorings. In other words, this *cornière* was essentially a room in the house left open for entrance from the square or movement along its sides.

Few very specific records of the structures built in these new towns of the Middle Ages survive, and virtually no accounts of life therein; we must infer from what facts we do have and the physical forms of the town just how life was carried on in the bastides. We have already noted their greater freedom. In France, bastidors seem to have been allowed to select from their own numbers a group of "consuls" who were given the right and the responsibility of governing the town. Similarly, the citizen of a bastide was permitted to select his daughter's husband; the lord had done so in the true practice of feudalism. The infamous *droit de seigneur* was apparently undemanded within the bastides. The sense we gain of the places is one much closer to the powerful towns of several centuries later than to the feudal countryside in which they were planted. Perhaps this fact as much as any puts in question any assertion of a central-place origin for these bastides.

The general practice of permitting the emancipation from feudal duties of a refugee villein from the country, after he had been resident in a city for a year and a day, seems as well to have adhered to the bastides. But Beresford states strongly, though in a different analytical frame, the argument against thinking of these places as having grown directly out of their native soil:

Useful as refugee villeins might be in providing an unskilled labour-force in a new town, its success depended upon a very different sort of immigrant: the man already possessing some knowledge of a craft or trade. If the project [for a bastide] was to succeed, the number of such immigrants would have to be substantial and their recruitment rapid. A numerous influx in the first months was not only a good advertisement to induce waverers, it provided the essentials of urbanism: sufficient specialists to be able to meet each other's needs; sufficient numbers to engender purchasing power that would attract sellers to their markets; and sufficient products to turn aside buyers from their accustomed routes to venture in new market places. Hence the insistence of many towns that burgage plots must be taken up within stated periods or else fall forfeit.

To recruit new townsmen with experience of crafts and trades it was necessary to draw on existing skills, and to lure men from other places where they were already practising them. Who could such men be? where were they to be found? and what liberties, privileges and franchises did the founders of the new town offer them?[25]

As Beresford admits, answers to the last of these three questions are easier than to the first and second. We know from surviving charters that wide privileges were given and most adult males were enfranchised in municipal elections. The morphological impact of such basic liberty and essential equality was considerable, as we shall see presently. We might first summarize the slight evidence that exists to explain who the immigrants were and whence they came, for in that explanation we can begin to see both the existence of a long-distance trading network and the early trials toward an urban economy to replace the feudal one.

Beresford suggests, "A likely source of recruits to the new towns—although there is no direct evidence—would be from among the younger sons of burgesses in the older towns. From at least the mid-twelfth century, and possibly earlier, general demographic conditions were favourable to migration from older centres, and it was possible for new towns to develop without destroying older towns by the loss of skilled and semi-skilled townsmen."[26] Numbers were sufficient as the population of the existing towns expanded, and the younger sons must have been well aware of the practices of trade and craft. By moving they might expect to engage in their occupation less fettered by their fathers or other members of the gild.

A number of historians, notably Bernard Bailyn,[27] have shown persuasively migration holds the possibility of establishing long-distance ties of family and friendship which might serve to connect merchants in distant towns within a trading network. In the case of the Florentine merchant Datini, the role played by family connections was undoubted. Though he did not operate in the bastidal part of Avignon, Villeneuve-lés-

Avignon, but in the older papal town, it seems a quibble to deny the use of this instance to substantiate a practice that seems to have been relatively common in filling bastides.

We may reason that the more successful merchants would tend to take up locations around the squares of bastides employing the *cornière* both to display the "trade goods" they used as tender and to collect the staple they might gain in return. Gold and silver were not in common circulation until the Age of Discovery opened the rich mines of the New World. Instead, the exchange of goods facilitated the trade of medieval times. The merchant exercised his function both as distributor and as collector, and his premises had to be sufficient to comprehend both activities.

If the leading merchants might be expected to take up plots on the frontage of the square, either when the town was being laid out or later, the lesser tradesmen might be assumed to come to occupy an intermediate economic and morphological position. How many merchants engaged in distant trade would there be in any one bastide? We must fall back on probability to venture that there were never more than could be accommodated in the houses with *cornières* surrounding the square. Lesser tradesmen, more in the class of craftsmen than of merchants, came to occupy sites within the town that would best accommodate what was clearly a compromise demand.

On the basis of this logical breakdown of locations within a bastide, we may envisage some characteristic divisions of the land-use within the town. Since virtually all these towns had squares, we may designate the first of these land-use divisions as that related to the market square. Within the square itself would be found a periodic market.

More to the point in explaining the origin of the bastide is the second half of the marketplace land-use component—the ring of merchants' shops fronting on the square and often giving on it by means of the *cornières*. Even in England where the *cornière* was little used, save in a very specialized form such as the second-story galleries found in medieval Chester, the symbiosis between merchant housing and open marketplace appears to have held. In Bristol's Old Market, the building that served as the piepowder court still stands to attest to this tie, and in many towns the more impressive burghers' houses survive or are recorded as having fronted on the marketplace.

[25]*Beresford, op. cit., p. 192.*
[26]Ibid., *p. 197.*
[27]*Bernard Bailyn,* The New England Merchants in the Seventeenth Century, *New York: Harper Torchbooks, 1964. [Reprint of Harvard University Press edition of 1955].*

Land-Assignment in the Bastides

In the bastide we are able to assert with fair confidence the initial importance of merchants based on their location around the square. In encouraging rapid and economically successful settlement, proprietors must have employed a reasonable strategy of "land-assignment,"[28] the evidence of which should suggest the relative ranking of various urban activities when weighted by town founders. Reasoning that the sites around the square or at the gates would be most prized, the unassailable presence of merchant housing (evidenced by morphological remnants) on the frontage of the marketplace must be taken as support for the highest ranks being accorded to that group. Neither the agriculturalist nor the craftsman stood in first place, but the man most likely to engage in long-distance trade for at least a fair part of his time.

Unlike the situation in the *bourg* and *faubourg,* in the bastide, the terrain was less likely a strong force to confuse the evidence or the stage-development that might be read in one of several ways. When a town, even one largely supported by distant mercantile activities, evolved over a long period, the writing of the past is not always so easy to read, because location of various activities within the town might stem from several different stages in past conditions and constraints. Not so in the bastide: "The planted town was not the architectural prisoner of its past, for it had no past. If the best was to be made out of the limited space available it was natural to be orderly and have a planned town,"[29] and we might add, *to assign land on some ranking of economic importance.*

How then was land assigned within the bastide? Broadly, it was done in terms of the rough model already sketched: at the town center stood the marketplace with its surrounding shops-houses of the leading merchants, often extended by *cornières;* farther away from the square but probably ringing it on all sides, save where a church might intervene, would be ordinary, rather simple, rectangular houses, sheltering the workshops of craftsmen producing for the local market or fabricating products for shipment to more distant buyers; finally, toward the edges of these towns, which were not very large even when they were quite

successful, would be the housing for men dealing directly with the agricultural hinterland, wherever one existed, who went out to the fields to supervise or themselves to labor. Probably no extensive, wage-employed, urban proletariat existed for whom a separate housing provision need be made.

The relatively small number of casual laborers who might have been found in the bastides were probably housed in odd spaces by chance left free in the broad structure of occupation districts that accounted for the shape of the social geography of the town. Thus, we may look at that occupation geography to gain a reasonable view of the nature of these places.

Occupations in the bastides were those of active workers, rather than capitalists and magnates. The gentry, who might have encouraged a bastide on their land for the wealth it would return, still lived outside it either in the older organic cities, where their *bourg* might have brought to their vicinity the first merchants, or more probably in the country castle, whose power symbolized and sustained their class distinction. The bishop was almost certainly to be found elsewhere; his see was normally in a town of antiquity, whatever other qualities it might lack. In a few places other ecclesiastical personages—priors or abbots and abbesses—might take up residence in the new towns, but usually only at the edge, as in the rather separate monastic institution at Beaumont. For the most part, the bastide presented a remarkable base for trying out relatively egalitarian land-assignment practices. The society was one in which great scalar differences were ruled out by the simple fact that men prospered finally from their own labor, not from inherited or bestowed wealth and distinction. The bastide became the nursery and laboratory for experimentation with a more egalitarian society, which depended upon hard work to break the power of inheritance, and which came to take over the town in the Mercantile Revolution of the fifteenth and sixteenth centuries. From such forefathers came the early settlers of America. Here at last we begin to see the conditions which fairly directly shaped our own heritage.

The basic land-assignment unit of the bastide was the actual plot held by a single bastidor. The tenure on which citizens of these towns held their land was characteristic of towns rather than the surrounding countryside, with its duties of furnishing labor in the fields. Instead, in the towns a quitrent *(cens)* was charged (commonly in England a shilling a year) which discharged the landholder of any further responsibilities to the landowner. The socage, which had begun as a return for labor in the countryside, was transformed to a return for money in the town. The freedom given the bastidor by such a shift must be fully appreciated. Although the actual land, whose early un-

[28]*James E. Vance, Jr., "Land-Assignment Practices in the Precapitalist, Capitalist, and Post-capitalist City,"* Economic Geography, *Vol. 47 (1971), pp. 101-120.*

[29]*Beresford, op. cit., p. 142.*

restricted use he enjoyed, was minute even by comparison with the small agricultural holdings of the time, his freedom in using it more than made up for its geographical restriction. He was a member of that group of outsiders called in the charters "hôtes," guests or visitors, who had been invited to the developing town to seek its prosperity and their own fortunes under a set of conditions contained in the *contrat d'hostice*.[30]

Though no precise dimensions can possibly serve for all bastides to show plot size, we can employ average ranges of dimensions to suggest the basic scale with which we are dealing. Beresford gives the common street frontage as "20 to 27 feet and a depth of about twice these dimensions.... Documentary references to the actual operation of laying out and assigning the building plots of a new town are few, but in compensation there is the dumb witness of the sites in England, Wales and Gascony that have the simply rectilinear grid of streets."[31] For the observer of urban morphogenesis, the term "dumb" appears neither precisely nor symbolically any more valid with respect to the evidence furnished by the urban landscape than by the urban document. Either reveals its record and the truth to be found there to the insightful reader. Following the practice of the Romans in their towns, the scribes of the bastide commonly referred to the street-blocks as *insulae* or îlots, "islands," though in the new bastidal town of Salisbury in Wiltshire they were called "chequers" apparently from the over-all pattern they formed. Within the *insula* the individual parcels were termed the *placeae*, themselves "also rectangular since it could most easily be marked out by lines drawn parallel to the sides of the Island. There was, however, no standard size of *placea*, and even in the most regular towns such as Monpazier there is more than one size apparent. In the most crowded quarters of the town [closer to the marketplace] the house frontages were short, but in the more open, residential areas the better off might take a whole Island. One whole Island was commonly assigned for the church and another for the market-place."[32] On occasion the individual houses were separated one from another by narrow passage ways, *androynes*, hardly wider than a man's shoulders.

Within the bastides the *hôtes* were given proportional lands, generally easily measured. As Lavedan noted, "To be easy to calculate an area, one needs a simple geometric figure: the simplest of all is the rectangle. The villages of the *hôtes* seem then to show us a layout of rectangular blocks more or less cleverly constructed.... The form of the *îlot* is only one ele-

ment in the plan, a stone in the ediface. How will these rectangular blocks be arranged? One can put them in a checker-board; one can also arrange them in a circle around a church or a central square. The material is so flexible it can take a thousand combinations."[33]

If we take perhaps the most representative of these new towns, Villefranche de Rouergue, as an example of how these lands were distributed, we find a significant pattern.

The plan of the bastide *of Villefranche was worked out in advance (the usual procedure for* bastides*). The territory consisted of three zones: the zone of the* bastide *proper subdivided into equal lots; the zone immediately surrounding the circumvallation, the* bari, *for gardens and vineyards, with the number of allotments corresponding to the number of families in the town; and finally, further afield, the rest of the acquired land for cultivation, since it was assumed that agriculture would remain for a long time the basis of existence for the majority of citizens.*[34]

Again, the idea was that of proportion among the *hôtes*. Each *hôte* was given (1) a town lot within an *îlot*, where he might carry on his trade, be it in a craft or in commerce itself, (2) a garden-vineyard holding in the *bari*, where he might raise much of his own food as well as the wine that came to be of ever-increasing importance to the functioning of the long-distance trading system of the region, and (3) a more extensive agricultural holding on which he might expand his vineyard or perhaps engage in grazing or field cultivation. In such a division none was favored, and none was disadvantaged, much as in the similar ternary division of lands in the early Puritan villages of Massachusetts.

The role of agriculture in the bastides is a debated point. E. A. Gutkind clearly thought it substantial to the point of domination; others have viewed it differently, restricting agriculture to the status of a specialized trade whence came the staple of long-distance trade.

Beresford makes the point that sharp division existed between townsmen and countrymen in terms of cultivation: "What inhibited the efficient exercise of a craft and the pursuit of trade was not the possession of land but the obligations that went with a [feudal] tenement if it were held by unfree tenure." If a man held land that required of him labor service, he was severely handicapped in the pursuit of his interests in trade.

[30]*Lavedan*, op. cit., *Vol. I, p. 286.*
[31]*Beresford*, op. cit., *pp. 146-147. Dimensions are cited on p. 330.*
[32]Ibid., *p. 147.*

[33]*Lavedan*, op. cit., *Vol. I, pp. 293-295.*
[34]*E. A. Gutkind*, International History of City Development: Volume V, Urban Development in Western Europe: France and Belgium, *p. 63.*

That was irksome enough for a peasant, but for a would-be craftsman and trader it was crippling. The place where bargains and sales offered themselves was the marketplace and not the selions of the lord's demesnes. The time when strangers might pass by, or for the market-bell to ring, might be just when the lord's reeve was calling for work on the demesne. Ships made port, commercial news arrived, and hungry travellers drew near according to a timetable that took no account of whether villeins were free that day from the demesne works. A craft might demand continuous application to a task or a manufacture might need continuous supervision of a process: a demand for carting services and harvest work would then be a fatal interruption. Of these demands the generality of burgesses were free. . . .[35]

We should not assume that either distant traders or the lesser entrepreneurs among the bastidors shunned land absolutely; they fled feudal service and their escape was made sure by moving from an older town to the new foundation established in freedom—the Villefranche, Sauveterre, Villeneuve, La Bastide, La Salvetat, or Castelfranc. Thus, in the burned ground of southern France, where the internecine Crusade had struck as heavily against the nobles as the common men, and where forest still remained to be cleared, the chance of a combination of commercial agriculture and the pursuit of an urban trade was probably greater than in England, about which more has been written.

This combination of agriculture and trade has direct bearing both on the shape of the bastide and upon its role in the emergence of the modern city. In essence *these planted towns became the instrument both of the occupation of undeveloped land and of its attachment to a geographically extensive trading system.* In the case of the bastide, there is no question that in many instances, perhaps most, these towns formed in economic terms as the germ around which the countryside developed. This use of the town as a developmental tool was an important contribution. The Romans had used towns as instruments of conquest and political domination, as the Spaniards soon would do in the New World. But the bastides of France, (in England they had less geographical scope) showed how towns might attach to one another in an initial economic bond which would strengthen into a firm political attachment.

[35]Beresford, op. cit., p. 210.

La Bastide, the Wine Trade, and Mercantilism

Though bastides themselves are fascinating, their role as a school for larger things introduces them to our attention. My basic thesis is that the French and the English experimented in the bastides with plantation settlement; through the bastides, the ministers in both kingdoms learned how profitable economic settlement could be; through the working of the bastides the rudiments of a national economic policy of planted settlement emerged. In its developed form, that mercantilist policy of the sixteenth and seventeenth century was the force that projected European settlement into the New World; and in the form of the bastide, *both social and morphological*, towns were introduced to North America.

The bastides were *planted towns* where it was necessary to offer the planters some very strong inducement to give up in one place and begin again in another. For some, failure would be sufficient *push to migrate;* for the more critical members of a planters groups, those with particular skills or necessary trading connections, *a pull* more than a push factor was required to bring about their shift. That pull had in general to be a breaking out of the society and economy of the Middle Ages, with an advance toward the modern era of social, political, and economic liberalism. Obviously the present liberal state was not reached in one move or a single generation, but the strategy commenced when the young merchant or craftsman passed through the gate of his birthplace on his road to the bastide, later to the colonial town, and in the nineteenth century, to the interior of the United States where Frederick Jackson Turner clearly understood the way such pioneering on the frontier affected men and society. Precisely, the role of the frontier in American settlement began with the founding of the bastides starting with the first, Montauban, in the year 1144. The signs were faint but they can be seen if carefully sought.

The inducement that the bastides used was remarkably simple. It was essentially equality: equal ownership of land within the town and in the *bari* and forests around it; equal participation in the economic life of the place with no established monopolies to narrow its scope; equal entrée to the political life of the place through the *contrats d'hostise et d'accensement,* which gave the settler a voice in government and a contractual responsibility for the tax to carry on the

Villefranche de Rouergue was founded in 1099 by Raymond IV, comte de Toulouse, but transformed into a bastide on the opposite bank of the river, in 1252–1256, by Alphonse de Poitiers, brother of St. Louis (Louis IX). As an important town, it was heavily fortified and possessed a cathedral (now only a church). The almost square houses, the basically orthogonal plan, and the great arcaded square make this perhaps the finest remaining bastide.

government he conducted.[36] Though movement to the bastide did not lead directly to religious freedom (the term was rather meaningless in the theological state of the time), it perhaps began to open the door. Certainly the Huguenot movement was remarkably successful several centuries later in the bastidal towns. It had its heroic last stand in a bastide, La Rochelle, which the Norman kings of England founded between 1130 and 1150 as a port to tap their southern domains. There we find the northern-most occurrence of the characteristic *cornières*. These towns grew up in the land devastated by early medieval religious wars and were absolutely central to the Wars of Religion of the sixteenth and seventeenth centuries that followed their foundation. If they did not give religious liberty, they at least were scattered about the battlefield where its cause was fought and finally lost at the bloody hands of Richelieu.

The form devised for the bastide was equally as "liberal" as were its social, economic, and political practices. That form was centrally concerned with offering equality to citizens. Lots were modest and proportional; streets were rather neutrally "equal" without the great disproportions so typical of the older medieval towns; the houses were highly functional and largely lacking the ostentation that was creeping into

the burghers' and bishops' towns. Even the "mansions" that Lucien Testut so lovingly sketched and studied in Beaumont-en-Perigord finally were the homes and workplaces of productive citizens, containing bakeries, dairies, and other relatively humble quarters.[37] These citizens earned a prosperity they reflected in the reconstruction of their houses but they seem always to have been democratic in the same high sense that Paul Revere, of a Huguenot family himself, was in eighteenth-century Boston.

The central morphological truth learned in the bastides was that *interaccessible and proportionate layout of the town is one of the more concrete expressions of a functional equality*, and a strong bulwark in its defense.

The social and morphological egalitarianism of the bastide was only one part of its contribution to the shaping of a model for New World settlement, though the most commonly understood. Equally significant was the proof the bastide offered of the ultimate *national and personal enrichment to be had from shaping*

---

[36]*See Lavedan, op. cit., Vol. I, p. 293. These contracts might be translated as those of occupation and assessment, of the right to run the town and of the responsibility to pay the costs thereof.*

[37]*The great French anatomist Lucien Testut was born at Beaumont-en-Perigord, one of the most unspoiled of the bastides. Testut in his study of Beaumont presents in his second volume the most detailed pictures of the houses of the bastide. As a famous anatomist, Testut drew surpassingly well and was more than almost any other observer clearly aware of the role of morphogenesis. Lucien Testut,* La Bastide-en-Perigord, *Bordeaux: 1920, 2 vols. The study of houses is in Volume Two.*

The market held in the square of Villeneuve-sur-Lot suggests the use that was made of these open spaces during the Middle Ages.

an interacting system of long-distance trade. Again, as with the inducement to settlers, the real need was to break away from the strictures of the traditional medieval economy. The bastides were particularly towns in a national framework. The English foundations in France, of which La Rochelle was only one of the larger, were encouraged both with the idea of defending the English possessions against the French and with making those lands valuable to the crown and to its supporters and agents. Although these lands were the personal possessions of the English king rather

than of his people, they were to be used for their collective prosperity, which in the end was indissoluble.

To test the strength of the argument that these bastides were particularly merchant towns for a distant trade, we may contrast the bastidal settlements which the Germans placed in the Slavic lands they were over-running at this same time with those in the Aquitainian Basin. We must distinguish between the defensible settlement planted by the German conquerors east of the Oder and the bastides of France. The differentiation extends beyond the relations between the town and the countryside surrounding it to the actual layout of the place. To understand the forms, we must look back at the traditional village morphologies of the Germans and the Slavs.

The villages that evolved in the German lands, those areas between the Rhine and the Elbe-Saale frontiers which remained outside the Roman *limes*, were of a particularly loosely agglomerate sort, the *Haufen-dorf*, in which the houses were in truth farmsteads collected into an open village. The buildings were physically separate, adjoined by gardens and barnyards, and little distinguishable from an isolated farmstead, save by being brought into loose proximity with other, similarly individual barn-house complexes. Farther to the west in what is now the Rhineland, the arrangement was slightly different. The assembly was made up of the same barn-house units but they tended to cluster in a line, along a street, rather than more compact morphologies. The *Strassendorf* of the Rhineland was what the French term a *village de route*, which in New England becomes a "string village." The *Haufendorf* was the French *village aggloméré*, and seems to be the rather imprecise equivalent of our village.

The difficulty of finding French or American equivalents for these Germanic forms is that in France and America the dispersed farmstead was a more common unit of rural settlement so the parallels are not too exact. In the French Midi, the characteristic rural settlement form is the *mas*, a Provençal word meaning "an isolated farmstead," derived directly from the Latin, apparently from *mansio* (dwelling), though the etymology is not fully agreed upon. In France south of the Massif Centrale, and in Armorica as well, the village is not apparently the original rural settlement form, quite in contrast to the rest of Europe beyond the Alps. This fact helps to justify the view advanced that the bastide in the French Midi was fundamentally an urban form, not a rural one. As Robert Dickinson notes, a difference arises between northern France with its rather open "market" villages and the Midi where "the compact, congested settlement is much more characteristic."[38] These towns show a strong preference for hilltop sites; Pierre Deffontaines found at least two-thirds of the towns in Aquitaine were so located.[39]

The contrast may as well show a different role for many of these southern towns, not that of local market center but rather that of collecting and distributing point in a much more geographically extensive trading system than found in the rural north. In the Midi the production of wine for distant shipment was important not merely economically but politically as well. As André Simon wrote in his unfortunately never-completed history of the wine trade of England, this trade was critical:

Abroad, the English monarch's continental possessions were more considerable than at any other time in this country's history. Henry [II] was at the same time master in the right of his father, of Anjou, Touraine, and Maine; in that of his mother, of Normandy; in that of his wife, of Guienne, Poitou, Saintonge, Auvergne, Perigord, Angoumois, and Limousin; these provinces which were amongst the most opulent of the French monarchy, were nearly all wine-producing and owed their wealth entirely to agriculture and commerce. The surest way for the Plantagenets to retain under their allegiance the subjects of these distant provinces was to attach them to their dynasty by bonds of interest, assuring them of a ready market, in England, for the sale of their wines, and granting them special privileges which might be termed, in modern phraseology, preferential tariffs. The result of this policy may be easily detected in the remarkable faithfulness of Bordeaux to the English Crown during the three following centuries, and the rapid decay of the Metropolis of Aquitaine after it was lost to England. Although Rouen was reunited to the French monarchy long before Bordeaux, the loyalty of its inhabitants to their English lord was very staunch; they offered a long and gallant resistance to his enemy and became French very much against their will.[40]

Because glass bottles were "then unknown, and the proper treatment of wine in casks only very imperfectly comprehended, wines were mostly drunk new, and custom had engendered a taste for their natural harshness. The stronger the wine the better it would keep, although the longer it would remain on tap the worse it would become, so that either light or old wines were always considered the worst by medieval consumers."[41] Speed in reaching the market was so important that a distinction was made between "wines of the vintage," which left Gascony for England in the fall of the year pressed, and "wines of the rack," which had been stored in Bordeaux for the winter, racked in the spring to remove their lees and then sent off to England. The wines of the rack were charged less freight because for them time was not so critical. We have already seen how in the London of Fitzstephen's time (just when the bastides were being settled) wine was often drunk directly on ships tied up at the Thames wharves so it would travel no farther than absolutely necessary and be drunk as soon as possible in the vintage year.

The combination of the longer political ties between Gascony and England, which were not fully broken until 1453, and the speed with which wine had to reach the market in those centuries certainly encour-

---

[38]*Robert E. Dickinson*, The West European City: A Geographical Interpretation, *London: Routledge & Kegan Paul, 1951, pp. 358-359.*

[39]*Pierre Deffontaines*, Les Hommes et leurs travaux dans le pays de la moyenne Garonne, *Lille: S.I.L.I.C., 1932, quoted in Dickinson, op. cit., p. 359.*

[40]*André L. Simon*, The History of the Wine Trade in England, *London: Wyman & Sons, 1906, Vol. I (all published), pp. 58-59.*
[41]Ibid., p. 261.

aged the creation of an elaborate trading system in the southwest of France. Even the wines of the rack could not tarry for more than a few months. The trade had a clear geographical structure; the vineyard areas closest to Bordeaux and Bayonne were the more important sellers in the London market, though wine was shipped from as far east in Aquitaine as Albi, Agen, Cahors, Cordes, Rabastens, Villeneuve-sur-Lot (Ste. Livrade), and Toulouse; thus most of the area wherein the bastide had become an important settlement form was included in this tributary region which produced wine that had, with great speed for the Middle Ages, to be sent on to a distant market.[42]

The great appeal of the Gascon wines in the English market, a greater appeal than existed for more northerly French wines, was the strong color and flavor they possessed and their abundance and relative cheapness. "The other French wines which were well known in England during the Middle Ages were those of Auxerre and La Rochelle," though they were consumed in far smaller quantities. The citizens of La Rochelle fought

The Chequers of Salisbury.

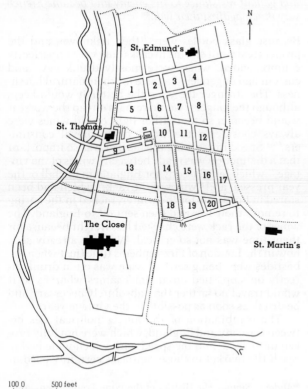

100 0   500 feet

[42]Ibid., pp. 270-271.

against the effort of King John (of England) to forfeit his title to the town to the French king but without avail so their trade declined greatly. Given all of the attendant conditions in the medieval wine trade, the ties between Gascony and England were assured by the strength and cheapness of the wine, its relative ease of shipment, the organization of the supply, and the adequacy of the commercial agriculture of the Midi to produce sufficiently and consistently.

The system of towns in Aquitaine and Languedoc (included because Montpellier and other areas of that province exported to England) must have reflected this large and particular trade. From that trade they may well have gained the support for the distinctive type of towns being planted anew in those parts, towns quite different from those emerging from the rural countryside of northern France.

André Simon's description of the Gascon wine trade of England in the twelfth century makes clear why the bastides could be different from small urban settlements elsewhere. To a degree uncommon to the time, the wine trade meant a long-distance movement, unique because it required careful organization and efficiency. Wool staple must be handled efficiently but not necessarily with dispatch. Other items, such as woad, might move as far and as quickly as wine, but not in the same volumes. In the three centuries during which England held major possessions in Gascony (from 1152 to 1453), this region produced one of the premier export products of the time and shipped it in quantities vast for the Middle Ages. A bit later, in the mid-fifteenth century, wine was imported into England at a rate of over three million gallons a year.[43] Although the traditional towns of Gascony were important in the trade, Bordeaux standing at the head as the port from which all wine must be sent on to England, the bastides seem to have played a vital role. Simon in his catalogue of towns from which wine was sent to medieval England lists many bastides—Libourne (the only port other than Bordeaux and Bayonne which might export directly), Castel Sargat, Castel Sarrazin, Cordes, Marmande, Mirabel, Montauban, Montclar, Rabastens, Ste. Livrade, Villeneuve d'Agen and others—to the extent that perhaps a third of the exporting towns were bastides. Thus, the wine trade seems to have been a critical element of support in many of these places, judging from the records that have survived.

The nature of agriculture around these towns no doubt aided in their attachment to long-distance trade. Because the townsmen held plots in the *bari* and beyond, they could and did raise grapes for the making of wine. In this way the prospective merchants could also

[43]E. M. Carus-Wilson, Medieval Merchant Venturers, London: Methuen, 2nd Ed., 1967, p. 271.

be vintners to assure their supplies, avoiding as well the rather rigid controls on winemaking in other areas where large estates and the church might well dominate the production. During the English ownership of Gascony, the area of the bastides was the area of the great expansion of wine production. If, as Henri Pirenne suggested in 1933 should be done, this wine trade were studied in full, likely we would see the first tentative steps toward a mercantile system tying one region with a distant region "overseas" and fostering in both the growth of cities. Bordeaux grew vastly in English hands, Libourne was founded along with the other bastides and waxed fat, Bristol in England began its great rise, and all told there seems most evidently to have been a major trading system at work causing this urban expansion. The bastide was a novel element in this system. The urban plantation served to develop the countryside and to handle the staple it was producing in a rapid and efficient onward shipment to the large metropolitan market—which was then, as later, England. Without the bastides I doubt that the vast increase in production, the rapid handling necessary, and the simple enterprise to make it all work would have been available.

The social, political, and economic experimentation that the bastide represented had a strong morphological base. The town of proportion and interaccessibility was not simply a coincidental associate with the social and economic liberalism, it was a fundamental part of it. In this role, the bastidal form became a model for later mercantile expansiveness, perhaps unconsciously but certainly powerfully. As we shall see in the next chapter, the mercantile city in England became a thing apart and the hearth from which New World urbanism spread. England would not so clearly have been the fountainhead of change without the historical accident of Henry's marriage to Eleanor of Aquitaine in 1152, and the experiments his subjects subsequently undertook to use her dowry in developing the national wealth. In the period that followed, an age of discovery may simply have been a historical accident, but the urbanization practices perfected in Gascony and the form of the bastide served even more handsomely to shape a New World once the English lost their French possessions and were forced to turn instead to trade pioneering across the western ocean.

6. THE PRINCE'S CAPITAL AND THE MERCHANTS' TOWN

"The close of the Middle Ages" sounds final and determinate, yet this epochal event was unperceived at the time, and the probable direction of change once the door was closed was uncertain. We need not be concerned just when the Middle Ages came to an end and what led to their demise; by the beginning of the seventeenth century a new world was at hand. The previous century had witnessed such a vast expansion of the horizon of western civilization that the new geographical scale alone would have made a new society necessary.

In the hundred years between the 1490's and the 1590's, such shifts of geographical perspective and political weighting had taken place that the European world of the Middle Ages was already "historical" and unreal. Germany and Italy became civilized backwaters where increasing intellectual and artistic refinement was harnessed to a local political treadmill that revolved incessantly but gained no perceptible ground. The English and Dutch during this century changed from medieval Europeans to modern world citizens, much to the surprise and ultimate dismay of the other members of what had been an intimately interacting society and generally coherent culture in the Middle Ages. France was racked with religious ferment which caused her economic shots to ricochet sometimes rather wildly; she entered this transition period along the same open and novel path as her Atlantic neighbors—the path to overseas colonization and conquest —and ended it treading the same grand road to nowhere followed by her overly aesthetic neighbors. Spain stood determined and medieval throughout, using her vastly expanded geographical horizon to show that the old order was the best, that the economic system of tribute and dynastic possession—devised by the Romans and perfected by the Normans and Angevins—could be made to work anywhere the Most Catholic King's flag could be flown.

Almost all the countries of western civilization set about expanding their geographical knowledge. The Norse and possibly the Irish began exploration even during the Middle Ages. Certainly the Norse were voyaging to Iceland and Greenland in the tenth and eleventh centuries. No doubt they visited North America, but their visit made little difference to history; they had no system for utilizing such a distant land and no desire to become lost in its vastness.

Only in the fifteenth century did the European economic frontier begin to expand. Until then, the East had been experienced only indirectly through a trade confined by Muslim middlemen to the eastern margin of the Mediterranean. But at the hands of the Portuguese navigators, following in Prince Henry's wake, the economic frontier moved quickly to the East, passing around the end of the Muslim barrier and making all of Europe deeply envious of Lisbon. As dynastic siblings of the Portuguese, the Dutch participated in that expansion, while the Spaniards, French, and English sought to join in the outward thrust of the European economic boundary. The English followed up on their early-sixteenth-century success in driving the mercantile frontier with the Italians from London to Livorno (Leghorn) and with the Germans from Southampton to Hamburg; they set out to project their trading realm across the North Atlantic. In this effort they were joined by the Protestant merchants of Rouen, St. Malo, La Rochelle, and other fishing and trading towns on the French Atlantic coast.

The Portuguese experience in reaching the Spice Islands of the East was a most inappropriate model for most of this economic expansion. In the East Indies, as slightly later in India and China, a highly developed land rich in products for trade was able to begin exchange almost the moment the Portuguese navigators reached its ports. In contrast, when the other Atlantic Europeans reached the New World they found an economic wilderness with few commodities they had experienced before and, in virtually all cases, little production of what was to be had. At first, nearly all that could be traded were wild pelts of deer in the south and of beaver in the north. Years of developmental activity and the education of European taste to a marvelous array of new products were required before trade could blossom. Even then, the native population of America was small and its economic organization ill-suited to the fiercely mercantilist society making a landfall on its shores.

To make the New World a second East meant far more diligent labor by the Europeans than had been required in the Far East, and the planting of towns and European populations to draw from the virgin soil the riches that might be had, but which were not directly at hand. In the West Indies, gold was thin in the rivers and the native agriculture still produced products not craved by Europeans. Instead the Spaniards carried to the New World a crop from the old—sugar. They had come to know it well in the preceding several centuries as its cultivation spread from the Near East through the Spanish possessions in Sicily and Andalusia to Moorish Morocco and newly discovered Madiera, which the cane reached in 1420. Only three-quarters of a century later (1494) sugar arrived in the Antilles, giving the Europeans their first realistic hope for profit from the strange New World. In the sugar boom that followed, all the Atlantic states of Europe planted colonies in tropical and subtropical America to gain a foothold in the trade. In those colonies, the first European towns appeared in the New World, towns of a peculiar and unfortunate sort. These towns of a caste-bound society came shortly to be characterized by the legal enslavement of large numbers of people. That most vicious of rank stratifications is the tie that connected these places more with the Renaissance towns of Italy and the Hapsburg lands than with the merchants' town of the European Atlantic shores.

In the tropical agricultural colonies, the town became the symbol of domination and the refuge of the overlord. Whether the agriculture depended upon enslaved natives or introduced blacks from Africa, the Europeans in the countryside were under constant threat of an uprising by the enslaved. In addition those Europeans were, of necessity, a small minority in any area of active production; both in the tropical plantation agriculture and in the mining that came to supplement it, hard physical labor was done by non-Europeans with the conquerors serving merely as supervisors and masters. The town in such an economic environment was the social refuge for the master class, who must resort to it at certain times to maintain themselves. Because of this association of the town with caste maintenance, we should distinguish two possible approaches to town building and occupation.

The first we might call an *isonomic* assignment, wherein persons living in the city have individual differences but no strong caste distinctions. Space would be assigned to them because they were individuals, and existing distinctions would be moderated by the basic philosophy of legal and social similarity, if not outright equality. In other towns, such as those in the tropical areas, caste was a fundamental and founding element. In such places, space assignment and even permission to reside would be based on caste and class. These towns may be called places of *eunomic* assignment, implying a structure based on rank order of merit, rather than equality of provision.[1]

The Renaissance town in Europe was clearly shaped in accord with eunomic principles. Its whole design was meant to provide impressive sites for buildings of pompous purpose—cathedral churches for absolutist prince-bishops; palaces for monarchs who had recently discovered their divine right to rule; tyrants of various stripe, be it commercial, ecclesiastical, or civil. These caste societies were often only moderately less repressive than the slaveholders' towns of the New World. Clearly, the Spaniards—slaveholders and subjugators of sometimes considerably advanced Indian "nations"—would adopt the Renaissance forms for the towns they built in America. A line dividing the

eunomic from the isonomic town in the Americas would pass between those areas settled by an overlord class intent upon indentured or enslaved labor, and those claimed by a merchant class committed primarily to the overseas expansion of social and economic liberalism, planted first in the medieval communes of Flanders and northern France, flowering in the bastides, and bearing mature fruit in Commonwealth London and the northern English colonies of America. Little wonder that when the New World sought liberty and freedom, the first shots were fired in Massachusetts, the most extreme of those merchant colonies. Considerable time was necessary to carry such an isonomic campaign to the areas of plantation agriculture and a caste society. John Adams conceived that a revolution was necessary and deliberately saw that Washington became commander-in-chief in order to involve the plantation aristocracy in this uncharacteristic destruction of the established order of classes.

The Two Cities of Europe and America

Europe in the sixteenth century was fast developing two patterns of city: the capitals of powerful princes desirous of creating great visual expressions of their absolute authority in a manner as close as practicable to the model of classical Rome; and the merchants' towns that grew from the economic replacement for medieval practices by mercantilism. Both the *capital* and the *merchants' emporium* were shaped along lines that emerged only in Elizabethan times to replace the order and balance so much the measure of medieval life. In matters political, absolutism came to substitute for the detailed definition of duty and privilege, which tied in mutual responsibility the sovereign and vassals of the Middle Ages. In matters economic, the broad and expanding horizon of mercantilism quickly replaced the bounded and rank-ordered "natural economy" of feudal Europe. Each shaped its own city, and like the *bourg* and *faubourg* in medieval times, those places tended to be separated from one other.

In the New World, the division was more than a local phenomenon. The realm of tropical agricultural development, with servitude of the masses, was the home of the Renaissance capital city transported to America, whereas the realm of colonization by the free

[1]*This division between eunomic and isonomic land assignment is based in part on J. P. Vernant's* Mythe et Pensée Chez Les Grecs *(Paris: F. Maspero, 1965). I wish to thank Professor J. B. Jackson of the University of California, Berkeley, and Harvard for bringing this work to my attention.*

merchant class led to the implantation of the merchants' town in temperate America. The European nations where mercantilism made greatest progress—France before Louis XIV, England, and Holland—were the planters of merchants' towns, while the countries where liberalism—economic, social, and religious—was fought to a stop in the Counter-Reformation were the planters of capitals with rigid social caste.

Europe during the Counter-Reformation came to be dominated by the administrative-political city. These cities were ordered and ranked by their administrative standing and assigned politically dependent territories, which have always shown a greater tendency for fixed geographical integrity than have the tributary regions of merchants' towns. Trading territories overlap, but political territories do so only by design and normally with fixed hierarchical relations. Significantly, in that part of Europe where the Counter-Reformation was strongest and liberalism was least advanced, the administrative-political order and its central-places were best developed. In such a region, the kingdom of Bavaria, Walter Christaller devised his central-place system; on closer examination, it stands more as a political-place system than one of trading places free to compete with each other.

peans in the East quickly began to exercise greater force than had been practical in the Middle Ages, and to seek an exclusivity of trade that came to mind only with the onset of mercantilist economic thinking. The trading wars of Holland and England in the East Indies, of France and England in India, and of France and England in the Ohio Country of North America were a direct outgrowth of competitive factory establishment undertaken by a mercantilist society.

This historical and economic context led rapidly to a conquest of trade through the use of planted towns, but often with a genuine reluctance to seek political domination of the area where the factory was sited. England placed factories in India just after the East India Company was founded (on December 31, 1600) but resisted asserting sovereignty for a hundred and fifty years. Similarly, the first English voyages to North America came in 1497 but nearly a full century intervened before any political claim was advanced—Newfoundland was claimed by Sir Humphrey Gilbert only in 1583—and a century and a quarter before any very effective settlement was achieved. At first, mercantile Europe around the North Sea sought not conquest but trade. Its towns were long in coming; when they arrived, they were simple merchants' settlements of distinctly isonomic structure.

Expansion in the Context of Trade

We must distinguish between the drive to advance a nation's economic frontier and the conditions under which advance was carried out. During the seventeenth and eighteenth centuries, most European countries—England, Holland, France, Denmark, Scotland, Spain, Austria, and Sweden—chartered "East India companies" not all of which showed much mercantile initiative; the best were more monopolistic in design than the free development of trade would have required. All were considered sufficiently risky to be vested with a geographical monopoly of trade thought sufficient to gain the necessary investment in their undertakings. The instrument chosen by the East India companies for engaging in trade was almost universally the planted "factory" where traders became resident in the distant land in order to facilitate ties with European trading partners. Under such a system, the factory took on a function of long standing in Europe, serving rather as the medieval "steelyards" served the *hanse* or the "English nation" in Antwerp. But Euro-

Expansion in the Context of Conquest

The Spaniards were conquerors and administrators from the very beginning. Columbus sailed in 1492; before the year was out, old style, Spain's first colony had been set up at La Navidad on Hispaniola. By 1498, the year of his third voyage, outright political domination of Hispaniola had been accomplished and a capital established at Santo Domingo. From then on, the history of Hispanic America was for four centuries (until the last colonies, Cuba and Puerto Rico, were liberated by the United States in 1898) one of political domination of subject peoples in the New World by a still partially medieval Spanish kingdom. From that political conquest, the world inherited a string of capital cities located to serve Spanish needs, and little urbanization that might advance the interests of the lands held subject to the monarch of the peninsular kingdom.

Crucial to the subjugation of the New World to the

Spanish kingdom was the extension thereto of an administrative system typical of Catholic Europe, the same that has been memorialized in Christaller's central-place theory in the guise of its Bavarian expression. The town was a critical feature of this administrative-political system, but one to be viewed only in an ordered, dependent role given by devolution of authority from above, in what the Middle Ages called the *Heerschildordnung*. The citizen of the Roman Empire had known it as imperial administration a thousand years before; the Spaniards termed it the "Law of the Indies" in the late sixteenth century. Authority remained at the top with *downward grants* for the carrying on of particular activities (Christaller's central functions): the decree of city form and function from afar, the creation of a caste-divided society to reside in the colony (with the town serving as the citadel and ultimate refuge for the overlord caste that would make up a minority of the total population), and the strong practice of symbolic and eunomic land assignment within the city.

All of these things strongly suggested the Roman conquest of Europe with subjugation of all to the imperial will, and its later modification to meet the more localized social and administrative structure of feudal Europe in the Middle Ages. As under feudalism, the economic base of Hispanic American development was rural and caste-based, with the town seen as the impressive capital and severe restrictions placed on occupational and geographical mobility for the indentured or enslaved "vassals" (of the rural activities of plantation agriculture and mining).

The Roman Empire Reaches the Western Shore

Occasionally history's evidence is so clear that we must suspect our conclusions, questioning whether we have been too easily persuaded by neat lines of evolution and descent. These lines may be so powerful because something of great importance that might controvert them has been misplaced with time's passage. Such is the case with the Spanish planting of towns and cities in the New World. This settlement seems so clearly the onward projection of the Roman colonization of ancient Iberia, modernized to the fifteenth century through the Spanish resettlement of the areas consid-

erably devastated in the campaigns against the Moors, and then carried clean and powerful to the Antilles as the accepted practice for Charles V's conquerors of the New World.

So the planting of Roman *castra* during the second Punic War had brought the western peninsula into the Latin world through city founding. The Romans perfected a rather standardized town model to pacify and control a conquered area, whether won through peaceful acceptance of inevitable domination by the powerful Roman armies or by actual fierce warfare with the native peoples. The *castra* were foursquare, regular, laid out all of a piece, with a land-use pattern determined as much by the symbolic activities the Romans assigned to cities as by defensive concerns, and generally lightly walled and constantly alerted to the needs for vigilance as the strongest protection.

What we know about those Roman camp-towns comes from many sources, but the most detail is furnished by the *Ten Books of Architecture* of Vitruvius, rediscovered in the early fifteenth century. They became the greatest literary guide to the recreation of the Roman world that became the objective of the Renaissance. At the onset of the Spanish conquest of the New World, the great force sweeping Catholic Europe and motivating the elaborate construction by her princes was the wish to recreate concretely the grandeur of Rome. To that end, the rediscovery of Vitruvius in manuscripts surviving from the tenth century was rapidly influential on the Roman pope and the Holy Roman emperor. Whether either had read Vitruvius is not important: we know that their architectural advisors had.

The parallelism between the Vitruvian manuscript[2] and the Laws of the Indies, the proposals made in 1573 in the name of the king of Spain, the violent and cruel Phillip II, is sufficient to suggest a conscious emulation at work.[3] Vitruvius begins (in Chapter IV, Book I) his prescription for the founding of a town with a note on its site: "For fortified towns the following general principles are to be observed. First comes the choice of a very healthy site. Such a site will be high, neither misty nor frosty . . . further without marshes in the neighborhood. . . . Again, if the town is on the coast with a

[2]*The standard translation is that of Morris Hicky Morgan* [Vitruvius: The Ten Books on Architecture] *published by the Harvard University Press in 1914 (reissued by Dover Publications, Inc., 1960). Citations are to the Harvard edition.*
[3]*A translation of those parts of the so-called "Laws of the Indies"* (Bulas y Cedulas para el Gobierno de las Indias) *dealing with the laying out of towns is furnished by Zelia Nuttall, "Royal Ordinances Concerning the Laying Out of New Towns,"* The Hispanic American Historical Review, *Vol. V (1922), pp. 249-254.*

St. Augustine (Florida) was laid out by the Spaniards under the "Laws of the Indies" in 1565, showing the response to those injunctions in a port city. The map is from ca. 1770, Library of Congress.

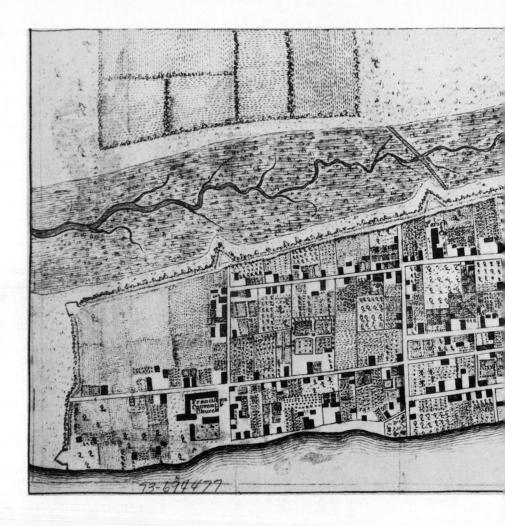

southern or western exposure, it will not be healthy, because in summer the southern sky grows hot at sunrise and is fiery at noon, while a western exposure grows warm after sunrise, is hot at noon, and at evening all aglow." In the words imputed to Phillip II, writing at San Lorenzo on July 3, 1573, "The chosen site shall be on an elevation; healthful; with means of fortification . . . .It shall be open to the north wind. If on a coast care is to be taken that the sea does not lie to the south or west of the harbor. If possible the port is not to be near lagoons or marshes in which poisonous animals and corruption of air and water breed" (Law 111, the second one dealing with cities).

In Chapter VI, Book I, Vitruvius goes on to deal with the question of the physical layout of the town:

1. The town being fortified, the next step is the appointment of house lots within the wall and the laying out

of streets and alleys with regard to climatic conditions. They will be properly laid out if foresight is employed to exclude the winds from the alleys. Cold winds are disagreeable, hot winds enervating, moist winds unhealthy. . . .

3. By shutting out the winds from our dwellings, therefore, we shall not only make the place healthful for people who are well but also in the case of diseases due perhaps to unfavourable situations elsewhere . . . will here be more quickly cured by the mildness that comes from the shutting out of winds.

To protect dwellings and other buildings from the effect of the wind, the Vitruvian town is to be oriented with respect to the winds, most ideally through the shaping of an eight-sided plan.

8. On this principle of arrangement the disagreeable

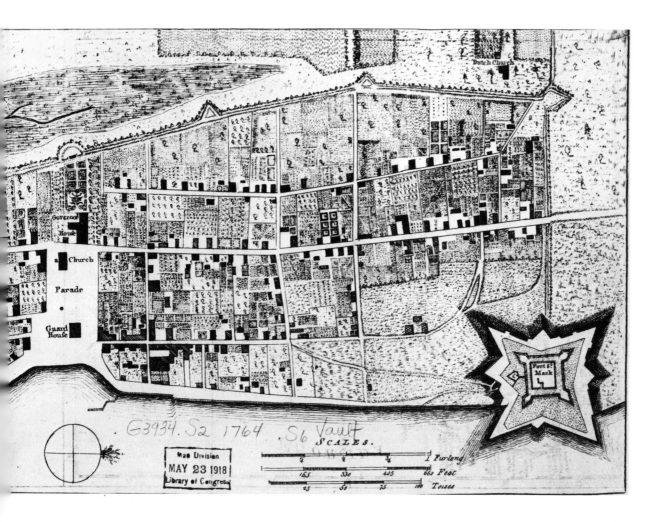

force of the winds will be shut out from dwellings and lines of houses. For if the streets run full in the face of the winds, their constant blasts rushing in from the open country, and then confined by narrow alleys, will sweep through them with great violence. The lines of houses must therefore be directed away from the quarters (cardinal points of the compass) from which the winds blow, so that as they come in they may strike against the angles of the blocks and their force thus be broken and dispersed.

In the Laws of the Indies the same principle is advanced, though far more succinctly than in the Roman's rather wordy tract:

114. From the plaza the four principal streets are to diverge, one from the middle of each of its sides and two streets are to meet at each of its corners. The four corners of the plaza are to face the four [cardinal] points of the compass, because thus the streets diverging from the plaza will not be directly exposed to the four principal winds, which would cause much inconvenience.

The town plat having been decided upon, Vitruvius urges in Chapter VII:

1. Having laid out the alleys and determined the streets, we have next to treat of the choice of building sites for temples, the forum, and all other public places, with a view to general convenience and utility. If the city is on the sea, we should choose ground close to the harbour as the place where the forum is to be built; but if inland, in the middle of the town.

Phillip II followed suit:

112. In the case of a sea-coast town the main plaza which is to be the starting point of the building of the town, is to be situated near the landing place of the port. In inland towns the main plaza should be in the centre of the town and of an oblong shape, its length being equal to at least one and a half times its width, as this proportion is the best for festivals in which horses are used and any other celebrations which have to be held.

In the Roman town, many public shrines and temples were ranged round the *forum*, but the multiplicity of gods required that others be built in the *emporium* (for Mercury, Isis, and Serapis), near the theater (those to Apollo and Bacchus), at the circus (Hercules), on the training ground (Mars), and at the harbor (Venus). Somewhat similarly, the Spaniards decreed that the cathedral should be on the plaza, in many instances, but elsewhere in an inland town, and that other foci of interest be placed elsewhere in the town:

118. At certain distances in the town smaller, well proportioned plazas are to be laid out on which the main church, the parish church or monastery shall be built so that the teaching of religious doctrine may be evenly distributed.

For the Romans, a similar spread was called for, though with rather different justifications (Chapter VII, Book I):

It is moreover shown by the Etruscan diviners in treatises on their science that the fanes of Venus, Vulcan, and Mars should be situated outside the walls, in order that the young men and married women may not become habituated in the city to the temptations incident to the worship of Venus, and that buildings may be free from the terror of fires through the religious rites and sacrifices which call the power of Vulcan beyond the walls. As for Mars, when that divinity is enshrined outside the walls, the citizens will never take up arms against each other, and he will defend the city from its enemies and save it from danger in war.

We might find further parallels between Vitruvius and the Law of the Indies but these suffice to show that the Roman prescript was updated for Christianity and adapted to the needs of a more clearly maritime conquest. Yet the fundamental practices are remarkably similar. The ordinances in both Rome and Spain were set out to secure the planting of towns to dominate a subject population. Thus, walling of sorts and protection internal to the town gained much greater attention than in the English and French colonies farther to the north. In both Mediterranean examples existed an ordering of land-use, reserving the *forum* or plaza for public buildings, and suggesting or decreeing the increasing exclusion of activities not thought appropriate to the town center, a remove established in order of their *pariah status*.

In each model, a clear statement set out physical design proper to all sites. For the Romans, it was the *castrum* (Vitruvius's octagon seems entirely to have been a utopian scheme) built on its rectangular grid with the street-block standing as the basic module for the city development. In Spanish America, a nearly identical grid was evolved. The very first law (110) dealing with city founding decreed that "the plan of the place, with its squares, streets and building lots, is to be outlined by means of measuring by cord and ruler, beginning with the main square from which streets are to run to the gates and principal roads and leaving sufficient open space so that even if the town grows it can always spread in a symmetrical manner." Perhaps borrowing from the bastides of southern France more than the Roman *castra*, the plaza was to be surrounded by an arcade, "for these are a great convenience for those who resort thither for trade" (Law 115). That plaza was to be the beginning of the town, just as the meeting of the *cardo* and *decumanus* was the base point for laying out the *castrum*. The morphological result was the same even if the Roman town evolved inward from its encircling *pomerium*, whereas the Law of the Indies town grew outward from its plaza.

117. [Beyond the arcades] [t]he other streets laid out consecutively around the plaza are to be so planned that even if the town should increase considerably in size it would meet with no obstruction which might disfigure what had already been built or be a detriment to the defense or convenience of the town.

The Laws say nothing more about the street plan, yet in virtually all cases a grid-pattern town grew up.

The strong parallel between Vitruvian notions of town planning and those of the Spanish king must have been apparent to the conquerors of America. They would have at least realized that the Romans colonized with the *castrum*, of which sufficient examples survived in Spain to serve as guide. Thus, though the Laws did not decree a grid-pattern town—merely an orderly, symmetrical, and convenient one—the concrete visualization of those town qualities would logically have reverted back to a Roman model; not among the conquistadors to the utopian octagon of Vitruvius, but rather to the workmanlike grids of the Roman legionnaires. This theory is conjecture. After all, no law among either Romans or Spaniards required the grid-pattern town, but observation of actual towns shows how universally they adopted it. The Spanish colonial towns were detailed under the several Laws already quoted and in a manner strongly suggestive of Vitruvian principles of town planning. But they did not follow the octagonal scheme of his writing any more than did the Roman camps in Iberia. Instead, both the Romans and the Spaniards seemingly had two classes of prescription for town founding: that guiding the location, land-assignment, and composition of the land-use of a town, and that for the overall platting of the town.

The Vitruvian principles and those of the Laws of the Indies detailed where the town should be sited, what it should contain, and, within that settlement, how the rank order of location should be carried out. From these Latin practices we derive three basic morphological processes: *settlement initiation* based on the specific purpose of the town, *land-assignment* within the town on some order of merit that reserves the more desirable or impressive sites to the more pompous uses, and *use exclusion* which places beyond the limits of the town certain activities, mostly those of a pariah nature, but not only those. Thus the two texts follow almost identical lines of reasoning as to settlement initiation: these places are to overawe and command a subject people tied to a distant suzerain first by the sea (the seacoast towns) and then by land (the inland towns). With nearly identical imperial designs, the Romans and the Spaniards came forth with nearly identical principles of initiation. Similarly, each practiced a basically *noncommercial land-assignment,* turning instead to a highly elaborated political and social ordering that must needs be reflected in the assignment of space within the town. Unfortunately beyond the prescription with respect to temples, little comes down to us from Vitruvius on the Roman ordering, though we appreciate from observation of the relics that such a conscious placement was at work. The actual prescription of the Laws has survived. It begins (in Law 120) with the plaza:

After the plaza and streets have been laid out building lots are to be designated, in the first place, for the erection of the main church, the parish church or monastery and these are to occupy respectively an entire block so that no other structure can be built next to them excepting such as contribute to their commodiousness or beauty. (Law 121) Immediately afterwards the place and site are to be assigned for the Royal and Town Council House, and the Custom-House and Arsenal which is to be close to the church and port so that in case of necessity one can protect the other. The hospital for the poor and sick of non-contagious diseases shall be built next to the church forming its cloister.

Only after such institutional provisions were carried out did assignment turn to individuals (Law 126):

No building lots surrounding the main plaza are to be given to private individuals for these are to be reserved for the church, Royal and Town House, also shops and dwellings for the merchants, which are to be the first erected. ... (Law 127) The remaining building lots shall be distributed by lottery to those of the settlers who are entitled

to build around the main plaza. Those left over are to be held for us to grant to settlers who may come later or to dispose of at our pleasure. In order that entries of these assignments be better made a plan of the town is always to be made in advance.

The rank-order assignment of space within the city became a distinctive feature of Roman towns, Mediterranean towns that came as successors, and finally, those towns in Hispanic America that followed in direct succession from Roman imperialism. In this method we find a great contrast with land-assignment practices in the North Sea realm and the colonies planted by its merchants. No free land-rent market was intended in the Hispanic towns. These towns were to be administered to make certain that rank rather than ability to pay determined where activities were located. In this way it became characteristic of Hispanic American towns that rank precedence was indicated by central location, with the reverse also the case. In the merchants' towns of the English and Dutch a merchant might pay a high land-rent for a central site not to elevate his social image but to increase his income. Thus, we find in these contrasting land-assignment practices —the Latin one socially derived and the northern one commercially based—much of the explanation of the contrast between the frenetic core and grim edges of the Latin American city and the decaying heart and prosperous suburbs of the Anglo-American one.

This contrast seems to have a strong and traditional base in the notion of land-use exclusion; the Laws clearly prescribed (in Law 122) that:

The lots and sites for slaughter houses, fisheries, tanneries, and such like productive of garbage shall be so situated that the latter can be easily disposed of.

This sensible provision seems to have been construed as placing these uses outside the town, thereby encouraging a further downgrading of the status of the area beyond the walls. No such wise provision was decreed in the northern colonization; neither did the low esteem for the edge of the city grow up so vigorously.

Within the Hispanic-American towns a residential morphology distinctly different from that of the medieval bastides grew up. "All town homes are to be so planned that they can serve as a defense or fortress against those who might attempt to create disturbances or occupy the town. Each house is to be so constructed that horse and household animals can be kept therein, the courtyards and stockyards being as large as possible to insure health and cleanliness" (Law 133). Again a clear division is made between the desirable qualities of the town center, and the threats existing beyond its walls. The last law dealing with the layout of towns (137) decreed that the Indians should be kept outside the place while it was being built, and gener-

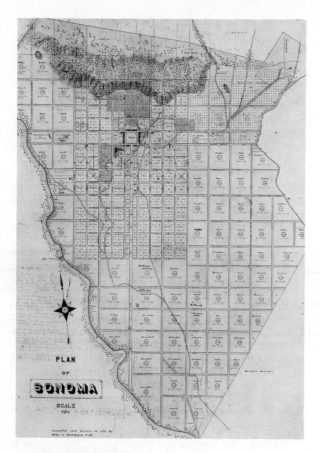

Sonoma, California, was
the last of the California
missions founded, and the
civil pueblo adjacent to it
was laid out by General
Vallejo in 1835 under the
"Laws of the Indies." The
distinction from the speculator's town in the
Middle West seems rather
slight beyond the accep-
tance of the essentially
40-acre, small-holders'
lots to be found surrounding the town plot in this
irrigated valley.

years before. Only as a "Spanish peace" was enforced
could the townsman look upon the countryside with
other than distrust and fear. Even then, he moved into
the rural area largely as a foreign overlord for a subject
people, normally required by this lonely role to keep
one foot within the city where during certain seasons
he maintained ties with his Hispanic peers. In this context the town was a very different thing socially and
economically from that in Anglo-America; as a result,
land-assignment within the place followed quite different practices.

The Emergence of Mercantilism
and the Mercantile City

While the past was conquering the lands that became
Hispanic America, Europe itself was experiencing
great changes that portended a new form of city in a
new form of society. The general ferment that accompanied the questioning of religious orthodoxy tended
to open lines of enquiry long closed by the strong barricades of established truth. The almost unrecorded
shifts began with the planting of bastides in the Middle
Ages, with the elevation of economic over dynastic concerns and timid steps toward a more democratic society. For those most questioning of nations, the ones
infected by Luther's and then Calvin's doubts, enquiry
could not be restricted only to religious questions.
Soon both the social ranking of men and the constraint
of their economic efforts to the narrow "natural" realm
of feudalism were cast in question.

In place of the "natural economy" of feudalism
came the "limitless economy" of mercantilism. Francis
Bacon believed of his time that "the jealousy of trade"
among nations was the economic rule; in that he was
expressing an idea that came formally to be advanced
by Jean Baptiste Colbert somewhat later. Inheriting
economic chaos from Richelieu and Mazarin, the two
cardinal-ministers who had preceded him, Colbert
proposed a system of protection for French industry
and trade, but active expansion of its economic frontiers. His real problem lay in establishing an economic
basis for the state at a time when several policies
seemed possible. To understand the quandary faced by
ministers of finance or the others concerned with the
king's purse during the sixteenth and seventeenth centuries, we must briefly recount the sharp change that

ally distinguished from the town residents so that
"They will consequently fear the Spaniards so much
that they will not dare to offend them and will respect
and desire their friendship." In this way the town became the instrument of colonial domination in the
same fashion it had for the Romans fifteen hundred

was taking place. Professor George Clark in his study of the seventeenth century summarizes the conditions with clarity when he defines mercantilism:

It was a system of political economy, that is to say it was a system for the regulation of economic matters by the state. It was, in Adam Smith's words, a system for "enriching the people", and its essence is that it was to do so by means of commerce. It starts from the assumption that a people is a community with a common wealth—the wealth of the nation—and that by proper measures this wealth can be increased. It is in fact the direct continuation for the larger unit called a "people" of the system of regulation by which in the Middle Ages the government of each separate town controlled the enrichment of the town as a whole. The aim of the multifarious ordinances of the medieval guilds and towns was, first of all, to ensure the provision of necessaries for the life and labour of its inhabitants. There must be a sufficiency of corn for consumption; there must be a sufficiency of raw materials for industry. A sufficiency meant not only an adequate total for all those who demanded it taken together, but also for each separate consumer or user an adequate quantity at a possible price. . . .These two elements of protection and regimentation remained throughout the mercantile epoch the fundamental principles of economic organization, but with this great difference, that now it was the state, no longer the town or its organ, the guild, which granted the privilege and protected against the unprivileged and the foreigner. That the state should have superseded the authority of the town in this matter requires no longer explanation: it was a consequence of the whole development of the power of the state which marks the essential difference between medieval and modern political history.[4]

The system was already developing before it came into full form and expression in England in the seventeenth century.

Another of Francis Bacon's aphorisms may serve to draw the contrast. He held: "The French are wiser than they seem, and the Spaniards seem wiser than they are" *(Of Seeming Wise)*. Statesmen of the late sixteenth century were beset by how to guide the course of their nations in a world wherein the Iberians, particularly the Spaniards, had gained great wealth and impressive power. The way to advance the wealth of the nation seemed to be to tread in the footsteps of the conquistadors. For a time, expeditions were sent out to search for other cities of gold, but few were found. By the time of Henri IV, the king's minister, the Duc de Sully, showed his understanding of modern economics and more liberal politics (he was one of the Protestants who

then, as now, show up unusually frequently as French finance ministers). Sully argued, *Pâturge et labourage sont les deux mamelles dont la France est alimentée, les vraies mines et trésors de Pérou* ("Grazing and arable faming are the two breasts by which France is sustained, her true Peruvian mines and treasures.").[5] The vast increases in French wealth and power in the succeeding two centuries, accompanied by the commensurate and never reversed decline of Spanish power, show us that the agriculture and labor of Frenchmen were indeed what nourished France and gave her a never-failing Peruvian gold mine.

The mercantilist system had several theorists, of whom Colbert is usually considered the first and Adam Smith the most important. But we see already at the turn of the seventeenth century that Sully was phrasing the ideas, but the Dutch and the English were proving better at practicing them. The monopolistic trading companies were one of the major instruments of such an economic policy, and they had come into existence sixty years before Colbert became a minister.

The canons of mercantilism were several:

First there was protectionism, by which a state restricted certain economic opportunities to its own subjects. . . . Its typical instrument is the tariff. . . . [Secondly] seventeenth century economists regarded some branches of trade as advantageous and others as detrimental. They favoured most highly those which brought in such goods as they could not supply for themselves, especially the precious metals, in exchange for manufactured articles which employed their labour at home. The colonial trades fulfilled these requirements, while much of the trade within Europe did not. Each country therefore tried to draw up its tariff, and its other protective arrangements such as navigation laws, in such a way as to reserve colonial trade and other paying trades for its own people, and to confine its own people to these selected channels.[6]

[4]*George Clark*, The Seventeenth Century, *New York: Oxford University Press, 1929; Galaxy Edition, 1961, pp. 22-23.*

[5]*Sully, as quoted in John Lough,* An Introduction to Seventeenth Century France, *New York: David McKay, 1969, pp. 111-112.*

[6]*George Clark*, Early Modern Europe, From About 1450 to 1720, *New York: Oxford University Press, 1954 (Galaxy Edition, 1960, pp. 196-201).*

The Mercantile City in Europe

The voyages of discovery of Columbus, Magellan, the Cabots, the Corte Reals, and others came at a time when Europe was ready to exploit their findings. The last half of the fifteenth century had witnessed the final resolution of several important medieval geographical conflicts, permitting nations which had not in any way lost the will to expand to turn their attentions elsewhere. When Columbus and Cabot returned, each told an eager Europe of the worlds to be conquered as much by trade as by armies. Such campaigns were particularly appealing in a time of an apparent balance of power among Europeans. Protectionism was bruited as early as the fourteenth century, as in the first English navigation acts, but could be actually accomplished only when the absolute and increasing national powers came into control in the fifteenth and early sixteenth centuries. Only then could trade wars emerge as the early modern replacement for the dynastic wars that dominated the Middle Ages.

At first it seems difficult to understand why Spain, the greatest of all the colonial powers in terms of domains, became, ultimately, so extremely backward in the operation of those domains and so little enriched by them. For the first century of expansion, gold and silver poured into Spain as never before seen by European eyes, yet she remained basically a poor country. The explanation is to be found in the several conditions that attended the Spanish conquest of the New World. A merchant class was notably absent in the Iberian kingdom, mainly as a result of expulsion of the Jews in 1492 and the Muslims in 1502, and of the severe repression of the Protestant tendencies most widespread among the mercantile groups.

Another contributor to this poverty in the face of riches came when Ferdinand and Isabella died without issue and the Spanish crown fell to the House of Austria, the Hapsburgs, who were deeply in debt to the Bavarian merchants, most notably the Függers of Augsburg. To profit from the trade of the Indies, the Hapsburgs decreed that all goods must pass through Seville under the supervision of the Casa de Contración, which levied high excise taxes. What profits were not already diverted by the Függers and their peers (from the Indies and Spain) tended to flow elsewhere. Because of the poor development of manufacturing in Spain, due to too great supervision and endless bureaucratic delay, the insatiable demand for manufactures in Spain and the Indies had to be projected farther into Europe—to The Netherlands, France and Germany. What profit Spain obtained tended in the end to enrich the rest of Europe and caused cities to grow in Flanders or Bavaria more quickly than in Iberia. And those imports came at a high price because the passage of the gold and silver farther into Europe inflated prices there, as Adam Smith demonstrated in his famous study on the "Digression of Silver."[7]

Spain learned only too well that the tools of a nation of men living by the sword and the crosier collected far less gold than did the pocketbook of the merchant or the hidden horde of the farmer. Excessive administration and the misunderstanding of the realities of trade plagued the Hapsburg Empire, as noted in the *Függer-Zeitungen*, private newsletters circulated by its bankers. From Seville on July 29, 1570, a correspondent wrote of a passenger from Cartagena in New Grenada:

He brings the unwelcome news that in Peru and Chile, that is to say the more distant settlements, numbers of people have rebelled owing to the severe taxes and imposts inflicted upon them daily. Moreover, they are furious because they are forbidden to plant vines, olives, corn and the like. Also all that they have been cultivating for some years past has been set on fire and destroyed. It is the King's will that all such articles should be exported from our own country and sold there, in order that his revenue and taxes both within and without the land may flourish exceedingly. The King was not a little put out that they should have thus presumed to be contumacious. This news at the present juncture is very bad, but not surprising, for if the load of a beast of burden is added to daily without regard to his strength but with thought of profit alone, he will lose heart and fall. Certain people who, except for the tribute in gold and silver which they pay to the King, desire to be free of all taxation, and have consequently often taken up arms against the King, walk freely abroad here, their only desire being to enrich themselves by war and disorder.[8]

If even heartless bankers could see the stupid rigidity of the Spanish policies, should we be surprised that they failed to produce an enduring commonwealth?

The age of discoveries seems to have had a very different course in western Europe north of the Pyrenees, where it was not so epic-making and as a consequence not so rigid. Voyagers were much more likely to sail on their own account, or that directly of merchants, so the same element of royal sanction and direction did not exist which seems in Hispanic-America to have perpetuated medieval economic practices well beyond their appointed time. When John Cabot set sail from Bristol in 1497 on the account of the local merchants, he was not the first to do so. In the middle

[7]*Adam Smith*, The Wealth of Nations, *Book I, Chapter XI.*
[8]*George T. Mathews*, The Függer Newsletters, *New York: Capricorn Books, 1970, pp. 37-38.*

of that century, merchants interested in the "Western Ocean" had sent into its unknown reaches ships to explore its trading and fishing prospects. In this action, the Bristol men were merely adopting the new sense of space characteristic of their time to the traditional trading purposes they had pursued in Ireland during the Middle Ages.

The Split Between the Merchants' Town and the Court Settlement

The motivating force in the shaping of the mercantile city was the opportunity that the Age of Discovery afforded to Europeans to expand their trading frontiers. That spatial spreading of trade brought the Middle Ages to a close with a sharp change in the scale of activity and a rapid transformation of the morphogenesis of cities. Germany and Italy felt little of the change, save among the likes of the Függers. In the absence of expanding trade, the only basis for town formation and enlargement in Italy and Germany was expanded or elaborated *courtly functions*. The Renaissance city emerged as the expression of such an administrative and political function, and saw relatively little use in the mercantile world of the North Sea countries and their overseas plantations. What Renaissance building took place in the New World sprang fairly directly from Spanish practice or its intended reproduction in the more caste-ridden slave colonies of the American South.

The expansion of the trade frontier reshaped urban form in two ways: first, it created an increase in trade that made necessary the enlargement of trading facilities—shops, warehouses, and counting houses. The medieval structure could not comprehend this change, and as a result gave way in the creation of new, post-medieval, urban forms. Second, the transportation facilities were elevated to a dominant postion as the acknowledged lifeline of urban existence. When we read Fitzstephen's account of London life toward the end of the twelfth century, the port on the bank of the Thames is portrayed with none of the bustle and urgency it gained with mercantilism. By 1550 the port functions dominated London life. Toward the end of the century, when Elizabeth sought to contain London's growth, she specifically exempted the port from further constraint.

The rupture of the medieval order came in the elevation of commerce to a position of absolute supremacy over the formerly more powerful artisan activities. Commerce needed a concentrated quarter in which to operate (where enlarged "business administration" could be carried on and where the information of trade was readily at hand). With distant trading, commercial intelligence was essential. The Függers had developed their *Zeitungen* to accomplish this flow of commercial intelligence, but they were exceptional only in the size of the realm in which they might operate. If you could not maintain the network of commercial correspondents such as the Függers did, then being in and of a bustling port was a good substitute.

Bristol had a flow of geographical intelligence that may have been the most widespread for any European port; in response to commercial and geographical knowledge, she sent forth expeditions financed by merchants whose windows looked onto the Avon's wharves. Even after the initial period of active exploration, the market still required constant attendance with regard to decisions to send more or fewer ships to fish the banks, whether and when to dispatch ships to the Spanish ports to sell the dried codfish returned from "New Found Land," and how to gain an effective auction market to set prices and anticipate prospects in distant marts. Only in an administered monopoly such as Spain's could such an *intelligence concentration* be avoided; even there, the king required clustering so he could keep his royal eye on the freebooting tendencies of traders. Seville dominated the trade of Spain as no northern city controlled the trade of England or Holland, but the merchants there could not exercise their collective judgment of the market, as in London, or their innovative skill, as in Bristol. Thus their results were grand only while the gold flowed, later becoming grim when the flow of bullion slowed, with little to substitute for it.

The mechanism of adjustment to needed changes in the physical structure of the mercantile town was a land-rent system wherein bidding for particular parcels of land took place in a market, with the highest bidder likely to gain possession of the site. At first the bidding must have been mainly for the choice site, with the building already standing upon it taken as a matter of course. We know that in the sixteenth and seventeenth centuries most urban buildings were merely survived transformations of the medieval house—tall and narrow if the city were walled, but somewhat less so if the place were effectively open, or little developed so as to make space relatively freely available. The mercantile city tended to reuse these properties in a variety of ways, with great ingenuity.

Members of the elite class described by diarists, travelers, and resident authors were not, in the long reach of history, the real forbears of the present world.

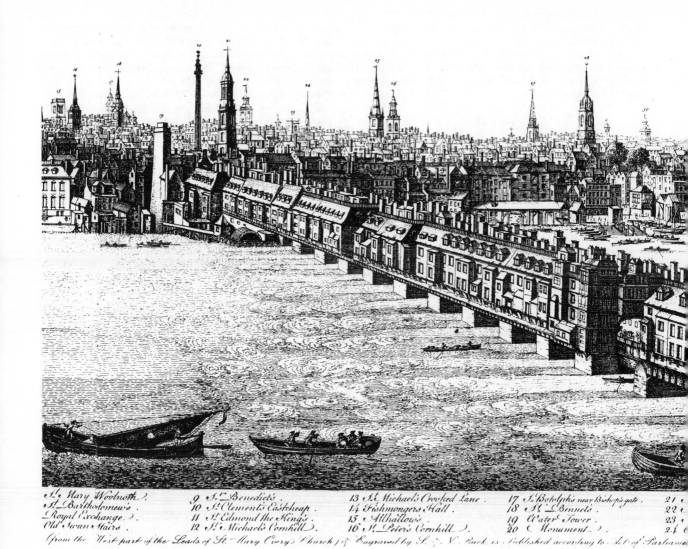

St. Mary Woolnoth.   9 St. Benedict's.   13 St. Michael's Crooked Lane. 17 St. Botolph's near Bishop's gate. 21
St. Bartholomew's.   10 St. Clement's Eastcheap. 14 Fishmongers Hall.   18 St. Bennets.   22
Royal Exchange.   11 St. Edmond the King's. 15 Allhallows.   19 Water Tower.   23
Old Swan Stairs.   12 St. Michael's Cornhill. 16 St. Peter's Cornhill.   20 Monument.   24

(from the West part of the Leads of St. Mary Overy's Church) & Engraved by S. & N. Buck is Published according to Act of Parliame

This view of London in 1749 is taken from the easternmost three panels of Buck Brothers' Panorama of London, 1749 (reprinted in 1972 by Sidgwick and Jackson, London). It suggests a closely built merchants' town even though it shows almost entirely a London rebuilt since 1666.

Most of the splendor that comes down to us in descriptions from the sixteenth and seventeenth centuries was nonurban, if not outright and consciously a rejection of the city. Kings became a suburban class well before the commonality, and the nobility trotted along in their enslaved fashion. London's Whitehall and Paris's Versailles may have differed in grandeur but not in fun-

damental location within the city pattern; they lay outside the merchants' town.

In the seventeenth century, some medieval houses were torn down to be replaced by the town houses of the powerful, as Antonio Canaletto's drawings of London in the early eighteenth century show us. In general, the housing for the aristocracy lay beyond the edge of the merchants' town,[9] as further confirmed in a

[9]*Adrian Eccles*, Canaletto, *London: Paul Hamlyn, 1967. Although painting in the 1740's, Canaletto was depicting the city as it stood just before the great changes that came to the British economy with the Industrial Revolution then beginning.*

25 St Margaret Patten's.
26 St Mary at Hill.
27 St Botolph's Aldgate.
28 St Dunstan's in ye East.

29 Billingsgate.
30 St Olaves.
31 Bear Key.
32 Allhallow's Barkin.

33 Custom House.
34 Tower Hill.
35 The Armory.
36 Tower Stairs.

37 St Georges in ye East.
38 Tower.
39 St Ann's Limehouse.
40 London Bridge.

No. 1. Garden Court, Middle Temple, London.

panorama of London drawn by the Buck Brothers and published in 1749.[10] Again the city represented is a bit later than the time we are considering, but it furnishes us with a summary useful in weighting the physical components of the city that resulted from mercantile conquest. The picture is of a town medieval in grain in the east, in the City of London, becoming increasingly Renaissance and ostentatious with westward move-

[10]*With notes by John Wellsman in 1972,* Panorama of London, 1749, *drawn by Buck Brothers. London: Sidgwick and Jackson, 1972.*

ment to Whitehall and Westminster. Few actual medieval buildings remain within the medieval town; most were destroyed in the Great Fire of 1666. But the scale and form of the reconstructions conformed reasonably well with what was there before, though rebuilt in more fire-resistant materials.

Paris and London had become, by the year 1600, the two largest cities of western society. Each was in the full sense a merchants' town, London more so than the French capital. In each, the court's presence served to stimulate a large-scale construction of town houses for the nobility, who were required (either by self-interest or by the king's will) to reside at court for part of the year. In London the requirement was less direct and the number of houses smaller; nonetheless the area west of Temple Bar became a region quite distinct from that to the east within the workaday city. In the Strand, "houses" were being built in even greater numbers than had been the case among the powerful bishops and dukes of the Middle Ages. Thus residential relocation of the wealthy was occurring in the late sixteenth and early seventeenth centuries.

Paris was the largest city of the West when Henri IV entered it in 1594, and certainly one of the more perplexed. The Wars of Religion had battered it about, particularly the suburbs outside the walls where many houses had been razed. But from around 1600 for another half century, Paris grew rapidly, expanding a third in size and prospering greatly, to such an extent that urgent calls arose for new building. King Henri IV played some role in that construction when he sought to have a silk factory set up near Le Marais, the marsh to the east of the city, and to bring Italian weavers there to complete their products. This plan was carried out on the unsold lots of a royal land speculation at the razed site of the former Les Tournelles Palace.

The scheme failed, but from it grew the Place Royale,[11] the first defined aristocratic development Paris was to experience. Around that square the important nobility just below the top rank took up residence. These lesser lights were seeking a compromise solution to a problem of aristocratic residence that had already been solved somewhat differently by the most powerful nobles and the *princes du sang*. Those proud courtiers had begun to build town residences of a distinctive sort—large, elaborately decorated buildings, often located on open lots but sometimes merely the largest building in a continuous street facade. These *hôtels* (perhaps best rendered in English as "great mansions") followed an aristocratic pattern fashionable at least since Jacques Coeur's time. They were comprised of a central block flanked by lower *pavilions* at either side enclosing a courtyard closed from the street by an impressive gateway. At first the *hôtels* were not notably concentrated in any particular quarter of Paris, if we may believe the maps of their location presented by Pierre Couperie for the reigns of Henri IV, Louis XIII, and Louis XIV.[12]

But particularly in the time of Louis XIV (when attendance at court was required, while the city of Paris remained as crowded and riotous as ever), the pattern began to change. The monarch had abandoned his several palaces within the city; Les Tournelles had been razed in favor of the Tuileries located outside the city wall in the west. As a result the districts of St. Germain and nearby St. Honoré were taken up by the aristocracy, a trend strengthened by the increasing rage for carriage driving. Within the old city, these vehicles were virtually stranded by the narrow streets and the press of pedestrians. But west of the Louvre, a carriage circuit—Cours-la-Reine—was set up for this folly of mobility without any geographical purpose. When an aristocratic quarter had been firmly fixed in the west, the former symmetry in the location of *hôtels* began to disappear, destroying along with it the social cachet of the Place Royale (des Vosges) and Le Marais in general. Only in the last few years has this area returned to fashionable approval.

The flocking of the aristocrats to be near the king became even more evident in 1680 when Louis XIV moved his government and ministries along with his retinue to Versailles. The clarion call of the court and fashion could not be overlooked; seventeenth-century Paris firmly adopted a practice which has been one of the prime dynamics of city growth ever since: the backstaying of aristocratic status by residence in the currently fashionable quarter of the city. This practice would have been incomprehensible to the medieval mind.

In previous times, most certainly in the Middle Ages, no clear evidence suggests that where one lived in the city was viewed as a cachet of social distinction. Housing choice was based on avoidance of unhealthy areas, clustering together of political factions, occupational association, and the search for the extraterritoriality of the steelyard or ghetto.

[11]*The Place Royale suffered a number of changes of name. During the Revolution it became the Place des Fédérés, in 1793 the Place de l'Indivisibilité, and under Napoléon the Place des Vosges, when Lucien Bonaparte sought in order to speed up the collection of taxes to conduct a contest, naming the square for the first* departement *to pay its taxes.*
[12]*Pierre Couperie,* Paris Through the Ages, *New York: George Braziller, 1974, Plates Xb, XIc, XId, and XIIc.*

The Form of the Merchants' Town

The towns that prospered during the Middle Ages were those of the merchants, so these seventeenth-century cities were in effect their direct descendants. Water had been the main practicable method of transport in the earlier period and remained so until the eighteenth century; thus no fundamental shift was made in the desirable location for such mercantile places. As its port grew, a city tended to divide between a working area of quays, warehouses, and shops and an area for upper-class housing. Behind this segregation lay a general principle that still holds true: the wealthy normally favor investing their money in structures, which show their wealth, rather than in excessively costly central land, which does not present its price to the naked eye. The wealthy, particularly the attenders at court, also became greatly concerned with style, adopting new fashions of architecture and new designs for housing to such an extent that the relict of medieval building remaining in the city held no appeal for them. But the merchants found these rather functional buildings readily usable for their purposes. The older sections in the heart of the city tended to convert to mercantile uses, broadly defined, which further encouraged the aristocracy to move out to their own "quarter" with its physical evidence of the leisured and wealthy life. Soon the notion grew up of *neighborhood reinforcement*, wherein the social standing of individuals living near one assumed importance lacking in earlier centuries.

The mechanism for change within the merchants' town was the *relative utility* of the site, measured by the bid-rent that potential occupants were willing to pay for its use. A separate bid-rent scale for residential locations, based on social esteem, did not grow up for some time. Within the mercantile component of the town, residence was based on the utility it offered for quick and easy access to the place of employment. Due to the scalar increase in commercial undertaking, no longer could the occupational household furnish lodgings for all workers. Some must seek rental housing; their search brought the introduction of a new bid-rent scale for worker housing based on utility of access.

By the late seventeenth century, at least three different rent scales operated in the city: (1) that for commercial premises predicated primarily on the quality of the site in the matter of access to transportation and exterior connections to customers, (2) that of the working people based on the ease of daily access to the workplace from the residence, and (3) that of the leisured class based on the levels of social cachet associated with various residential streets and neighborhoods. This classification, although neater than fact, serves to clarify the forces of separation at work in the city with the onset of major growth in commerce and population in the seventeenth century.

Some measure of the need for city enlargement is furnished by the growth in shipping use of the port of Bristol during the seventeenth and eighteenth centuries. "In 1687, 240 ships cleared from Bristol, thirty years later in 1717 the number had increased to 375 and in 1787, 448 vessels left Bristol in the year." Ships entering show a similar growth. "But these totals understate the growth of trade since the size of vessels rose during the century. In 1701 the average tonnage of ships owned by Bristol merchants was 105 tons, by the end of the century it was 144 tons." In 1700 Bristol received 19,878 tons inbound shipping while in 1790 it received 76,000 tons. This eighteenth-century growth was merely following a trend begun with the Commercial Revolution two centuries earlier, which meant that the medieval urban structure came less and less to suffice.[13]

Response to scalar increase in the trade of cities was both demographic and morphological. Populations increased rapidly. Bristol grew from 20,000 in 1700, as the third city of Britain, to 64,000 in 1801, as her second city; in America, Boston already ranked fourth or fifth among cities of the British dominions at the end of the seventeenth century with a population of ca. 7,000, exceeded in size probably only by Norwich, Bristol, and London.[14] The ports of the Atlantic fringes were the scene of the urban revolution of the Mercantile Era. Some places had already been large because of medieval trade; Antwerp, for example, had stood as the greatest trading city of Europe in 1560. Guicciardini, the Venetian envoy, then described the port, noting that sometimes 500 ships passed in a day (no doubt boats on the Scheldt as well as those by sea) and 2,000 carts entered the city each week. Antwerp had taken the trading crown from the Mediterranean and Venice, and it remained on the Western Ocean shore never again to leave, though Antwerp was eclipsed for over two hundred years when the Dutch choked off her ac-

[13]Walter Minchinton, "The Port of Bristol in the Eighteenth Century," in Bristol in the Eighteenth Century, edited by Patrick McGrath, North Pomfret, Vermont: David and Charles, 1972, p. 129.
[14]Carl Bridenbaugh, Cities in the Wilderness, The First Century of Urban Life in America, New York: Alfred A. Knopf, 1960 [originally published 1938], p. 143.

cess to the sea by denying her navigation on the lower Scheldt, a sorry state that ended only in 1863.

The list of European ports becoming great cities between 1500 and 1800 is considerable. Antwerp was the first, but was soon followed by Amsterdam, Rotterdam, Rouen, and the north German ports. Even more spectacular was the rise of the marine cities of Britain and America. So many towns rose to large size and great economic activity that we can look in detail at only a few representative examples—Amsterdam and Rouen on the Continent, Bristol in England, and Boston and the other Atlantic ports in America.

Amsterdam as a Mercantile City

Amsterdam had been a medieval port of modest importance greatly exceeded in influence by Antwerp and even Bruges. Through her opening via the Zuider Zee to the North Sea she entered into the Baltic trade in herring and grain; as the sixteenth century saw the swift decline of the *hanse*, that Baltic trade increased. The city's rise was furthered after the cruel reconquest of the southern Hapsburg Netherlands by the Spaniards, when a number of skilled workers—Protestants and Jews, for the most part—came to Amsterdam, bringing trades and skills essential to the growth of a great merchants' town. Still, for much of the seventeenth century, Amsterdam's real financial prosperity came from the traditional grain trade. Local merchants bought grain in the Baltic, brought it to the port on the Amstel for storage in great high warehouses until the market price rose, then sold it to make a speculator's profit. Such activities fitted far better in a Protestant city than they would have under the economic teachings of the medieval Catholic church, with its concern for just price and its abhorrence of regrating—which this storage in anticipation of a price rise really was. Once free of Spain and the *hanse*, Amsterdam entered earnestly into the carrying trade, building larger ships. These *fluiten* came by the end of the sixteenth century to be the leaders in merchant marine activities. The dangers of navigation led to the creation of insurance, and the city on the Amstel became a great insurance center, even insuring Holland's enemies in time of war. Refugees from the final reconquest of Antwerp by the Spaniards brought the glass, diamond-cutting, jewelry, and damask weaving trades to Amsterdam, adding further to her wealth.

Amsterdam and the "Fixed Cake of Commerce"

The greatest contribution to the prosperity of Amsterdam came from her rather oblique entry into the trade of the Indies. Throughout the sixteenth century, effective ties had existed between Portugal and Holland while both were greatly interconnected through ties to the Spanish royal family. After 1581 and the onset of the "Sixty Years' Captivity" of Portugal by the Hapsburgs, these ties were strengthened for a few years, and at least tenuously maintained until Holland became independent in 1609.

Seventeenth-century mercantilist thought held that only a very finite amount of "trade" could be had. Nations therefore sought viciously to guard what they held and to steal increments from others. In our time, this notion has been called the "fixed cake of commerce so that one nation's gain therein must be at the expense of another's loss." Along with the "fixed cake of commerce" went the idea that "the objective is always the development, from an agrarian base, of an industrial, commercial and maritime superstructure coupled with an attempt to secure a bigger share in the profits of international commerce for one's own citizens."[15] Even a secret slice of the cake, such as Holland gained in a secret treaty with Spain in 1609, was indeed of value. Perhaps the most valuable component of trade at the beginning of its development is the simple knowledge of the market and its sources of potential supply. In a time of trading monopolies, this desire to gain a piece of the previously forbidden cake of commerce lent considerable support to movements for local independence.

The Dutch in their protracted negotiations before 1609 had held out first for freedom of religion but equally for freedom of trade. In the American Revolution, the priorities were reversed; freedom of trade came first to the minds of American revolutionaries, as Professor Arthur Schlesinger and his students have fully demonstrated during the last forty years.

---

[15]*Jacob van Klaveren, "Fiscalism, Mercantilism and Corruption," in D. C. Coleman,* Revisions in Mercantilism, *London: Methuen and Co., 1969, pp. 140-161.*

The merchants' port of Amsterdam in 1544 shows the relatively small size, and compactness within its walls, of even the leading late medieval cities. Amsterdam was tightly built up with narrow linear houses (on older burgage plots) that did not have the height of those in interior cities where the bearing capacity of the ground was greater. But Amsterdam had the great virtue of door-to-door delivery of goods to the merchants' houses along the five canals that served the city.

The Form of the Dutch City

What sort of town grew from the rapid expansion of the Dutch trading horizon? In an interesting study of Holland at the time of Rembrandt, during the seventeenth century, Paul Zumthor tells us:

For the most part Dutch cities were constructed according to one or the other of three typical plans: rounded, with more or less circular streets, as in Leiden, Haarlem, and Gouda; or nearly quadrangular, with rectilinear streets: as in Delft and Alkmar; or finally a point, often of unequal sides, between two arms of water, as at Dordrecht or Medemblik. Along the principal canal, which forms an axis, irregular facades are aligned with stalls (for selling) sheltered by penthouses; there is then a

bridge like the back of donkey, another canal, here a long market-place dominated by the building of the Public Weigh House; a market of meat, the city hall, itself the testimony of a municipal charter; and higgledy-piggledy around all this are ranged the steep gables, and the spire of a tall gothic church, as at Gouda. This marketplace is the center around which the daily life is organized.[16]

At the beginning of the seventeenth century, the streets of the marketplace were first being paved to overcome the nuisance of mud and grit tracked in from the sand and clay plains on which these Dutch cities were built. (Sir William Temple, British ambassador of this time, brought back the tale of a man who visited the mistress of a Dutch house whose sturdy maid hoisted him to her shoulders and carried him to the staircase within to avoid the scuffing of polished

[16]*Paul Zumthor,* La Vie Quotidienne en Hollande au Temps de Rembrandt, *Paris: Librairie Hachette, 1959, p. 18.*

floors.)[17] Streets were paved as much to make commerce easier as to limit the grime for in the Dutch pantheon, trade and cleanliness already stood equal. By 1650 most public streets had been paved, to such an extent that the Calvinist ministers viewed this as a most questionable luxury.[18] On the alignment of many streets flowed a canal, sometimes bordered by paved ways on either bank; the more elegant streets were lined with trees. These conditions held in the newer or more wealthy districts.

In the poorer quarters life was different, as were the physical conditions under which it was lived. Streets were unpaved, with sewers running down their centers, houses were built of wood, following the architecture of the Middle Ages. Upper stories hung successively farther over the street until, when no canal separated the houses, the occupants of the attics could shake hands across the way. Zumthor tells us, "A heterogeneous population swarmed in these quarters, at least in the larger cities. The housing problem, continuous during the seventeenth century as a result of demographic growth and the speculation in rents, had made virtual barracks of these medieval hovels. Traffickers in rent bought such houses to cut them up into small pieces to increase the number of apartments, only to let them in turn at usurious rents."[19]

Dutch houses came to be built from brick with stone trim, and were low if space were available. But normally they were fairly narrow, though not exceptionally high. An unusual feature was that they normally stood separate, even if the gap between them might be little more than an inch or two. Structures in areas outside the slums were usually occupied by single families, and when more housing was needed it came in the outward spread of the city rather than in pushing upward within existing quarters. No doubt a large part of this spread resulted from the difficulty of securing good foundations in a city such as Amsterdam, which had of necessity to be built on piles driven into the argillaceous muck of the polder belt. Three or four stories became the norm, though in Amsterdam some houses reached as high as five to eight.[20] But even so, height in housing came to be associated with wealthy bourgeois residents rather than with crowding in the poorer quarters.

Four or five windows sufficed for lighting the interiors of most houses, which were often quite deep. The facade frequently bowed out to protect a lower part from the rain. Below the street level was a cellar, reached through an areaway closed by a grating.

Raised a few steps up was the first floor. Along its front just above the tops of the windows ran a *luifel*, or awning, of painted wood under which an artisan might work or his family might take the air in warm weather. When the building was used for selling, the single large window of the first floor would give way to a large door opening to a shop.

At the top front of the house, the basically triangular gable was likely to be handled decoratively with an attic window and a rather fancy outline sometimes effectively masking the actual roof-line. Four or five distinctive facades characteristic of mercantile Amsterdam still define the skyline of the heart of the city. Some have sinuous curves typical of the baroque, others are stepped in clean sharp angles, others are slanted or scroll-like. These facades have been the distinguishing feature of Amsterdam from "the golden century," the seventeenth, when simplicity was still a virtue but wealth was flooding in from the Baltic, the merchant marine, and the Indies trade.

Amsterdam houses differed greatly. The facades of the houses of the wealthy were decorated with insets of marble or faïence, pilasters and deep window embrasures, and shutters rather than the covered *luifel*. Among the most modest class the houses were of single story, and the only luxury was the careful varnishing of wooden surfaces. In a climate so damp as Holland's, this feature was not simple vanity.[21]

In the seventeenth century, the occupational districting of Dutch cities was still very clear. Trades lived together in specific streets. As Zumthor notes, "The concentration of similar activities in the same place makes simple and most effective the right of supervision which rests in the different 'corporations' [gilds]. . . . A city is thus a conglomeration of small worlds each of which has its own complexion, its gossip, and its odors. From house to house one spies, keeps watch, and maintains an order based on tradition. The masters of a trade give their name to a street, or a square: the canal of Glazers, the port for Wine, Cheese Street, Flower Street, that for Spices, and the Blacksmith's Brook; Amsterdam has its Canal of the Lords."[22]

With their prosperity the Dutch began to beautify their cities, particularly by laying out some of the earliest public parks (called *mails*), in the form of promenades. Utrecht's *mail*, established in 1637, was nearly half a mile long.

The true nature of the seventeenth-century Mercantile Revolution emerged in Amsterdam, which remained in the center of the Dutch trading empire. One of the largest cities of the West, it was undoubtedly the most wealthy and orderly of its time. It ranged along

[17]*Geoffrey Cotterell*, Amsterdam, The Life of a City, *Boston: Little, Brown, and Co., 1972, p. 190.*

[18]*Zumthor, op. cit., p. 19.*

[19]Loc. cit.

[20]Ibid., p. 20.

[21]Ibid., p. 21.

[22]Ibid., p. 22.

concentric canals by which the city had expanded outward from the medieval dam where it began. A great wall of brick surrounded the place, beyond which the poor lived in hovels that suggested even at this time the vast contrast found in our day between Paris and her *bidonvilles*. Wealth and squalor have always cohabited in great cities.

Amsterdam became a cosmopolitan city, perhaps the first since Constantinople, and grew apace. By 1600 the city was so crowded that new building space was badly needed. Within a few years, its area was increased three-fold, to 726 hectares, which still proved insufficient. A ring of new suburbs was added, with wider streets radiating out from the old city center along which new shops were opened. Growth continued, finally far distant from the medieval core, which had been largely transformed by replacement structures. In these outlying quarters, rectangular street patterns, introduced in the "Plantage," formed the city extension of the late seventeenth century.

While the city grew, another change became visible that was to have great effect on the building of civic monuments and churches—the increasing demoratization of urban society which showed up in both secular and ecclesiastical structures. To take two examples: the great City Hall in Amsterdam, built between 1648 and 1656, startled contemporary observers both by its vast size and by its absence of monumental and ceremonial entrances. Seven equal and small arches flanked its front on Dam Square. Within the building all sorts of municipal services were carried on, ranging from the Bank of Amsterdam through the arsenal, the courts, and the jail. This city hall was no longer a ceremonial "gild hall," but rather a municipal service building, however grand its frescoes and reliefs. Similarly, with the Reformation, Protestant churches became houses of preaching to a far greater degree than even the preaching barns of the twelfth century that brought on the marvelous innovation of Gothic architecture. The Dutch Reform church rejected Gothic architecture and the church of nave, crossing, and choir in favor of a much more austere neoclassicism and a basically circular preaching hall. As Zumthor has it, "It was no longer important to turn the eyes of the faithful toward the East but rather their ears toward the center, toward the pulpit."[23] For this goal, the linearity of the Gothic church was a nuisance fast overcome in so pragmatic a place and time as seventeenth-century Holland.

Holland in the seventeenth century possessed a peculiar blending of power and parsimony, of display and thrift. Italian architecture with elaborate or even excessively extravagant ornamentation was rapidly introduced. But still Amsterdam was a merchants' town

[23]Ibid., p. 29.

with housing plots to match. Even wealthy merchants' houses seldom gained great width—Amsterdam's average at the time was 20 to 25 feet with a depth of no more than 200 feet, sometimes even including fairly extensive gardens. All large houses must still have access to the canal, as attested even today by the pulleys affixed to their gable ends over which ropes may be thrown to raise large items to storage in the attics. In a city that grew from 100,000 population in 1600 to some 150,000 at midcentury, the combination of a more widespread distribution of wealth, or at least fairly general sufficiency, with a desire for material comfort meant that housing was to be solid and even ostentatious but rather democratically modular in scale.

Rouen: The Town of Mercantile Failure

Certainly one of the better tests of the role of mercantile support in the shaping of the modern west European-North American city is furnished by the contrasting experience of Amsterdam and Rouen. Josiah Cox Russell in his study of medieval population at times adjusts his figures to match his assumed rank-size rule, but at least his relative standings usually seem justified. He

The seventeenth-century housing in Rouen still gave great evidence of medieval practices, such as timber framing, the filling of walls by scantlings and lath and plaster, the overhang of upper stories, and the persistence of burgage plots.

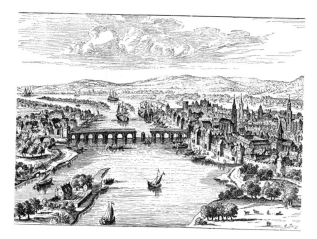

shows Rouen with a late medieval population of some 25,000 to 34,000, whereas that of Amsterdam in the early fourteenth century stood at less than 10,000.[24] Thus, the picture we have seen of seventeenth-century Amsterdam as a large and powerful place is a superb portrait of the mercantile city. In contrast, Rouen stands as the city second only to Paris in northern France during the Middle Ages, and certainly the classic example of a medieval trading town.

We will not recount all of the glories and vicissitudes of medieval Rouen. It remained strongly attached to England while Normandy and the island kingdom were one realm, and gave greater loyalty to the descendants of the Plantagenet kings of England than to the Capetian kings of France. With great reluctance the Rouennaise were forced to become part of France, whose geographical concerns were different from theirs. Even before the Norman conquest of England, a law of Ethelred II's in 979 exempted wine from Rouen and spices brought through there from import duties at London. And the *hanse* at London counted a number of Norman merchants from Rouen and Caen among its members. "By way of Rouen England received wines from France, fish from the Baltic, fruits from Portugal. By way of Rouen Holland imported furs from Ireland, leather from England, metal from Spain, and wine from France."[25] The outward-looking quality of the town was strong in the Middle Ages but:

The discovery of the New World stimulated even more the activity among the Rouennaise merchants. They were among the first to take part in the great discoveries. They were as active as the Genoans and Venetians, and again as the Amsterdamers and men of Lisbon were at a later time in founding colonies; it was in truth from these counting houses of maritime commerce, generally by sons, that trading enterprises were undertaken in each of the distant continents. Rouen multiplied these dépôts. *Her ships left every year in November-December for* la grosse aventure. *They returned in February-March loaded with new provisions of which only a very small part remained in France, the bulk being reexported to foreign lands. Newfoundland supplied cod; Canada furs and beaver pelts for hats; the Îles [of the West Indies] sugar and cacao; Brazil and Guyane dye woods, indigo, leather, and tortoiseshell; Guinea and the Coast of Africa loaded slaves; oil nuts for pressing, and above all spices. Rouen had long possessed the privilege of undertaking commerce with the ancient ports of the Ponant (West): Nantes, La*

Rochelle, and Bordeaux, but, in 1549, Henri II gave them a monopoly on the importation into France of spices and drugs coming from overseas by water. This royal privilege listed 218 different articles.[26]

Despite a start equal with other mercantile towns of northwestern Europe, several subsequent events and conditions served ultimately to defeat Rouen in a race possessed of the most relentless competition. Even before political events intervened to restrain her trade, Rouen suffered from her location nearly fifty miles from the sea on a river hardly adequate even for medieval trade. As ship size necessarily increased with the venturing forth on the sometimes cruel Atlantic, the Seine proved a difficult approach for the port; at least four days were required to come from the open ocean, and sometimes as long as ten days to gain it again against a stiff west wind. In addition tolls on the lower river were levied under privileges remaining from the Middle Ages. When winds were adverse, ships had to be hauled to the town along a tow path commonly in a ruinous shape. Even so, in the late sixteenth century the progress was great; Rouen became the entrepôt for Canada and undertook to carry on trade with Spain, Portugal, and Italy to the south and Flanders and Holland to the north. J. Levainville tells us, "The mastery of the sea was disputed by Amsterdam and Rouen: the time of London had not yet come." But when France's war with England intervened, the English began to buy directly the goods previously imported via Rouen. "In spite of her commercial monopoly of trade with the colonies she experienced active competition from Holland in the spice and coffee trade and from Le Havre in the handling of heavy goods."[27] Other hands at the table began to clutch more determinedly their pieces of "the cake of commerce" until, by the end of the seventeenth century, most of the great overseas empires were forbidden to Rouen, which a century before had truly been a "world entrepôt."

The fabric of Rouen still preserves many medieval forms, serving notice that the quickened pace of the late sixteenth century lasted too short a time to reform the city. The typical Rouennaise house was built of timbers erected in a post-and-lintel frame; the spaces between the timbers were filled with lighter material, such as laths, and surfaced either by lime plaster or slates. Slates, introduced from Flanders, still distinguish the ancient port town on the Seine. Doors and windows were few and narrow and closed only with shutters. The windows at first had no glass; even after the introduction of glazing, they were no larger. Houses were dark and drafty; as the ancient posts and beams dried out, gaps were left through which the wind blew

[24]*Josiah Cox Russell*, Medieval Regions and Their Cities, *Bloomington: University of Indiana Press, 1972, p. 117 and p. 148.*

[25]*J. Levainville*, Rouen: Étude d'une Agglomeration Urbaine, *Paris: Libraire Armond Colin, 1913, p. 146.*

[26]Ibid., *p. 148.*

[27]Ibid., *p. 149.*

in bad weather and along which rats, those vectors of the plague, could scamper at any time. To this dreary picture we must add the frequency of stairways and passages along which fire could race so quickly in this city of old and powdery wood. "Rouen the museum city was often in fact the city of death."[28]

Just as in Amsterdam, the houses in Rouen were built on long narrow lots with gardens behind, often ranging from 25 to 30 feet in width and 60 to 100 feet in depth. The entrance was always in a gable on the narrow frontage which looked upon the street.

The long narrow farm lots, *boëls* in an old Norman word, had perhaps been defined by the Danes; they certainly existed in the countryside and were still used in the expansion of the city of Rouen even in the eighteenth century. "The very narrow facade of the Rouennaise houses shaped their structural uniformity. For the most part the oldest residences were gable to the street and built up to the utter limit permitted by their material and the decrees of the archbishop. . . .Besides the gable-end houses, which were the most common, one still found more modest houses, restricted to a single story and with a deep overhanging roof." These uncomfortable houses were built as lean-tos by "bourgeois owners (who) leased them to the poor specifying that they could keep neither hogs nor sows. They were occupied by urban workers who had to live at the center of town. Gable houses and lean-to houses were the most common types at the beginning of the growth of the city."[29] Such simple structures were little changed even during the short-lived trading prosperity of the late sixteenth century. "In the seventeenth century the great families rebuilt their *hôtels* but the alignment of the streets changed not at all. Many were without air, dark and tortuous."[30]

Slack trade during the reign of Louis XIV froze the city in this form. "Engravings of Rouen in the sixteenth century and in 1830 show us almost identical quarters." The revocation of the Edict of Nantes, which had given the French Protestants—so numerous in shipping, trade, and skilled manufacture—some toleration in the practice of their religion, played its part. "If the revocation of the Edict of Nantes was of religious origin, its consequences were indisputably economic. Seven thousand five hundred Protestants left the city, but the workers they employed left as well. The Intendant de la Bourdonnaye estimated at 20,000 the number of inhabitants lost by Rouen at the end of the seventeenth century as a result of wars and the revocation."[31]

The Mercantile Revolution of the seventeenth cen-

[28]Ibid., *p. 305.*
[29]Ibid., *pp. 309-310.*
[30]Ibid., *p. 332.*
[31]Ibid., *p. 369.*

tury brushed Rouen only lightly and did not transform it. The loss during that century of trade with Spain and Portugal and then with Holland and England was the result of the great upsurge of doctrinaire mercantilism which naturalized shipping and trade to subjects of a particular king, leaving those formerly trading as middlemen under a ban. French settlement efforts in Canada never matched those of England in what became the United States; in 1763 France turned her back on Canada, a situation that remained true until Charles de Gaulle rediscovered New France two centuries later in 1967. With the reactionary trend of France under Richelieu and Louis XIV, the decline of Rouen was complete. She settled back toward the past as a *ville-musée* where the Middle Ages survived until nineteenth-century industrialization finally broke the lassitude. As an industrial city, Rouen finally gained an improved waterway to the sea and retrieved some of her medieval commercial importance.

The Form of Bristol: The Emerging Residential "Environment"

No more revealing picture of the distinction between the city as the workshop of man and as the monument to enshrined and narrowly-held power could be furnished than by comparing Bristol in the West Country of England with the several dozen princely towns in Germany and Italy possessed of similar regional status. Most past observers drew conclusions quite unfavorable to the port on the Avon, though few were as acid as those of the poet Thomas Chatterton who in the eighteenth century could see only:

Bristolia's dingy piles of brick,
Lovers of mammon, worshippers of trick . . .

He was seeing a city of vigor but little self-conscious design, a combination never understood by aesthetes who possess too little of the first and too much of the second.

Embedded in this contrast is a truth of the character which became, as the years passed, one of the basic forces at work in the shaping of cities: the sensitivity of the prosperous and powerful toward the nature of their physical environment, and their ability to command its change. That morphogenetic process was best demonstrated in the cities of the seventeenth and eighteenth centuries. In the Renaissance cities of the Continent, princes and haughty prelates looked upon their capital as an expression of their own environmental taste; consequently, they had to remake the town in the image they thought intellectually flattering. Würzburg, Karlsruhe, Nancy, and Mantua, to cite only better developed examples, were shaped into *internalized environments* desired as a setting for the power of their prince or bishop. Because the town already served as the capital, it could be thus internally transformed without vitiating any economic purpose of the place.

In merchants' towns, similar motives might affect the powerful, but they were shrewd enough to see that their prosperity must be somewhat distinguished from their taste. The wealth that made them powerful was to be earned at the docks, in the assembled workshops that became factories, and within the growing capacity of warehouses where trade goods were stored. Continued earning might require a further enlargement of the city's working space, often at the expense of civic display and the self-conscious shaping of an environment for residence.

Bristol furnishes us some useful glimpses of how the merchants' town dealt with the morphological dilemma of growing economically and at the same time providing for the rich and powerful merchants the residential environment in current fashion within western civilization. By the time of the Renaissance, a consciousness of physical environment had awakened in the European mind, and its impact on cities depended primarily on where the rich and powerful chose to live. On the Continent, the town as the seat of nobility and power was still well entrenched, though lurking in the background was the Roman tradition of the *villa*, which in Italy gained lasting identity with Palladio's villa *La Rotonda* near Vicenza begun in 1567. Suburban villas became relatively common during the Renaissance, standing as adjuncts of the nearby town rather than a separate geographical base for aristocracy. In England, from Norman times on, the towns had been left primarily to the merchants, while the countryside was reserved for, and dominated by, the aristocracy. Thus, when we look for the Renaissance in Italy we find it both in the town and in the rural areas around some cities. But in Britain the picture was reversed. Because the aristocracy was so strongly countrified, the great Renaissance buildings were placed in the lawns of an Oxford or Cambridge, or the "parks" of "great houses" such as Longleat, Hardwick Hall, and Hatfield House.

Why was the rage of European urban fashion so feeble in England's towns? Even in London, Renaissance building was largely confined to the West End precincts of the royal court in Westminster and its extension along the Thames to the Savoy. First we must understand that one secures within the city *the consciously designed environment* so desired by the wealthy

of the time through being able to create a visual entity which conveys the impressions sought. In the countryside a single "house," even of relatively modest scale, could do the job, as did Lord Burlington's Chiswick Villa (1725) just outside London. When a large estate could be so developed, as at Blenheim Palace (1705) in Oxfordshire, it was indeed impressive; the farm buildings could be given a neoclassic facade, thereby making a regal show of what was merely a Very Big House. But in the town, only major reconstruction of an extensive quarter, or the creation of a totally new quarter at the edge, could gain the visual integrity so prized in the Renaissance.

Within the context of the merchants' town, the reconstruction of an area for visual effect alone was unthinkable unless catastrophe had cleared the site. In London a classical architecture so typical of the Renaissance was attempted in the Royal Exchange (1671), a rather formless and out-of-place structure that had the grace to burn in 1838. More in place was the simpler Georgian architecture, distinctive to England and quite obviously the creation of a mercantile society. The merchants' town of Britain and the court towns of the rest of Europe stood in sharp contrast. "The work of the world" was the guiding concern of the mercants' town while in the court town it was conferral of an elite status through strict adherence to the fashion of "high architecture."

Let's begin our view of Bristol through the eyes of Celia Finnes toward the end of the seventeenth century:

The Buildings of ye town are pretty high, most timber work, the streets are narrow and sometime darkish because the roomes on ye upper storys are more jutting out, so Contracts ye street and the light. The suburbs are better buildings and more spacious Streetes.[32]

The general description of seventeenth-century Bristol supports Finnes on the morphology of the place but some found greater fault than she:

When we consider Bristol as a place of trade and riches we are greatly surprised to find the houses so meanly built, and the streets so narrow, dirty, and ill paved. This is in some measure owing to an ill-judged parsimony; for the houses being mostly built in the same manner as those in London before the fire of 1666, with the upper stories projecting in the streets, are patched up and repaired from time to time—But this is a very impolitic measure; for besides the expenses attending the different repairs, and the low price of the rents, were a fire to happen in Bristol, it would be attended with as dreadful

[32]*Celia Finnes*, Through England on a Side Saddle (*Griffiths edition of 1881*), p. 200, quoted in Peter T. Marcy, "*Eighteenth Century Views of Bristol and Bristolians*" in Patrick McGrath, op. cit., *p. 230.*

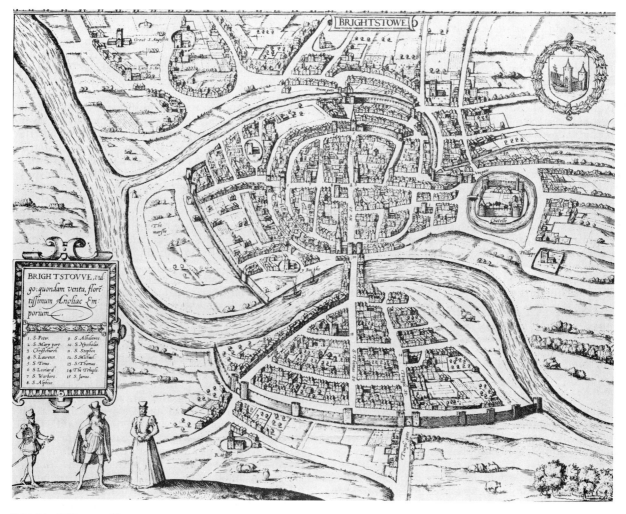

BRIGHTSTOWE

BRIGHTSTOVVE, vul
go; quondam venta, flore=
tiffimum Anoliae Em=
porium

1. S. Peter.   9. S. Albalowes.
2. S. Mary port.   10. S. Nycholas.
3. Chrifichurch.   11. S. Stephen
4. S. Laurence.   12. S. Michael.
5. S. Tomas   13. S. Thomas
6. S. Leonard   14. The Temple.
7. S. Warbors   15. S. James.
8. S. Alphius.

Bristol in 1581 was still
a compact medieval town,
nearly circular in outline
as it focused on its port
and castle.

consequence, in proportion to the number of inhabitants,
as it was in London.[33]

Perhaps Bristol is best summed up in the comments of
the editors of the eighth edition of Defoe's famous
Tour . . . when they noted that "The internal and trading parts of the City are partly antique, high, irregular
and projecting, and built of wood and plaister . . . ."

[33]Ibid., p. 24. The quotation is from R. J. Sullivan, Observations
Made During a Tour Through Parts of England, Wales, and
Scotland, *London, 1780.*

Having visited in our course the medieval city, we
should have no difficulty in identifying the origin of
this pattern and the nature of the processes that shaped
it.

What emerges new to our tale from the descriptions
of Bristol is the presence of "squares" and more open
housing areas on hills near the cathedral where "your
merchants have their little County Seats in the adjacent Eminences'" and suggesting the commencement
of a new form of city structure. The picture is that of an
attention to location rather little known in the Middle
Ages. With the great growth of trade, merchants tended
to be evicted from central premises by the needs of
their businesses, and to be drawn to specific housing
areas by the environmental qualities obtaining in those
places. In Bristol we see the two normal expressions of
this trend toward the discrete housing quarter: *the*

square laid out on the edge of the existing city, and the more distant *suburban development*.

Through the time of the English Civil War, Bristol had been walled after a fashion, though extensions to the enclosures were relatively easily made to include the expanding town. A district of wealthy and powerful merchant's houses grew up at Redcliff across the river Avon, where already in the fifteenth century growth was taking place and the most glorious parish church in England was being built through the merchants' benefactions. But in the seventeenth century, the practice of *class separation* in residence began to become widespread, and was expected of those who might afford it. In 1702, in the marshes between the rivers Frome and Avon, outside the medieval walls, a new residential quarter was set out around a large square named for the queen regnant with houses of three stories, a consistent roof-line, and an amplitude that allowed their occupants to possess and store carriages. The contrast between these new quarters and those of the medieval core is succinctly given by the subsequent Loyalist Thomas Hutchinson upon his visit to England in 1775:

> *I had formed a pretty just idea from the long-continued accounts of people who had been there, but it rather fell short: the houses are meaner, the streets narrower and dirtier, and except the buildings in three or four small squares (or rather some of these buildings), and some of the Company Halls, there are no elegant houses, scarcely fit for a first-rate tradesman to live in.*[34]

Hutchinson seems to have revised his view when he finally departed New England during the Revolution, loyal to his king but appreciative of New World society and its commercial accomplishments:

> *Yesterday took a full view of Bristol from Brandon Hill, where they say Cromwell erected his battaries and beat down their houses. I think, take in all circumstances, and I should prefer living there to any place in England. The manners and customs of the people are very like those of the people of New England, and you might pick out a set of Boston Selectmen from any of their churches.*[35]

The two morphological solutions to the creation of a residential environment for the upper-middle class—the in-town square and the suburban development—would reflect differences in occupation as much as in-

come. Doubtless the most well-to-do probably took to the suburbs as the most convenient morphological approximation of the "County Seats" of the gentry. For men actively engaged in trade, the city house would best suffice; for the rentier class less intimately involved in the daily life of the business world, the suburb was perhaps better, avoiding the bustle of the merchant class and the responsibilities of the truly landed gentry. In England, the successes of trade in the seventeenth and eighteenth centuries joined with the later successes of factory industry and transportation investment to create a fairly sizable upper-middle class freed of toil but not tied to the land, as the medievally-based upper class continued to be. For these urban men without daily business concerns, the suburb was the "Ideal City." For the urban man with business concerns, the consciously-established middle-class environment of the designed square or terrace of row-houses was equally an "Ideal City."

While the merchant class was moving into this new environment, their older residences were being put to more economic uses. Accounts tell us that carts were forbidden in Bristol because of the possible disruption they might cause in the vaults dug even beneath the streets in the older medieval core for the laying down of wine. Some argue the actual cause for the embargo, but none contest the existence of such distinctive storage facilities, which signal the rise of the port on the Avon to a preeminent role in the wine trade, an office it still performs. On a wide scale, late medieval properties were transformed to uses of the Mercantile Era. The vast expansion of the sugar trade in the middle of the seventeenth century led to the reuse of some of these buildings—even quite impressive houses of medieval origin—as sugar-houses. The pattern in the times of simpler technology was the reuse of older properties fully as much as the construction of new and specialized premises. Some new structures were necessary, as in the case of the thirty glass-houses strewn about the town that stood as pyramids belching smoke,[36] but this degree of particularization in structures was probably unusual.

The ties between the working quarters of the merchant and his residential districts had to remain close, even if less so than in the case of the manual workers in his warehouse or on his dock. The relationship was determined by the working day. "[H]ere even the wealthiest worked with admirable energy. The business day, in 1700 began at 5 or 6 A.M. and continued until 6 P.M. Then came supper, an hour or so at the tavern, and then to bed. The beer-houses shut at 9 P.M. in winter, at which late hour the curfew rang from St. Nicholas."[37]

[34]Ibid., *p. 26. (The quotation is from P. O. Hutchinson,* Diary and Letters of Thomas Hutchinson, *2 vols., London, 1883-1886, I, p. 346). The description of the Queen Square is from C. M. MacInnes and W. F. Whittard,* Bristol and Its Adjoining Counties *(British Association Handbook for 1955), Bristol: 1955, p. 261.*

[35]Loc. cit. *(The quotation is from Hutchinson, op. cit., II, p. 148.)*

[36]Ibid., *p. 15.*

[37]MacInnes and Whittard, *op. cit., p. 233.*

Little chance arose in such a system to move far during the course of an already crowded day.

We know relatively little of the lot of the actual working class in these merchant towns. Likely, their housing provision came largely through the operation of a process commonly thought normal: housing filters down from previous, more economically elevated, users to those closer to the bottom of the social heap. In Bristol, such a practice transformed the normal medieval house—as an occupational and residential unit for the extensive household of the merchant or master craftsman—into a structure more specifically used for housing. London presents more evidence than Bristol, showing the subdivision of previously prosperous dwellings, or their enlargement through the adding of ells, lean-tos, and other physical attachments.

As M. St. Clare Byrne noted in general, but specifically in the context of London at the turn of the seventeenth century, "Nothing creates a slum quarter more quickly than old houses that have come down in the world. The palace that was originally designed for some nobleman and his enormous establishment becomes first the tenement house and then the rabbit-warren, the plague spot, crowded from garret to cellar with dirty, poverty-stricken wretches." Notably in London, "The tide of fashion, ebbing westward, had left stranded many such city houses. Elizabeth tried to enforce the rule of 'one house one family', but not even a Tudor could arrest this inevitable process, whilst others of her measures literally forced such cohabitation upon the poorest section of the community." The measures most contributory to this crowding were those of Elizabeth and her successor James, seeking to control the growth of London's commercial and political power by constraining the expansion of "the Great Wen" they felt the city to be. "(T)heir legislation forbade the erection of new buildings upon hitherto unoccupied sites in the City, and also within a three-mile radius beyond the gates."[38]

The physical world of the slum was initially little different from the physical world of the medieval occupation quarter so vividly portrayed by Brueghel in the previous generation. The change in the social mix more than any other single thing transformed the districts. Slums come first in the mind, and only later in directly responsive physical forms. The medieval house was crowded, not too sanitary, and possessed of a mixture of work and residence. But it brought together all strata of the medieval urban population. When the leaders of that society began to move elsewhere, to be joined in the next generation by the less socially dominant but still somewhat elevated groups, the making

of the slum had begun. Finally, such districts are more the product of the principles of social geography than of the study of urban morphogenesis in which we are engaged.

The Renaissance City: The World of Inequality

While the merchants' world of the fifteenth and sixteenth centuries was fairly rapidly transforming itself into the Industrial Age in which we live, a corresponding movement occurred among those possessed to traditional distinction. They sought to crown their world of privilege and aristocracy with surpassing monuments only newly available through enhanced technical competence. The discovery of the aesthetics of visual perspective, probably first in the West and in early-fifteenth-century Italy, combined with improved technology to encourage great and ostentatious building. Filippo Brunelleschi (1377-1446) and Leon Battista Alberti (1404-1472) are generally credited with the first effective use of the concept of visual perspective, in their efforts to record on flat paper the carefully proportioned image of the Roman ruins which were entering anew into the concern of western civilization.[39] The logical follow-up to the discovery of how to represent a three-dimensional building on a flat surface was to design buildings to be seen as a totality, presenting a designed, three-dimensional impression.

During the Middle Ages, three-dimensionality of design of building space was in terms of the interior of the building, not of its exterior. Space in the medieval building was functionally intended, while the outside of the structure was left to evolve as it would, generally as a flat and functional plane on which existing decoration would be in mural form, or at most low relief. Even the great works of the Middle Ages, the cathedrals, tended on occasion to have fairly uninspiring exteriors, saved usually by the superb qualities of the building structure, which in Gothic architecture could not fail to be in evidence. But the surfaces were often "exceeding plain" (as at Albi in southern France where a fortress church looks almost modern in its functionalism), or were treated as two-dimensional, to be decorated with basically painterly designs rather than architectural

[38]M. St. Clare Byrne, Elizabethan Life in Town and Country, New York: Barnes and Noble, first edition, 1925, revised 1961, p. 79.

[39]Bates Lowry, Renaissance Architecture, New York: George Braziller, 1971, pp. 13-14.

ones (as at Orvieto in Tuscany where the mosaic "facade" of the cathedral is a superb picture but a rather unimpressive building exterior).

Only with the introduction of visual perspective did the exterior of buildings begin to take on a designed visual quality, often, in fact, rather divorced from the handling of the interior space. One may look at the facade of St. Peter's basilica in Rome and learn little indeed about the nature of the enclosed space, something that never happens when you look at the exterior of Chartres, Salisbury, or Albi.

The emergence of *the cult of the exterior* plays an important role in the morphogenetic analysis. For the first time since Roman days, and due in large measure to the great concern that Alberti and his contemporaries had for a "rebirth" of the Classical Era, buildings were designed from the outside in, or at least with the two concerns given equal weight. The result was an attention to exterior spaces unknown since classical times. The Middle Ages had witnessed market squares and other working open-spaces, but little that existed simply for the visual impression it presented. With the Renaissance, as the high-art world of western civilization beginning in the fourteenth and fifteenth centuries came during the last century to be called by historians, open-space became a design necessity. If perspective were to be used, space outside buildings must be introduced so the visual qualities of that perspective design could be appreciated. Cathedrals did not change greatly; even in the Middle Ages, they commonly fronted on market squares since the medieval church served as the watchdog of consumer concerns, keeping careful watch on the operation of the retail market. But for private houses, even rather large ones such as Jacques Coeur's palace, the Renaissance was truly revolutionary.

As the concern for the visual surface of the building increased, the appeal of sites outside the city grew. The creation of villas outside Italian cities, the beginning of the chateaux in the environs of Paris and in the Loire valley, the creation of the great houses of rural England all stem from the full expression of the cult of the exterior. It is a short step from designing the outside within the city to doing so in a carefully worked out landscape outside the city. The final exterior design arrived in the seventeenth century when the palaces in great parks came to every monarchy seeking to borrow the ultimate grandeur of Louis XIV, who at Versailles had combined the greatest house ever built with the most impressive gardens.

A morphological concern pulled the aristocracy out of the city and made their life increasingly distinct from the life of the rich merchant or craftsman. In the Middle Ages, those rich city men had sought social distinction through civic benefactions. During the Ren-

aissance, they had of necessity to take up country residence, building a great house which could furnish both the reason and the title for the barony to which each aspired. Only in the last decade or so has any Englishman shown the affront to tradition of adopting a title based on a city neighborhood.

The Renaissance as a historical period has been characterized by rather consistent exaggeration, particularly as to the role played by high art and architecture. In an era so heavily turned toward the rebirth of a classical model of the city, with the new component of employment of visual perspective, self-conscious design had to take precedence over any other morphogenetic process. In concentrating on the designer's city, scholars have dealt with the essence of the place. They have not, however, dealt very effectively with these cities as the homes of ordinary men. The basic problem is that of institutionalized inequality: to allow a small group to design and create the city of their own elite conception, other interests must be subjected to that narrow goal. The Renaissance would be most fully developed, and least interrupted by features jarring to the self-conscious design, in cities with the weakest and most subservient economics. *The merchants' town and the absolute ruler's would be rather polar extremes.* Rome of the Renaissance popes was a feeble place economically, living on the tribute of a vast ecclesiastical empire, but was constantly growing as a grand urban design. In contrast, London became the capital of a vast empire long before she gained much that was imperial in design.

My purpose is not to denigrate high art or architecture, but to put it in human perspective. Because the Renaissance was so strongly concerned with a formal city, only those persons in society who could predetermine formal components had much bearing on design. The church could play a vastly important role in the rebirth of the classically-ordered city, as could the increasingly absolute rulers. One of the clearest expressions of the Renaissance came when Brunelleschi set about redesigning the quarter south of the Arno in Florence to serve as the proper setting for his newly designed church of S. Spirito.[40] In this action he was following in the footsteps of the Roman emperors, who in presenting a new basilica to imperial Rome had it placed in a new *forum* adequate for its setting. Bates Lowry tells us of Alberti, who must stand as the true exemplar of the Renaissance in architecture and design:

Shortly after Brunelleschi's death in 1446, Alberti began to put his ideal of architecture into material form by following closely the model provided both by the

[40]Ibid., p. 18.

The most extravagant urban design of the Renaissance was probably the piazza laid out in front of the rebuilt St. Peter's basilica, which in the sixteenth century replaced Cluny as the largest church in Christendom.

Roman ruins and by the writings of Vitruvius, the only existing classical treatise on architecture. His approach to the creation of a work of architecture was a natural extension of the general concept Alberti held about the nature of a work of art. Any work of art was envisaged by Alberti principally as an object to be judged in terms of its relationship to a model taken either from the world of Nature or from the work of her most accomplished interpreters—the artists of the classical era.[41]

In this work, "Alberti sought the creation of an image—painted, sculptural, or architectural—that would be as 'lifelike' or perfect a rendition of the model as possible."

Renaissance design requires a *model*, preferably harking back to a precedent of appropriate antiquity and grandeur. The fact that the social connotation might be narrowly authoritarian carried no negative weight in the decision of an all-powerful church or civil administration. "Immediately upon becoming Pope in 1503, Julius II began the most grandiose building program undertaken in Rome since the time of the Emperors. These architectural works were intended to help create the image of a Papacy equal in grandeur to Imperial Rome."[42] His architect, d'Angelo Bramante, devised an "oriented space as a means of controlling the observer's experience of the building" that clearly led to the creation of vast and complex spatial designs in the Renaissance city, which dealt arbitrarily with that place as a workshop or *emporium*. The "common man" entered not at all into the scheme of things, save to experience the building within an oriented space. Crowds were needed as evidence of power, but having served to exalt the ruler, they must disperse into a city where their physical comfort or economic productivity were of most minor concern. This was a city of vast inequality.

In our present world, despite massive problems, equality is nearer realization than ever before. The precedent of the Renaissance has relatively little application, and consequently rather little interest. The Renaissance was a time utterly weighted down with a concern for precedent—every building, whatever its ostensible purpose, must offer a clear physical expression drawn from a classical or natural precedent. In rejecting the era of classical rebirth as of much concern to us, we merely accept the standards the time itself set. If our purpose were the study of the designed city, we could not dispatch the Renaissance so briefly.

[41]Ibid., *p. 21.*

[42]Ibid., *p. 36.*

The Georgian City: A Scene for Man

How did the modern world come about? What produced a society wherein equality and democracy have taken on overriding importance? If we look at the past through elite eyes, the change to popular control breaks largely unheralded and quite unexpectedly some time in the middle of the nineteenth century. Yet the abruptness of that change is due more to suppression of knowledge of its origins than to the rapidity of its successes. Change was a long time in coming, but was far less revolutionary and restricted to the nineteenth century as it might seem.

Already in the late Middle Ages, in the bastides, the roots of equality, popular sovereignty, and the whole context of liberal thought were to be found. In the merchants' town of the seventeenth century, the sapling was healthy. In the successor mercantilist city of Restoration and Georgian times, the tree grew large enough to produce the seeds of the great change, which came quickly with industrialization and the nineteenth century. The notion of the Georgian city is itself partially elite in form and origin; still, if we project that Georgian image so as to encompass all urban people, the emerging pattern far more clearly explains present urban life than it projects the life of the Renaissance city then slowly withering away on the Continent. The Georgian city held a functional competence lacking in the Renaissance: it was designed as the home of a productive society. The Renaissance city stood as an intellectualized setting for a dogmatically unproductive society founded on a thousand-year history of traditional order and complex social, economic, and even geographical immobility.

We are fortunate in having a classic study of the Georgian town in John Summerson's *Georgian London.* He summarizes that city's morphogenesis:

Another conclusion to be drawn from our bird's-eye view [of Georgian London] is the rather obvious one that London has never been planned. Beside other 18th-century capitals, London is remarkable for the freedom with which it developed. It is a city raised by private, not by public, wealth; the least authoritarian city in Europe. Whenever attempts have been made to overrule the individual in the public interest, they have failed. Elizabeth and her Stuart successors tried bluntly to stop any expansion whatever. They failed. Charles II and his pet intellectuals tried to impose a plan after the Great

Fire. They failed. Nearly every monarch in turn projected a great Royal Palace to dominate at least part of his capital. All failed until George IV conspired with [the architect] Nash to cheat Parliament into rebuilding Buckingham House. The reasons for all this are embedded deep in England's social and political history. London is one of the few capitals where church property and church interests have not been an over-riding factor; where Royal prestige and prerogative in building matters have been set at naught; where defense has never, since the Middle Ages, dictated a permanent circumvallation to control the limits of development. London is above all a metropolis of mercantilism. The basis of its building history is the trade cycle rather than the changing ambitions and policies of rulers and administrators. The land speculator and the adventuring builder have contributed more to the character of the Georgian city than the minister with a flair for artistic propaganda, or the monarch with a mission for dynastic assertion.[43]

Thus, a contrast in morphogenetic process existed between the mercantile towns developing in England and by extension in the English colonies in North America, and the towns of autocratic rulers and their courts on the Continent. Summerson has merely suggested the contrast in process: we shall concentrate on that difference. The fundamental distinction to be drawn is between a city shaped by land speculation and land-and-housing market forces in the English world, and a city far more clearly the product of design decisions taken for purposes of "taste" and ostentation on the Continent. Because speculation has such a black name in the modern world, this battle might at first seem to be one of darkness with light. Though that may in part be true, I suggest that the forces of light were those supporting speculation and those of darkness were the proponents of authoritarian practices within the city.

Beginning as a rather typical medieval town based heavily on its port and governmental functions, by the year 1600 London had begun to show the signs of giving birth to a wholly new existence, particularly in the City itself. A rapidly increasing role was being played by a morphogenetic process long present but until then merely one of a number of forces at work. That process, which seems most appropriately called *congregation,* led to the concentration of activities and social groupings in particular places within the City. Instead of the medieval occupational clustering, a specialized form of congregation according to the work carried on, the merchants' town that London so strikingly represented

[43]John Summerson, Georgian London, *New York: Charles Scribner's Sons, 1946 (more readily available in a Penguin paperback). The following quotation is from pp. 9-10, emphasis supplied.*

tended to develop an economic-class structure associated with particular places in the urban fabric. This clustering had long existed as an exceptional force—as in the Savoy suburb of magnates' houses found even in medieval times—but in London after 1600, the exception became the rule. The social complexity that had characterized the medieval town tended to disappear in favor of two separate post-medieval "towns," each partaking to some degree in the Middle Ages as well as anticipating modern times. The inheritance from the past was the extended "occupational" household; the anticipation of the future came in the more clearly emerging *economic-class districts* that were earlier largely unknown.

The occupational households of London in Stuart and early Georgian times were of two main sorts: those still carrying on the medieval tradition of the master, with his apprentices and journeymen living together under one roof in a house he held, and a new form of occupational household based fundamentally on what Thorstein Veblen characterized much later as a "leisure class." In this upper-middle-class or aristocratic household lived the blood relations of the family head, as well as a sometimes surprisingly numerous corps of servants. Characteristically, these households were not headed by someone directly and constantly employed. Instead the head might most likely be the holder of capital either in the form of rents and shares or in rural estates that before the expansion in the New Lands in the nineteenth century might be highly prosperous. These men might hold offices under the crown or parliament, but the day-to-day orderliness of the true businessman was not required of them; thus they could live in places more removed from their work than was possible for the real worker. In contrast:

The substantial merchant who lived about Cornhill, Throgmorton Street, Lombard Street, and the close purlieus surrounding the Royal Exchange, or, having shipping interests, resided in Thames Street, had the apartments devoted to his counting house on the street level, and his warehouse very likely built in the rear or at the side; he dwelt with his household in the rooms above. The mercer of Paternoster Row, and, indeed, the shopkeeper everywhere, traded indoors. Sometimes he built out a pent-house to the street, but he did not make his great display in front, nor did he expect his goods to be seen from outside....

It was not a pleasant place to live in, this City which was more than full of people. Where a man had business, there his life was spent, and with him were his wife and often a large family of children, and his assistants and apprentices, all in one household. This made every street populous. Stuart London was, too, excessively noisy. London's vibrating note, which Lowell

likened to "the roaring loom of time," has been attuned to many keys, but never has this been a silent city.[44]

Alongside this teeming, solid, and traditional working population was an even more numerous class of urban poor, which had grown up as the mercantile city expanded and become badly housed in "meaner dwellings, built back to back," commonly "a mere casing of weather boards fastened to their shaking frames" with "a smear of black pitch made the only water-proofing. These were the homes of thousands of London's toiling populace—two rooms or at most three, dark, stuffy, and horribly insanitary. Narrow and filthy alleys, without pretence of paving and often ankle-deep in mud, gave the only access. Wanting even such accommodation as this other thousands were forced to find refuge in underground rooms. Others, again, were herded into tenements, falling rapidly into ruin by wilful destruction and want of repair."[45]

The Great Fire of 1666

Is it any wonder that even before the Great Fire of 1666, which physically swept most of this structure away, the leisured classes were moving out of the City? As Summerson tells us:

In Tudor times, when Britain's mercantile strength was in the making, the City of London became the main fortress of mercantilism; and as the merchants increased their riches and influence the aristocracy shifted westwards towards Westminster. By the end of the Civil War, the sturdy wealth and coarse puritanism of the merchants had won every inch of the ground. The old mansions were demolished or split up, their gardens covered with tenements. The gentry, the luxury traders and the upper layers of the professional classes followed the aristocracy westwards. The City became a mercantile stronghold, inhabited by its freeman, the manufacturers and merchants, and ruled by livery companies, in the persons of their elected representatives–aldermen, sheriffs and Lord Mayor.[46]

So, when that most misbegotten Stuart monarchy was restored in 1660, London was already actively pursuing a clearly separated congregation of merchants in

[44]*Walter G. Bell*, The Great Fire of London, 1666, *London: The Bodley Head, 1920 (revised edition, 1923), pp. 11-12.*
[45]Ibid., *p. 14.*
[46]*Summerson*, op. cit., *p. 36.*

the City, and of the leisured class in the until then open "liberties" of the City along the Strand and in the royal city of Westminster. The great plague first visited upon this two-part city in 1665, removing by death over 55,000 souls from the jurisdiction of the Lord Mayor; the Great Fire burned in September, 1666, removing some 13,200 houses, about 80 per cent of the City within the walls and a considerable district that had grown up in its liberties to the northwest and west. In all, 373 acres within the walls were divested of their buildings.[47] Relatively little aristocratic property was destroyed beyond that held for rents within the City or that occupied by lawyers in one of the Inns of the Court. As a result, the Great Fire was a harrowing experience for the working City of London, leaving a nearly vacant slate on which to build a new, *truly mercantile City;* in contrast, the world of the gentry was little affected. The act of rebuilding London perhaps did more to create a "modern" class within the increasingly out-of-date social class structure in England than any other event before the First World War. Walter Bell in his classic study of the Fire shows how the split between the landowners, who were particularly firmly ensconced in the countryside, and the merchants, the true city-men, was increased by the catastrophe.

Wealth was restricted to two classes, the landowners and the merchants, between whom the cleavage was sharp; where the landowner spent his money in ostenta- *tious display, the merchant saved. Time and again, as the long experience of City loans has shown, the merchants' hoard bore the national burdens, and now it came out to restore the burnt city.*[48]

For the merchants, the Fire was a crushing financial blow, matched by the chance to shape a City more suited to the needs of an economy expanding rapidly with the overseas spread of the mercantile realm. In addition, the building experience it necessitated was in the end of great use to the freemen of the City, whose numbers expanded rapidly with the final abolition of the severe gild restraints on entrance to a trade. As an emergency measure, parliament removed the constraint of trade, the fundamental basis of medieval gild law, by enacting the following:

All carpenters, bricklayers, masons, plasterers, miners; and other artificers, workmen and labourers to be employed in the said buildings [in the reconstruction of the City after the Great Fire] shall for the space of seven years next ensuing, and for so long time after as until the said buildings shall be fully finished, have and enjoy such and the same liberty of working, and being set to work in the said building, as the freemen of the City of the same trades and professions have and ought to enjoy; Any usage or custom of the City to the contrary notwithstanding. And that such artificers as aforesaid, which for the space of seven years shall have wrought in the rebuilding of the City [of London] in their respective arts, shall from

Contemporary map showing the extent of the Great Fire of London in 1666. The medieval wall is clearly visible, so we can see that in the northeastern part of the city some buildings survived and that west of the wall there was destruction in the Liberties.

---

[47]*Bell,* op. cit., *p. 266.*

[48]Ibid., *p. 284.*

*and after the said seven years have and enjoy the same
liberty to work as freemen of the said City for and during
their natural lives.*[49]

After the Fire

Conditions for rapid economic growth could hardly
have been better once the blow of the Fire itself was
met. A new fabric was introduced which provided
somewhat better streets for the city; along those ways
ranged buildings far sturdier and more suited to the
growing trade of London than those swept away in the
first four days of September, 1666. Along with this
physical improvement came a considerable social
change that at first did not seem too radical; in the end,
it proved as transforming as the actual physical reconstruction of the City. Trades were opened to outsiders
and in considerable numbers as never before. The
sharp losses of population experienced during the
plague the year before were considerably made up, and
the City was on the whole somewhat more healthful as
a place to live than when it was still a creaking relict of
medieval times. Finally, the experience of large and
active works and the more productive employment of
capital in development of lands and buildings gave to
the city-men skills found nowhere else in the kingdom.

Strangely, the physical separation of the aristocratic from the merchants' city came at a time when the
differences in wealth between landowners and merchants were probably less than they had been previously, or were to become when coal mining and speculation in lands on estates near London and the provincial cities gave noble landlords incomes beyond the
expectations of all but the most eminently successful
merchant. But the separation had come, and for more
than a hundred years the City was the fortress of mercantilism that Summerson has described so fully.
Thus, we may look at Fire London, that is London Rebuilt, as perhaps the first modern city. It was a really
large town, approaching a population of probably half
a million people, increasingly organized for productive
and expansible economic activities, in sharp contrast
to the rigidly constrained economy of medieval times.

[49]*This clause is from the Rebuilding Act enacted by the House of
Commons in 1667.* Ibid., *p. 254.*

The Origin and Form of the Expansible City

We have noted the efforts of Elizabeth and the early
Stuarts to stop London's growth. Significantly, the one
activity not constrained—the functions and occupations associated with the port—led most directly to the
growth they sought to obviate. The great expansion of
the mercantile frontier of England directly produced
the growth of the port of London, in the specific guise of
the various monopoly trading companies resident
there, and made new docks essential and storage of
goods from distant lands a necessity. A backward
glance clearly shows Elizabeth's policy to be indeed
ill-conceived, whether or not one agrees with her goal
of limiting growth.

We can understand the fatal flaws in crown policy
toward London as a natural outgrowth of normal political processes. Two main alignments of power were
emerging within London—the court and its minions,
and the merchant class of the City. Each had an increasingly characteristic purlieu: "the West End" of
Mayfair and Westminster for the gentry, the City and
its environs for the merchants. Each group argued the
absolutely essential nature of expansion of the city in
their individual interests. Elizabeth's proclamation of
1580 bears quotation:

*The Queen's Majestie perceiving the state of the city of
London (being anciently termed her chamber) and the
suburbs and confines thereof to increase daily, by access
of people to inhabit the same, in such ample sort, as
thereby many inconveniences are seen already, but many
greater of necessity like to follow, being such as her
majesty cannot neglect to remedy. [As]. . . .where there are
such great multitudes of people brought to inhabit in
small rooms, whereof a great part are seen very poor, yea,
such as must live of begging, or by worse means, and they
heaped up together, and in a sort smothered with many
families of children and servants in one house or small
tenement. . .if any plague or popular sickness. . .enter
amongst those multitudes. . .a great mortality would
ensure. . .[and] the infection would be also dispersed
through all parts of the realm. . . .[Thus] her maj.,. . .doth
charge and strictly command all manner of persons, of
what quality soever they be, to desist and forbear from any
new buildings of any house or tenement within three
miles of from any of the gates of the said city of London,
to serve for habitation or lodging for any person, where no
former house hath been known to have been in the mem-*

ory of such as are now living; and also to forbear from letting or setting, or suffering any more families than one only to be placed, or to inhabit from henceforth in any house that heretofore hath been inhabited.[50]

Two functioning exceptions to this embargo on building were permitted: (1) housing for port workers was allowed in the Act of 1592 which implemented Elizabeth's proclamation, and (2) housing for the middle and upper classes might be built through special permissions granted specifically by the crown (as in the case of Bedford's development of Covent Garden beginning in 1630). The merchants' interests were guarded through permitting an expanding port function; the gentry's needs were cared for through the tolerance, under exceptions, of the aristocratic housing development growing up north and west of the City and in the environs of the government quarter in Whitehall.

The Rise of Land Speculation

A string of misfortunes—the accession of the Stuarts to the throne in 1603, the conflict between the king and parliament, the Dutch War, the Plague of 1665, the Fire of 1666, and the general disarray of the short reign of James II—served in a sense to delay the collapse of the policy of containment for London. With a sharp setback to population and commercial activity in the 1660's, the issue was somewhat masked, particularly as the rebuilding after the Fire must have made it difficult to establish the niceties of building control envisioned under Elizabeth's proclamation. Quite the reverse: the large-scale effort at reconstruction brought greater numbers of construction workers to London, removed the excise on the import of timber from the Baltic for several years, and generally simplified the process of construction. These factors must have encouraged an expansionist viewpoint that lodged uncomfortably in a city supposedly contained.

Both centers of political power—the noble landowners of the West End and the great merchants of the City—applied strong pressure to drop the embargo on building. Taking the two groups together we find the introduction of a concept of land-speculation that was

not new but certainly was previously unknown for such scale as now obtained. The Tudors had had to call on the support of a number of energetic men and had, in return, both ennobled them and rewarded them with confiscated lands taken from ecclesiastical foundations at the time of the English Reformation. These lands were widespread geographically, but many were in and around the capital, where bishops had always had large houses and abbots town mansions to facilitate their more direct roles in the life and intrigues of the court. Thus, the suppression of the powerful churchmen led easily to the creation of a set of powerful nobles holding similar properties, if sometimes for rather different purposes.

The beginning of the seventeenth century was a time of rapidly increasing wealth among the merchants of the City. Their enrichment cannot have left the great landowners unimpressed. They were envious, wishing to gain the rewards of a system of invested capital that was beginning to become rationalized and evident. The merchant had his trade to enlarge and intensify but the landowner, at least while remaining within his own sphere, had only his estates to develop. Probably for this reason, and because of their greater ease in gaining the king's ear and, consequently, his indulgence, the nobles (rather than the great mercants) first initiated speculative building. This fact is odd, since the gentry held a certain distaste towards the building over of the rural lands which formed the sign and support for aristocracy. But the law of entail which restricted the sale of such lands was in common practice. Mark Twain, with his usually sharp eye and clear head, appreciated this practice as the main reason that the British aristocracy had not earlier been beggared by their extravagances and general lack of ingenuity.[51] Under such an institutionalized protection of the financially incompetent, only the "use" of the property could be varied; for that purpose, speculative building on ground leases that preserved the entail was ideal.

---

[50]*Steen Eiler Rasmussen in* London: The Unique City *(New York: The Macmillan Co., 1937) discusses at length in chapter four the attempts to contain the growth of London. The quotation is from Rasmussen, pp. 67-68.*

[51]*In discussing his mother's prideful assumption of descent from the English Lambton family (Earls of Durham) and of their occupation of their estates for some nine hundred years, Twain held: "I argued—cautiously and with mollifying circumlocutions, for one had to be careful when he was on that holy ground, and musn't cavort—that there was no particular merit in occupying a piece of land for nine hundred years with the friendly assistance of an entail; anybody could do it, with intellect or without; therefore the entail was the thing to be proud of, just the entail and nothing else; consequently, she was merely descended from an entail and she might as well be proud of being descended from a mortgage."* The Autobiography of Mark Twain, *ed. by Charles Neider, New York: Washington Square Press, 1961, pp. 30-31.*

The Georgian Residential Estate: Covent Garden

Henry VIII in the exercise of his absolute power confiscated the properties of the church that were no longer needed for the practice of religion after his split with Rome in 1534. Among these were most of the monastic and conventual establishments in the kingdom, many of which were forthwith granted to powerful minions of the crown. John Russell was such a man. In 1552 he was given a leasehold of seven acres of the convent garden located on the Strand. On this site he built a great mansion—Bedford House, named for the earldom he was given in 1550—comprising many rural estates as well as several in the liberties of the City of London. In the gardens behind Bedford House, the fourth Earl decided to lay out a grandiose housing estate which Summerson viewed (in what seems an oddly myopic frame) as "the first great contribution to English urbanism."[52]

Perhaps at the insistence of the king (on granting a license to build in a time when growth was legally disallowed), Bedford had Inigo Jones lay out an Italian *piazza* with houses on the west and north side, a church to the south, and the Bedford gardens to the east. Development was slow; evidently the land was not quite ripe or else the Italianate row houses of considerable size were ahead of their time. Eventually the land was built upon. The houses were of generally uniform style, certainly with fixed elements of the facade—notably the roof-line, the arcades that came to be called "piazzas" (thus contributing a splendid Americanism to New England speech which democratically gives this title to even the common man's front porch), and a general level of upper-class accommodation.

One of the major elements in the ripening of land for speculative profit was the creation of a fashionable quality in these districts. Covent Garden was probably slightly too early; the City had not yet fully lost its social image and the country gentry had not yet fully accepted the need to occupy a town mansion for a part of the year. But by the time of the Restoration of 1660, the world of London was divided. Steen Eiler Rasmussen tells us how it came about:

When the [country] magnates purchased houses near London it was not town-houses in narrow streets but country-houses with a service of different buildings and vast gardens. The arrival of each noble family increased the population not only by the family itself and its many servants with their relatives but also by merchants, artisans, and others who lived on the aristocracy. Besides London, the town of producers, the capital of the world-trade and industry, there arose another London the town of consumers, the town of the Court, of the nobility, of retired capitalists. Where a little room was left between the big mansions the middle classes settled in groups of smaller houses which sprung up as best they could. But very soon the proprietors discovered the chance of using the areas for considerable housing enterprises which would provide suitable quarters for people of quality. In the long run the development of the town made it impossible to leave large areas as private gardens. On the other hand, when an earl or a duke did turn his property to account he wanted to determine what neighbours he got. The great landlord and the speculative builder found each other and together they created the London square with its character of unity as it is by dignified houses, all alike.[53]

The City was firmly in the hands of the businessmen. The West End had become the world of "quality" and "fashion" to the extent that to live too far east was a social solecism. With respect to a later development of the (then) Dukes of Bedford, "The Right Honourable John Wilson Croker once solemnly propounded the question in the House of Commons: 'Where is Russell Square?'" in a classic put-down of London's second largest residential square. It became the silly fashion of the Quality "to affect a superior ignorance of localities not actually within the purlieus of Mayfair."[54]

The two worlds of the City and Mayfair operated under quite different morphogenetic processes, contrasting in the nature of speculation, in the style and form of buildings and the way they would be assembled into "contributions to English urbanism," in the lifestyles they engendered, and, finally, in their transferal to other cities and other lands. The speculation practiced in the West End was geared to a very concerted effort, expressed over considerable areas, to shape a social definition of land-use. One use of land was obvious: the housing of the ever-growing city population. But beyond that, the selection among potential tenants came largely by design. A fair number of great landowners were seeking to develop their estates—the Russells, the Grosvenors, the Cavendish-Harley alliance (Dukes of Portland), Lord Burlington, Lord Southampton, the crown on its own account, the Rugby School as well as Harrow and Eton and Westminster colleges, Marquis Camden, and a number of others.[55]

[52]*Summerson, op. cit., p. 13.*

[53]*Rasmussen, op. cit., pp. 165-166.*
[54]*E. Berresford Chancellor,* The History of the Squares of London, *Philadelphia: J. B. Lippincott Co., 1907, p. 211.*
[55]*Summerson gives a map of the earlier estates to develop (op. cit., fig. 22, p. 149); while Coppock and Prince, ed.,* Greater London, *London: Faber and Faber, Ltd., 1964, gives a map of the nineteenth-century estates (fig. 20, p. 96).*

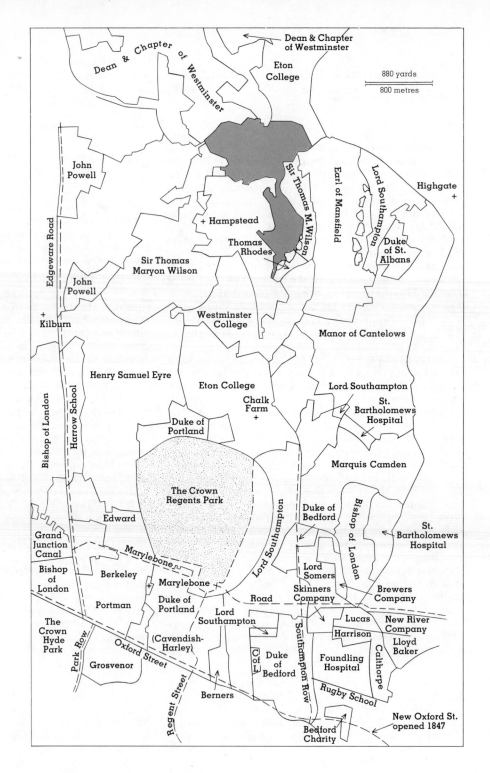

Map of London Estates on which Georgian housing was built.

Dean & Chapter of Westminster

Dean & Chapter of Westminster

Eton College

880 yards
800 metres

John Powell

Sir Thomas M. Wilson

Earl of Mansfield

Lord Southampton

Highgate +

+ Hampstead

Thomas Rhodes

Duke of St. Albans

John Powell

Sir Thomas Maryon Wilson

+ Kilburn

Westminster College

Manor of Cantelows

Henry Samuel Eyre

Eton College

Lord Southampton

Edgeware Road

Chalk Farm +

St. Bartholomews Hospital

Bishop of London

Harrow School

Duke of Portland

Marquis Camden

The Crown Regents Park

Lord Southampton

Duke of Bedford

Bishop of London

St. Bartholomews Hospital

Edward

Grand Junction Canal

Lord Somers

Brewers Company

Bishop of London

Berkeley

Marylebone

Marylebone

Skinners Company

Lucas

New River Company

Portman

Duke of Portland

Road

Harrison

Lloyd Baker

The Crown Hyde Park

(Cavendish-Harley)

Lord Southampton

Foundling Hospital

Calthorpe

Park Row

Oxford Street

Grosvenor

C of L

Duke of Bedford

Southampton Row

Rugby School

Regent Street

Berners

Bedford Charity

New Oxford St. opened 1847

Each sought to shape a particular social image within a minutely class-bound society in order to "ripen" the land not merely in time but as well by social class.

The square became the device by which the speculator sought to gain the highest "quality" of patronage to follow the lead of one or several aristocratic families who might be encouraged to take up residence "in the square." The Dukes of Bedford, as experienced speculators in land "values" and properly accustomed to the ermine, shaped such a social grouping at Bloomsbury Square around Bedford House.

The prototype came from Paris, where Henri IV sought to develop land in the Marais, the former swamp that lay inside the extended walls of the city. In 1607, the area was designed as a great square—the *Place Royale* (later *des Vosges*)—321 feet on a side, surrounded by 38 "pavilions" (that we would term "row houses") intended for occupation by upper classes. The fourth Earl of Bedford's *piazza* at Covent Garden was a pale image of this design. But when William, Lord Russell married the daughter of the Earl of Southampton and came into possession of his landholding northwest of the City, the development of a square such as was to be found in Paris could begin in earnest in the fields about Southampton (later Bedford) House.

Henry Jermyn, First Earl of St. Alban's, had several years before laid out St. James's Square in Mayfair, probably on the model of the Place Royale, which he would have known as a wealthy royalist refugee living in Paris during the Commonwealth. At first this speculation faltered, as Jermyn held only a lease from the crown. When subsequently he talked the king into a freehold title to the property, he managed slowly to

The Place Royale (present Place des Vosges) was completed in 1615 at the instigation of Henri IV, becoming the first great public square in Paris and the model for such residential designs in London and other western cities.

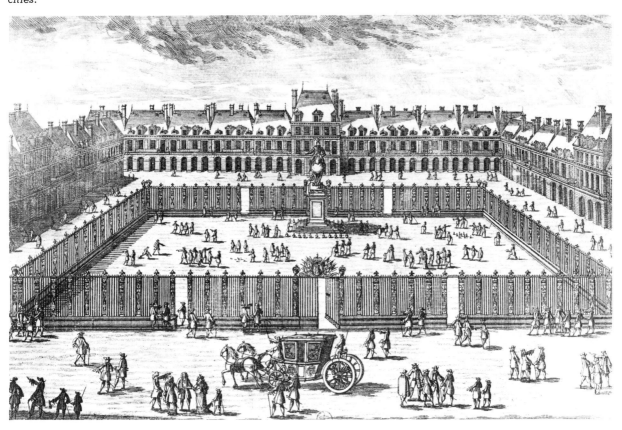

develop it into the square with the highest social cachet of the time.[56]

These aristocratic landowners and speculators no doubt gained the pick of the social roster in those class congregations they managed to draw to their squares.

The Concept of Class Congregation

The general concept of class congregation was of far wider application and of more enduring force in shaping the city than just these land-speculations in Restoration London. The massive growth of the City of London's business activity had caused the congregation of merchants and manufacturers, of dock workers, hawkers, clerks, and a hundred other tradesmen. The City was crowded and increasingly alien to the traditional country-based society that still clung to the aristocracy. Not surprisingly, when the Restoration came in 1660 the gentry had literally disappeared from the City. The process was one of separation rather than segregation: enough wealth had fallen into the hands of the great merchants so they could command their own district within the city, and, as well, sufficient power and privilege attached to the nobility to assure that their purlieus would be those of their choice rather than eviction. Two groups may show strong separation without the one-sided push of segregation.

This separation by class into two distinct social and economic congregations created distinctions in lifestyle and the practices of speculation that were to have great bearing on the settlement of America. Let us summarize the contrasts in land development practices and city forms that grew out of them.

[56]These developments are detailed in Summerson, op. cit., p. 23, and in Chancellor, op. cit., in the section on Bloomsbury Square, as the development around Bedford House came to be known.

London Rebuilt

In the City an increasing domination of development by business requirements and the reconstruction made necessary by the Great Fire meant the creation of a new physical form. The medieval pattern was swept away by the Fire, but also by the City's changing needs. After all, the town could have been rebuilt in a medieval form. Instead the great merchants, the men with the money and power to do the job and thus the group who decided how it would be done, settled on a moderate reshaping of the medieval morphology. A numerous body of commentators bemoan the failure of London to adopt one of the grandiose and highly Renaissance plans for the rebuilding proposed by Dr. Christopher Wren, John Evelyn, and Robert Hooke. They argue that London would have been so much more impressive a city, and a fitting physical skeleton on which to place examples of great architecture, if one such overall design had been adopted.

The critics overlook the fact that after 1666 the City was the epitome of a merchants' town; a quite different set of demands took precedence then over those of national image and refined taste. As Summerson tells us, "Taste in architecture reached London about 1615: taste that is, in the exclusive, snobbish sense of recognition of certain fixed values by certain people. Taste was a luxury import from Italy, received and cherished by a small group of noblemen and artists whose setting was the not very polished Court of James I. [Thus] Architecture was a late comer to this little circle of intelligence in a still half-medieval England."[57] The City retained more of the medieval than did the West End, but not in any pejorative sense; rather, in the City, the concept of "form follows function" in urban design and house architecture was carried over from the Middle Ages to the modern world. In the West End, the tyranny of visual design arose and began its increasingly arid course.

The rebuilding of the City came in two basic programs. The first tried to improve the conditions of circulation about the place; the second attempted to devise houses both more fire-resistant and more structurally appropriate to the times than were the old and frequently tinkered-with medieval gable houses the Fire had swept away. The street-improvement program had few grand accomplishments but many quietly significant ones. For the first time, wheeled vehicles could move rather generally about the town as

[57]Summerson, op. cit., p. 11.

most streets, other than cul-de-sacs and simple alley-ways, were made broad enough for wagons and carts. Carriages were less maneuvrable than carts and the tale remained that the City was closed to wheels; in truth, it was opened to the workman's wheels if not the nobleman's. Other changes came in widening and improving the alignment of a few arterial streets—those leading to London Bridge and the more important gates—such that the commerce of the place could grow and continue to function.

The Fire meant the beginning of building specialized with respect to both location and function. The commissioners entrusted with guiding the rebuilding established the use of four types of houses, the choice among them depending upon the width and importance of the street on which each fronted:

The first and least sort were to be built in bylanes, two storeys high, irrespective (as in all cases) of cellars and garrets;

The second sort in streets and lanes of note, to be three storeys high;

The third, fronting high and principal streets, of four storeys; and

The fourth type, the merchant's mansion houses "of the greatest bigness," not built to the street front also not to exceed four storeys.

For each type of house the thickness of brick walls, heights from floor to ceiling, depth of cellars and sufficiency of party walls, scantlings of timber and much other detail were set out in scheduled tables, to which the builders were required to conform.[58]

Unspecified in law but the outcome of the rebuilding process was the increasing rationalization of land-use within the City. Thames Street, along the river, was enlarged, straightened, and given a fully constructed quay between it and the river (perhaps Dr. Wren's greatest contribution in the reconstruction other than his wealth of churches and the reconstructed St. Paul's cathedral). For the first time, ships could tie up at a dock and gain access to cranes for lifting cargo and to warehouses just across the quay.

Such improvements of economic activities are hard to demonstrate at this late date, but seemingly the general form of the post-Fire house was more conducive to efficient manufacture and commerce than had been its medieval predecessor. These square, small but essentially modular buildings tended to present a common roof-line on the street frontage and a common height for stories: these aspects would have made opening one house into the other more straightforward. Also, although the housing of the poor was hardly a priority concern, probably some improvement was made over

[58]*Bell, op. cit., p. 251.*

the worst conditions of the pre-Fire town, if only because the terribly modest new housing for the poor was probably more healthful than that it replaced.

In the absence of a full study of the workaday world of London at the end of the seventeenth century, we must depend largely on quite indirect evidence. That evidence suggests that the City as rebuilt after the Fire was fully a commercial town, dominated by economic activities and with economic tests of spatial allocation. Although it was not designed for specific trades, save in the docks and the areas where the noxious trades were finally driven outside the City walls, for the time, the best physical conditions for economic activity were to be had there. Thus, within a few decades of the crushing Fire, the City of London became the world's *emporium.* Because of that, the metropolis that grew around it became the greatest city on Earth until the beginning of this present century.

The World of the West End

The world of the West End was very different. There, rule was by privilege and social congregation. The squares were merely the diamonds of clearest privilege in a setting that was class-bound wherever experienced. The aristocratic developers came to realize that theirs was a socially complex society dependent for order upon the top but for comfort on the bottom. This society required shops for trading, housing for servant classes, mews in which carriages, horses, and their attendants could be housed, and other expressions of the social pyramid. The upper-middle class, gripped by the notion that social mobility meant occupational inactivity, sought doggedly to take up residence near the gentry, and to be equally unproductive. Thus, the squares were adjoined by streets in which the uniform facades hid housing of lesser ostentation, but still commodious beyond basic necessity. Those in the side streets had few servants (though they were many by present-day standards). The rise of this extensive and increasingly leisured middle class shaped the extensive housing areas in Bloomsbury, Mayfair, and Kensington.

A recurrently separative process was at work in both the City and the West End. As merchants gained increasing wealth, they could afford to ape the aristocracy; in a class-bound society, their doing so was almost inevitable. As generations succeeded to commercial wealth, their ties with the City became less burdensome and more periodic, if not in actual fact abstract. In such a situation, the commercial middle class began to take up residence in nearby Bloomsbury (no doubt explaining the unawareness of the haughty members of Parliament as to that district's whereabouts). Lawyers from the Inns of the Court to the south also moved into this area, when they married and left the bachelor quarters the Inns afforded.

The result was the creation of an extensive class possessed of considerable capital but, at least in the first generation, engaged in productive labor. For them, a social rise meant a shift in residence out of the City. The line was fuzzy between the leisured middle class and the gainfully occupied component of that same economic stratum. Likely a careful study would show that, as the broad class grew in size, internal congregations evolved within the middle class, based on such distinctions as work or leisure.

Hanover Square in London was one of the earlier Georgian copies of the Place Royale in Paris.

Class Structure of English Cities

To understand the nature of urbanization in England, with its strong class identification of housing quarters, we must look at class division of the English population both in the seventeenth century and later. Fortunately, Gregory King set forth in 1688 a rough description of "the Pyramide of English society."[59] To summarize King's conclusions, the titled classes accounted for less than .5 per cent of the total English population; adding important landowners (squires and upper freeholders) at 5.5 per cent and middle-class professionals (merchants, clergy, civil servants, army and navy officers, practitioners of the liberal arts, and lawyers) with 4.4 per cent, still less than 10 per cent of the population was in the landowning or "house commanding" class, even including the servants of these families in the population totals. The other 90 per cent made up the working or unemployed group who tilled the fields, operated the looms in domestic manufacture, manned the forges, carried goods on the docks, or did the multitude

[59]*G. D. H. Cole and Raymond Postgate,* The Common People: 1746-1946 *(London: Methuen & Co., 1938, revised 1946) present this material. King's estimate was undertaken at the time of the "Glorious Revolution," while Patrick Calquhoun's estimate, subsequently referred to, covered England and Scotland at the time of the Napoleonic Wars, pp. 70-71.*

of jobs that soon allowed Britain to become the world's first industrial power. Even inclusion of King's "lesser merchants, clergy, and civil servants and small freeholder, farmers, shopkeepers, and innkeepers" added only 30 per cent, leaving 60 per cent of the population in the lower classes of hard manual labor or unrelieved poverty.

A similar classification of the "pyramid of United Kingdom Society" was made at end of the Napoleonic Wars by Patrick Colquhoun. Using roughly the same grouping employed by King, he found the titled classes were slightly less large in relative terms (0.31 per cent), though Britain's population was three times larger than in 1688. The upper-middle class had dropped from 5.5 to 4.6 per cent; the lower-middle classes had become proportionately most reduced, from 30 down to 15 per cent. The manual working and pauper classes now constituted 80 per cent of the population.

While the numbers in the lower class were growing massively, absolutely and relatively, little was done in housing for that group. English urbanism had certainly been an unbelievable failure in human terms. Engels and Marx, observing this society and its urban morphology in the 1840's, found the explanation in the matters of class conflict and economic system. Without denying the truth to much that they wrote, I would argue that a fundamental misunderstanding and misapplication of urban morphogenetic processes during the Georgian times played a large part as well.

The Failure of English Urbanism

The failure of English urbanism through its negative impact on Marx and Engels can certainly be said to have remade the course of human history. To establish its background, we must return to the period following the 1666 Fire when the two approaches to urban development were being worked out—by the City merchants in the much-enhanced commercial structures that rose out of the ashes, and by the gentry in the leisured life in the West End. In each case occurred a major transformation of the morphogenetic processes at work during the Middle Ages. In the merchants' town, a *revolution of scale* began, brought on by the rapidly expanding trading frontiers of a successful mercantile policy and encouraged physically by the reorganization of the society and structures within the town. The nonproductive classes had moved out, opening space to those who labored, and allowing an unobstructed land-rent market to come into being without the impediments usually introduced by politically and socially powerful families. Further, the types of houses built after the Fire proved highly adaptable to transfer from a joint workshop-residence function to a total use for business activities, as attested by the number still in use even at late as the 1940 "blitz" of London.

So long as merchants continued to live in the City, serving as masters of occupationally organized households with apprentices and journeymen living in, the housing of the working class was probably improved by the Fire. But as the straightjacket of class became more binding, both through the merchant's own financial success and through the increasing use of social-class congregation among the wealthy, the successful merchant felt the need to move his family to a "proper" neighborhood. This urge was greatly intensified in succeeding generations when money tended to be inherited rather than earned. The out movement of the merchant class from the City would be further encouraged by the good commercial use that could be made of their former houses, or the growing demand for working-class tenements into which those houses could be divided. Perhaps initially, the merchants' exodus made things better, but in the long run it undoubtedly encouraged the deterioration of working-class housing. So long as the merchant lived among his workers, we may assume that concern for public health and simple humanity would obviate the worst housing conditions; once a strong class division of housing existed, no such

enlightened self-interest may be automatically assumed.

Much as crowding increased in the City because of the economic successes of the area and its merchants, responsibility for the aggravation of housing conditions must seemingly be placed on the doorstep of the gentry rather than the merchants. In a society where the pinnacle of esteem is reserved for the unproductive, the economically successful tend toward indolent descendants. This generational transfer from the business community to that of "taste" and "refinement" necessitated a geographical migration within the city. Summerson, observing the gulf between the City and the West End, tells us that the merchants' town "was a city built by generations of closely organized carpenters and masons, a city of gables, mullioned windows, carved barge-boards, corner posts and brackets, a city in which architectural novelty consisted in exceptional feats of carpentry, in curious enrichment of extravagant use of stone." This City seemed to the refined of the social elite a curious place, not made less so when reconstruction after the Fire met the demands of a commerce increasingly isolated from their own "brisk order of an age of intelligence and expense" then growing up in Mayfair.[60]

London did not grow evenly between these two social components with their separate districts. In 1700 London is thought to have had "about 674,500" people and not to have increased appreciably in the next fifty years (with a 1750 estimate of 676,750). But there was a considerable difference of demographic experience by class. Before around 1800, "the earlier building booms appear to represent chiefly the expansion of particular classes of Londoners, expansion in the sense of families moving from smaller to larger houses—rather than a net increase in population. On the other hand, it should be remembered that increase in the upper classes of Londoners was off-set by an enormous death-rate in the lower classes, especially during the first part of the 18th century; and this, too, may be held to account for the considerable increase in the west at a time when the northern and eastern contours of London hardly changed."[61]

Probably as the economic activity in the City expanded, which it demonstrably did, a continuing inflow of migrants from the countryside both enlarged the operations of the port and trade, and filled the worker places frequently made vacant by fatal or disabling disease and a generally short life-expectancy among the laboring classes. There must have been relatively little incremental provision of working-class housing after the reconstructions undertaken at the time of the Great Fire. The structures built then, and for

[60]*Summerson*, op. cit., p. 12.
[61]Ibid., p. 9.

a long time thereafter, were truly *modular houses*, usually two or three stories high and of narrow frontage, with the building line flush with the sidewalk. If the building was a residence or domestic workshop, the ground floor would look like an ordinary row-house. When selling was carried on therein, "Shops and Shop-fronts emerged slowly from the mere contrivance of extra large sash windows to full architectural consciousness." By the middle of the eighteenth century, "bowed fronts were beginning to be preferred to straight-up-and-down framing; and the 'pent-house' projections prescribed in the Rebuilding Act (of 1667), having been rendered unnecessary by the compulsory introduction of rain-water pipes, were giving place to elaborate classical cornices" to decorate the shop-front.[62] Still the workplace and the residence remained in intimate physical association so long as the units of business were not too large in size.

As the trade quickened, accommodation of the increasing number of workers needed became difficult, creating a growing body of people seeking rental lodgings apart from a workshop secured for any trade they might practice. As wage labor increased, so did demands for lodging. But little growth in the working-class housing provisions was to be noted in a city heavily penned in by the class-specific housing estates of the growing leisured class, and in an investment climate wherein building for the lower elements of society would not have seemed too wise an undertaking without the careful daily supervision of those workers by a master, such as had existed in the medieval occupational household. Instead, the existing increments to the labor force seem to have been cared for casually and probably badly. Odd corners not taken up by the middle class—Southwark across the Thames and small areas amidst the more elegant estates—were for the thrifty and continuously employed working class, not for the "masses." For the casual workers so necessary to the operation of a great port and its docks and warehouses, little was done.

In a physical quarter of the City where the modular structures built after 1666 could easily shift from residential to commercial use, added pressure on the supply of housing was consequent upon such losses of housing to shops, domestic or larger manufacturing establishments, or warehouses. As the thrifty working class moved to Southwark or Camden Town, the middle class to Bloomsbury, and the magnates to estates in the Home Counties, the poor were left the deteriorating and shrinking body of residence within the City. And few persons other than those so confined gave the matter much thought.

The situation in the West End was very different indeed. There, new forms of "urbanism" were being devised and built, as Summerson has it. But these were forms for a great metropolis with a large body of people living at least in part on unearned income, even when some might practice a managerial role in business, serve in the law, or engage in the loftier professional or civil service roles. This type of upper-middle-class district could attain only small size outside London, and was of so little consequence in America as to be important in only a few towns. The *West-End model of housing* was distinctive to London and of relatively little transfer value to other cities. Yet, it shaped many of the accepted urban attitudes, particularly with respect to the desire to attach a distinctive social identification to a city neighborhood and to the architecturally proper form that such housing estates should take.

Because style and taste were so intricately interwoven in those efforts to create a social identity for an area, two things followed: people of similar social status and intellectual and political identification tended to congregate together and, given that fact, changes in fashion could quickly create or destroy the social cachet of such a geographical congregation and outdate its morphological expression. Once a housing area lost fashionable attributions, the group still seeking those qualities was forced to migrate where the proper image was still to be found.

This search for the whilom cachet began *the generational shifts* that Summerson noted. And the elevation of architectural style and geographical location of residence to determining roles in the social acceptance of families gave the land speculators a weapon of utmost edge in forcing the market to respond to their prodding. But to operate such a system as that found in London's West End required a moneyed class of a size to be found in very few places. Novelists and architectural historians have never tired of telling us of Georgian squares and their residents, but as a pandect for the study of urbanization in the industrial era, this story is a narrow and parochial outline.

[62]Ibid., *p. 249.*

The West End Model

The physical complex that became the basic morphological component of the Georgian city was inextricably related to the social desires of the middle and upper classes at that time. To assure the desired surroundings when the lands about a previously suburban great house—such as Bedford (Southampton) House—were developed for the income that could be secured from urban housing, it was essential to try to give a specific quality to that project. Much of the land in London's West End was entailed, forbidding sale of the freehold. Thus the practice became to develop "estates" wherein title to the land remained with the landowners, who offered leaseholds, originally of fairly short duration but ultimately commonly around sixty or ninety-nine years in term. At the end of the lease period, the land and all improvements on it would revert to the landowner. No more effective device could have been found to control the long-term use of land in an era when the concept of zoning was unimagined.

Because these developments were often adjacent to aristocratic mansions (though as time passed most of the mansions were torn down to be replaced by more intensive urban housing), great effort was made to maintain an elevated tone for the neighborhood. Forced construction of housing of sufficient size and cost guarded against the encroachment of "other classes." But the tone of a housing estate was conferred even more by the architectural style decreed for its construction. In these attached row-houses, a common facade presented to the street was essential. First, the frontage of each "house" was predetermined. They were usually fairly narrow in width and normally limited to three construction bays—perhaps 16 to 40 feet at the outer limits.

As a matter of fact there arose only a few types of buildings, which with their characteristic features were repeated over and over again in long rows of streets and they only varied in scale and in interior decoration. Facing the parks–St. James's Park and Hyde Park–houses were built as very narrow and very deep buildings .... In the squares and places of Bloomsbury where the street front is the best the houses were less deep. The largest room on the first floor was a broad room facing the street, and facing the yard there were two deep rooms side by side .... This Bloomsbury house with its three bays we find in large scale in Bedford Square. Here each room is as large as a ballroom, but in streets near by the same type of house is also to be found in smaller scale, down to quite small

dimensions, as for instance the houses in Doughty Street where Charles Dickens lived in No. 48 (1837-39). Houses smaller than these have become two-bay buildings, but little by little the composition of facades as systems of bays was abandoned and one large window for each room was considered sufficient.[63]

Rasmussen's description speaks of the London house in the mid-nineteenth century when Londoners had a bit more social range in their occupation, but it serves well to present the type of house and the standardization that came quite early to the housing of the moneyed classes. The facades along a single street-block frontage were made uniform with roof-lines, and the height of individual stories was kept consistent. Normally the three bays were revealed by three large windows in the upper stories, and two windows and a doorway on the first floor. Cellars were increasingly used as builders sought to enlarge the accommodation of the houses without making them visually too tall. The main cellar (a subcellar below it might be used mainly for storage of coal and other household needs) was built at ground level, affording windows to the back; at the front, the street was raised on a causeway-like feature, bordered on each side by area ways that allowed some light to reach the fronts of the cellar, and access to the first floor was more or less on a level. Most commonly, these were really four-story houses with the true ground floor (cellar) hidden at the front by raising the street one level upward to give entry directly into the public-entertaining rooms of the first floor.

This feature of city row-houses in England was not widely copied when the form was brought to the large cities of America. Perhaps London's poor drainage conditions (brought on by the underlying layer of clay) encouraged what was really an "above-ground cellar," a feature unnecessary with the commonly superior drainage found in American cities, where cellars could be occupied even when dug well below the natural surface of the land.

The range of class variation within Georgian housing was kept fairly narrowly bounded. The squares were the most desirable spots, sporting the largest houses and the wealthiest occupants. Wider streets leading out of the square came next in order of precedence and would be occupied by the firmly established middle class. Their houses were less commodious than those fronting on the square but were still impressive in their architectural presentation to the street. In lesser streets or near the small cluster of shops commonly built into these developments to save servants' shopping time, the housing would be relatively modest. In these lower-middle-class infillings, working authors such as Dickens might find lodging.

[63]*Rasmussen, op. cit., pp. 233-234.*

The Georgian world was all "front;" when one turns to the rear elevations of these buildings, the disappointment must be extreme. Their rear walls are grubby and cluttered beyond common practice, even in the most architecturally condemned of American housing tracts today. Mews for the housing of horses and the storage of carriages were sometimes accommodated at the back. There, too, were frequently found somewhat haphazard outbuildings for the overflow of household storage.

The small open space behind the main building seems to have been provided entirely for sanitary purposes, to admit light and air at the rear and to contain cesspits used by the household "closets." The kitchen garden of the medieval burgage plot was gone, and the landscaped yard of the American house had not yet been discovered. The aristocracy required landscape gardening to be formal and a bit bleak, certainly space-consuming and stylized. It was associated with the sort of landscaping found in big country houses; for that, one needed lawns, sheep, carefully placed clusters of ancient trees, and all sorts of things impossible in the city courtyard. Apparently the middle class drew the gauze curtains on the back yard and gave up. A family was known by what street or square its house was "in," so the rear was yet another of those Victorian unmentionables. As Rasmussen had it, house fronts were Georgian; their rears were Gothic.

The Town Outside London

So far we have considered London as the exemplar of urbanization during the seventeenth century. Even for

Englishmen this was hardly the full truth. Many settlers coming to America during the Great Migration of that century had had far more experience with Bristol or Norwich than with the Great Wen. In his study of the social and economic climate of England at the time families were driven to leave for the fearsome New World, Carl Bridenbaugh describes the nature of these English provincial towns:

Some of the new construction went up on vacant sites; occasionally old houses were demolished completely and replaced; in other instances, medieval structures were enlarged or modernized. Everywhere the richest merchants lived in three-story houses of ten to fifteen rooms; the most prosperous tradesmen inhabited four or five rooms on two floors. Because party walls, which served two buildings, could not be breached for windows, light entered a town house from the front and rear only. Consequently, in urban rebuilding after 1600, there was widespread replacement of latticed windows by glazed ones to insure not only better lighting but better ventilation, an important consideration to the townsmen, who spent more of their days indoors than did their rural neighbors. The house of a retailer often had a large "shop window" covering most of the front of his place, and if there were a pent-roof above it, it could be removed in the morning to open the shop to passing customers. Fire hazards prompted the Exeter authorities to proscribe thatched roofs in 1603, and subsequently slate and tiles began to replace the picturesque and familiar thatch in new houses, but many of the old roofs remained intact for decades.

The fact that many new or rebuilt private houses graced every city and large town did not drastically alter their medieval appearance. The High Street of Exeter illustrated the transition in the principal provincial cities from the accession of King James (1603) to the calling of the Long Parliament (1640). Nearly all buildings were of timber construction; only here and there was there a stone structure; most of the roofs were of thatch, the law notwithstanding. The two- and three-story buildings, low-pitched, small, far from convenient, and crowded together, were only occasionally relieved by some substan-

Clifton in Bristol still preserves some of the finest Georgian buildings of England. This "South row" in Brunswick Square was constructed on lease-holds by the house-carpenter, Edmund Workman, who let them out in 1771. Of the seven houses in this row only the middle is double-fronted, though the end houses have their entrances on the inter-secting streets (and thus are not shown in this drawing). From Walter Ison, The Georgian Buildings of Bristol, London: Faber & Faber, Ltd., 1952.

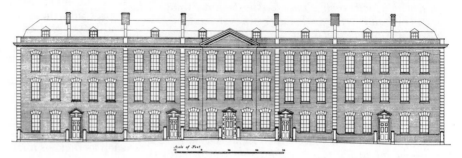

tial merchant's fine residence–a spectacle of the rich and the poor living side by side. [64]

Thus, in these provincial cities, which were to become the model for the New World towns, class division was a social but not a geographical fact. The build of the place showed the slow transformation of a fabric, originally medieval, under the gentle but continuous pressure of the mercantile system. In America the medieval component was reduced, as it was already seen to be passing away, and the more modern elements were increasing, but the town was fundamentally functional, organic, and rather modular in form.

Perhaps as central as any feature in determining the build of the provincial English towns was the fact that their structure had been organically evolutionary rather than initially designed and fixed. This growth pattern showed up in the alignment of the streets and the placement of buildings, as well as in the restriction of open spaces to clearly functional purposes. In most instances the houses had probably come first, with the streets standing only as open paths of variable width winding their way amidst the buildings—the main fiber of the city's fabric. Streets were made by the serial collection of many individual wills in the placement of houses, not always a very proportionate or orderly process. Even on flat ground, these paths could wander badly, and on hilly terrain they could be sinuous and indirect indeed. But unlike the later grid-pattern streets, made to march over ground regardless of its character, the collective-will streets of the Middle Ages were seldom impracticable of traverse.

The houses placed at functionally appropriate locations were typically medieval, wooden-frame structures with "jetties" that carried upper stories outward to gain more space. Where space was not critical, as in the country houses of Suffolk and Essex, the jetties simply gave some protection to the weather-boarding of the lower story. In towns, the gable was normally to the street so that in the face of the close juxtaposition of buildings, or even their attachment along party walls, the greatest amount of light could be admitted to the structure front and back, where the only windows could be let into the wall. In England the lesser constriction of towns by defensive walls meant that houses were not normally so tall as on the Continent, particularly in the provincial towns that must have seemed the most appropriate model for the settlers going to the mercantile frontier.

The open spaces of the late medieval town of England were obviously the outgrowth of need rather than show; they were the marketplaces for the most part. Seemingly only where an ecclesiastical estab-

lishment stood in a tiny town—such as Ely—would it have space about it not strictly for practical use. In Salisbury, with its great lawns, we deal with a bastide the overall design of which was worked out before foundations were laid, and where the civil and ecclesiastical purposes of the town were well known before construction began.

Two Models of Urbanism for Transport to America

Clearly two forms of urban development were available to the persons who crossed the Atlantic during the Great Migration of the seventeenth century. The first was that associated with the aristocratic districts in London and a few other cities, most notably at Clifton outside Bristol. That well-to-do settlement is perhaps the best remaining example of the integrated social congregation and its attendant buildings.[65] It was growing up in the same period as the American colonies which had continuing associations with the port on the Avon, so we may reasonably assume its model to have been fully as well known as London's, and probably somewhat more adaptable to the colonial needs.

The other model that must have been known well was that of London Rebuilt, the commercial town risen from the ashes to become the most important economic place on earth, and the previous home of Boston and Philadelphia settlers. Because of the social class of those migrants and their purposes for going to America, this London Rebuilt model was the more important. It was a working place of relatively moderate reforms in society, politics, and religion and, above all, it was a city. The holds of the small ships in the Great Migration contained far more townspeople than would a representative sample of the English population; their first act on reaching the western shore was to attempt to reproduce the town life of the England they had left in search of a more perfect world. Part of that quest for perfection was the improvement of the city; they did not abandon it, as so commonly modern reformers do.

---

[64]*Carl Bridenbaugh*, Vexed and Troubled Englishmen: 1590-1642, *New York: Oxford University Press, 1968, pp. 134-135.*

[65]*Walter Ison*, The Georgian Buildings of Bristol, *London: Faber & Faber, Ltd., 1952.*

The Planting of the American City

We are fortunate indeed that Carl Bridenbaugh a generation ago set out to dispel the myth that the European settlers in America were coming as countrymen and agricultural pioneers. In his two classic volumes on colonial urbanism—*Cities in the Wilderness* and *Cities in Revolt*—he covers the American city experience up to the time of the American Revolution.[66] That experience was rather different in contemporary view from what it seems to have become in retrospect today, rather reversing the notion that hindsight is the more perceptive. Bridenbaugh states at the very beginning of his book:

Cities rise and flourish in proportion as their natural advantages correspond with the demands of a particular age. This correspondence may be either accidental or the result of preconceived purpose, but history provides many instances of towns which, lacking this harmony between the physical and economic environment, have despite artificial efforts of founders or promoters remained condemned to comparative unimportance, outdistanced by more fortunate rivals. In the seventeenth century material greatness was commercial, not industrial. Those towns prospered, therefore, whose sites commanded certain vital trading advantages–the possession of good natural harbors, the control of avenues of trade and communication, or the dominion of a productive countryside. When in this period the Old World began to plant its colonial settlements on the North American continent, commercial considerations as such largely dictated their locations. Design rather than accident endowed the principal offspring of seventeenth century colonizing impulses with situations favoring the pursuit of trade and navigation.[67]

In the minds of the promoters of North American colonies, the advance of the trading, mercantile frontier shaped their actions; otherwise their efforts would have borne little economic return. Many merchants, and perhaps more settlers, were of dissenting religious view or of unhappy social or economy status. Still the men who put up the money for the voyaging and held out some hope for a continuing economic support of the plantations once established saw this venture as one of economic trade.

[66] *Carl Bridenbaugh*, Cities in the Wilderness (1625-1742) [*original edition 1938*], New York: Alfred A. Knopf, 1955; *and* Cities in Revolt (1743-1776), *New York: Alfred A. Knopf, 1955. Republished jointly in 1955 as* Urban Life in America.
[67] *Bridenbaugh*, Cities in the Wilderness, *p. 3.*

This classic problem is part of most migration movements. Pushing factors must propel settlers against the resistance that distance always interposes, but attractions must draw them out as well. For religious and social outcasts, the gain might be personal satisfaction and a sense of a better psychic existence. But the merchant paying their way must have some reasonable anticipation of, mainly, economic return. He would back their venture, or even originate it and subsequently recruit their association with it, basically to extend the economic system in which he was functioning. In seventeenth-century England and Holland, this system of mercantile endeavor was fairly simple and certainly most effective. In France the same economic motives were involved. But a resolution of the Wars of Religion in favor of the Roman church had meant an unbridgeable gap between the court and government on the one hand, and the most effective merchant group and potential population for recruitment to migration on the other. The less than impressive history of French colonization in Canada owes as much to that schism as to all other causes combined.

If we accept a commercial motive for all colonies, and that only some as an additional concern were religious commonwealths, then we can see that the trading entrepôt must be the logical model for the developing towns. Plantation of settlers came first in just such towns with "the dominion of a productive countryside." The European peopling of America came from the initial coastal towns outward rather than, as frequently imagined, from the growth of the towns serving the needs of an earlier developed countryside. History in America utterly contradicts the assumptions of central-place theory, whose role on her stage must wait for the third act, when the nation had become as densely settled and politically and administratively complex as the medieval Germany in whose relics this special system was conceived.

The wave of European plantation came as a town-founding effort with great similarity to the conscious spread of economic towns—bastides—into the wasteland parts of Europe in the twelfth, thirteenth, and fourteenth centuries. The purpose was closely similar and the *dramatis personae* nearly the same, given a few elements of changed costuming. As in the Middle Ages, the notion existed of a sovereign capable of asserting a claim based on assumed divine support. The Spaniards and the Portuguese drew straight from the past when they secured a papal decree dividing the unknown world into two spheres wherein each of the Iberian kingdoms separately might explore and claim lands. Other Catholic powers bridled at this act, though only the French did so effectively. The Protestant kingdoms treated the matter with the reverence it deserved, ranging the seas and claiming land not actively defended by another European power. But once an area was claimed, whether by the Protestant English and Dutch or the Catholic French, Spaniards, and Portuguese, the notion of national sovereignty was in operation. Subsequent development within the claimed area was controlled by royal grant, much as it had been in the Middle Ages.

French Colonization in America

When Champlain established his *Habitation* at Québec in 1608, his purpose was seemingly rather complex—imperial in politics, proselyting in religion, and mercantile in economics. That rather bureaucratic quality remained throughout the French sovereignty of Canada, until 1763. In seeking colonists for the Laurentian settlements, the French reverted directly to feudalism rather than to the more evolved social and economic system of their own bastides. The king granted basically feudal estates to a group of *seigneurs* (persons and ecclesiastical foundations) whose jobs it became to secure settlers for the colony of Canada. In return, the *seigneur* was allowed to collect a feudal quitrent (such as we have already seen in the bastides), a *cens*, from the residents on the holding, thus termed *censitaires*, as well as other forms of excise taxation characteristic of the feudal economy. The result was the creation of a rural society and an agricultural economy quite distinctly different from that emerging across the Appalachians in New England, New York, the Jerseys, and Pennsylvania.

Seemingly because the Huguenots were forbidden entry to Canada by a militantly Counter-Reformation government in France, the colony that resulted was economically stunted and productive of a feeble and somewhat artificially maintained urbanization. Québec was a proper town, though unbelievably priest-ridden, even when compared with the rather grim religiosity of Boston. The combination of bishops as the religious rulers and the rural feudalism of the seigneurial system produced a limping economy, while the economy of the English colonies dashed forward under the aegis of the merchant class working from London and the West Country ports as well as resident in the New World. To change matters, the French government began, in 1663, the operation of a royal government for Canada, guided by another viceregal figure alongside the bishops of Québec, the Intendants of the crown. The crown monopolized the pelteries of the forest, the one trade that showed much hope of producing profits, setting back the course of city building by further committing Canada to a peculiarly rural economic base. The commercial agriculture then developing in Maryland and Virginia or the resident mercantilism growing up in New England were obviated by Canadian dependence upon the production of gathered products from the forest, fish that might be caught by fishermen coming seasonally directly from France, or the rather subsistence farming practiced on semi-feudal holdings by a basically peasant agriculture. What towns might grow in this barren soil were those of administrators and viceroys—ecclesiastical or royal—more than merchants. Québec, Trois Rivières, and Montréal became the only towns, but were *towns of control* more than commerce. Their glory was found in their seminaries rather than their *depôts* of trade.

To complete the picture we find the one North American instance of the seige castle being built by the royal administration of Canada to defend the colony against the depredations of the merchants of Britain and British America. At Louisbourg on Cape Breton Island, a great fortress was built between 1720 and 1740 to defend the frontiers of the colony, as the Nor-

The city of Québec, founded in 1698, was more an administrative and ecclesiastical town than the entrepôt of merchants. This seventeenth-century view shows the upper town of institutions and the lower town of shops and warehouses.

man seige castles such as Château-Gaillard had done in the Middle Ages. Like them, Louisbourg proved less than invincible, falling after seige to a body of New England merchants and their henchmen in 1745. As a frontier fortress it was a failure. A certain allegorical quality attaches to the seige of Louisbourg in 1745; then, perhaps more clearly than at any other time, the supremacy of the mercantile era over the feudal era was signalled. The expedition that captured the fortress was almost entirely American, made up of men whose families had lived for several generations free of the yoke of Europe's traditional social order. And the anger felt in New England over the return of the place to the French at war's end was an attitude that a people long used to the peculiarities of dynastic warfare—as were all Europeans—would have been unlikely to entertain.

If Canada represented the effort to project an incompletely evolved mercantile Europe into North America, as I believe it did, then the failure of France's policies there can be read not merely as the early warning of the collapse of the dying monarchical system, which came in France herself not more than twenty-five years after the loss of Canada. France's failure may also serve as evidence of the disastrous policy of "ruralization" practiced in royal Canada. The conquest of Canada by the British in 1763 led to two events that tell us much about the role that cities have played in the broad history of North America.

Once sovereignty shifted to the British, northward migration of city-men from the English colonies to the south was considerable, to the extent that Montréal was a predominantly English city throughout much of the nineteenth century, and Québec had a considerable English minority population at the same time. The English in Canada became the denizens of the towns and the French tended to retreat into social, political, cultural, and religious isolation in the protective realms of the countryside. The "habitant" became the French Canadien, rural, parochial, devout, politically and socially conservative, and economically stagnant.

In the meantime the English were acting like their merchant forebears, building and dominating towns, expanding their economic interests over the vast realm Canada became, and generally acting like the hated Americans south of the border. Only since the Second World War have the French Canadiens turned to the cities in great numbers, taking over control of those urban clusters within their own province, gaining stature as businessmen, and becoming increasingly typical North Americans. But the rustication of the Canadien for almost two hundred years after the Conquest has placed a grim economic inheritance on Jean Baptiste's shoulders. We might well interpret the Québec nationalism of the present generation as an effort to recapture from "les Anglais" the cities of the province of Québec for the use of the dominant population group which had never given up the countryside around them.

The City in the English Colonies

In the thirteen English colonies south and east of the Appalachians—which for simplicity we may call the American colonies—a very different situation was found. Perhaps at the very beginning, the distinction between the English and French colonies was not so striking but it evolved into a fundamental contrast. Again we may best turn to Bridenbaugh's characterization:

> Pursuit of trade and commerce was the all-embracing activity of the early colonial villages–the very basis for their existence. These little seaports served as the focal points at which immigrants and manufactured articles from the Mother Country converged for redistribution in the New World, while through them the produce of rural and frontier settlements found its way to distant markets. The colonial town was primarily a commercial community with its daily exchange of goods–a community of market places, warehouses, wharves and shops.[68]

These towns were dominated by a merchant group whose ties were not with the bureaucracy of England, as those of Québec were with the church and state in France, but rather with the merchant class in London and the West Country port towns. As Bernard Bailyn has clearly shown, ties were constantly reinforced between the merchant groups in the English towns on both sides of the Atlantic; the motivations of the economic life of London or Bristol were immediately reflected in Boston or Philadelphia. Cities on the Charles or the Delaware constantly resisted any highhanded assertion of a hierarchical subjugation of New World activities to rural production alone, or even in the main.[69] If the employment of mercantile economic practices for the production of wealth was the right of Englishmen, it was so in each geographical world they might reside in. The result was that the towns were the key to the use of the American colonies as a settlement

[68]Ibid., p. 26.
[69]Bernard Bailyn, The New England Merchants in the Seventeenth Century, New York: Harper Torch Books, 1964.

for English migrants. Those people came to the New World mainly as freemen, seeking greater personal liberty—as much economic as religious. Thus, the analogy with the medieval bastides was most direct. *Stadtluft macht frei* was not the motto of these pilgrims because they did not think in German, not because the concept was foreign to them. The perpetuation of feudal servitude as found in the Laurentian colonies of France would have destroyed whatever "pull" the New World offered to English settlers. Where assisted passage was necessary, it was accomplished through indentured servitude for a fixed period of years rather than by the direct transfer of continuing feudal practice to America, as in Canada. In Maryland, for example, the Calverts' attempt to recreate the manorial system with feudal duties came to nought.

holding into manors held by lords of the manor, who owed them fealty and paid, in turn, quite substantial rather than symbolic quitrents, in perpetuity. The lords then let out to their own tenants parts of the manor to be held in fealty and payment of a very substantial part of the produce of that land. The manor would as well have its own farming lands cultivated directly by the lord with his own servants—indentured to begin with, but soon enslaved Africans. This feudalism was not pure, but certainly its intent was distant from the world of the city merchant who shaped the New England colonies. Thus, we see the perpetuation in the American colonies of the two traditions of social and economic organization then found in England, and the two models of the city then found within London.

Feudalism Aborted in America

When the Calvert family was granted land to found a colony in southeastern Newfoundland, near Ferryland, they encountered conditions utterly unamenable to the extension of the rural-estate economy of England to America. Consequently George Calvert, the first Lord Baltimore, petitioned the king for a replacement grant in the neighborhood of Virginia, which was given him to the north of the Potomac River in 1632. In that region the Calverts were provided a proprietorial province wherein they could collect quitrents (nearly identical to the French *cens* collected in Québec), levy taxes, appoint all officials, establish and appoint the pastors of churches, and generally control matters. Their charter stated "that at all times, and in all things, such interpretation be made thereof, and allowed in any of Our Courts whatsoever, as shall be judged most advantageous, and favorable unto the said now Lord Baltimore, his heirs and assigns."[70] This charter attempted to extend rural feudalism to the American colonies; the failure of that effort tells us much about the real social and economic nature of that planting effort.

The legal organization of Maryland was basically feudal. The Calverts *held* their land as a grant from the king for which they paid annually at Windsor Castle a symbolic two Indian arrows. The Calverts divided their

[70]*R. V. Coleman, The First Frontier, New York: Charles Scribner's Sons, 1948. The quotation from the charter is contained on page 219.*

Strong Town, Weak Town

To borrow Cromwell's phrase in a slightly transformed context, the "New Model" city won hands down, as his "New Model Army" had at Naseby (1645). In the Chesapeake Bay colonies of Virginia and Maryland, two distinct forms of settlement initiation occurred, with consequent differences in the governmental organization of the areas. Both forms led to a peculiar deficiency of towns that John Reps has remarked upon.[71] The two forms were the colony planted by the trading company, such as that set out by the Virginia Company beginning at James Town in 1607, and the colony as the creation of a single proprietor, as in the efforts of the Calverts in Maryland.

Governmentally, three English institutions were transferred to the New World: "As the ancient English town meeting reached a high development in New England, as the system of close vestries was very thoroughly worked out in Virginia, so the old English manor was best preserved in Maryland."[72] But only the town meeting appears to have fitted very well with the creation of cities; more accurately, where cities were needed in the fundamental settlement fabric of the

[71]*John W. Reps, The Making of Urban America: A History of City Planning in the United States, Princeton, N.J.: Princeton University Press, 1965, pp. 95-119.*
[72]*John Fiske, Old Virginia and Her Neighbours, Boston: Houghton, Mifflin and Company, 1899, Vol. II, p. 146.*

area, they must be accompanied by a civil governmental organization at the lowest level that could serve the urban needs. The civil organization of Maryland did not forbid the growth of towns but the society that produced the civil organization of Maryland was not particularly aware of the needs or uses of towns. This society was drawn from the petty country gentry of the British Isles—Baltimore was a small village near Cape Clear on the southwest coast of Ireland—and was desirous of perpetuating a rurally based economy. Tobacco made such a course seem rational in colonial Virginia and Maryland, notwithstanding that such a base would have seemed wildly unsound in New England which also could and did raise tobacco.

In New England, urbanization began with town settlement, based on practice of trade and shipping. The development of the countryside was only one of several economic supports, and was characterized by a strong civil foundation based on local municipal organization in the enduring New England town. In the Chesapeake Bay area, initial and continuingly rural settlement took place in large agricultural holdings ("plantations" and manors), resting on a single base of commercial crop production. The development of cities came only quite late in the history of the area, as a response to an increasing demand for quite specialized retail and trading services, and characterized by a strong civil foundation based on county units. We will summarize the full story behind these two approaches to urbanization in America.

The Origin of the "Strong" County in America

In his classic study of Virginia and her neighbors, John Fiske dealt with the characteristics of the Chesapeake Bay pattern of settlement and political and social organization, particularly with the debt that Maryland bore to the counties palatine in England. When the Normans conquered England they devised, as we noted in Chapter 4, an administrative system that divided the holdings of grand feudatories among many counties. Thus the crown would have no effective rivals, as had the kings of France with their great dukes of integrated provinces. Instead manors were given in many different counties, usually well distributed. In three places where such a system would not be safe, where

the threat of invasion required a strong local agent of the crown—at Kent in the southwest where French invasion was always possible, Durham in the northeast, and Cheshire on the Welsh border—a county palatine was organized and given into the care of a single powerful lord. But William I was astute indeed in giving Cheshire and Durham to their respective bishops, then as now without legitimate issue, and Kent to his brother Odo. The practice within these counties, and a few others that joined the palatine ranks from time to time (Pembrokeshire, Lancashire, and Hexhamshire), was to give virtually full autonomy to the count palatine. He was permitted to organize his own system of feudal dues and fealty, collect his own taxes, run his own law courts, and be captain of his own troops. Only the direct tie between the king and the count palatine served to represent the area to the court, to the extent that Durham was unable to send members to the House of Commons until the reign of Charles II in 1675; she stood as a quasi-kingdom more the peer than the subject of Westminster.

Fiske shows that in organizing the Ferryland colony in Newfoundland (1623), George Calvert's "province in Newfoundland, which received the name of Avalon, was to be modelled after the palatinate of Durham, and the powers granted to its lord proprietor were perhaps the most extensive ever bestowed by the English crown upon any subject."[73] The strength of those powers allowed the Calverts to bring to the New World so clear a manorial system. In turn, the creation of a "strong county" was made necessary to take the place of the leadership of the town in administration, which was fairly characteristic of the later Middle Ages in England and of the Roman church organization throughout its existence in Britain, an administrative system largely taken over by the Church of England after the break with Rome. But neither the Anglican nor the Catholic church had an episcopal organization in America until the eighteenth century, so we may disregard the church as an early force in the creation of an urban base of administration. And in the rural settlement of large producing units, towns were little required to provide the local and everyday services that might elsewhere be demanded of them. Just as the medieval manor had been a closed, natural economy free of daily needs for markets, so the manors of Maryland and the plantations of Virginia needed trade only once or twice a year when hogsheads of tobacco were to be sent to Bristol or London and when they received a return of manufactures from England or from Boston, the trading *emporium* of the American colonies.

The outcome was the creation in the Middle Atlantic colonies, of the county as the dominant and even

[73]Ibid., *Vol. I, p. 260.*

sole political unit once the manors lost their status in the eighteenth century. The county court, for administration as well as ajudication became the dominant administrative body, the sheriff the main county officer, and the county the basic unit for representation in provincial legislatures. The existing towns were small and relatively impotent. But strangely they tended to be rather elaborate in layout. That seeming inconsistency explains more than we might at first expect. But the urbanization of the middle and southern colonies came only at the very end of the seventeenth century, continuing into the eighteenth in many cases, specifically Baltimore. Thus we may turn first to the early settlement of New England, where the town arrived with the original settlers in Massachusetts Bay.

The Planted Town in New England

"Provincialism" is a term that has lost virtually all of its meaning in modern America; every region has its distinctive qualities but none is enclosed, distinct, and sufficient unto itself as were the English counties and colonies in the seventeenth century. Additionally, today we do not find the sharp contrasts in degree of development that once existed. Few now would think Boston the cultural "hub," or New York the fulcrum for commercial concerns, as they were in the eighteenth and nineteenth centuries, and the rest of the land a provincial backwater. Yet in the early years of American settlement, the province was far more real than was "America" as a concept of spatial integration. "The conditions of settlement and of development within each colony meant that each evolved its own individual legal system, just as each evolved its individual social and political system. Geographical isolation, the date and character of the several settlements, the degree of absence of outside supervision or control—all had their effect in ultimately developing thirteen separate legal systems."[74] We might add further to Professor George Haskins' catalogue by holding that the contrast in urbanization among the Thirteen Colonies was so sharp that the more earnest efforts of

the middle colonies to copy England in her laws could be related to the like efforts of the Chesapeake country to reestablish the social basis on which that English law was originally founded—the concept of the landed estate, the landed elite, and the geographically-bound working class.

In England, as in Europe in the Middle Ages, attachment of a labor force—and thereby a potential military levy—to a rural area was written into law, broadly as serfdom but with local variants almost without end. In the Chesapeake and Carolina colonies a similar attachment was eagerly sought, first through the indenture of agricultural "servants" brought to America from England, Scotland, Ireland, or the Continental possessions of her monarchs but ultimately by actual enslavement of forcibly-transported Africans. Certainly the ability to enforce continued rural residence and legal attachment to a local commercial-agricultural estate made slavery attractive beyond any moral resistance found in the economic and social traditionalists of the South. In such a context it is not surprising that Southerners, with a semi-manorial economy, resisted the building of towns, took on most energetically the manorial system of England, with its particular law and courts for its enforcement, and shaped a fundamentally anti-urban society.[75] Whether or not they knew the phrase *Stadtluft macht frei*, they certainly knew the concept of a city's providing freedom, and resisted the creation of cities for that reason.

In New England the law reflects a very different practice. Two interesting innovations took place. Instead of depending upon an English common law drawn from a kingdom run with paramount concern for the landed economy and its aristocracy, "Massachusetts law was not common law at all, but a new-made system of law based on the Bible."[76] The biblical commonwealth was envisioned as actually operating there, starting in 1629 when the Puritans established their settlement, more than a decade before that biblical polity became a reality in England.

The other innovation was that Massachusetts came well ahead of England in incorporating commercial law into its judicial concern. "When the colonies were first settled, the *law merchant*—the rules and practices of commercial law—had not been fully 'received' into common law, that is, by the royal courts of England." Yet as early as 1647 Massachusetts began to enforce that law merchant as it was not enforced in England.[77]

[74]*George L. Haskins*, Law and Authority in Early Massachusetts *(1960), quoted in Lawrence M. Friedman*, A History of American Law, *New York: Simon and Schuster, 1973, pp. 30-31.*

[75]*For a discussion of the manorial law and courts of Maryland see Friedman, op. cit., p. 40, which notes that even a truly medieval piepowder court was organized at St. Mary's, the first provincial capital.*

[76]*Ibid., p. 30.*

[77]*Ibid., p. 69.*

Thus, Massachusetts, and by emulation its neighbors—New Hampshire, Rhode Island, and Connecticut—became biblical commonwealths of a merchant class. For them geographical attachment of labor was anathema, for its irrationality in an entrepreneurial society. Only indolence and sloth need be condemned. As a result laws were quickly adopted against idleness,[78] leading to the "warning off" of uninvited migrants from afar,[79] and generally against the powers of wealthy leisure as contrasted with earnest labor and productivity.

Laws of Property

When the English plantations in the New World were bruited toward the end of Elizabeth's reign, and undertaken in Charles's, two rather contrasting property practices were introduced in America. When the merchant class of London and the other ports set about founding the New England colonies, they used freehold ownership of land as the basic property practice. In the planted towns just as much as the Puritan villages, the householder normally owned the plot on which his dwelling stood. And in the countryside, "the family farm" became the universal form. This landowning tradition was to have surpassing importance in the social geography of America and the form and location of the Industrial Revolution in the United States. The

[78]*The* Laws and Liberties of Massachusetts *of 1648 required that no person shall "spend his time idlely or unprofitably under pain of such punishment as the Court of Assistants or County Court shall think meet to inflict" (quoted in Friedman,* op. cit., *p. 70).*

[79]*The resistance to newcomers was in part a fear for the welfare responsibility they might ultimately pose. After a residence of three months they had created an "establishment" entitling them to poor relief. To avoid this the newcomer might if of questionable estate be "warned out," thus removing the local responsibility. (Josiah H. Benton,* Warning Out in New England, *1911, quoted in Friedman,* op. cit., *p. 77). Much as this was a concern under the poor law, we may reasonably infer that if labor were much desired the concern thereof would greatly outweigh the unease with respect to the poor law. After all, in such a grim frontier society as Worcester County, Massachusetts, in the eighteenth century 6,764 persons were "warned out" between 1737 and 1788 (Benton,* op. cit., *p. 59), when the numbers of those physically unfit for labor must have been small indeed.*

mercantile tradition brought to the northern colonies seems to have assured this freeholding of property by the average man in a truly isonomic land-holding pattern.

The southern colonies of America were the purview of the petty aristocracy of England and its hangers-on. These "proprietors" were gaining lands in America denied them in England. As a result, the cadet branches of gentle families tended to take up settlement in the New World. They were joined by Quakers, who might eschew the currently worldly, but showed remarkable consideration for future security. Both groups looked upon land-holding as a speculative venture wherein raw land granted to them, or bought from a proprietor, could be "developed" for a current profit. At the same time, such land might serve as a deposit against the future if let out at leasehold, or at least for a quitrent. In Maryland an outright feudal system was attempted, accompanied by quitrents in the countryside and leaseholds in the towns. Similar practices were employed only to a somewhat reduced degree in Pennsylvania. All told, the Middle Atlantic colonies were an outgrowth of the property notions of the English gentry, quite in contrast to the concepts of land-holding and property practices typical of the City merchants and their sons and cousins who settled New England. Admiral William Penn had speculated in lands in London after the Fire, so we should not be surprised that similar interests gripped his son William in his proprietorial colony on the Delaware.

From this strikingly different quality of landed property in the northern and southern colonies in America, two traditions of city formation emerged. The quality of land-holding in New England was isonomic; each man had sufficient land for his needs but relatively little increment for use in increasing his rank. Class distinction did exist in New England—John Hull held much of the Narragansett Country, as Samuel Eliot Morison has shown—but, in general, land in Puritan New England was held for use, not speculation. And the towns that grew up there were organic places whose form was clearly predicated on practical needs and isonomic land-assignment.

In the colonies from New York on south, conditions were strikingly different. The Dutch *patroons* of the Hudson valley were lords of manors and holders of vast properties desirable only for speculation. Similarly the proprietors of the Jerseys, of Pennsylvania, Maryland, and Virginia looked upon land as a commodity for sale more than for use; transactions took place long before any possible productive employment of the holding could be undertaken. Accounts of the Virginia frontier make special mention of the tendency for landowners to sell out their first plantation and move toward or beyond the margin of settlement to shape a new land-holding. Even George Washington, the richest man of his time, bestowed a lifelong attention to speculating in frontier lands. In contrast, the frontier of settlement in New England moved very slowly. Land was made available by the General Court, the sovereign in that nonproprietorial colony, only as a group of cultivators could be assembled and dispatched to take up productive residence.

A Biblical Commonwealth of Towns

When the Massachusetts Bay Company was chartered in 1629, its purpose was to initiate trade for England with the New World through the settlement of a colony somewhere in "northern Virginia," which meant simply somewhere south of the French Laurentian colony. Initially, as a trading colony, no distinction was made between Virginia and Massachusetts, but quickly differences arose. Virginia was possessed of "proprietors," who quickly became "landed proprietors" rather than "merchant proprietors," as those in Boston. Virginia's charter remained in England, as did most of her proprietors, whereas the organic act for Massachusetts Bay was brought to Boston when that town was founded in 1630, in the company of most who held rights from the crown to create a colony. By this simple "domestication" of charter and company, The Bay managed to gain a degree of operating freedom absent in the other colonies, and the company fiercely resisted efforts to have the charter returned to England for amendment or abrogation. The stance taken was essentially that of the medieval towns in their fights with episcopal and feudal overlords. The outcome of the fierce patriotism of the communes of the Middle Ages had been the gaining of a humanist society and the freedom of the individual in a society until then characterized by the view of persons as no more than members of classes and corporations. In the New World, the results for American liberty were as important.

Fundamental to the shaping of New England was the transfer, along with the charter, of the concept of mercantilism then widely espoused by the commercial classes in Britain. For the practice of mercantilism as an economy, with its wide-ranging commerce, towns are essential. So the first settlers around Massachusetts Bay created germinal urban places. In their time in

England, the town had become an institution of hope in an otherwise dark world. "A substantial amount of unemployment in the rural areas was normal, but during periods of crisis, such as 1622 and 1629-31, it rose noticeably. Furthermore, wages in husbandry failed to keep up with the rise in prices of necessitites."[80] Initially the resort in such times and circumstances was migration to the city.

"During the sixteenth century many people left their manorial villages or open farms to settle in some larger place nearby. Ordinarily the impetus for this internal migration, symbolized by the enclosures, is discovered on the land. Almost as important, however, was the urban lodestone." Not current adversity, but the long-continued social subjugation of the rural laboring class gave the spark to tinder that flared into migration. "To many a man, woman, or youth, the lure of town life as they glimpsed it on market days or during the visits to annual fairs sooner or later became irresistible. Year by year the attractions grew more compelling, socially quite as much as economically."[81]

These towns were not greatly impressive in physique, but they were burgeoning in economy by comparison with many rural areas. The attraction of employment and the possibility of escape from the largely frozen social orders of the countryside were compelling. And as Bridenbaugh notes, the women first of all saw the light. "At the least, many a 'queen of curds and cream' employed feminine cajolery to sway the family's decision to move townward, for 'Rusticus' frankly confessed 'they are our wives that first sollicite and perswade us to come to your Cities.'"

The Form of the New England Town: The Bastidal Model

Although the settlers on the wild western shore of the Atlantic were experienced of both the bastidal form (Salisbury, Hull, and the London-towns in northern Ireland) and the organic town, they tended to make their choice on the basis of terrain. Because the Shawmut peninsula, where Boston was placed, was outlined by coves and possessed of sharp rises up the side of

[80]*Carl Bridenbaugh*, Vexed and Troubled Englishmen: 1590-1642, *p. 210.*
[81]Ibid., *pp. 120-121.*

drumlins, an irregular siting of houses grew up along easily traversed paths. Thus Boston's essential design was set as organic. At the same time, in Newtown (Cambridge) a short distance away, the bastidal form was adopted on a flat site.

In New England, particularly in Massachusetts, we must distinguish between the universally used basic modular component of town founding—the house of essentially late medieval form constructed of wood— and the way those units were collected together into a town. That act of collection could conform to terrain and to readily apparent functional assemblies—as at Boston—leading to a truly "organic" layout so much the norm for the merchant towns of Europe in the Middle Ages.

These places were not formless or shapeless, and they most assuredly were not laid out by cows, as is so inaccurately asserted. Rather they were places where the functional needs of the time were given absolute rein and where the guiding concern must have been to furnish for the greatest number of settlers the closest and most equal access to the one essential part of the town—the waterfront. If we reflect on the Boston pattern at its beginning in 1630 and immediately thereafter, *the point of initiation* was one of a series of coves where land-sea connection was made first on the beach, and soon at the sides of wharves extended out to adequately deep water. From that cove, houses stretched back along a *path of collective will*, rising up the sides of the drumlins that surrounded the landing place.

A test of this concept of morphogenesis is fortunately most ready to hand in the towns of the Avalon peninsula of Newfoundland—Calvert's first colony. The same ethnic stock is involved with fairly similar economic concerns and the same freedom to evolve a pattern to meet the specific contemporary needs. The persistence of squatting tenure down to the present, the practice of fishing and trading connection with the West Country of England until the Second World War, and the drawing of a major part of the population from English stock all contribute to a good reproduction of Boston's conditions in the seventeenth century.

From these Newfoundland towns on the "Southern Shore" below St. John's and around Conception Bay, a *beach-oriented pattern* of town layout is obvious, wherein the control feature is the beach, or a series of beaches, along which houses are ranged in close proximity. Their rather free-siting disregards front-lines and absolute parallelism of structures; often basically rural house forms are used in a physical fabric still more urban than rural. Not insignificantly, the only remaining seventeenth-century residence in Boston— Paul Revere's House—is actually such a rural form, with the roof-slope parallel with the street and the

number of windows thus somewhat restricted. The house in the Newfoundland fishing towns is rural by way of its physical separation, but strangely urban in form. Thus, the street layout is seemingly the distinctive feature of these beach-controlled towns, more than any particular house type.

If we look at Salem and Cambridge, the first of the Massachusetts Bay towns (Plymouth was settled by a different group with contrasting background and interests), we find an important element not to be observed in Boston, "established" more than laid out formally a year earlier. When Salem was laid out in 1629, a proportional quality in the assignment of lands became even more clearly evident when a "Newtown" was set out on the Charles River upstream from Charlestown in 1631.

The "beach layout" of Boston is clearly shown in John Bonner's map of 1722, nearly a century after the town was founded in 1630.

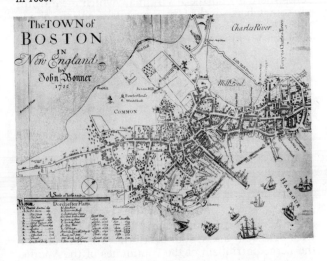

This new town was soon called Cambridge; it combined proportional land-assignment with a street patterning that would encourage functional equality. "The average home lot measured about 100 by 80 feet. Most of the streets were 30 feet wide. The market square in the northwestern part of the village was approximately 150 feet by 200. Midway along the principal northwest-southeast street stood the meetinghouse on a plot only slightly larger than those allotted for houses. Virtually the entire village with its little gridiron of streets occupied a site hardly more than 1,000 feet square. In its scale and the clear distinction between village and countryside the Cambridge plan resembles the tiny *bastide* towns of southern France or the similar settlements in Britain like Winchelsea, Flint, Salisbury, or Hull."[82] Cambridge was not a port; later, Cambridgeport developed to the east to fulfill that function, and the site was fairly level so the bastidal form was consciously or unconsciously adopted.

Even where the bastidal layout was missing, as at Salem and other places that came to reflect the elongated (linear) town pattern first established there, fairly narrow limits to lot size were found, with none of the obvious class distinctions present in the Renaissance town. Furthermore, whichever of the two "community forms" common to New England—the bastidal or the linear—was undertaken, the layout was equally predicated exclusively on practical needs, with open space restricted to usefully employed units.

New England saw the town common elevated to the role of a standard component, but the space was distinguished by common use rather than by abstract visual design. Thus it was normally termed in New England "a common," not "a green," as outsiders consistently misname it. It existed to provide for grazing "in common," for the drilling of a militia drafted by universal conscription, and for the multitude of *uses* that a functioning community makes of adaptable open space. That latter-day churches came occasionally to be built on the common says merely that with the sapping of their original austere role as meetinghouses for civil and religious purposes, and their consequent adoption of a modified English Renaissance architecture, churches began to have visual pretensions that could not be served by location on a house lot as they were when Cambridge was a "newtown."

To reiterate a critical point, the *layout* of these New England towns differed from English precedent, save in the odd instances of the bastidal forms that existed in odd places in Britain. The towns of New England had no Big Houses, no churches on imposing sites, no designs of dominance or subordination. When Boston became the capital of the Massachusetts Bay colony, little thought was given to constructing pompous buildings. Even when a "state house" was built in 1658 it was placed in functional, not visual, perspective. It stood in the middle of King Street and consisted of no more than the upper floor above a covered market used for daily and mundane needs. It is historically fitting indeed that Boston's Old State House, which stands even today, has in its basement a subway station for the use of Everyman. No Williamsburg Capitol this, in landscaped grounds that create isolation from the people.

[82]*John W. Reps*, The Making of Urban America . . . , *Princeton, N.J.: Princeton University Press, 1965, p. 126.*

Colonial New England buildings were those of the very end of the Middle Ages transferred across the ocean in the form being built just before the Great Fire of London. But the street layout of the small merchant towns being placed on the harbors of New England was different from that in the mother country. These towns were orderly in one of two ways, neither of which would have been particularly at ease in the English countryside. The structure of the *linear town* was usually given by some elongated natural feature—a strand-line on the shore, a river-front inland, the alignment on a river terrace (as in the Connecticut Valley towns), or a deeply incised valley site (as in Worcester or Fitchburg). The second layout was the simple and usually *small rectangular grid reminiscent of the bastide.* Linear towns sought constantly to adopt the basic features of the grid layout and more common arrangement of streets, the fundamentally bastidal form which became the American grid-pattern town. Most linear towns had thin and elongated grids aligned along with the initial strand or valley-strike street. Constraint of the physical site usually limited the expansion of the grid, rather than any turning away from that pattern. Towns such as Worcester or Providence are gridded where and to the extent possible.

The only real exception to this classification into two types of towns by street plan came where a simple road intersection in the countryside was subsequently struck with urbanization, causing the town to grow, logically, out along the roads intersecting there at acute angles. Even when the resulting pattern was one of a star-like branching of main streets, gridded infilling usually occurred between those major arterials. American towns constantly turned toward the egalitarian, economically productive bastidal layout wherever possible, even when the major skeleton of the town began as strand- or star-like.

The real character of the New England town was to be found in its vernacular architecture. This was shaped by culture and terrain, rather than by overall design of the city as in the Renaissance and Georgian "quarters." The house-forms developed in Salem and Providence were essentially rural frame houses, made fashionable by a bit of Renaissance decoration, placed within small gardens sufficient to allow this urbanization of basically bucolic architecture. A rough bastidal grid, as on Federal Hill in Providence or west of the Derby Wharf in Salem, was adequate for the placement of these structures in small yards that would permit the opening of all sides to the admission of light and air and the maintenance of a basically rural architecture.

In Boston, because of the expectation of greater growth on a small peninsular site, the architecture soon began to adapt a *closed-in building style.* The Paul Revere House of 1676 was a country house, showing some adaptation to the city with its blind side walls; the brick row-houses soon emerged to make better use of a confined site. Already in the 1630's we find the General Court of Massachusetts adopting legislation permitting the building of party-walls, a necessity for this sort of construction. The house in Boston evolved over the early history of the town, becoming truly urban in form. But the street system retained permanently its initial strand-line quality, however urbane the houses might become. In the same way the bastidal towns, much the more common sort in colonial times, still might maintain a rural-seeming style in the houses that lined their regularly gridded streets. A continuing interaction between houses and streets, in towns like Salem, Providence, and Newport, shaped a distinctive, organically evolving merchants' town as the model for New England.

The Emerging American Grid-pattern Town

The bastidal form that rose in New England, when nature permitted, must be understood in cultural terms. Although the Roman towns will not serve as the most basic prototype—little military and political domination characterized colonial Anglo-America as it had Rome's and Spain's empires—we still may cite the bastide as a form akin in purpose and layout to the planted towns of colonial America. The absence of open space for visual (as opposed to practical) purposes, the modular division of towns lots, the relatively egalitarian urban society and government, and the heavy economic dominance by trade all support the role of the bastide as the prototype for American town building. Particularly in New England, the historical similarities were heightened by a great tendency toward Protestantism and what Max Weber called "the Protestant ethic" in business practices, and the wish to advance the "commonwealth." These were religious congregations in the guise of New England "towns" but they were above all else economic places. Only a relatively small fraction of the population actually belonged to the Puritan "consociated" churches of "visible saints," but all residents seem to have shared the belief in the "Protestant ethic" of hard work, honest dealing, and personal enrichment as a sign of God's grace.

The role of port was so strongly the urbanizing force

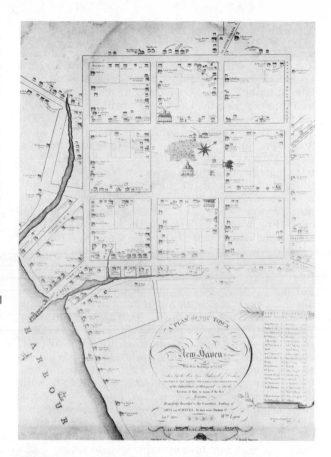

New Haven, as it was laid out in 1638, was a bastide in America with a distinctly isonomic land-assignment and an orthogonal plan. The map shows the modest development in 1748.

in New England that the strand-line alignment of streets was perhaps most common in the coastal towns. Boston, Newport, the earlier parts of Providence, and Strawberry Banke (Portsmouth, New Hampshire) display this pattern. The dockside was the point of initiation of the town; by 1645 Boston had fifteen wharves for its trade,[83] and had become the largest town in all the English colonies. New England was rich in organically patterned towns—Boston, Worcester, Fitchburg, Portsmouth, and Portland—or sections of towns—the older parts of Salem, Hartford, Providence, and Newport. The bastidal layout was even more common, particularly away from the coast—in Cam-

[83]*Bridenbaugh*, Cities in the Wilderness, *p. 23.*

bridge and Springfield—or as later increments to ports—in Salem, Providence, Newport, and even Boston. New Haven had stood a splendid example of the bastidal layout from its beginning in 1638.

Which pattern was to be adopted seems to have depended largely on (1) the presence or absence of a strand-line point of initiation, and (2) the availability of a relatively level site if an inland place. The houses dotted along these streets, of whatever pattern, were initially late medieval in form and wooden in construction. But as the material prosperity of the New England colonies advanced, and London was rebuilt into what became a Georgian city, the architecture of that reconstruction was adapted "in wood" for many port towns, notably Newburyport, Salem, and Providence.

The Development of Philadelphia

By the time William Penn and his neighbors in the Jerseys and recently captured New York were setting about town founding, the models had changed from those employed two generations before in New England. Because the pattern they adopted became so dominantly the one that was spread across a continent, as the American frontier advanced, the "London Rebuilt" model is worth describing in some detail.

Philadelphia was surveyed in 1682 and laid out as a town along the Delaware River, only to be expanded almost immediately, at Penn's order, to reach to the Schuylkill River to the west. Between the "Front Streets" at either river, a rank of twenty-two blocks was set out spreading for eight tiers north-south, or a total of 176 street-blocks in an area measuring one mile by two. One main street of one-hundred-foot width, then labeled High Street, though subsequently called Market, extended from river to river. Eleven blocks west of the Delaware, and eleven east of the Schuylkill, a north-south street of the same width, Broad Street (then as now), was run. The center of the town was at the crossing of these hundred-foot streets, which were twice as broad as the ordinary ways. "In the Center of the City is a Square of ten Acres; at each Angle (of that square) are to be Houses for Publick Affairs, as a Meeting-House, Assembly or State-House, Market-House, School-House, and several other Buildings for Publick Concerns. There are also in each Quarter of the City a Square of eight Acres, to be for the like Uses, as the Moore-fields in London; and eight Streets (besides the High-street), that run from Front to Front, and

twenty Streets (besides the Broad-street), that run across the City, from side to side; all these Streets are of Fifty Foot breadth."[84]

At first glance this layout might seem to be the adoption of a Renaissance visual city as the "American standard," but such an impression would be highly deceptive. Philadelphia was regular and proportional, and offered sites for public buildings. But from the number of "Houses for Publick Affairs" listed for siting around the main square, clearly they could be only fairly modest individually. The four other squares were specifically intended for public use, rather than restricted to access by householders living around them, as were the residential squares of London.

Moorfields had originally been a swampy area beyond the walls of the City of London where refuse was dumped throughout much of the late Middle Ages. When its surface rose to the point the land drained reasonably, the "moor-field" came to be used for bow shooting and other sports engaged in by the city populace. "The citizens (of London) acquired the right of prescription to the fields, although they were not by any means the property of the City." Yet by 1592 Parliament determined "That it shall not be lawful to any person or persons to inclose or take in any parte of the Common or Waste Groundes scituate lienge or beinge within thre(e) Myles of any of the Gates of the saide Cittie of London . . ." ['An Acte against newe buyldings,' 1592].[85]

So the squares of Philadelphia were for no different purpose than the Boston Common. That area had been set aside at the settlement of the town and guaranteed against further diminution in size four years later when the Town Meeting decided on March 30, 1640, that no further encroachment by gardens or buildings could be cut out of "the open ground or Common field."[86] The "squares" of Quaker Philadelphia were more regular but their purpose was that which had kept open ground available around medieval London, and had brought it at the heart of Boston a generation before. To read a great Renaissance "design" purpose into the squares of Philadelphia seems hardly justified by contemporary intentions.

Philadelphia's orderliness was that of a merchant seeking to rationalize his units of sale and make them of sufficiently standard form that purchases could be made sight unseen. Penn was anxious to sell lots to Englishmen never departed the island's shores, as well as to those migrating. His desire was greatly

[84]A Short Advertisement upon the Situation and Extent of the City of Philadelphia and the Ensuing Plat-form thereof, by the Surveyor General (London, 1683), quoted in Reps, op. cit., p. 161.

[85]Rasmussen, op. cit., pp. 81-82.

[86]Bridenbaugh, Cities in the Wilderness, p. 21.

aided by the standardization of house lots in the new town, whose plat he had largely decreed if not surveyed. In this concern for distant disposal of land, Penn was truly the father of the American speculative town, and the originator of a lineage of development quite distinct from that of the medieval bastide and the New England town. In those places, strong pressure was exerted or it was outright required that the landowner be a resident of the town where his land stood. Penn importuned his absentee landowners:

> *The Improvement of the place is best measur'd by the advance of Value upon every man's Lot. . . . And though it seems unequal that the Absent should be thus benefited by the Improvements of those that are upon the place, especially when they have serv'd no Office, run no hazard, nor as yet defray'd any Publick charge, yet this advantage does certainly redound to them, and whoever they are they are the great Debtors to the Country. . . .*[87]

Thus, the order and system of Philadelphia's layout was that of the merchant class addressing at a distance an investing class of capitalists, rather than, as in Boston, a merchant class seeking to found a New World mercantile system such as was carried by those coming across the ocean to set up in Massachusetts Bay. Such a difference most likely explains the contrast between the morphogenesis of the New England town—be it linear or bastidal—with its resident commonwealth, and that of Pennsylvania with its strong admixture of Quaker theology and Quaker capitalism. Theology was present in New England, but capitalism was somewhat muted in a society of more isonomic land-assignment, which clearly assumed that land was bestowed for and at the time of use, not as a speculative commodity, as in the Quaker town.

William Penn seems at first to have envisaged an open place when he decreed, "Let every house be pitched in the middle of its plot so that there may be ground on each side for gardens or orchards or fields, that it may be a green countrie towne that will never be burnt and always be wholesome."[88] But Philadelphia did not grow that way. As laid out, the blocks in the Quaker City measured usually 425 feet wide east-west and between 500 and 675 feet north-south, with the shorter blocks located adjacent to the High Street.[89] The lots seem to have been fairly small; those in the second block back from the Delaware River averaged around 48 feet in frontage, while those on the waterfront—which were to be used for warehouses—

were similarly around 100 feet in frontage. Along High Street, original frontages seem somewhat more ample, perhaps between 140 and 150 feet. Everywhere the sense given by the 1682 map of Philadelphia[90] is that of a town with fairly small lots and a great degree of standardization. At first the lots were the site of such modest structures that crowding was not great. But soon, "In older sections large three-storied brick houses and other buildings began to replace the 'mean and low' frame or brick structures of earlier years. A sign of overcrowding in these areas was the gradual appearance of tenement houses; in 1772 four of them were erected on Front Street and two on Second." The evidence is not extensive but subdivision of lots must have taken place, and certainly before long the row-house was introduced, filling the street frontage with a continuous facade of buildings. Land was increasing in value and Christopher Saur told in 1724 that, "House rent is high because the houses are all built of bricks . . . ."[91]

The Nature and Intent of the Philadelphia Model

All the faults of speculative town development in America during the three succeeding centuries cannot be blamed on William Penn and the plan he so earnestly fostered for Philadelphia. His plan had virtues, and many others have contributed less well-intentioned changes to the "Philadelphia model" of urbanization. Nonetheless, the fairly hardheaded developmental notions first advanced in the Quaker City were adopted enthusiastically and applied widely. Penn's writings do not omit even the notion of profiting from the development of a religious haven. He castigates Pennsylvania for what it has cost him, tending to disregard the fact that the sales of land there even in his lifetime were very considerable—over $100,000 alone for lands outside the city on a grant he secured in recompense for a debt of £16,000, a debt hardly likely to have fetched a full return if sought in money. This proprietorial colony was run from England, and characterized by the practice both of leasehold and the as-

---

[87]*William Penn*, A Further Account of the Province of Pennsylvania [*London: 1685*], *quoted in Reps, op. cit., p. 167.*
[88]*Quoted in Struthers Burt*, Philadelphia: Holy Experiment, *Garden City, N.Y.: Doubleday, Doran & Co., 1945, p. 37.*
[89]*Information contained in Reps, op. cit., p. 163 and fig. 97.*

[90]*This map*, A Portraiture of the City of Philadelphia in the Province of Pennsylvania in America, by Thomas Holme, Surveyor General, *is well reproduced in Reps as fig. 97.*
[91]*Bridenbaugh*, Cities in the Wilderness, *pp. 305-306.*

sessment of quit-rents. Whatever his philanthropic purposes, Penn also sought to enlarge his competence; in doing so, he devised a system of town founding that could be widely used by others who might have unalloyed interests save for gain. Again the contrast with New England is sharp. Philadelphia became a town of small lots with continuous ranks of houses, rather than the open, far more green, towns of New England Puritanism.

What then were the elements of the Philadelphia model? First, it permitted the rapid, simple, and determinate division of larger land holdings into small parcels which might be verbally described and sold to others. In New England, *land-utilization* seems to have been the main test of the forms of land-division; in Philadelphia, *land-sale* probably determined the form. Furthermore, land was raised to the status of a *commodity*, which might be standardized, precisely described, and reasonably appraised as to value from afar. That factor dominated the design. Quite unlike the situation in the medieval bastides, or their successors in Cambridge and elsewhere in New England, Philadelphia was a promoter's town, of a size completely different from the milieu in which it was set. When Boston and New York were tiny places half a mile across, Philadelphia was laid out 2 miles deep and a mile wide, a size not the least inferior to that of large

European cities, and twice that of the City of London. It is usually said that Philadelphia had its extensive form with the purpose of providing an open, healthy, and green town over an extensive area. Yet the scale of lots even in 1682, and certainly more apparently a few years later, suggests that the conservative consumption of economically valuable land was intended, as if it were clear in the Proprietor's mind that land was the main commodity on which he might hope to recoup his investment, and quite probably gain a vast enhancement of his fortune.

The basic layout of Philadelphia, and thereby the model based on that town's founding, had reasonably but not excessively wide streets. London reconstructed after the Fire had streets nearly as wide as those of Philadelphia. We must infer that William Penn's father, who was engaged in a speculation to bring wooden deals from Scotland to London to be sold in supply of the reconstruction,[92] knew all about that reconstruction. The committee established to determine the regulations for the rebuilding of London settled upon a series of street widths between 16 feet for alleys and 100 feet for the "high and principal streets," figures similar to the 50- and 100-foot widths in Philadelphia.[93] Although we cannot argue that Penn foresaw the continuous facades with uniform front lines that became typical of Philadelphia, he would have known

Philadelphia was laid out in 1681 on a plan that was probably the original speculator's design for an American city, a plot that measured one by two miles and was easily divided into lots that might be sold at a distance. Map is from 1682.

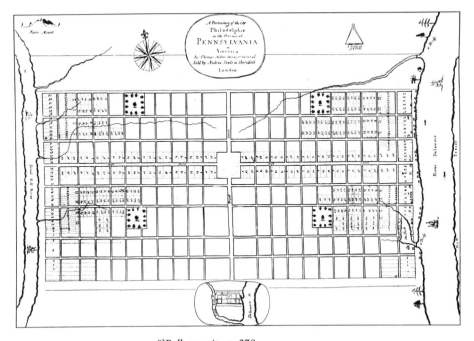

[92]*Bell, op. cit., p. 279.*
[93]*Rasmussen, op. cit., p. 119.*

what the reconstruction of England's metropolis had produced.

Houses rose singly, as landowners or tradesmen were able to find money [for rebuilding]. With here a finished building standing alone and next to it uncovered sites, the town for some years wore the appearance of a crazy patchwork; but the work was good. The houses keyed correctly one to another in continuous streets, precaution having been taken that all breast-summers should range of an equal height house to house, breaking only where ordered by the Surveyors. Roofs in the same way were made uniform.[94]

Certainly the scale of the lots in the New World metropolis seems more appropriate to this continuous band of houses than the detached house found in New World towns, where the lots were generally wider. As has been shown by the architectural historian William Murtagh, "The regularized facade which resulted [from the reconstruction of London] is startling close to the type of domestic architecture associated with colonial Philadelphia." Murtagh notes that both pre- and post-fire types of buildings were employed by settlers in Pennsylvania, but row-housing emerged less than a decade after foundation when, ca. 1691, Budd's Long Row was constructed on Front Street between Walnut and Dock streets. John F. Watson writing in 1830 had described these:

The houses of Budd's row, were all two stories, were first framed in heavy timber and filled with bricks the wood was, however, concealed and only showed the lintels or plate pieces over the windows and doors, which were covered with mouldings; the uprights for windows and doors were grooved into that cross timber, and looked like ordinary door and window frames.[95]

These houses were essentially medieval style, but their assembly into blocks was a harbinger of the modern city, quite likely founded on practices begun in earnest in London after the Fire. Workmen constructing these row-houses would probably have been trained in the construction of the past, but the landowners and surveyor were cognizant of the way the rebuilt City of London was being shaped. The key to Philadelphia's morphogenesis was not so much building technique as the plot and block assemblages that came to be the American "norm" founded on a "Philadelphia model," which was in truth the *London Rebuilt* model.

Penn had laid out a city of vast extent broken into super-blocks of long frontages. Soon those blocks were subdivided by cutting additional streets and narrowing the individual frontages. From the early colonial period, evidence survives of a merging of construction style and land-division; we know what was done but not exactly why it came about. The colonial houses of Philadelphia were "seldom more than sixteen feet on any dimension" and they might be assembled two to the initial lot, the one lying behind approached by an alleyway. "With the rapid growth of the city, the large blocks of Holmes' original plan were subdivided into smaller portions by secondary streets. The urban lot which resulted from further subdivision of these smaller blocks was the same narrow lot which also existed in England [sic] after the Fire." The lots were not merely narrow, but also quite deep. Murtagh found them four to five times as deep as wide in a random sample.[96] If we accept the value of around 16 feet as the construction module in these colonial houses, it is easy to understand why the 16-foot frontage became the modal figure for towns laid out on the Philadelphia model.

The tight packing of houses along street frontages came early in Philadelphia history, and stood quite in contrast to New England practices. Save for Boston, the Puritan towns still were characterized by houses of broader base, almost certainly detached and standing in a fairly ample garden, and constructed of wood. The medieval technology using heavy corner-posts with morticed beams let into them, with weather-boarding covering ("clapboards" in New England), was used in the northern colony well into the nineteenth century. Thus, it seems hard to believe that in an even better-timbered Delaware Valley, brick building was required by the shortage of readily and relatively cheaply available lumber. Instead, the speculative recourse to narrow lots seemingly made necessary brick building in order to avoid too rapidly recurrent fires.

Once such brick row-housing had evolved, the standard construction and layout of the city in the Middle Atlantic colonies (and subsequent states) was fixed. Ranging from New Brunswick and Trenton on the north to Philadelphia, Chester, Wilmington, Baltimore, and Georgetown on the south, the *row-house towns* were developed. Similar assemblages of houses on lots and street frontages were to be found in the Hudson Valley, along with some inheritance from Dutch city building, which was, as we saw in Amsterdam, equally dependent upon narrow lots built up in brick row-housing. But in the New Netherlands, brick building was probably carried on more from habit brought from Holland than from the absolute needs of fire protection and the utilization of narrow frontages introduced by land-speculation. In time, however, the

[94]*Bell, op. cit., p. 292.*

[95]*John F. Watson writing in 1830, quoted in William John Murtagh, "The Philadelphia Row House,"* Journal of the Society of Architectural Historians, *Vol. XVI, No. 4, p. 8 (Dec., 1957).*

[96]*Murtagh, op. cit., p. 9.*

speculative urge must have arrived, encouraging the use even on Manhattan of the Philadelphia (London Rebuilt) model of town layout for maximum land capitalization.

The English Renaissance in America: The Third Model

We have already noted the great problem southern proprietors experienced in creating towns within their colonies. The first real town built south of the Mason-Dixon line was located at the confluence of the Ashley and Cooper rivers in South Carolina where, in the reign of the second King Charles, a town was precisely laid out in his honor. Around the year 1672, Lord Anthony Ashley-Cooper, for the Carolina proprietors, instructed the governor of the colony to lay out a town on the peninsula between the two rivers. As at Philadelphia a few years later, this instruction was issued from afar by a land developer rather than by a group of planted settlers. The intention was to create a port through which goods could pass to and from the large landed estates being set out on the Carolina coastal plain. On those plantations the proprietors were attempting to establish a direct and highly self-conscious extension of feudal England under a plan whose social and political organization came from the reactionary pen of John Locke. Attempts were made to create a neofeudal class of "landgraves" and "caciques" supervising a serfdom of "leet-men" who would plow the fields and raise the crops that were to support a new rural aristocracy in leisure.

Fortunately much of this plan failed to come into being, but on its malign foundation grew the slavery for which South Carolina became the most ardent spokesman, and, as well, the political and social domination of the colony by a small rural oligarchy, which made true democracy unknown in this part of the South until the last few years. In this clearly eunomic society, land-assignment was made in the same spirit.

With such a rural domination, towns might never have emerged in the South without the need for import of luxuries for an increasingly wealthy rural "aristocracy" and export of the commercial crops of rice, indigo, and, later, cotton, which paid for such refinement to be brought from England. At first, Charleston was little needed when, "Prior to 1710 the produce of the [South Carolina] colony was considerably diversified, the principal exports being deerskins to England, and pork, corn, a few naval stores and lumber to Barbados."[97] But the provisioning trade for the West Indies could prove very profitable even in the early years. And the deerskin trade was of utmost importance until interrupted by the Yamassee War in 1715, which not only cut off the peltery but also threw many outlying settlers back upon the protection of Charleston. Despite these problems and fluctuations, the Carolinians were wealthy enough to import £150,000 worth of goods, largely from England, in 1718. And when the rice trade between the Carolinas and the West Indies began in earnest soon thereafter, the base was created for a port concerned with the shipment of a staple and the return of manufactures—usually in fair quantities if of a most basic material such as cloth, or in tiny lots for the luxuries of the planter class.[98]

Given the Lockean grand design for the Carolina society and the proprietorial quest for return on investment and privilege, a town must be built. On Ashley-Cooper's orders, Charleston was laid out:

> The Town is run out into four large streets. The Court house which we are now building is to be erected in the middle of it, in a Square of two ackers of land upon which the four great streets of 60 foot wide doe center, and to the water side there is laid out 60 foot for a publick wharfe as also for other conveniences as a Church yard, Artillery ground, etc., and without there is care taken that the front lines be preserved whereby wee shall avoid the undecent and incommodius irregularities which other Inglish Colonies are fallen unto for want of ane early care in laying out the Townes.[99]

Certainly this early Charleston was the germ of the "designed" city then gripping the aristocratic mind of England. But it was not the true speculator's town, such as Penn laid out a couple of years later, wherein a vast area out of all proportion to any as yet experienced demand in the New World was set out and made ready for sale. The Carolina proprietors seem to have had in mind a "Grand Modell" for the town but were never willing to make the investment it would require. Instead they urged orderly design upon the residents, and kept their own purses firmly closed. Only when the Carolina plantation economy began to burgeon could the exhortation be taken up in earnest and effected, by a native aristocracy who anxiously sought the approbation of the class in England from which the proprietors were drawn. Like that English oligarchy, they were forced into the city during a "Season," a periodic

[97]*Bridenbaugh*, Cities in the Wilderness, *p. 32.*
[98]Ibid., *pp. 177-178.*
[99]*Maurice Mathews in 1680, quoted in Reps, op. cit., p. 177.*

migration for which a new "Grand Modell" had grown up in London's West End.

Why must the Carolina planters repair to the city during a Season? The expansion of field cultivation in that province came first in dramatic terms through the production of rice to supply staple food to the sugar islands of the English and Dutch in the West Indies (and to Surinam). Given the hot, very humid summer climate of the Carolina coastal plain, malaria and other fevers were encouraged even further by the water-logged cultivation of rice; those of wealth and leisure, who might, sought to leave the plantation during the fever season, shaping a periodic social congregation at the better ventilated and somewhat drier town near the coast. The Charleston merchants, already trying to create a local-aristocrat caste, were aided by this seasonal influx of the planting aristocracy, the class most revered in the neofeudal society of South Carolina. The impact on city design is obvious: they sought to create a subtropical "West End" fronting on the Cooper River, with large houses built in a consistent pattern on sites which could clearly be ranked, as to precedence, by those carefully erecting the social pyramid Charleston society became. As so rarely occurs, the merchants' town lost out to the aristocrats, but only because the merchants wished to be included in that class.[100]

The shaping of the aristocratic quarter in London, Bristol, and other English county towns had created the layout and house design that architectural historians call "the English Renaissance" in its earlier phases and "Georgian" in its later. These quarters were quite consciously "designed," with careful determination of the accepted architecture, lot and street-frontage assembly, and overall form of the quarter. These morphological elements were impressed upon the city from above, rather than evolving through the actual functioning of the place. In this way the classic division between the merchants' town and that of the leisured class had to come about before the Renaissance design could be erected into a social necessity, which could be used as a measure of the worthiness for admission to status, class, and culture of a particular group. In London's West End, the system reached its most evolved form, taking on subdivisions probably found nowhere else. But as the American South developed (with its all-too-conscious effort to borrow distinction through emulation of the English gentry), *the morphology of social acceptance* was ready to hand. The transformation of Charleston, particularly in the one hundred and fifty years between the Yamassee War (1715) and the Civil War, demonstrates how social striving could shape a city. The number of examples

that we might find in England—Brighton, Bath, Buxton, Eastbourne, Harrowgate, and Cheltenham to name only the more obvious—is great but, to America's more egalitarian good fortune, the number there was far smaller.

The English Renaissance town in colonial times was probably the only form taken by these *towns of emulation;* later in our history, others arose such as the "shingle style" house of Newport, Narrangansett Pier, Bar Harbor and Pasadena, which created a new architectural expression of the social striving. But we shall examine the English Renaissance town of the colonial South. In that era and region, four towns must be noted as conforming most strongly with *English Renaissance* model—the two Chesapeake Bay capitals, Annapolis and Williamsburg, and the two South Atlantic neofeudal "towns," Charleston and Savannah.

In the history of Virginia and Maryland many efforts were made to found towns during the first half century or so of settlement, most of which proved stillborn and all of which were stunted. Jamestown, the oldest English settlement in the Thirteen Colonies, was certainly one of the feebler. In 1662 orders from England sought to make the town more presentable as the capital of a colony already half a century under development. An "Act for building a towne" was passed and Jamestown was ordered to be so recast:

> *That the towne to be built shall consist of thirty two houses, each house to be built with brick, forty feet long, twenty foot wide, within the walls, to be eighteen foote high above the ground, the walls to be two brick thick to the water table, and a brick and a halfe thick above the water table to the roofe, the roofe to be fifteen foote pitch and to be covered with slate or tile.*

> *That the houses shall be all regularly placed one by another in a square or such other forme as the honorable Sir William Berkeley [the governor] shall appoint most convenient.*[101]

The individual Virginia counties were each expected to build one of the Jamestown houses, and all sorts of subventions and exertions were envisaged to accomplish the creation of a proper provincial capital. But in 1676 the embittered small-holders of Bacon's Rebellion burned Jamestown to the ground, putting an end to a notoriously unsuccessful experiment at town founding. When Bacon's forces were defeated after their captain's untimely death, Governor Berkeley viciously hanged thirty-seven of their leaders, causing that none-too-timid monarch Charles II to comment, "That old fool has hanged more men in that naked country

[100]Bridenbaugh, Cities in the Wilderness, *p. 417.*

[101]*William Henning,* The Statutes at Large . . . of Virginia, *New York, 1832, Vol. II, p. 172, quoted in Reps, op. cit., p. 93.*

than I have done for the murder [sic] of my father."[102]

This grim farce had only one fortunate consequence—the final destruction of Jamestown which, in its seventy years of trying to be a town, had been uncomfortable, unhealthy, and notoriously ungrowing. In its place, a new capital would have to be laid out; that job was done by Berkeley's more astute and intelligent successor, Francis Nicholson, who had just completed a similar job for Maryland where previously he had served as governor.

When Nicholson became governor of Maryland in 1694, he had behind him a considerable knowledge of the fashionable quarters of London (he is believed to have been the natural son of the Duke of Bolton) and of Paris (where he went frequently as a diplomatic courier). Arriving in Maryland, he secured passage of legislation establishing two new towns, one of which was named originally for Lord Baltimore's wife, Ann Arundel, but was subsequently named instead for Princess Anne, soon to reign in her own right. Annapolis, the new town, became the provincial seat, and Nicholson assured that its design would befit the capital of an aristocratic province of landed manors.

The plan of the town may well have been Nicholson's; we do know that he superintended the construction of a town with two massive "circles" and a "Bloomsbury Square" of 350 feet on a side. The "Public Circle" was over 500 feet in diameter and soon became the site of the provincial capitol, while the "Church Circle" was one of about 300 feet. Streets radiated from these circles, though Reps points out that they did not always line up with the center of the circle, assuring the visually impressive focus so desired by Renaissance planners. Nonetheless, the town of Annapolis was an obviously visual construction, set out to impress with its plan and to assert a haughty dominance of those entering from the countryside. The place was small compared to Philadelphia, about 25 rather than 176 blocks within the initial design; some blocks were quite small in contrast to the super-blocks of the Quaker City. The town plat was about 3000 feet by 2500 feet, little more than a quarter of a square mile, in the face of the 2 square miles of Penn's capital. The lots were large in Annapolis—outside the nine unnumbered lots ranged round Bloomsbury Square, only 108 numbered lots were included in the original layout.[103]

Clearly Lord Baltimore's capital was more a town for the gentry than one to meet the vast expectations of

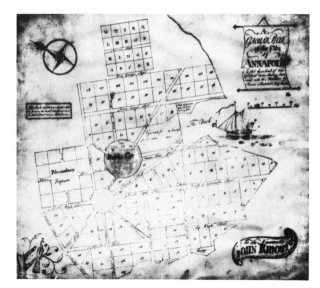

This eighteenth-century map shows the complex orthogonal design of Annapolis as it was laid out in 1695. The large size of the lots and the clearly "neo-renaissance" layout of streets demonstrate the eunomic quality of this plan and its land assignment.

the merchant class. A Maryland law of 1695 had specified "that when any baker, brewer, tailor, dyer, or any such tradesmen, that, by their practice of their trade, may any ways annoy, or disquiet the neighbors or inhabitants of the town, it shall and may be lawful for the commissioners and trustees . . .to allot and appoint such tradesmen such part or parcel of land, out of the present town pasture, as . . . shall seem meet and convenient for the exercise of such trade, a sufficient distance from the said town as may not be annoyance thereto . . . ."[104] The adoption of such a provision would have been most unlikely in Massachusetts, and its implementation (as was the case in Annapolis), highly unthinkable. But the Maryland capital, as a town of social collection and emulation, must be, as was Georgian London's West End, sheltered from the merchant's world. The plan, the background of the designer, and the early history of Annapolis all support

[102]S. E. Morison and H. S. Commager, The Growth of the American Republic, New York: Oxford University Press, 1942, Vol. I, p. 80.

[103]These computations are taken from the "Plan of Annapolis, Maryland: 1718" given in Reps, op. cit., as fig. 62.

[104]"An Act for Keeping Good Rules and Orders in the Port of Annapolis," quoted in Reps, op. cit., p. 106.

the view that the town was set out in the English Renaissance style for the housing of the socially elevated.

Before the layout of Annapolis was completed, Francis Nicholson was appointed governor of Virginia. With Jamestown (or what had not already rotted away from neglect of an initially misplaced town) largely destroyed by the firebrands of the rebelling farmers, he could plan a second capital, at Williamsburg, near the college he had earlier aided in founding. Nicholson persuaded the legislature to place its new capital at Middle Plantation between the James and York rivers on a site with a design on which he almost certainly exerted the dominant influence. Two impressive buildings—the Capitol and the Governor's Palace—were set at the end of open vistas, the first at the eastern closing of Duke of Gloucester Street, 99 feet wide, and the second at the north end of the Palace Green, 200 feet wide and about 1,000 feet long. Houses fronting on Duke of Gloucester Street were to be uniform in facade and impressive in design.

Throughout the description of the town (in the specifications of the act creating the capital and in contemporary accounts) runs the desire to make this as strutting a place as its small numbers of inhabitants would permit. It was to be a government town, laid out to serve that purpose, and intended only for the social class that had much voice in the running of a proprietorial province before the American Revolution. Thus, not insignificantly, in 1779 (while the war was still going on) the Commonwealth of Virginia deliberately abandoned Williamsburg in favor of Richmond. In part, this move was the result of the shift of the economic heart of Virginia westward into the Piedmont, but it was as well a turning away from the town so ostentatiously the seat of an arrogant king's haughty lieutenant. Richmond grew rapidly and in much more characteristic clothing for an American city—in the working attire of the merchants' town, where the government met only occasionally and not for too long.

The final English Renaissance town in the South was Savannah, which grew up to support the cotton kingdom that emerged after Eli Whitney's invention, in that city, of the cotton gin. Savannah did not begin in the form of a trader's town but rather as an English Renaissance place to serve a social experiment. James Oglethorpe sought to salvage the debtor class from the barbaric practices of eighteenth-century England by combining humanity with defense of the realm and expansion of the settlement frontier. Resettling debtors would take them out of English prisons, provide a market for English goods and a source for staples for English manufacture, and defend rich Carolina from the Spaniards of Florida. "In June 1732, King George II, convinced that the new colony would be good politics as well as good works, granted the vacant lands south

of Carolina to twenty-one Trustees for twenty-one years and modestly gave it the benefit of his name, Georgia."[105]

An enthusiastic effort was made to shape a new society through the imposition of a utopian morphology: six "wards" of the town were confidently expected to be needed as the colony grew. Savannah's wards were an intellectual creation distinctly different from the design of the speculator's Philadelphia. The ward as adopted was some 600 feet on a side, little larger than Penn's original super-blocks, and divided sensibly into four residential blocks of 300-foot length, called "tythings," whose depth of slightly more than 200 feet was, in turn, divided by an alleyway of 22.5 feet. Between the two ranks of two blocks bounding the ward, a square was delimited at its ends by four small blocks ultimately intended as the sites for public buildings. This assemblage of the ward was square in outer form, with straight streets; great care was given to the creation of vistas. This was the first expression of an effort that became common in nineteenth-century America —the use of a strongly physically-deterministic model to "improve" the social condition of man. Clearly Georgia was the first American instance of "social refuge and reform," as opposed to religious congregation.

The houses of Savannah were small clapboard affairs not appreciably different from the simpler houses of the West Indies. The great planters' houses from those islands, which had been copied in the impressive mansions on Charleston's Battery, were originally absent from her southern neighbor. Savannah was characterized as "an agglomeration of rural hamlets" as originally laid out, but when the rise of Savannah as the premier cotton port brought wealth, similar mansions were built and Savannah in turn became a place of summer refuge and social congregation for the inland planters. As such, the port remained an island of the English Renaissance in an otherwise mercantile America until it began to decline in the years following the Civil War. When mercantile activity came strongly to Georgia, it grew along the rail lines, notably in Atlanta, which was set up at the terminus of the Western and Atlantic and clothed in the garments of a proper speculator's town, copying Philadelphia rather than London's West End.

[105]*Ships of the Sea Museum, Savannah*, Savannah Revisited: A Pictorial History, *Athens: University of Georgia Press, 1969, p. 6.*

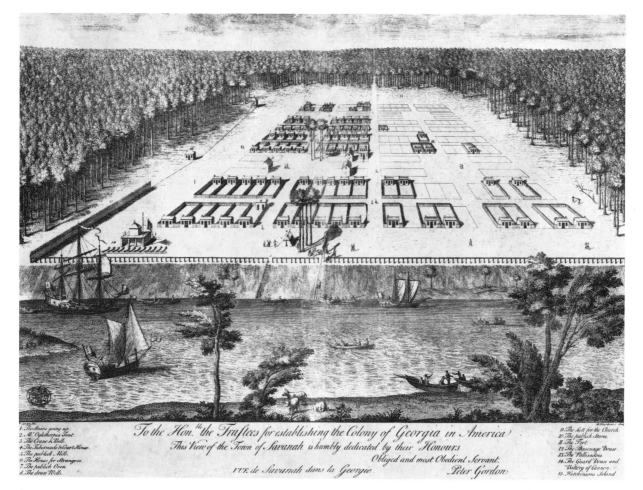

To the Hon.ble the Truftees for establishing the Colony of Georgia in America · This View of the Town of Savanah is humbly dedicated by their Honours Obliged and most Obedient Servant, rue de Savanah dans la Georgie Peter Gordon.

1. The Stairs going up.
2. Mr. Oglethorpes Tent.
3. The Crane & Bell.
4. The Tabernacle & Court House.
5. The publick Mill.
6. The House for Strangers.
7. The publick Oven.
8. The draw Well.
9. The Lott for the Church.
10. The publick Stores.
11. The Fort.
12. The Personage House.
13. The Pallisadoes.
14. The Guard House and Battery of Cannon.
15. Hutchinsons Island.

Savannah, shown in this 1734 view, was in the process of foundation on an elaborate plan comprised of wards, of which four had then been laid out. As the city evolved, it became the most eunomic in its land-assignment of any American city.

A Useful Model for American Cities

Three broad models were used for the creation of towns in the Thirteen Colonies. The earliest used was the late-medieval, pre-Fire London and provincial-English-town model adopted in New England. These places were economic towns but free in America of most of the trappings of class to be found in England. In physical form they owed a great deal to the bastide, having on reasonably level sites a forthright rectangularity, or on more broken locations greater linearity in alignment with the terrain. What distinguished either physical expression was the *isonomic land-assignment*, relatively small, reasonably equivalent-sized lots adequate for a family residence and workshop but not showing any "reserve" for speculative purposes. Like the bastides, these were cities of workmen at work rather than plattings of open land in search of urbanization and speculative profit.

In social terms, the bastidal nature of the New England town became the useful, and employed, model for American urbanization. But as a physical form, the New England town was laid aside beyond the Connecticut valley, even by those migrants to upstate New York, the Western Reserve of Ohio, and the upper-lakes states who took in their emigrants' wagons the concept of the biblical commonwealth represented by Massachusetts and her daughters.

The physical pattern for the American city had to be found among the other two models brought from England: the English Renaissance model used in the few large towns which grew up in the South, and the London-Rebuilt model used in the mercantile quarters after the fire of 1666. In the New World, the rebuilt-form of London could be made regular and expressed in a true grid-pattern, looking more like the "perfect" bastides than did Cambridge, New Haven, and the other New England towns shaped in their image. The form was true in Philadelphia but not the social structuring. As a speculator's town the Quaker City lacked the fundamentally isonomic land-assignment that had characterized the bastide, and became the backstay of the New England biblical commonwealth.

The great mass of urbanization took place in America west of the Appalachians. The first trans-Appalachian towns were Lexington and Louisville (1779), Pittsburgh (1784), Marietta (1788), and Cincinnati (1790), and in them a particular pattern became fixed, that of Philadelphia, or London-Rebuilt. In Pittsburgh, the Penn heirs copied William's speculator's town laid down first in Philadelphia. This town was rectilinear with relatively small blocks, narrow and equal size lots, and with only a single public square. Its regularity was despite a most constrained site at the confluence of the Allegheny and Monongahela Rivers, where the Ohio begins, and within a deeply incised valley. The original plat[106] had ninety-four blocks, but only one open space was left; even the spectacular riverbanks were given no visual design. So much for the Penns' alleged passion for baroque design. Just as Philadelphia, its several squares notwithstanding, had less open space than

"late-medieval" Boston, Pittsburgh had less open space than Louisville.

Louisville was laid out by settlers rather than speculators and, like the bastides, showed a craving for isonomic order and proportion. The first meeting of the prospective residents, held in April 1779, ordered

. . .that a number of lots, not exceeding 200 for the present, be laid off, to contain half an acre each, 35 yards by 70 where the ground will admit of it, with some public lots and streets.

That each adventurer draw for only one lot by chance. That every such person be obliged to clear off the undergrowth and begin to cultivate part thereof by the 10th of June (1779), and build thereon a good covered house, 16 feet by 20, by the 25th of December. That no person sell his lot unless to some person without one, but that it be given up to the Trustees to dispose of to some new adventurer on pain of forfeiture thereof.[107]

Unlike the Penns' towns, Louisville was not a speculator's town, yet its design was nearly the same. The Kentucky town showed strikingly the two components that were coming to make up the American model of urbanization: (1) a regular grid of small lots and moderate size blocks, easily described, occupied, and transferred (useful to speculator and occupant alike), and (2) an urban society given to isonomic land-assignment and the generally liberal social, economic, and political practices characteristic of the medieval bastide.

Louisville's physical form is contained in a plan drawn in 1779, showing twenty-one blocks of house lots and twenty-one parcels of fairly equivalent size, noted as public. Seemingly the settler's bastide could be more liberal in its provisions for the future than was the land speculator's, however grand his stated or imputed motives. The emerging town of Louisville tended toward the lesser standards of the marketplace but let us not confuse the relative initial generosity of popular and proprietorial intentions on this matter.

Cincinnati serves to clinch the argument for an American norm—the amalgam of bastide, London Rebuilt, and speculator's town. Dr. Daniel Drake, frequently called "the Benjamin Franklin of the West," set out in 1815 to present a *Natural and Statistical View, or Picture of Cincinnati and the Miami Country*. In the forthright manner of his mentors, Franklin and Dr. Benjamin Rush, Drake establishes the tie:

Philadelphia seems to have been the model after which the portion of this town first laid out, was planned. Be-

[106]*Figure 121, in Reps, op. cit., reproduces a plan of Pittsburgh for 1787, which is the one determined some three years earlier by the Penns.*

[107]*Quoted from original minutes of the meeting in Reuben T. Durrett,* The Centenary of Louisville, *Filson Club, Publication No. 8, Louisville, 1893, p. 34.*

tween Broadway and Western Row there are six streets, each 66 feet wide, running from the river north 16° west, and lying 396 feet asunder. These are intersected at right angles by others of the same width, and at the same distance from each other; except Water and Front streets, and Second and Third streets, the former of which are nearer, and the latter, on account of the brow of the Hill, more distant. Not a single alley, court, or diagonal street, and but one common, was laid out. The blocks or squares were each divided into eight, lots 99 by 198 feet, except those lying between Second and Third streets, which were made ten lots each. . . .[108]

Although these lots originally sold for $100 each, by 1814 "the lots in Main, from Front to Third streets, have sold at $200 per [front] foot . . . ." On a 99-foot lot, such a speculator's gain would indeed serve to increase the capital of the original owners and argue for the virtues, in a capital-deficient nation, of town speculation as a national economic endeavor.[109]

The role of such speculations in city life is well shown by Cincinnati's history as an administrative town. First bruited in 1789, the town began its existence during the nineties. It gained the palm of a true "city" by being constituted a county seat and the site of a courthouse, built on the waterfront Common in 1802. When the courthouse burned in 1814, the county commissioners decided to move the building site nearer to the heart of the emerging town and, in turn, "sold out, on perpetual lease, the whole of the public ground." The little public space included in the original plan was thereby lost.[110] The town, like most in the Middle Atlantic states, was possessed of market houses—"the two older are supported by a double, the newer by a triple, row of brick pillars"—which somewhat made up for the absence of public space. They showed as well how much the growth of the surrounding countryside sprang from the existence of the town. Cincinnati prospered as a distant-trading town, as was clearly shown by its most impressive building in 1815:

The most capacious, elevated and permanent building in this place, is the Steam Mill, erected in the years 1812,

'13, and '14, under the direction of William Green, an ingenious mason and stone cutter, on a plan furnished by George Evans, one of the proprietors [of this rental property]. . . .Its height is 110 feet, and the number of stories is nine, including two above the eaves. . . .Through the building there is a wall dividing each story into two unequal apartments—the one designed for manufacturing flour; the other for receiving wool and cotton machinery, a flax seed oil mill, fulling mill, and and several other machines.[111]

As the agricultural economy of southern Ohio quickly matured from clearing the forest to exporting its field products, the need for processing before shipment was obvious in a nation where transportation was primitive and costly. Cincinnati fulfilled that processing role, and took on a form that was to be repeated westward to the edge of the vast Middle West agricultural realm and in favored economic spots all the way to the Pacific. Lest there be any question as to which came first, the town of Cincinnati or the countryside that supplied its raw materials, we may wisely return directly to Daniel Drake who had observed the truth at the time the town began.

As this town is older than the surrounding country, it has at no time had a surplus of laboring population or of capital. The former have been required to assist in clearing and improving the wilderness; the latter has been invested in lands, which from their low price and certain rise, have held out for the capitalists a powerful inducement. The conditions which are said to constitute the basis of manufacturing establishments, have not, therefore, existed in the same degree as if the town had been younger than the adjoining country.[112]

Thus we see in Cincinnati the true nature of the town as it became a general form in the growth of the American republic. After a colonial period, when three main urbanization models were adopted (along with a fourth if we accept as a model the absence of towns found for so long in the Chesapeake Bay area before government efforts finally bore a sickly but showy fruit in Annapolis and Williamsburg), the pioneers knew what the appropriate model for settlement should be. Many of them, such as Daniel Drake's father Isaac were crossing the Appalachians just before the Constitutional Convention to settle in Kentucky in 1788, thus entering the first "West."

That model was the speculator's town drawn largely in morphogenesis from Penn's Philadelphia but fortunately shorn of the late medieval trappings of rural feudal tenure that never quite disappeared in the

[108]Daniel Drake, Natural and Statistical View, or Picture of Cincinnati and the Miami Country. Illustrated by Maps. With an Appendix Containing Observations on the Late [New Madrid] Earthquake, The Aurora Borealis, and Southwest Wind, Cincinnati: Looker and Wallace, 1815. Extensive portions of this rare book are reprinted in Henry D. Shapiro and Zane L. Miller, eds., Physician to the West: Selected Writings of Daniel Drake on Science and Society, Lexington: The University Press of Kentucky, 1970, pp. 66-129. Quotation is from p. 80.
[109]Ibid., pp. 81-82.
[110]Ibid., p. 84.

[111]Ibid., p. 86.
[112]Ibid., p. 88.

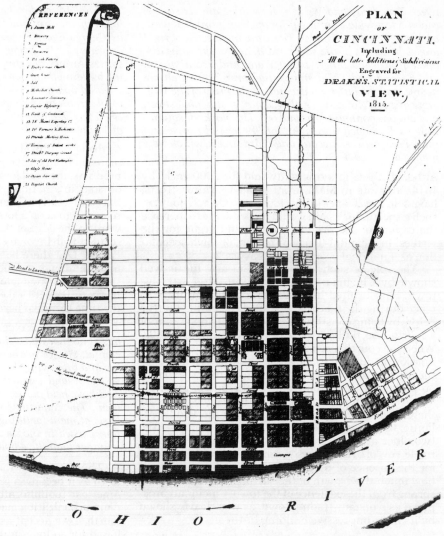

Cincinnati, as sketched in Drake's Statistical View of 1815, was a recently established speculator's town with the rigid and fine-grained orthogonal qualities that role assumed in the American Middle West.

Keystone State. The role of speculation so castigated today was perhaps the most hopeful tool they carried in their wagons, or on the riverboats such as Isaac Drake used to reach the West. The rise out of frontier poverty was made more rapid by the hoped-for increment of pioneering, which was the speculator's profit. But in this American model the actual settlers most commonly gained, as Louisville's first town ordinances sought to assure, rather than the distant and leisured landowners who had emerged as the social elite at the end of the Middle Ages. Their efforts to shape America as a New World extension of that rural class system of Britain and France were largely failures. Québec struggled to little avail; the middle colonies leaned too

heavily on the land and the undesirable social stratification found to be required in the pioneer plantations; and the towns of the South sought to reproduce an economic social system truly foreign to the emerging society and economy of the Great Republic.

In the end, a combination of New England social and economic institutions and the speculative practices initiated in the wealthy proprietors' towns of New Jersey, Pennsylvania, and Maryland was carried westward. Daniel Drake did not comment on that social and economic synthesis, probably because his father was moving westward to get away from just such an area developed for speculators from the English gentry. Isaac Drake left Plainfield, New Jersey, because as

Daniel said, "My father and his brothers were not contended [sic] with their position,"[113] which was that of landless younger sons. The father sought improvement in the countryside but his son, Daniel, could see how much more hopeful was the future in the town. As he tells it, "I was in a stage of transition from one state to another; from the rural to the civic, from the rude to the refined, from obscurity to noteriety! . . .The conception of this change was less my own than my father's. . . .His poverty he regreted; his ignorance he deplored. . . .In consulting the traditions of the family he found no higher condition than his own as their lot in past times; but he had formed a conception of something *more* elevated, and resolved on its attainment; not for himself and [my] mother, not for *all* his children—either would have been impossible—but for some member of the family. He would make a beginning; he would set his face toward the land of promise, although, like Moses, he should never enter it."[114]

To gain his end, Isaac Drake, "On a cold, damp and dreary day of December 1800 [took] fifteen year old Daniel Drake, a timid, home-loving country boy from Kentucky . . .to the home of the leading physician in Cincinnati, Ohio," to be apprenticed to a trade and to come to enjoy the fruits for which he had fought during the Revolution and which had drawn him to the frontier, but not to his hoped-for security that would permit a reasonable level of life and learning.[115] Only in the city could true social mobility, with its premium of education and the broader view, be secured in this time on the frontier. Thus, we may close our consideration of the planting of the city in the American lands on this note of hopefulness that the city engendered in the minds of our ancestors, in this case in the person of my own distant grandfather, Isaac Drake. For them, the accomplishment of the general promise betokened by the physical generosity of the New World came in the social and intellectual advance to be had only in the cities of the Great Republic in the years before they became industrial metropolises.

The onset of the Industrial Revolution, which we take up in the chapter, came first in rural areas well supplied with water power and those older cities well served by water-borne transportation. Liège, the capital of the Prince Bishops shown in this early nineteenth-century engraving, was first served on the Meuse River by small sailing vessels (such as those shown at the left), but soon after 1800 steamboats (as at the right) came to provide for the greater demands of an industrial society.

[113]*Daniel Drake*, Pioneer Life in Kentucky, A Series of Reminiscential Letters, *Ohio Valley Historical Series, No. Six, Cincinnati: The Robert Clarke & Co., 1870, p. 6. Reprinted with extensive comments by E. F. Horine, New York: Henry Schuman, 1948.*
[114]Ibid. [*Horine edition*], p. 110.
[115]*Horine, op. cit., p. xiii.*

MANCHESTER
AND
SALFORD.
WITH THE ADJACENT PARTS,
SHEWING ALSO
THE DIFFERENT ALLOTMENTS of LAND
PROPOSED TO BE BUILT ON.
AS
communicated to the Surveyor by the respective Proprietors.

By C LAURENT, Engineer.

MANCHESTER and SALFORD

Published for L Pigg by C Laurent, Geographer.

A Plan of MANCHESTER and SALFORD taken about 1650.

A Map of the

7. THE REVOLUTION OF ECONOMY AND EVOLUTION OF THE CITY: URBAN MORPHOGENESIS IN THE INDUSTRIAL AGE

Although the city has changed greatly in the last two hundred years, we should not forget that human culture is characterized by evolution more than revolution; human adaptation is generally less violently cyclical than that of an economy. The Industrial Revolution was a reality of the economy; due to mankind's more balanced course, the events ensuing in urban morphogenesis were rather more evolutionary, depending more heavily on the structure and culture of cities prior to industrialization than is often appreciated. Thus, to the extent that cities are comprised of economic institutions and systems, the change was so radical as to be virtually revolutionary; to the extent that cities are physical, social, and cultural entities, the change was evolutionary. Contrasting processes of change divide economic from social and cultural events.

Not only a change in economic conditions shaped the Industrial Era and the city which became its most obvious manifestation. Above all else, the change in scale of economic activity transformed the shape of the western world. The change in scale was both absolute and "geographical"—absolute in the sense that the totality of productive and trading activity increased rapidly, geographical in the sense that Adam Smith used the term to reflect a geographical specialization of labor.

The argument as to when the Industrial Revolution began has been extensive and long-continued. Between 1760 and 1785, the production of coal and the consumption of raw cotton in Britain expanded remarkably, indicating the rise of industrialization and of the effort to gain some degree of geographical freedom in the location of industry. The development of the steam engine by Mathew Boulton and James Watt, starting from their partnership commenced in 1775, was perhaps the most signal event of the Industrial Revolution from a geographical viewpoint, for it allowed the siting of factories in response to factor endowments other than waterpower. For our purposes we may logically date the "revolution" from that time.

As Jérôme-Adolphe Blanqui, who first proposed the term in his *Histoire de l'Economie Politique* published in 1837, said: "The end of the eighteenth century was distinguished [in England] by wonderful discoveries, destined to change the face of the world . . . .The conditions of labor underwent the greatest modification they have experienced since the origin of society." The change was particularly in the application of powered machinery to the manufacturing process. The result was that "hardly was the industrial revolution born from the brain of those two men of genius, Watt and [Richard] Arkwright [who improved spinning techniques], when it took possession of England. . . . No age has seen such economic revolutions accomplished in so

little time, and it is not surprising that such unusual changes should have disconcerted all [previous] systems."[1]

The system most disconcerted was that associated with the balance and order of the medieval city. During the previous age, economic activity had been administrated in such detail that privileges of production and sale were carefully laid out, through charter provisions granted to a gild or a town. Similarly, the feudal rights associated with rural production and consumption enforced a like constraint on collection, production, or trading in one or a few places. In a time when government and church were supported by various localized exactions—excises and tithes in particular—geographical concentration was resisted by those with a sufficient power to enforce their will and to defend their geographical monopoly.

In his highly personal view in *Cultural Foundations of Industrial Civilization*, John U. Nef argued that the industrial transformation began much earlier, probably at the very end of the Middle Ages when, notably in France, the royal court encouraged the establishment of factories for the production of goods in an orderly and supervised manufacture. But these factories were given over to the productions of tapestries and porcelains for an aristocratic market. This was a factory economy, but in no sense an *economy of scale*, which had to await the advent of English industrialization. In the island kingdom, the Renaissance had had little development; the large increase in the production of goods by traditional hand methods began the "industrialization" that had reached radical proportions by the time Blanqui describes.

The creation of the French factories led to great involvement of the crown in the nascent industrialization, which accounts as much as anything for the aristocratic market intended for the *articles de Paris*. While this court influence was going on in France, "In England the effectiveness of the economic regulations of the Crown and of its participation in manufactures diminished. At the same time the royal revenue which had increased notably under Henry VII and Henry VIII, hardly grew at all in terms of capital purchasing power during the reigns of Elizabeth I, James I and Charles I. Meanwhile the real revenue of the French crown had at least doubled."[2] The increase in absolutism and the continuing role of the church in economic affairs in France stood in contrast to England, where Henry VIII's confiscation had created a much more flexible

[1] *Jérôme Adolphe Blanqui*, History of Political Economy in Europe, *New York: G. P. Putnam's Sons, 1880, pp. 430–433. This is a translation of the 1837 French edition.*
[2] *John U. Nef*, Cultural Foundations of Industrial Civilization, *New York: Harper & Brothers, 1960, pp. 40–42.*

and adaptable scene for economic change. Thus Britain was a much more likely site for the first campaigns of the Industrial Revolution.

England was the first nation to expand her coal production to any degree, and the first to replace the use of wood and charcoal as fuels for home heating and the smelting of iron. At Coalbrookdale in Shropshire in 1735, Abraham Darby managed to produce iron successfully with a coke (coal) charge along with his iron ores. The outcome was both rapid and highly dynamic. "The significance for industrialism of the changing nature of iron metallurgy in the north of Europe did not consist mainly in the movement towards larger iron-making establishments. It consisted rather in the orientation of iron-making away from products wanted primarily for their beauty and durability, in the direction of products wanted for their utility."

In the Middle Ages iron had been produced by repeated heatings and hammerings of the ores themselves; thus very rich ore was required to produce iron with a reasonable amount of labor. Furthermore, that forging process produced a considerable waste along with the wrought iron. With the introduction of smelting in a furnace with a coke fuel charge, cheaper, leaner ores might be used. Germany and Sweden possessed rich ores while Britain had only much leaner ones. Thus the coke smelting process was a greater boon to England than to the medieval iron producers.

Cheaper iron meant that iron could be used for products other than those mainly for the wealthy. "By the mid-seventeenth century, partly as a result of the growing use of cast and pig iron and coal, England had obtained a lead over all other countries in the production of common commodities, in which quantity and utility rather than quality and elegance were the main concerns of the makers and the consumers."[3]

Production for the common people as a road to wealth came as a novel idea. Throughout classical and medieval times, a strong attitude of elitism in craftsmanship held that the desirable objective was to improve the quality of products, to make them literally works of art, with normal occupations being considered arts. The logic of that view is rather strong: since manufacture was by hand, each item could differ from the previous one based entirely on the increasing skill of the workman. In such a situation, "freezing" production at a particular level of skill would have been undesirable, as the workman would then set his "wage" at that level and forgo further "raises." Under hand operation, he was less likely to expand his volume of production than his quality. Thus, by recovering the increasing value of skill through enhanced prices for his work, he would maximize his income.

Machine manufacture operates differently. The level of "skill" must be frozen in setting up the machines. That level may not be too high, or, in many cases, recovery of the increased cost of machines by higher prices for the goods would prove difficult. Machine production could increase its return only in two intimately related ways: (1) by expanding the potential market for the particular good by producing it at a cost far below that possible to the handworker, and (2) by maintaining the price level for the product at such a figure that a mass market would be secured. Finally, in machine production recovery of costs of production on the sale of only a few items was totally impossible. The modern aircraft industry has shown to the English and French the grinding truth of that fact.

The machine was the logical instrument of what John Nef called "a quantitative economy." The search for a quantitative economy led first at the end of the sixteenth century to "a new and extensive use of cast and pig iron and coal fuel."[4] At first, coal was used mainly for heating. After Darby's experiments, it became the backstay of the iron industry and the true motive force of the quantitative economy that grew out of the Industrial Revolution. The shaping of that quantitative economy brought on two distinctive geographical conditions so central to the shaping of the modern world that they must be considered fully.

Concentration of Production

The first geographical product of the quantitative economy was the collection of manufacture into one or a few sites in sharp distinction to the normal wide spread of craftsmen making similar items during the Middle Ages. Initially much of the quantitative production took place in the countryside—in Europe commonly to avoid the legal strictures imposed through the gild system of earlier times (whose realm of control was particularly the towns) and in America because of the heavy dependence upon waterpower.

Two different stages of industrialization are involved: in Britain the movement of quantitative production into the countryside came already before any extensive application of power to the operations. The number of partially idle hands in rural areas as well as their standing outside any gild system drove the early

[3]Ibid., pp. 50–53.

[4]Ibid., p. 50.

"factors" to set up their organized and relatively standardized production in a series of farm workers' cottages. There, wives and children, and the agricultural workers themselves in quiet periods in the tillage, would produce pins or nails or other simple fabricates. An individual, the factor, was the organizer of this trade, bringing simple iron sheets or wire to the cottage and collecting at the end of the week the nails and pins produced in rural domestic "industry." Adam Smith left us a detailed account of these activities[5] in which he shows how the concentration of production of simple items easily subject to mass selling can be evolved into mass production.

The evolution of the quantitative economy is well shown in the transformation of the nail trade. Ephraim Bell told of its geographical conditions in the early nineteenth century.

> . . .the manufacture of hand-made nails is carried on at the workmen's own homes, where they have a small workshop, which is termed a nail shop. A few years ago a nail shop was frequently attached to small farmhouses, in which the farmer and his family made nails when they could not work on the farm. . . .
>
> When a nailmaster commences business, he opens a warehouse (in an area where nails are already widely produced); but, to carry on a large trade in all descriptions of hammered nails, he must have supplementary warehouses in several districts. At each of these warehouses, on certain days in the week, nail-rod iron is delivered to the nailmaker sufficient for him and his family to work up in a week, and at the expiration of that time he is expected to return the iron made into nails, when he receives a further supply. A nailmaker, his wife, and all his children above the age of nine years, are generally engaged in his small nail shop making nails; children, both boys and girls, are generally put to work in making nails at the early age of nine years.[6]

Already this form of production was different from that of the late seventeenth and early eighteenth centuries. As iron became more plentiful, and thereby cheaper,

[5]Smith's description of the "division of labour" revolves around the pin and nail trade (The Wealth of Nations, Book I, Chapter I). A further geographical description is available from the middle of the nineteenth century, reflecting earlier conditions, in Samuel Timmins, The Resources, Products, and Industrial History of Birmingham and the Midland Hardware District, London: Robert Hardwicke, 1866 (actually the Handbook for the British Association for the Advancement of Science meeting held in Birmingham), which has sections dealing with "The Handmade Nail Trade," "On the Manufacture of Needles and Fishhooks," and "The Pin Trade."

[6]"The Handmade Nail Trade" in Timmins, op. cit., pp. 110–111.

fairly traditional practices could be expanded without technical transformation, as happened with nail making. By 1830 in the area between Stourbridge on the middle Severn and Birmingham, and westward to Dudley, 50,000 people were estimated to be "employed in the manufacture of hand-made nails" in a trade that supplied 120 tons a year to the East India Company (90 tons in tea-chest nails alone) and 640 tons to the Admiralty. Even in 1851, the handmaking of nails in Belgium was estimated to amount to "about eight to nine thousand tons per annum." When one thinks of the number of tea-chest nails in a ton, the existence of at least a "paleo-quantitative economy" seems evident.

Geographically, this quantitative economy in an initial stage had created a *workshop district in the countryside* near the iron workings in the West Midlands of England and those on the coal fields of Belgium in the Principality of Liège. The extraction from the city led to a rough concentration in the countryside, where a great number of farmhouse forges could be set up. For that purpose two staples were needed: relatively cheap iron and fuel of low cost. The coal fields of Belgium and the West Midlands supplied both, even to the point of having coal measures intimately interbedded with clay-band iron ores. The existence of such a resource base was sufficient to extract the industry from the towns, and the manual skills the nailors developed could for a time keep the production in handworking. By building up their skills, they could increase their daily production, thus increasing their "wages," so long as raw materials could be kept cheap and local.

Also, as Adam Smith pointed out, virtue could be found in giving up agriculture entirely and concentrating on a careful division of labor.

> . . .It is impossible to pass very quickly from one kind of work to another, that is carried on in a different place, and with quite different tools. A country weaver, who cultivates a small farm, must lose a good deal of time in passing from his loom to the field, and from the field to his loom. When the two trades can be carried on in the same workhouse, the loss of time is no doubt much less. It is even in this case, however, very considerable. A man commonly saunters a little in turning his hand from one sort of employment to another. When he first begins the new work he is seldom very keen and hearty; his mind, as they say, does not go to it, and for some time he rather trifles than applies to good purpose.[7]

Production will increase and at least in theory the return to the worker will be enhanced.

But such an absolute division of labor within the countryside came only with the glimmerings of the Industrial Revolution, when the conditions were set that

[7]Smith, op. cit.

This factory in Ashton-under-Lyne in Lancashire was located on a stream to obtain process water for washing but was operated by hand, as shown by the absence of a mill dam or a mill race. From Aikin, The Country Round Manchester, 1795.

permitted a man to earn a living within a rural area from a single occupation. Raw materials were needed in sufficient quantity to allow concentration of the efforts of a number of men on a single occupation, as production in the country required the use of factors and other wholesalers to collect and forward the goods being produced well away from a consuming market. Thus, the agent, or factor, became a critical element in this industrializing process, and his interests were not exactly identical with the workman's. Increasing scale of production was independent of the factor's own labor. He could sell more and more without reaching any ceiling beyond which human limitation could not be pushed. So long as he had agents in large markets—cities and ports—he might sell more and more. To do so, he needed more and more production, preferably within a geographical area sufficiently confined as to allow him to supply it with nail-rod and to permit him to gather at week's end a product for sale at a distance.

In such a context the interests of the factor were strongly driven toward ever-increasing production. This drive was obviously matched by one for the application of machinery to the process, as the geographical realm from which the factor could collect, or to which he could distribute staple iron, would be severely limited. Also the ability to collect, house, and feed more workers in such a neighborhood would be limited. All needs pointed toward lending greater productive power to the hand of the workman. Again Adam Smith tells us why.

It is naturally to be expected, therefore, that some one or other of those who are employed in each particular branch of labour should soon find out easier and readier methods of performing their own particular work, wherever the nature of it admits of such improvement. A great part of the machines made use of in those manufactures in which labour is most subdivided, were originally the inventions of common workmen, who, being each of them employed in very simple operation, naturally turned their thoughts toward finding out easier and readier methods of performing it.[8]

Smith's condescension toward the common man seems hardly warranted in England and certainly ill-advised with respect to America. At the time of the Exhibition of 1851 in the Crystal Palace, one of the great shocks to British manufactural pride came in viewing the large number of very complicated self-acting machines exhibited by Americans—sewing machines, gun-making machinery, all sorts of shoe-making and small hardware fabricating machines, and a wealth of others. In the Midland Hardware District, many trades were fundamentally transformed in the 1850's and '60's when these American machines were introduced. These machines were not the product of the ingenious but plodding mind Smith describes, nor were they simple. While simple machines were normally the first to be developed and used, they were soon followed by machines where various processes could be executed by a single integrated system.

If the division of labor led to a concentration of the first stage of industrialization in defined regions in the countryside, the application of machinery brought still further geographical consequences. Because machinery implied in most cases, though not in all, the application of nonhuman power to the manufacturing processes, the location of the power became a critical locating force. In Britain most of the rivers were short and normally already appropriated for waterpower even during the Middle Ages (to run the wheels of grist and other millers). As the quantitative economy expanded into a full Industrial Revolution in the mid-eighteenth century, relatively little basis remained for such growth if it were to be driven by waterpower. Prior appropriations of mill powers, conflict with navigation improvements, and the relative absence of extensive reservoirs in natural lakes, which were most uncommon in England, all made waterpower rather inexpansible.

Although not specifically a matter of the availability of power, another significant factor to consider for an understanding of the expanding industrial economy of England is the source of workers for en-

larged factories. The pattern of land ownership in the English countryside concentrated freehold possession in a few hands, notably those of the landed gentry whose claims were based heavily on medieval vassalage to the king. Yeoman farmers of lesser rank still represented a relatively small component of the rural population. In no sense was the family farm the English norm; instead agricultural tenentry was common and agricultural labor perhaps even more widespread. As a result of this concentrated land ownership and the separation of most rural people into a landless labor force, any shift away from *traditional* farming practices, which are usually highly labor intensive, toward the quantitative economy of staple production of wool and mutton or cattle was likely to create a surplus labor force in the countryside.

This surplus is exactly what occurred during the enclosure movement, at work from Tudor times on into the nineteenth century. *Enclosure* was the shifting of common lands into individual ownership, again a force concentrating land ownership, the social impact of which was the shaping of a class of landless unemployed. As the workers and their families lost their jobs on the farms, they also lost any legal or functional basis for rural residence. To a considerable degree the landless unemployed had to gravitate to the city, partly in the hope of finding a new and even better life, as we saw in the last chapter, but also of simple necessity. They had lost their functional role in the countryside, and they had no residual ties to property that might have held them there, as took place later in New England. The upshot was that the English countryside was rich in neither available waterpowers nor in potential employees.

But before the rather fruitless countryside could be abandoned by the incipient industry which had grown up there in odd spots—the nail working on the outskirts of Birmingham and in southern Lancashire and the early textile "factories" of the Stroud valley of Gloucestershire and around Trowbridge in Wiltshire, for example—some means of gaining two distinct objectives had to be devised. The first objective was to expand the market for the goods produced; the other was to shape some source of power other than falling water.

We can begin to understand the attainment of a quantitative economy by looking briefly at the woolen industry of the southwest of England. The central force in domination of that trade by the southwest was the quality of the wool raised on the Cotswolds and other hills of the area. With such a staple for production, the fiber could be exported as far away as Prato in Tuscany, where the merchant Datini was paying the highest of all prices for fleeces from the Cotswolds. As time passed, local wool was increasingly used in local manufacture, largely in established towns during the Mid-

[8]Loc. cit.

dle Ages. "It was evident by the early fifteenth century that the old urban industry was incapable of producing sufficient cloth. The gild system was essentially restrictive and unsuited even to the idea of an expanding market."[9]

The gild was so rooted in the medieval notion of ordering of economic life that it could never adjust and had ultimately to be done away with; but first it had simply to be avoided. "During the period 1350-1500, the cloth industry moved away from its traditional urban centres and out into the country. The main reason for this was the need for increased supplies of water to drive the new mechanised fulling-mills. So long as the [fulling] method was to tread the cloth in a trough, the towns were able to provide such water as was needed." With increasing demand for cloth this most arduous process was the first to be mechanized. Both process water and falling water were required to turn the millwheels that gave the force to beat the raw cloths into a finished shape. "Fulling-mills were found occasionally in England at the end of the thirteenth century, but at that time there is certain mention of them at only twenty-six places in Wiltshire, Somerset and Gloucestershire."[10]

In his pioneering work on industrial archaeology, Kenneth Hudson goes on to characterize "the medieval industrial revolution" as "long drawn out." "As ever more cloth was needed especially for export, in the fourteenth century, the weavers could not keep their looms constantly busy without resorting to the services of spinners in the country districts. As soon as the point was reached when a high proportion of both the spinning and the fulling was being done in the rural areas, it was reasonable for the weavers to establish themselves there as well."[11] Thus came the shift from the medieval tradition of urban craft manufacture to the quasi-modern practice of mechanization. The countryside could hardly have provided either the power or the labor for a vast, truly modern production. But in this transitional stage, the locale was ideal, enjoying the further benefit of entrepreneurial freedom from the gild system and its narrow horizons.

With the shift outward from the city, particularly into the country near Bristol, the role of the factor as an organizer and facilitator of trade was greatly enlarged. When, in the fourteenth century, London replaced Bristol as the main exporter of cloth, conditions were set for the emergence of the class of traders who ultimately, in the sixteenth century, became factors. "The London exporters wanted to deal with a few middle-men, not with the multitude of individual weavers. These middlemen, the clothiers, consequently rose to be the leading figures in the rural cloth industry. The men best placed to become clothiers were those who had already established a fulling-mill, which could easily be made to serve as a central depot . . . ."[12] The clothiers became the great organizers of manufacturing providing wool to the spinners, receiving the spun yarn, and subsequently putting it out to handweavers. When the rough cloths were again returned to their mills (which came ultimately to be called "factories" —the place of operation of a factor), these clothiers had them fulled and then dispatched to London to the exporting merchants with whom they generally maintained rather close association.

The factor's role grew even more important when the "character of the trade changed fundamentally during the seventeenth and eighteenth centuries. Before about 1650 the main export was of undyed broadcloths to be finished in Flanders. By 1750 the local industry was mainly concerned with the manufacture of coloured cloth, and dyeing, like fulling, was a capitalist enterprise."[13] Such capitalist enterprises commonly showed a careful and continuous supervision of the processing by the manufacturer, regardless of the actual use of machinery. But once the factory had been created not merely as a depot for the organization of the production but also as its actual site, a strong force urged the use of as much machinery as could with economic wisdom be employed. The capitalist had the money for its purchase, the organization of trade sufficient to bring on a quantitative production, and thus the ability to justify its purchase.

The ability to command a larger market made machinery a wise investment; the use of machinery made the wide introduction of power economically and institutionally astute. In the Middle Ages the master of a craft earned his living in two ways—from the planning of his trade over a period of time, and usually more heavily, from the actual labor he put into it, skilled as it commonly was. Essentially, he was selling skilled labor from which his return was gained by degree of skill and time expended. But with the introduction of a capitalist organization to manufacture—timidly in the fulling mill, subsequently in dyeing, and finally in all steps of production—the master's earnings came from organization, on a much vaster scale than that of his medieval ancestor, and from invested capital.

Strictly, the master no longer earned any wage for labor; he did none. But capital, unlike labor, could be accumulated to an almost infinite degree, and earnings from it could similarly be expanded beyond the mea-

[9]Kenneth Hudson, The Industrial Archaeology of Southern England, Dawlish [Devon]: David and Charles, 1965, pp. 82–83.
[10]Ibid., pp. 82–83.
[11]Ibid., pp. 82–83.

[12]Ibid., pp. 83–84.
[13]Ibid., pp. 83–84.

sure of labor. Thus, the master of the Industrial Era, who by then was commonly called a "master manufacturer," could use his capital more productively by expanding his market than by improving his product. In this context one of his great concerns was to push outward the mercantile frontier to enlarge the potential market he might tap.

The introduction of application of power to manufacture came early in industrial history but was a very long time in coming to full development. Basing our brief appraisal on British experience alone, we find that the Romans used water mills during their occupation of England and that the "Saxons used water-mills extensively, and more than five thousand are recorded in those parts of England which were covered by the Doomsday Survey [of 1086]."[14] These mills were almost exclusively, if not actually so, used for the grinding of grain. But still as early as 1185 waterpower was used for the operation of a fulling-mill, which along with forging iron, pumping water from mines, and crushing ore were the main uses to which waterpower was put before the eighteenth century.

As Hudson shows, "As industrial demands grew during the seventeenth and early eighteenth centuries the provision of adequate power supplies from rivers and streams became an increasingly difficult problem. Today the power available to the early industries appears ludicrously small." This smallness of provision was particularly daunting in face of the fact that investment capital was scarce indeed until the Industrial Revolution had gotten well underway. After building a dam, a millrace, sluices, and the wheel itself, the eighteenth century millowner "might supply a factory with less power than could be obtained from a modern two horse-power electric motor, power which might fail completely in a dry summer or frosty winter."[15]

Britain was a poor and impoverished land in the matter of waterpower. Unlike New England where the Industrial Revolution first took place in America, in England glaciation was so feeble that its scars had largely disappeared when human history began. The few lakes, most diminished at that (such as the Norfolk Broads), were commonly in such flat country as to be powerless to encourage industry. Only a few small glacial valleys, as in the romanticized Lake District, held reservoirs of even incidental importance.

By comparison New England had a vast string of interconnected natural reservoirs divided one from another by sharp accidents in the ground that grew from glaciation (through its disruption of the preglacial drainage). Small, narrow, cheaply-built dams could produce both high heads of water and extensive ponding to carry the power over dry or cold periods.

The history of waterpower in Industrial Era Britain was the ingenious development and modification of mill wheels—from undershot to overshot and then into several kinds of turbines in the refinement of earlier pioneering French work on those smaller and more productive water machines. In the United States, the Industrial Era for waterpower was much longer and more generously defined. Instead of experiencing a cramped need for technical ingenuity, America sought to develop *the water-power city* of which there were a number of striking examples, beginning with Paterson (New Jersey) and growing more elaborate in Lowell and Holyoke (Massachusetts) and Rochester (New York). Britain and the Continent saw no such development.

The essential poverty of Britain and Belgium with respect to waterpower sites turned attention there instead to the development of steam power. The early history of the steam engine is much discussed, but we may agree that Thomas Newcomen built the first economically successful steam engine in 1712 at Dudley Castle in Staffordshire. With respect to industry, however, the improvements that Watt made to the engine were decisive; for the first time the steam engine was efficient enough in fuel use to be a source of power available beyond the pithead of the collieries. In 1765, Watt first developed the separate condensing chamber. In 1775, he joined Mathew Boulton at the Soho Works in Birmingham to build his engines in fair numbers, some five hundred beam engines by 1800.[16] All told, the engines produced about 7,500 horsepower, something like that of the most modern diesel-electric locomotive in the United States, which itself may be coupled with two or three others to move a full freight train. Nevertheless, this capturing from nature of the ability to produce power when and where wanted created the true economy of quantity.

Before this, power had been where nature put it, while the potential market for goods was commonly far away. As Colin Clark showed, in the era before steam, transportation of those goods to the market depended essentially on the whim of nature blowing on the sails of a ship. Muscle power, either of men or animals, came at too high a cost in food consumed to be used for transport of goods over great distances. The initial role of the steam engine developed by Newcomen was to aid the production of mineral ores and fuels so that a quantitative economy might begin; Boulton and Watt's engines permitted the introduction of large scale in manufacturing independent of the vagaries of nature's winds and falling waters. The later steam engines of Oliver

[14]*Kenneth Hudson*, Industrial Archaeology: An Introduction, *London: John Baker, 1963, p. 90.*
[15]Ibid., *p. 91.*

[16]Ibid., *p. 98.*

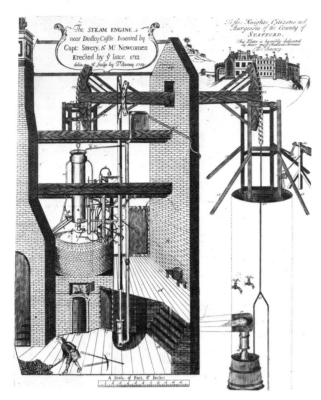

The Newcomen steam engine of 1712 was the first successful application of steam to the operation of machinery, ushering in the geographical mobility for industry that was essential for the onset of the Industrial Revolution.

Evans and Richard Trevithick allowed the concentration of manufacture in a few places by at last shaping a transportation system that could carry inexpensive goods in large quantities cheaply to national and international markets.

England: Industry Comes into the City

One of the more surprising myths about the Industrial Revolution is that this wrenching change in economic practice took place in England outside the traditional manufacturing areas. To the extent that industrialization collected the domestic labor of country cottars into cities, this myth might be true, but the flow of work and workers to the city was so slow as to take at least a century to complete. We have seen that, even as late as the 1860's, nails, pins, and other traditional domestic products were still being forged in sheds behind farmhouses in Worcestershire and Lancashire. Eventually machine production took over completely, but hardly by storm. Instead the quantitative economy placed such demands on traditional trades that they could not cope, and increments to production had to come in factories. Because incremental labor was more readily available in cities than in the English countryside, those new factories tended to be urban once Boulton and Watt's engines made that a possibility.

Nor were the great industrial towns of Britain all, or even dominantly, the creation of the Industrial Revolution. Birmingham was the second town of Warwickshire in the thirteenth century, exceeded in size only by Warwick, the administrative center, with its castle. Similarly, Nottingham was a county and a city in medieval times, as the tale of Robin Hood shows us; he tangled with the sheriff of Nottingham, not of Nottinghamshire. Manchester we know from its name owes its origin to the Romans, and certainly Bristol, another county-city, was well known before the Industrial Revolution.

There is some truth in the view that the Industrial Revolution shaped the urban geography of Britain outside of London. A few new cities rose to extreme importance under industrialization, but to a considerable degree they were less true factory metropolises than additions brought on by the expanding system of long-distance trade and transportation. Liverpool is an undoubted child of the Industrial Revolution, starting as a small port on the west coast in 1700 and outdistancing Bristol as the port of the West by 1800. After the formal union of Scotland with England in 1707, and its grudging and dilatory implementation of commercial equality for Scots in the English realms, Glasgow grew greatly as a port. We should not, however, forget that the city on the Clyde had been important even in the late Middle Ages for its university and cathedral.

To understand the relationship of the Industrial Revolution in Britain to the location and form of cities requires a more analytical view than is commonly employed. One cannot, for example, quote Daniel Defoe out of context, as so many do. His comment is familiar: "Manchester, one of the greatest if not really the greatest meer village in England." We must add, as he did directly: "It is neither a wall'd town, city, or corporation; they send no members to Parliament; and the highest magistrate they have is a constable or headborough; *and yet it has a collegiate church, several parishes, takes up a large space of ground, and including the suburb, or that part of the town called* [Salford] *over the bridge; it is said to contain above fifty thousand people. . . ."*[17] Seemingly what mattered to the British mind was the rank and political standing of a town rather than its actual function. And Manchester had not enjoyed the political respect its economic importance warranted. Defoe argued that his population estimate, "though some people may think [it] strange, and that I speak by guess, and without judgment, I shall justify my opinion so well, that I believe, it will convince you my calculation is at least very probable, and much under what fame tells us is true."

Defoe goes on:

The Manchester trade we all know; and all that are concerned in it know that it is, as all our other manufactures are, very much encreased within these thirty or forty years especially beyond what it was before; and as the manufacture is encreased, the people must be encreased of course. It is true, that the encrease of the manufacture may be by its extending itself farther in the country, and so more hands may be employed in the country without any encrease in the town. But I answer that though this is possible, yet as the town and parish of Manchester is the center of the manufacture, the encrease of that manufacture would certainly encrease there first, and then the people there not being sufficient, it might spread itself further.

But the encrease of buildings at Manchester within these few years, is a confirmation of the encrease of people; for that within very few years past, here, as at Liverpoole, and as at Froom in Somersetshire, the town is extended in a surprising manner; abundance, not of new houses only, but of new streets of houses, are added, a new church also, and they talk of another, and a fine new square is at this time building. . . .

If then this calculation is just, as I believe it really is, you have here then an open village, *which is greater and more populous than many, many, nay, than most cities in* England, not York, Lincoln, Chester, Salisbury, Winchester, Worcester, Gloucester, no not Norwich itself, can come up to it . . . .[18]

How very deceiving is Gordon East's summary of Defoe: "To Defoe, however, Manchester was only 'one of the greatest if not the greatest mere [sic] village in England.'"[19] This evidence makes it appropriate to take a new less traditional view of the urban impact of the Industrial Revolution in Britain.

The First English Industrial "City": A Countryside of Segmental Labor

The greatest problem confronting us in viewing the urbanization of England as a result of industrialization comes from the narrow, excessively "historical" view of the city entertained by British observers. To them, a city must be an important medieval creation, even though it might also have Roman roots (as Manchester did), be possessed of a royal charter (as Manchester was not), be normally the site of a cathedral and a surrounding wall, and serve as part of an administrative-military system intended to maintain the king's peace and sovereignty. In such a context the towns Defoe cites as smaller than Manchester in 1725 gain great significance. He is saying that even before the real onset of the Industrial Revolution, Manchester was larger than all but London and Bristol among the traditional British "cities." Perhaps we should examine anew the notion that Manchester, Birmingham, Leeds, and the other "factory towns" had no historical underpinnings and grew only with the development of machines and steam engines.

We must first recognize that the Industrial Revolution had several stages, extended over some two centuries. The first stage—an outward turning from the city at the end of the Middle Ages—Defoe mentions with respect to Manchester. It has been thought of as an escape from the constraints of the gild and other civic regulations, but may also have been the initial effort to create a quantitative economy. The emphasis under

[17]Daniel Defoe, A Tour Through the Island of Great Britain (1724-1726), London: G. Strahan, in Cornhill (1st ed.), 1727, Vol. III. Emphasis supplied and excess capitalization removed.

[18]Ibid., p. 262. Emphasis supplied.
[19]Gordon East, "England in the Eighteenth Century," in H. C. Darby, An Historical Geography of England before 1800. Cambridge, England: Cambridge University Press, 1951, p. 499.

the gild system in medieval cities was to maintain quality and, not incidentally, prices. By projecting manufacture into the surrounding countryside, both increase in production and, to a considerable degree, reduction in the cost of the finished product could be accomplished.

Sweating labor was very real, but not necessarily the central force in reducing production cost. That reduction came as well from tapping the unused labor of the agricultural population, potential productive effort that remained after the necessary farm work had been done. The first stages of "industrialization" in the Cotswolds and other areas active under the "putting-out" system took on this pattern.

A further encouragement for this rural domestic manufacture was the survival of manor practices under which an earnest effort was made to create localized self-sufficiency on the estate. Country people determined the products they consumed mainly by what they themselves might produce. Existing "trade" tended to be between rural neighbors. Thus, the notion of manufacture had always existed in the countryside; the emerging quantitative economy in the sixteenth and seventeenth centuries could turn to supplying long-distance trading demands, once a system of trade organization and improvements in internal transportation could be shaped. Particularly in the seventeenth century, the explosive spread of Britain's trading empire shaped a mass market, while the turnpike and river navigation improvements substantially bettered internal communications. For light items or modest volumes of goods, these initial improvements, the first in transportation since Roman times, could suffice.

Segmental Labor

This incremental work, a part-time employment that went along with basic agricultural work, may be called *segmental labor*. We need anticipate the time of full city industrialization and distinguish *time*-segmental labor such as this in the country from *family*-segmental labor, which came when families were housed within the city and under conditions where only the father or the male members of the family might be employed in a particular industry. With time-segmental labor, the whole family likely worked on the land for a period of the year and in the nail-shed or weaving-shed at other times. If, however, the trades were specific to a particu-

lar age and sex, family-segmental labor was the practice. The occupation of spinster was so characteristically family-segmental as to supply us the term reserved for unmarried adult women, a state which the Scots seemingly consider irremediable when women reach their majority unmarried.

Industrialization: First Stage

During the first stage of industrialization, the demands for goods (in a quantitative economy) were projected from the cities, where that new economy was understood and implemented, into the countryside surrounding them. In the countryside, the existence of vast amounts of time-segmental labor combined with the vestiges of the manorial economy made for easy expansion of hand-production of goods into a full rural domestic industrialization.

Industrialization: Second Stage

The next stage of industrialization began when the quantitative economy expanded beyond the competence of rural domestic industry, into a situation where some application of powered machinery was needed. We cannot easily select a date for that event. Already in the twelfth century, fulling-mills were at work. The first waterpowered fulling mill, in 1185, became for England the first known application of waterpower to a process other than grinding grain.[20] So the use of power even in textile manufacture had medieval roots.

The application of power to the making of yarns ushered in what we think of as the Industrial Revolution. We must look at the textile trade of the early eighteenth century to see what made the application of power a necessity; in doing so, we see the critical difference in system and form between medieval industrialization

[20]*Hudson, op. cit., p. 90.*

and that under a quantitative economy. In the Middle Ages, most manufacturers (we have called them craftsmen to this point) took raw staples—furs, fibers, leathers, and the like—and completed from them a finished product. If they used a partially processed staple, it was, as was to be their own work, a product of hand labor. Thus, the scale of handworking was universal and the chance for great discrepancies in the rate of production among the various processes was somewhat held down. But with the development of a mass market, such as the one the Mercantile Revolution of the sixteenth and seventeenth centuries saw, the pressure to produce in quantity encouraged innovation. The efforts were diverse, affecting a number of trades. By looking at the most historically important, the textile industry, we may see how innovation in one aspect of production forced change in another.

The Evolution of the English Woolen Industry

Before the middle of the eighteenth century, woolen and worsted manufacture was Britain's most important industry, as well as perhaps the most dispersed. Three major areas were heavily involved in producing woolens: the West Country in the Cotswolds and Somerset, centering on Bristol; East Anglia with the greatest focus on Norwich; and the West Riding of Yorkshire, where Leeds and Bradford had been centers of the trade for several hundred years.

In the West Country and East Anglia, "the organisation and the capital were provided by wealthy merchant clothiers. They bought the raw wool from the farmers, they passed it on to the spinners, they sent the yarn to the weavers. Once the cloth was woven the merchants either had it taken to other specialists for finishing or else undertook the bleaching and dyeing themselves on their own premises." Production was organized but manufacture was not collected in a single village or even a single premises. "The spinning and weaving were easily done in the workers' own houses, without the need for expensive equipment. The finishing processes, even before the introduction of power-driven machinery, were more efficiently and cheaply carried out in larger units, because a good supply of water and more elaborate buildings were essen-

tial."[21] The geographical pattern produced by this industry was one of rural domestic production, with spinning at the cottage door and weaving in a shed built on behind. Interspersed within this industrial countryside were mill sites and places where process water could be secured, at which a fulling-mill or a bleachery would be found in a small "mill building" that might be little larger than a house. Clearly two different location systems were at work: the segmental labor of the agricultural areas determined the location of spinning and weaving activities, whereas the sources of water for power and processing served to locate the "mills."

"The system in the West Riding was different. There, in the earlier part of the eighteenth century, the workshops were 'embryo factories without steam-power.' The industry was in the hands of master-craftsmen, who bought their own wool, spun it, wove it, dyed it and eventually sold it." This manufacture was not at all located by the availability of segmental labor: instead it was a self-contained production depending on hand labor. And we know that the availability of process water and small wagon pits for coal (to be used for heating the workshop and the waters used, not initially for power) served, along with available village or country housing, to locate the "manufacture." Because the workplace was determined by the traditional location of the master, and the processing was under his direct control, masters "employed assistants, [and] they were in direct contact with the market and they controlled all the capital needed to convert raw wool into finished cloth." Even before the creation of steam-powered factories the geographical pattern of the woolen industry of the West Riding was clustered and rather specialized as to the particular woolen cloth produced.[22]

[21]Ibid., p. 53.
[22]Loc. cit.

Map of Yorkshire, from
Aikin, The Country Round
Manchester, 1795.

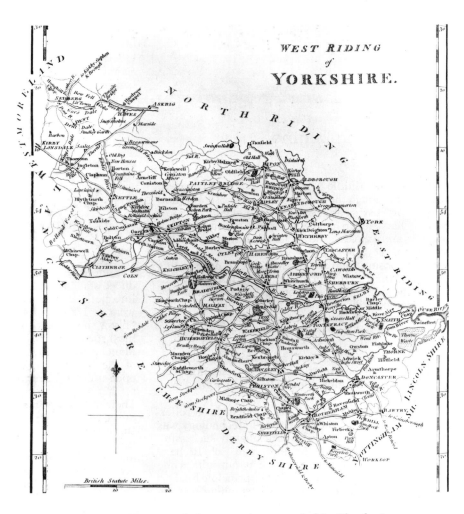

A Bottleneck in Weaving

The strongest force at work in bringing the locational shift from domestic to factory industry was the invention of the flying shuttle. Weaving was perhaps the most constraining process in the traditional textile manufacture. The weaver's need for daylight in which to work limited his productive hours, but as well he could only weave at the rate his hand could throw the shuttle across the loom. Light was hard to improve, but John Kay, in 1733, accomplished a great advance in throwing by his invention of the "flying shuttle" which

speeded up weaving remarkably. The device was comparatively simple, but it halved the labor input in weaving, allowing the same labor force to produce twice as much cloth. Before the flying shuttle, two men were required to operate a loom—they stood on either side to throw the shuttle back and forth across the warp—but now one could do the job. Kay developed the process at Colchester in Essex, but met with such resistance from the local weavers that he was driven from the town, which led him to the West Riding.[23] In the north, where the primordial "embryo factories without steampower" existed, the invention was rapidly taken up by the masters who were themselves

[23]F. George Kay, Pioneers of British Industry, London: Rockliff, 1952, p. 97.

workers. And the flying shuttle forced upon textile production a new shortage.

The Spinning Engine

Already in the Middle Ages, when England began to attempt to staunch the outward flow of wool staple and force its processing and weaving in England, a disproportion had shown up between the productivity of spinners and weavers. The ancient distaff spinning was so slow that several spinsters were required to keep up with the consumption of a single weaver. To aid in this difficulty, the English in the fourteenth century imported the spinning wheel from Italy, where to a considerable degree English wool was then being woven into cloth at Prate and Florence. More yarn could be spun and the industry could grow without a vast enlargement of the labor force. Again in the mid-eighteenth century a new disproportion had arisen, requiring a further improvement in spinning. The authorship of that improvement has been argued ever since that time.

In 1738, Lewis Paul took out a patent for a roller-spinning device and the basic shift in technology was begun. Paul's machine was not ultimately successful, but its principle was. In the hands of Richard Arkwright, who some argue stole it outright while others say that he "developed" Paul's principle further, a successful machine for automatic spinning was devised and patented in 1769. If any date deserves to be counted as the first year of the Industrial Revolution, it was 1771, when a mill was set up to use this machine. Because Kay and others had encountered so much opposition in the introduction of their machines, Arkwright and his partner, Jedidiah Strutt, established their mill in rural Derbyshire, at Cromford, where a small waterpower was available from the outfall of the drainage of the nearby lead mines. Fortunately that first Cromford mill still stands so we can learn directly from its physical evidence.

The improvement in spinning came rapidly thereafter, particularly as Arkwright's patent was soon thrown out for several irregularities and by the simple greed of potential manufacturers who fought its remaining in force. James Hargreaves, a weaver at Standhill near Blackburn in Lancashire, found that his wife could not spin fast enough to keep up with his loom, so he invented a machine named in her honor.

On it, he could simultaneously spin at first eight, but ultimately 120 threads. The "spinning jenny" became a successful machine, to be shortly improved by Samuel Crompton into the "spinning mule," which combined features from Arkwright and Hargreaves' machines.

Too Much Yarn Leads to Machine Weaving

The increased ability to spin yarn by machine produced such a flood of yarn that it could not be woven into cloth. A Lancashire minister, Edmund Cartwright, went in 1784 for a summer holiday to Matlock Bath, only a short walk from Arkwright's second and then most successful mill. There, in conversation with some Manchester millowners, he learned of this overtaxing of the hand-loom weavers. In the innocence of the open-minded, he remarked, "Then Mr. Arkwright must set his wits to work to invent a weaving machine." Their assurances that it could not be done further induced a curious man to make the attempt, which was successful. Thus, Cartwright established the notion that technical improvement was generally possible, and that disproportions which arose in a continuous process must be dealt with by technological experimentation and improvement.

The Coming of Steam Power

In such a context, the problem of power came up for solution. The notion of powered machines was neither new nor unsuccessful. Obviously the quickening pace of the quantitative economy had first introduced traditional forms of power to the manufacturing process. We have already seen that waterpower was introduced to fulling in the Middle Ages. Strutt and Arkwright had used horses for power at Nottingham during their experiments there, turning to waterpower only at Crom-

Map of Derbyshire. Note the location of Matlock, Cromford, and Belper on the Derwent River at the middle of the county with the Duke of Devonshire's estate at Chatworth just to the north. From Aikin, The Country Round Manchester, *1795.*

ford in 1771. Since England is not well supplied by waterpower, the use of steam for power had been toyed with for more than a century when the need within the textile trade became urgent. The Greeks had appreciated the power inherent within the expansion of steam, and had used it as had the medieval Chinese for rather frivolous purposes (opening temple doors and

producing "magic" effects). But only in the seventeenth century was a purpose equal to steam's power given to the medium in the pumping of water from coal mines. Initially the steam was used directly to create a vacuum into which the water was drawn. Thomas Savery in 1698 patented an engine "for raising of water and occasioning motion to all sorts of mill works by the impellent force of fire."[24] Through this device for the first time in human history water was raised more than the 24 feet at sea level that natural law determines.

A French refugee, Denis Pepin, was first to employ the piston, which was to prove the central element in the generation of steam power. But only the pressure-cooker, which he also invented, proved a success, as he demonstrated in a dinner tendered to the Royal Society in 1680. Final success in devising a steam engine came when Thomas Newcomen built a practical "atmospheric engine," possibly in 1705 but certainly by 1712. From that time on, many improvements were made, but the steam engine was a practical device in increasingly wider use. James Watt's great advance came not in "inventing" the steam engine, as is so commonly supposed, but rather in making it a generally economic engine which could be used to create power independent in location from the winds and falling water.

The West Riding of Yorkshire: An Industrial Landscape

In the West Riding of Yorkshire, we may see in what fashion the steam engine shaped the geography of the Industrial Revolution. Given the local integration of all processes that go into the production of finished textiles, it is not surprising that steam power was to play a larger role in the West Riding than in the other traditional textile areas—the West Country or East Anglia. "When steam power became available, the Yorkshire clothiers were able to convert their workshops into factories with little difficulty and to push their Southern competitors out of the market. This, rather than 'Because they were closer to the coalfields,' seems to be the answer to the classic question, 'why did the woolen textile industry transfer its headquarters to the West Riding?'"[25] The West Riding manufacturers had found it greatly to their benefit to invest in machinery. Now they found it both within their financial resources and greatly to their profit to apply steampower to their works. In this way the Industrial Revolution could take

[24]Ibid., p. 28.
[25]Hudson, op. cit., p. 53.

what were small process-integrations located in villages or small towns and allow them to become great factory cities.

Since the Middle Ages, the western section of the great county of York, West Riding, had been an area of woolen textile production. "Clothiers" had evolved a system of operation which saw their "factories with handworking" located in the small valleys or larger dales on the east side of the Pennines. These workplace extensions of their houses usually were served by water led along ditches from the streams plunging down the slopes from the soaked peat mosses that capped the hills. The water was particularly used for processing, but in a few places for power as well. A clothier's shop was usually surrounded by a small-holding of a few acres on which the proprietor could keep a cow or two and some sheep, but most importantly on which he could spread his woolen cloths for bleaching, stretching, and finishing. The "factory" itself employed a few "hands," who worked in the fashion that term suggests. Within the towns farther down the valleys—Bradford, Wakefield, Huddersfield, and especially Leeds—lived other clothiers whose job was to buy semi-finished cloths, see to their final processing, and arrange for their shipment to distant customers.

In the early eighteenth century when Daniel Defoe passed through the West Riding, he found a *landscape* of industry more than an industrial town.

After we had mounted the third hill, we found the country, in short, one continued village, tho' mountainous every way, as before; hardly a house standing out of spealing distance from another, and (which soon told us their business) the day clearing up and the sun shining, we could see that almost at every house there was a tenter, and almost in every tenter a piece of cloth, or kersie, or shalloon, for they are the three articles of that country's labour. . .yet look which way we would, high to the tops and low to the bottoms, it was all the same; innumerable houses and tenters, and a white piece [of woolen cloth] upon every tenter.

But to return to the reason of dispersing the houses, as above; I found, as our road passed among them, for indeed no road could do otherwise, wherever we pass'd any house we found a little rill or gutter of running water. . .and at every considerable house was a manufactury or work-house, and as they could not do their business without water, the little streams were so parted and guided by gutters or pipes, and by turning and dividing the streams, that none of those houses were without a river, if I may call it so, running into and through their workhouses. . .[and] the dyeing-houses[, s]couring-shops and places where they use this water, emitted the water again, ting'd with the drugs of the dyeing fat, and with the oil, the soap, and the tallow, and other ingredients used by the clothiers in dressing and scouring &c. . . .

Then, as every clothier must keep a horse, perhaps two, to fetch and carry for the use of his manufacture, (viz.) to fetch home his wooll and his provisions from the market, to carry his yarn to the spinners, his manufacture to the fulling mill, and, when finished, to the market to be sold, and the like; so every manufacturer generally keeps a cow or two, or more, for his family, ...But now, to speak of the bounty of nature again, which I but mentioned; it is to be observed, that these hills are so furnished by nature with springs and mines, that not only on the sides, but even to the very tops, there is scarce a hill but you find, on the highest part of it, a spring of water, and a coal-pit. I doubt not but there are both springs and coal-pits lower in the hills . . .and the coals in the upper pits being easie to come at, they may chuse to work them, because the horses which fetch the coals, go light up the hill, and come loaden down.

Having thus fire and water at every dwelling, there is no need to enquire why they dwell thus dispers'd upon the highest hills, the conveniences of the manufactures requiring it. Among the manufacturers houses are likewise scattered an infinite number of cottages or small dwellings, in which dwell the workmen which are employed, the women and children of whom, are always carding, spinning, &c. so that no hands being unemploy'd, all can gain their bread, even from the youngest to the ancient; hardly any thing above four years old, but its hands are sufficient to it self.

This is the reason also why we saw so few people without doors; but if we knock'd at the door of any of the master manufacturers, we presently saw a house full of lusty fellows, some at the dye-fat, some dressing the cloths, some in the loom, some one things, some another, all hard at work, and full employed upon the manufacture, and all seeming to have sufficient business.[26]

If any landscape could be considered industrialized before the Industrial Revolution, it was the one in the West Riding. All houses and all hands were turned toward the woolen textile trade. In this dispersed housing-workplace pattern, most of the processes of cloth manufacture were handled. The fulling operations and the marketing of cloths tended to be missing; both were carried on in the "towns" of Huddersfield, Wakefield, Bradford, and Leeds. Leeds in fact was second only to London in the distant trading in cloth. In general, "the towns were not the centres of manufacture, but were chiefly engaged in the finishing processes, in the marketing of raw material, cloth and foodstuffs, and in providing accommodation for mer-

[26]Defoe, op. cit., 1st ed., Vol. III, pp. 97–101.

chants, clothiers and travellers."[27] Only as the quantitative economy grew into full scale, calling to use the steam engines that might easily be fed from the local coal-pits, did the manufacture tend to collect toward the valley bottoms where sites were more ample for large factories and where the coal from the concealed coalfield could be used more readily. Even so, as the valley towns grew in size, the factories crept up the lower hills and the housing of workers moved even higher, to the edge of the moor that Defoe viewed as forming a "frightful country."

Manchester: The Spreading Open Village of Manufacture

The growth of the woolen trade of the West Riding came in a sense before the onset of what we normally recognize as the Industrial Revolution. Remember that Defoe was describing Yorkshire in the 1720's when the scale of production was rising rapidly with "all hard at work, and full employed upon the manufacture, and all seeming to have sufficient business"—strong proof that the use of steam power was the result of an upswing in demand rather than the other way round. But how could demand first be demonstrated and then focussed on a restricted geographical area such as the West Riding or Lancashire? After all, in the Middle Ages, much of England's land and labor was being used to produce the golden staple and work it up into cloths.

In 1795, John Aikin, a physician, published a book containing *A Description of the Country from Thirty to Forty Miles Round Manchester*, providing us with an invaluable record of the topographic and economic conditions found in the earlier years of the industrial age. Of particular use was Aikin's summarization of the stages in the evolution of the textile trade in and about Manchester.

The trade of Manchester may be divided into four periods. The first is that, when manufacturers worked hard merely for a livelihood, without having accumulated any capital. The second is that, when they had begun to acquire little fortunes, but worked as hard, and lived in as

[27]H. Heaton, The Yorkshire Woollen and Worsted Industries (1920), p. 289, quoted in W. G. East, op. cit., p. 509.

Map of canals, rivers,
and roads in the region
where the English In-
dustrial Revolution
began. From Aikin, 1795.

plain a manner as before, increasing their fortunes as well by economy as by moderate gains. The third is that, when luxury began to appear, and trade was pushed by sending out riders for orders to every market town in the kingdom. The fourth is the period in which expense and luxury had made a great progress, and was supported by a trade extended by means of riders and factors through every part of Europe.

It is not easy to ascertain when the second of these periods commenced; but it is probable that few or no capitals of 3000l. or 4000l. acquired by trade, existed here before 1690. However, towards the latter end of the last century and the beginning of the present, the traders had certainly got money beforehand, and began to build modern brick houses, in place of those of wood and plaster. For the first thirty years of the present century [the eighteenth], the old established houses confined their trade to the wholesale dealers in London, Bristol, Norwich, Newcastle, and those who frequented Chester fair. The profits were thus divided between the manufacturer, the wholesale, and the retail, dealer; and those of the manufacturer were probably (though this is contrary to the received opinion) less per cent, upon the business they did, than in the present times. The improvement of their fortunes was chiefly owing to their economy in living, the expense of which was much below the interest of the capital employed. . . .

When the Manchester trade began to extend, the chapmen used to keep gangs of pack-horses, and accompany them to the principal towns with goods in packs, which they opened and sold to shop-keepers, lodging what was unsold in small stores at the inns. The pack-horses brought back sheep's wool, which was bought on the journey, and sold to the makers of worsted yarn at Manchester, or to the clothiers of Rochdale, Saddleworth, and the West-Riding of Yorkshire. On the improvement of turnpike roads waggons were set up, and the pack-horses discontinued; and the chapmen only rode out for orders, carrying with them patterns in their bags. It was during the forty years from 1730 to 1770 that trade was greatly pushed by the practice of sending these riders all over the kingdom, to those towns which before had been supplied from the wholesale dealers in the capital places before mentioned. . . .Within the last twenty years the vast increase in foreign trade has caused many of the Manchester manufacturers to travel abroad, and agents or partners to be fixed for a considerable time on the Continent, as well as foreigners to reside at Manchester. And the town has now [1795] in every respect assumed the style and manners of one of the commercial capitals of Europe.[28]

[28]J. Aikin, M.D., A Description of the Country from Thirty to Forty Miles Round Manchester, London: Stockdale, 1795, pp. 181–184.

From this analysis emerges a picture of the separation of textile manufacture in two ways: that between woolens and cotton goods, which transpired in the hundred years of which Aikin wrote, and that of various functions within the making and selling of textiles. This functional separation within the sphere of business operation had considerable geographical implications beyond the simple one of the location of the market for sales. What emerged was the division between the making of cotton textiles, which was carried out into the country towns around Manchester, and the organization of the trade and the selling of its products, which continued in Manchester, becoming, in the end, Manchester's main function. Meanwhile, manufacture grew in size in Oldham, Bolton, Ashton-under-Lyne, and the other towns-become-cities that lay up to twenty miles away.

To understand the evolution of Manchester's city form, we must consider the mid-seventeenth century when, as a result of the creation of the East India Company monopoly, trade with India was being encouraged. Part of that trade centered on the import of cotton textiles from the East, uncommon indeed in the Middle Ages. Cottons—lighter, brighter, and more fashionable than woolens—were taken up by the increasingly fashion-conscious upper classes of England. That shift worried the woolen manufacturers. So they began what proved a long but futile campaign against the import of cotton products.

First they gained parliament's support in forbidding printed cotton calicoes, restricting the trade to "grey cloths" to be printed in Lancashire and the Clyde Valley where the finishing trade grew up, replacing to a considerable degree the older but not-too-vigorous woolen manufacture. Then the woolen manufacturers succeeded in gaining the embargo of grey cloths and further limiting the import to cotton yarn. At last in 1721, parliament even forbade the import of cotton yarn. But at that juncture, two realities turned aside the impact of that partisan legislation. The first was the increasing production of cotton in the West Indian and American colonies, outside the monopoly of the East India Company with its sensitivity to legislation, and the other was the established interest of the calico printers of Lancashire and the Clyde Valley. Cotton fiber could continue to be imported so the real problem was getting it spun into yarn. To do so required two things not in great supply: a segmental labor force, and the greater skill needed to spin cotton as opposed to wool.

Woolen yarn was normally rather coarse and weak, gaining its strength through the normally greater thickness of woolen fabrics and their frequent "finishing" by felting and fulling. Cotton yarns were normally finer and the fabrics were seldom as radically "finished," so the spinning problem became acute after the Indian yarns were forbidden. In this context, the efforts to develop a spinning machine took place. And when Richard Arkwright, in 1769, patented the water-frame spinner the campaign was well started. In 1774, Arkwright's mill at Cromford opened, producing a great quantity of yarn, superior in strength and fineness to anything that could be made by English hands, and he made it with a small and untapped segmental labor force—the orphans wards of the county of Derby.[29] The timing was critical as it was in 1758 that the flying shuttle, originally invented for woolen weaving, was introduced to the production of cottons, thus greatly increasing the demand for cotton yarns.[30] The conjunction of these two developments expanded the production of cotton textiles very rapidly, encouraging still further technological development—most notably the introduction of machine weaving, of which the first example in Lancashire was only in 1790. The complex history of the textile industry is a tale of interacting technological advance leading in the end to the first unquestionable quantitative economy. To serve that vast industry, with its hundreds of thousands of employees, the new geographical settlement, the *industrial metropolis*, was first evolved in and about Manchester.

The nature of the transition from the Middle Ages to modern times in England helps explain the morphogenesis of that new settlement. In their classic study of the Industrial Revolution, J. L. and Barbara Hammond present us a surpassing summary of the events of the time. "The disappearance of the medieval economy was the essential stage in the Industrial Revolution. It came earlier in England than elsewhere; it led to great technical improvement and a rapid increase in production; it took a different course and its ultimate consequences were different."[31] For these reasons the English Industrial Revolution is of great importance and interest, but hardly serves as a universal model for industrialization. For that we must eventually establish other distinct models that are as valid as the English but rule elsewhere.

[29]For a discussion in greater detail of this industrial emergence of cotton spinning, see James E. Vance, Jr., "Housing the Worker: The Employment Linkage as a Force in Urban Structure," Economic Geography, Vol. 42, 1966, p. 294–325.

[30]Arthur Louis Dunham, The Industrial Revolution in France: 1815—1848, New York: Exposition Press, 1955, p. 269.

[31]J. L. and Barbara Hammond, The Rise of Modern Industry, London: Methuen & Co., 1925, p. 90.

Land Owning and the Industrial Revolution

The Hammonds find the critical difference between England and the Continent in the manner of the destruction of the peasant villages, where the death throes of the Middle Ages were felt. "On the Continent the peasant as a rule survived. The commercial motives that gave such encouragement in England to headlong enclosure [of previously common lands] had less play elsewhere: reasons of State that had once made all Governments wish to keep a peasant population still counted in countries with a land frontier: [and] the enclosing class nowhere else made the laws [as they did through their control of the English Parliament]." They argue that on the Continent the absolute monarchies tended to check the power of the aristocracy. In England, however, the aristocracy was supreme, managing to establish its pattern of land ownership as the most powerful one. "Consequently England alone emerged from this revolution as an agrarian society without peasants or the obstacles a peasant economy presents to an industrial system based on concentration of power and specialization of tasks. In other countries the capitalist system was confined for the most part to industry: in England it began by overspreading the village as well as the town."[32]

The most striking contrasts existed between France and England. In France the demise of the medieval economy came through political revolution, and in England, through the usurpation of common rights by a tiny and arrogant minority. "Thus when the medieval village disappeared in France the peasant became an owner, whereas when it disappeared in England he became a labourer. This happened because the relationship between lord and peasant was abolished in France in a revolution that made the peasant more powerful than the lord, whereas in England it was abolished when the lord was supreme."[33]

The aristocracy's fierce drive for control of the land had several stages, all leading to a common goal—the capitalization of farming. The Hammonds cite the rise of the merchant class to wealth and its display as forcing upon the traditional aristocracy the practice of capitalism. "In the sixteenth century the chief motive

[32]Ibid., p. 90.
[33]Ibid., p. 89.

for enclosure was the stimulus given to farming for the market by the rise in prices and the expansion of the cloth industry. When commerce increased its profits and the classes engaged in it stepped into a more lavish style of living, the landlord found himself in a world in which he had to make drastic changes if he wished to maintain his social prestige. [This was a change from] feudal times [when] the lord's pomp and state depended on the number and condition of his tenants." To more democratic observers, simple social arrogance seems as likely an explanation of the narrowing of English land ownership. Even the Hammonds admit, "As domestic order became more secure, the command of men counted for less and less; as wealth grew and all classes [sic] acquired more expensive habits, the command of money counted for more and more."[34]

As landowners sought to increase their incomes, they began a systematic theft of the rights of the common people to common lands, and introduced the practice of the farmer's holding land under a lease rather than common rights. In the end the landowner succeeded in capturing the use value of most land, and created a situation in which "He believed that the best work was done by labourers who depended on their wages and had nothing to distract them from their duty to their employer. This relationship he considered the best for production, and production was everything."[35] The result was the capitalization of farming, and the creation of a rural proletariat which might remain in the country only so long as it served the financial interests of the aristocratic landowners; it could hardly become a major source for securing segmental labor.

This rather harsh indictment of the landed gentry has not been the common view: instead it has been argued that "Public spirit and private interest seemed to draw the landlord to the same conclusion. The population was growing faster than its resources; the Industrial Revolution was throwing up towns where food was consumed and not produced . . .[grain] growing was immensely profitable to the landlord and urgently necessary for the State."[36] One might as well argue that making cotton textiles was "urgently necessary" for England, but it produced no more than grinding poverty for its laborers. And those laborers had not even the slight protection that access to land has furnished to the working class in other lands—as in the peasant holdings of France and Germany and the homesteading of the United States.

[34]Ibid., p. 84.
[35]Loc. cit.
[36]Loc. cit.

Land ownership proves a somewhat disregarded aspect of the Industrial Revolution. In the West Riding, it produced a distinctly different geographical cast to industrialization from that found in Lancashire, where the small-holding was less common and the proto-factory was not the normal business organization before the introduction of machinery and waterpower or steam. Yet our standard view of the coming of the Industrial Revolution tends to be projected from the conditions in and about Manchester—a fascinating and important instance of the industrialization process but not the only form or indeed the universal model.

The Industrial Revolution rapidly came to be widespread, and early affected three other nations—Belgium, France, and the United States—in its earlier stages, particularly within the general textiles trade. We will look at the pattern as evolved in Lancashire and at three other patterns equally as different as that in the West Riding from the Mancunian experience: those in the Principality of Liège that became part of Belgium, in northern and eastern France, and in New England.

The Formation of the Mancunian Metropolis

The pattern of trade and manufacture in southeast Lancashire, the purlieus of Manchester, was much older than the Industrial Revolution. "Enlightened self-interest, however, if not warmer feeling, induced the [medieval] lords of Manchester to foster the growth of the little community dwelling behind the church and hall. It is not possible to fix precisely the date when its urban character was fully recognized by the grant of tenements on burgage tenure, free from servile dues and services, and (with some restrictions) saleable and bequeathable by will . . . ." The problems attendant to the emergence of the somewhat free burghers' town have been discussed during our consideration of the Middle Ages. "All that we can say is that these privileges were probably acquired before 1222, when Robert Grelley [the lord of the manor] obtained a grant of an annual fair for the town from Henry III. By the end of the century the town contained about 150 burgage tenements, and the mention of a fulling mill shows that

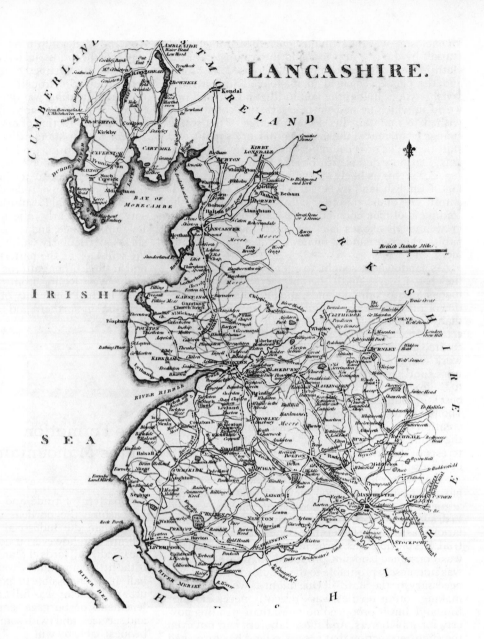

Map of Lancashire, from Aikin, The Country Round Manchester, *1795.*

cloth-weaving had already established itself there.[37] Thus Manchester entered the economic scene as a trading place for woolen cloths produced by hand-loom workers, most likely both within the emerging town and on farms in its environs.

[37]*James Tait, "A Brief Historical Sketch", in British Association for the Advancement of Science,* Manchester in 1915, *Manchester: The University Press, 1915, p. 3.*

The existence of a fulling-mill seems to indicate the same collecting process at work in Manchester that was to be found in the West Riding right down to the nineteenth century. But Lancashire was a less grim land than the West Riding; as a result, landed estates—manors—came earlier to the scene. Already in the Conqueror's time, Lancashire was a county palatine, one of those frontier counties (like Cheshire and Durham) where feudalism was exaggerated in the effort to provide a defense of the realm from outside intruders (for which in Manchester we must read "Scots," whose last invasion of the city came as late as 1745). In the counties palatine—true marchlands—powerful lords were set up and given large estates to provide them with potential fighting men to aid in the defense of the borders. Throughout the history of Lancashire, right down to the present, and certainly most critically until the middle of the nineteenth century, aristocratic ownership of the countryside meant little freehold ownership among the common people; the small-holding was far less legally defended than in the West Riding.

The import of this situation is that when the scale of production began to grow, in the general increase in English cloth-making and distant trading in the sixteenth and seventeenth centuries, growth took place in a rather specific settlement context. The large landholdings in aristocratic estates were sprinkled with medieval "towns," whose purpose was particularly to serve as collecting centers where handweavers could bring their cloths for fulling and trading. "During the sixteenth century the prosperity of Manchester seems to have suffered no such set-back as was experienced by many English towns. The demand for 'Manchester cottons' (i.e., woollens) continued to grow, and a new and fruitful material had been found for its looms in 'a kind of bombast or down, being a fruit of the earth growing upon little shrubs or bushes, brought into this country from Smyrna, Cyprus, Acra and Sydon, but commonly called cotton wool.' But the new cotton trade did not begin to attain great dimensions until after the middle of the seventeenth century."[38]

But the cotton trade did not really give its geographical structure. That structure originated earlier when the city began to play its role as merchants' town. We have noted the stages in the evolution of the Mancunian "manufacturer" from a cloth-maker using largely his own labor and that of his family and apprentices to that of international trader in goods made by others. The change came most observably in the early eighteenth century, though it seems highly unlikely that the roots were planted only then. The creation of a fair at Manchester as early as 1222 suggests strongly that some weavers, those with more commercial than manufacturing abilities, might have weighted the balance of their labor towards the selling end, leaving to others the production of the cloths in which they traded. In any event, we know from an account of Manchester published in the first year of American independence that the role of factor or wholesale agent was then firmly established in the city only two years after Richard Arkwright had set up the first steam mill in the

[38]Ibid., *p. 5.*

area (for spinning and making textile cards) within the woolen, not the cotton, trade.

James Ogden in describing Manchester in 1783 noted:

Fustians [originally a linen and then a cotton cloth] were made about Bolton, Leigh and the places adjacent, but Bolton was the principal market for them, where they were bought in the grey by Manchester chapmen, who finished and sold them in the country. These Manchester chapmen went over regularly on market days to buy the fustian pieces of the weavers; every weaver then procuring yarn [woolen] or cotton as they could, to make another piece, which subjected them to great positions and inconveniences. The buyers were disappointed, and suffered in their turn, when the demands of the trade were brisk. To remedy this inconvenience, some of them furnished warps and wool to the weavers, and employed persons to put warps out to the weaving, by commission; and encouraged many weavers to fetch them from Manchester, endeavoring to secure the honesty and care of their workmen, upon bringing in the piece, by the force of good usage and prompt payment; but reserving to themselves a power of abatement, for deficiency in the spinning and workmanship."[39]

The Obliteration of Small-Holdings and Rural Exodus

The industrialization of southeast Lancashire occurred in an area rather different in its preindustrial conditions from those found farther east in the West Riding. In the county palatine, the mixture of agricultural work with what has been called a "bye-industry," the domestic production of textiles, weighed more heavily toward farming than in Yorkshire. In Lancashire textile production was domestic but with a greater dependence upon agricultural employment, perhaps because the land was commonly occupied by lease or tenantry

[39]*James Ogden,* A Description of Manchester. . .with a Succinct History of its former original Manufactories, and their Gradual Advancement to the Present State of Perfection at which they are arrived; *reprinted as* Manchester A Hundred Years Ago, *ed. William A. E. Axon, Manchester: John Heywood, 1887, p. 74.*

rather than freehold. George Townsend Warner gives us a picture of a Lancashire village, Mellor, under traditional domestic production.

Here there were fifty or sixty farmers, of whom there were not more than six or seven who raised their rent directly from the land, "all the rest got their rent partly from some branch of trade, such as spinning or weaving woollen, linen, or cotton. The father of the family would earn from eight shillings to half a guinea at his loom, and his sons, if he had one, two, or three alongside of him, six or eight shillings per week. But the great sheet-anchor of all cottages and small farms was the labour attached to the hand-wheel; and when it is considered that it required six or eight hands to prepare and spin yarn sufficient for the consumption of one weaver, this shows clearly the inexhaustible source there was for labour of every person from the age of seven to eighty years . . .to earn their bread, say one to three shillings a week, without going to the parish" [for poor relief]. This example, dating from 1770, is drawn, as has been said, from Lancashire, where the by-industries clustered most thickly; and here, in the midst of the new machinery, the hand-spinners of cotton were soonest driven from the field.[40]

Indeed, when in Lancashire the earning of the rent from domestic production became difficult or impossible, the family was forced off the land and into the towns that were rapidly growing to be factory cities.

This particular aspect of land-holding drew a contrast between the two Pennine textile areas. In the West Riding, the manufacturers owned their small-holdings, secured water (for power and processing) on the site, and generally used the plot as the basis of trade. This trade remained dispersed much longer; concentration came only in finishing the cloths and in selling them in the "piece halls" of Bradford or Wakefield. In southeast Lancashire, the enclosure of lands previously held in common, in order to provide more arable land and more productive sheep runs, had produced a pattern of large land-holdings. Land was rented to the hand-loom weavers, but always with the landowner's lurking desire to recapture the land and turn it toward the increasingly profitable "scientific farming" that had come to England in the eighteenth century. That farming called for the cultivation in rotations of larger units of land, beyond the ability or the purse of the cottager. Thorold Rogers in a study of large and small holdings considered the plight of the "small holder." He noted that England and Wales in 1688 had 310,000 small freeholders and farmers. These were the rootstock both of farming and of the domestic industries of the countryside, and in that second bye-

industry they concern us greatly even in a study of the origin of cities.

The decline of the rural small-holder came only in the eighteenth century, just before the Industrial Revolution. The creation of the small-holder class of occupiers of land had come at the end of the Middle Ages, with the awareness that the "old order" of feudalism was fast departing and during the search for a new order. Elizabeth proved the instrument of much of that change; she not only tinkered with city size and form, but also she acted with respect to small-holding. Elizabeth's age was similar to our own New Deal period, in that social planners sought to use settlement policies to right human ills. Unfortunately in both cases a heavily romantic view of the countryside meant that the social planning was not very effective with respect to cities, placing its heavy reliance on a sort of refuge in rural areas. As America seems again to be taking this tack in her social thinking, a brief look at the outcome of Elizabeth's policy toward small-holding may not be untimely.

In 1589, "Elizabeth's government passed an Act, under which four acres of land were to be annexed to every new labourer's cottage which was built, and crowding in cottages was prohibited, by inflicting very substantial penalties on owners who permitted more than one family to inhabit the same tenement. . . .The Act did not annex these plots to existing cottages. . . . But as time went on, the Act was operative. As population increased it became a substantial obligation, . . .[and to landowners] a substantial grievance, which Parliament removed by abrogating the Act early in George III's reign," just at the time the Industrial Revolution was in full spate.[41] Such small-holdings badly interfered with the eighteenth-century wave of enclosing common lands and open-fields, and with the subsequent adoption of the "new farming," with its complete emphasis on increased "production."

This concern with the quantitative economy was as strongly marked in the agricultural sphere as in the industrial. Referring to a social movement current in the late nineteenth century, when he was writing, Thorold Rogers concluded, "Perhaps it is new to some of you, that the doctrine of three acres and a cow—for near two centuries four—attached to the labourer's cottage, has so respectable an antiquity as an Act of Elizabeth, a date which precedes the creation of any existing dukedom and most peerages." In our words, but hardly the deferential ones of Britain at the turn of the century, the small-holdings had a more ancient base than the privilege of the men who greedily de-

[40]*George Townsend Warner*, Landmarks in English Industrial History, *London: Blackie & Son, 1898, revised 1924, p. 248.*

[41]*James E. Thorold Rogers*, The Industrial and Commercial History of England, *New York: G. P. Putnam's Sons, 1892, pp. 256–257.*

stroyed them as the Industrial Revolution vastly enhanced the value of farm land by creating an urban proletariat ready at hand to consume the products of those fields in the "new farming."

The Arrival of the Cotton Manufacture Through Long-Distance Trade

In cotton, a long-distance trade was essential, extending initially to Syria and Cyprus but subsequently to the West Indies, Brazil, and the American colonies. To organize such trade required the skills and offices of the wholesaler, so we find nineteenth-century Manchester becoming the center of organization of what came to be both a massive industry and a world marketing system. The cotton trade differed greatly from the traditional woolen industry of the West Riding, with its internalization of staple and production. Even when the Yorkshire woolen industry had to turn outward for wool, which it did not do for a long time, it still conducted the trade on a far less massive scale.

In the end the handling of cotton was further split, with Manchester serving more as the trader in cloths while Liverpool, the port that grew from the trade, traded in cotton fiber. In a study of the Liverpool merchants and the cotton trade from 1820-1850, D. M. Williams shows that, "If the entire period . . .is examined, certain trends are plainly visible. Most outstanding is the fact that in the twenty years from 1820 to 1839, a period of very rapid expansion, the cotton trade became more and more concentrated into the hands of a small group of merchants. . . .Thus up to 1839 the increase in imports was not met by a greater number of importers but by an expansion in the leading merchants' scale of operation. . . .Clearly, after 1820 the cotton trade became the preserve of large operators dealing in United States' cotton."[42]

That group of large merchant firms dealing in raw cotton included several from the United States (Nicholas Biddle in his guise as a speculator in cotton

among them) and from Scotland. In any trade needing long-distance connections, the requirement of temporal and geographical intelligence is such that a few specialized dealers will come to the fore, and they are as likely to come from the areas supplying the staple as from the consumers thereof. Like all such operations based on commercial intelligence, a strong force operates within such a trade to congregate its practitioners in one or at most a few cities.[43] The Lancashire cotton trade came in the end to have two types of distant intelligence—that with respect to the supply of the cotton staple, and that with respect to the selling in a world market of the cotton textiles produced around Manchester. The trading center for cotton staple rapidly became Liverpool, whereas that in textiles came strongly to be Manchester, which drew to herself the selling functions of a complex producing region whose manufacturing soon departed the metropolitan core.

The External Evolution of the Industrial Metropolis

This external evolution of the manufacturing phase of industrialization was present in most of the early factory districts. Manchester was followed in turn by Boston in Massachusetts, Rouen, and Verviers in Belgium, as centers of commercial intelligence around which factory towns would be ranged. As time has passed, the links have been further lengthened, as when cotton textile production was shifted from New England to the American South, in a final movement during the 1920's. Boston and more strongly New York remained the centers of commercial intelligence from which textile factors worked to finance production and whence the market for textiles could be appraised and production and sales efforts initiated. More recently, the same linkage has been further extended, as so-called "multinational corporations" push production even farther away—to Korea, Taiwan, Hong Kong, or Singapore —while maintaining the factoring, organizing, and selling functions in the commercial heart of the indus-

[42]D. M. Williams, "Liverpool Merchants and the Cotton Trade, 1820-1850", in Liverpool and Merseyside: Essays in the Economic and Social History of the Port and its Hinterland, edited by J. R. Harris, London: Frank Cass & Co., 1969, pp. 189–191.

[43]For a more detailed and processional view of this creation of wholesaling towns, see James E. Vance, Jr., The Merchant's World: The Geography of Wholesaling, Englewood Cliffs, N.J.: Prentice-Hall, Inc., 1970.

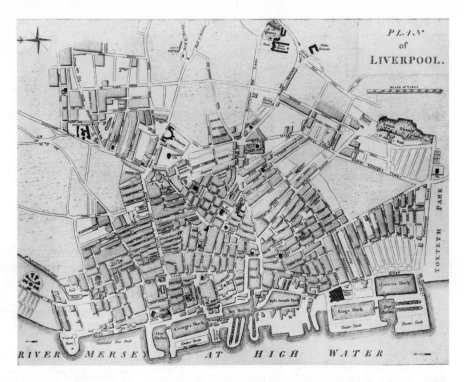

Map of Liverpool, from Aikin, The Country Round Manchester, *1795.*

trial system of cities. The system began in Manchester in the early years of the Industrial Revolution, changing not in basic relationship but simply in the geographical extent of its external evolution and the length of the linkages.

Towns Become the Support of the Countryside

The Industrial Revolution is seldom considered from the perspective of the countryside; in fact, we tend to think of industrialization as almost a destructive element sapping the strength of the rural areas and seeking to encroach upon their long-established purlieus. Yet such could hardly be further from the truth, either in Britain or America, though the two countries experienced sharply different settlement consequences of industrialization.

In Britain, a new practice of farming could come

into existence only as a result of industrialization and urbanization. The chance afforded rural landowners to rationalize economically their land-use and cropping practices came as a result on the one hand, of the ability to encourage surplus rural population to migrate to the rising industrial cities and, on the other, of the establishment in those metropolises of a large and protected market for English agricultural produce. Enclosure of common land into privately held pasturage, expansion of the land given over to wheat production for an enlarging urban proletariat, and agricultural reform of a sort impossible if the traditional rural economy had persisted, all made farming far more profitable as a result of industrial urbanization than it would have been without those cities and their factories and workers. If it had ever been as true, as some believe, that towns can only grow out of the countryside, it certainly was demonstrably untrue once the Industrial Revolution was in full effect. Not without significance, von Thünen's study of the economics of agricultural land-use was city-centered, and was a system of land-assignment based on the city as the originator of farming practices. Von Thünen was writing in the decades of the early nineteenth century when industrialization was in full sweep, even if not directly so in the area near Tellow, his estate, in what is today East Germany. In his study of the "isolated city" written in 1826,[44] von Thünen leaves no doubt that the town shapes the economic life of the country in the modern world of industry.

The rise of the industrial city restored economic vitality to rural England and the land-owning class became wealthy as a result, though they showed no gratitude toward the cities that made them so. Instead political lines were drawn between Tories, raised to great power by rural wealth gained within a rejuvenated farming system, and Whigs, first made wealthy and powerful with the rise of commerce and industry in the eighteenth and nineteenth centuries. The split came to be one between the country and the town because the first attempts at powered industrialization, which came in the country, tended in Britain to be short-lived and succeeded by a massive development of factories in cities.

In a study of Ashton-under-Lyne, the manor lying directly east of Manchester, Winifred Bowman showed that already in the fifteenth century that manor had the privilege to hold two annual fairs at which wool fleeces and cloths might be traded. As the manufacturing component of the metropolitan industrialization began to concentrate outside Manchester, Ashton rose to great importance as a manufacturing place and rather soon after cotton came to dominate in southeast Lancashire. The first cotton mill was established in Manchester in 1781 and the first in Ashton-under-Lyne in 1785.[45] Initially these mills were powered by water. When the endowment of waterpower was soon taken up, attention had to turn to Boulton and Watt's steam engines.

The ease with which power was adapted to spinning was probably a result of the critical need for more yarn to support the expansion of the textile industry along basically traditional lines of domestic production within a quantitative economy. The technical improvement in one process was not necessarily directly or rapidly followed by a change in another as the case of the powered-loom shows beyond question. First developed in the 1790's, the power-loom was violently opposed by the weavers of Lancashire. Ashton was so in the forefront of that group that the town of Manchester had established the precaution that her church bells would be rung to warn that the potentially riotous Ashton weavers were marching on the organizational hub of the metropolis.[46] In face of that opposition

power was not brought for many years to the weaving of even fairly cheap textiles, with the result that Lancashire displayed a mixture of hand- and machine-weaving even as late as the middle of the nineteenth century. Thus, the great early application of steam power as a supplement to the fully utilized waterpower came in the carding and spinning phase of textile production, which led to a much greater concentration of yarn production than that of cloth making. Again this fact was a force creating the complex metropolitan area with distinct industrial satellites surrounding a dominant center of organization and commercial intelligence.

Weavers tended to continue to operate in outlying industrial towns but to secure the yarns to be woven in their looms through Mancunian manufacturers' "putting-out." This organization continued the vast need for workers greater in numbers than might have been called for in a fully mechanized operation. At Ashton and a dozen other places lying just beyond Manchester's boundaries, great housing tracts of very cheap houses were laid out, often by aristocratic landowners such as the earls of Stanford and Warrington who owned much of Ashton. In those tracts, hand-loom weavers operated a little-appreciated form of what might be called "collected domestic production." Unfortunately, this domestic production was shorn of the backstay of the "weaver's plot" of earlier Lancashire or the small-holding of the Yorkshire woolen manufacturer.[47]

In addition, these tracts of small row-houses served as the home for families—often further crowded in their housing by boarders—employed in the spinning mills and the machine-weaving establishments that came into being after about 1825. In essence, this housing supply was made available by private investment to allow the concentration of workers coming from the surrounding countryside or, in the case of southeast Lancashire, from the south of England where the economy after the Napoleonic War was none too healthy. The flow of in-migrants also included a number of Irish who were fleeing that verdant land of hunger in the 1830's and '40's. All these groups crowded into Ashton, and Lancashire in general, and the landlords provided tiny houses for them. The Royal Commission Studying the State of the Large Towns and Populous Places in the 1840's brought out evidence that these

---

[44]Published as Johann Heinrich von Thünen, Der Isolierte Staat, with an introduction by Heinrich Waentig, Jena: Gustav Fisher, 1910.

[45]Winifred M. Bowman, England in Ashton-under-Lyne, Altrincham [Cheshire]: John Sheratt for the Ashton-under-Lyne [City] Corporation, 1960, p. 425.

[46]Ibid., p. 439.

[47]This view of Ashton is based on a careful appraisal of the manuscript 1851 census of England for Ashton-under-Lyne which I undertook sometime ago. Unfortunately too many of the enumerator's books have been lost to make a detailed study possible. But on the basis of the evidence available to me, I became convinced that this notion of the "collective domestic manufacture," even as late as 1851, is valid.

houses were so modest, if not outright mean, that they could be built for as little as £50, perhaps $250 in American money of the time. But in this collection of domestic manufacture into a new industrial metropolis, we have a peculiar and rather unappreciated stage in the industrialization of cities.

Friedrich Engels on the Morphogenesis of Manchester

Decrying the tendency to use Manchester as the sole example of industrialization, one can never avoid it as a fascinating and critical pillar in what was a somewhat more encompassing ediface. Such a wealth of material has come down to us about the Industrial Revolution in the city that we cannot turn away from it, yet we must take Manchester as a prime example, hardly a universal one. A case in point is furnished by the detailed and perceptive analysis of the society and form of Manchester gained by Friedrich Engels from twenty months' residence there in 1842-1844, just at the onset of full factory development. On his return to Barmen in the Rhineland, Engels wrote *The Condition of the Working Class in England*, publishing it in 1845 and thereby establishing his credentials as one of the fathers of socialism and communism. Because his picture of England was painted in such dark hues, for more than a century his book tended to be viewed as a political tract, which it was. But the accuracy of its description of those "conditions," which seems incontestable from a wealth of less doctrinaire writing that has subsequently been made public, was disregarded.

No one, it seems to me, looked upon Manchester as an Industrial Era city with the perceptive morphogenetic eye that Engels seems to have possessed. The great criticism lodged against Engels is that in this first application of dialectical materialism, well before Marx used the term of analysis, he romanticized the quality of rural life in the preindustrial era while painting the Industrial Age even blacker than it was. I would incline toward the view that the hues of his Manchester in 1843 are those of a careful realist, while the color with which he paints the domestic production before the development of factories are far brighter and more cheerful than reality would have required. As the editors of the recent retranslation of the book point up, the lot of earlier nail workers in Willenhall in the Black

Country and the sewing girls of London's East End was certainly no better than that of Manchester's "little piecers," the most depressed workers in the cotton mills.[48] The apprentices in the Willenhall lock trade are graphically described by Benjamin Disraeli in his *Sybil, or: The Two Nations* (of 1845) wherein a basically "domestic trade" is presented in colors equally as dark as those employed by Engels.[49]

Engels begins with a description of "The face of the country [which] has been completely changed as a result of the Industrial Revolution." Painting perhaps too strong a contrast with the past, he finds southeast Lancashire "an obscure, poorly cultivated bog" before industrialization, which had "increased ten-fold in 80 years" with many large towns growing up there. "Liverpool and Manchester, for example, have together 700,000 inhabitants. Near [Manchester] are Bolton (50,000 inhabitants), Rochdale (75,000), Oldham (50,000), . . . Ashton and Stalybridge (40,000)."[50] The vast expansion of numbers in the industrial cities came as a result of the initial need for workers when industry was mechanized. To gain that labor, wages were increased over those to be earned in domestic production in the countryside, drawing to the emerging cities hordes of workers, under- or unemployed in the country, as well as those simply seeking financial improvement. Signaling a proclivity of the Irish population that we may recognize, but mixing up its cause, Engels tells us: "Meanwhile, in Ireland, where law and order had only been fully established at the beginning of the eighteenth century, the population—formerly decimated by English barbarity—was expanding quickly. With the expansion of English industry many Irishmen migrated to England to seek work there. These [together] are the reasons for the expansion of the great factory towns and commercial centers in the United Kingdom, in which at least three-quarters of the inhabitants are members of the working classes."[51]

It was essential to establish the rapid growth of population in the cities through massive in-migration from the country because the conditions Engels describes were so grim that the expansion in numbers in the working classes could never have been accounted for by localized biological growth. Also those rapid increases in population serve to explain why, after an initial inflation of wages through migration to the city,

[48]*Friedrich Engels*, The Condition of the Working Class in England, *translated and edited by W. O. Henderson and W. H. Chaloner, Stanford, Calif.: Stanford University Press, 1968 (original English edition, London: Basil Blackwell, 1958), p. xii.*
[49]*Benjamin Disraeli*, Sybil, or: The Two Nations [*1845*], *Harmondsworth [Middlesex]: Penguin Books, 1954.*
[50]*Engels, op. cit., p. 16.*
[51]*Ibid., p. 24.*

the working classes experienced a rapid decline in those same wages to the point that former hand-workers might very well have their wages reduced well below what they had earned in rural domestic industry. Essentially, though Engels never states the case, the oversupply of the labor force answering the call to the city created, at least in considerable measure, the deterioration of social and economic conditions there. Thus, to blame the entire decline on the process of industrialization and the "middle classes," as he repeatedly does, is to whitewash the evidence. Fully as guilty—perhaps more so, depending upon your point of view—was the rural land-ownership system, which forced the rural unemployed into cities as rural land was outright concentrated into a few, generally aristocratic hands.

I think this tendency to internalize the Industrial Revolution to the city alone—finding there both its victims and its oppressors—is rather a case of partisan pleading and bad historical geography, particularly when we attempt to analyze and understand the effect of the industrialization process on the common people. In justice, we cannot deny the very considerable mistreatment of the working class by the manufacturers, but to think that the malign intent of a single small, though powerful, group produced such misery is too simple. Instead, responsibility lies both in the events taking place within the city and the forces outside the city that were causing people to move into them and, once there, contributed to their hunger. The rural landowning class must bear as much responsibility for the evils of the Industrial Revolution as do the actual final agents of oppression—the factory managers.

The Economic Transfer from City to Country

The evidence is strong that the rural landowning class, basically aristocratic in social status, desired to reduce the numbers of rural people. In part, they wished to increase the field and pastoral agriculture of the landowner through enclosures, and in part they wanted to keep down the taxation for the support of the local poor. We know that much of the flood of migrants to Manchester and the other industrializing towns came with a firm "push" rendered by parish authorities in the countryside and the south of England, and soon in Ireland, administered with the view of freeing the rolls of financial responsibilities. Once there, the now-urban proletariat was still to experience the oppression of that same landowning class in two other ways at least. First, landowners were very reluctant to see their properties given up to urban uses because social status in English society was heavily based on ownership of rural lands. In the case of Nottingham, Birmingham, and a number of other growing industrial cities, this effort to keep the countryside for the underpinning of the system of aristocracy was so strong that the city could not easily grow in area to accommodate its burgeoning population. The urban working class was forced to live windward of the factory chimneys in part because the estate owners must continue their febrile interest in foxhunting, undiminished by the human suffering it brought. Similarly the notion of the "proper" landscape was so narrowly that of the gentleman's park that the city must be kept at bay to maintain that preserve.

The second way in which the system of rural aristocracy played a dark and direct role in the oppression of the urban proletariat came in the social cancer it fostered among the industrialists themselves. Because high social status in England was so artificially and narrowly defined in terms of ownership of rural estates, the cotton magnates sought rather quickly to buy rural lands to advance their search for the ennoblement that might ultimately come with it. With the notable exception of Robert Owen, whose mind ran always in terms of the urban community, admittedly not vast in size but still urban rather than rural, the cotton magnates succumbed to the desire to be accepted among the gentry, which could only be accomplished by sedulous copying of their ways. A recent study of the Arkwrights has shown how very significant that diversion of interest and capital from the cotton trade may have been. That study might as well have included the Strutts, Samuel Oldknow of Manchester, the Cromptons, and a number of iron masters who fell before the same idol. The association was not one-sided; for the aristocracy, the cotton magnates had the great virtue of possessing liquid capital. Georgiana, the Duchess of Devonshire, whose husband's estate, Chatsworth, was just up the road from Cromford, learned this fact to her comfort already in the 1790's when she borrowed £6,000 from Arkwright to pay off a gambling debt. The Duke's intercession probably kept Arkwright out of court when his too-casual mill building at Bakewell infringed the downstream riparian water rights of the Duke of Rutland. But even accepting that manufacturers and dukes could scratch each other's backs, the dominant position of the rural aristocracy was what counted. In seeking so earnestly to be like them, the cotton manufacturers diverted capital from their factory undertakings and the possible improvement in the lot of their operatives.

The tale is fairly clear from E. L. Jones' account. [52] Richard Arkwright had bought estate land around Cromford as early as 1776 but, in seeking to expand his mill building, he had to sell this land to raise ready capital. The social advantages of land ownership seem always to have been played off against the business advantages of ready capital for investment in machines and the conduct of the business. In the earlier stages of the development of the cotton industry, the business had to take precedence not merely over the craving for social elevation on the part of the manufacturer but also in the matter of treating the emerging factory industry as an occupational household in the same way that the medieval masters of crafts had done. At Cromford and Belper, Arkwright and Strutt had acted like medieval masters in providing housing for their workers. But once they began to expand their factories and trade, they soon dropped that general social responsibility in the interest of making the maximum use of their capital in that expansion.

Unfortunately they found it impossible to shed the social pretensions that gripped their hearts. While the lot of the workers in their factories was declining and their housing was becoming more and more grim (as the long-standing and hidden subvention from the employer to his workers was removed by throwing the rental relationship entirely into a general market situation), the lot of the countryside was being improved. Not only did the cotton magnates "bail out" the Georgianas, but also they saved their male relatives as well. Richard Arkwright the younger, in buying Hampton Court in Herefordshire, essentially salvaged a main part of the fortunes of Lord Essex. In this operation alone, Jones figures that Arkwright invested around £230,000. Comparison with the total investment in the fixed capital of the whole cotton textile industry in Britain in the same year (1809) of only £400,000[53] shows how much capital was diverted from the conduct of the cotton trade and the welfare of its workers, who actually earned the return, as a subvention to maintaining the artificial "economy" of the countryside.

This question is not involved only with the diversion of money from the highly productive urban industries to the increasingly uneconomic rural establishments but is as well one of political and social estimation. Daniel Defoe saw the relationship clearly when he

held, "An estate is but a Pond, but Trade is a Spring." From the time of the Industrial Revolution on, the English countryside was the ward of the labor of the factory workers. Their sweating came in considerable measure not only from the necessary privations imposed by the industrial processes, but as well from the enslavement of English society, culture, and economy to this haughty relict of the medieval economic system. Economic organization and social order had during the Middle Ages been based on agriculture and the manpower for defense it offered. But by the late eighteenth century, the defense forces were mainly those of merchant seamen, and the economy was increasingly urban. Yet the dead hand of the past ruled Britain, maintaining an artificial support for agriculture in the Corn Laws, a nonfunctional order of precedence in the gentry, and the utter fiction that the cities were the product of the countryside. Manchester, by depending upon an imported staple, effectively denied that assumption to any with open eyes to see.

Throughout the late eighteenth and nineteenth centuries, the ever-expanding "beautification" of the countryside pumped money earned in the cities into the creation of new estates or the support of existing ones. This era saw large numbers of new "country houses" of an unrelieved ostentation and the creation of a vast acreage of new "parks" for the wealthy, wherein a synthetic English landscape was developed. If we take into account the sweat of the working classes that went into them, those morally atrocious creations might gain less adulation than they now receive. Finally, "the economic interests of the truly affluent and most powerful in trade, industry, and land did overlap in England. Moneyed interest and landed interest could not fatally bifurcate in a country where so many great landed proprietors were aware that their true roots lay not in coats of arms cash down, as it were, from the College of Heralds, but in discreet remittances from warehouses, mines, or mills, and where, since socially the landed gentleman was king, so many successful manufacturers would aspire to his crown."[54]

It seems to me that two great misfortunes resulted from this association of the cotton magnates, and other manufacturers and "moneyed interests," with the landed interests. The first was the intolerable exaction that propping up the decayed social and economic system of the medieval aristocracy (even late elevations accepted that moribund system in using their titles) made on the truly productive classes of England, those who worked in "warehouses, mines, or mills." The lot of the working class was demonstrably less good for the transfusion of their productivity to the countryside, quite in contrast to the infusion of strength that Ameri-

[52]E. L. Jones, "Industrial Capital and Landed Investment: The Arkwrights in Herefordshire, 1809–43," in Land, Labour, and Population in the Industrial Revolution, London: Edward Arnold, 1967.
[53]Ibid., p. 68.
[54]Ibid., p. 50.

The Market Place in Manchester was, in the late eighteenth century, still a very modest affair, beginning to show the rising prosperity of the city but demonstrating the continuing poverty of the working class.

can workers received from the presence of a productive and democratic countryside, as Professor H. J. Habakkuk showed.[55] The other misfortune is that Friedrich Engels viewed Manchester at the time he did through a vision that must have been strongly tinted by nineteenth-century romanticism so common among

[55]*H. J. Habakkuk*, British and American Technology in the Nineteenth Century; The Search for Labour-Saving Inventions. *Cambridge: Cambridge University Press, 1962.*

German intellectuals. Taking Peter Gaskell's book *The Manufacturing Population of England* [1833] as the proper picture of rural life and industry, Engels used dialectical materialism to blame the lot of the working class entirely on the industrial system. He overlooked or was unaware of how very much the countryside influenced city life through physical constraint of growth, overpriced food, transport thence of rural welfare problems, sirening away of urban wealth to support rural decadence, and the creation of an antipathy towards the city so typical of the weak toward the strong. If only he had known more, and had seen how large a role the rural society and economy of England played in creating the lot of the city workman: if only he had been aware of how, with a different kind of countryside in America, the situation was different, we might have had a quite different development of communist thought, and thereby of world history.

The Morphogenesis of an Industrial City: Manchester in 1843

What then was Manchester like when Engels went there in 1842? In the classic mold of travelers to the north, he begins by descending upon the city from the crest, the Blackstone Edge of the Pennines, noting "a beautiful hilly countryside ... intersected by the charming green valleys of the Ribble, the Irwell, the Mersey and their tributaries" on the lower courses of which is to be found "the most densely-populated part of England. In Lancashire—particularly in Manchester—is to be found not only the origin but the heart of the industry of the United Kingdom." Engels held that with good endowment of the "three factors that are the essence of modern industry"—the application of water and steam power, the use of self-acting machines, and the division of labor—"the evolution of the modern system of manufacture has reached its climax in Manchester." Because of this climax position and his intimate knowledge of the place, Engels proposed to look at Manchester. "In the circumstances it is to be expected that it is in this region that the inevitable consequences of industrialization in so far as they affect the working classes are most strikingly evident."[56]

In this sober fashion we learn that in the mind of this young German visitor, Manchester was to be erected as a model of the "inevitable consequences of industrialization" in changing for the worse "a beautiful hilly countryside" and a reputedly humane domestic industry (so romanticized by Gaskell), which Engels seems to have taken as his Eden before the industrial fall.[57]

With these cautions in mind, we may still gain a most useful picture of the classic industrial town just after its time of greatest growth. "Manchester proper lies on the left of the Irwell, between this river and two smaller streams, the Irk and the Medlock, which flow into the Irwell at this point. Salford lies on the right bank of the Irwell in a sharp bend of the river ...." Round about are a number of places which have fully grown together with the city during its rapid development. Slightly farther away, but generally continuous with Manchester, are the satellitic towns—Ashton, Oldham, Stalybridge, Stockport, Bolton, Rochdale, and several others. "In the centre of Manchester there is a fairly large commercial district, which is about half a mile long and half a mile broad. This district is almost entirely given over to offices and warehouses." Quite in contrast to the medieval city, the Manchester of Engels' time anticipated modern conditions: "Nearly the whole of this district has no permanent residents and is deserted at night, when only policemen patrol its dark, narrow thoroughfares with their bull's eye lanterns." This quarter, which today we would call a central business district, lay near the medieval core of the town and was "intersected by certain main streets which carry an enormous volume of traffic. The lower floors of the buildings are occupied by shops of dazzling splendour. A few of the upper stories on these premises are used as dwellings and the streets present a relatively busy appearance until late in the evening."

"Around the commercial quarter there is a belt of built up areas on the average one and a half miles in width, which is occupied entirely by working-class dwellings. This area of workers' houses includes all Manchester proper, except the centre, all Salford and Hulme, an important part of Pendleton and Chorlton, two-thirds of Ardwick and certain small areas of Cheetham Hill and Broughton [all of these former outlying villages now continuous with Manchester]. Beyond this belt of working-class houses or dwellings lie the districts inhabited by the middle classes and the upper classes." Thus we see that even in the early 1840's the notion of a social class stratification outward from the center, accompanied by a rise in status with outward shift, had become characteristic of the English city. This point is important to appreciate when we come to the modern city, as it has direct bearing on the question of so-called "white-flight."

The middle-class districts "are to be found in regularly laid out streets near the working-class districts—in Chorlton [on-Medlock] and in the remoter parts of Cheetham Hill." Obviously these housing "estates" were built by speculative builders who were laying down monotonous carpets—perhaps doormats is a better image in the case of Manchester's modest-size middle class—of uniform and eminently "respectable" row-houses along carefully identical streets of stultifying "order" and "correctness." Engels elsewhere speaks most critically of the absence of plan in the working-class areas but, a true son of a class-

[56]*Engels, op. cit., p. 50.*
[57]*A number of observers, including the translators and editors of the edition of Engels being cited, have pointed out the German's uncritical acceptance of Gaskell, leading through its overly sanguine view of England's past to a rather fundamental exaggeration of the "inevitable consequences of industrialization." To accept Engels' view of the future, one must first overlook the real conditions in the past, accept dialectical materialism, and rule out any possible improvement within the capitalist system. As he, perhaps unwittingly, but still rather doctrinally, mistakes the degree of change wrought by capitalism, one may question the singleness of solution he perceives for this situation.*

ordered society, he smiles on the picked-up dullness of the middle-class terraces.

Beyond these regimented accommodations lay the suburban landscapes of the well-to-do. "The villas [detached houses] of the upper classes are surrounded by gardens and lie in the higher and remoter parts of Chorlton and Ardwick or on the breezy heights of Cheetham Hill, Broughton and Pendleton." Apparently this outward movement from the city was fairly recent, as it was observed by L. M. Hayes, "In Manchester about the year 1840 and onwards, the middle classes began to realize that town life was not very desirable, and families began migrating and settling in the various suburbs."[58] The nature of the undesirability of the central area was apparently largely a matter of public health, not either of personal safety or chance association. The slow emergence of the idea of contagious disease had done much to condition persons with money that their "duty" to their family was to move out, shielding the family from possible contagion. This notion was strengthened when cholera struck Britain yet again in the 1830's.

In a tantalizing reference to the use of public transportation, which he simply does not amplify, Engels continues his discussion of the villa areas. "The upper classes enjoy healthy country air and live in luxurious and comfortable dwellings which are linked to the centre of Manchester by omnibuses which run every fifteen or thirty minutes. To such an extent has the convenience of the rich been considered in the planning of Manchester that these plutocrats can travel from their houses to their places of business in the centre of town by the shortest routes, which run entirely through working-class districts, without even realizing how close they are to the misery and filth which lie on both sides of the road." One wonders whether this arrangement was planning or land-and-transportation economics. Truly only the well-to-do could use horse-drawn omnibuses; many recent studies have confirmed fairly conclusively that "mass transit" until the coming of the electric trolley was a rather ironic term. This transit was shared among the relatively small and well-washed numbers of the fortunate classes. But it may have been the result of little conscious planning. A capitalist society need not plan that way; the market brought the situation about. Perhaps this quibble is academic, though I think assertion of cause and proof of cause are equally essential elements in a single act of support; to assign the cause wrongly does put in doubt statements of the process at work.

This argument is further developed by Engels when he holds that "even the less pretentious shops adequately serve their purpose of hiding from the eyes of wealthy ladies and gentlemen with strong stomachs and weak nerves the misery and squalor which are part and parcel of their own riches and luxury." Still we have seen that in more humane expressions of capitalism and in socialist societies this "facade" of shops does develop. Interestingly, it was observable as much as 140 years ago. "These shops have naturally been greatly influenced by the character of the population in the area which lies behind them. Those shops which are situated in the vicinity of commercial or middle class residential districts are more elegant than those which serve as a facade for the workers' grimy cottages. . . .[One of Manchester's main arteries] Deansgate, for example, changes in character as one goes due south from the Old Church. At first there are warehouses and factories. Next come shops of a somewhat inferior character and the street becomes dirtier, while taverns and gin palaces become increasingly frequent. When he reaches the end of the street the appearance of the shops can leave no doubt in his mind that no one but the workers would dream of patronizing them."

Engels does not support his original contention very effectively when he looks at another artery, which we would tend to call "a radiating business street." Market Street ran southeasterly from the Manchester Exchange, "the thermometer which records all the fluctuations of industrial and commercial activity" in the metropolis and in England; it ran first into Piccadilly "with its huge hotels and warehouses" in an association we will see become particularly related to railroad stations (Manchester *Piccadilly* in this case), but its further continuation, as London Road, "which lies near the river Medlock, has a very different appearance. Here are to be found factories, public houses and shops which cater for the needs of the lower middle classes and the workers. By the time Ardwick Green is reached, the street has changed its character yet again, and is flanked by residences occupied by the upper and middle classes."[59]

The pattern emerging in Manchester by 1840 was very strikingly that of the modern city, with separation of one function from another and the separation of one social class from all others. Following the Anglo-Saxon model of housing that we saw in Chapter 6, the city showed an increasing elevation of social status as one moved out from the center, with the "Old City" in Manchester standing as a slum even in 1840. Scattered around that Old City, intermixed with poor housing, and spreading out along the valleys of the Irk, the Med-

[58]*L. M. Hayes*, Reminiscences of Manchester and Some of Its Local Surroundings from the year 1840 [1905], *p. 51, quoted in Henderson and Chaloner's translation of Engels. Quotations from Engels are from pp. 54–55.*

[59]*Engels*, op. cit., *pp. 55–56.*

lock, and the Irwell, were the industrial quarters—grimy, noisy, plagued by smoke and stench, but finally the source of employment for most of the population, a group without the earnings to pay for any transportation to and from work. The streets that ran through Manchester came to be lined with shops, as they have remained to this day despite a socialist social revolution and the introduction of automobiles.

One item—working-class housing—has changed most strikingly; with that change, we must believe both in the improvability of society and the tempering of the worst features of capitalism. To understand that change we must turn to Engels' most perceptive and valuable description of Manchester. His descriptions of the working-class housing areas are so graphic and so detailed that it is hard to find the best summation of his writing. His account covers the several working-class quarters, which though much the same in character, were diverse when described individually.

Taking as perhaps the worst extreme "the district near the 'Old Church' . . .one sees immediately on the right hand side a row of antiquated houses where not a single front wall is standing upright. This is a remnant of the old Manchester of the days before the town became industrialized. The old inhabitants and their children have left for better houses in other districts, while the houses in Long Millgate, which no longer satisfied them, were left to a tribe of workers containing a strong Irish element." Engels noted that even the shopkeepers and publicans in this district "make no effort to give their establishments a semblance of cleanliness . . .[as it] is quite obviously given over entirely to the working classes . . . ." Not only were the old houses deteriorating but also they were being crowded by the filling in of what little open-space they had had by the building of additional houses on the tiny lots. "The condition of this street may be deplorable, but it is by no means as bad as the alleys and courts which lie behind it, and which can be approached only by covered passages so narrow that two people cannot pass. Anyone who has not visited these courts and alleys can have no idea of the fantastic way in which the houses have been packed together . . . . And the fault lies not merely in the survival of old property . . .[for] Only in quite modern times has the policy of cramming as many houses as possible on to such space as was not utilised in earlier periods reached its climax." What was no doubt the case for Manchester certainly was not true for London, where already before the Fire such crowding could have been found without any recourse to industry, or in some Italian medieval cities, without any reference to capitalism.

This sketch will be sufficient to illustrate the crazy layout of the whole district near the River Irk. There is a very sharp drop of some 15 to 30 feet down to the south

Diagram from F. Engels: The Condition of the Working Class in England. Reprinted by permission of Stanford University Press.

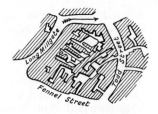

bank of the Irk at this point. As many as three rows of houses have generally been squeezed on to this precipitous slope. The lowest row of houses stands directly on the bank of the river while the front walls of the highest row stand on the crest of the ridge in Long Millgate. Moreover, factory buildings are also to be found on the banks of the river. . . .To the right and left a number of covered passages from Long Millgate give access to several courts. On reaching them one meets with a degree of dirt and revolting filth, the like of which is not to be found elsewhere. The worst courts are those leading down to the Irk, which contain unquestionably the most dreadful dwellings I have ever seen. In one of these courts, just at the entrance where the covered passage ends there is a privy without a door. The privy is so dirty that the inhabitants of the court can only enter or leave the court if they are prepared to wade through puddles of stale urine and excrement. . . .Several tanneries are situated on the bank of the river and they fill the neighbourhood with the stench of animal putrefaction. . . .The first court below Ducie Bridge is called Allen's Court. At the same time of the cholera [1832] this court was in such a disgraceful state that the sanitary inspector evacuated the inhabitants. The court was then swept and fumigated with chlorine. . . .If one looks at the heaps of garbage below Ducie Bridge one can gauge the extent to which the accumulated dirt, filth and decay permeates the courts on the steep left bank of the river.[60]

Engels' view of the slums of Manchester is undoubtedly correct: we must judge whether this phenomenon was geographically restricted or was the general pattern of working-class life in an industrial city. Engels himself, as well as other observers, suggest that we should divide the question: What were the general qualities of housing and life for the working class in Britain as a whole? Was variation to be found within the housing of this working class in industrial cities? Crowding within the worker's cottage was considerable even in the countryside. Families tended to be fairly large—they had numerous children, and households were commonly composed of several generations living together—with the result that the accommodations of most working-class households—whether of agricultural or factory workers—must have been rea-

[60]Ibid., pp. 58–60.

sonably crowded. No doubt the operation of urban land economics assured that workers' "houses" in the city were more certain to be small and cramped than were those in the country. But since most of those in the working class, in country as well as city, were renters rather than freehold owners, small scale in housing provision was seemingly their common lot.

Building on observations elsewhere and later in history, we may argue that part of the problem was one of acculturation. Rural people, used to living in open country, were collected into cities, and failed to adjust to that new environment. To take one example: the common practices of reutilizing broken items, which are stored for repair and reuse in the country, becomes intolerable in cities. With no open space for storage, the broken items which may look to be "thrifty storage" in the farmyard become "garbage and junk" in the city. Similarly the privy and pigsty that stood for sanitation in the farmyard could, with the tightly packed numbers of the city, become absolutely intolerable. But is this presence of filth and poor health conditions the result of capitalism rather the simple necessity in certain economic activities to cluster people together? The urban landowners and factory operators do not bear all of the blame.

Finally the habits of the rural proletariat when transferred to the city and collected into working-class neighborhoods can produce fairly hairy conditions without the reach either of capitalism or industrialization. Both classical and papal Rome faced these problems in the absence of both of these economic institutions; the difference came rather in the existence of an absolutely powerful government which could command the resources, and the use of urban land to bring water to the city and remove the wastes so easily dealt with in the open country and so nearly intractable in the city. Yet biologically and socially, the people are pretty much the same in both areas. The simple Irish peasant remained relatively little changed between Galway and Manchester or Boston, but practices that remained unremarked in the peasant cottage were quite valid housing and health problems in the city.

The Concept of the Generalization of Housing

This picture of slums raises a second question: Did the working-class areas of these industrial cities differ? The answer begins to emerge as we introduce a new concept—the *generalization of housing*—a simple but useful idea. Throughout most of economic history before the Industrial Revolution, the basic unit of housing in both the country and the city was the occupational household. On a farm, the farmer and his biological family were joined by hired hands—either single men or men and their families. In the city the medieval master of a craft brought together in his house not merely his own family but as well the production and sale of the goods of trade and the housing of the apprentices and journeymen most commonly producing them. We know that some renting of housing occurred in the medieval city. Though the evidence as to the proportion is not readily available, probably little outright rental housing existed apart from the occupational household of the master. Until the Industrial Revolution, one normally gained housing through gaining employment. This pattern of housing provision was probably traditional from the very beginning of permanent residence in cities.

One of the fundamental changes wrought by the Industrial Revolution was the shaping of a substitute for the occupational household. This change was not at first apparent when Richard Arkwright set up a factory to utilize his water-frame for spinning yarn. He turned to several waterpower sites on the river Derwent in the Peak District of Derbyshire where, in partnership with Jedidiah Strutt, he established a mill at Cromford in 1771 and downstream at Belper in 1776. In 1783, a year after the partnership was ended, Arkwright built his own mill at Cromford, just upstream from the original mill of 1771.[61] In each situation, the occupational household was used in one of two ways. The original Cromford mill depended heavily on segmental labor drawn from the adjacent villages and farms, mostly the children of lead miners at nearby Wirksworth, farm children, or orphans who were wards of the county of Derby. In the case of the orphans, Strutt and Arkwright accepted the responsibility for housing their workers. This same responsibility was increased when they built

[61]*The dates of these several mills are from Nikolaus Pevsner,* The Buildings of Derbyshire, *London: Penguin Books, 1953.*

the Belper mill in 1776; at that site they took over an existing waterpower, previously used to drive the hammer of a forge, which had a mill village adjacent to it. That village was enlarged to house Strutt and Arkwright's workers. Thus in a specialized sense the "occupational household" can be considered to have survived the first stage of the Industrial Revolution.[62]

When the mills began to move into larger cities, to be powered by steam engines, the change came. Those larger towns already had an urban labor force, a proletariat if you will, which could be secured without having to provide housing. Particularly as the Industrial Revolution began to pick up speed with the introduction of steam power, more machinery, and larger scale of production, the manufacturers found this abdication of responsibility for housing provision highly desirable. Instead of having to invest part of their never-sufficient capital in workers' housing, they might concentrate it all in building factories and financing the purchase of staple raw material and in the various stages of manufacture. But by abdicating responsibility for housing, the capitalists fundamentally transformed the conditions of employment. Essentially they threw their workers onto the general "market" for housing in a change I have called the *generalization of housing*. With that generalization, subvention from the manufacturing process to the housing, as had probably occurred throughout much of economic history came to an end. Instead the worker had by his wages to buy housing. Even if those wages remained unchanged, which they did not in the early nineteenth century, the worker would probably have experienced an actual cut in his disposable income as the housing provisions shifted to a market transaction between the worker and an independent and distinct investor in housing.

No doubt the expectations of investors rose with the Industrial Revolution. They could see Arkwright and other manufacturers, as well as aristocratic landowners whose estates were underlain by coal measures, becoming extremely wealthy. It must have seemed the normal course for investors in housing properties to gain equally. Certainly in many cases those investors were the great landowners, who had shown no compunction at sweating the coal miners or evicting the rural working class, so we could hardly expect otherwise with regard to housing. Even when the landowners did not themselves engage in building, their leasing practices frequently contributed to the

deterioration of housing. In what was perhaps his most deadly accurate shot at English legal and social practice, Engels showed the tie between leasehold and shoddy construction and rapidly declining upkeep on rental housing.

The English practice is to lease building land for twenty, thirty, forty, fifty, or ninety-nine years. When the lease falls in, possession of the land and the buildings on it reverts to the ground landlord [who was commonly a member of the aristocracy], who does not have to pay for unexhausted improvement. The builder, therefore, constructs the cottages of a type unlikely to survive beyond the period of the lease. Since some of the leases are as short as twenty or thirty years it is easy to understand that builders are not likely to sink much capital into cottages built on such land. Moreover, the owners of the houses who are bricklayers, joiners and carpenters or factory owners are generally not prepared to spend very much money on repairing or maintaining their property.[63]

An often-disregarded problem is that this shift from the occupational household to the generalized provision of housing led to the shift of housing cost from one beyond the discretion of the workers to one within his control. Thus, when wages proved insufficient, as they commonly did then as now, the worker had to choose between various ways of disposing what was an inadequate income. How did the worker spend his money, and was this a factor in the deterioration in the quality of housing? Winifred Bowman quotes testimony given before the royal commission of 1843 with respect to the expenditures of "cotton operatives" in Ashton-under-Lyne.[64]

Expenditures of Cotton Operatives in
Ashton-under-Lyne in 1843

Item	Expenditure in Pounds Sterling	Percentage of Total Income
Food	185,720	64.32
Clothing	26,410	9.15
Fuel	9,350	0.32
House Rent	33,870	13.24
Sundries	8,180	2.83
Education	2,220	0.77
Ale and Spirits	14,430	5.00
Medicine and Medical Aid	6,160	0.06
Savings Bank	2,410	0.84

[62]*For a detailed discussion of Cromford, Belper, and the whole matter of segmental labor and housing generalization, see James E. Vance, Jr., "Housing the Worker: The Employment Linkage as a Force in Urban Structure,"* Economic Geography, *Vol. 42, 1966, pp. 294–325.*

[63]*Engels*, op. cit., *p. 69.*
[64]*Bowman*, op. cit., *p. 433.*

No doubt the most startling "budget" feature is the large part taken up by the cost of the food. This testimony was given at the very time Engels was resident in Manchester observing the conditions of working-class life. We can see that the cost of food truly impoverished that working class. Once housing became discretionary, it would probably rank in almost any person's mind as second to food, as it does in these figures, and clothing would follow in order, as here. Then the exactions of the high cost of food become clear in their bearing on the amount of money available for housing. The high cost of food was very much the outgrowth of policies adopted by Parliament for the benefit not of the industrial capitalists but of the land-owning aristocracy.

In the interest of maintaining and increasing the income of the rural landowners, no doubt in a political response to the growing wealth and power of the commercial and industrial interests, severe restrictions were determinedly maintained on the import of grain from overseas. The resulting high price for basic food consumed nearly two-thirds of the income of the working class, if the figures from Ashton were at all representative, and they seem to have been. In response to this large exaction for food, other expenditures, particularly those for housing which now fell within the category of discretionary assignment, tended to be of necessity reduced. Out of this came the practice of spending only around 15 per cent of the income on housing. At first, the workers had no alternative; food

was so costly that all else had to yield to its demands. But after 1846, when the repeal of the "Corn Laws" rapidly brought down the cost of some foods by permitting the import of cheaper American and Argentinian products, the practice of assigning no more than 10 to 15 per cent of working-class income to housing persisted. Right up to the present, the notion has been firmly held that such a part of the family budget was sufficient for housing. The result has been that British workers' houses have been much more modest than those of Americans of the same class. The poor quality, though certainly better than the state described by Engels, continued up to the time of the First World War when, at the close of hostilities, it became obvious that the government must adopt a comprehensive program of public housing to improve on the quality that the workers could, or would, buy for themselves.

Ashton-under-Lyne in 1794, as the ancient textile town was changing over to steam-powered machine operation.

The Row-House "Terrace" and "Back-to-Backs"

In the satellitic industrial towns surrounding Manchester, the basic pattern of working-class housing that was to serve Britain until the 1920's was nearly evolved by Engels' time. This pattern was the row-house, in England usually called a "terrace" of houses, with party walls between adjacent houses and small backyards behind, which were held separately and fenced one from another. As the years passed, certain improvements were made. A small front yard might be added, a few square feet tacked on to the rear as sheds or later as a closet off the garden in which a flush toilet was placed—the water closet—but in general the pattern of the row-houses was highly consistent. The frontage might vary, but it generally ranged between about 15 to 20 feet, with 16 feet probably the most common width of the facade. That width would contain a front hall, normally quite narrow, with a "front room" beside it which would be used for daily living. Behind these, a kitchen opened on the backyard, where the coal-shed and privy (or later the water-closet) would be found. A narrow set of stairs led from the front hall to two or three "chambres," as chill and damp as the mind may imagine, where the family slept. This example would have been good working-class housing where land was not too expensive, wages were reasonable, and the family could and would spend perhaps a full 15 per cent of their income for housing. Where any of those factors was less favorable—land too expensive, wages low, or discretionary expenditure for housing less, all quite likely occurrences—the housing might be far more austere.

The most typical form of housing austerity was the so-called "back-to-back house." These structures had only one wall open to the outside; two houses on adjacent streets would share a rear party wall, leaving neither with any back yard. The savings on land costs and construction—the sharing of yet another wall—were such that these houses could be built, and as a result rented, for less. The Royal Commission studying the State of the Large Towns and Populous Places found that these houses might, in the 1840's, be built for as little as £50 each. As a result literally hundreds of thousands of back-to-back houses were built, and they became the basic component of the housing stock in most of the larger industrial cities. In 1919, the city of

Birmingham had some 150,000 working-class houses[65] of which more than half must have been back-to-backs, as in 1939 some 75,000 back-to-backs still stood, even after the city had built 50,000 working-class houses in the inter-war years.

Whether back-to-back or the more ample single-depth terraces, these row-houses were assembled in similar fashion along fairly narrow streets with sidewalks on each side and in street grids that were either truly rectangular—as they were most likely to be in back-to-backs—or slightly curving but with streets basically parallel to one another. The density of land coverage was very high, perhaps because almost universally the houses were of two stories without either cellar or attic. In the back-to-back areas, the streets had, of necessity, to serve as the existing open-space. Until flush toilets were introduced, a line of shared privies stood down the middle of the street. One day a week, the street was closed to vehicles so that washing lines could be strung across it for housewives on both sides to use for their laundry. Commonly after cars were introduced and were beginning to be owned by the working class in the years after the Second World War, the system was for alternate streets to be so obstructed. Before then, seemingly all washed on Monday, as was the long-standing British tradition.

The 1843 budget figures of the Ashton cotton operatives suggest several other components of the industrial housing area as it emerged by the middle of the last century. Very basic food needs could be met at the small shops which tended to be scattered about the working-class housing areas. Opinions differ greatly as to the merits of the various types. One of the worst in virtually all minds was the "truck" or "tommy" shop run by the factory owners. Trading was in exchange for a script given instead of currency by the mills in the workers' pay envelopes. This system is generally believed to have further victimized the workers both by forcing them to trade only in the truck shop (the only place accepting the script) and by so monopolizing their trade that excessive prices could be charged for the goods exchanged for script. When a neighborhood housed workers from a single plant, the chances for the successful operation of the truck shops were great, particularly as they often offered small advance credit that firmly tied the necessitous or improvident worker to the truck shop, seemingly forevermore.

Even in those areas where truck shops were not present, or after legislation had caused them to be removed, the small shops that served the workers were

[65]Herbert J. Manzoni, The Production of Fifty Thousand Municipal Houses, Birmingham: City of Birmingham, 1939, p. 17.

probably not on the whole the cheapest place for them to shop. But the small shopkeeper's role is not as yet finally determined; I shall leave that argument to others. The use of such small shops carrying a very limited range of goods fitted well physically into these working-class neighborhoods. A shop could be slipped into a row-house or a back-to-back—commonly at the end of a block—without any special morphological provision. Within the neighborhood, another form of retail trade, that of the street hawker, assumed considerable importance. Vegetables and fruits, fish, meat, and other fairly common and often perishable commodities were sold from barrows. Markets beyond the neighborhood—in ancient marketplaces in all parts of England, in market halls in the more carefully planned towns, or in street markets in Lancashire and some other highly industrialized areas—served special needs or particularly the demand for perishable products. These markets would be the most likely place from which to seek to buy clothing and the very basic household demands such as dishes, pots and pans, and bed coverings.

Pubs and Public Conveniences

The 1843 figures for Ashton suggest yet a different need that was met within each neighborhood, that for ale and "spirits," normally gin. In that era, the production of ale was most likely to be *within* an inn or the farmstead, with a brewhouse in the yard. Thus, in the pattern of production and consumption at the beginning of the Industrial Era, brewing was domestic. As industrialization spread and factory towns became larger, the opportunity arose for a brewery in the town to supply a number of possible drinking places. Inns might continue to produce their own ale, but working-class areas held few traditional inns though a normal Englishman's thirst remained. Town breweries solved the problem of supply by establishing "public houses" where their product was sold to the general populace living in the vicinity. These pubs came to serve relatively small neighborhoods, particularly when several breweries in a city each sought a set of "tied houses" that sold only their own ale, and later beer. Thus, the frequency of pubs was in part a function of working-class thirst, itself related to the general drabness of

industrial life, but also a function of the pattern of intense competition among breweries. The early nineteenth century had seen much drinking of gin, when a dram could be had for a penny; the gin shops were often little more than a room in a house within a working-class district. The effort to reform the habits of the poor led to the imposition of ever higher taxes on gin. By mid-century, gin and other hard liquors had become much more the downfall of the prosperous than of the poor; beer and ale had become the nearly universal drink of the working class, save on special occasions. And the brewing and handling of unpasteurized beer (all that was available at the time, and much the English preference until the last decade) required some basic level of organization that the small publican could not easily provide. Thus the city brewer interjected himself into the picture; he set up a large brewery, the products of which were fairly consistently and rationally distributed in his own wagons to his own public houses within the metropolitan area. The English came to drink almost exclusively in public and at the neighborhood pub, which became a critical component of the social geography of the working-class areas.

This practice led fairly quickly to the provision of public conveniences to make socially acceptable and sanitary the homeward journey on chilly damp evenings of the men who had congregated in the pub until it closed. These "public conveniences" are a striking feature of British urban morphology, which is understandable mainly in terms of the concentration of drinking in working-class areas to men and in public houses, one of the odd social outgrowths of the Industrial Revolution still reflected frequently in the comic strip of "Andy Capp."

Districts Within the City

The fundamental assemblage of buildings and uses in the English industrial city was the working-class district comprised of row-housing ranged round about one or several factories and served by quite local shops and pubs. The locating factor was the factory, because the hours of labor were long and the virtually universal way of going to work was on foot. The result was the creation of a city, or even a metropolis, of small, very

This "pub" at Ghent in Flanders is there called an Estaminet, but it shares with those in nineteenth-century England a largely male clientele and a concentration on the sale of beer.

definite neighborhoods, which contained the life of most people save for weekly or less frequent visits to the market square, the market-hall, or the street market for the buying of items of clothing, house furnishing, or perishable food. This parochial existence was enforced by conditions of work and housing and the economic unavailability of access to mechanical transportation. Only later in the nineteenth century, when the bicycle, the trolley, and finally the cheap excursion to the seaside by train began to come into the life of the working class did any appreciable breaking out of this narrow geographical frame of life occur.

The factories built in English cities were for the most part rather tall and compact structures, requiring relatively little land and occupying sites quite comprehensible within the standard street grid of the city. The height came from the use of mechanical distribution of power, largely by gears and shafts, from the rotative motion of the steam engine, which forced the general compaction of the plant. Only where specific processes, such as glass making, brass founding, or chemical manufacture required specialized sorts of buildings, were particular sites required. Even then, the chances were good that the plant would be located well within the built-up fabric of the city where the firm would have begun at an earlier time, with the growth of worker housing coming around it.

The central area of cities in industrial England tended to be the province of the middle and upper

classes, as Engels saw it. There were clustered the offices of bankers, solicitors, and other persons dealing specifically with financial interests; stores for the more well-to-do—jewelers, tailors, dressmakers, and other lines of trade beyond the reach of the working class; and governmental and ecclesiastical offices. Shops were on the ground floor and offices in the stories above, though only to a height of two or three floors. Interspersed amidst these newer undertakings would probably be a few old inns, a railway hotel or two, the stations of the separate railroad companies serving the place, and some remnants of the preindustrial town. In back courts, small alleys, and hidden spots were quite commonly found "stews," where tiny deteriorated buildings housed the very poor who served as the casual or most menial labor in the central activities. In few industrial places had any overall design guided the growth of the towns, so buildings tended to stand as individual conceptions of what a city should look like, showing stages of fashionable "architecture," parsimony or generosity as the landlord felt, and a generational mixture of structure—some virtually medieval, others essentially modern. Because of such a mixture of things, and the absence of the orderly plan made fashionable by the Georgian city, a constant craving arose to promote "development schemes." These schemes sought first to sweep away the stews and the corners occupied by the interests of the poor, replacing them with grand streets with proper facades and "appropriate" uses. Joseph Chamberlain began his political career in masterminding "the Corporation Street Scheme" in Birmingham, which in 1876 provided that ancient place, but rather recently incorporated city, a new "main street." In other growing industrial towns, improvement likewise was heavily equated to physical reconstruction into genteel uses of the former purlieus of the poor. A strong strain of physical determinism argued that bad houses made bad people, so razing the slums would raise the people.

Railroads and the City: The Right to Mobility

This notion was so confidently held that an avid welcome was often extended to railroad companies when they sought to build into or through the center of the city. They were asked merely to pass through the neighborhoods of the poor, for the dual purpose of razing some of the worst of that property and for shielding the middle- and upper-class quarters from the smoke and noise of the trains. The force that railroads exerted on urban land-use, removing from other uses large areas and destroying working-class neighborhoods without a general practice of replacement elsewhere, has been well covered in John Kellett's *The Impact of Railways on Victorian Cities.*[66] As he points out, the railroad companies were given two unusual privileges— that of being a corporation allowed to raise capital from more than six persons, a privilege industry did not possess until the 1860's, and that of being allowed to exercise the right of eminent domain (compulsory purchase). In return for these vastly important privileges, social responsibility was not as well developed as one might have hoped.

Giving evidence before a royal commission on the Metropolitan Railway Termini, the great social commentator, Charles Pearson (solicitor to the Corporation of London), stated the problem succinctly: "A poor man is chained to the spot; he has not the leisure to walk, and he has not the money to ride." And the intrusion of rail lines in the dense working-class neighborhoods of inner London aggravated that situation. "They are crowded together still more, they are pressed

together more densely in a similar description of houses to those which they formerly inhabited."[67]

Quite simply, little was done to care for those evicted. Instead, they were forced upon an already overcrowded working-class housing supply, aggravating its existing plights. In such a way does the destruction of bad housing, without other actions, lead to even worse people, to the extent that increased crowding leads to increased crime and social disintegration. But the royal commission study buried action on the problem, if not the truth of its existence.

Voices were raised in objection to the snobbish and condescending policies of the railroad companies and their parliamentary spokesmen. Those gentlemen argued that lowering the price of travel was against the best interests of the companies. Those able to pay first- and second-class fares might travel a class lower just to save money. James Smithells, Traffic Manager of the Lancashire and Yorkshire Railway, testified in 1866 (in answer to the question, "would it not be an advantage to the public to attach third-class carriages to all trains?"), "I should scarcely call it an advantage. Our district is full of men who have risen by their own industry and energy, but their economy is such, although they occupy a respectable position in life, that if third-class carriages were put on with every train they would avail themselves of them. I think that many persons who take advantage of third-class trains ought not to do it . . . ."[68] Similarly, they held that, though third-class travel paid its way, it took a much larger increase in numbers in that class than in higher classes to enlarge the profit of the company. The great Daniel Gooch of the Great Western Railway argued that the working class had not the time to travel. William Cawkell held that offering low fares to the working class was "an inducement for a great many people to take advantage of them and take long journeys which they can badly afford to do." That exemplar of the established order, the Duke of Wellington, believed that railroads might become "a premium to the lower orders to go uselessly wandering about the country."[69]

None among the upper classes believed that the poor should have mobility, daily or periodically. Best they stay in their quarters in the central city, even if those places came to be yet more crowded by increasing influx of migrants to the city and by the absolute reduction in the supply of working-class housing, as it was destroyed to provide routes and stations for rail lines entering the city. In 1844, William Gladstone had sponsored an act that finally held "that each company be required to run over their line on each weekday at

[66]*London: Routledge & Kegan Paul, 1969.*

[67]*Quoted,* ibid., *p. 37.*
[68]Ibid., *pp. 89–90.*
[69]*Quoted,* ibid., *p. 91.*

least one train conveying third-class passengers in carriages provided with seats and protected from the weather, at a speed of not less than twelve miles an hour, including stoppages, and at a fare not exceeding one penny a mile for adults, children under twelve half price, and under three free, 56 lb. of luggage to be allowed without charge."[70] Thus, for the first time the notion was accepted that the laboring class had the right to mobility along with the more fortunate members of society. After 1871, when the Bank Holidays Act finally made a few days a year available to the workers for recreation, these third-class fares could take on greater importance. The railroads even found it both possible and financially profitable to offer excursions to the seaside from Manchester, Birmingham, London, and the other large industrial towns on the Bank Holiday Mondays.[71] The business view was far from favorable in many cases. Jack Simmons quotes the general manager of one company: "The London & North Western company have hitherto held the belief that society in this country, for all purposes, naturally divided itself into three classes, and that the wants and tastes of the community are best served by their present practice" of sticking to a truly subservient third-class, tolerated mainly by government order.[72]

Within cities we can hardly expect that the views of such managers would be at all favorable to providing cheap transportation to workers commuting to work. Only in 1854, when the Great Eastern Railway sought to extend its lines into the northeastern part of the City of London to Liverpool Street Station, was the working class given any regard in the matter of intraurban transportation, and then only because that extension destroyed so much working-class housing that parliament would not authorize it unless the company provided "workingmen's trains" early in the morning and after five or six in the evening. The destruction in Shoreditch and Bethnal Green in East London was to be compensated for by providing access by train, for a fare of a penny for workingmen, to the newly emerging working-class suburbs of Edmonton and Walthamstow. For the distance of eight miles these trains were truly cheap, but for twenty years they had no reflection in the practices on other London rail lines. As the pressure on central-city housing grew, and the quality of those areas deteriorated, an Artisans' and Labourers' Dwellings Act of 1868 required that "the obligation placed upon the Eastern Counties (Great Eastern Railway) system of railways out of London to provide trains for artisans at the rate of a penny for each passenger per course of seven or eight miles should be extended to other suburban railways as opportunity may offer."[73]

Only as these cheap workingmen's trains became more available was there much impact of the railroad on the life of the industrial class, and even then mainly in London. In the provincial cities, the use of train commutation was much less for the whole population and apparently of very little significance among what we would today call "the blue-collar workers." Seemingly their wages were sufficiently low so the cost of transport, by whatever medium, was too great to be borne save for the odd excursion to the seaside during Bank Holidays or the later "wakes weeks" of industrial Lancashire and other areas in the North. These vacation periods apparently represented the modern version of the medieval "wake" of the local parish when a festival was held in honor of its patron saint. In northern industrial towns, as wages and working conditions improved, the local mills would close for a summer week, and all workers would be free to go to Blackpool or other seaside resorts during the specific wakes week for Bolton, or Rochdale, or the other parishes.

Abandonment and Succession

The effect of the train on the middle- and upper-class housing pattern was very different indeed. These were the two of the three orders envisaged by the manager of the London and North Western Railway (LNWR) for whom the railroad was a true emancipator. As cities grew, formerly desirable housing felt the pressure for change through crowding and the possibilities of the wealthier classes realizing large returns on capital by abandoning those premises in favor of new ones more distant from the city center. Doubtless it was not the social pressure from below that caused the middle and upper classes to move; rather their desire to move came to be paired with the chance to sell leaseholds or freeholds closer to the center (with no great loss or even a considerable gain), bringing about the creation of the suburb. As early as the 1820's omnibuses had been introduced to London and other cities (we have seen them by Engels' time in Manchester). These original mass-transportation vehicles came to be used by

[70]Quoted in Hamilton Ellis, British Railway History: 1830–1876 [Vol. I], London: George Allen and Unwin, 1954, p. 129.
[71]Jack Simmons, The Railways of Britain, London: Routledge and Kegan Paul, 1961, p. 26.
[72]Ibid., p. 26.

[73]Ellis, op. cit., 319–320.

middle-class men in commuting back and forth to central offices and warehouses. The "villa" or detached house began to be the ideal of the upper social strata, who had the money necessary to cover the increased cost of commutation. As the London and Birmingham Railway (later the LNWR) was finished in late 1838, "halts" near London became possible, around which villa communities might be laid out.

Such a rather unexpected, and certainly unplanned for, growth of suburban commuting traffic began to emerge on the other rail lines built out of London. Generally the development of this traffic depended rather on the social status of the housing areas along the line. The LNWR, frosty toward workers on its own account, was further dissuaded by the elevated status of the suburbs in the northwestern quadrant of London's growth. There, for several reasons that Hugh Prince has identified, the housing was middle and upper class, particularly to the west of the London and North Western lines.[74] The railroad tended to fix in all-too-firm masonry and nearly as rigid social practice, the division of London into "two cities." The working-class city lay mainly to the east of the LNWR, and the city of the "quality" lay west of George Stephenson's overbuilt line. The LNWR reached London from the provinces; some would question how long it would have taken the Metropolis to make use of railroads had not the greater "drive" of industrial Britain to the north projected lines to and into a rather reluctant London to the south. The London and Birmingham and the later lines to the north continued to have poor connections to the workplaces of the Metropolis, which lay in the East End.

Intraurban Railroads

To remedy the problem of connecting London's mainline railroad stations with the City and, as a result, affording use of the railroads for the suburban commuting of City men, two schemes were developed which ultimately made London a city of vast commuting flows. The first proposal grew out of the initial failure, on the part of the LNWR, to profit from its ostensible connection of Birmingham with London's docks for the export of the vast array of goods produced in the West Midland metropolis. As originally planned, the London and Birmingham reached Camden Town just beyond the built-up limits of London, where the railroad established a junction with the Regent's Canal to be used for carrying export products to the docks on the Thames in London's East End. The service was slow and difficult, thus failing to develop as foreseen. To improve on this situation two things were done: the London and Birmingham was carried to Euston Square at the edge of the built-up heart of the City of London, and a rail line was built to the docks and, at a slightly later time, into the edge of the City at Broad Street Station, which was opened as the North London Railway in 1865.[75] This line to the docks and the City, which came to be known as the North London Railway, provided after 1865 an easy and efficient access from the business heart of the City to the potential suburban areas located along the LNWR, and subsequently along the Great Northern Railway (whose mainline station was King's Cross). This easterly line of both railroads made the mainlines and metropolitan branches a great system for well-to-do commuting back and forth to emerging suburban areas. Already when the London and Birmingham was built, London's northwest was the socially elect area: the North London with its mainline connections made certain the survival of the pattern already shaping in this quadrant—the rise of probably the largest suburban district of any city in the world. That great suburban band made Broad Street Station, despite its obscurity, almost the busiest station in London (more people passed through there daily than through Isombard Brunel's Paddington and Stephenson's Euston combined).

The other solution to the problem of making the railroads useful for suburban commuting was the creation, under the aegis of Charles Pearson, of the Metropolitan Railway, an underground line beginning at Paddington on the west to provide a City connection for the Great Western Railway. It passed near the other mainline stations (Marylebone, Euston, St. Pancras, and King's Cross) to the City at Farringdon Street, where the authorities had recently cleared the site of the offensive meat market. It was assumed, as was the practice for many years, that mainline steam trains would pass through Paddington and King's Cross to go on to Farringdon Street, where they would gain better access to the City.

When the line opened in 1864 it proved highly successful, but along with the North London line to Broad Street, its patronage was largely that of the middle

[74]Hugh C. Prince, "North-west London 1814–1863" and "North-west London 1864–1914," in J. T. Coppock and Hugh C. Prince, Greater London, London: Faber and Faber, 1964.

[75]A detailed account of the reason for, and the construction of, all the London stations is given in Alan A. Jackson, London's Termini, Newton Abbot [Devonshire]: David and Charles, 1969. Also in paperback, Pan editions, London, 1972.

class. "Until 1875 indeed, the North London Railway was exempt from the obligation to carry third-class passengers; the stockbrokers and merchants travelled first-class, and the clerks a respectable second."[76] Again the improvement of the travel of the middle class showed little benefit filtering downward to the working class. Only after 1900, when the American notion of true mass transit was brought to London by Charles Tyson Yerkes with the Central London Railway, did the working class gain much thought or benefit. Then the Tupenny Tube began a transformation of the lower-class housing areas that was a radical, and a frightening, vision to the proper classes west of the LNWR.

What sort of suburbs did the railroad bring to London and other English cities? Already in Engels' words we have seen the broad outlines. Strong class division existed among the residential areas, based fundamentally on "the ability to pay" for suburban rail service. London and the industrial metropolises that grew rapidly in the nineteenth century tended to be surrounded by rolling countryside, sometimes, as in the case of the land on the London clay, rather gentle in slope. On these lands surrounding most cities grew up a belt of "large houses" and market-gardens where wealth was able to maintain or secure convenient access to the city. As pressure for intensification of land-use grew, the high productivity of the fields planted to crops of a perishable nature could ward off for one further generation the expansion of housing areas. But as the economic return to be gained by "urbanizing" the estate or the vegetable field grew large enough, as it usually did once convenient and direct rail service was locally available in the journey-to-work to the central area, then breaking up of the large parcels into "housing estates" was so common as to be almost the universal practice. These estates could range over a fair social spectrum, but they did not reach very close to the bottom of the social heap. Instead the poorer members of society had either to depend upon deteriorated housing of the middle and upper classes or had to seek housing in the cramped and mean workers' housing developments close to mills or the casual employment found largely in the city center. Those working-class housing developments were dense in population and truly constrained in form—both tiny in ground area given to each house and limited to generally undesirable sites where no one but the most socially disadvantaged could be expected to live.

This social stratification was the most significant feature of the Victorian suburbs. The society housed was unbelievably concerned with image and address to the point that the dreary conventionality of these areas can hardly be imagined if unexperienced. Streets were

[76]Ellis, op. cit., p. 318.

Map of Sultan St., Camberwell, 1871.

classified in an urban social taxonomy clearly perceived by the Victorians of the upper two classes. "It is worth noting, incidentally, that since the right suburban address was to the resident primarily a social requirement, it was nearly as much a matter of nomenclature to him as it was of the site or of architecture, and sophisticated builders knew this. The monotonous but purposeful recital of Debrett['s Peerage]—Burlington, Montague, Addington, Melbourne, Devonshire, Bedford, and so on—was, therefore, a special characteristic of the pre-Victorian and early Victorian suburban address."[77] As each large parcel was committed to development, the builders operating there tried to appraise the market and determine the most profitable use to be made of the land in terms of total return. Surprisingly, construction for the lower-middle class or even the upper working class might prove more profitable than that for the more elevated. H. J. Dyos in

[77]H. J. Dyos, Victorian Suburb, Leicester, England: Leicester University Press, 1966, pp. 170–171.

his classic study of Camberwell, a mixed suburb in south London that housed elements ranging from the upper working class to the upper middle class, adduced evidence that found, size for size, working-class housing paid considerably higher rents than did that for the middle class.

The social compositon of this area was very mixed. Between Oakhurst Grove and Peckham Rye and on parts of the British Land Company's estate farther south was a number of well-to-do streets occupied most by professional people, but the majority of the houses in East Dulwich, some of them designed for two families and others used as though they had been, were occupied by the working classes. A seven-roomed house, with bath and garden, could be had here at the end of the period for £30 a year plus taxes, but in the poorer streets a seven-roomed house cost 13s. a week. The difference between renting rooms in such localities was similarly slight—four rooms for 9s. a week in the better, three rooms for the same rent in the poorer streets.[78]

At first we might assume that therefore everyone might avail himself of the chance to rent in the better-class street, but the sharp social discrimination of Victorian class structure was such that few landlords would have rented space to the working-class family in the better area. Certainly those lower-class people would never have "presumed" to rise "above their station." For these reasons English economic life had a strangely regressive quality, with the poor paying more for housing than the wealthy just as they actually paid more for transportation, in terms of the space and speed of transport furnished, than did the rich. As this subsidy of the rich by the lower classes is still the case with first-class air travel, our surprise should come only from the persistence of such practices.

The houses built in these suburban areas were of two sorts—detached villas on rather sizable lots and row-houses ranged continuously along a street frontage. The terraces of row-houses were much the more common. The villas were often the remnant of an essentially semi-rural pattern when they housed within the limits of an outlying village persons of urban culture but independent income not necessitating a daily journey-to-work to and from the city. They were within easy periodic reach of the city but not truly a morphological part of that place. Only as rail transportation was extended to the villages of the surrounding country would daily commuters of considerable wealth take up these villas, and as the city grew the villas would form merely an enclave within the generally expanding carpet of terrace housing.

Those terraces were structurally rather similar, though scale and architectural detailing might vary

[78]Ibid., p. 185.

Houses (a) on Trafalgar Avenue, built in 1852; (b) in Vicarage Grove, built between 1866 and 1868; and (c) on Ivydale Road, built in 1900, show the changes in style as well as the diversity of classes found in the south London suburb of Camberwell.

somewhat. The most expensive row-houses would be of three stories and a cellar and of reasonable width, perhaps 20 or even 25 feet. Such a household would hold public rooms on the first floor, with the kitchen and other servants' quarters in the basement. Family bedrooms would occupy the second floor, and servants' rooms the third. Normally the house had the front door and the stairway to one side, with the rest of the space given over for use in entertainment as well as family life. Beyond a reasonable number of villas, the upper-middle class depended most heavily on the row-houses: "The two-storeyed brick terrace was the almost standard component, even for fairly substantial houses, which might signify their superiority by an extra storey (if only an attic with a dormer window) or by a wider frontage."

Class did not show in the basic plan, but rather in the architectural detailing. Normally a shallow door-surround produced a basic porch which might be pushed outward from the front wall to convey a greater sense of elegance. Pilasters and columns, more elaborate surrounds for windows and doors, and the introduction of a one- or two-story bay window gave higher class to the house in a clear and visible fashion, something which along with the proper "address" became matters of intense concern to the socially imprisoned Victorians. "The principal roofing material was blue Welsh slate, sometimes cut in a petal shape or surmounted by a fretwork of ornamental red ridge tiles, and terminated at the gable ends by narrow wooden or even leaden barge boards; on the larger houses the barge board almost became a piece of architectural millinery, an elaborate frippery which was intended 'to do something' for the whole appearance."

Brick was so universally the building material that only its color remained in question. Color depended mainly on the geographical source of the clays used, and ranged from grey through blue to yellow and red. Sometimes the red was rather fierce, as in the University of Birmingham. There the immoderate intensity of the color gave the whole class of provincial universities the sobriquet of "Red Brick" as their most instantly apparent quality, and one intimately tied up with Victorian building not so dominant at Cambridge or Oxford as in Birmingham or Leeds. Those areas with blue brick, particularly favored it seems for small city halls and public conveniences but not unknown in rather unhappy residential areas, stand as the epitome of Industrial Revolution building, commonly holding up the rafters of Methodist chapels or giving security and strength to police stations in working-class areas.

The fronts of houses were adorned by "distinctive embellishments" in the better order of construction normally in "the form of plaster mouldings to make sham balustrades to unusable balconies above the bay-windows, or to form tooled columns which were often of absurdly bulky or slender dimensions. It was no rare thing for each of the capitals to these—usually composed of fossilized fruit and unidentifiable foliage—to be quite different from each of its fellows on the same house, but to be repeated (in a different permutation) a few doors away."[79]

Uniformity in substance was matched by novelty in

completion in a harness fairly typical of Victorian material life. Identical houses were more common in the cheapest streets and the "geometry of the ground plan tended to settle some of the social issues from the outset, for the longer and straighter and flatter the street the fewer the pretensions it normally had." Most cultures seemingly make some qualitative association with regularity and irregularity. During the Renaissance the orderly and straight was most respected, but though the romantic Victorians thought highly of conformity in social behavior, slight irregularity in civic design gained a certain desirable cachet. "The choice of trees, too, had its social overtones: planes and horse-chestnuts for the wide avenues and lofty mansions of the well-to-do; limes and laburnums, and acacias for the middle incomes; unadorned macadam for the wage-earners." A society of established order must of necessity assign symbols of rank. "Within such limits, however, the occupiers themselves also had plenty of scope for little acts of symbolism, as, for example, in the furnishing of the front windows or the arrangement of the front garden." The corsetted order of the Victorian garden pains us, but it told its contemporaries much about that almost central question, the social rank of the occupants.

. . . The aspidistra half-concealed by carefully draped lace curtains, the privet hedge of carefully determined height, the geometrical perfection of the minute flower-beds edged with London Pride, the window-box trailing fern and periwinkle–these were some of the elements in one situation. Ivy-scaled walls, great round clumps of laurels, rhododendrons, lilac, and laburnum, lawns infested with sparrows and set with pedestalled urns, and gravelled drives–these were the elements of another. It would be a mistake to think of these features solely in terms of personal taste. They gave scope, it is true, for the outward expression of romantic idiosyncrasies, but they were equally emblems of different shades of respectability, some of suburbia's badges of rank, and their collective expression was a subtle acknowledgement of a locality's status in suburban society.[80]

The railroad brought the development of such housing areas as suburbs outside of London; they were more extensively developed there than elsewhere, but not very differently. In a society obsessed with class and fearful of misapprehension as to personal status, the housing combined an unbelievable timidity with just enough distinction to gain the ranking of people as regards "respectability." The terrace of houses could shelter the grave-diggers of northern Camberwell just as it did the barristers of her more select streets but, with the practiced eye of the class-divided society,

[79]Ibid., pp. 186–188.

[80]Ibid., p. 189.

there was no danger of stumbling blindly into inappropriate surroundings. The "little acts of symbolism" were fully as important as the fundamental acts of providing shelter.

The Geographical Limits of Non-Intercourse

We have considered the emergence of industry in Manchester and Britain in general; we now must look at the pattern of the city given to industry in other countries. The Industrial Revolution era witnessed in the city the most salient of the changes in morphogenesis. Writing in 1842, W. Cooke Taylor, a commentator on the evils of the Corn Laws, argued "that the geographical limits of non-intercourse established in Manchester are the greatest of the special evils connected with that town. The isolation of classes in England has gone far to divide into nations as distinct as the Normans and Saxons." His conclusion was echoed most effectively two years later when Disraeli published his *Sybil or: The Two Nations.*

Taylor saw this separation of the classes as conducive both to callous disregard for the welfare of the workers and as destructive of any acculturation process to be worked on immigrants to the city. Because Manchester required such massive in-movements of unskilled labor, it "does not afford a fair specimen of the factory population . . .and that outward aspect of the place affords a very imperfect test of the state of trade in South Lancashire . . .there is always, and must necessarily be, considerable distress in a place where there is a large demand for untrained labour." In a caveat that Engels might well have practiced that same year as he observed Manchester life, Taylor noted clearly, "It is a very common error to attribute to the factories the evils which really arise from an immigrating and non-factory population . . . ." He continues, "I took some pains to ascertain the character of this immigrating population, and I found it such as to account, in a very great degree, for the high rate of mortality and the low condition of the morals in the township of Manchester. It appeared that peasants inadequate to the fatigues of rural toil frequently come into the towns with the hope of finding some light employment suited to their feeble strength, and that persons whose charac-

ter is blighted in the country seek to escape notice in the crowd of the town."[81]

Then the "geographical limits of non-intercourse" combined with the implosion on the city of a rural population to contribute immeasurably to the deterioration of urban life. The in-migrants were not always of the best abilities and practices, and were so divided from the accomplished urban population in both the working and the middle classes as to be isolated from its improving influences. To demonstrate his point, and as well to serve almost as the text for our analysis of the impact of industrialization on American cities, Taylor takes note of the continuing mill villages standing self-contained outside the city center. First, those places were not flooded with the vast numbers of unskilled labor he notes in Manchester. In addition, those self-contained factory towns were characterized by the manufacturer serving two roles, that of factory manager and that of landlord for the housing of workers. Taylor reasons that in such a joint undertaking, the best interests of the landlord are served by as continuous a period of employment as possible, which he sees as considerably alleviating the rigors of industrial life, notably when some paternal relationship existed between the manufacturer and his workers. We may question the social wisdom of such a tie but we need not question the practical benefits in housing to be gained from it. In essence, Taylor describes the situation before the generalization of housing that we have here proposed as an essential analytical concept.

In sum, the Industrial Revolution in Britain brought about two new morphogenetic processes of great strength: *"geographical limits of [social] non-intercourse"* arose, creating at least the Two Nations that Disraeli discerned; in turn, *housing was generalized within cities,* thus abolishing the introduction of a subvention from the manufacturing process to housing. In any event, two distinct groups of capitalists were created with nonconvergent interests, in contrast to the traditional situation. Other morphogenetic processes have been discussed earlier; the forces exerted by the countryside and its social elite on the city led to *the implosion of rural evictees on the city, the constraint of the physical spread of the city by aristocratic landowners, and the beggaring of the urban working class by high food prices* artificially maintained by the rural gentry, prices which made it impossible for the urban working class to buy adequate housing for itself. Thus,

[81]*W. Cooke Taylor,* Notes of a Tour in the Manufacturing Districts of Lancashire: In a series of Letters to his Grace the Archbishop of Dublin *(2nd edition, 1842), extracted and reprinted in* The Idea of the City in Nineteenth-Century Britain, *edit. by B. I. Coleman, Boston: Routledge and Kegan Paul, 1973, pp. 83–86.*

the process of industrialization was only one of several forces shaping the city of the Industrial Age.

Belgian and French Industrial Landscapes

In the seventeenth century, Belgium and France were more the home of industry than was Britain. France, under the active encouragement of the monarchy, had set up factories in the seventeenth century and had evolved a fair understanding of the organization of large productive facilities. Unfortunately most French factories were established to supply luxury items to a minute market drawn from the royalty and top nobility. Tapestries, porcelains, and other fine manufactures were particularly the French product, and depended almost entirely on skilled handworking. Innovation was present in business organization, but the introduction of power was not.

In Belgium, then known as the Austrian Netherlands, two industrial traditions were well-established. In Flanders, medieval textile towns such as Bruges, Ypres, and Tournai were surviving, but not necessarily prospering, while in the east in the nearly independent Prince-Bishopric of Liège, the textile trade was joined to metallurgical industries dependent upon the local coal mines. In the seventeenth century, the Liège mines were more productive than those of England. The Flemish towns showed little change when the Industrial Revolution began slowly, joining with France in a cautious period of waiting that pushed initial industrialization largely into the nineteenth century. Only the Principality of Liège showed much activity during the eighteenth century. Two factors assured that this rather small region would become the second area to be transformed by the Industrial Revolution (after the industrial districts of England): the presence of coal deposits and an established metallurgical industry (in copper at Dinant and in iron at Namur and Liège), and the rapid establishment of ties between the Principality and England in the matter of technical advice and investment. "In the eighteenth century the Prince-Bishops of the virtually independent ecclesiastical territory of Liège were active in fostering the economic development of their coal and iron resources at a time when the Hapsburgs [in the Austrian Netherlands] were losing interest in their possessions in the Low Countries. . . .British influence upon the industrialization of Belgium was particularly significant since in the early days of the industrial revolution it was only from Britain that the most modern machinery and information concerning the most recent advances in technical knowledge could be secured."

Despite stern laws forbidding the export of machines or plans for them, and the emigration of skilled workers, all of these reached Belgium, as they did the United States, before the end of the eighteenth century. Perhaps the most significant of those emigrés was William Cockerill who, with his sons and son-in-law, was "largely responsible for reorganizing on modern lines the carding and spinning of wool and the weaving of woollen cloth in Belgium." His son John Cockerill was the great developer of the iron and steel industry which grew up rather incongruously on the

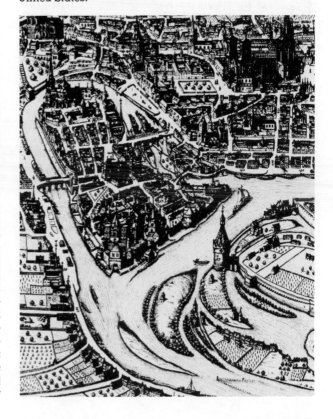

Liège became the hearth of the Industrial Revolution in Belgium, much as Manchester and Providence were for England and the United States.

Prince-Bishop's estate at Seraing just outside Liège to become "the largest integrated engineering concern in the world in the 1820's . . .[with] the production of coal, pig iron, machinery, steam engines, river steamboats, locomotives, railway rolling stock, rails and armaments . . . ."[82]

The Principality of Liège affords us a view of what is often conceived of as the classic situation in the Industrial Revolution—new industry is forced out of the city into the surrounding countryside where the laws of constraint and order, inherited within cities from the Middle Ages, did not rule. In a sense, this was the Liègoise case, but without the degree of simplicity that generalization suggests. Instead we find that some of the trades (where it was more a case of reorganization of business practices than of new technical processes) moved out to gain freedom from the gild constraints. In others, such as the iron and armaments trade enlarged by John Cockerill, the innovation came directly within the *faubourgs* of the city of Liège itself.

This same distinction must be made, though less clearly, in England. New industries or strikingly new processes did not automatically lead to rustication of manufacturing; instead the mass industries of the Middle Ages—most notable textile making, which was the era's largest employer of hands—fought change. Change was resisted because it was so wrenching to the social fabric that had supported the commercial life of the medieval city. Just as the Reformation swept away the overly elaborated and self-serving hierarchy and administration of the Roman church (or the anti-clericalism of revolutionary France did the job where the Reformation was unsuccessful), and political revolutions sought the same end of the established medieval order in government and social-class division, the destruction and replacement of the medieval industrial order became an effect of the Industrial Revolution. When efforts were made to introduce totally new industries and processes, the medieval social fabric was less disturbed, and therefore, the urban society was less unwelcoming.

In textile manufacture, however, little welcome was given to new organization of the trade. In Yorkshire the wide spread of proprietorship meant that change came by general acceptance; in Lancashire the cotton textile industry had no medieval roots that must be attacked. But in the Principality, conditions were different, as Henri Pirenne showed. Starting in the

fifteenth century, the textile trade was dominated by the masters of Liège so that country production came only in coarse woolens based on the fleeces of Ardennes sheep. But as the Middle Ages waned, particularly in the Vesdre valley east of the city, a group of weavers began to seek to improve their product. They sent apprentices to the finer textile industry of Leyden in Holland, and began to import the finer Spanish fleeces. The Liège masters fought back, ultimately without success.

The country weavers began to create a new textile town at Verviers where "the calcarious property of the water in the Vesdre, the abundance of fuel thanks to the proximity of the coal mines and above all the cheapness of hand working" gave an increasing competitive advantage.[83] In the seventeenth century, the village became legally a town and the countryside round about was fast filling up with weaving sheds as "All the country which surrounded it was industrialized . . .[as] the women spun the wool and the clack of the looms extended ever farther into the silence of the countryside. In the town there arose a confusion of shops, fulling-mills, shearers, dyers, and storehouses," a confusion no less true of present-day Verviers. The town of Verviers had only a small bourgeoisie; most of the capital was directly absorbed in the manufacturing process.

Along with that relative absence of a leisure class went a numerous industrial proletariat divided into the specialized crafts of preparing and processing wool into textiles. As Pirenne tells us "Nothing here recalls to mind the gilds which still survived in the old urban centers. . . .The originality of the Verviétoise industrial structure consisted precisely in its complete independence with respect to this [medieval] corporate regime. Verviers was born and developed in the most complete liberty." But "in the course of the XVIII century, capitalism became sufficiently powerful to bring about a change in commercial organization. The merchant was changed to the manufacturer who brought together in large buildings all the machines and their workers who manufactured the finished cloth, from the washing of the wool to the dressing [*toilette*] of the cloth. Thus, the modern factory appeared and began to draw to its hierarchical factories and to put under its direction workers from the domestic workshops. In 1789 a plant was described that employed no less than a thousand workers."

If the Verviétiose industrial district began in "complete liberty," it soon lost that boon. As the numbers of in-migrants increased, their liberties were lost to an extent. In the end, the plenitude of possible workers meant that manufacturers controlled wages, forcing

[82]W. O. Henderson, Britain and Industrial Europe, 1750–1870, *Leicester, England: Leicester University Press, 1965 (Second Edition), pp. 102–106. In his chapter on Belgium, Henderson discusses mainly the career of the Cockerill firm but presents in passing one of the more up-to-date accounts of English influence on Belgian industrialization.*

[83]Henri Pirenne, Histoire de Belgique, des Origines a Nos Jours, *Bruxelles: La Renaissance du Livre, 1948, Vol. III, pp. 187–189.*

them downward. They lengthened the work day, and began the increasing overcrowding of housing, in a narrow valley at the edge of the Ardennes, until as many as six persons occupied a single room. The paternal regard for the workers that Taylor imputed, perhaps romantically, to the rural factory owners of Lancashire was hardly present in the growing town of Verviers. Conditions became progressively worse, particularly in housing, so a strike was called in 1759 only to be met with a lock-out by the employers. When the Austrian government attempted to introduce arbitration, it proved ineffectual; from then on, the employers had rather complete control of working conditions. But in the matter of housing, in what was the first instance of municipal concern expressed effectively, the city of Verviers in 1795 studied the construction of a *"cité ouvrière,"* which stands as the first case of municipal socialism in housing in Europe.

In Verviers the logical outcome of the Mercantile Revolution of the sixteenth and seventeenth centuries could be perceived. "Capitalism, originally commercial in origin, became industrial with ever increasing investment in machines. The capitalists sought to augment the production and reduce the cost price of manufacture without loss of technique."[84] Also improved mechanical manufacture made it possible to use cheaper raw materials—*queues et pennes* (wings and tails, the local people termed it). From 1797 on, efforts were made by John Cockerill, backed by the

most important manufacturers of the place, to introduce English textile machinery. As in Lancashire, home of the technical innovation, spinning was the first to be improved. Machines allowed eleven workers to produce what had formerly required the labor of a hundred, and at a great reduction in cost. But this mechanization meant the loss of livelihood for the country spinners, who were forced to move to the town, thus preventing any rise in the pay of the workers already there. The influx of cheap labor joined with technical advances to make Verviers and its surrounding area a great textile center, particularly after the French invaded and conquered Belgium under Napoléon, opening up the large market of a France engaged in continent-wide warfare with England.

After having suffered isolation and the imposition of economic barriers first at the hands of the Austrians and then the monarchial French, the Verviétoise textile district now saw rapid expansion. Cheap labor, new mechanization, and finally a great expansion of the market through an expanded mercantile frontier created the three conditions necessary for the onset of the Industrial Revolution. "In 1810, eighty-six large factories in the Verviétois employed at least twenty-five thousand workers."[85]

Now we may try to project these conditions in eastern Belgium to the scale of industrialization found in France and Belgium as a whole. In the Middle Ages, Flanders had dominated the textile trade. The cities of

The woolen textile town of Verviers grew along the Vesdre River starting in the fifteenth century, becoming a legal town in the seventeenth century. It gained great prominence when, in the mid-eighteenth century, the absence of gilds there made the valley an early scene of the Industrial Revolution. Today Verviers is a complex industrial town still heavily engaged in textile production.

[84]Ibid., *p. 378.*

[85]Loc. cit.

Flanders had become the largest in northern Europe; Antwerp, their port, was the greatest trading town of the north. But as the Mercantile Era advanced, the markets open to Flanders tended to remain static, or to shrink, as did her near neighbor, Rouen. Thus the Dutch and the English benefited most from the mercantile expansion beyond the bounds of Europe, and thus the Dutch and English cities grew. The Flemish towns stagnated, as did those of Normandy in France where the eviction of the Huguenots proved a fatal blow to the entreprenuerial spirit so necessary to the transformation of the medieval to the industrial economy. Only when the French Revolution destroyed the clericalism and trade corporatism of France and Flanders was Belgium ripe for industrialization. First the monarchy and the powerful ecclesiastics of France were toppled; then the French captured the Austrian Netherlands and the Principality of Liège. Earlier the groups who now make up the Belgians had sought the destruction of the Austrian and ecclesiastic rule on their own but had failed to bring it about. Suddenly the climate of economic thinking on the Continent was transformed. Efforts were made to introduce the English industrialism to France and Belgium. As has been shown, despite laws to the contrary, English workers and machines were carried to the Continent; during the last decade of the eighteenth century and the beginning of the nineteenth, industrial districts dependent upon modern machinery manufacture began to grow rapidly in France and Belgium.

Two areas were industrialized under this program: the old textile towns in Flanders and Normandy—Bruges, Ghent, Ypres, Lille, Amiens, and Rouen—began to grow anew, and the traditional rural textile areas spread throughout the "middle kingdom" of medieval Lotharingia—the Prince-Bishopric of Liège, Limburg, Lorraine and particularly Alsace and the Franche Comté—began to show transformation of rural industry rather on the pattern of the Verviétois. Thus two models of industrialization and urbanization growing out of it could be discerned. One model was the rejuvenation of long-standing cities when the destruction of the gild privileges and the growth of potential markets made new processes available to them. In this model, the city was already in existence. The main product of the Industrial Revolution was the crowding, and ultimate overtaxing, of the medieval urban form by a new scale of manufacture and clustering of people that would have been impossible and unimaginable in the Middle Ages. Very bad conditions tended to attend this form of industrial urbanization, as we know from the grim accounts of industrial Lille, Ypres, and other textile towns in Flanders and Normandy that come down to us from the end of the last century.

The other model of industrial urbanization comes from the "middle kingdom," where the growth came much as Pirenne described it for Verviers. A rural textile industry was first swept up in a general expansion of handworking production. Small towns, without significant medieval roots, became the locus of the new capitalists. As their markets grew along with their capitals, mechanization could be introduced, further expanding the population of the new towns and forcing upon them considerable problems. Yet even so the conditions in Montbéliard, Belfort, Mulhouse, and Verviers were probably not so bad as those in Flanders. Since the form of the town evolved mainly in response to the needs of an industry, it might lack the historical

The industrial towns of Belgium, as shown in Liège were often crowded into narrow valleys forcing worker housing to be placed on steep slopes reached mainly by stairways.

associations and splendid buildings from the past, but it avoided some of the physical constraints and inefficiencies of trying to modernize a medieval city form.

For Americans, the most interesting industrial district in Lotharingia may be Alsace and the Franche Comté, where factory towns grew up in the foothills of the Vosges and Jura, respectively. These areas were extracted from the complex political geography of the middle kingdom, and annexed to France between 1678 and 1680, bringing with them traditions of urbanization and textile production only slightly less developed than in Flanders. Within the mercantile frontiers of France when the Industrial Revolution broke on Europe, Alsace and the Franche Comté developed a waterpowered industrialization remarkably similar to that growing in New England at the same time.

Out of the east side of the Vosges, where it drops steeply into the structural valley of the middle Rhine, a number of rushing rivers fell in a series of steps which might easily be tapped for units of waterpower manageable under the technology of the early Industrial Age. In this area, particularly along the Vosges, fleeces were ready to hand. That supply was made possible by the practice of shifting cultivation (the English call it "swidden"), which meant that fields were cleared, commonly by burning, and cultivated for seven or eight years. When productivity declined, they were withdrawn from cultivation to be replaced by new clearings. "But although now left undisturbed the ground was by no means unproductive; having been a field it now became a pasture . . . ."[86] Thus, in the Ardennes and the Vosges where such shifting cultivation was practiced, the acreage of pasture normally equalled that of cultivation, encouraging the pasturing of flocks in large numbers. In the Jura, in the County of Montbéliard, four new towns were created between 1562 and 1690. There, much of the land had remained undeveloped by medieval assarters, or was destroyed in the wars of the seventeenth century which wracked the lands formerly Lotharingia.[87] This creation of new towns, presumably endowed with some of the economically liberal inclinations of the bastides of southern France, was also accompanied by a complex of circumstances that dispersed rural settlement into farmsteads, rather than collecting it into villages, as was the common practice in that part of Europe. Thus, the age and nature of settlement in this area was more akin to the conditions found in New England than might at first be suspected.

[86]Marc Block, French Rural History, Berkeley: University of California Press, 1966, p. 27.
[87]Ibid., p. 19. An assarter was a man whose job was to grub out trees and shrubs to clear fields or pastures.

In Alsace, settlement was in villages but the area possessed a dynamism lacking elsewhere in France. "The skill of the Alsatians in manufacturing textiles and in construction of machines and the motors to run them enabled them to keep pace with the rapid and extensive progress of England, as scarcely any other part of France was able to do, and to specialize to a considerable extent in the production of both fine yarn and fine cloth."[88] The use of power was so great in fine textile manufacture, because machines had to move rapidly, that good waterpower sites were crucial to the conduct of the manufactory. The several valleys east of the great rounded crest of the Vosges—from south to north the Doller, Thur (with Thann), Lauch (with Guebwiller), and Fecht (with Munster)—became dotted with textiles factories, initially of woolen production but later mostly in cotton. High-quality production grew first from the need to find a product that could stand the cost of shipment over a considerable distance to market and subsequently from the need to import the cotton fiber over greater distances than did its competitors—in England, Normandy, and Belgium.

The settlement pattern associated with the Alsatian textile industry was that of the *river alignment of towns*. The limits were established toward the head of the stream by the first waterpower site of sufficient volume to permit economically useful components of power, and toward the lower reaches of the valley by the place where the flat plain of the Rhine graben reduced the head of water to too low a figure to be of much value. Water was needed, too, for processing and finishing, as printed fabrics were particularly the specialty of this area. Thus, the higher quality of water toward the heads of the streams was also significant to the location of industry. In addition to the river alignments, later industrial development grew up away from the foothills, in Mulhouse and Belfort for the most part, where coal for steam-power factories could be secured by canal. These *steam-powered cities* were similar to those that comprised most of the industrial base in England, and those to be built in New England, as at Fall River and New Bedford, when coal became cheap and plentiful in the United States.

While the Alsatian industry was dividing into these two geographical components, industry in the Franche Comté was taking a different form. Some was associated with steam (as at Belfort, which is actually in the Franche Comté, though industrially more akin to Alsace). Montbéliard took on a distinctive geographical pattern. There and farther south in the foothills of the Jura, a number of charcoal iron workings had been active for several centuries before the Industrial Revolution. Thus, when the pace of production quickened

[88]Dunham, op. cit., p. 110.

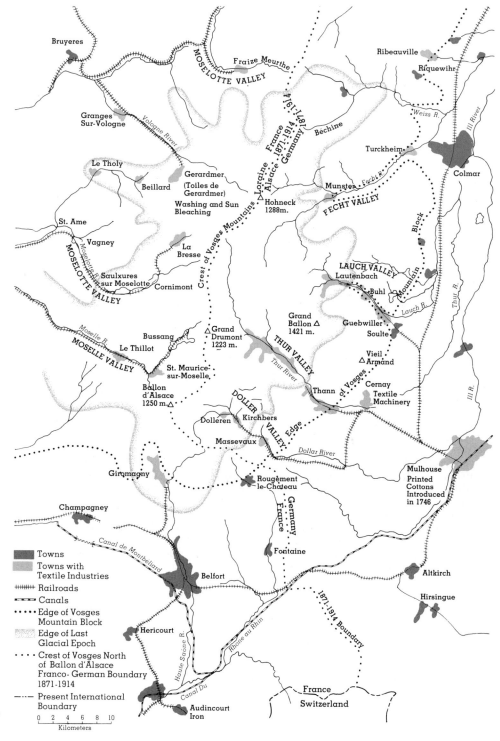

Bruyeres

MOSELOTTE VALLEY

Fraize Meurthe

Ribeauville

Riquewihr

Granges
Sur-Vologne

Vologne River

Béchine

Weiss R.

Ill River

Le Tholy

Beillard

Gerardmer
(Toiles de
Gerardmer)

Washing and Sun
Bleaching

Hohneck
1288m.

Turckheim

Colmar

Munster

Fecht R.

FECHT VALLEY

St. Ame

Vagney

Moselotte R.

MOSELOTTE VALLEY

Saulxures
sur Moselotte

La
Bresse

Cornimont

Crest of Vosges Mountains

Lorraine France 1871-1914
Alsace Germany 1871-1914

Block

Mountain

LAUCH VALLEY

Lautenbach

Buhl

Lauch R.

Thur R.

Moselle R.

Bussang

Le Thillot

MOSELLE VALLEY

Grand
Drumont
1223 m.

St. Maurice-
sur-Moselle

Grand
Ballon △
1421 m.

Guebwiller

Soulte

THUR VALLEY

Thur River

Vieil
Armand

Edge of Vosges

Ballon
d'Alsace
1250 m.△

Dolleren

Kirchbers

DOLLER
VALLEY

Thann

Cernay
Textile
Machinery

Massevaux

Dollar River

Ill R.

Giromagny

Rougement
le-Château

Mulhouse
Printed
Cottons
Introduced
in 1746

Germany
France

Champagney

Canal de Montbeliard

Fontaine

Altkirch

Hirsingue

Belfort

1871-1914 Boundary

Hericourt

Haute Saône R.

Rhone au Rhin

France

Switzerland

Canal Du

Audincourt
Iron

Map of Alsatian textile
region.

Towns

Towns with
Textile Industries

Railroads

Canals

Edge of Vosges
Mountain Block

Edge of Last
Glacial Epoch

Crest of Vosges North
of Ballon d'Alsace
Franco- German Boundary
1871-1914

Present International
Boundary

0 2 4 6 8 10
Kilometers

in the early nineteenth century, a number of conditions encouraged the development of a manufacturing area distinctive from all others in the former middle kingdom.

Many of the towns in the County of Montbéliard were new creations in the late Middle Ages, and much of the surrounding agricultural settlement was in dispersed farmsteads. To add yet a further difference, this area was a Protestant island in the midst of a basically Catholic sea. Soon after the county was attached to France in 1793, it became an important manufacturing place, producing cotton textiles and hosiery, then textile machines, wire, nails, and other iron goods. When bicycles became fashionable in the 1870's, Montbéliard took up their manufacture, shifting then to automobiles. She stands as perhaps the most exceptional "Detroit" in Europe, with factories spread among a number of smaller towns in a very rural setting (as are the engineering works for Peugeot). The impression is rather that of a French Massachusetts with a thorough industrialization of a previously dispersed farming and small town region. With the success of those industries, based initially on small increments of power (from charcoal and water for forges) gained in a widely spread manufacturing pattern, a great *industrial region with fairly small cities* has grown. The economic liberalism of Protestantism, the ingenuity of a free rural population with a craft tradition, and an established tenure for those rural small-holders seem to have created this industrial settlement form.

Europe experienced several basic forms of industrial settlement, though basically they divided into two process groups: those industrial towns which were true metropolises, starting from a major nucleus of production and spreading outward into the country round about—as in Manchester, Bruges, Lille, and Rouen; and those countrysides where industry grew up rather independent of towns of any great size but with sufficient general success to shape an industrial region, coming together in the end into an industrial *sympolis*—as in the West Riding of Yorkshire, the Verviétois, the valleys of the southeastern Alsace, and the County of Montbéliard. This same division occurred in the industrialization of the United States, to which we now turn.

The Peculiar Case of the Industrial City in America

Until the shots were fired at Concord in 1775, most types of manufacturing were forbidden in the English colonies in America. The Thirteen Colonies had been set out with the notion of furthering the mercantile development of England. As a result, an active effort was carried on to stop or severely restrict any production of manufactured goods outside the mother country.

Not all production could be stopped; a few items, it was recognized, must be produced in the colonies for their own essential needs, or for the needs of England. From the beginning, elements of local handicraft were accepted, rather akin to those produced locally within the manorial or "natural" economy of the Middle Ages. Woolen cloth was woven in the home for family use; in Rowley in Massachusetts from the 1630's on, a modest quantity of these cloths were handwoven for sale in New England. Much of this manufacturing activity could exist in the obscurity of distance from the king's agents, but expansion of the scale of production beyond that intended for the local consumption was difficult. Any noticeable flow of American goods to England or her Newfoundland or West Indian colonies would have brought anguished cries from the home manufacturers. In 1699 a Woolens Act "forebade colonial woolen cloth to be sold outside the place or plantation where it was woven; but as most rural families carded, spun, and wove their own wool, this caused no hardship in America."[89]

The colonies were always permitted to process the agricultural products for which they were first set up. Molasses could be distilled into rum (though the Americans illegally imported molasses from the French colonies where it was more cheaply bought than in the English islands). Tar and turpentine, barrel staves, box boards, and a number of other forest products were fabricated quite legally. Along with a booming trade in salt fish, flour, rice, indigo, tobacco, potash, and several other simply-processed staples, America could support an active merchant community and the ships to carry their goods to the West Indies and Newfoundland, even on occasion to England.

But England's example was not lost on the colonial

[89]*Samuel Eliot Morison and Henry Steele Commager*, The Growth of the American Republic, *New York: Oxford University Press, 1942, Vol. I, p. 102.*

merchants who were fully as enterprising, and perhaps somewhat more ingenious, than their English colleagues. They wished to try their hand at manufacturing just as they had at trading. The English sought to control the Americans' entry into manufacturing in several ways, of which the most effective was not the embargo placed by parliamentary acts, easily overlooked by those at such a distance, but instead the tight control that England exercised on the availability of specie in America. The situation became so desperate that the legislature of the Massachusetts colony issued promissory notes to finance Sir William Phips' expedition against Québec. These notes, with the possible exception of similar paper uttered in Sweden at this time, were the first paper currency ever issued and they did serve, though with certain awkward qualities.[90] The colonies found it difficult to operate in foreign trade or with England, where the balance of that trade was normally against the colonies, but internal to America the paper began to make possible the accumulation of bills of credit which became the main medium of exchange, in the end giving us our "dollar bill" in contrast to Britain's pound "note." With these bills, merchants could begin to assemble capital and look toward the creation of manufacturing establishments.

We cannot speak in detail of all of the early mills, but we may note their general use. Grist mills had existed from the beginning of the colonies, and from 1645 iron smelters were operating, beginning with one in Massachusetts.[91] Fulling-mills, sawmills, and a few other simple waterpowered operations were carried on before the Revolution. But in general only the iron making industry showed much development. Until 1750, iron exports from America had been forbidden, though by then a number of smelters were at work in Massachusetts and the other colonies. The colonies had been self-sufficient in iron making perhaps as early as the beginning of the eighteenth century; certainly in 1750 when the British market was opened to colonial pig and bar iron, a surplus of around 3,000 tons remained for export.[92] When that legislation had been adopted by the British Parliament, one of its provisions was that Americans could not develop any further works for producing finished products. Yet we know that such an embargo was largely disregarded. By 1775, "There were actually more 'furnaces' [where pig iron was produced] and 'forges' [where pig iron was resmelted into bar or wrought iron] in the Thirteen Colonies than in England and Wales . . .[and although] most of them were very small, employing but a few

dozen hands at the most . . . the average annual production—300 tons of pig iron for each furnace, and 150 tons of bar iron for each forge—was about the same as in England."[93]

In 1700, the American colonies were producing around 1,500 tons of iron annually, about 2 per cent of the estimated world production. In 1750, the figure had risen to around 10,000 tons annually, and then to 30,000 tons in 1771. "In any case, the production of iron in America on the eve of the Revolution may have been as high as 15 per cent of world production, a proportion that was not again equaled until well into the nineteenth century. And while this high production was largely for domestic consumption, the colonies were net exporters of unfinished iron."[94]

Even from a very early time, at least as early as 1645, industry was not unknown to the new colonies, nor was it necessarily carried on at a trivial scale. But certain overriding conditions were imposed from outside that *may* have given American industry an unbalanced development during its first 150 years. We know that the English parliament sought to ward off virtually all manufacturing in the Thirteen Colonies; we know as well that they were not wholly successful in their efforts. Without such restraints, what would have been the amount of actual production? Only by looking at two facets of production—of iron and of textiles—can we guess. On the basis of existing bits of evidence, we can assume certain industries in America would have developed on a large scale well before the Revolution if the English parliament had not ruled otherwise. Distilling, ship-building, some basic kinds of textile production, and anything that would have benefited greatly from cheap and vastly plentiful waterpower might well have grown up in the Thirteen Colonies, as did iron making. But in this realm of conjecture, we should not lose sight of the fact that to a point well in advance of what parliament wanted, the settlers in the New World participated in Britain's emerging eighteenth-century Industrial Revolution.

Writing in 1916, Rolla Milton Tryon set out to study the nature of *Household Manufacturers in the United States*.[95] He proposed the notion of the "family factory," historically a peculiar concept, but one that helps us understand the great amount of "manufacture" done in America before the formal Industrial Revolution, as Phyllis Deane has shown there was in

[90]Ibid., p. 104.
[91]*Peter Temin*, Iron and Steel in Nineteenth-century America, *Cambridge: M.I.T. Press, 1964, p. 13.*
[92]*Morison and Commager*, op. cit., *p. 102.*

[93]Ibid., *p. 103.*
[94]*Temin*, op. cit., *pp. 15–19.*
[95]*Rolla Milton Tryon*, Household Manufactures in the United States, 1640-1860, *Chicago: University of Chicago Press, 1917. For a discussion of the English Industrial Revolution before 1760 see the early chapters of Phyllis Deane*, The First Industrial Revolution, *Cambridge: The University Press, 1965.*

England. Tyron shows with impressive statistics that the scale of production in farm homes could be very impressive indeed—one family made more than eight hundred yards of textiles of various sorts in one year, as well as possibly other tools of agriculture and the general necessities of life. A distinctive unit of "manufacture," the family sought both to maximize its product and to care for a diversity of needs. The agricultural implements were simple but usually sturdy and homemade, as were most furniture and household goods.

The *process of self-provision*, the Yankee commandment, prepared a fertile ground in which invention might germinate. We have seen how Eli Whitney's chance visit to Savannah produced first the cotton gin and ultimately a vast social and economic transformation of the western world. Immediate ingenuity, so typical of New England in the nineteenth century, created a flood of machines from a basically rural area in central Massachusetts, the valleys of western Connecticut, and the hill areas of Vermont. The cotton gin, effective and cheap firearms, the sewing machine, and a whole string of somewhat more complex textile machines came from what might seem a nonindustrial population. Yet when we look into their daily life, these inventors had always had to be builders of things to carry on the "family factory." If that fact had been appreciated by the rather parochial English historians of technology, American technical accomplishment would not have broken upon England as such a surprise as a result of United States displays at the Exhibition of 1851.

But the formal history of the industrialization of America usually begins only with Samuel Slater and the first cotton spinning mill he set up in 1790 on the Blackstone River just outside the colonial port of Providence. We know that Slater had just completed a seven-year millwright's apprenticeship to Jedidiah Strutt, Arkwright's partner, at Belper. As a trained millwright, he was freed of that indenture, but not permitted on pain of death to leave England, even for her own colonies—and certainly not for those which had just won independence. Yet Samuel Slater secretly set off for New York hoping to interest American merchants in furnishing him the capital with which to set up a mill. Manhattan proved a poor site for a water-powered mill, so he accepted the offer of Moses Brown and other Providence merchants to come there and literally "set up shop," as it fell first to his lot to reproduce the machines he had worked with in Belper. This direct transfer of textile machines from the hearth of the English textile revolution suggests quite logically that America's industrialization was introduced by Slater, and was totally derivative of English technology. At best, that truth is only partial.

Slater did journey to America and reproduce the machines in use in England. But this act was not the birth of American industry, as is so commonly alleged. The United States was at that very moment producing something close to one-sixth of the world's iron output. In addition, the textile "manufacture" of the United States was a very large enterprise, despite the fact that most of it came from family factories. In 1790 the city of Providence and its vicinity produced 30,000 yards of woolen cloth, while in the first nine months of 1791 Providence city produced 25,262 yards of linen cloth, 5,858 yards of cotton, 3,165 yards of woolen cloth, 512 yards of carpeting, 4,093 pairs of stockings, 859 pairs of gloves, and 260 yards of fringe.[96] With respect to Manchester and southeast Lancashire, we have noted that only a well-developed domestic industrial district could take in and employ the product of a machine spinning mill such as Arkwright had established at Cromford and Belper and Slater had brought to Providence (Pawtucket in later years).

The introduction of spinning machines in America came in a context rather different from the one found in Britain, both in legal constraints and in corporate controls. Gilds had never been effective in America, so corporatism was not a feature of American industry, and most assuredly not of the family factory. For this reason the family factory unit tended to handle all processes involved in the production of a cloth, save perhaps for the act of fulling, which in the Thirteen Colonies as in England was the most difficult and unpleasant job, already "mechanized" in the late Middle Ages. Otherwise, *the American family factory seems to have been based on the integration of processes within a single extended biological family residing on a single farm.* I mean specifically to draw a sharp contrast with the conditions within the domestic textile industry of Lancashire, and only to a lesser degree of the West Riding. Because of this integration of processing within a single American farm, no dependence was placed upon merchants (later factors) to organize and "put-out" the goods, as was found even in Yorkshire. Textile production thus became a universal feature of rural America, particularly in the area north of Maryland where free labor dominated. Those colonies dependent on slave labor tended not to be so heavily involved in this type of production, yet Tryon argues that during the American Revolution even slave labor was widely used in such household manufacture, reverting to field and servant employment once peace returned.

As household manufacture was so widely spread in the Thirteen Colonies, no specialized towns were given over to facilitating this manufacture. Instead merchants in various towns bought or bartered for cloths and other textiles and sent them on for trade in cities, in the insular possessions of Britain in the West Indies

[96]*Tench Coxe's report on manufactures, quoted in Tryon, op. cit., pp. 133–134.*

Photographs of the pre-revolutionary family factory are nonexistent, but this turn-of-the-century shot taken by Jacob Riis in New York City, showing a Bohemian family making cigars at home, suggests many of the colonial conditions of the manufacture of goods at home. All available hands were used.

and Newfoundland (but not in Britain herself, where these goods were strictly forbidden entry). In return for home-produced cloths, farm families and those city ones that made textiles gained the items of trade for which they had neither specie nor sufficient bills of credit. Thus, handwoven textile products furnished a medium of exchange in a land starved, by antiquated economic practices in England, for a basic supply of coins for simple trade. Under such a circumstance, cloth making was both widespread and earnestly pursued.

Household manufacture did not require any charter of privileges as had so long been necessary in parts of England. Because England had failed after the mid-1640's to supply manufactured items to the American colonies in any quantity commensurate to their needs, people had had to develop certain types of "manufacture" in almost ubiquitous distribution. The notion of the specialized area of production, and consequent distant trade, was foreign to American experience, save in the most important of raw staples—rice, indigo, tobacco, lumber, potash, fish, deerskin, furs, and the like—that traded to England. But as the scale of export increased, notably in the southern colonies, local self-sufficiency began to decline, and food began to move into the southern area from elsewhere in the colonies.

Class distinction had always colored importation; the more pompous members of colonial society had traditionally favored imported English textiles over those produced in America. The very adjectival term "homespun" suggests a certain bucolic naivete that would hardly flatter the self-esteem of the Boston merchant or the Virginia planter; they seem to have avoided those fabrics when they had their portraits painted, and as well probably in most public places. But the country people and the working class did not shun the native, so most of the durable fabrics—the linsey-woolsey, jeans, ducks, fustians, and the like—were made here well before 1775. In 1775 the patriots of any class rejected British textiles to such a degree that the trade virtually disappeared except in those areas held during the Revolution by British forces—New York City and parts of the coastal South. The effect was striking indeed when a "nonimportation" policy was introduced in 1774 and remained in effect until peace was near. For New England the imports dropped from half a million pounds sterling in the period Christmas, 1773, to Christmas, 1774, to £71,000 in 1774–1775, £55,000 in 1775–1776 and nil until 1782–1783, when, with the restoration of peace in 1783, imports quickly rebounded before Christmas to £200,000.[97]

After the war, the strong belief arose that if the nation were to survive economically it must do two things that had immediate and vital bearing on the effort toward industrialization. First, it must integrate the thirteen separate local economies, previously firmly attached for the sale of staples and the purchase of manufactures directly to England, into a "national economy" now strongly excluded from the British market. Second, it must encourage the emergence of household manufacture from the family factory into full-scale factory development. With the lifting of the yoke of king and parliament, the United States was free to engage in any manufacturing it could sustain, and to trade its goods to any port that would have them.

This political emancipation brought almost immediate industrialization. If we date the effective nation from 1789 and the adoption of the Constitution, we may perceive the clear foundation of a national industrialization several years before nationhood. This economically critical step could be taken so soon and so

relatively surely because of the quantity of "quiet manufacturing" before 1776.

It was soon apparent to the American merchants trading now with the wide world that to practice their trade properly they needed access to manufactured goods to be exchanged for raw materials, which have always been the ballast, economic as well as physical, of any healthy merchant marine. The need for manufactures to exchange for needed raw materials combined with the general enterprise and ingenuity of the New England Yankees (there being really no other true Yankees) to encourage efforts to make use of that region's main factor endowment, the great disruption of its preglacial river drainage by that relatively recent geologic event. Most places in New England had not, since the glacial age, drained properly. Water was plentiful in swamps and ponds of glacial origin, and streams were filled with rapids. These sites could be easily and cheaply developed into mill sites by building only small dams.

Waterpower was plentiful north of the southern limits of American glaciation, which reached southward to include all of New England and New York State and a thin fringe in northern New Jersey and Pennsylvania. That glaciated area had held the traditional water mills for sawing boards, grinding grain, and fulling cloth since the arrival of the English. Parenthetically, though the United States ultimately proved to be vastly rich in coal deposits even within the Appalachian states, at the close of the Revolution virtually no coal production had developed, and that which was soon to develop came only in anthracite mining. Thus, though coal could subsequently shape the American economy, in 1790 it had yet to do so.

Waterpower had at first to furnish the muscle of any American Industrial Revolution. The nation was fortunate in its natural endowment beyond any level found in Britain or Belgium. The glacier had disrupted the drainage in a hilly land with a moderately heavy rainfall—around forty inches a year—producing many natural reservoirs, as well as the rapids and falls at which the descent of water could be transformed into power. In fact, the very name given to North Providence when the site of Slater's Mill became a separate town—Pawtucket—was an Indian term for a place of falls. Later the first true industrial city in America, Lowell, was set up by "The Proprietors of the Locks and Canals at the Pawtucket Falls of the Merrimac River" in Massachusetts. With plenty of ponds and dam sites to be had, New England was an ideal physical location for an Industrial Revolution.

Such transformations of the economy also take place within a specific economic context that exerts a force toward scalar increase in production. The search following the Revolution for a "national economy"

[97]*Tryon, op. cit., pp.* 58–59.

made industrialization desirable. Not only had the need arisen to create domestic production of products for which the money would no longer be available to purchase from Britain but also the nation also strongly desired to secure domestically a group of staple manufactures—cheap and durable textiles, small metal products, wooden wares—that would provide trading commodities for exchange at the tropical African and Asian ports. Thus, as the merchants of the New England ports began fitting out ships to trade more widely than had been their privilege under British economic planning, they felt a strong need as well to secure an increase in American manufacture. To begin with, they could rely on the massive "family factory" production, but its competence to deal with an expanding trade was limited by the fact that such production was incidental to other occupations. In any event, that form of production was severely restrained by the small expansibility of handwork in a labor-deficient land.

American economic history has established the truth that the capital earned by the merchant ship-owners of New England in overseas trade paid for the early factories, which came ultimately to make New England the first industrial district. Certainly the money that the Quaker Browns of Rhode Island had earned in the whaling industry paid Samuel Slater's costs in setting up his first mill. And the pocketbook of the Boston China Traders bore the brunt of Francis Cabot Lowell's experiments at Waltham that created the first true factories found anywhere in the textile industry, in Europe as well as America.

The Early Textile Factories

The stage was set for the emergence of the New England industrial city by several false entrances. The earliest use of spinning machinery in America seems to have been in Philadelphia in 1775, "when probably the first spinning-jenny ever seen in America was exhibited in that city." This jenny was the earlier hand-operated one, not the Arkwright water-frame that Slater built in Providence in the fall of 1790. Mills were established in the Quaker City but they prospered no more than did one set up in Worcester in Massachusetts in 1780. These efforts sought to tap British technology at a great distance and, in time of war with that country, hardly under the best of circumstances. "The first establish-

ment, however, which can by any interpretation be considered a textile factory was erected at Beverly, Mass., in 1787. The legislature aided this enterprise. The factory continued in operation for several years, but its career as a cotton factory was brief, and it did not meet with much success."[98] In fact that Beverly factory was more successful than is generally acknowledged, surviving until 1807 when it was put out of business by an embargo.[99] The modest pretensions of this factory show up clearly when we note it produced bed tickings.

The earliest phase of the Industrial Revolution in America was strikingly different from that epoch in England, as was the second phase. In England the earliest factory industrialization—at Cromford and Belper—was in the countryside, utilizing small groups of segmental labor and avoiding the legal constraints to innovation that existed in cities with their survival of medieval corporatism. In America the earliest factories were in the nation's largest towns—Philadelphia, Boston, Beverly, and Providence, which all fell within the twenty largest places in the new nation—depending upon one of the few pockets of segmental labor to be found in that over-employed land. But quickly each country shifted its locale for factories. Those in England grew up mainly in the towns, while in America factories sprang up mostly in the countryside, though often quickly developing a city outside their gates. Two main facts seem to account for this peculiar reversal. America had never experienced urban corporatism, so the city need not be shunned even in the earliest phase of industrialization. Also America's general shortage of labor meant that the tiny available groups were more likely to be encountered in the city than in the countryside, where cheap land meant that wide ownership and full employment were possible.

The necessity of establishing this relationship with scarce labor led to the evolution of the American factory system into a heavy dependence upon segmental labor drawn ultimately from the land, thus turning the prospective manager's attention there. Along with the growing need for waterpower, which could only in the very earliest phase be supplied in adequate quantities in or near port towns, the pull to the countryside came ultimately to be very strong in America, while it withered in Britain, because of an almost immediate eviction of any rural population which became surplus and the poor waterpower resources of rural England. Only New Lanark, built by David Dale and Robert Owen on

[98]*Caroll D. Wright*, The Industrial Evolution of the United States, *Meadville, Pa.: The Chautauqua-Century Press, 1895, pp. 121–125.*
[99]*Harold Underwood Faulkner*, American Economic History, *New York: Harper and Brothers, 1931, p. 298.*

the upper Clyde, proved to be similar in locating forces to a hundred mill-dam sites in New England.

In America, a number of forces exerted pulls that ultimately resolved into a factory location. The availability of raw materials, power, labor, capital, market, and transportation all entered into the decision. No doubt the availability of capital was initially most important, operating to cluster the earliest factories around the important trading ports where capital was being accumulated in trade. This geographical leash had considerable reach. Factories were set up within a day's journey of Providence, Boston, and Baltimore, so that the capitalists could exercise fairly direct supervision of their plants in a preelectronic era. The next question was, where were sizable waterpowers available? Only when that question had been favorably answered would labor availability be considered. And once capital, power, and labor had been brought together, it was reasoned that further capital inputs would furnish transportation of raw material and finished product to the burgeoning factory city.

This formula worked. Several of its phases are of interest and importance to us in understanding the evolution of the tie of industrialization and urbanization in the United States.

American Industrialization and Urbanization

The first phase of industrialization-urbanization is represented by the earliest mills already noted. The large towns were all ports (Beverly was both a port and the nation's eighteenth "city" in population), where capital, potential market, available transportation, and small units of segmental labor were available. Power was in shortest supply, though initially, as in England, hand operation and the use of horses to turn machines masked that poverty. But in Providence and Baltimore, which both lay almost directly on the Fall Line, this first phase of industrial-urbanization could be extended over a longer period before recourse need be taken to more inland siting of factories. The Blackstone and Pawtuxet valleys adjacent to Providence and the Jones Falls valley at Baltimore became early homes to American industry. In New York City no first phase industry based on waterpower gained much growth. Manufacturers had to look farther afield, by turning to

the high falls of the Passaic River where, in 1791 and under the aegis of Alexander Hamilton, the Society for Establishing Useful Manufactures was organized to develop the primary manufacturing town for the new United States. Using the 50-foot fall as a power source, the Society was authorized to lay out a "manufactory" within a six-square-mile reservation. The first plant to be built was for cotton textile production but under governmental operation not much was accomplished. Only slowly, and along strange routes, did Paterson become an important industrial town, adding steam-locomotive production and silk weaving and dyeing in the 1830's, and subsequently many other forms of industry associated with the needs of a large metropolis.

Successful and continuing cotton textile manufacturing began with the factory Samuel Slater set up on the lowest falls of the Blackstone River in the northern part of the city of Providence. There, where previously a forge had been operated by waterpower, Moses Brown and William Almy financed and organized the firm that supported Slater's efforts. "In the years between Slater's arrival in America in 1789 and the passage of the Embargo Act, December, 1807, the industry adopted English machinery, imitated England in the type of labor employed, took advantage of the cheapened product of the cotton gin, and gained for itself a wide and expanding market. At each step the lead was taken by Almy and Brown of Providence, the first successful machine spinners in America."[100]

Samuel Slater's first mill at North Providence (Pawtucket), built in 1793.

[100]*Caroline F. Ware*, The Early New England Cotton Manufacture: A Study in Industrial Beginnings, *Boston: Houghton Mifflin Company, 1931, p. 19.*

To understand the progress of the American cotton textile industry, we must distinguish among the three types of "machines" used in the earlier spinning efforts. The first developed, James Hargreaves' *spinning jenny* of 1764, did not lend itself to powered operation, as it had several somewhat discontinuous operations. This machine produced a soft yarn excellent for filling but not for use as the necessarily stronger warp threads. The second machine was the *water-frame*, which Richard Arkwright claimed he invented and which he patented in 1769. The process involved was continuous and could be carried out by mechanical power, producing a fairly stout yarn that was able to stand the strain of use for the warp in coarse fabrics such as those first produced in the Slater mills. The third type of spinning machine was the *mule*, so called because it combined features of the Hargreaves and the Arkwright machines. It was developed by Samuel Crompton in 1779. This mule could be hand-driven, and produced a stronger, finer thread that could be used successfully for the warps in fine cotton textiles. But the mule was such a heavy machine that it required the labor of strong men rather than children or women, who commonly operated both the jenny and the water-frame.

When Slater's first mill, built specifically as a "factory house" to avoid the inconveniences of the previous dwelling houses where Almy and Brown had experimented with cotton textile production, started production in 1791, it employed eight children, and one adult supervisor. This use of child labor was a practice brought directly from Belper in Slater's head and widely used during the earlier decades of cotton production. Even as late as 1801, Slater was employing "over one hundred between the ages of four and ten" in his Pawtucket Falls mill.[101] This factory was so successful that it was producing great quantities of yarn that required ingenious selling to whatever market was available. In the earlier years this market was found in the small domestic shops of handweavers of woolen textiles. The early cotton threads spun on the water-frame were fairly coarse and were desired mostly to provide the warp threads in mixed woolen-cotton fabrics. To sell from the Pawtucket mill, it was necessary to have the truly massive domestic market provided by the "family factories."

Quickly following on his success in the first mill, Slater and his partners had a new building, specifically designed for cotton spinning, erected at the same falls. Fortunately, this 1793 mill building still stands, so from it we may gain a clear picture of what facilities were needed at that time. The descent from the New England barn is obvious; this two-story clapboard building is constructed with heavy timber framing and topped with an attic lighted by a clerestory, making three floors available for working. The waterwheel operated in a well just under the front door with the power taken by belts to the several machines. At the front, a tower contained the stairs for the building and the ever-present bell loft, where the signal that began to regulate the lives of the workers, as never before, came to be hung. Within these buildings, real constraints were introduced both by the need to transmit power mechanically from the millwheel and by the use of wooden framing. In 1793 three cards and two frames with 72 spindles were at work in this mill. When more production was desired, the tendency was less strong to enlarge an existing mill than to build a second one. Thus American mills tended to differ from English ones by being somewhat more spread out along feeder canals that brought the water to several individual mills with independent waterwheels, or later turbines.

Once the power at the Pawtucket Falls had been fully engaged, Slater and his partners looked elsewhere, developing true mill villages at some remove from Providence. In 1806 Samuel Slater and Company began the development of a town on the Branch River, a tributary of the Blackstone, which became Slatersville, one of the earlier of the "Arkwright Villages" that sprang up around Providence.[102] Yet the demand for cotton thread still increased. So in 1811 the company had to reach out even farther from Providence, into the southern tier of Massachusetts at South Oxford (which became a separate town named Webster shortly after Slater developed his mill there). At Webster, "The property in 1817 consisted of one cotton factory of 2,000 spindles, a woolen mill, a grist and saw mill, 16 dwelling houses, and 700 acres of land." But even that establishment was not the limit to which the firm could expand, though it had begun to see that the small increments to waterpower represented by the 1793 mill at Pawtucket, the mills at Slatersville and Voluntown (Connecticut), and that at Webster were becoming out of date. The large integrated factory was emerging, so the Slater Company looked outward and "purchased an estate consisting of a small cotton mill, several tenements, and a fine water-privilege at Amoskeag Falls, on the Merrimac River. This was the foundation of the great manufacturing city of Manchester, New Hampshire."[103]

The Congress sought a report on the cotton textile

[101]Ibid., p. 23.

[102]For a detailed discussion of these Arkwright Villages, see James E. Vance, Jr., "Housing the Worker: The Employment Linkage as a Force in Urban Structure," Economic Geography, Vol. 42, 1966, pp. 304–307.

[103]Frederick L. Lewton, "Samuel Slater and the Oldest Cotton Machinery in America," Smithsonian Report for 1926.

industry after it had been underway for a quarter of a century.

According to a memorial presented to the United States Congress there were reported to be at the close of the year 1815, 99 cotton mills in Rhode Island, with 75,678 spindles; in Massachusetts, 57 mills, with 45,650 spindles; and in Connecticut, 14 mills with 12,886 spindles; making a total of 170 mills operating 134,214 spindles. The average capacity of cotton mills at that time was only 500 spindles. The "Old Slater Mill" (of 1793) at Pawtucket up to this time the largest in the country, contained 5,170 spindles.[104]

The picture of the second phase of industrial-urbanization shows a number of relatively small mills scattered in the environs of the large colonial port cities at small waterpower sites which came normally to be surrounded by an "Arkwright Village." In those villages, the manufacturer provided housing for his workers, recruited from nearby country in part by the offer of housing as well as employment for the entire family, down even to children of rather tender years. The Pawtuxet valley southwest of Providence still furnishes us with an example of this sort of settlement, which we might with some justice term "village urbanization." The people taking up residence there were mostly from rural areas, gaining their first experience at urban life in small mill villages such as Hope or Lippet.

This second phase of village industrialization had followed on a first which, set at the edge of the port city, was little able to be expanded as the market increased. But like the first phase, the second was given over almost entirely to the spinning of yarn and thread for use as warps in handweaving. Under that narrow development of industry the labor demands in any one place were reasonably met by attracting to the village a modest number of families from which the several classes of workers could be drawn. The men and older boys served often as mechanics, maintaining the machines and dealing with heavy loads. The wives worked as supervisors of machines and operatives of the more complex processes. The children from 6 to 12 or so could aid the machine tenders or tend their own.

[104]Loc. cit.

The Third Phase of Industrialization: Urbanization

Repeated reference has been made to fundamental changes that came in the third phase of industrial-urbanization in the United States, which are critical to our story for two reasons. This third phase was a distinctively American experience. It was the first period of industrial development in this country when true city-forming and filling took place.

The first-phase mills at the edge of the colonial port had had only very modest impact on those places, mainly by supplying some trade goods to fill the holds of the burgeoning merchant marine at home in those ports. The Arkwright Villages of the second phase had greatly expanded the flow of goods, but they still lay sufficiently far from the city that they had doubtful impact on either its retail trade or its housing market. No doubt wholesaling in those port cities gained as this market for consumer goods in the surrounding country increased, but we should not overestimate the impact. Some evidence exists that the level of consumption of goods was then so small, compared to the present, that trade would have been mostly in food. And much of the food still came directly from the country into the villages without passing through the warehouses of the city wholesaler.

With the third phase came the creation of true industrial cities distinct to America. They stood as essentially self-contained new urban creations, because American technology and business organization were innovative and imaginative to a degree well in advance of Britain, and because they still had a large factor endowment of waterpower. When American industry sought to expand in the textile trade, it would still continue for some fifty years to turn to waterpower. In the third phase the search was for large components of waterpower, not so much because the spinning mills were becoming larger, which they were, but because in America a strong campaign was aimed at creating *integrated factories* for the production of textiles from raw material to fully finished product. Quite in contrast, in the textile areas of Britain (either in the cotton trade of Lancashire or the woolen trade of Yorkshire), the complex urban integration—the "conurbation," as it came to be called in the 1920's—was needed to secure production. We have already examined this pattern at length.

In America no inheritance of established interests need be dealt with, so the sorts of process divisions found in the north of England (where towns had their time-honored specializations that carried over into the

Industrial Era) could be avoided. Also America's shortage of labor meant that mechanization rather consistently was held as a national goal. The whole resistance to machines—Luddism—that swept England in the early nineteenth century was absent in this country, where the family factory was a reality but not a totality. Those "factories" were located on family farms where basic support was provided by agriculture, so a decline in the domestic textile production would not totally impoverish the workers. Industrialization of textiles into factories did affect the family factories; that effect led to the successful recruiting of segmental labor from just such farms into the factories that shaped the "Waltham System." But there was a difference. In America the part-time supplement to the family support was wiped out by industrialization: in Britain the rural cottar's nearly total livelihood disappeared. In England a settlement and demographic revolution was wrought in the early nineteenth century, with the social and economic consequences that Engels witnessed and described. In America change came more by the industrialization of the countryside than by the full transformation of the national society and economy.

The Waltham System of Industrialization

The effort to create an integration of industry at one place was initially undertaken by a small group of Boston capitalists, most notably Francis Cabot Lowell and Patrick Tracy Jackson, brothers-in-law seeking to invest in local industrial development money earned in the shipping trades. Lowell went to Britain in 1811 to recuperate from an illness, found himself there when war broke out in 1812, and improved his time during the conflict by visiting cotton mills in Lancashire and Scotland. On those inspections he saw the earliest powered-looms at work but was unable to purchase one, or even the plans therefor. On his return to America in 1813, Lowell set about building such a loom. With the help of a mechanic, Paul Moody, he successfully completed a power loom that is commonly called the Waltham loom with power applied to the weaving frame through a cam action. Starting in 1814, he and Jackson organized the Boston Manufacturing Company which immediately sought a site for a mill as close to Boston as possible, finding it at a 5-foot fall on the Charles River nine miles west of the city at Waltham.

When the Waltham factory opened in 1814 it was the first of its kind in industrial experience; it was truly the world's first process-integrated plant. Starting with baled cotton bought from Southern dealers, Waltham workers carded, cleaned, roved, spun, and wove cotton into cloth, which in turn was finished for the market and transferred as a total product to a single wholesale dealer whose job was to sell and distribute. The Waltham company did not seek to match the finer products of Britain, turning instead to "plain, coarse, white sheeting made from number fourteen yarn which the power loom could turn out easily and which could be used for almost all purposes, especially by the western pioneers." The market proved so good that by 1822 the investors in the Boston Manufacturing Company had earned 104.5 per cent on their capitals. Such a performance obviously courted envy and emulation which assured that the Waltham System would find frequent competitors.

The original Boston Manufacturing Company grew apace during the nineteenth century, as this 1884 photo shows. The original plant forms most of the western section of the taller buildings in the background.

Certainly most fundamental to the Waltham System was the integration of the processes within a single plant, an act that led to the necessary clustering of a fairly large work force at one spot. No longer could the casual segmental labor—Slater's eight children at Pawtucket—suffice. Instead workers must be recruited, particularly while the use of waterpower often determined the establishment of the plant outside the existing cities. Even the Slater mill had outrun its easily accessible labor, and had to seek large families and encourage their residence near the mill. In Waltham, conditions demanded both numbers and skills, so Lowell and Jackson devised a justly famous recruiting system. To tend their power looms they found young women the most adept and reliable, particularly those between about 18 and 22 years of age. The city of Waltham had precious few candidates as the mills were increased in number ultimately to three, with a bleachery added, so recruiters were sent into country areas seeking to hire young women for a determinate stint in the Waltham factory. Their success in gaining recruits was striking, but to understand the reasons we must look both at the treatment of those recruits in Waltham (the pull factor) and the eagerness of those young women to leave the farm (the push factor).

Massachusetts agriculture, and that of New Hampshire to the north, was beginning to show its limited future by the time of the War of 1812. Endless springtime clearing of stones from the fields seemed not to reduce the next year's stone crop and the soils thus freed for cultivation were far from bounteous in production. The short summers did not foster too full an array of crops. In all, the New England farm seemed to produce more character than wealth among its cultivators. An increasing restiveness grew on those hill farms, which by the early nineteenth century were perhaps more "over-populated" than any other section of America. The "Yankee Exodus" to the Middle West was one symptom, while the flooding of rurally born young women into Waltham and its successors was another.

Francis Cabot Lowell had observed English industry with an analytical eye and come away determined not only to reproduce the factories but also to do it without the worst social features associated with them in the older industrial nation. His idea was to use a periodic labor force, which would maintain one foot on the farm while working for a few years to earn money in the factory. Caroline Ware believed "furthermore, about half of the workers, those in the group of largest mills, did not really move to the milltowns but maintained their connection with their home farms during the period of their work in the factory. Even the other group of workers who came to the mills with the intention to remain could never give up the possibility of returning to the land."[105] In contrast to Britain, where land ownership was narrow and aristocratic, in New England it was general, and remained a constant refuge in times of economic difficulty. "Consequently mill labor became an impermanent group, as it often does where agriculture remains dominant while factories develop."[106]

Whether the outcome was fully understood or merely fortunate, in any event throughout much of the nineteenth century, industrialization was not associated directly with the creation of a permanent urban proletariat. Only in the years after the Irish famine and other agricultural collapses in Sweden, Germany, and elsewhere in Europe did the conditions change. The immigrants who went to work in the textile towns of New England could not find refuge in a destitute Ireland or in a socially rigid Sweden. They were an American proletariat produced not by native conditions but instead by the conditions of a Europe still weighed down by a feudal class system.

During their early years the factories of the Waltham System provided a novel, quite useful physical solution to the problem of periodic worker residence. The boardinghouse was established, built and maintained by the factory owner, and kept a place of moral rectitude by carefully established rules. These houses were required by "a large body of unskilled labor continually drifting into the mills, forming a stream of fresh, vigorous country workers rather than a permanent factory class. The boardinghouse system of housing and controlling these workers was the skillful and popular adaptation which the early American manufacturers made to the limitations placed by the social and economic conditions which they had to meet."[107] So long as the recruitment of labor for the Waltham type mills came through "factory nomads," this system of boardinghouses served quite well. But with the turn to immigrant labor in the 1840's and '50's, it became inadequate.

An important distinction must be made between the Slater- or Arkwright-type mills of Rhode Island and the ones under the Waltham pattern that spread across northern New England. The Arkwright mills were slow to progress to weaving as well as spinning, depending for many further years on putting-out of yarn to hand-weavers, who generally produced more complex fabrics—either finer in quality or with stripes and plaids. The soft weft yarns produced on the Arkwright frames were combined with fine strong warp threads

[105]Ware, op. cit., p. 65. *The smaller the number of a yarn (that is, the number of hanks per pound), the coarser it is. Number forty would produce a fine cotton, number fourteen would not.*
[106]Ibid., p. 13.
[107]Loc. cit.

produced on hand-operated spinning mules to create a better class of fabric but one less cheaply manufactured.

What has this distinction to do with the evolution of the industrial city? Mule spinning required the labor of men while water-frame spinning could be done by children, with the result that in and around Providence, where the Arkwright mills and Villages were clustered, the pattern was that of families living permanently in an industrial life-style. Because the waterpowers available were small at any one place, the great integrated factories with their larger need for power did not develop. Perhaps this natural factor endowment kept the Providence textile development in the Arkwright rather than the Waltham stage. But with only a part of the industrial production clustered in factories—the weft yarn spinning—while warp thread production and actual weaving both remained domestic activities, the basis for urbanization was kept small. This industry was much closer to the English prototype than what came to be the American.

Providence was the great center of the textile dyeing and finishing industry in America and to it came grey cloths from the domestic looms fed by the Arkwright Villages round about. Ultimately this area became the true Lancashire of America, with the same attractive force for the unfortunates of other lands and the same creation of an industrial proletariat. But the southern New England textile district languished in this second phase of industrial-urbanization for several decades in the first half of the nineteenth century, while the Waltham System spread over much of northern New England, creating the nation's first industrial cities.

The Waltham System was not merely one characterized by process integration and a particular source of workers living in boardinghouses. In addition, it was the first clear demonstration of the industrial "multiplier effect." The Waltham company from the very beginning had manufactured most of the machinery used in their mill and as a second and a third mill were built at the falls of the Charles, they constructed more looms and spinning machines. They also initiated the practice of building such machines for others, thus establishing the strong tie that has subsequently existed between the manufacture of a consumer product and the making of machines for that production.

Lowell: The First American Manufacturing City

In Waltham the Boston Manufacturing Company entered upon an established town. The impact was obviously considerable in physical terms, but the town was not the product of the Industrial Era more than in the rapidity with which it grew during the first quarter of the nineteenth century. But soon the needs of the market could not be met from the Waltham mills, nor could they be enlarged. All the power of the 5-foot fall was employed in running the machinery of those three brick mills, "comprising eight thousand and sixty-four spindles, and two hundred and thirty-one looms." This machinery took the labor of "about four hundred persons, mostly females, working up seven hundred thousand pounds of cotton, and making two million yards of cloth per year."[108] But Waltham had met its limit so long as water was the source of power.

The Rev. Mr. Henry Miles has left us a starkly factual account of how America's first industrial city was born:

In 1820, Mr. Paul Moody had charge of the Waltham Mills, and a friend of his, Mr. Ezra Worthen, a former partner in business, was connected with the manufacturing establishment at Amesbury. From his childhood Mr. Worthen had been acquainted with the neighborhood of Pawtucket Falls [of the Merrimac River] and when the profitableness of the [Waltham] manufacturing business led to inquiries for water power, the immense advantages which this place held out soon struck his eye. While on a visit to Waltham, he expressed a wish to Mr. Patrick T. Jackson, one of the principal Directors of the company there, that they would set up works in some new place, and give him employment conducting them. Mr. Jackson replied, that they would willingly do this, if he would find a good water power. Immediately Mr. Worthen named the Pawtucket Falls; and with a piece of chalk drew a map of the river and canal on the floor. The rude sketch was sufficient to give Mr. Jackson a favorable impression, who requested Mr. Moody to visit, with Mr. Worthen, the place which the latter gentleman had described. It was not long before they explored this whole neighborhood, tracing the course of the canal [around the Falls built in 1797], surveying the adjoining land shores, and satisfying themselves that the place afforded great facilities for build-

[108]Rev. Henry A. Miles, Lowell, As It Was, and As It Is, *Lowell: Powers and Bagley, 1845, pp. 21–22.*

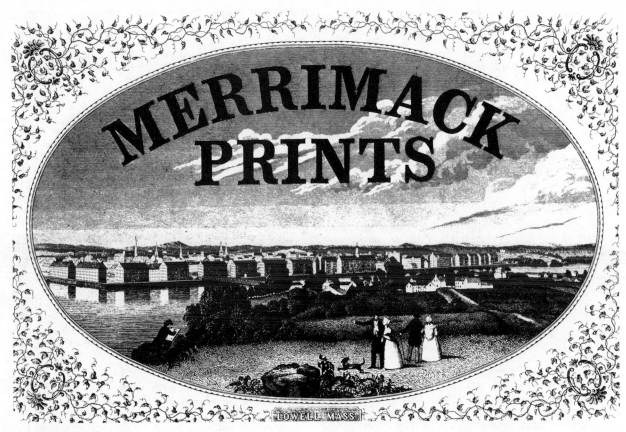

MERRIMACK PRINTS

LOWELL MASS.

This vignette of Lowell shows the city in the mid-nineteenth century as it was represented on the label of the Merrimack Manufacturing Company.

ing up a large manufacturing town. Soon after the reception of their highly favorable report, the Directors of the Waltham Company resolved to procure this eligible site.[109]

This site was on the forty-eight miles of the Merrimac River between the New Hampshire boundary and the sea, in the course of which the water drops 90 feet; "a little more than one-third of the total fall occurred before the location of dams on the river, within a distance of about one mile at Pawtucket Falls, nine miles south of the New Hampshire boundary." Those falls were of a considerable potential as the "river has a mean discharge of 8,020 second-feet, producing in a descent of 30 feet a theoretical motive force equivalent to about

[109]*Ibid., pp. 22–24.*

27,000 horsepower,"[110] something like four times the power produced by all the Boulton and Watt steam engines built during the eighteenth century.

To develop such a massive power source, a new form of industrialization had to come into existence. Initially the Waltham interests had organized the Merrimack Company to buy the canal at the falls and the adjacent land in order to establish a new factory but soon the scale of the waterpower was seen to be much greater than that needed for a single plant. In 1826 the Merrimack Company transferred all its holdings in machine shops, canals, waterpowers, and lands to the Proprietors of Locks and Canals, a separate company that subsequently furnished feeder canals and waterpowers to nine other major mills constructed in Lowell up to 1839. Unlike Slatersville or Waltham, this city was to have public utility waterpower as its foundation stone.

[110]*Margaret Terrell Parker,* Lowell: A Study of Industrial Development, *New York: The Macmillan Co., 1940 (A Wellesley College Publication), p. 60.*

The mills built in Lowell could be more massive than any before seen, because little question of power shortage existed. To begin with, the mills were not too much larger than those at Waltham. Over the years, the buildings were heightened or extended until they became some of the larger structures in the country, running for hundreds of feet along the canals and rising to five, six, or seven stories. Miles in 1845 described a typical mill yard:

On the banks of the river, or of a canal, stands a row of mills, numbering, on different corporations, from two to five. A few rods from these, are long blocks of brick boarding-houses, containing a sufficient number of tenements to accommodate the most of the operatives employed by the Corporation. Between the boarding-houses and the mills is a line of a one story brick building, containing the counting room, superintendent's room, clerk's and store rooms. The mill yard is so surrounded by enclosures, that the only access is through the counting room, in full view of those whose business it is to see that no improper persons intrude themselves upon the premises.

Thus the superintendent, from his room, has the whole of the Corporation under his eye. On the one side are the boarding-houses, all of which are under his care, and are rented only to known and approved tenants; on the other side are the mills, in each room of which he has stationed some carefully selected overseer, who is held responsible for the work, good order, and proper management of his room. Within the yard, also, are repair shops, each department of which, whether of iron, leather, or wood, has its head overseer. There is a superintendent of the yard, who, with a number of men under his care, has charge of all the out-door work of the establishment.[111]

In 1845, thirty-three of these large mill buildings ranged along the canals and the bank of the Merrimac, making Lowell the largest cotton town in America and one of her few great industrial cities, with a population of 30,000. A full third of the population was engaged as operatives in the mills or their workshops, though female employment remained disproportionate, with 6,320 females and 2,915 males. Clearly the Waltham System of recruiting women in the country had still to operate but soon thereafter the European immigration changed that pattern most distinctly.

The boardinghouse built by the millowner was very much a part of these towns. The recruitment of labor required such a provision, and the siting of the factory cities at waterpower locations in the country left no alternative housing supply, as might have been the case in a port city. So long as boardinghouses were the

manner of sheltering the workers, the basic quality of housing was probably equal to that beyond the narrow world of the mill yard, even though the supervision and moral policing must have irked anyone with a free spirit. The houses were normally of brick, built in rows along carefully laid out streets. The crowding of the site was yet to come in its worst aspects. Short of the fact that individuals had relatively little personal space in these buildings, a condition found as well in the farmhouses of the time, few contemporary criticisms were made of the boardinghouses.

Already in 1834 Lowell had a "main street," Merrimack Street, with shops for the sale of "clothing, shoes, dry goods, silks, shawls, linens and laces, china and hardware, West India goods, groceries, confectionary, drugs, books, and 'fancy goods,'" to satisfy the needs of a population no longer self-sufficient. As Lowell's business community came quickly into existence, several hotels—the Merrimac House, the American House, and the Washington Hotel—were built. Contemporary observers noted that this burgeoning city had no office buildings, as the administrative functions (more elevated than those carried on in the counting room) were pursued in Boston, whence came the capitals for the mills and the decisions that ruled the lives of those mills and their workers. Lowell exemplified for the first time an industrial city distinct from the center of long-distance trade that the colonial ports had been.

The newness struck Charles Dickens when he visited Lowell in 1842. "It was a very dirty winter's day, and nothing in the whole town looked old to me, except the mud, which in some parts was almost knee-deep, and might have been deposited there on the subsiding of the waters of the Deluge. In one place there was a new wooden church, which having no steeple, and being yet unpainted, looked like an enormous packing-case without any direction upon it. In another there was a large hotel, whose walls and colonnades were so crisp, and thin, and slight, that it had exactly the appearance of being built with cards. I was careful not to draw my breath as we passed, and trembled when I saw a workman come out upon the roof, lest with one thoughtless stamp of his foot he should crush the structure beneath him."[112]

Dickens, despite his great contempt for America and dislike for her people, still applauded the factories and by implication drew most flattering contrasts with Lancashire. "The rooms in which [the Lowell operatives] worked were as well ordered as [they] themselves. In the windows of some there were green

---

[111]*Miles, op. cit., pp. 64–65.*

[112]*Charles Dickens,* American Notes *[1842], New York: Fawcett Publications, Inc., 1961. Chapter 4. As a lower middle-class Englishman he found it essential, and fun as well, to abominate everything American, but he was impressed by the Lowell mills.*

plants, which were trained to shade the glass; in all there were as much fresh air, cleanliness, and comfort as the nature of the occupation would possible admit of." Despite the heavy reliance upon the Waltham System factory labor had not the pathetic quality so common in Britain. "Out of so large a number of females, many of whom were only then just verging upon womanhood, it may be reasonably supposed that some were delicate and fragile in appearance: no doubt there were! But I solemnly declare, that from all the crowd I saw in different factories that day, I cannot recall or separate one young face that gave me a painful impression; not one young girl whom, assuming it to be matter of necessity that she should gain her daily bread by the labor of her hands, I would have removed from those works if I had had the power."[113]

as possible in England (save for the inhumane land-owning system which shed so many social responsibilities from the account of the country where it belonged to the city, which could not possibly cope simultaneously with the sins of the English and Irish gentry)? In New England a democratic society, which greatly irked Dickens by its crudity, and unmannerliness, and general lack of understanding of "station," had far better dealt with its social responsibilities than had his own country. Thus the early industrial cities of America demonstrate how successful urban life might be, if unencumbered by the responsibilities shed by the rural areas.

Only when great numbers of landless, destitute European emigrants—from Ireland, Britain, Sweden, Germany, and other countries where a rural aristoc-

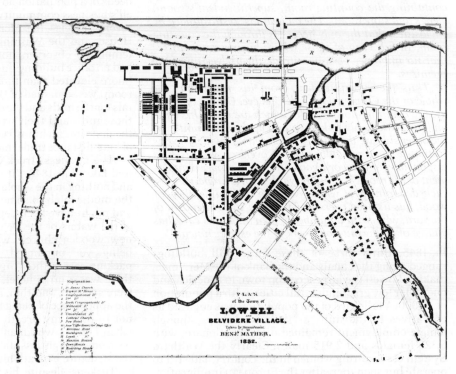

The nature of the early mills with their mill yards and associated housing rows can be seen in this 1832 map of Lowell. From the Proceedings of the Semi-Centennial . . . of Lowell. Lowell: Penhallow Printing Establishment, 1876.

Dickens abstained from drawing a direct contrast between the virtues he found in Lowell "and those great haunts of desperate misery" at home, arguing instead that "there is no manufacturing population in Lowell, so to speak: for these girls (often the daughters of small farmers) came from other States, remain a few years in the mills, and then go home for good." Certainly this was true. But would it not have been equally

[113]Ibid., p. 85.

racy proved both cold-hearted and incompetent in dealing with the economic and social problems of the mid-nineteenth century—came in a flood did these American industrial cities begin to deteriorate. In place of the boardinghouses, "tenements" were built. These great wooden barracks occupied their lots so completely that in Lowell's neighbor, Lawrence, that developed at the middle of the century, women commonly hung their pots and pans on the wooden wall of the house next door to gain more space in their overcrowded kitchens.[114] These tenements were the response to a need to house large families, many members of which would at least seek work in the factories and shops of the city, rather than the workers alone, as under the Waltham System.

Speaking of Lowell in its earlier years, Margaret Parker showed that, "Place of residence in the 1834 directory is indicated, in many cases, not by streets, but by corporations; '32 Hamilton corporation;' '27 Appleton corporation;' '2 Suffolk blocks,' '22 Carpet blocks' are typical addresses."[115] The securing of a job in one of the mills made housing provision available. "Each of the long blocks of boarding-houses is divided into six or eight tenements, and are generally three stories high. These tenements are finished off in a style much above the common farm-houses of the country, and more nearly resemble the abodes of respectable mechanics in rural villages. They are all furnished with an abundant supply of water, and with suitable yards and outbuildings."[116] Some of the boardinghouses and apartmented houses were of brick, though as time went on wood seems to have become the common building material. In the boardinghouses, "The front room is usually the common eating-room of the house, and the kitchen is in the rear. The keeper of the house (commonly a widow, with her family of children), has her parlor in some part of the establishment; and in the same house there is a sitting-room for the use of the boarders. The remainder of the apartments are sleeping rooms. In each of these are lodged two, four, and in some cases six boarders. . . ." Although on the whole, housing was satisfactory, the Rev. Mr. Miles found that, "In many cases, these rooms are not sufficiently large for the number who occupy them; and oftentimes that attention is not paid to their ventilation which a due regard to health demands. . . . At the same time, it should in justice be added, that the evil alluded to is not peculiar to Lowell, and will not probably appear to be a crying one, if the case should be brought into comparison with many of the apartments of milliners and seamstresses in the boarding-houses of our cities."[117] But despite this crowding, "The rents of the company's houses are purposely low, averaging only from one third to one half of what similar houses rent for in the city. In times of pressure a part of this low rent, and in some instances the whole of it, has been remitted.

[114]For a detailed account of this tenement-house problem in Lawrence, including the situation mentioned, see Robert E. Todd and Frank B. Sanborn (under the advice of Francis H. McLean), The Report of the Lawrence Survey, Lawrence, Massachusetts: The Trustees of the White Fund, 1912.
[115]Parker, op. cit., p. 73.
[116]Miles, op. cit., p. 67.
[117]Ibid., pp. 68–69.

There is no intention on the part of the Corporation to make any revenue from these houses. They are a great source of annual expense." Thus, the existence of the Lowell boardinghouse, and its fellows in other Waltham System towns, was encouraged by manufacturers, in a continuation of the medieval practice of assuming some social responsibility for workers. Self-interest was apparent; the discipline in the houses made for better discipline in the mills, and the more healthy qualities of life there lent benefits to the employer as well as the worker. But doubtless the physical quality of life in these boardinghouses was probably not inferior to that in the country whence came the boarders.

The Boardinghouse in Nineteenth-Century America

The flood of migrants to the rapidly growing cities of the nineteenth century came commonly from rural areas where the extended family was perhaps the norm. Certainly in Europe, this large social grouping was standard, as it was in many rural sections of America. When they married, sons merely built ells on the family farmhouse, making it housing for several generations and several nuclear families. As daughters left for Waltham or Lowell, they would hardly have expected more than a boardinghouse-type accommodation. Similarly, as sons went to become mechanics, they would have eagerly sought these boardinghouses. At home they probably had relatively little individual space and certainly would in most cases have found living alone distasteful and impractical. Our present-day notions of the space needed by individuals and the virtues of privacy are recently-acquired culture traits which we should carefully avoid projecting backward into the last century. Then people lived much together, in small space, with few physical possessions.

Because of that way of life, moving into the city commonly led individuals and even families to take up residence in a boardinghouse or, with more money, a hotel. Life in the nineteenth-century city was in a very literal sense "mobile;" people commonly moved on during their lives from one city to another, keeping their baggage to the minimum and living often in what we would think of as transient accommodations. A couple, even with children, might occupy one or two

This view of the street leading to the cotton mill in Lowell in the mid-1830's shows the boarding-house rows in which "female operatives" employed in the mills lived. In the left fore-ground are houses for foremen or superintendents and their families. The size of the people in this engraving should not be taken literally. The rail line was the normal 4' 8½" gauge.

rooms in a boardinghouse or hotel. Certainly before having children such accommodations would be quite standard. Thus, when we read of these cities we find far more hotels than we would expect by their size, and boardinghouses in great numbers. The impact of these rather dense housing forms on the city can be easily perceived. So long as the conditions within the buildings were reasonable, and large families were not crowded into spaces previously used by one or two individuals, an efficient form of city for the pedestrian era was provided. But as the flood of immigrants overpowered the physical form of housing that had been established for individuals or couples, the pedestrial city became a slum.

The Spread of Third-Phase Industrialization

By 1839, the ten textile companies that made up the main body of Lowell's manufacturing had been built. In addition, the Proprietors of Locks and Canals had grown from a beginning as a builder of textile machin-

ery to the largest engineering works in the United States, building steam engines and steam locomotives among other forms of machinery. Lowell had little more power from water, and was not yet ready to supplement it with steam. The search for additional power had to come at other falls. Rather quickly in the fourth and fifth decades of the last century, factory cities were set up by Boston capital in Manchester and Nashua in New Hampshire, at Biddeford-Saco, Lewiston-Auburn, and Augusta in Maine, and at Lawrence, Chicopee, and Holyoke in Massachusetts. In most cases, fairly complex hydraulic works had to be established distributing power by canal to several plants. Both Lawrence and Holyoke, particularly the second, were great waterpower cities. Interestingly:

The mill communities which developed in northern New England as a consequence of the Waltham enterprise had their antithesis in the Providence region. Even though the Rhode Island mills had been denied the use of the Lowell loom, the southern region was not to be out-done in the matter of technological improvement. The adoption of the Scotch crank loom, which had been built by William Gilmour, a Scotch immigrant, by a large Rhode Island concern already in 1817 showed that the manufacturers were keenly interested in vieing [sic] with their northern competitors. As a consequence, the contrast of systems of manufacture and industrial adjustments between the two districts is the more significant.

The major factor making for this distinction is geo-

graphic. The type of water power in the Rhode Island-Connecticut Region determined the make-up of these localities: small but numerous. But few of the communities had sufficient power wealth to serve more than one or two mills. The Blackstone Valley with its ninety-four cotton factories in 1844 illustrates the situation. Then, too, the ascendency of Slater meant British rather than American practises should dominate. Thus, the constituency of the small factory villages was a collection of families dependent exclusively upon wages earned in the village mill, as opposed to the groups of young people recruited from the farm homes in the vicinity of Lowell and other northern mill towns.[118]

This then was the pattern in New England industrialization, the nation's nursery of manufacturing, at the middle of the last century. A continuation of the second-phase industrial-urbanization in southern New England produced regions of rather dense manufacturing population in a quasi-urban pattern of mill villages spread along a dozen separate river valleys, of which the Blackstone was merely the first and the most classic in its settlement pattern. These valleys with their mill towns encouraged the growth of the cities of Providence and Worcester through projecting upon them a diversity of demands for textile machines, engineering works of many forms, supplies of consumer goods, and food. Providence was the port where cotton was received and transhipped, first by canal up the Blackstone valley to Worcester and subsequently by the railroad net that developed in the area only some five years later than in Lancashire. In many ways this Rhode Island-Connecticut pattern of industrial-urbanization, the "second phase," shared notable characteristics with the pattern of the north of England. Considerable specialization by towns occurred with respect to manufacturing processes and function; the organization of the trade centered on Providence and, to a lesser degree, Worcester. Grey cloths moved about the area from one town to another; transportation needs were critical. Thus the Blackstone Canal was opened October, 1828, to Worcester. But to secure that canal, water was diverted from the mills, and soon great conflict grew up between the demands for process and power water and that for lockage.[119] Finally the Providence and Worcester Railroad built between 1844 and 1847 solved this problem.[120]

If the second phase of industrial-urbanization in New England led not to new cities but rather to an industrialized countryside, the third phase, as represented by the Waltham System cities, was fully urban. Perhaps the population was only periodically resident within the city, but the city itself was fixed and real. It differed from the older Atlantic ports mainly in the absence of the great mercantile functions. As noted, office buildings were in Boston rather than Lowell or Lewiston, and most of the wholesale functions remained in Boston or Portland (Maine). But as money came to the workers, retail shops were opened in the Waltham System cities, and the towns became sizable by contemporary standards. In 1850 Lowell, with a population of 33,383, ranked twenty-third in the country in population, the same size as San Francisco and larger than Chicago, Detroit, or Cleveland. Boston was third, exceeded only by Baltimore and New York, while Providence stood seventeenth. Throughout the second half of the nineteenth century as the urbanization of America was very rapid, New England, and Massachusetts in particular, showed the strong impact of early industrialization. With an area only slightly more than a third that of Ohio, the three southern New England states in 1900 had twice as many cities within the first fifty cities (eight) as did Ohio (four), commonly thought the state of the most good-sized cities.

---

[118]*J. Herbert Burgy*, The New England Cotton Textile Industry: A Study in Industrial Geography, *Baltimore: The author, 1932, p. 27.*

[119]*Edward Chase Kirkland*, Men, Cities and Transportation: A Study in New England History, *Cambridge: Harvard University Press, 1948, Vol. I, p. 85.*

[120]*Interestingly the Providence and Worcester disappeared into the New York, New Haven, and Hartford Railroad already in the nineteenth century but emerged from it in 1973 when the owners of shares in the Providence and Worcester voted to end a long lease of the line and operate it themselves. As a result the P & W was a tiny bit of line that survived in solvent state the great debacle of the Penn Central Railroad that had absorbed the New Haven when it merged the Pennsylvania and New York Central in 1968. Edward A. Lewis,* The Blackstone Valley Line: The Story of the Blackstone Canal Company and the Providence & Worcester Railroad, *Seekonk, Mass.: The Baggage Car, 1973.*

The Industrial City Comes of Age in America

By the middle of the nineteenth century, industry had become a sizable factor in American life, though we cannot determine its precise contribution until 1870, when the first census data on manufacturing employment appear. Then 17.41 per cent of the labor force was hired in factories while still a full half was employed in agriculture. But despite the considerable changes that have occurred during the century for which we have data, manufacturing employment has increased in percentage contribution only from 17 to 24 per cent in a full century. Thus, by the end of the Civil War, the general role of industry was well determined and its proportionate share in the national economic life established. For that reason, we may summarize the conditions about the time of the Civil War as the coming of age of the industrial city in America. Most subsequent changes affecting manufacturing workers were part not so much of an industrial urbanization as of the general evolution of urban life and culture, and the physical transformation of the residential structure of

were accompanied by the creation of distinct *industrial organization cities*, as in Providence for the second stage or Boston for the third. In these cities, the complex business and banking services were carried on; various goods were supplied by wholesalers to the largely industrial places. As time passed and industrial development within the textile towns matured, engineering functions initially carried on by the Boston Manufacturing Company in Waltham or the Proprietors of the Locks and Canals in Lowell tended to become separated out. We find Lowell, Taunton (Massachusetts), and Paterson becoming important machine and metal-working centers. With the spread of markets for textiles, the financial and wholesaling functions tended to be located in larger cities.[121] Thus, with respect to the large cities, we must distinguish two phases of industrial urbanization: the first when the administrative and financial functions of the factory era began to be expressed in large central cities grown from the colonial ports, certainly in the first several decades of the last century, and the second when actual industrialization of the port city itself took place, notably from the time of the Civil War on, when steam power became dominant. These two phases supply the last in our brief catalogue of expressions of industrial-urbanization.

Two forces were conducive to the large-city phases of industrialization: the introduction of steam power, and the large-scale immigration of Europeans into the

Table One. Employment by Selected Industries in Five Census Years

Census Year	Total Labor Force in Thousands	Percentage of Workers Employed in Specific Industries				
		Agriculture	Manufacture	Trade and Finance	Transportation	Construction
1870	12,920	49.77	17.41	6.42	4.95	6.05
1880	17,390	49.51	18.23	7.02	4.95	4.77
1890	23,740	36.27	20.01	8.38	6.45	6.07
1900	29,070	36.84	21.81	9.49	7.22	5.71
1970	78,597	4.40	24.64	23.68	5.73	4.30

cities. Finally, by around 1875, most cities had industry as an integral component of their support so the actual process of industrial-urbanization became part of the general process of urban growth and evolution.

What then were the forms that industrial-urbanization took in the United States up to the close of the Civil War when manufacturing became a general component of most American cities?

We have already seen three stages of industrial-urbanization in New England, the last two of which

[121]*Allan Pred has written extensively on this period of American industrial-urbanization, expressing particularly the role that the great port cities played in this economic development.[Allan R. Pred, The Spatial Dynamics of U.S. Urban-Industrial Growth, 1800–1914, Cambridge: M.I.T. Press, 1966.] The discussion here diverges genetically somewhat from Pred in viewing the first three phases of industrial-urbanization before turning to the large cities. In this it is indebted in part to recent unpublished work of David Meyer, who argues the case of the locale of the impact of the employment multiplier.*

United States at the middle and the end of the last century.

The United States is almost as old in the development and use of steam engines as is Britain, and is possessed of an independent line of advance running parallel in time with that of the Boulton and Watt engines. In America in the late eighteenth century, Oliver Evans began his ingenious efforts to develop a steam engine. He did so quite successfully, and with more courage and imagination than the careful Scot had done in Britain.

Evans began his inventor's career in his early twenties when, employed in making textile cards, he devised a machine that could produce 1,500 cards a minute. By the 1780's he was dreaming of creating a steam engine light enough to propel itself—something the low-pressure engines of James Watt could hardly do—but he lacked the money to carry out his ideas. In 1803, however, when the United States purchased Louisiana, gaining sovereignty over the mouth of the Mississippi, a group of investors commissioned Evans to build a steam-driven boat to operate on the great river. He did so very successfully, employing a double-acting, vertical-type steam engine with 30 rpm, which was heated by a copper boiler with iron ends wherein the pressure of steam was raised to 50 pounds (per square inch). It was greatly in advance of the Watt engines, and was able to produce far more power for its weight than could those from Birmingham. Mounted on a hull at New Orleans, the Evans engine worked well. Unfortunately, it was almost immediately caught in a flood, transported half a mile inland, and left stranded by the receding waters. Nevertheless, the engine did yeoman but unnoticed service for many years, powering a sawmill that cut 3,000 feet of lumber daily.

Evans engines did, however, come into rather wide use before he died in 1819. In 1803 he had begun to work his own shop with steam power,[122] and in 1805 he was commissioned by the city of Philadelphia to build a steam dredge to clear its docks of mud. This Evans did, first deliberately building the hull a mile and a half from the docks and there mounting tons of brickwork and the engine on this scow. With this load to transport, Evans then had the scow propel itself through the streets of Philadelphia to the waterfront. Even then he insisted on navigating the dredge on the open Delaware River before setting it to work in the docks. One wonders what would have happened if Evans had had Boulton's money behind him to develop his ideas. In any event, his dredge unquestionably worked, and was one of the earliest steamboats, as well as being probably the first self-propelled land vehicle in American experi-

ence.[123] Evans was merely the first of a number of experimenters with steam power, who included many, among them John Fitch, James Fulton, Nicholas Roosevelt in steamboats, John Stevens, Peter Cooper, and Ross Winans in locomotives, and George Corliss in stationary engines.

The first application of steam power to manufacturing in the United States remains in doubt. A steam-powered sawmill existed in New York in 1803. We have seen Evans' involuntary sawmill application in Louisiana the next year; in 1808, he went west of the Alleghenies to set up a most ingenious flour mill run by steam. By 1811 Evans was producing high-pressure steam engines capable of 70 horsepower. By 1830 steam was fairly widely employed in the United States but not so much in the cotton textile trade as elsewhere, most notably in river transportation. The 1830 census showed that "57 out of the 161 plants in Pennsylvania used steam, although the factories enumerated in New York, New Jersey, and all of the New England states with the exception of Massachusetts used water power. Of the 169 plants in that state, 39 used steam."[124] Clearly Pennsylvania with its proximity to coal deposits, and no doubt the impressive example of Oliver Evans, had put steam to use early in the last century; interestingly enough, Massachusetts was beginning to do so.

Only as higher pressure engines were developed, more in America than in Britain, could the cost of fuel be borne for installations in factories as distant from the mines as they would be in most American industrial cities of the early nineteenth century. Only Philadelphia was near enough the mines to make early economic use of coal. All other cities where steam might have been employed could hardly have done so with the inefficient Boulton and Watt engines until improvements were made. Only as canal and rail lines were opened to the coal fields in eastern Pennsylvania, mostly in the third and fourth decades of the century, did coal begin to become cheap enough to use for steam-power production at considerable distances from the coal fields. At that time, of course, once the coal was brought to the Delaware or Hudson rivers, its further shipment was made by water, thus favoring sites on or accessible to tidewater; New York City, Philadelphia, the ports of Long Island Sound, and southern and eastern Massachusetts all became potential sites for steam-power production.

Caroline Ware tells us, "Steam did not come to supply energy for cotton manufacturing at all generally until railways made transportation of coal convenient

[122]John W. Oliver, History of American Technology, New York: The Ronald Press, 1956, p. 136.

[123]James Thomas Flexner, Inventors in Action: The Story of the Steamboat, New York: Collier Books, 1962, p. 237.
[124]Faulkner, op. cit., p. 299.

and cheap after the Civil War." Samuel Slater constructed a "steam mill" in 1828, perhaps the first in the country, at Providence.[125] In 1839 the Naumkeag Steam Cotton Company was organized in Salem and remained in business until 1953, nearly bracketing the history of steam cotton production in New England.[126] Certainly as the waterpower at both the Arkwright and Waltham sites proved insufficient to meet the demands, coal would be brought in if at all possible and used to fire steam boilers. The Blackstone Canal carried a lot of coal and no doubt played a role in keeping some of the mills in the villages of the valley after water proved insufficient.

The great impact of the introduction of steam power came when the steam engine allowed any city to industrialize, even the large colonial ports which until then had had to shun most mechanical production. We see the clearest case of this in southeastern Massachusetts, where New Bedford had been a major port in the early nineteenth century, depending on the whaling trade. Much given to enterprise and trade, the town had lacked the factor endowment to engage in the earlier phases of New England industrialization.

But in 1846, New Bedford men set about creating a cotton mill in a truly scientific fashion.[127] They sought by market and manufacturing analysis to determine what kind of cotton textile would best reward them and how its manufacture should be established. "They figured that they could make fine sheetings at a cost of twelve cents a yard and sell it for fourteen cents. 'All other calculations that we have made', their committee reported, 'show only from half to three-quarters of a cent profit.'"[128] Given this desire for fine sheetings, the proprietors needed mule-spun yarn which, in turn, fairly determined where and what kind of mill establishment would be needed. We have already seen that throstle-spinning, as in the water-frame and its derivatives under the Waltham System, can be carried out by women workers, but mule-spinning, as in most of Rhode Island mills, requires male labor.

Thus, the incorporators of the Wamsutta Company in New Bedford faced a very different labor situation from that in the Waltham System towns. Men were critically needed; the city of New Bedford could be depended upon to provide the segmental labor force of men more than women and children. An urban location with a generalized supply of housing was far more useful to their purposes than the boardinghouse system begun in Waltham. Basing their factory design on the Hope Mill in the Pawtuxet Valley of Rhode Island and their labor source on the city of New Bedford, Wamsutta became highly successful and showed the way toward the large steam cotton mill that depended upon cheap fuel and massive labor available in a port city, particularly one of declining sailings. In contrast, when Lowell sought at the same time to expand, it reproduced itself and its parent, Waltham, at Lawrence, where at least in the beginning, the boardinghouse became the norm. Most graphically, Lawrence and New Bedford, both industrialized in the mid-1840's, demonstrate the two distinct forms of industrial-urbanization produced by contrasts in power sources and in labor recruitment.

Fall River followed on the New Bedford pattern but only after a somewhat equivocal start as a waterpower town. On the site, the Quequechan River falls over 130 feet in less than a mile and a half between a good natural reservoir in the Watuppa Ponds and tidewater. Hardly a better congregation of factor endowments could be envisaged. The first mill was established in 1811, depending upon one of the several falls, and others were set up with fair rapidity. Fall River came to specialize in calico printing, and also undertook the manufacture of a distinctive set of textile machines for that trade. As skill improved, and the basic cloths that had begun the Waltham factory in 1814 began to lose customers in favor of the fancier printed goods, Fall River continued to expand until the Quequechan could no longer power the city.

In 1859, a radical change occurred in the local industrial pattern. Steam was introduced as a power source, and the mills moved away from the river and onto the shores of the several local ponds where boiler water of good quality could be secured from reservoirs produced on a granitic surface by glacial disruption and damming of preexisting drainage. At the same time mills were spread along the waterfront where the coal could be discharged directly from coastal schooners to the coalyard of the mill. "Localization in Fall River is thus primarily due to the tidewater location which made possible the receipt of cheap fuel. The situation of the city, however, in a region where manufacturers had a propensity for textiles, and its accessibility by water to markets were accessory in establishing its pre-eminence."[129] And preeminent it indeed became. By 1875 Fall River had a third of all the spindles in Massachusetts, and stood the largest textile city in the country.

[125]Ware, op. cit., p. 82.
[126]Dirk J. Struik, Yankee Science in the Making, New York: Collier Books, 1962, p. 304.
[127]Burgy, op. cit., p. 28.
[128]Ware, op. cit., p. 107.

[129]Burgy, op. cit., p. 34.

The National Pattern of Industry

As in New England nationally the first three phases of industry had revolved around the availability of waterpower, initially at small dam sites near Baltimore and Philadelphia and other colonial mercantile towns, next near larger falls on the Mohawk River or the upper Hudson, and finally at large "waterpower cities" such as Paterson and Rochester. In the Middle Atlantic states the use of steam was early and more rapid in coming. Industry in the New York-Brooklyn-Jersey City-Newark area, in northern New Jersey, and in eastern Pennsylvania was heavily reliant upon steam power long before the older and more industrialized New England had to turn in that direction. And in the fourth phase, when steam power was introduced, the focus in the Middle Atlantic states was more heavily upon the industrialization of the port cities—New York, Brooklyn, Jersey City, and Newark—of Philadelphia and the numerous suburbs it had already swallowed up by 1854, and of Baltimore and the growing nexus of industrial-urbanization around Pittsburgh at the forks of the Ohio.

The concentration of steam-powered industry in the large cities was certainly in response to the opportunities for long-distance trade available there, as well as the very considerable local market they furnished. Pred has cited a number of forces that encouraged "Urban-Size Growth," among them "endogenous natural increases" in population, the "absolute increase of wages and real buying power" in the second half of the nineteenth century, urban "agglomeration economies" not yet matched by sharp rises in the cost of urban factory sites that would in our time force manufacturing into the suburbs or industrial satellites, and what stand as a mass of "circular and cumulative growth processes" that encourage the expansion of the city as a market for manufacturers.[130] To these we might add one of great significance and another of somewhat less importance.

[130]*Pred*, op. cit., *pp. 41–46.*

The Great Immigration and Industrialization

The more significant added factor was the great flood of immigrant labor into the port cities which, for the first time in the late 1840's and succeeding decades, made labor fairly plentiful and thus somewhat less costly in relative terms and certainly easier to assemble there in large blocks. The notion of untapped local segmental labor pales before the onslaught of great masses of immigrants wherein all members of the group were seeking work and were, in a particularly striking way, "footloose" as to the site of that employment. Nonetheless, the immigrants were initially found in the port cities, or in their environs, and there they were most likely to remain, all things being equal. Some groups, particularly the Germans and the Scandinavians, were moving toward distant ties in the Middle West, in a much more directed migration than affected the Irish and the Italians, and later the Russian Jews. Those three groups found themselves arrived in coastal cities rather bereft of an onward objective, and tended to

The clustering of workers' residence by ethnic congregation is clearly shown in this map. The dominant French Canadian population is shown occupying the traditional "rows" adjacent to the older mills.

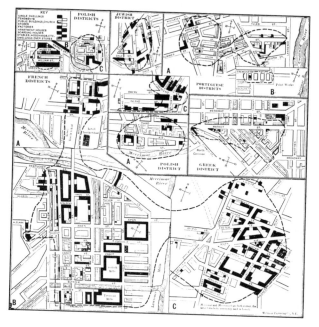

Table Two. Immigrants Arriving in the United States, 1821–1900

Years	Total Immigration	Yearly Average	Country of Emigration				
			Great Britain	Ireland	Scandi-navia	Germany	Italy
1821–25	40,503	8,100.6	8,890	12,926	97	1,394	251
1826–30	102,936	20,587.2	16,189	37,798	163	5,367	158
1831–35	346,631	69,326.2	32,182	72,257	693	45,592	1,895
1836–40	346,627	69,325.4	33,628	135,124	1,562	106,862	358
1841–45	430,336	86,067.2	80,186	187,095	4,909	105,188	674
1846–50	1,279,915	255,983.0	186,858	593,624	9,533	329,438	1,196
1851–55	1,748,424	349,684.8	235,981	694,683	15,511	647,273	3,668
1856–60	849,790	169,958.0	187,993	219,436	9,169	304,394	5,803
1861–65	801,723	160,344.6	247,089	176,359	16,738	233,052	3,448
1866–70	1,513,101	302,620.2	359,807	239,419	109,654	554,416	8,217
1871–75	1,726,795	345,599.0	329,793	295,179	119,688	508,394	27,060
1876–80	1,055,395	211,079.0	178,250	141,692	123,328	209,868	28,699
1881–85	2,975,683	595,136.6	784,636	345,399	352,334	709,390	109,504
1886–90	2,270,930	454,186.0	422,719	310,083	344,160	492,950	197,805
1891–95	2,123,879	424,775.0	195,362	227,202	244,599	397,640	288,235
1896–1900	1,563,685	313,737.0	76,172	161,214	126,913	107,512	363,658

remain there unless they had specific individual ties to persons of the same ethnicity in more distant cities. Unlike the Scandinavians and the Germans, the early influx of Irish and Italians had not gone to the interior; thus their ties were less likely to be there.

The scale of migration to the United States was rather radically changing during the nineteenth century. From an annual average of just over 8,000 immigrants in the period 1821-25, the numbers rose relatively consistently to ten times that figure in 1841-45. But the late '40s witnessed a flood of desperate Europeans unheard of in any previous migration, reaching a yearly average for the period 1846-50 of 186,858, and in the next five years of more than a quarter of a million a year. Perhaps no other statistic from the last century shows more graphically how badly European social policy had failed, most notably in Great Britain and Ireland; the western isle had always been the largest source of migrants in every period up to 1855, but Britain took over and stood at the head until the '80s when Germany came to lead the pack.

We emphasize these figures for two reasons. First, they go far toward explaining the fourth stage of industrial-urbanization in the United States. Second, they serve as most concrete evidence of how complete was the collapse of the traditional feudal-rural social structuring of Europe that took place at the middle of the nineteenth century, however much the failure of the revolutions of 1848 may have seemed to argue otherwise. The effort to maintain a rural and aristocratic dominance in Europe could continue for another sixty-six years, until 1914. Political power rested with the landed aristocrats, who could use the emerging industrial cities of Europe as a dumping ground for social and economic problems first nurtured in the country. America existed as a safety valve for overpopulation, underproduction. Those weary of the defunct but not replaced social system that Europe had inherited from the Middle Ages could go there. By going to America this mass of emigrants from Europe took the same course that the new settlers in the medieval bastides had done seven hundred years earlier. Europe's history has been one of a "repression in the country" as the German aphorism has it. *Stadtluft macht frei* recounts the medieval escape from serfdom to the city, later to the bastides in the twelfth and thirteenth century and by the vast flood to American cities in the nineteenth century. A commonly-held European notion has been that the nineteenth-century migration was simply a dash for economic gain; certainly it was that, but freedom in the nineteenth century required money most critically, as the intellectual and political freedom of Europe's upper classes showed so clearly. And whatever intellectual advance Britain's higher social classes made came more from their leisure than from their genes.

The Fourth Phase
Came in the Great Cities

The rapid growth in size of the immigrant force, which came particularly after 1845 as these figures show, went along with the switch to steam power to allow the larger mercantile and transportation cities to become as well industrial places. The history of American urbanism shows this trend strikingly when we discover that large components of the growth in population of cities in the nineteenth century came from the great increase in a few very large places—New York, Philadelphia, Chicago, Boston, St. Louis, Baltimore, and their environs—fully as much as from the spread of city growth through the nation. The advantages of concentrated population for labor and for consumption, of superior transportation connections, and of readily available capital all plumped for the big city to be the site of the fourth phase of industrial-urbanization. We can think of the Northeast, Middle Atlantic, and eastern Middle Western states as the region dotted with mercantile cities dating from before 1850. In those cities and their environs, manufacturing concentrated. In the second half of the last century, a new settlement form arose, that of the industrial satellite, which should be distinguished from the residential suburb.

An *industrial satellite* was a town, fairly close to a major administrative city, where the specific manufacturing processes were carried on, usually under the financial or corporate control of the central town of the industrial complex. Lowell was clearly an industrial satellite of Boston in the same way that the Arkwright Villages of Rhode Island were of Providence. A region centering on a mercantile-transportation city (most commonly a colonial port) commonly had these satellites spread around it for a distance of 50 to 100 miles. These satellites were served by the central city's wholesaling establishments both for the needs of the people and for those of the plants, provided with financial, medical, legal, and other services by the dominating city, attached to the outside world by railroads converging on that city, and generally in the orbit of that place in terms of political control, newspaper publication, and what small number of cultural events were made available. In truth the fourth phase had two settlement components: *the dominating mercantile-transportation hub*, now heavily industrialized and vastly expanded in population as the city of assimilation for a massive immigration, and the surrounding industrial satellites, connected to it by rail and ties of corporate control. Along with its metropolitan role in cultural, political, and servicing matters, the central city maintained an integrated system of dominant city and industrial satellites.

The American Industrial City in 1860

At this point in history, industrialization had become an aspect of most larger towns, particularly those of great size or long standing, and it was commonly assumed that the extended industrialization of the metropolis would care for most of the manufacturing needs of the nation. A dichotomy no longer existed between the city and the factory town: cities were industrializing and factory towns were fast becoming urban, at least on a limited scale. Just before the Civil War, a number of regional centers already available to serve the various parts of the United States rose to true metropolitan importance. This rapid growth came in part from quickening of industry related to a fast spreading network of rail lines, the continuing inflooding of European migrants, and the increase in America's trade with the rest of the world. The "cities of the United States" had previously been on the East and Gulf coasts or aligned along the Ohio River; now, truly metropolitan places were growing up in the Middle West and the Far West.

Initially the cities of the East Coast and the Ohio grew to metropolitan size, but by 1860 railroad towns with important components of manufacturing (Chicago and St. Louis) had risen to that status. In the three censuses taken after the Civil War in the nineteenth century, the common advance of population and industrialization was clear. In 1870 the cities were important regional transportation centers but they were as well heavily industrialized for their time and region. Only Washington, no doubt a metropolis as a result of the growth during the war, stood in a different category. The cities to reach full metropolitan status in 1880 were so dominantly industrial as to need no further explanation. By that year the necessity of an industrial base for rapid urbanization was accepted; only as industrialization spread to other regions did metropolitanism also arrive there. In 1890 most of the newly arrived metropolises were in, or more precisely

The Census Year in Which Cities Reached 100,000 Population

1820
New York

1830
Philadelphia

1840
Baltimore
New Orleans

1850
Boston
Cincinnati

1860
Chicago
St. Louis

1870
Buffalo
Louisville
Newark
Pittsburgh
San Francisco
Washington

1880
Cleveland
Detroit
Jersey City
Milwaukee
Providence

1890
Denver
Indianapolis
Kansas City
Minneapolis
Omaha
Rochester
Scranton
St. Paul

1900
Columbus, Ohio
Fall River
Los Angeles
Memphis
New Haven
Paterson
St. Joseph
Syracuse
Toledo
Worcester

1910
Albany
Atlanta
Birmingham
Bridgeport
Dayton
Grand Rapids
Lowell
Nashville
Oakland
Portland, Oregon
Richmond, Virginia
Seattle
Spokane

1920
Akron
Camden
Dallas
Des Moines
Ft. Worth
Hartford
Houston
Kansas City, Kansas
New Bedford
Norfolk
Reading

Salt Lake City
San Antonio
Springfield, Massachusetts
Trenton
Wilmington, Delaware
Yonkers, New York
Youngstown

1930
Canton, Ohio
Chattanooga
Duluth
Elizabeth, New Jersey
El Paso
Erie
Evansville
Flint
Ft. Wayne
Gary
Honolulu
Jacksonville
Knoxville
Miami
Oklahoma City
Peoria
San Diego
Somerville, Massachusetts
South Bend
Tacoma
Tampa
Tulsa
Wichita

1940
Charlotte

1950
Austin
Baton Rouge
Corpus Christi

Little Rock
Montgomery
Phoenix
Savannah
Shreveport

1960
Albuquerque
Beaumont, Texas
Columbus, Georgia
Greensboro
Hammond, Indiana
Jackson, Mississippi
Lansing
Lincoln
Lubbock
Madison
Newport News
Niagara Falls
Portsmouth, Virginia
San Jose
St. Petersburg
Topeka
Torrance
Tucson
Wichita Falls
Winston-Salem

on the edge of, the Great Plains, where meat packing, the handling of grain, and the carrying out of transportation functions brought workers and the growth of cities. In the latter part of the last century, the status of "metropolitan city" virtually always implied also the role of major manufacturing center.

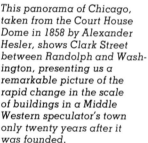

This panorama of Chicago, taken from the Court House Dome in 1858 by Alexander Hesler, shows Clark Street between Randolph and Washington, presenting us a remarkable picture of the rapid change in the scale of buildings in a Middle Western speculator's town only twenty years after it was founded.

With the advent of that correspondence, we need no longer think in terms of the city during the Industrial Revolution. As cities were industrialized, urbanization was largely an outgrowth of two forces: mercantilism, which shaped the urban revolution of the seventeenth century, and industrialization, which wrought an even more profound change in the nature and size of cities during the nineteenth century. Since that time the fundamental form and structure of the city has not experienced any radical upheaval and transformation such as

took place during those two periods. Subsequent to the Civil War, and in other countries to a similar degree, the changes in cities have come largely from increases in the scale of trade and manufacture, from growth of population, and from fairly radical transformations in the technology of transportation. Thus, in the next chapter we may view the city of the present not largely as a fundamental transformation of past cities, as has been the case up to now, but rather as the evolution of the Industrial Era city that came into full form about the middle of the last century. For this reason our method of looking at that modern city may change. We no longer need deal with periods and historical procession: instead we may seek a process model searching to explain the structure and utilization of the modern city, particularly in America, but generally in western civilization.

8.   URBAN FORM IN THE MODERN WORLD:
A POSTSCRIPT ON MORPHOGENETIC PROCESSES

Our analysis of the role that cities have played in human history has been largely chronological. We have traced the many distinctive uses made of urban places, and noted the slow evolution of the physical build of the city. Both the history of the city and its physical evolution have been continuous, with new roles growing out of past experience. New uses to accomplish different human purposes for this critical human institution were always being found, and the forms of the past have been adapted rather than abandoned. The most primitive shelter is still understandable to us as a house, with features found as well in the most recent constructions; the earliest city has qualities that we find in the most modern. When we use the term "new town," the adjective refers more to the settlement's period of establishment than to the form it takes. "New towns" in Britain, France, Poland, and Hungary look suspiciously like places shaped by bastidors in the Middle Ages and by large American industrial firms in the late nineteenth century. The nature of urban life and city form requires another view than that the present is sufficient unto itself, and that what is "new" is always previously unknown. I hope this book has served to show how much we learn from the past, and how we may use experience as a pandect for future action.

By the close of the more disrupting and transforming phases of the Industrial Revolution—by about 1850 in Britain and perhaps 1870 in America and Belgium—a common urbanization process had grown up that has not changed so fundamentally during the last hundred years as it did during the previous century. The urban system has experienced transformations rather than replacements. Thus we may deal with the past century rather as a unit, observing the forms and functions of cities without specific reference to time, and noting the fundamental urban *processes* at work, most of which have operated fairly continuously for that period, or longer. *Functional processes* are those which grow out of the roles of cities; *form processes* can be viewed in terms of morphogenesis.

By looking at the last hundred years as a unit, we can see both the roles that cities now play in western civilization and the common physical features to be found in urban places from the Black Sea westward to the Pacific in the northern mid-latitudes. Most of the lesser-developed countries of Africa, Asia, and Latin America turn for a model to these heavily developed

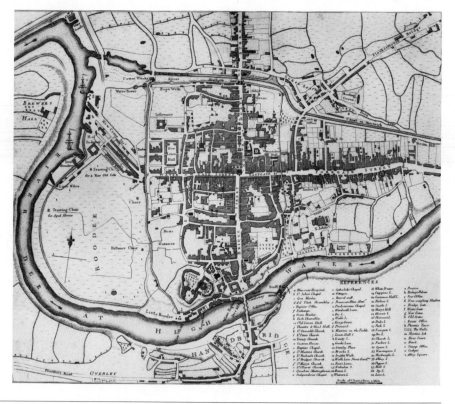

In 1794 Chester still showed the medieval redevelopment of a Roman castrum with the cardo and decumanus forming the medieval high streets and burgage plots, clearly suggesting the centuriation of Roman times. The Roman wall, transformed only moderately over the centuries, can still be seen, and the small change in the scale of the city over nearly two millennia perceived. From Aikin, The Country Round Manchester, 1795.

urban areas when they attempt to modernize their economies and urbanize their lives. Setting aside any qualitative or moral judgment as to this model, we cannot question its surpassing importance in the world today.

The vast growth in city size during the last hundred years, as well as the great proliferation in the number of cities, makes impossible the sort of analysis attainable for earlier times. Antebellum America had dozens of cities; now the nation has hundreds, for which we have vastly more information. Thus a detailed analysis of modern cities must wait for a later volume. For now, in this postscript on the continuing application of historically significant morphogenetic processes, we will instead identify certain processes at work in the modern metropolis that account for the most striking forms of morphogenesis.

Emerging Urban Realms and Systems of Cities

The morphogenetic processes at work during the last hundred years have been most fundamentally affected by two things: *the great growth in population and areal extent of cities* has led to the creation of urbanized belts, frequently among closely related systems of cities; and *the introduction of mechanical transportation as a universal good* available to virtually all city persons has created cities no longer simple in structure, without the focus on a single center and a unitary set of internal ties. These new metropolitan regions are now comprised of a set of *urban realms*, each self-contained for everyday living. The ties among them take on an abstract quality, and their maintenance is the responsibility of a small minority of the metropolitan population. Electronic communications have fostered this parcelling out of the city into urban realms, but have not replaced the personal contact still critical for the operations *within* an urban realm. At the same time that the development of relatively fast mechanical transportation has permitted interrealm movements of commuters and goods, economic and time constraints have limited the practice of journeys beyond the realm.[1]

[1]*The first analysis of the "city of realms" is presented in my monograph on the San Francisco Bay Area City; James E. Vance, Jr.,* Geography and Urban Evolution in the San Francisco Bay Area, *Berkeley: Institute of Governmental Studies, 1964.*

The new geography of cities comprised of urban realms and interrelated cities within an extensive system became necessary when distances within the metropolis became too great to permit easy daily interaction across the whole area, yet distances among cities in a system were "contracted" enough to allow frequent movement between them. When that daily interaction could comprehend only a geographical fragment of the metropolis, the forces for the resorting of the location of functions became strong.

During the past hundred years, we have witnessed the massive separation of functions formerly carried on within a single contained and comprehensible city area. Central business districts have arisen as a distinct land-use unit, from which wholesaling has largely been removed. The scalar growth of cities has meant that residence has become a separate and congregated activity, largely unmixed with economically oriented activities. And as growth in size of cities and advances in the application of mechanical technology have come to bear on this resorting process, further divisions within the congregations of a particular land-use have taken place. Shopping has divided between the central business district and a number of nearly identical outlying shopping centers. Industrial districts of different sorts have grown up. And offices divide among several clusters—those in skyscrapers at the very heart of the city, those spread along radiating business streets nearer their dispersed customers, and those in sylvan office parks located in the outer suburbs. From these offices, control may often be exercised over a vast national or international system of cities. The specialization of functional locations has been the morphological history of the last hundred years, first allowing cities to grow beyond the extent that would be practicable for the daily interaction of all metropolitan residents, and then encouraging the congregation of related functions into urban realms, discernible on the ground and demonstrable as integrated systems in the daily movement within the metropolis.

The ties among the realms within the metropolis bear some resemblance to the ties among the cities in an extensive system: local integrity of specific functions exists within both urban realms and the urban regions that focus on the major regional center at the heart of a specific system of cities. At the same time, a well-defined but limited systemic relationship operates among those same realms or regions. In either case, only a small minority of workers will have reasons to cross with any frequency the boundary of their realm or region. In metropolitan areas today, the most common movement is within outlying realms, just as the clusters of more distant travel show strong focus on the *regional cities* such as Atlanta, Oakland-San Francisco, Minneapolis-St. Paul, Dallas-Ft. Worth, Phoenix, Seattle, Denver, and Los Angeles. Large numbers of people seldom "go downtown" in the larger metropolises. Within urban regions, most people find it unnecessary to visit the regional city with any greater frequency. But the administrative-supervisory workers in most metropolises constantly journey back and forth to the central office district; similarly, within the large systems of cities, members of this same class relatively frequently journey to and from the regional city.

The introduction of extensive space within the metropolis led ultimately to the creation of urban realms which showed a certain level of functional integrity. A reverse dynamic has been at work in the matter of urban regions. There, space has been "contracted" through the introduction of electronic communication and fast air travel. The geographical outcome appears to be the introduction of a new level of geographical association intermediate between the *metropolitan system*, which has been evolving for nearly a hundred years, and the domination by a very small number of "primate" or *nationally dominant cities*.

For a long time, the Northeast, particularly New York City, dominated American life in education, culture, economics, and social matters. Chicago exercised a smaller but still dominant role in the Middle West. Today, however, we discover that metropolitan cities are still the urban milieu for most people. But in the matters mentioned—education, culture, and the like—the regional cities have grown in importance, and bid fair to remove a very considerable part of the domination of New York, the Northeast, and Chicago. The three levels of American urbanization today are: (1) the metropolis, (2) the regional city, and (3) the old dominant city. The first two forms are growing in importance, while the third is declining, as has the central business district in the affairs of the metropolitan area. Thus, cities have experienced devolution downward from the city core to the urban realms, and from the old dominant city to the regional cities and the urban regions themselves.

The history of American metropolitan existence is replete with the rise of the old dominants, which were mostly either colonial- and federal-period ports—such as Boston, Providence, New York, Philadelphia, and Baltimore—or early industrial giants—such as Pittsburgh, Buffalo, Cleveland, Detroit, Chicago, and St. Louis. That history is now becoming equally characterized by the decline of the dominants, always in absolute terms if they are viewed separately from their suburbs, and always in relative terms when we compare them to the new regional cities of the South and West. Growth in American urbanization is coming (1) in the suburbs, often quite distant ones at that, of the older dominant cities, and (2) in both the heart and the suburbs of the newer regional cities. Thus we find inter-realm contrasts much stronger in the older cities and the interregional contrasts stronger between the older dominant metropolises and the newer regional cities.

A Concentration on American Cities

The two great forces at work in western cities—great scalar growth and the introduction of mechanical transportation—both found their clearest and most forceful expression in America. Skyscrapers were invented in America—either in Chicago or New York, according to their respective partisans; cars were first widely owned in America. The small size of American cities at the onset of this period of growth allowed most of the urban fabric to be in that sense "modern," and the United States has the most balanced pattern of urbanization of any western nation, with no regions seriously devoid of large cities and no one city dominating, as is true in most of western Europe or the underdeveloped world. Not all urban experience is best read from recent American experience, but in this postscript, the forces and processes at work can most efficiently be discerned in America. To the extent that European practice is strikingly different—as in the case of the London greenbelt, or the policy in Paris of encouraging working-class housing development in great walls of apartments in the peripheral "Red Ring"—that contrast will be noted. But in general terms of morphogenetic processes, this chapter will be concerned with the evolution of the physical structure of the American city during the last hundred years. To understand that evolution, we must look first at the changing role of the city in the western world.

The Role of the City in the Western World

Much conjecture and argument has attached to the origin of cities. Two notions have gained dominant acceptance: the city originated as a place of religious congregation, out of which came other functions requiring the close assembly of people; or the city began as a mart of trade, around which it was necessary to throw a wall for protection against nomadic marauders and alongside which came other cluster functions such as the conduct of government and the exercise of the priesthood of a religion. In either case, rather quickly the conduct of trade came to be the fundamental *economic* role of the city, so that we may view the trading town as the historically primate economic place.

In the conduct of trade, certain elements of fabrication would occur, particularly near the end of the line of trading connection where the ultimate consumers would make use of the products. Thus, we can seldom divide trade from manufacturing, *sensu strictu*, but we can argue that the trade was the initiator, and fabrication the outgrowth thereof. Until the Industrial Revolution, in most western countries the restraint of institutionalized geographical proportioning kept manufacturing in scale with the local or regional body of consumption.

The Industrial Revolution was a fundamental transformation of the role of cities because it shattered the established geographical order of production in proportion to regional market. Cities with extensive trade connections had always been able to grow in contrast to those with truncated ties, but now also towns with superior manufacturing establishments could grow at the expense of those poorly endowed. The geographical projection of a city's long-standing influence in trade could become even more dominant when manufacturing could be added as a further backstay to economic power. Manufactures did move in medieval trade, and cities did grow because of fabrication as distinct from trading—Florence, Venice, Bruges, and Ghent are examples—but, without question, such manufacturing tended to concentrate on luxury items sold widely but to a very thin market. The events of the Industrial Revolution that proved so radically transforming of urban geography were particularly those associated with mass manufacture for a mass market; the ability of manufacture to encourage urban growth was vastly enhanced in comparison with the medieval pattern.

A frequent assumption is that during the Industrial Revolution factories were sited near "natural factor endowments" of raw materials or power, even of labor, with little reference to existing lines of trade or capabilities of distribution. Recent research has begun to demonstrate fairly concretely that a certain affinity (perhaps even a stronger tie, as it may develop) existed between the ability to distribute goods and the locale of manufacture. Providence, for example, became one of the important merchant towns of colonial America, and the Brown family there a powerful trading group. We know that as early as the middle of the eighteenth century, they were engaged in the manufacture of sperm candles derived from the products of their whaling interests. We may hold that trade led to manufacture, which in turn led to elaborating a wholesale distribution system that added further to the wealth of the Browns and the growth of Providence. In this context, a later Brown, Moses, called Samuel Slater to Providence, financed his establishment of a factory, and exacted in return an exclusive contract to sell in wholesale trade the product of that and later mills. In very similar ways Boston and Baltimore, both early centers of manufacturing, tied together the establishment of industry and the conduct of trade. Finally more waterfalls remained to be developed and the ones across which dams were thrown tended to be in the environs of the existing trading ports. In this way, early manufacture became a backstay of established trading dominance. One is encouraged to conclude that the presence of a trading network was necessary to make possible the initiation of mass manufacture; otherwise, the medieval practice of geographical proportioning would have been difficult to break.

Thus under the Industrial Revolution the role of cities obviously changed from a domination by trade to a balance between trade and manufacture. Those cities that could do both grew to dominant size; those restricted to a single activity were less dynamic in their expansion.

The Industrial Revolution was a time, as Paul Mantoux and others have shown, when the ability to get about and carry goods was greatly enhanced.[2] This fact certainly was significant in bringing about industrialization. In addition, it led to a transformation of the local pattern of industrial development. In place of the close association of factories with wharves and riverfronts so common in the past, the increased mobility made possible by canals and railroads led to the shaping of a city system in which the manufactur-

[2]*Paul Mantoux*, The Industrial Revolution in the Eighteenth Century: An Outline of the Beginnings of the Modern Factory Systems in England. *New York: The Macmillan Company, 1961. Revision of the original translation of 1928.*

ing was carried on in outlying satellites. Lowell was the classic example, one that must be distinguished from the decentralized inheritance from the late Middle Ages found in England.

In Lancashire and Yorkshire, the Industrial Revolution was a time of scalar increase, *in situ*, within a pattern of industrial dispersion introduced by process separation. Towns grew where villages had been previously engaged in a specific process in the production of textiles. But the goods themselves had to be moved from town to town before they emerged as finished products.

Starting in Waltham in 1814 and coming to full flower in Lowell in 1824, *the American system of manufacture* became one of a complex urban system, with satellites, where integrated industrial production took place, ranged geographically around the central trading city. This system has been particularly well demonstrated with respect to the growth of Boston and the "Boston Associates," whose capital built mills in a dozen different places in New England in the middle of the last century. The Associates organized the trade and built the factories to furnish the goods which moved in Boston bottoms to a hundred ports on all the seas.

The vast accumulation of wealth in the Hub, Boston's preferred sobriquet, during the last century came because those Boston merchants were among the first men and women to understand the true nature of the tie between trade and manufacture. They understood early the critical nature of the lines of connection between the port city and its productive hinterland. Boston financed and encouraged the first important canal in America (the Middlesex Canal of 1804), as well as the first net of railroads built outside of England (Boston had more rail lines entering it in 1835 than did London or any other city). This conception of the contribution of improved transportation made possible the creation of the geographically complex *urban region*. Lowell could not have existed without a Boston to sell its goods, and it became increasingly apparent that Boston could not grow to major world status without a Lowell or two to fill its warehouses of distant trade.

The separation of factories from the traditional core city came not merely in the creation of satellites placed some distance from the center (26 miles in the case of Lowell), but also in the movement of factories to outlying sites in the city itself. This shift was dictated by the increasing scale of production, which could no longer be carried on in the cramped and commonly inherited premises of the city core. The medieval pattern of production was so undemanding of special construction that we generally cannot distinguish the occupational-unit housing of the time by actual artisan

trade. But with the industrialization of the last century, processes of manufacture became sufficiently distinct and demanding of special facilities that it became reasonably easy to distinguish a textile factory from a shoe factory or a glass works. In meeting these special demands, a vacant site near the edge of the city often became important—even in the absence of any very particular power demands, as in the case of the shoe factories. Simple size became an element as it seldom had been in the earlier artisan manufacture.

The consequences of these two separations—of core-city factories from the center of that place, and of industrial development from the central city to satellites—were great indeed in the matter of housing. No longer was the general growth of the city fabric necessarily sufficient for the needs of the manufacturing population. They were moved away and increased in number to such a degree that a critical need arose for a separate industrial housing policy, yet little or none developed.

The City as the Prime Producer

Pastoralism and agriculture provided the occupation and support for most of the world's population until very recently. We have seen that the "natural economy" of the Middle Ages was rurally based, institutionalized in feudalism with its yoking of political power to land-owning in a situation completely predictable for an economy where the main source of wealth was in control of land and its pastoral and agricultural production. The Commercial Revolution of the sixteenth and seventeenth centuries came when the parochial "natural economy" was first questioned and then faced with an active competition, based in cities and encouraging the growth of those places. The eighteenth century added an even more powerful demographic force, the tie between industrialization and urbanization. By a hundred years ago, the city was fast becoming the "prime producer" of wealth in the world.

Wealth and prosperity as we view them today come not from the basic production of raw materials but from their fabrication into the goods man uses. Until 1973, it was commonly believed that the "conditions of trade" were consistently unfavorable to raw material-producing nations and advantageous to those shaping manufactures and furnishing services. The events set in train by the third Israeli-Arab war, with the rise to power of the nations joined in the Organization of Petroleum Exporting Countries (OPEC), have put in doubt the absolute validity of the one-sided favor of the conditions of trade. Nevertheless, even the oil producers seem convinced of the ultimate victory of the fabricators as shown by the efforts of OPEC members to reproduce such a manufacturing-serving economy within their own boundaries, in anticipation of the ultimate depletion of their oil.

The greatest significance of this revolution against the long-dominant element in the human economy is perhaps best shown in the command economies of the socialist countries of eastern Europe and Asia. Most East European countries, and those of Asia, carried forward the traditional practices of the "natural economy" well into the twentieth century. Poland and Hungary remained dominantly agricultural countries up to the Second World War, as did China and Indo-China. Feudalism had legally disappeared in much of the area only during the nineteenth century, and the large landed estate survived as an economic unit in much of the socialist world until the chaos of the Second World War finally disrupted these traditional backstays of the economy.

When the Communist governments in eastern Europe were established in 1945, they inherited territories largely rural in economy and settlement. The common pattern was that of one major city where political activity centered and consumer-oriented light manufacturing took place. Otherwise, collecting centers for the agricultural produce were likely to be the main component of urbanization in a dominantly rural world. Hungary furnishes us a particularly striking example even today. Budapest is a city of some two and a half million people; no other city in the country reaches a population of one hundred thousand. This pattern is changing, largely in response to the nearly universal assumption made in command economies that the low state of industrialization leads to their "lower standards of living." Consistently throughout the Comecon countries of eastern Europe—those in the Soviet economic bloc—and in other countries endeavoring to develop the more radical forms of socialism, as in Africa and Asia, the turn to planning is truly a turn towards active and offical urbanization.

The basis of this strong drive for urbanization tied to industrialization is the observation that, since the middle of the last century, the largest component of growth in the national economies of the advanced countries has come in those activities associated with city life. In the western world, the high GNP is earned in the cities; the less-developed nations seek to gain this level of prosperity by emulation. They observe with a clear eye that the growth element in the countries they seek to copy is not to be found in the countryside, but in the cities. Whether careful analysis would always result in an unfavorable comparison of city and country is rather beside the point: the perception of the world at large is that "cities pay." In a hundred developing countries, the rapid growth of urbanization is not viewed with half the disfavor it earns in western Europe and North America.

Thus in the present world the city is viewed as the fundamental element in the national economy—a direct reversal of the medieval pattern, when cities were thought to be parasitical and were normally greatly underprivileged in political affairs. Only in very recent years, and then far from completely, has this political discrimination been reduced. The famous "one man-one vote" decisions of the United States Supreme Court were the culmination of a reversal in practices that had begun when the countryside was dominant in the Middle Ages. Even those decisions have failed to overcome all of the discrimination that arose when there was some justice to the view that the countryside supported and defended the nation. Although most informed persons today would grant the economic significance of cities, many still look upon those large clusters of people as physical and psychologically stressful places to be abandoned by those with the money to do so.

A certain polarity in the view toward the countryside may be found in the capitalist and socialist worlds. We have noted the strong campaigns in the radical socialist countries of eastern Europe and elsewhere to industrialize and urbanize in a search to improve the qualities of life. In the capitalist world of western Europe and North America, a reversal is taking place: there, those individuals (and the society in general) who have gained capital have shown a strong proclivity to use the money to buy periodic or permanent rurality for themselves. This striving follows upon the suburbanization and ruralization movement of the nineteenth century, when prosperous Londoners, New Yorkers, and Bostonians first moved out along rail lines for suburban residence in search of a physically more healthy environment than was to be found in the cities.

Adna Weber, in his classic study of the creation of the nineteenth-century metropolis, concluded in 1899 that the only salvation of man in the city from a health viewpoint was to be secured through the creation of suburbs. He held that in the "rise of the suburbs" was to be found "the solid basis for hope that the evils of city life, so far as they result from overcrowding, may be in large part removed. If concentration of population seems destined to continue, it will be a modified concentration which offers the advantages of both city and country life. It will realize the wish and the prediction of Kingsley (*Miscellanies:* "Great Cities"), 'a complete interpretation of city and country, a complete fusion of their different modes of life and a combination of the advantages of both, such as no country in the world has ever seen.'"[3]

It followed that as the prosperous looked toward the suburbs, the wealthy or the retired tended to look toward the actual countryside. In part this was the search for class mobility where within a structure the higher levels of society were associated with the rurally-based aristocracy. To rise socially, it was widely believed rural residence was essential for at least a part of the year. The "estate" became the tag that told of social distinction; even more modest strivings required a move out of the city. Thus several forces led the prosperous and wealthy of the capitalist countries to turn toward the countryside: the established leaders of society had always resided there; the health conditions in the nineteenth century encouraged rural refuge from diseases that were common and virulent in cities; and the culture of northwestern Europe and North America had been freighted with the notion that the countryside was a more worthy, patriotic, natural home of man than was the city.[4]

In the socialist countries the striving for industrialization still continues unabated and virtually unquestioned; thus we witness a rapid and enthusiastic urbanization. Given the staunchly egalitarian and industrial orientation of these "people's democracies," another great appeal to urbanization is to be found in the much greater facility toward the industrialization of housing provision to be found in urban rather than in rural areas. These Communist countries have learned from the Commercial and Industrial Revolution of the West that capital formation comes most readily and most rapidly in cities; they seek to apply this lesson in a search for a similar prosperity. In the capitalist West, that accumulated capital is used instead to buy the qualities of life that are, often erroneously, attached in the minds of people to the preurban rural existence.

Social commentators, even those such as Lewis Mumford who show considered regard for cities, often tend to think of the proto-city as vastly preferable to the full-blown model found under industrialization. A quality of "necessary evil" lurks constantly in the background of much that is written and said about cities in the West, with the escape to the countryside viewed as the emancipation that money or retirement buys. Thus, the role of the city has changed from the medieval one where ordinary men believed that cities made men free to a more current view that only the money to be earned in cities could provide that liberty, and then only through flight to the country.

The radical socialist world holds a very different view of the situation, but even the elite of the egalitarian society show their distinction through the possession of a dacha or a cottage in the countryside around Moscow, in the foothills of the Polish Tatra, or in the hills northward from Budapest toward the Danube Bend. Perhaps in another generation the polarity of socialist and capitalist on this matter of attitudes toward the city will disappear.

The relationship of industrialization to urbanization has changed slowly but fundamentally during the past hundred years. Originally much industrialization came in the countryside where waterpower and freedom from legal restraints might be found. While such productive efforts remained small in scale, the countryside remained reasonably untouched. But as the simple act of manufacturing came to envision truly mass production, it was no longer possible for industrialization to be unaccompanied by urbanization. Plants employing a thousand workers came to support fairly large towns or small cities when the so-called "industrial multiplier," which led to service employment often larger in numbers than the actual factory employment, came into play. And the tendency to develop associated and derivative industries in factory towns further encouraged this trend. Only when and where workers could continue to live in a rural settlement pattern and commute to work in a rural factory could these consequences be avoided. As such freedom to commute depended both on efficient individual transportation and upon freehold ownership of rural housing, the necessary conditions were found in relatively few places—the American and Canadian "Middle West," Belgium, and parts of France, notably the Franche-Comté. Elsewhere, the likelihood was that transport was missing, as in eastern Europe, or that land was held by large owners, as in Britain and much of the Mediterranean.

[3]*Adna Ferrin Weber*, The Growth of Cities in the Nineteenth Century: A Study in Statistics, *Ithaca, N.Y.: Cornell University Press, 1963, p. 475. [This edition was a reprint of the 1899 Columbia University edition.]*

[4]*For a general discussion of the anti-urban attitudes so prevalent in the United States in the nineteenth century (and at the present), see Morton and Lucia White,* The Intellectual Versus the City, *Cambridge: Harvard-M.I.T. Presses, 1962. For a more particular discussion of the tie between the classical revival of the last century and the denigration of towns see James E. Vance, Jr., "The Classical Revival and Urban-Rural Conflict in Nineteenth Century North America,"* The Canadian Journal of American Studies, *Vol. IV (Fall), 1973, pp. 149-168. For an interesting statistical account of the considerable shift of demographic growth in the United States to nonmetropolitan areas see Wilbur Zelinsky, "Nonmetropolitan Pennsylvania: A Demographical Revolution in the Making?,"* Earth and Mineral Sciences, *Vol. 45 (1975).*

Other Changes in the Role of Cities

If the introduction of large-scale industry accounts for the most fundamental change in the role of cities in recent history, that event does not stand alone. Many other factors have contributed to the existing new pattern of activities and attitudes toward urbanization. Certainly one of the more important changes appears in the matter of attitudes toward the physical expansion of cities. We have noted Adna Weber's final conclusion from a detailed study of nineteenth-century urban demography that only through recourse to suburbanization could cities survive biologically. He was expressing the view of the majority of housing reformers of his time—starting with A. T. Stewart a generation before and to be followed within a decade by Ebenezer Howard and his "First Garden City," which was in fact far from the first such place. To the post-Civil War American and the Victorian in England, the "interpretation" of city and country was a high ideal. In America from the close of the war on, a number of garden suburbs had been built, both by private development companies and by industrial firms. Garden City, Long Island, has been noted; Pullman, Illinois, and Hopedale, Massachusetts, and half a hundred other

workers' satellites could have been found when Weber was writing. For the middle class, numerous garden suburbs combined features of town life with the environment possible at the edge of the country. These included Brookline and a dozen other towns outside Boston; Llewelyn Park, the towns of Westchester County, and other places around New York City; the towns of the Main Line west of Philadelphia; Roland Park in Baltimore; the towns along the Des Plaines River west of Chicago, notably Frederick Law Olmsted's Riverside; and those circling St. Louis and adjacent to San Francisco on her peninsula.

"Right thinking" supported this "interpretation" for all classes of society and, given the American ability to accomplish goals practically rather than doctrinally, the spread of United States cities into suburbs was rapid and extensive. Generally up to the 1960's this accomplishment was thought to be positive, even when it extended commuting time. But recently the view has changed; Malthusianism has particularly gripped America, and the borrowing of English planning attitudes has been shameless and unthinking.

Americans have clearly perceived that population growth is out of hand, and that something must be done. Instead of dealing with the problem head-on—seeking to stabilize the national population at its current level and to limit immigration from those lands that show completely improvident population policies—many social activists have proposed limiting the physical growth of cities, an act of demographic

Riverside became an elegantly designed suburb of Chicago, laid out according to plans of Frederick Law Olmsted drawn up in the 1870's. The Burlington Railroad furnished the connection to the city and this was their station, with its romantically disguised water tower, in 1887. Both the greater element of design and the greater cost of commuting by train made Riverside a sound middle-class suburb.

restraint equally as ineffective as that proposed by Soranus in classical times.[5] The attacks on "urban sprawl," "slurbs," and other vividly-termed demons represent a reversal of the long-standing liberal stance that called for suburbs.

The Fall from Grace of the Suburb

In part, this attack grows out of a misunderstanding of British planning practices which has suggested that that policy has much bearing in America, or for that matter other than exceedingly costly success in Britain. "Greenbelts" were proposed by Patrick Abercrombie's wartime plan for London, largely to accomplish a morphological transformation of the city, cutting off the interwar spread of the working-class into the green countryside around the city, and placing the workers instead in detached industrial satellites or in more densely built-up housing "estates" inside the greenbelt. England is a tiny, heavily populated land with widely scattered towns that have grown from two centuries of industrialization. A real chance existed that on some vectors London could become continuous with the Midland industrial cities and with Reading. In addition, the social and symbolic role of the countryside was much greater in Britain than in America; a powerful drive, similar to that during the Industrial Revolution, aimed to "preserve the countryside," which meant "keep it for a highly elitist way of life." Whether these causes were just the Briton must decide, but they were certainly alien concerns for Americans.

Given sufficient land, a stabilized population such as we now seem to be approaching with respect to natural increase, Americans have no reasonable need to worry about the cohesion of cities. Similarly, America is fortunately free of the feudal past that makes of the countryside a social and class cachet, which powerful groups can seek to limit to their own use. Thus, the reversal of the traditional liberal call for suburbs has grown in America out of the borrowing of inappropriate external examples, as well as the failure to deal with the root cause of city expansion without which no effective land-use policy is possible. Until population is stabilized and illegal immigration from

[5]*Soranus (A.D. 98-138) proposed that at the critical moment in intercourse, contraception would be secured through the woman's holding her breath.*

Latin America and elsewhere is dealt with sternly, no amount of inveighing against "slurbs" will hold back the tide. Still we must give full weight to the changed planning notions that have taken over, which seek to constrain the physical growth of cities. In such a climate of opinion the physical transformation of the city can be very fundamental.

The election of the city to the role of receptacle for a rapidly expanding world population is fully in keeping with its already established office of caring for the acculturation of the rurally dispossessed. Society in western countries ever since the Agricultural Revolutions of the seventeenth and eighteenth centuries has faced the problem of what to do with a surplus population found in rural areas. In part that surplus grew out of the higher life expectancy in the country; the population there, unlike that in cities, was more than reproducing itself even two centuries ago. In part the surplus came from technological changes in farming which reduced the demand for labor, thus creating rural unemployment. So long as cities were biologically unable to maintain their populations, the influx from the country served two useful purposes: to reduce rural overpopulation and to maintain the urban population in spite of a high local death rate. But soon after the turn of the last century, the health conditions in cities were so considerably improved that the influx of rural people began to shape a rapid and massive positive growth in urban populations.

Along with this growth in cities went a continuing overpopulation in the country, a surplus further expanded by mechanization of agriculture, which in turn reduced the demand for field labor. This situation was particularly true of the American South where, in the years just before and just after the Second World War, a radical transformation of agriculture led to a massive surplus rural population among black field hands. Following a tradition of long standing, those rejected by the rural economy flocked to the cities—to Detroit and other Middle Western industrial cities in the 1930's, to New York and the Northeast and West Coast in the post-war decades. In each of these receiving areas, the cities bore the brunt of the in-migration and the economic and cultural problems introduced. In these areas, improving technology was making increased demands on labor skill, and improving health was increasing the ranks of the unskilled, creating a severe and chronic unemployment situation. Nevertheless, the tradition of exporting people, and thereby problems, from the country to the city was so firmly established that despite the absence of need for labor in the city, migrants continued to arrive, finding a situation only slightly less desperate than the one they left behind.

The role of host to large unskilled populations—

from the country or from overseas—which was functionally essential for the economic and social health of cities up to the time of the First World War, came in later decades to bring to those cities problems that are only now being seen to be beyond the ability of urban places alone to handle. American national social and economic policies have failed to perceive and deal with this changed role for cities, creating several "urban crises" of the mid-seventies, most notably that of New York City where an incredibly inept municipal administration combined with a massive flow of legal and illegal migrants of little skill to inflate welfare costs beyond the ability of even a well-run city to handle.

This role of the city as a refuge is not restricted to the United States, though it perhaps reaches its highest and most harrowing expression there, where it is an "internal" problem. Many European countries host in-migrant peoples—the Algerians of France, the Yugoslavs and Turks of Germany, the Yugoslavs of Sweden, the Spaniards and Moroccans of Belgium, and the Spaniards of Switzerland. In time of full employment, the labor of these "guest workers" is critical to the economic health of those lands. In the best of circumstances, they are well housed and well cared for, but in the worst, in the *bidonvilles* of France or the shack towns established on squatting tenure elsewhere, conditions can be very bad indeed. Throughout the lesser-developed world of Africa and Latin America, such extralegal settlements are common when the desperate rural population moves into *favellas* at the edge of Brazilian cities or shack towns outside African towns.

In modern society, the city becomes the dumping ground of social and economic problems, perhaps most often not of its own making. But illogically and unfairly, dealing with those conditions is commonly viewed as an urban rather than a national responsibility. Europe has practiced a deceptive "avoidance" of those problems, in the sense that permanent residence for "guests" is normally restricted; in times of depression, their welcome is revoked and the problem population is returned to the place of its origin. In the United States, that course is not available, fortunately, so the problem remains to be dealt with.

Connectivity among Cities: The Decline under Air Travel

One of the less widely perceived shifts in the role of the city has come in the matter of the connectivity among such places. In times past, particularly during the period before the Second World War when rail transportation was dominant, the connectivity among cities reached a very high level of geographical comprehensiveness. All cities of any size were provided with an essentially complete web of service to nearby and distant places. Trains that carried people or goods from Boston to New York went directly on to provide service to all eastern cities and, with minor changes, to all North American cities. Some places had better-than-average rail connections—Chicago, St. Louis, Kansas City, and the like—but once underway, the pattern of train movements and of rail lines kept sharp contrasts in service to a minimum.

The great change has come in the introduction of air transportation, which oddly plays favorites far more than did the railroads. In a sense all parts of the Earth's surface are available by air in a way they were to no single transportation medium in the past. But given the economics of air transport, possibility and actual service are two distinct qualities. The terminal costs of landing or taking off, and loading while on the ground, are such that it pays to stop only in a few places. And unlike the case in rail transport, intermediate service by air is costly and destructive of efficiency on the main connection. The geographical result has been to raise a few cities to a dominant position in air transport and to relegate others to a costly and irksome dependence.

The New Junction City

Any examination of American air transport will show that, in the flush of enthusiasm at the close of the Second World War, airline companies began to offer service to a vast array of places, with fairly frequent schedules and the sort of complex interconnection characteristic of the rail competition. Planes were small, flew fairly low, and could land and take off from modest airports. The technical changes in aircraft have transformed that pattern. Jet planes are efficient but they fly high, are expensive to land and take off, and require both large landing facilities and large increments of payload to operate in economic efficiency. The result has been that the airline companies, particularly during the economic squeeze of the mid-seventies, have "rationalized" routings so much that a few cities are afforded vastly superior air service, whereas most places have lost much of the advantage they formerly held. In place of the service of intermediate cities has come the notion of the "connecting plane" from one of a few super-airports. On the Atlantic Coast, New York, Washington, Atlanta, and Miami have become hubs of a great number of connecting flights. In the interior of the country, Chicago, Dallas-Ft. Worth, and Denver have assumed this function, while on the Pacific Coast only Los Angeles stands at the highest level, though San Francisco and Seattle are major hubs. Elsewhere in the country, the major cities—Boston, Cleveland, Pittsburgh, Detroit, Minneapolis-St. Paul, Houston, and the like—are served rather indirectly. Airlines will offer direct, sometimes nonstop flights to a few major cities, but more service will be provided via the *new junction cities* such as Dallas-Ft. Worth, Denver, Atlanta, Los Angeles, or New York. The advantage afforded those junction cities in a cost-conscious time is obvious, notably when it comes to those functions of corporate supervision which depend upon constant travel. The advantage of locating a headquarters office in a junction city needs no great explanation.

The impact of this hierarchical separation of functions only now emerging in the air-transport industry is not as yet fully clear. Likely it will exert a strong force toward concentration, not necessarily in a single city, but toward a few cities in the growing element in American economic life—the provision of high-level financial and administrative services. The evidence is at hand to suggest this concentration into a rather new category of *supervisory-service cities.* Atlanta, recently for a short period the nation's busiest airport, has blossomed as the center for the South. Dallas and Ft. Worth are seeking earnestly to use air transport as an aggressive weapon against the pretensions of Houston. Los Angeles and San Francisco are greatly sensitive to the importance of air connections in the maintenance of their self-established roles as "the City" on the West Coast. And Phoenix tries amidst severe obstacles to gain junction-city status to match its efforts to become a major center of supervision and service.

The impact of air transport on European and other cities is less straightforward because air transport there, and on other continents, tends to be carried on by subsidized national airlines highly subject to national planning. Most European countries have such a discrepancy between the service to the capital and that to other cities that the strengthening force of this concentration of service in a few world cities merely reinforces the already strong collecting habit of the capital. Paris and Brussels, Vienna and Budapest, Prague and Warsaw, London and Lisbon all show this trend. One wonders if the plans for France, for example, which constantly state the desire for decentralization of functions, might be advanced as much by deconcentration of air service from Paris as by the holding of cabinet meetings in Lyon. Only in Germany and Italy is there any serious parity among cities in air service, and there only Milan and Rome and Frankfurt and Düsseldorf show much strength.

Amenities as a Force in City Support

Along with the concentrating tendency that air transportation has introduced to cities has gone an important role in elevating amenities to a higher place in the organization of life. Environmental amenity has never been entirely absent from the thinking of city builders and those individuals whose position allowed them consideration of other than most pressing wants. The villas of the countryside of Latium or the Mediterranean coast near the mouth of the Tiber, the abbeys and manor houses of the Middle Ages, and certainly the chateaux of the Loire valley from the sixteenth century on, all show how the nature of the site and the ambience of the local environment were considered when building structures raised above the plane of the most basic need. But for any great number of individuals, only fairly recently has amenity become a major factor in the decision process. The English aristocracy joined their French cousins during the eighteenth century when the introduction of landscape architecture became well developed in England. Gardens were laid out and the natural vegetation was brought sternly in line with the educated conception of beauty. The countryside was made beautiful where it was not naturally so endowed. For increasing numbers of middle-class families, the view out of the window and the quality of the breeze that entered it became matters of concern.

Perhaps the ultimate in amenities existed in the almost totally transformed surroundings of the French Châteaux, as this one near Alençon.

The Resort

The suburb was an early satisfaction of this concern but, in time, increasing leisure and greater ease of movement brought the resort to more distant places for reasons of health or environmental amenity. Apparently the search for health was the first attraction for the visit to thermal and mineral springs, having origins at least as early as Roman times. The coastal beach resort gained prominence only during the last century, a timing it shares with the mountain summer resort of the White Mountains in America and the Massif Centrale and Alps in Europe. We cannot easily begin to distinguish the concern for health from that for aesthetics until the nineteenth century. In general, Continental Europeans were still then, as now, more concerned with health. They favored the spa, which gained its name from the Belgian health resort of that name made famous and fashionable by Peter the Great, rather than the place of more direct environmental amenity, which was favored by the English and Americans. In the United States the combination of a basal population of English extraction with a recently migrant population from the European Continent meant that both watering places and seasonal resorts became popular during the last century.[6]

In America and England the coastal resort became for the prosperous a definite adjunct of urban life even before the end of the last century. The New England coast, seaside New Jersey, and the Delmarva peninsula all had beach resorts; those in New England showed distant connections to interior cities such as that of Pittsburgh with the Rhode Island Coast and that of Cincinnati with Bar Harbor in Maine. In America the mountain resort gained an equal favor, though England seemed singlemindedly committed to the "seaside," a term that was far from always the "beach" the Americans favored, as the shingle of many a Nice or Brighton attests. In all these earlier cases, however, we are dealing with a vacation residence in the mountains, at the shore, or on the Riviera. Only on the Riviera was winter rather than summer "the season."

The European habit of winter holidays entered but slowly into more Puritan America. In the late nineteenth century, the coast of the Carolinas and Georgia began to be taken up for winter resorts, as did parts of southern California, but only the very well-to-do or the sickly could enjoy these reliefs from the grim northern winters. In writing on this migration to California, Carey McWilliams termed this a "Pullman car migration" that entered the Los Angeles basin in the

[6]For a discussion of the several reasons that people left the city during the last century, see James E. Vance, Jr., "California and the Search for the Ideal," Annals of the Association of American Geographers, Vol. 62 (1972), pp. 185–210. A general discussion of Wilderness and the American Mind by Roderick Nash (New Haven: Yale University Press, 1967) presents the special role that wilderness plays in our national view of amenities. Other useful titles on this subject are: Roland Van Zandt, The Catskill Mountain House (New Brunswick: Rutgers University Press, 1966); Richmond Barrett, Good Old Summer Days (New York: D. Appleton-Century Co., 1941); Earl Pomeroy, In Search of the Golden West (New York: Alfred A. Knopf, 1957); Billy M. Jones, Health-Seekers in the Southwest, 1817–1900 (Norman: University of Oklahoma Press, 1967); and the late Edward Ullman's seminal article on the role of amenities in location decisions: "Amenities as a Factor in Regional Growth," Geographical Review, Vol. XLIV (1954), pp. 119–132.

1870's.[7] Only as time went on did the lesser folk make it there, and then only when fierce competition between the Santa Fe and Southern Pacific railroads lowered fares to such sums as a dollar or two between Chicago and Los Angeles. Great changes in the social structure of America and other western countries were necessary before the attraction of amenities could find expression in more than the vacation journey.

The Location by Amenities

The change came in the years after the Second World War when a panoply of new industries made possible the adoption of new productive locations more possessed of amenities than had been those typical of the earlier phases of the Industrial Era. In addition the facilitation of travel by jet aircraft was such that many activities formerly held in rather tight clusters near the dominant cities of the economic ecumene could begin to move outward. Firms that before the war would have tended to have headquarters in New York, Boston, or Chicago, the old dominant cities, began to locate in Los Angeles, Atlanta, or even Boise and Salt Lake City, the emerging regional cities. Particularly in those industries dependent upon mental activity largely divorced from the consumption of raw materials—research and development, publishing, and aerospace activities—amenities could be used as a drawing card for recruiting highly skilled employees. Given jet air travel, people, documents, and small components could be delivered in New York or Washington nearly as quickly from the San Francisco Peninsula as by automotive transportation from Philadelphia or Richmond.

In this way, air travel has joined with amenities to shift large elements in the working population. And the great improvements in pension, social security, and other retirement schemes has meant that more people retire with enough money to move to a warm and pleasant climate than was ever possible in the past. Certainly the vast increase in the population of Florida, and the Southeast in general, of Arizona, and of the West Coast has meant a new base for urbanization essentially unknown until the nineteenth century, and then only seasonally important. For every Brighton or

[7]Carey McWilliams, Southern California Country: An Island on the Land, New York: Duell, Sloan & Pearce, 1946.

Atlantic City encouraged by the railroad, a dozen Sun Cities or Orlandos have been supported by social security, good geriatric medicine, and the ease of jet plane travel.

when the Industrial Revolution in England had grimly degraded the older commercial cities on which it settled in the nineteenth century.

The Rise of Service

The rise of what have been termed tertiary economic activities, which we have defined as supervisory and servicing, has been an additional transforming force in cities. The medieval town was mainly concerned with trade and artisan occupations, a configuration of economic activity that was joined by large-scale manufacturing after the Industrial Revolution. Only in recent decades has that dealing in and fabrication of tangible goods lost dominance in the productive activities of mankind. Now, in the most developed countries, fully half the population may be engaged in "services," as exemplified by the 53 per cent of the United States population now so employed. Given this vast body of workers, we should not be surprised that the physical form of the city has experienced a Service Revolution to match the earlier Commercial and Industrial Revolutions.

Most notably, the Service Revolution has come to dominate the central parts of the largest American cities. Trade, both retail and wholesale, which initiated the economic town and occupied its center until the time of the Second World War, has moved out of the core to a most marked degree. In turn industry, which in the nineteenth century was most heavily concentrated near the heart of the city where were the easiest access, the best external connections, and the largest in-migrant population of potential employees, has also moved out.

The fact that the supervisory and service occupations now fill the majority of buildings in the city's heart results from the negative force of relocation of other activities to other areas than the core, and the positive force of the rapid expansion of these service activities as a proportion of the total productive labor. It is a great social misfortune that the in-migrant unskilled population that proved so essential to early industry is little needed in this service activity, which itself has almost nothing to sell but the intangible results of education and training. For this reason, cities have faced problems as critical under the Service Revolution as those described, and decried, by Engels

Transport Differentiation: Purpose of Journey

A final dynamic element currently at work in transforming the role of cities is that of transportation differentiation by the purpose of the journey. Medieval and early industrial cities knew little alternative to pedestrial transport; only the very wealthy could afford the sedan chairs or carriages used in cities, and few townsmen strayed far from their native city save for those ecclesiastical and lay aristocrats possessed of country estates. For them, carriages or carts provided transport for the seasonal shifts between town and country.

When industrialization brought great population to towns, a need arose for transport for those living toward the edge of the city. In Mediterranean Europe the poorer classes tended to reside near the city's edge, so little was done there. But in northern cities, the more prosperous tended to keep to the edge as settlement expanded. Thus, in Paris and London and other large northern towns, omnibuses were introduced in the 1820's to carry the middle classes from their peripheral residential areas to the center of the city. In America only New York was extensive enough, mainly because of its elongated insular location, to need much internal transport that early. In the thirties, horsecar lines were built northward from lower Manhattan toward the residential areas developing in the open country near Murray Hill. By mid-century, other large American cities had developed their own horsecar lines. In all cases, however, public transportation was first undertaken to tie the middle-class residential areas to the city core. Recent studies have shown how relatively costly public transit was, and how little it was used by the working-class population of nineteenth-century cities.

As the middle-class areas continued to advance with the settlement frontier of the city, steam-train lines came to furnish the connection to the center. It became an integral part of middle-class life to use public transit for the journey to work while attempting to make private provision for recreational movement.

Those families that could afford them had horse-drawn vehicles for movement within the suburbs or for recreational travel in the nearby countryside. Because horse-drawn vehicles were always relatively expensive to own and operate, a latent demand urged a more efficient form of personal transport in suburban areas. That demand was met in the 1870's by the invention and manufacture of the safety bicycle which could be used in local areas with reasonably good streets and roads, as the suburbs had. The great desire of suburban dwellers to use their bicycles in the adjacent country led to the first "Good Roads Movement" in America, and the first efforts at macadamizing or hard-paving country roads. In the early 1880's the typical American suburban family would have been characterized by a railroad commutation to work by the head of the household, and the movement of the children and the younger adult women about the suburban town on their own bicycles.

The late eighties and early nineties were a time of considerable change. In the suburbs and between the suburbs of smaller cities and their core, the steam railroad was not a notably efficient or practical form of commuter transport. For those particular areas, a mechanized "horsecar" was needed so that costs could be reduced and distances of practical travel somewhat increased. The first efforts came with true mechanical traction, provided by cables drawn by winding engines located in district engine houses. Starting in San Francisco in 1873, cable cars came into widespread use in America, and rather more restricted employment in Britain and on the Continent. But cable lines were not very easily worked in cold wet climates, where the conduit for the cable tended to fill with water and then freeze, so efforts continued to find a better form of mechanical horsecar. Battery-operated cars were introduced, compressed air was employed, and a diversity of tractive mediums came into use.

Paris in 1900 had nearly a dozen different kinds of track-guided transit lines—the first, le Chemin de Fer Américain organized in 1853, used rails west of the Cours-la-Reine but free-running wheels east thereof to the Louvre.[8] Compressed-air cars were introduced in 1887 on the Vincennes line, steam-power cars were used for the Exhibition of 1889, and hot-water cars were used soon thereafter on the Courbevoie-Étoile line. In 1891 a cable car line was run from the Place de la République to the Église de Belleville, and battery cars began to run in 1892 from the Madeleine to St. Denis. Joint steam-compressed air services were run outward from the Odéon in 1893, and several other combinations were attempted before the first live-contact electric line was opened in 1896, between the Place de la République and Romainville.

Frank Sprague's trolley system came into nearly universal use both in America and in Europe, to the extent that it, rather than the 1853 horsecar line, gained the title Chemin de Fer Américain. For small cities and suburbs, the trolley lines were physically and economically an ideal form of transit, one that is at the present time being reexamined by planners with more than a nostalgic bent. These trolley lines could be built cheaply, on fairly narrow streets, and run economically with only moderate patronage. "Light rail transit" of current planning vogue is merely the trolley line somewhat brought up to date.

The trolley made mechanical transport available to a much wider spectrum of the population than could have been served either by steam trains or horsecars. But it still failed to care for the recreation needs of the upper classes. For the working class, the trolley outing to the amusement park built at the country end of the line by the traction company held a strong appeal, but not so for the middle and upper classes. They wanted great freedom of destination and timing, and more privacy. For them, the bicycle builders began to experiment with a mechanized bicycle, ultimately transformed in the late eighties and the nineties into the automobile.

When cars became practical contrivances after the turn of the century, they were taken up quickly and fervently by the middle and upper classes, first for recreational and suburban travel. With that adoption, a new complexity of transportation existed for this group—steam trains for commuting, and automobiles for personal recreational and household travel. Until the decade of the 1920's, the working class had to content itself with the trolley as a means both of commuting and of gaining access to recreation. But in the United States in the years after the First World War, mass-produced Fords and other cars dropped in price sufficiently that many working-class families could afford them, adding that group to the existing population that could command two types of transportation—a mass form for commuting, and an individual one initially for recreational purposes. After only a short time, however, the blue-collar workers realized that car ownership gave them the possibility of occupying housing no longer restricted to the proximity of the plant or within trolley access to it. When the worst years of the Depression of the 1930's were over, and when the Federal Housing Administration(FHA) program of mortgage support for lower-income house purchasers was introduced in 1934, the American working class showed the same penchant for moving away from

[8]Jean Robert, Les Tramways Parisiens, Paris: R.A.T.P., 1959, p. 11.

Only with the introduction of elevated railways, on which steam trains could first be used to provide mass transportation, were fares sufficiently reduced to permit the working class to commute to and from work and to travel into the central business district. This photograph shows Chicago's South Side elevated railway in 1893 when it still operated with steam engines.

both its workplaces and its characteristic mass transit for commuting that the upper classes had demonstrated.

At that time, just before the Second World War, a new form of residential structure was clearly about to be created in the new and large housing tracts that individual mobility, mortgage guarantees, and a potential mass market had called to the drawing boards of developers. All that was lacking was a new form of arterial highway on which the flow of cars from the suburbs to the central city could operate without the impedences normally introduced by the older, preautomobile inner suburbs. In 1940 the state of California opened the Arroyo Seco Freeway between Pasadena and downtown Los Angeles, thus creating an experimental "freeway" (the first) which proved that such a highway transformation could open vast peripheral areas to daily commuting by private automobile.

Unfortunately the turn to freeways narrowed the choice of transport open to many people to that of the automobile alone. The economic distress visited upon commuter railroads and trolley lines by the shift of housing farther out from the center, the construction of housing tracts on sites well removed from mass transit facilities, and the creation of freeways to allow daily commuting by car rapidly killed the trolley lines in the 1940's and '50s, and severely reduced the barely mar-

ginal position of rail lines. By the 1960's only a few cities could boast any survivals of the previously extensive system of a rail-guided rapid transit. Suburban commuter railroads were restricted to Boston, New York, Philadelphia, Chicago, and, less significantly, Baltimore, Washington, Cleveland, Detroit, and San Francisco. Trolley lines disappeared from most cities, surviving only where trolley cars were used extensively in subways, as in Boston, Pittsburgh, Philadelphia, and San Francisco, and in New Orleans, where the St. Charles line took on the quality of a tourist attraction. New York and Chicago continued their subway and elevated routes but did away with their surface lines. Thus, significant fixed-plant transit was to be found in only four cities in the United States—Boston, New York, Philadelphia, and Chicago—with bits in a few other places such as Newark, Pittsburgh, Cleveland, New Orleans, and San Francisco.

The history of urban transportation has tended toward a cycle of simplicity followed by complexity only to be reduced again to simplicity. Initially, walking about was the main and virtually the only way to accomplish "transportation." With the advent of large urban populations, and the consequent areal spread of the city, the more well-to-do began to seek vehicular transport, thus creating a complex provision pattern. The introduction of the trolley brought that choice to most of the class elements in American society with direct and fundamental influences upon the residential structure of cities. The years after the Second World War witnessed a return to the simplicity of the early city, with in this instance a universal dependence upon automobiles for transportation. Those elements of society unable to command the use of a car were severely disadvantaged; the housing pattern had been established mainly in terms of car use, so the pedestrial alternative was difficult or impossible.

We find American cities at that state at the moment when many factors give urgency to a return to transportation complexity. The increasing cost and scarcity of energy, the heightened social responsibility that comes out of a better understanding of the role that mobility plays in economic advance and prosperity, and the late realization that dependence on a single way of getting about—be it jet planes or automobiles—is seriously constraining to individual freedom have all encouraged a conscious reform of the current transportation provision in cities. In seeking to understand the role that cities play in our lives, we must take account of the change from complexity to simplicity during the postwar decades, and consider as well the likely changes that will come in the next couple of decades when we must seek consciously to reverse that narrowing choice.

The Processes of Urban Morphogenesis

Although cities play changed roles in the modern world, a consistency remains between the past and present, and that consistency of process furnishes the best descriptive and analytical tool for understanding how cities are shaped.

For a number of years, my own research interests have centered on this question of urban morphogenesis and its consistent processes. I shall therefore lean heavily on my previous work, not from conceit, but from simple expediency. Up to now, few geographers or other urban scholars have shown much interest in the subject of *physical process* in city shaping, so little work by others may be turned to for support; what exists will be used. Otherwise this section must stand as a brief summarization and integration of ideas I have expressed elsewhere in a wide variety of publications, not always easily available to a general audience.

Urban Initiation and the Central Business District

It is common practice in the western world to think of the "heart of the city" as what is today called the "central business district." Good morphological justification supports this view, but it tends to mix up cause and effect. The central business district is the site of the oldest buildings in most cities; we may demonstrate through historical-geographical research that where the central business district is found today, the original city was found, and often the total medieval city. This evidence might at first seem to suggest that the central business district originated the city, that retail trade was the initiating force which brought the town into existence. From such unresolved areal associations, misconceptions of universal process, such as central-place theory, have arisen. But looking, as we have in this book, at the evolution of role and form in the cities of western civilization, clearly long-distance trade was more significant as an earlier initiator of cities than was local-market trade.

But why *is* the central business district, a retailing structure, now at the heart of the city? The answer is both simple and fundamental to the creation of a body of thought on urban morphogenetic processes. Concisely stated, the greatest characteristic of urban physical structure is the separation of form from function, which may be slightly amplified to include the notion that locations do not shift but the "best and highest" use of locations may.

In our example of the *faubourg*, the protection provided by the castle was sought first, and the sheltering of distant traders. As the town grew, often building high walls for its own protection, adjacency to the *bourg* might no longer be needed. In that event proximity to the gates of the cities might be more advantageous to the conduct of distant trade than would be location under the castle in the center of the city's area and population. If such a simple case evolved, the retailing functions of the city marketplace might well encroach on the distant merchants' area surrounding that square, *not because the merchants had been forced out* but rather because they had taken up residence in a new quarter better served geographically for their purposes than the original one.

The history of cities is replete with instances of voluntary migration of functions, with subsequent occupation of the previous quarters by another function. The whole concept of land-use succession is founded on such a process. To account for present-day locations in the city by either (1) current locations of activities, or (2) rigid land-economics explanations is far too simplistic. The fault with the first argument is its circular reasoning; in the second case, the amount one is willing to pay for a site is not the same at all times in urban history. If land-economic reasoning had been active at the advent of medieval cities, distant traders could undoubtedly have outbid retailers for the most protected sites. In the same way, when distant traders no longer needed the *faubourg* site, they were quite willing to yield it to others. A new site closer to the port or the gate better served their needs, and they might increase their operating capital through selling their former central site to a retailer for whom centrality within his market—the city and the immediate countryside—gained increasing value. But if the distant trader reasoned otherwise, as was sometimes the case, then he could and would continue to occupy the central site.

Finally, the ability to occupy the most expensive site is the ability to earn enough to pay its rent. Economic history suggests to us that in capital-accumulation and profit-creating matters, the distant traders were far superior to the local traders. If they chose to occupy a cheaper site, it was because it served their current best interests.

We must then distinguish between the initial location of activities in urban history and their subsequent shifts. The present occupation of the heart of the city by the central business district says mainly that given present conditions, the complex of activities found there today *currently* gains the most from such a location. The phrasing of that statement is considered and deliberate. Notice it does not say that retailing necessarily gains most from such a location, or that the economically most productive forms of retailing locate at the center. Neither of those statements would be fully true today. In the years since the Second World War, incremental growth in retail trade has come almost exclusively outside the central business district. Many cities have experienced a fairly catastrophic absolute decline in central retail trade. We may logically conclude that the same economic and noneconomic forces which encouraged the distant traders of the Middle Ages to look beyond the marketplace are today encouraging the successors to the retail traders of the late nineteenth and early twentieth century to look beyond the central business district.

Quite unlike the thinking in sociology, which may not be very true even in that context, this process is not one of "invasion and succession" but rather of *departure and replacement*. The retailing core of cities has been declining in relative, sometimes in absolute, importance, and in area. Thus, the function that still needs the core location has a free field in which to expand without having very vigorously to outbid retailers for sites. The full test of that assertion is furnished by cities like Detroit, where central-area retail decline has led to land vacancy. If the land valuations in the core were more than the historically-justified fiction that they are, vacancy of land would hardly last for very long. In many cities, however, a deintensification of land-use has occurred in the last 25 years, save where quarters for the supervising-and-servicing component have been put up at a rate equal to that of retail decline, as in San Francisco.

The central business district of American cities has come to be dominantly a *central office district*, with retail functions increasingly assuming a dependent role: dependent upon the captive market of the office workers or the daily or periodic visitors to the city core, and dependent in absolute importance. When we look at cities in the United States today, we find that those with major regional or national office roles—Boston, New York, Washington, Chicago, Atlanta, Dallas, Houston, Los Angeles, and San Francisco—have "healthy" central business districts, whereas those with weak office functions—Cleveland, Detroit, St. Louis, Baltimore, and a string of medium-sized cities—show weak central districts. In almost all cities, retailing has lost its ability to pull many people to the center; only the increase in nonretail activities gives vigor to the core. Only New York seems to follow an independent course, with retailing still very important in the support of the central area, though with an evident shift from the former peak near Herald Square (Macy's and Gimbel's) to an emerging one in the East Fifties. Perhaps New York differs so because of its rather untypical housing pattern and the obsession of its residents with style and display (to the degree that travel convinces you that New Yorkers are the most overdressed people in western society).

What are the processes at work today in shaping central business districts? Odd though it might seem to some, they are very much the forces that have always been at work. The central business district presents one of the few examples, and certainly the most striking, of the continuing role that pedestrial movement plays in the city. Before the Industrial Revolution the practical limitation on the size of most cities was that posed by the feeding, housing, and keeping in health of too large a population. Paris, London, and Milan were so large as to pose real problems but most other towns managed without too much struggle. Even in the giant cities, the scale still permitted most urban activities to be carried

The central office district
was a result of mechanized
transport which allowed
extended journeys to work.
Its form was radically
transformed in the late
1880's when "skyscrapers"
were constructed. Initially these were tall buildings
supported by masonry walls,
as in the Monadnock Building
(the building without a
cornice shown to the right,
designed by Burnham and
Root). Two years later in
building an extension of
the building (the section
in the left foreground,
designed by Holabird and
Roche), the owners added
a steel-framed building of
the same height and general
aspect but with great
contrasts in actual detail.
Note the elevated railway
station in the lower left
corner of the photograph.

on by walking from one place to another. Within any one functional district of a city, walking was relatively easy and certainly universal. As economic quarters evolved into office districts (London's "City" is the clearest example), shopping areas, and wholesaling and manufacturing sections, the interchanges among establishments and the access by the public to shops and offices remained on foot, thereby introducing an area limitation on the growth of a particular district. Throughout the nineteenth century, few economic dis-

tricts grew larger than could be handily served by pedestrial movement, a general truth that was particu-larly correct with respect to the central shopping area.

No absolute value for the largest possible shopping district is valid for all sizes of city but it seems reason-able to say that only where massive population allowed an economic-class breakdown within the whole range of shopping districts—as in Paris, New York, Boston, Chicago, Los Angeles, or London—would the districts expand over an area greater than that easily covered by walking. Internal to each price class of shopping, the district that remained would still be manageable on foot. Thus, the upper limit to what John Rannells called "the linkages" within central districts remained not very different in round scale so long as men had to walk among the shops or offices.[9] If more space were needed, one of two processes intervened: either buildings were built higher to pack more activities into the same walkable ground area, or a separation of functions took place. As an example of the first intervention, we may cite the late-nineteenth-century hotel, department store, or office building, where the elevator developed at mid-century came into its own as an expansion agent permitting the enlargement of the district without consequent extension of its area. The separation of specialization can be observed in a number of instances within late-nineteenth-century central business districts. In that period, wholesaling and retailing were generally divided from one another. Wholesaling was moving away from the center to sites near the railroads that became the lifeline of its existence.

Similarly, in the post-Civil War period, offices and shops began a separation that today is nearly complete. Shops built upward; offices dealing directly with large numbers of people were brought down from upper floors. In the post-Civil War period, banks, stockbrokers, and other customer-oriented offices began to show up on the first floor in cities. The separation meant that the shopping district could grow without losing its potential customers at the outer edges, and the same could be true for financial districts with their expanding numbers of offices.

The processes shaping the central business district fall naturally into two classes—those internal to the district and those related to the external relations of the district. The real constraint imposed by pedestrial movement, the upward extension to allow growth in volume of the district without accompanying ground expansion, and the separation through specialization are all internalized processes, working in any central business district and independent of the conditions of land-use surrounding that area.

Other processes grow out of the relations of the district to its neighbors. The two most fundamental of these external processes are in truth opposite sides of the coin; one—assimilation of previously noncentral-area land—is normally matched by another—discard of central-area land—in such a way that the location of the central business district may change, but its real extent will remain relatively consistent.[10] In the case of the separation between wholesaling and retailing, the process of discard played an important role—in a number of cities, the wholesalers remained in place while the retailers moved away from them to create a new shopping district on land assimilated from urban space previously used mainly for housing. In similar fashion small, labor-intensive manufacturing has shown a tendency to occupy the buildings cast off by the central business district, because the intensity of labor use often implies having to site the factory near the center of urban mass transit, a system normally built to provide access to the central retailing and office areas from the suburbs. With that mass transit in place, as at Pennsylvania Station-Herald Square in New York or the intersection of Main and Fourth streets in Los Angeles, collecting nearby the number of workers for a garment industry was greatly simplified, thus explaining the location of the garment districts in those cities.

The process of discard suggests abandonment. But in the traditional core of the American city, other businesses—largely in wholesaling and manufacturing—were usually waiting to take up the space. Recently, unfortunately, with the radical shifts in the desired location characteristics of those two economic undertakings, little subsequent use has been made of the buildings in the zone of discard. Governmental policy has been forced to devise a program of urban redevelopment to care for what previously the market mechanism for urban land handled successfully.

So many small-scale processes are at work in the central business district that a discussion of all of them is impractical. We find within the area a strong process of association among types of shops and offices. Specialized clusters will occur of department and clothing stores, travel agencies and airline offices, stockbrokers and stock exchanges, banks, shipping companies, and other types of office occupations. Although competition among firms in the same trade may be keen, considerable comparison of their wares and services occurs, and they share dependence upon ancillary sales and services. Lawyers tend to cluster both around the courts and the law libraries and bar association clubrooms. Medical offices today normally cluster tightly together, depending upon adjacent medical specialists and laboratories. Over and over in the city, the process of clustering reflects either shared needs for ancillary facilities or the search for direct competition with other firms in the same activity.

One factor that plays more than an incidental role

[9]John Rannells, The Core of the City: A Pilot of Changing Land Uses in Central Business Districts, New York: Columbia University Press, 1956, particularly chapter three which describes establishments and their linkages.

[10]R. E. Murphy, J. E. Vance, Jr., and B. J. Epstein, "Internal Structure of the CBD," Economic Geography, Vol. 31 (1955), pp. 41–44.

in drawing businesses to the center is the availability of partially or fully amortized properties; rents can be quite low within the central district—certainly lower than in many of the outlying shopping and office districts that seek to compete, areally, with the core. We still tend to think of the heart of the city as the most expensive place to locate, as is true of the most desired parts of the center. But toward the edge of the district in older shopping and office buildings, rents may be quite reasonable. For the firm engaged in a highly specialized activity, either in servicing or retailing, the mere fact of being in the heart of the city may be critical. To that firm, taking a peripheral site in the central business district may be more desirable than taking the most centrally located position in an outlying center. Where the degree of specialization is high, quite probably the entire market of the metropolis is needed to support the firm or shop, and that entire market can normally be most easily tapped in the central business district, even at its edge.

Distinction should be drawn between the appeal of outlying shopping and office facilities to visitors to the metropolis and the appeal to its residents. For the visitor, "the city" is likely to be the core of a metropolis—Manhattan, the Loop and the Near Northside in Chicago, or downtown San Francisco—whereas for the metropolitan resident, "the city" is increasingly any part of the physical extent of the place. Because the needs of the distant visitor tend to parallel those of the office community—access to good external transportation, the availability of highly specialized and fashion-conscious shops for men and women, the availability of elegant and commonly expensive restaurants, nearby provision of public entertainment and public convening facilities—cities have shown a strong tendency for the core to become the purlieus of those in office occupations and of visitors to the metropolis.

Because many cities lack any very strong appeal for office clustering, they seem as well to lack any strong appeal for visitors. Exceptions occur, but generally where the city has been successful in holding onto downtown offices, it has also been successful in appealing to visitors. New York, despite an overwhelming array of negative qualities, has remained a city in which to locate offices and the city to visit. Chicago and San Francisco share in this pairing of functions. In Los Angeles the poor development of an office district—that which exists is currently heavily overbuilt, with rather high vacancy rates even in quite new and prestigious buildings—seems paired with a poor appeal of the city core to visitors. Not downtown Los Angeles, but Disneyland, Knott's Berry Farm, and all sorts of amusement facilities at the edge of the city seem to draw visitors from afar.

The special case of Los Angeles introduces one caveat essential to our consideration of the office building in cities. It is commonly argued that large amounts of new office-building construction serve as evidence of maintenance or growth in the functional importance of the central business district. This notion is very shaky. In a number of cases special conditions of taxation and investment policy encourage the building of new structures in a city where there is no demonstrable shortage of office space. Both Minneapolis and Los Angeles offer fairly strong evidence that massive new skyscraper construction has merely created large amounts of vacancy in still quite usable older buildings in other parts of the core. And in every city—New York, Chicago, and San Francisco as cases in point—new construction probably shifts occupancy from one part of the core area to another, leaving a zone of discard for office buildings not so different from that previously experienced for shops. And as was the case for the earlier zone of discard, the market does not take up these abandonments. Thus, a public policy of urban redevelopment must try to remove these discards from a market situation where declining use causes severe physical deterioration. Somewhat illogically, these redevelopment policies frequently encourage caring for the problem of declining retailing by subsidizing the construction of new office buildings in that zone of discard; the new structures there siren tenants from older office buildings, creating a subsequent zone of office building discard. Who can be found to move into that vacuum? Many cities now propose a "sports complex," a "convention center," or, if all else fails, government buildings. Perhaps a little more awareness of the urban morphogenetic processes might make these policies more logical and effective, and certainly far less catastrophically expensive.

Prestige plays a very strong role in site selection by office-using firms. Because offices make little use of physical commodities, and today relatively less use of routine labor, the physical location and properties of the building seem less important than its business cachet. New buildings, particularly architecturally distinctive ones, tend toward a more positive image than those built just before or after the Second World War. As new buildings open and old leases run out, the shift of tenants can be very considerable, due to intangible, prestige considerations.

Another expression of this concern with cachet, perhaps one of the few positive benefits of style, has been the recent craze for reusing buildings, particularly those of distinctive architectural style or historical association. Perhaps the earliest example occurred when Bonwit-Teller refurbished a dusty museum building in Boston to serve as a fashionable women's wear store. The most influential reuse was probably that of the Ghirardelli chocolate factory in San Francisco, which was turned into a shopping center in the early 1960's. The practice has been widely adopted elsewhere—Boston's old City Hall has been turned into restaurants and highly desired offices, and other old buildings have been intelligently transformed to a startling variety of uses for which they were not built. Along with the rush to new buildings, this shift to the distinctive and historically interesting old building has meant, however, that the "modern" office buildings of the 1930s, '40s, and '50s tend to show a high rate of discard in many cities. Will their time ever come?

Time has been an essential factor in the shaping of the downtown areas of most North American cities in the same way it has been in western Europe. North Americans tend to feel that their cities are distinctly different from those of Europe, and sharply to be distinguished from those places by newness. More careful analysis of the relationship between the two sides of the Atlantic shows that the contrast is not half so striking as it may seem at first. Cities in North America, particularly in French Canada or the United States, date from the seventeenth century, when Québec (1608), Albany (1624), New York (1626), Boston (1630), Hartford (1635), Providence (1636), New Haven (1638), Montréal (1642), Norfolk (1670), Philadelphia (1681), and Charleston (1688) were established. By the end of that century, several of the colonial towns ranked among the largest cities in the English realms, with Boston probably fourth or fifth in size of the towns under the British crown.

No very critical difference exists between the North American and the European cities, save for the presence or absence of a medieval core. These cores are missing in American cities, but they also are exceeding small and subsequently rather unimportant in a score of the larger cities of Europe—such as Birmingham, Manchester, Leeds, Berlin, Madrid, Brussels, Essen, Milan, and Livorno. In relation to current concerns, then, how different is the age of urbanization between Europe and America? The settlers in the New World had great experience with older cities; culturally, no break was produced by the seventeenth-century migrations across the sea.

Finally, if we examine the demographic history of most cities in Europe, we find the places very small, with less than five thousand population in all but a relatively few cases, until the year 1600. Growth tended to be rapid everywhere (in Europe as well as America) in the seventeenth, eighteenth, and nineteenth centuries.

It is important to establish the relatively strong identity of cities in western civilization if we wish to consider the general dynamics of growth in central districts of these cities, because the "historical" part of all cities now remains as little more than the core. Only London, Paris, and Milan were large enough in the Middle Ages to shape a pre-Commercial Revolution city greater than the extent of the present downtown. Elsewhere, what became the business district was the main substance of the medieval city.

Are there, then, stages, with associated processes, that account for the creation of the present city core? I believe there are, and that those stages can be seen in the history of European as well as American cities. Elsewhere I have sketched the "normal" course of evolution of the central business district,[11] and will now summarize those stages.

The seven processes at work in the shaping of the core area of cities begin, as might be expected, with the *process of inception*. As we have seen, the city plays many different roles, and cities are founded for a number of different reasons, even if caring for long-distance trade may be the dominant purpose they serve. As most cities quickly took on trading functions, the inception of the city core commonly came as a "business district" for all types of trade and the services soon called into being by that trading activity.

The location of the initial core of the city can be considered under the notion of the *point of attachment* of the city to a long-distance trading system. This relationship of the city to distant places and the movement of her merchants and traders among such economic partners make it essential to see the role of cities as more than that of serving the localized, natural economy (because most frequently the precise location of the original city can best be understood as a complex compromise between the needs of local defense and supply and the practice of distant trading).

The point of attachment is strongly affected by transportation technology. In the Roman world (the Roman road net in the interior and the rivers and coastal routeways) transportation was more externally oriented, and it fairly determined where the towns would be attached. This was no central-place system, but it was most assuredly a transportation-derivative system. With the collapse of the large empire, the desired points of attachment changed, most notably to elevate the role played by rivers. In the Middle Ages a river location became of surpassing importance; the river provided the only economically feasible transport in a time of political disintegration, with its accompanying neglect of roads used mainly in distant movement. The medieval city growing up for economic purposes, as opposed to those primarily for defense or religion, was so characteristically a river town that few controverting examples may

[11]*James E. Vance, Jr., "Focus on Downtown,"* Community Planning Review [*Canada*], *Vol. 16 (1966), pp. 9–15.*

be found. Bourges in central France, Aix-la-Chapelle in the Rhineland, and tiny Birmingham in the West Midlands of England might be notable exceptions.

Paul Mantoux and other historians concerned with the Industrial Revolution have rightly emphasized how much improvement in transportation was required before large-scale manufacture could be undertaken. That improvement came first in the amelioration of natural obstacles to river navigation, soon to be followed by the creation of artificial waterways, canals. With these transformations a new system on which points of attachment could be located came into existence. The change in the geographical pattern of cities was considerable; Birmingham, Sheffield, Leeds, and Bradford could grow to great size, as did Liège and Namur with the improvement of the Meuse. Particularly in America, the canal era provided a new system for attachment. Chicago is merely the largest of a network of cities that began as canal towns. Others are Ottawa, Cleveland, Buffalo, Toledo, in a special sense Pittsburgh, Cincinnati, and Evansville, and—through diversion of the effective mouth of the major river of the region—Boston and Charleston.

The railroad provided an even more ubiquitous net for such attachments, though its impact in America was infinitely greater than in Europe, where most of the possible city sites had already been taken up by the early nineteenth century when the railroads arrived. In the American interior the railroad initiated fewer towns than it ultimately came to sustain. Being a very easily expanded form of transportation, the railroad could readily be employed as a backstay for an already established but not prospering town. Chicago beat out St. Louis to become the metropolis of the interior by making more astute use of rail connections; Kansas City bested its Kansas rivals by building a railroad bridge across the Missouri River in 1869 and parlaying every possible rail connection that the mind might imagine. Again and again, the railroad provided a different system for attachment *to*, which plucked many plummeting cities from a grim destruction when their previous supports gave way.

Thus, the first process we need be concerned with in the shaping of the city core is its initiation, which carried with it a concern for the act of deciding upon a point of attachment to some extensive transportation system.

The second force that worked upon the city core was *the process of exclusion*. The early town would have small components of a number of different land-uses, sufficient for the time, but ultimately too small to serve and too much in the way to remain. As towns were so consistently trading places, merchants' houses commonly forced other activities toward the edge of the built-up area. This exclusion was less active during the Middle Ages, because the highly "efficient" system of urban land economics had not yet been fully developed, but it must have been present, as shown by the shifts in use that did transpire. As the modern city developed from the Industrial Revolution onward, the process of exclusion assumed major importance. Business districts grew by encroaching upon housing—thus functionally forcing it out—and transportation lines were cut through cities using this same process.

During the past hundred years, once any town has been founded, its residents commonly wait impatiently for growth to take place. Such an expansion occurs in the frame of the former town, and operates through the mechanism of the rent-gradient, under which a lot at the very heart of the city has the highest value and all lots grading out toward the edge of the city have successively less value. This gradient means that the location of any activity tends to be primarily determined by the rent-paying ability of the function. Similar activities tend to have similar abilities at rent-paying, so the high-rent area of the city tends to become ever more exclusive in its content. Notably, housing is pushed outward, and industry and wholesaling can remain at the center only in the depreciating zone of discard left in the wake of the geographical shift of the core of the downtown. The wholesalers probably could pay more for their location if it served any purpose for them to do so. But because so much of the wholesalers' business is conducted indirectly, through orders received by mail or phone, their physical site has nowhere near the same requirement for "centrality" as has the retailers'.

The result of this agency of exclusion, rent-paying ability, is the creation of the "downtown" or central business district as we know it. Before exclusion has time to accomplish its first resorting, the "town" and the "downtown" tend to be identical in area and somewhat unstructured. Once the grading mesh of rent has done its job, the central business district has both reality and structure, as retail trade and various service functions can buy the more elevated slopes of the rent-gradient, leaving for the manufacturers, wholesalers, and house-seekers the lower, less narrowly-limited slopes.

In the beginning, just after the preliminary sorting has taken place, the core tends to have a number of inherited buildings, built originally for housing, manufacturing, or wholesale trade. As these buildings are taken over by central business district functions, they may either enjoy a continued life with a new function in an old form, or they will be reconstructed, normally unit by unit, in form as well as function.

This evolution of central use and buildings must be distinguished from the revolution wrought by urban renewal. The evolution of the core of the city is tradi-

This etching of South Station, Boston, by Margaret Philbrick (1937) shows the conflux of public transportation that supported most large-city business districts. Shown are the station (at that time the busiest in the world), the elevated railway, and the subway system (the first to be built in the western hemisphere).

tionally a cell-by-cell replacement, similar to the process in wood petrification, while the revolution of the core destroys the structure of the past, reducing it to ash and a cleared site.

Because exclusion of noncentral functions is the result of a limitation in the supply of central land, evidence of the beginning of exclusion (as a structural dynamic) serves as a fair indicator of the shift of a city from a minor status to a major one, particularly as a regional trading center of wholesale and retail activity. The measure of a city may be taken by the prevalence of exclusion from various land-use districts. Exclusion stands as an essentially negative element in the shaping of the core; it throws things out but it does not in itself reform the structure of the city. But the same general forces that worked to reserve the downtown primarily for selling and service also worked to create a completely new structure within the core.

The third force at work in the creation of that core is the *process of separation*.[12] An important aspect of location is association. Most things in the city stand in relation to other things, and the links between things may be as important as the outright location. Thus, the tie between a shoe store and a department store assures that the shoe merchant will pay not only for a central site but also for a close linkage with a department store. Exclusion drives uses away from the center, but separation merely drives groups of uses apart when they seek to congregate either with their competitors or with complementary uses. The location of the group may be no farther from the center in separation and subsequent congregation than its individual members were before the split, but that group will occupy only a small sector of the core.

As the cluster of any particular type of activity in the core grows, the chances for separation increase. If one activity gains a very strong base—such as the financial service functions have in New York, the City of London, or San Francisco—it may so dominate an area that the other central functions move farther away. Financial activities took over lower Manhattan to such a degree that the shopping district moved first to 12th Street, then to 34th Street, and, currently, to 57th Street. In London the shops left the City to cluster in new quarters on Oxford Street or Knightsbridge. By 1970, San Francisco shops had moved well away from the financial district, leaving a zone between, into which that growing component of the city core, offices, could expand, as it has. We may conclude that separation takes place when the number of identical or related activities is sufficient to occupy a large enough area to make that part of the city center undesirable for unrelated or otherwise clustered activities.

This consideration of the dynamism of the city core leads directly to the fourth force at work there, the *process of extension*. We have noted the existence on the line of advance of the central business district of a zone of assimilation where buildings and areas formerly used by noncentral activities are being taken over by the advance of the growing center. The growth of the downtown through extension came when some things

[12]*A much more complete discussion of the process of separation and its pair, congregation, is contained in my introductory essay for Volume One of the Publications of the National Science Foundation Comparative Metropolitan Analysis Project, published by Ballinger Press in 1976. James E. Vance, Jr., "The American City: Workshop for a National Culture," in John Adams, ed.,* Contemporary Metropolitan America, *Cambridge: Ballinger Press, 1976.*

we now take for granted were new, and when cars made access to them more widespread. The sale of automobiles, of food in composite supermarkets, of meals and drinks outside central hotels, and of business machines and equipment were introduced in the dawn of intraurban mobility. New businesses tended to be set up on those streets that lay in the vanguard of the advance of the downtown—that is, in the zone of assimilation where the cachet of style was higher than the level of the rent. In the half century since the automobile really began to play a role in downtown areas, the arms of central use extending well beyond the previous limit imposed by pedestrian movement have grown long and strong. No longer may we think of the core as a completely compact area; along certain streets, distinct land-use districts represent separated clusters of activity, which may serve the whole metropolis and which are reached almost exclusively by auto transportation. Business services and equipment seek such locations, as do automotive sales.

As the city grows in size and becomes more populous, certain of the central functions begin to show up in outlying areas. These replicas occur most often in outlying shopping centers or in massive, detached headquarters in office blocks. In such a way there emerges the *process of competition* between the city core and possible replacement locations for its activities in other parts of the city. This process may actually cause a decline in the space needed at the center, even in a healthy, growing metropolis. Only if the functions that remain in the center grow apace, filling the space that becomes available through the process of competitive replication, will still another process at work on the core—the *process of readjustment*—be directly avoided.

Readjustment normally takes the form of decline in the economic value of the sites and their buildings to the extent that physical deterioration is allowed to begin to consume the buildings. At that time, the readjustment is physical as well as functional, and two ultimate courses seem foreordained: either a carefully-thought-out policy of use change will allow the buildings to regain a sufficiently valuable employment that they can be maintained from earnings, or the buildings will have to be pulled down. The current fashion for reused buildings makes the first alternative much more likely today than it was throughout much of the era of industrial cities. Even so, some buildings, for which no one can conceive of an economic use, will decay to the level they must be destroyed.

At that juncture one of the great quandaries facing cities becomes operative; seemingly, in urban areas, the space most in demand is empty land at the edge of the city, suitable for development. The absence of preexisting structures and fixed uses offers the developer both a handsome speculative development profit and the freedom to shift as the economic market for urban structures shifts. The search for open-space within the city has also concentrated at the edge, as has the concern for all other increments to the city; yet, as we have seen, the greatest likelihood of naturally occurring open-space is to be found at the center. But we cannot rid ourselves of the notion that the core of the city is a place where the scarcity of space makes any land too valuable to be opened anew as parks and playgrounds. If we were willing to let the land-rent system take its normal outcome, we might well find our cities opening up and "greening" at the center, where in truth we do have a great need for that change.

The difficulty of allowing the land-rent system to operate unfettered is that it might severely restrict the availability of property-tax funds in just that part of the metropolis that has inherited the greatest number and severity of social problems. Thus, planning has called for trying to reverse the trend by returning to the stage of initiation, when space was unfettered at the center and no ruling prior conditions could mess up the new uses. Under the *process of urban redevelopment*, land is cleared at the center, usually reassembled into large blocks, and sold at a massive discount to private developers who are restarting the development process in the city. The objective is not necessarily wrong, but the large subsidy to the wealthy developers, the heavy-handed and unyielding destruction that comes from complete clearing, and the loss of values—both human and morphological—through the bulldozing nature of urban redevelopment are unfortunate outcomes. One feels that if some solution other than the singleminded attempt to start the central-area development cycle all over again could be found, attempting smaller changes would be of greater virtue than larger changes.

Two ways to break out of the straitjacket of declining taxes and increasing social welfare demands seem possible. Those social welfare costs could be spread around "according to the ability to pay," by putting the housing for social welfare responsibilities in the taxing constituencies in proportion to their average wealth. This system would create great resistance, not in itself a fault, but it would also deal with the poor as pawns, which is unacceptable. The other solution would seem to avoid this cavalier attitude toward the desires of the poor while accomplishing the goal of assigning tax responsibility where it belongs. Broad taxing constituencies could be created where the ability of the wealthy suburbs to pay taxes could be matched with the responsibilities of the poorer inner cities to furnish social welfare. Certainly the metropolis would be the geographically smallest defensible taxing constituency, while the nation-state might not be too large. This plan

does not suggest that metropolitan government must be introduced or that the small-area government be abolished. It does propose that tax refuge from problems of metropolitan or national origin must be stamped out, and responsibility established to the level of society which produces such social welfare problems. At that point, the automatic and often cruel process of urban redevelopment could be reexamined to see how much it is needed in human and morphological terms, the main measure we should apply.

The Core of the City in Europe

The dynamics outlined so far have been particularly characteristic of Canadian and American cities and somewhat less valid for Europe, though the basic processes probably apply in any normal city on either continent. In Europe, the fact that the city core is also to a considerable degree the medieval city *in toto* means that the growth processes tend to be obscured by having taken place in the cell-by-cell replacement of medieval buildings, frequently located on burgage plots which preserve to the present certain aspects of the occupational household and its space needs. The fixity of the street pattern and the lot outlines, both of which are tied closely to the definition of land ownership, one of the most immutable features of urban form, is such that the freedom for modern development comes within very narrow spatial limits. Only when, as in the empire of Napoléon III, a massive transformation of the urban fabric is undertaken by the state will these medieval constraints disappear. But even in the Paris that Baron Haussmann built to Napoléon III's orders, the insides of blocks bounded by the major avenues and boulevards cut through the medieval city (which existed to that time) contain a fabric still suggestive of the distant past. The Marais district between the cleared site of the city markets (Les Halles) and the Place de la Bastille shows more of the Paris of Louis XIV than of Napoléon III. Because Paris was relatively so small in the Middle Ages, and now holds so very much that was built during the past hundred years, Parisians and their planners have felt a strong and conscious desire to rediscover, restore, and preserve this medieval or Renaissance district of Le Marais.

In most European cities, the modern needs were such that one of two things happened: either the

Passage de l'Opéra.   Café Mulhouse.   Opéra. Rue Drouot.   Jockey-Club.   Cercle Montmartre.

BOULEVARD DES ITALIENS (côté sud).

Rue Favart.   Opéra-Comique.   Rue Marivaux.   Café Anglais.   Rue de Grammont.   Bazar.

BOULEVARD MONTMARTRE (côté sud).   BOULEVARD DES ITALIENS (côté sud).

Rue Vivienne.   Maison Frascati.   Rue Richelieu.   Café Cardinal.

15 Cent. LA LIVRAISON. — 10ᵉ Livr.   Aux bureaux de l'Illustration, rue de Richelieu, 60.   TYP. DE FIRMIN DIDOT, RUE JACOB, 56.   20 C. par la poste.

Paris as rebuilt at the order of
Napoléon III by Baron Haussmann.

378   *Urban Form in the Modern World*

medieval core was so reworked in the nineteenth century as no longer to offer an impediment to the growth in size and variation in function, or the core for business purposes shifted elsewhere. In Paris a bit of each took place. The avenues that Haussmann opened, such as the Boulevard de Sebastopol, the Rue de Rennes, and the Boulevard Haussmann, served to connect the newly constructed railroad stations to important parts of the city, particularly the former core. Meanwhile, the center of gravity shifted from the area to the east of the Louvre—around the Hôtel de Ville and in the area of the Palais Royale—westward toward the newer constructions around the Avenue de l'Opera and the Place Vendôme, where the streets were generally wider and more direct in their routing.

In city after city this same pattern was followed. New sections were added in Lyon, Marseille, London, Brussels, and most other cities that grew rapidly during the nineteenth century. In this way the multi-centered core became more characteristic of European cities than of American ones, though New York developed along that line, and many cities in England and on the Continent had but a single continuous core. Where the core had separate parts, the shopping district strongly tended to occupy one and the office district the other, as in the financial district of Lower Manhattan and the shopping district of Midtown, the City in London and the West End shopping district, and in the greatly complex Paris, with department stores on both the Right and the Left Bank and shopping streets greatly distinguished by price class. But, if complexity in the core is more typical of Europe, it is most typical of the larger towns, with the medium and smaller cities generally having a single continuous shopping-office area. As in Rouen, that shopping area may occupy a medieval quarter and even medieval buildings; in Lyon, the two segments of the core occupy eighteenth- and nineteenth-century streets and buildings; in Bristol and Cologne, the shopping districts are of post-World War II construction due to bomb damage that removed previously medieval shopping quarters.

Tall buildings have been rare in Europe until very recently, and even now they are scattered, perhaps more commonly well away from the traditional core than in it. Instead functional separation has permitted a number of adjacent areas to operate reasonably successfully with pedestrial movement at a time when the total district would have been too large to be served in the same way. In part, the subway systems of London, Paris, Berlin, and Budapest were built around the turn of the century to permit a "pedestrian city" to continue to operate when only the construction of tall buildings (as in Chicago) would have allowed it to operate without transportation internal to the core itself.

In most European cities, class division in shopping is much more characteristic than in America, with the poorer classes getting by largely by patronizing local shops, leaving the great shopping streets and department stores to the middle classes. Similarly, the very wealthy would use a separate shopping system, such as that in the Faubourg St. Honoré or the Rue de Passy. The local shop still remains very important in the shopping pattern of Europe as much because of strong price maintenance practices as for any other reason.

The practice still remains among a number of professionals in Europe to maintain an office in their home, a practice which has largely gone out in America. Thus, in Paris or other Continental cities, lawyers, physicians, and even business firms often take premises in the middle of a basically residential quarter, leaving the office functions of the city core less numerous and certainly less obvious to the casual observer. The view we are presented when visiting the heart of a European city is one of shops almost exclusively in ground-floor space, save in the most elegant or impoverished residential quarters. There, more frequently than in America, small professional offices may occupy what are simply first-floor flats. In turn, the four to six floors of space above the shops may be given over to smaller office premises than are commonly to be found in the tall buildings of North America, or to hotels that "occupy" several floors of a building, rather than standing as a distinctive structure in the American fashion.

If we move out of the core area, the use of upper floors will change to permanent residence, but the buildings themselves will not be distinctly different in form from those at the center. The intense build-up of structures in the core is far less characteristic of European cities, but at the same time the number of stories of buildings in residential areas will normally average much higher there than in America. To a considerable degree, the build of the European city was set before all but a small minority had much access to mechanical transport within the city, so the coverage of land came at about the maximum height possible before mechanical elevators were commonly used. Even after they came into use, the pattern established in the early Industrial Era tended to be continued until the last ten to twenty years, when emulation of America and planning beliefs in the ultimate shortage of building space led to the introduction of the skyscraper to Europe.

The skyscraper in a European city has been employed in a very different geographical pattern from that found across the Atlantic. In America skyscrapers began as a means of making growing cities viable while mechanical transport was still in shortage, or in situations where a functional district became too large to be walked about unless tall buildings were built. The financial districts of Chicago and New York, the hotel sections of most large cities, and the premises of large

Rue de la Paix, place et colonne Vendôme.

BOULEVARD DES ITALIENS (côté sud).   BOULEVARD DES CAPUCINES (côté sud).

Rue de Choiseul.   Bains chinois.   Rue de la Michodière.   Pavillon de Hanovre.   Rue Louis-le-Grand.

BOULEVARD DES ITALIENS (côté nord).

Café de Paris.   Rue Taitbout.   Tortoni.   Maison-Dorée.   Rue Laffitte.   Café Riche.   Rue Lepelletier.

The Rue de la Paix and Boulevard des Italiens were among the most fashionable streets under the Second Empire.

department stores were all built upward to care for concentrated demands by greater numbers. Only in the case of the department store did Europe follow a similar practice. Europe had fewer highly integrated concentrations of offices, though not by any means fewer offices, and hotels were small in the number of rooms and far less a feature of European than American cities. The dominance of so many countries in Europe by their capital city, the generally less mobile nature of the population, and the much narrower spectrum of the population that might afford the luxury of travel and of

overnight accommodations all kept the supply of hotel rooms smaller in European cities.

Paris invented the department store in the 1840's, when the Bon Marché grew to be a true example of the diverse seller: but Boston invented the modern hotel. The Tremont House was the first hotel clearly built for transients and possessed of the general features we still associate with such accommodations: a considerable number of rooms, dining facilities, space for public assemblies, and something European hotels were very slow in adopting—bathrooms. As James

The Bon Marché is considered the first department store, opening in Paris in 1852. It is shown here in a photograph from 1857.

Marston Fitch notes, the Industrial Era in America introduced a number of new building forms: "Typical of these was the great metropolitan hotel, a type which appeared in full flower with Boston's Tremont House" of 1828-29.[13]

We will not add further to the distinctions drawn between European and American city cores. The differences are considerable but the processes at work seem shared across the ocean. In part, difference of staging in city growth made the differences as great as they are. Where new starts have had to be made in Europe—as in the cities severely damaged by bombing in the Second World War—the results have been similar indeed, supporting the view that the processes of morphogenesis are the common property of western civilization. But the site on which they are brought to bear can differ not merely by political and geographical distinctions, but by the nature of the prior settlement on which the processes must work. In America only a very small number of places had much development before the Industrial Revolution, so only in that handful of places is the comparison with Europe very genuine or meaningful.

A Metropolitan Pattern of Wholesaling

In the medieval city the merchants, who were primarily wholesalers, commonly lived and traded in the center of the town in houses near the marketplace. As we have seen, events consequent upon the Industrial Revolution began to change the location desires of wholesalers. In large measure this change was a positive response to the rapid growth of the money economy which threw ever larger parts of the working population into a position of having to buy virtually all their needs. They might well have to turn to normal wholesaling-retailing channels to secure for their own use even the products they were producing in the mills. I would argue that wholesaling was always the dominating element in trade; it merely became even more commanding and extensive with the shaping of an industrial society, wherein even the farmers would find it hard to subsist on their own production. The

industrialization of life certainly led directly to the commercialization of farming; now all elements of society were forced into a money economy and the consequent dependence upon established channels of trade, notably those of the wholesaler. The farmer would sell his goods directly to wholesaling firms and would buy his seed, chemicals, and many other requisites directly from them. Thus, large customers might achieve short-circuiting of the retailer, but little likelihood existed that the wholesaler could be effectively circumvented.

Thus the Industrial Revolution elevated the role of wholesaling fully as radically and rapidly as it did that of manufacturing. To produce goods in mass quantities meant the creation of agencies to distribute those goods to a mass market, necessarily geographically dispersed. The rise in the scale of wholesaling was great, and the need for the relocation of this activity away from its traditional center placement was considerable. No doubt at first the pressure to move was only modest; expanding the size of the building in which the trade was carried on might well suffice for another generation in the traditional location. We know that wholesalers remained in the heart of the city, often combining a growing wholesale trade with a growing retail trade. In the long run, the scalar expansion of both retail and wholesale trade seems to have made necessary the separation of the two functions and a congregation of each in a new clustering.

The history of Marshall Field as a retailer-wholesaler in Chicago serves as a case in point. Field took over a combined operation from Potter Palmer in 1865 at a stage in the commercial development of Chicago when merchants were loath to place all their faith in either retailing or wholesaling.[14] For many years thereafter, Field maintained both a retail and a wholesale department, but by the early seventies they were separated in location. The retail store led the shift of Chicago shopping from Lake Street, where it began alongside the noisome Chicago River, to a widened State Street where the focus has rested until today, though doubtless it will not remain there much longer. A comparison of the locations of the two departments is interesting. State Street was adjacent both to the elevated lines and to the Illinois Central Railroad tracks on the east side of the central district. The wholesale department came to occupy one of the seminal architectural structures of the nineteenth century—Henry Hobson Richardson's wholesale house, constructed in 1887 on the full block bounded by Adams Street, Quincy Street, Franklin Street, and Fifth Av-

[13]*James Marston Fitch*, American Building: The Historical Forces That Shaped It, *Boston: Houghton Mifflin Company, 1966, p. 122.*

[14]*Lloyd Wendt and Herman Kogan*, Give the Lady What She Wants! The Story of Marshall Field & Company, *Chicago: Rand McNally & Company, 1952, p. 67.*

enue on the west side of the loop near the Chicago River amid the greatest cluster of railroad stations in this city, now the world's greatest rail hub. In such a split of location we can see the basic elements that were repeated over and over again throughout America, and only somewhat less frequently in Europe.

The great scalar increase in wholesaling, along with the transformation of transportation, made a new location for wholesaling a necessity. Wholesalers had always demonstrated the ability to expand their market area in a fashion utterly untypical of retail trade; thus when the railroad lowered the cost of goods transport and provided an integrated net of lines extending over a quarter of a million miles in the United States, the wholesaler was presented with an opportunity he was able to exploit if he would. Marshall Field and a hundred others of similar stripe demonstrated how wide an area a wholesaler might dominate—in Field's case, the whole interior of the United States in some lines of goods—and therefore what large premises were needed. To have continued the physical association of retailing and wholesaling was simply not practical. In the late nineteenth century, most joint wholesale-retail operations were abandoned in favor either of specialization on one or the other, or, as in Field's case, through the creation of what were essentially parallel firms with distinctive locations, each within the congregation of establishments distinctive either to retailing or to wholesaling.

Can we then generalize about the location of wholesale trading in American cities? I have done so in *The Merchant's World: The Geography of Wholesaling*.[15] When the separation of wholesaling and retailing became clear-cut by the 1880's and '90s, the former merchants showed a strong attachment to the city's rail facilities. In the late nineteenth century, the shipment of goods took two basic forms: carload lots were dispatched from one shipper to another, normally a manufacturer to a wholesaler but on occasion from a wholesaler to a large retailer; or shipping was by packages, sent particularly by "express company" or by railroads accepting less-than-carload-lot shipments. Because wholesalers normally had to send goods to their customers in less-than-carload lots, the location of express offices and freight stations became critical location factors in the siting of their warehouses. When the shopping district tended to move away from the riverfront, as in Chicago's shift from Lake to State Street, or the railroad passenger terminal, as was almost universally the case, the land

left in the zone of discard became highly usable for wholesale warehouses. Freight stations and express offices were normally nearby, while railroad sidings could be led directly to the unloading doors of the warehouse for receipt of carloads of goods from the manufacturers.

This *railroad station district* location for warehouses became the first "typical" site in American and Canadian cities. A number of towns still have massive quarters of five- and six-story buildings filling whole blocks and served by railroad sidings. Omaha, Kansas City, Chicago, Denver, Dallas, and Winnipeg—each made a major city by the coming of railroads—show clearly such late-nineteenth-century districts. Even in London and Paris, the warehouse location is not unknown, as demonstrated along the lines out of the Gare du Nord and Gare de Lyon in Paris and those adjacent to Paddington and Euston in London. Because in the interior cities of North America the railroad came essentially contemporaneously with the first startling growth of the town, the warehouse districts are compact, coherent, and generally very central in location. In Europe, the railroads came much later in the morphological history of the city. Thus the warehouses are more spread around the city, generally less continuous in area even along a single rail line, and certainly not so obvious a feature of the urban landscape.

To this point, we have treated all wholesaling districts as the same, yet we know that that is hardly the case. A number of districts depend upon "customer access" in ways similar to those true of the central shopping district. Unlike the conditions in the shopping district, in wholesaling access to what might be termed professional shoppers is what matters. As an example, we may take the produce wholesaling district of the city.

There, chefs from restaurants, small retailers from the central city, the purchasing agents for institutions, and the agents of large, more distant customers come together to buy perishable produce whose price is strongly influenced by an auction market adjusted to conditions of supply and demand. Because the goods cannot be kept, because describing their quality is difficult, because suppliers as well as customers are likely to be numerous, the auction market with most customers participating is a critical feature of successful buying and selling of produce. The result was that, in the late-nineteenth-century city, the produce market was quite centrally located, often near the railroad yards or the city's wharves. In the case of Les Halles in Paris and Covent Garden in London, even these good transportation links were at some distance away from the produce market, but the customers were located close by and were commonly best served at locations that now seem badly availed by distant transport. Only

[15]James E. Vance, Jr., The Merchant's World: The Geography of Wholesaling, *Englewood Cliffs, N.J.: Prentice-Hall, Inc., 1970. Specific reference is made to Chapter Six, "Wholesaling within Cities, A Brief Postscript."*

as the number of central-city customers has declined in favor of larger and more distant purchasers have the markets moved out to Rungis or the south bank of the Thames.

Other *customer-access wholesaling districts* occur in cities. Commonly, a cluster of establishments serve the remaining artisan groups at work there—the plumbers, carpenters, and other building trades; the automobile repair shops; the electrical and other repair facilities. In these trades, the need for parts and items used for work is great but the capital available to the artisan is usually small, and the ability to stock the "right" part is limited. What we might call *stockroom wholesalers* cluster near them, whose sale of items to artisans makes the workers' trade possible.

The *product-comparison district* is another example of necessary customer access even within wholesaling, and one particularly characteristic of the clothing and furniture trades. In each, the buyers for stores go to a fairly narrowly defined area in a particular city seeking to compare the products offered by different manufacturers and their agents. New York's garment district in the thirties of midtown Manhattan is a classic example, which shows the associated features of bars and entertainment places, hotels, and theaters that seem allied to a wholesale market drawing buyers from distant places. Furniture marts in Grand Rapids, Chicago, High Point (North Carolina), and San Francisco demonstrate the same specialized clustering of wholesal-ers' establishments, in these instances mainly in massive buildings constructed specially to house the exhibits of a number of manufacturers and their agents. One of these, the Merchandise Mart constructed in Chicago in the late 1920's, was, until the Pentagon was built during the Second World War, the largest building in the world.

Several other customer-comparison districts can be found in American cities. The recent proliferation of record labels as well as the very high component of "timeliness" in recordings has meant that most large cities have clusters of phonograph record wholesalers where retail dealers can quickly replenish their depleted stocks to meet a larger or an unexpected demand for a particular "hit." In certain manufacturing districts of the city, notably those making clothing, clusters of wholesalers will sell the findings and buttons used in cutting and tailoring. Because of the great array of shades and hues used in clothing, no one manufacturer could hope to stock the thread, binding, buttons, and other findings to be used in a normal season's manufacture. In printing areas, the availability of paper of different size, weight, finish, and color poses a similar problem which is met by having specialized paper wholesalers who serve all printing establishments, so that those manufacturers need not provide their own stocks for unexpected needs.

In a number of other wholesaling operations, complexity of demand and specialization of need has

H. H. Richardson's great mercantile building, Field's Wholesale House, was constructed between 1885 and 1887 to provide for the separation of Marshall Field's wholesaling business from that of his retail store. Perhaps no other American building in the last century was as admired and copied, showing up in Richardsonesque wholesaling establishments in cities from Boston to Los Angeles.

meant that wholesalers must be fairly approachable by their customers. In electronics, business machines, computer machines and "software," and a number of other highly technical demands, the potential customer often wishes to view the product before buying. Unlike the style-conscious clothing and furniture trades, where being at the height of fashion is critical and therefore buyers must congregate seasonally in one of a small number of style centers, in these technical fields, ease and frequency of access count. Thus the business machine, electronics, and computer companies have among the most extensive networks of manufacturer's sales agencies.

Some central-area wholesalers deal only in the titles to goods, selling a product unseen to be shipped directly to the customer from the manufacturing plant. Such fully defined *manufacturers' sales agencies* commonly occupy general space in the office part of the central business district. As that area normally has unusually good communications facilities, as well as broad-ranging customer access, the office district is their best location for serving as a go-between for the customer—many of whom would call in orders but some of whom would visit the sales office—and the manufacturer located at some distance from the city.

The same dynamism that first led to the separation of retailing and wholesaling, and which drew the warehouse congregation toward the rail terminals of the cities, ultimately caused that clustering to move out of the city core. The motor truck probably affected the geographical pattern of wholesaling more than any other economic activity in the city. Once trucks came into wide use, wholesaling firms found that outlying sites were far more economical for their purposes. Single-story construction on ample lots was cheaper than the multistory construction required when firms clustered into a wholesaling district near the downtown. With single-story buildings the palletizing and mechanical handling of goods became feasible, adding another economy, as well as scale-increases in their operations. An ideal site might be gained for wholesaling of bulky commodities (sold by abstract orders secured either by phone or by traveling salesmen) at the junction of major arterial highways and major rail lines. As cities developed circumferential by-pass roads, the crossing of these with the rail lines entering the metropolis became a particularly favored site where boxcars could be spotted easily by the railroad company and the trucks of the wholesaler could be rapidly underway in the distribution of sales to distant cities. Even within the city where the firm was located, distribution from the edge inward was frequently quicker and easier than from the center outward. The food-wholesaling firms, particularly the great distribution warehouses of chain stores, saw the greatest virtue in these outlying warehouses, though other mass distributors using distant ordering joined in the movement out of the city core.

The Mail Order House and Its Location

In the years just after the First World War, a specialized form of "wholesaling-retailing" grew up in a string of American cities. The great warehouses of the mail-order firms—Montgomery Ward and Sears, Roebuck—were located toward the edge of the city at this time. The explanation for this form was complex, but one of the key elements was the institution of rural free delivery and parcel post; parcels could be sent through the mails to customers located at a great distance from the warehouse. These warehouses could be freed of their previous reliance on express shipment. Not only did the volume of sales vastly increase, but the warehouses could be moved away from the center, so long as they could be furnished postal facilities on their new site.

After 1945 the creation of small mail-order retailing firms, particularly in the exurban environs of the large eastern cities, added the trading in often highly specialized, and expensive, items to what had initially been a postal purchase of rather basic and workaday commodities. Many magazines seem to subsist on advertising for such exurban mail-order firms, replacing the catalogues of Ward's or Sears. The general principle that we should note is that parcel post, introduced by Postmaster General Wannamaker, gave much greater choice of distribution sites than had been possible with express shipments, previously the main means of distributing relatively small bundles of goods. With parcel post at work, a wholesaler could operate anywhere there was a U.S. Post Office. Given the political nature of that bureau, operation was possible wherever any appreciable clustering of people occurred. Only the cheapness of distributing goods in their own trucks acted as a strong force to hold those distribution warehouses near large metropolitan cities.

In recent years the American pattern of wholesaling has been further elaborated with the creation of a series of planned "industrial parks" where small to medium-sized firms can set up warehouses with considerable ease. In many of these industrial parks, the main tenants are in fact wholesalers. The relatively low employment totals found in wholesaling in addition to the advantage gained in so transportation-oriented an undertaking by good planning of access, rail lines, parking facilities, and wide streets have encouraged such location.

Firms engaged in distribution also are very sensitive to the local level of taxation. With sometimes vast inventories of goods, personal property taxation affects them critically. Thus many wholesalers have been more interested in the local tax rates than in any other consideration, scrapping all the vaunted advantages of being close to a major market or well sited on freeways or rail lines in favor of a low tax bill. The considerable development of wholesaling in Reno can be explained by the fact that Reno and Nevada have adopted very low rates of personal property taxation; with these, they are the closest "tax refuge" to the burgeoning northern California market. Connected to Sacramento and the Bay Area City (that continuous metropolitan area which completely surrounds San Francisco Bay as well as much of San Pablo Bay) by a major interstate highway and a mainline railroad, many wholesalers find it cheaper to send their goods onward to their customers from 200 miles away, rather than storing those goods nearby in a city and state with high taxation.

Industry Within the Metropolis

The modern city, though very much the product of the Industrial Revolution, is not specifically the product of local industrialization. Some great cities of the world are heavily industrialized—Chicago is the most notable example—but in a goodly number, factories play a relatively minor role, as in the Bay Area City that surrounds San Francisco Bay. The general quickening of economic activity, the rapid turn to the money economy, and the increasing importance of transportation and financial and supervisory activities that the turn to industry brought, all served to enlarge and elaborate the structure of cities even in the absence of local industry.

As we have seen in the last chapter, the construction of early factories often came in the countryside, more likely so in the United States, France, or Belgium than in Britain, but not uncommonly in all industrializing countries. As a result, two rather distinct location analyses of industrial location are possible—one for the national pattern, and another for the siting within cities. The main body of the literature concerns the first of those analyses with notable contributions by Alfred Weber, August Lösch, Allan Pred, and others.[16]

Location within the city has by comparison received relatively slight attention, with the major work available being Edgar M. Hoover and Raymond Vernon's *Anatomy of a Metropolis*.[17] The most notable locational feature that Hoover and Vernon found was the decline of central-city employment in manufacturing. "In some cases these relative declines have been so marked as to emulate Manhattan's pattern and to produce an absolute decline in number of jobs. In the period from 1947 to 1954, for instance, this has been the case for Boston, Philadelphia, Chicago, Detroit, Pittsburgh, St. Louis, and San Francisco."[18] Quite logically, they conclude that the forces at work in Manhattan are not unique to that city.

The cause for the outward shift is perhaps most frequently termed as "the search for space" in an argument that the central city is too crowded for modern industry. That search is related to "One of the most universal changes in factory processes over the past 30 or 40 years [which] has been the widespread introduction of continuous-material-flow systems and of automatic controls in processing."[19] Currently, because of these changes, the "common practice in many lines of manufacture [is] to find a site which imposes the least possible restraints on the shape of the structure; to plan a production layout suitable for modern processes; and then to wrap the building around the layout." In such a situation, "the shape and size of city block grids. . .have become a powerful restraint on fac-

[16]*Alfred Weber*, Theory of the Location of Industries, *Chicago: University of Chicago Press, translated with an introduction and notes by Carl J. Friedrich, 1929; August Lösch, The Economics of Location, New Haven: Yale University Press, translated by William H. Woglam and Wolfgang F. Stolper, 1954; and Allan R. Pred, The Spatial Dynamics of U.S. Urban Industrial Growth, 1800–1914, Cambridge: M.I.T. Press, 1966; Edgar M. Hoover, The Location of Economic Activity, New York: McGraw-Hill Book Company, 1948.*

[17]*Edgar M. Hoover and Raymond Vernon*, Anatomy of a Metropolis, *presents the main locational findings of the New York Metropolitan Regional Plan study conducted in the late 1950's. Also in the series is Roy B. Helfgott, W. Eric Gustafson, and James M. Hund, Made in New York. All the volumes were published by the Harvard University Press.*

[18]*Hoover and Vernon*, Anatomy of a Metropolis, *Garden City: Doubleday Anchor Books, 1962, p. 24.*

[19]*Ibid., p. 27.*

tory location." Not only has demand increased for unfettered space, but an absolute increase in the space requirements per employee has also occurred. In the New York Metropolitan Region, "pre-1922 plants stand on 1,040 square feet of plot space per worker, while the plants built from 1922 to 1945 occupy 2,000 square feet and those built after 1945 occupy 4,550 square feet of plot space per worker."[20]

This general trend suggests that the town-country relations in manufacturing have been very different from those associations in other economic and residential activities found commonly in both areas. In the early stages of industrialization, factories were located in the countryside mainly to obtain waterpower. In America, notably New England, a considerable body of segmental labor was also made available as the productivity and comparative advantage of New England farms declined after the opening of the Erie Canal in 1825. First the spinsters and then the sons of farmers went to work in the factories, so the "labor problem" was not great until the middle of the century or later. At that time it was discovered that the main increment to factory workers was coming from immigrants—from Europe in the cities and from French Canada in rural or small-city New England. This flood of potential workers drew some industries to the city, along with the improving and ramifying rail lines which could bring coal and raw materials as well to the city as the countryside, and in turn could distribute their product to a thousand towns and a million farms. The late nineteenth century was the era of city industrialization when the relative positions of town and country were reversed and the great industrial proletariat of cities created. So long as processes were individualized and heavily labor-intensive, the cities held the edge over the country. But with the trends Hoover and Vernon noted, the balance returned to the rural or at least outer suburban areas.

Transportation went along with manufacturing technology as a great force for change. "The search for space, in 1860 or 1960, has always been conditioned by the manufacturer's need to assemble his materials and distribute his goods at reasonable cost. If the railroad and the truck had never been invented, America's manufacturing centers would have developed very differently. Great multistoried factories would probably have lined the nation's riverbanks in order to hold down transport costs."[21] But railroads were invented long before good and cheap internal transport was available to passengers within cities. This technological disparity in timing forced the creation of the large city slum and the industrial satellite located some distance outside the nineteenth-century city. The slum was the way workers could be housed within walking distance of mass employment within the city; the satellite was the alternative solution for a factory that could remain reasonably self-contained and at a distance from the central city. For those trades depending upon seasonal expansion of employment, the city was essential, as it was for those trades (such as clothing manufacture) that depended upon subcontracting, style, and factor-financing of production. In other instances, as in the hosiery industry of Reading (Pennsylvania) where style and factor-financing were perhaps less critical, the necessary female segmental labor force could be secured in a small city, surrounded by coal mines and an excess of male employment.

So long as water transport was the controlling form, as it was before about 1840, a riverfront or canal-front factory siting was characteristic. "At that time, the Manhattan shores of the Hudson River and the East River were lined with shipbuilding, slaughtering, grease-rendering, and soap-making plants, with iron works, engine works, and plants of many other kinds." Brooklyn's waterfront was similarly lined, as were the banks of the Morris Canal in Newark and the shores of Long Island Sound in Bridgeport and of the Hudson in Yonkers and Poughkeepsie.[22] Every important manufacturing city in America before the Civil War was strongly characterized by such factory alignments, as around Boston and Baltimore harbors, lining the Chicago River and its several branches, fronting on the Ohio River in Cincinnati and Louisville and the Mississippi in St. Louis, and the small industrial towns upriver from it. Even San Francisco industry, when it sprang up in 1848-1849, lined the Yerba Buena Cove and North Beach.

In the beginning, railroads did not much change this alignment because they were built first to serve existing shippers. We should not forget that the Boston and Lowell was the first well-financed railroad to be finished in the United States, and that heavy construction and easy availability of capital came because Lowell provided the certain market and the Boston Associates and their business allies furnished the capital to build a proper and enduring double-track line. But once the original and established shippers had been served, the railroads' common practice was to build branch and spur tracks to open new land and to try sometimes to divert shipments from a rival line. "The advent and spread of railroad spurs in the [New York Metropolitan] Region had two major effects on the location of plants: plants were freed from waterside locations and were allowed to spread out from the old cities into the surrounding towns; and the New Jersey side of

[20]Loc. cit.
[21]Op. cit., p. 32.

[22]Loc. cit.

the Region obtained a major transport advantage over the New York side." Because of the barrier of the Hudson River, nine intercity railroad lines had their termini in New Jersey but only three in New York City, and one of these, the Long Island Railroad, was by far the most deadended of all American lines. New Jersey then gained the advantage of better transportation to add to its existing advantage of greater proximity to the main body of American markets and to the coal fields which increasingly provided the power for industry. Until the 1920's, New Jersey had two coal-carrying canals—the Morris, and the Delaware and Raritan—to add further to its locational advantage.

The conditions found with respect to wholesaling when trucks came into general use also obtained in manufacturing. "Beginning about 1920, as this new mode began to be adopted for haulage inside the large metropolitan areas, additional forces favoring the newer areas were set in motion. Now a quicker and more flexible means existed for moving bulky goods for short distances, reducing the disadvantages of settling away from the railroad lines and harbor piers."[23] Factories could now be built not merely in suburbs and satellites but as well on sites unserved by rail lines.

Particularly for those plants producing small and fairly valuable items, bringing in the materials by truck and sending on the products by truck was entirely practical. Trucking worked in two ways to encourage manufacturers to locate factories outside the central cities. Initially, it offered a greater freedom in the choice of the place they might engage in manufacturing. Subsequently, as traffic on the obsolescent central-area streets became snarled, it made the shift almost essential.[24] Time taken to enter the central city could be costly both in the tying up of equipment and the paying of truck drivers, who were far more costly per ton of goods carried than were the railroad engineers and firemen who had previously done the job.

The greatest impact of the truck has been visited upon those industries selling most of their product fairly locally. "The industries which ship to local customers are a familiar group; they include such establishments as newspapers, bakeries, breweries, bottling works, and milk plants. Their distribution problem typically has two aspects: deliveries must be closely timed at the peril of missing sales; and the cost of transport must be held to a minimum because of the comparatively low value of the delivered product."

The Ford Motor Company's River Rouge Plant was the first of the giant integrated manufacturing plants that created a total separation of housing and workplace.

[23]Ibid., *pp. 34–35.*

[24]Loc. cit.

Newspapers have continued to locate near the central business district—though that practice has begun to change, as the relocation of the *Boston Globe* shows. The other local-consumption manufacturers have found that they need a site which produces the minimum aggregate distribution cost, usually in the central city but hardly in its core. Newspapers will probably also come to such a location, as the delivery cost continues to rise as a proportion of the total production cost. The main problem in resolving this point of minimum distribution cost is that the size, area, and settlement pattern of the city are all changing, in turn producing a changing answer to the question of where the minimum distribution point is.

Another dynamic that has affected the intrametropolitan location of manufacturing is the differential in wages. Until the advent of massive unionization of labor in the 1930's, distinct contrasts were common in wage levels even within a metropolis. The central city was commonly organized before the suburbs or the industrial satellites so the differential worked as an additional incentive for out-movement. Today, that differential is not likely to be very great within a metropolis, but interregional contrast is still considerable, with the South and Southwest characterized by considerably lower wage levels than the Northeast and eastern Middle West. Still a net migration moves from the highly-paid to the less-paid regions. Within metropolises the movement is also present, but for somewhat different reasons. Within the metropolis, the greater attraction of the outlying areas as a residential site makes recruiting workers there sometimes easier than in the city. Particularly in skilled and scientific trades, the appeal of suburban or even country living is enough in some cases to make firms seek locations in those areas in order to find the class of worker they wish.

Hoover and Vernon in their study of New York found that smaller firms within a specific type of manufacturing were more likely to locate near the city core than were their larger competitors. This contrast came from the greater need for services external to the firm in the smaller establishments. Over the nearly twenty years since their studies, this factor has assumed less importance because mergers and "take overs" by large firms have been frequent. The small firm has no less need for those external services, but considerably fewer small firms exist today than even a score of years ago. And the *raison d'etre* of most mergers, to gain access to more capital, has further encouraged the outward shift of production to new plants with adequate space, more mechanized and automatic production lines, and, in a number of instances, a location well away from the original home of the firm in states possessed of cheaper labor and lower tax levels. Because most central cities have become the highest taxers, they have been par-

ticularly shunned in the construction of new plants, further elevating the taxes that must be levied there to meet the ever-growing social welfare cost imposed upon the city as the nation's place of acculturation and social refuge.

The simple notion of a return of industry to the countryside would be too inclusive to be fully true: the notion of the exodus of large amounts of industry from the central city is not. Today the factory is as suburban as everything else, save for the rather specialized plants that occupy rather traditional sites. These depend heavily upon the congregation of plants in the same line—as in the garment trade—or of those serving the same group of central-city customers—as in printing, baking, and other consumer goods. If the political limits of the central city are extensive, as in Houston, Los Angeles, or New York City, many of the suburban-type factories may actually be located within the municipality. In other cases where the limits are tight—in Boston, San Francisco, and St. Louis, for example—the seeming flight of manufacturing will be exaggerated. In all cities, the pattern of morphological change is fairly similar.

In the years since the Second World War, a new and distinctive transportation system has been created, as different from the traditional city street pattern as were the railroads. Starting in Boston in the late 1940's, the practice of building circumferential or by-pass highways around cities has taken hold, providing a new set of distant connections for sites in open country around the city. Massachusetts Route 128 furnished the first clear indication that the desired post-war factory site was where rail and freeway came together with plenty of land and the possibility in adjacent areas for large increments of tract housing capable of sheltering a considerable workforce. Workers were encouraged to migrate—not for great distances, but internally within the metropolis.

The chance for a new blue-collar life-style was a not unimportant consideration in the appeal of this type of factory employment. For many workers, taking up residence in industrial suburbia represented a much-sought-after escape from the crowding and deterioration of the central-city working-class quarters; for others from the surrounding rural areas, it represented a shift to "the modern way of life" that was suburban in its popular expression.[25]

In morphological terms, the siting of industry in the suburbs of the metropolitan city and in a location in the satellites some miles from the metropolis is little dif-

[25]*For this, see the following section dealing with residential land use and Bennett M. Berger's* Working-class Suburb: A Study of Auto Workers in Suburbs, *Berkeley: University of California Press, 1960.*

ferent from its location in the smaller cities and towns of the Manufacturing Belt of the Middle West; all these areas represent small-city, nativist America. The popular press, women's and household magazines, and the general social institutions of the United States and Canada tended in the post-war years to treat such an environment as the norm for man and an improvement over a more definitely urban or rural past. Critics differ in their viewpoint; I would argue that despite its faults, this small-city nativist America was better than the past. And doubtless most people wanted it to exist, as we shall see.

In western Europe the same general forces were at work as in America, though the more recent changes lagged a little behind North America, just as North America was behind Europe in the earlier shifts in location. In the earlier phases of industrialization, factories and cities were intimately associated in Europe. There, far more surplus labor was available in cities than in the country, and the use of steam rather than water-power was greater, allowing the taking of the factory to the existing city. Often a larger scale of production occurred at an early time than in America, such that if the factory did not move to the town, as it did not in the West Riding of Yorkshire, a city grew up around the factory sites.

Mobility for workers was, until very recently, perhaps the last ten years, far lower in Europe than in America. The high cost of intraurban transport kept most workers on foot until well into this century, and the low wage expectations in comparison with the cost of automobiles kept them on bicycles and trolleys or buses until the 1960's. This "immobility" was joined by conscious national housing policies in Britain, France, Scandinavia, and Germany which envisaged housing workers in large blocks of flats close to the traditional sites of factories within the city itself. The juxtaposition of housing and production was much slower in changing in Europe than in America; the "garden city" of great parochial fame, for example, was more a radical proposal than a reality until the late 1920's, and even then it remained a strongly working-class compound shunned by the upwardly mobile population to whom the acceptance of housing in a Council Estate that became the public housing project in Britain was an admission of defeat. So long as workers lacked individual mobility, the Council Estates became a form of central-city housing to care for central-city factories, and other employers of physical labor.

Only in the years after the Second World War was there striking change in the location of factories. The considerable destruction of plants through bombing, the rise in scale of production, the modernization of processes, and most notably the tremendous increase in the use of motor trucking for the transport of materials and products all encouraged the outward shift of plants, found a generation earlier in America. Today, though the central parts of European cities still hold more manufacturing premises than do American central cities, the larger, more modern, and more significant plants in both areas have taken toward the edge of the city.

Europe tends to divide somewhat along transportation lines. Belgium and France continue to use canals to a greater degree than Britain. Germany comes only slightly behind her immediate neighbors. On the Continent the railroads assume moderate importance as freight-haulers, though trucking seems to be gaining at a fairly rapid rate. In Britain, it may surprise some to note, the truck is god. More than 90 per cent of the intercity transport of goods is by truck, a figure vastly greater than in the United States.[26] The result has been peculiar indeed. In Britain the use of trucking has seemingly permitted the maintenance of older plants, with perhaps rather unfortunate consequences when it comes to international competition, because a truck can reach essentially any plant and in turn bring materials from any source and distribute goods to any market. The befouling of the British highways by diesel fumes is appalling even to a Californian. Conservationist land-use policies, as exercised by planning agencies, may have encouraged this maintenance of past location practices. Certainly the freeway (motorway) policy adopted by post-war British governments has furthered that trend by making highway transportation easier, and trucking more appealing.

A further contrast between Europe, particularly Britain, and America comes in the matter of the "suburbanization of industry." Because suburbs have been rather severely restrained by the planning establishments of most west European nations, no place remains in which to carry out this dispersion. Europe has tended to view the countryside in a highly traditional, rather elitist fashion, reserving it for the agriculturalist and the prosperous. The result seems to have been a repression of the technological urges to disperse found in American manufacturing. As we have seen, this repression has been secured at the cost of a radical transformation of the more-efficient into the less-efficient modes of transporting goods. One can only wonder whether some of the seemingly insoluble British economic problem does not come from such doctrinaire land-use planning, constraining the location of factories but improvidently freeing the highway to oversized trucking, itself an inflationary force as the mainstay of the manufacturing economy.

[26]*In 1970 in the United States railroads still carried nearly twice as much volume as trucks (39.97 per cent to 21.44 per cent), while inland waterways approached trucks (15.98 per cent) and pipelines surpassed them (22.43 per cent). Even air transport carried a measurable percentage (0.176).*

Evolution of the Residential Structure

The main constituent of most urban structures is housing. In that fact lies the difficult problem that residential land-use poses when we seek concise generalizations. Not only is housing the largest user of urban land, but also in housing we find the greatest nonrational complex of qualities. Houses are intensely cultural creations, reflective of men's psychological and historical imperatives fully as much as their practical needs. In all societies, much of the housing is economically unrational. So most of the tests we use to determine the nature and location causation of economic activities fail badly when it comes to residential location and use. Culture determines the nature of housing, and culture has a critically historical quality about it.

Throughout our discussion of cities, we have seen a series of closely related dynamics of land-assignment that began as the expression of tribalism (in the synoecism that produced Greek cities), became a political role in the city and state of Roman times, an ecclesiastical office or service in the Dark Ages, and then an aspect of gainful occupation and nationality in the Middle Ages. Cities in these several times were shaped into tribal areas, political-class districts, monasticized religious foundations accompanied by the attached "communities" (such as those of "Orientals"), or occupation quarters. Each was a basis for residential structure, but only a few were even primarily economically determined.

Since the Industrial Revolution the practices have changed fundamentally. As noted earlier, the generalization of housing, which turned it into an economic commodity, began with the Commercial Revolution and gained full flower with the Industrial. Thus, in the past hundred years, economic class has played the dominant role in shaping residential areas. Nevertheless not only income is important. Within the general pattern of income division, other considerations count most heavily, among them race, language, education, religion, and a complex today called "lifestyle." But these elements all operate within a broader structure that is divided by economic class. We have poor and middle-class black areas, wealthy and poor Jewish areas, French- and English-speaking quarters divided in turn by income. We have, of course, described the social geography of cities. But, unlike the search of social geography itself, our search is not for social distinction but instead for the physical expressions of all these elements of modern urban society.

The five levels of Parisian life (by Edmond Texier in 1854) portrays an interesting urban morphology. In Paris before the introduction of elevators the "French flat" had come into existence as the ancestor of modern apartments, but it was vertically stratified in such a way that social class declined sharply with increasing elevation, just the reverse of the situation when elevators were introduced at the end of the century.

The city throughout history has witnessed a net inflow of population from the countryside, such that all such places have had to develop social and economic institutions serving to acculturate the rural person to urban life. Initially, city residence may have been periodic rather than continuous; the necessary adjustments to be made were less severe. In Roman times, the whole political system emphasized the city dweller as the fundamental prop of government; the greatest honor that might be bestowed upon a man from the provinces was to appoint him a citizen of Rome. In that context, city life was such a desirable objective that the whole Roman civilization was aimed toward emulation of the life of Rome. And when Rome herself began to lose the urbane attributes (through the barbarian invasions), the center of urbanity and city living shifted to Septimania in southern France, which served until the Albigensian Crusade as a repository of those enlightened attitudes toward cities. But in the end, the feudal system overpowered the Roman urbanism, and the destruction of the Cathari was more than a brutal and blood-thirsty orgy on the part of the church; it was the final defeat of the idea of the Roman city.

In the nearly eight hundred years since the preaching of the Albigensian Crusade (1207), the country has tended to be held as the "ideal" in most western societies outside the Mediterranean, and the firm base for political power in most countries until very recently. In such a situation, the city has had to face the oddly conflicting role of serving as the heart of economic development while standing itself as rather a badly tolerated "nuisance," Elizabeth I's "great wen." In such a climate those persons who constantly resorted from the country to the city came badly prepared for urban life. So long as serfdom survived, the marvelous freedom the city afforded must have made the immigrants' efforts toward urbanization more earnest and successful, but with the end of serfdom and the rise of industrialization—which tended to be contemporaneous events—the problem of urban acculturation became much aggravated. The numbers flooding into the city grew greatly, and the distinction between rural and urban life was made more radical.

This preface is necessary to an understanding of one of the basic structural features of modern cities, the distinction between the *in-migrant city* and the *nativist city*, with the term nativist bearing two related meanings. First, in the nativist city reside those individuals and families accustomed to city life and acculturated to its institutions and practices. And second, in this city is practiced the *national* culture, as opposed to ethnically specific or deliberately distinguished cultures.

A few examples explain the division between the two cities, a term deliberately modelled on Disraeli's notion of the "two nations." In the nineteenth century,

the great influx of foreign-born persons to major industrial cities in the United States was on a scale never before known. And in England, the influx of Irish to the industrial cities was in like measure, save for their technical status as subjects of the monarch. The hearts of cities became "little Irelands," "German town," or what have you, with American-zone cities showing far greater diversity than those in Britain. As yet, most of the Continental cities had experienced far less industrialization and little foreign in-migration. Instead, the existing in-movement was better described as a rural implosion on the city. The provincial French came to live in Paris; the Belgian peasants moved in a daily cycle between small-holdings in the countryside and industry in Namur, Liège, and Antwerp or Brussels. In northern Italy, the poor rural families came to reside in grim workers' quarters in Milan and other industrial cities.

Friedrich Engels well described what was happening in Manchester in the 1840's: the Irish and other in-migrants from the impoverished countryside took up the older and heavily deteriorated sections of the city while the natives of the place moved out to "villa districts" toward the edge of the city. Engels did not draw the distinction between the in-migrant and the nativist city, but we may use his evidence to show its existence fairly early in the development of the industrial city.

A wealth of description from the last century shows the existence in America of the "two cities," and the impact of the distinction on the morphogenesis of housing areas. The classic "Chicago Model" of social organization within the city, proposed by Robert Park and Ernest Burgess in the 1920's, is strongly expressive of this differentiation, terming the core "the zone in transition."[27] "In the zone of deterioration (in transition) encircling the central business section are always to be found the so-called 'slums' and 'bad lands,' with their submerged regions of poverty, degradation and disease, and their underworlds of crime and vice. . . . The slums are also crowded to overflowing with immigrant colonies—the Ghetto (for Jews), Little Sicily, Greektown, Chinatown—fascinatingly combining old world heritages and American adaptations. Wedging out from here is the Black Belt, with its free and disorderly life."[28]

Far removed from the deterioration and transition would be a "residential zone," and at the edge of the city a "commuters' zone." Burgess, in his specific proposal of this concentric-zone hypothesis of urban residential organization, tells us nothing about these

[27]*Robert E. Park and Ernest W. Burgess*, The City [*first published in 1925*], *Chicago: University of Chicago Press, 1967.*
[28]*Ibid., pp. 54–56.*

areas. We may infer, though, from the general tenor of his arguments that in this area, socially-upward mobility had acculturated the peoples involved, shaping what I have called a nativist zone, largely shed of ethnic and rural denotations.

In the nineteenth and the earlier years of the twentieth century, the common assumption was that all in-migrants sought acculturation to the city and social mobility toward the nativist city. The American melting-pot culture was the result of the acculturation and the social mobility resulted in the American suburb. Because the fashion among today's aesthetes is to denigrate both, I must point out that each of these goals was viewed with vast approval by social "reformers" and the sensitive critics of the years before the Second World War. When the choice was seen as between perpetual relegation to the class engaged in menial work, denied social integration, and heavily discounted as a political force and therefore consistently denied admission to the main body of American society, few voices were raised for ethnicity and separation. It was considered, quite correctly I believe, that the wonder of America and her cities in comparison with Britain and Europe was the rapidity with which people could change social standing and economic class.

In America, the birthright elistism of Europe found little support; instead a staunch belief arose in the need for an open, integrated society—the two qualities seemed to be essential elements of the same ideal. In the American mind, one might not be both slave to the past and free in the present; one could not be both an imperial German and a republican American. In this context, the great social effort in American cities, which became the main crucible for acculturation of immigrants, was toward an integrated native culture, and away from the pluralism that had led to the medieval ghetto and the endless tribalism of language and religion in Belgium, Germany, and England. In the contemporary mind, as American cities were growing wildly in the late nineteenth century, pluralism in culture and separation in residence were viewed as vestiges of all that led several million aspiring common people to abandon Europe to the elite and seek a more perfect social system across the Atlantic. Many believed, as I still do, that if a "new America" was to be created, rather than merely "another Europe," both cultural pluralism and residence based on ethnicity, like-mindedness, and externally enforced segregation had to be replaced by a social and residential mobility that can only practically take place within a society of acculturation.

A strong association sprang up between social and morphological structure as American cities grew. So long as the merchants were the leaders of society and government, and engaged in active trade focussed on the port, the center of the small city tended to maintain itself as a desirable place to live. But once those merchants became capitalist investors, the functional tie to the center lost its strength, and they could move to quarters somewhat more removed from the economic scene.

In Boston, the shift was to Beacon Hill, which to us today seems "downtown" but to them suggested open pastures and estates before these were broken into lots around the beginning of the nineteenth century. Allen Chamberlain, in his detailed study of the area, noted, "Someone in a whimsical mood once defined the social-geographic distinction between the south and the north slopes of the Hill as the 'nabob' and the 'bob' sides."[29] On the "nabob" side, the rich and powerful of the nineteenth century took up residence; on the "bob" side, the Negro slaves freed in Massachusetts at the close of the Revolution set up their modest wood-frame houses. Both a class distinction and a morphological contrast existed between the two. On the south side of Beacon Hill, row-houses highly reflective of Regency terraces in London were constructed. But no great geographic distinction was made. As the slaves were emancipated, they sought to move to a "better" (more peripheral) location, as did the Cotton Whigs in Boston who were no longer economically tied to the wharves. This American way of advancing socially and economically motivated the powerful as well as the poor.

So long as all groups could aspire to this American way of living and moving, a single dynamic could be imagined for cities: the Park and Burgess model assumed both validity and the status of a national goal and policy. Unfortunately in recent decades, two forces have infringed that status badly: (1) for the black Americans, integration was a vicious mirage which seemed never attainable, and (2) certain ethnic groups, perhaps most notably Jews but to a lesser degree Hispanic-Americans, experienced an increasing reluctance to abandon their transported culture in favor of the traditional American culture. These ethnic groups began to argue strongly for a "plural society" in which it became almost essential to maintain social separation in order that language might be perpetuated (as among the Hispanics), or transported culture might be left more intact than seemed possible in an integrated society (as among the Jews). There were, and remain, differences of opinion in all these groups. Some blacks think that integration will place them at a permanent disadvantage politically; they argue for a distinct black culture, which they hold could not survive if true

[29]*Allen Chamberlain*, Beacon Hill: Its Ancient Pastures and Early Mansions, *Boston: Houghton Mifflin Company, 1925, p. 42.*

integration took place. Some Hispanic-Americans hold with fervor that they should continue to operate in Spanish, and that any pressure to substitute English is an infringement of their rights as a minority. In such a situation, it is hard to think of the creation of a truly integrated residential society.

Similarly, the hierarchy of the various Jewish rites has recently shown great concern for any decline in their strong ethnic identity. This concern is combined with assumptions of religious discrimination which make a rational resolution of the question neither easy nor likely. Instead, rabbinical groups have called for an increase in the Jewish birthrate, on the strange argument that, because they form such a small proportion of the world population, Jews should be excluded from the general concern about overpopulation and, in any event, the maintenance of Jewish identity is too important to do otherwise. Could the Maine Yankees not argue in similar vein and validity? Nevertheless, the signs are strong that the American ideal of a native, integrated, socially and economically mobile society, moving out of the city to take up a stance of improvement in the suburbs, is far from the broad consensus it once was. In that, we find a significant change in urban morphogenesis that applies particularly to the United States.

The occupational household of the merchant, the artisan, the knight, or, in only a slightly transformed sense, of the ecclesiastical foundation of one sort or another, was the basic unit of both social and economic life in the Middle Ages. Only with the coming of the Commercial Revolution of the sixteenth and seventeenth centuries did matters begin to change so that the balance swung against such establishments toward the nuclear, noneconomic housing unit. These noneconomic units had existed in the Middle Ages, though we know relatively little about them, as they were not the important element in either economy or society. But when commercial cities grew in size, soon to be enlarged further by the results of the Industrial Revolution, *the rental market for housing became the dominant one.* Housing was generalized and economic measures began to apply in determining its size, location, quality, and form of occupance. For a time this trend toward an absolute split between the provision of employment and the provision of a job was fairly slow. Early mill villages witnessed the employer providing housing for his workers just as the earliest department

Solid working-class housing on High Street, Bristol, Connecticut, around 1900.

stores in Paris, and notably the Bon Marché, felt the responsibility to provide dormitories for their clerks. But such humane medieval practices soon disappeared, leaving the city residential structure mainly the outcome of normally asocial and quite frequently antisocial market forces. This adoption of a laissez faire attitude toward housing brought on a strong reform movement in the late nineteenth century, out of which grew the concept of socialism, which was to sweep the world in the succeeding hundred years until today it stands as very much the most common economic system.

Socialism and Planning: Responses to Poor Housing

Socialism has meant to housing what the Industrial Revolution did to manufacturing: it has made housing a mass commodity subject to industrialization, planning, and "equalization" to a few standard models. Even in the non-socialist countries, the manufacturing process (called tract development) has become "rationalized," streamlined into planned flows, and productive of a few basic, and a number of illusory, choices. Given this *industrialization of housing*, the locational demands have become critical—many acres or many floors are needed to make the manufacturing process efficient and economical. From that fact have come the two basic modules of present-day housing—*the tract*, and *the high-rise apartment structure*. In all probability, it is also responsible for the sense of anomie and regimentation that seems to affect many people in the western world.

The ultimate phase in the industrialization of housing construction may well be represented by the conditions in socialist eastern Europe, particularly Hungary, where in seeking to industrialize a formerly rural area, urbanization has had to be rapid and sweeping. Given such a strong campaign, the need for mass additions to the housing supply of Budapest and other Hungarian cities has been extreme, leading in turn to efforts to provide the greatest amount of housing at the least cost and the most intense use of the skills of building trades.

Post-war Hungary learned, as did interwar England, that national housing policies may fail not merely because of a lack of funding, but as well because

too few workers are trained to construct the housing needed and authorized. England found relief from this bottleneck by turning away from the almost unquestioning use of brick masonry, which had come with the Great Fire of 1666 and the spread of the industrial city in the nineteenth century, toward poured concrete for Council Estates. Hungary in the years after 1945 turned toward the establishment of factories where major prefabricated concrete components of apartment blocks could be shaped before being transported to the actual construction site.

Rather interesting consequences of this development plan may be seen today. The first is the necessary dependence upon massive and rather uniform apartment blocks of six to ten or twelve stories, in areas where before 1939 most housing was of only a single story. A second consequence was the need to concentrate construction within an area relatively close to the actual housing factories, since moving the components farther had proven too costly. Finally, the housing factory approach seems particularly geared to an eastern socialist regime where much emphasis is placed on "equality": the modular apartment must necessarily be at a fairly modest level, so only where a mass market can be created and *maintained* for such basic housing does the factory for houses seem practical. As developed in Hungary, that market has been almost entirely for high-rise blocks of flats; in England and France, socialist planning has equally been founded on these barracks of houses, which Le Corbusier termed "machines for living" when he first proposed them in the 1920's and '30's—as such he made them when he built *Unité d'Habitation* near Marseille between 1945 and 1952.

This matter of a residential policy adopted by the government, and advanced by public appropriation and control on private development, is an aspect of housing that has entered the scene essentially only during the hundred years we have under discussion. We saw the general collapse of private housing provision for workers sometime at the middle of the last century. The degradation of the living standard and social institutions was such that the more humane contemporary society called for housing reform.[30]

Socialism came first as a city policy, undoubtedly for two basic reasons: first, cities were the location of

---

[30]*Elsewhere I have discussed this evolution from laissez faire to public policy in the matter of housing in more detail, so here I will merely attempt a most brief summary. See my chapter on governmental and financial constraints and encouragements for housing, mainly in America and Britain during the last hundred years, in R. J. Johnson and D. T. Herbert*, Social Areas in Cities, *Vol. 1, London: John Wiley and Sons, late 1976.*

the most glaring social and housing problems in the Industrial Era; second, it was politically more possible to create reform governments within cities than within nations as a whole. The early philosophical searches for a socialist ethic could be attempted in actual practice within a city, when the local council could be convinced of the need for, and the wisdom of, the effort. Before cities themselves could become so motivated, private philanthropists took on the task. Rather interestingly, the first effective reformer in Britain was George Peabody, an American financier who had taken up residence in London in the middle of the last century. The first effective urban housing reformer in America was an immigrant from northern Ireland, A. T. Stewart, whose department store in New York was the most successful of its time and whose model "housing project" at Garden City, Long Island, was the origin of that much used name. But neither the Peabody Houses in London nor Garden City could possibly solve so massive a problem. Thus efforts were made to involve city governments in remedial measures.

By the late 1880's, the situation in London was ripe for the adoption of a public housing policy; an umbrella government had been created for the whole city with the establishment of the London County Council (LCC) in 1889, an act that finally made a public housing plan practical, so almost immediately the LCC started building blocks of flats for working-class residence. Over the succeeding years, British cities in general undertook this activity, though a consistent national policy was not adopted until the close of the First World War. Then the appalling nature of working-class housing broke upon the consciousness of the middle and upper classes, as did the sobering democratic truth, long held back in this class-ridden society, that the aristocracy had not fought the war, as it had before Napoléon, but the British working class. Thus, the post-war government called for "homes for heroes," and began a major public housing program.

During the interwar years, more than a million dwellings were built in public housing, more than a hundred thousand in schemes of the LCC alone. In addition, construction subsidies of a modest sort were offered to private builders so as to lower the purchase price of their houses. This subvention was needed to counteract the high cost of securing development land from its aristocratic owners. Thus, even before a socialist government came to power for a period long enough to effectuate real plans, as it did in 1945, the British government was massively involved in housing. Most other European countries were similarly engaged, though none to the same degree as Britain, no doubt because she was the most urbanized of all European countries other than Belgium.

In the years following the Second World War, it became established practice in European countries for the government to take responsibility for providing housing for the working class. So-called "New Towns" were built outside of London. These areas were very much like American suburbs developed in the interwar years, save for the fact that they were totally in public housing and were used almost entirely by the working class, taking on a narrow class orientation that some found undesirable. In Paris the several French governments adopted a policy of building gigantic walls of working-class apartments in a band surrounding the interwar suburban areas, themselves heavily working-class in orientation, but mainly in small, frequently privately-owned houses. This band of post-war working-class residence was equally as class-specific as the English "New Towns" and came, in the political confrontations of the 1960's, to be known as "the Red Ring," through its support of Communist candidates. Le Corbusier, who was far left in politics, had been most influential in shaping this proletarian circumvallation of Paris and other French cities in the post-war years. In country after country, the policy evolved, as the public took responsibility for workers' housing, that those developments were relegated toward the edge of the city into class-specific housing projects. The great, grey, rather grim *megastructure* of apartments was generally adopted as the actual form of residence. Little conscious concern was directed to groups other than the working class; instead, a somewhat dogmatic objection was raised in some countries against the private ownership of housing.

Mixed Enterprise and the Interwar Suburb

In the United States, this policy debate between public and private provision of housing had a very different history. Similar concern arose for the plight of the slum dwellers in the nineteenth century, but virtually all efforts until the 1930's came through (1) trying to raise the income level of those people so they might effectively enter the private housing market, (2) seeking to forbid the worst features of free-market housing through health, safety, and general welfare provisions of the general body of American law, and (3) attempting to shape a market-provided body of housing that fell within the possible purchase or rental of most people. In this effort, the United States had one great advantage over Britain, and some other European countries.

As we have seen in our discussion of nineteenth-century Manchester, land was always a requisite of high social status in Britain, so strong social, essentially noneconomic, reasons existed for keeping land in rural, aristocratic use. Thus the growth of cities was often inhibited, or made difficult, by the narrowing of the supply to the point that prices of available land were inflated. This problem was attacked in the interwar years when the British governments attempted to subsidize land to lower its price to the working class, though in general this attack did not solve the problem. In America land was vastly available and had never, save in the English-mirror societies of Chesapeake Bay, assumed a major role in status conferral. Thus, no artificial, noneconomic narrowing of land supply occurred, nor did the consequent rise in prices. Normally land was relatively cheap outside American cities, and working-class housing could be built more cheaply than in Europe. Several other factors contributed to that cheapness of land—greater geographical mobility for the lower classes than for those across the Atlantic, which meant the earlier creation of a mass market, and much cheaper construction, through a greater use of wood and much more efficient construction practices.

The "three-decker" was a means devised to provide housing for three families in what were little different from three single-story cottages. Because hours in the mills were long and transport was little used by wage workers, these buildings provided a rational solution to housing an urban proletariat in spacious and airy quarters.

In the 1930's the United States began to work toward a definite national housing policy, arriving in 1934 at a joint program of public and private construction. Of the two, the private was vastly the more important and effective when the Federal Housing Administration (FHA) was created to encourage the building of private housing for persons of lower income. We will not detail the several, and changing, provisions of United States housing legislation in the 1930's and '40's. But we may note that millions of houses were built for the working class, and all other classes. America felt no antipathy toward private ownership (quite the reverse, in fact), so the market mechanism served splendidly to meet the needs of the majority of people. Unfortunately it did not meet the needs of everyone. So, as is all too common, the larger successes are often faulted for the smaller failures.

The American housing policy was rather unsuccessful in providing good accommodations at reasonable rents for those persons unable or unwilling to adopt the established path toward suburban life within a melting-pot culture. Most notably, a failure came in the poor housing of the thousands of southern blacks who were forced by the extreme poverty of the rural South and the decline of cotton cultivation in the traditional Cotton Belt during the 1930's to migrate to northern cities. When that migration led geographically, as was common, to segregated slums in New York, Philadelphia, Detroit, or Chicago, the absence of an effective public housing policy produced dreadful conditions.

The black migrants were discriminated against in housing to the point they could not gain anything like free access to the suburban solution that was sought through FHA financing and its accepted construction. They were forced into older, central-city apartments, not replaced or improved by any national or local program, and kept there by rigid segregation. Other groups "passed through" these slums on their course toward social mobility, but the blacks could not get out until the mid-1950's, when the highly discriminatory features of the original FHA legislation began to be thrown down by the courts. Even then, free access to suburban housing was largely a myth for another ten years, and remains heavily restricted by clandestine practices in many areas even today.

When public housing was built in far larger quantities during the post-Second World War years, it took on a most unfortunate social complexion of failure and segregation. The blacks and the Hispanic-Americans were not segregated by outside forces into these housing projects. Rather, because of low incomes among those groups, discrimination against blacks in suburban housing, and the necessary dependence of these floods of unskilled in-migrants to the northern metropolitan areas on such public housing, blacks and Hispanic-Americans tended to bulk very large in such

A black community, such as this one in East Oakland, California, tends to occupy housing of an earlier generation of white working class. The shopping center in the center of the picture, Eastmont Mall, is typical of the integration of shops found in these large developments of the 1960's but untypical in having a dominantly black clientele.

projects, remaining longer than any other wayfarers on their road toward social advance: the blacks stayed due to lack of skill, discrimination, and the general problems of acculturation in the city; the Hispanic-Americans remained mainly due to lack of skills and their inability to use English. Had such public housing been built in the late nineteenth century or the years before the 1930's, successive masses of Germans, Irish, English, Scandinavians, Poles, and Italians would have occupied these projects, and our history would have shown the heavy reliance on such subsidized shelter by new arrivals to the city. Because projects existed in no great numbers before the 1950's, most of the "older immigrants" had passed beyond them before they were built. Still the failure of the black population to be able to get out and into the suburbs is a serious blemish on an otherwise quite exceptional record of providing good housing, with great personal choice, a level of privacy unknown elsewhere, an adequacy of space envied among the European working class, and a timeliness of availability that startles English, Swedish, or French applicants for public housing.

Recent changes in the cost of housing in relation to the level of income have made a reexamination of national housing policy essential. No longer can the lower-income levels of society hope to buy houses; even the middle class can be severely strapped in doing so. While the inhabitants of Council Estates in England commonly assume that 12 to 15 per cent of their income is all that they should be expected to spend for

housing, members of the white-collar middle classes in America commonly spend 30 to 35 per cent of their now less-relatively-elevated incomes on housing. With rises in other costs—notably food and gasoline—this high proportion of income can hardly be raised further. The rapidly inflating costs of housing are setting an ever higher threshold on the relative income necessary in order to use the "traditional" American solution to housing provision, the private ownership of a suburban house. Not only do we need to deal effectively with the stagnation of the poor in the central city, but soon we will as well have to deal with the failure of the established system to take care with the housing of the majority of the American population.

The years since the Second World War have witnessed a radical change in housing everywhere, even in the United States, from a basic reliance upon private initiative and provision of housing to a necessary governmental policy to gain that end. No longer, or certainly only for a very short time more, are we likely to be able to treat the morphology of urban housing as an aspect of economic and social geography. Rather, it will become a dependent feature of public policy, lacking both the testing mechanisms of satisfaction and effectiveness furnished in the marketplace and the variety of choice and general personal freedom that individualized housing has made available to us.

The main reason for the change is simple necessity in a democratically responsible society. Large elements of the population cannot secure acceptable housing in the private market-generated sector, so government has had to step in. A less fundamental but still contributing reason for the intrusion of public concern into what had traditionally been an economic activity rather on a par with trading, agriculture, and manufacturing was a growing concern for the role of "speculation" in the spread of the urban landscape, particularly in the construction of suburban residences.

The concern with speculation is hardly new; Henry George with his proposals to "capture the unearned increment" of land values through a "single tax" shaped his ideas while viewing the frenetic speculation in lands in the San Francisco Bay Area in the 1860's.[31] A strong philosophical objection has always been raised against the rapid rise in value of land, which is widely thought to result from a lack of effort on the part of the owner. In the nineteenth century, the great focus of this objection was in the creation of town-plats in the little-settled parts of the American Middle and Far West. Mark Twain and Charles Dudley Warner satirized such speculations in *The Gilded Age: A Tale of Today,* published in 1873. Yet, in part, the urge to speculate in town sites made a widely dispersed and heavily regionalized urban structure available to twentieth-century Americans, thus avoiding the urban overcentralization found in France, Spain, and much of eastern Europe.[32]

Speculation in land gained even darker regard among social and environmental critics in the 1960's, when this grossly selfish activity was widely alleged to be destroying the countryside and making cities vast, formless places. I would not question the philosophical objection to speculative gain; I share it, in a moral sense. But the facts do not seem to bear out the evil consequence seen in land development.

Finally, urban residential land-use spread so rapidly because cities grew so rapidly due (1) to a generally great increase in population in western industrialized countries, and (2) to the increasing dependence that was made upon urban areas "as the home of man." The abandonment of the countryside played a major role in expanding the cities, so to take the stance the city was raping the country is as unanalytical as it is rhetorical.

To cite a few figures for the United States: the American population increased by over one-quarter, more than fifty million people, between 1950 and 1970. During this same period, the urban population of the United States increased by almost two-thirds (64.6 per cent), while the rural population decreased absolutely by 343,000, or a bit less than 1 per cent. Given the vast increase in numbers, nearly fifty-two million, which essentially had to be taken up in urban growth, how can we think that speculation was the basic reason for the spread of cities?

Finally, speculation is a parasite that waxes fat on the growth brought by other causes; it does not cause that growth. Even using only Standard Metropolitan Statistical Areas to approximate the truly urban areas of the country, the increase in the period 1950–1970 was from 62.5 to 68.6 per cent of the national population, with a corresponding drop in percentage contribution by the nonmetropolitan area. Short of draconian birth-control measures or a forced return-to-the-land movement similar to that instituted by the victorious Khmer Rouge in Cambodia, cities could not have failed to expand in the post-war period, even without a single speculator. This is not an academic quibble but a necessary caution, as we saw grimly portrayed when a confused young lady convinced of the rape of the countryside sought to assassinate the President of the United States in Sacramento in the summer of 1975. Her view of development as an evil plot of a few capitalists missed the point that the nation's population has doubled in the last sixty years.

The Morphology of Residence in Cities

Taking all of those forces consistently at work in shaping the urban pattern of residence, and adding the recent changes of great magnitude, we may attempt a simple model of housing in the city. The first component we need deal with is the relatively small *survival of nineteenth-century housing;* the growth of the central business district tended to invade those residential areas and lead to their demolition. In very slow-growing cities, some nineteenth-century housing may remain, built when most people had to walk to work. But in the more dynamic places, such housing is largely gone, save for that built at the very end of the century when trolleys had begun to encourage a rapid outward expansion of housing and some decline in the average density of residence.

[31]*Henry George was a printer and newspaper editor in the Bay Area; he published there in 1871* Our Land Policy, *whose basic ideas he revised and elaborated in his classic* Progress and Poverty *in 1879.*

[32]*For a more thorough development of this argument see James E. Vance, Jr., "Metropolitan America: Evolution of an Ideal," published in the report on the First Hungarian-American Seminar in Geography by the Hungarian Academy of Sciences, Institute of Geography, 1976.*

This "trolley city" largely survives as the slums or ghetto of such cities as Chicago, Philadelphia, New York, and Boston. Walk-up apartment houses, tenements, and "three-deckers" tend to make up this area, termed by sociologists the "zone of assimilation." The foreign immigrants of the late nineteenth century came to be acculturated with that zone, and the black and Puerto Rican (and more recent Hispanic) in-migrants have shown a less rapid cultural assimilation there.

In a number of metropolitan areas the "central city" has become a section where those groups consciously opposing inclusion in the broad "national" culture have sought to create their own "turfs" with an accompanying narrowly circumscribed life-style. Elsewhere, I have called these *opposition areas*, and shown them to be deliberate efforts at separation instituted by the residents themselves, so that to talk about "discrimination" or "segregation" is merely self-serving political rhetoric.[33] In Berkeley, a large "South Side Community" grew up with a strong siege mentality and the belief that the rest of American cities were largely filled by the benighted or the philistine. This area was the home turf of the nihilistic Symbionese

Liberation Army. In other cities with strong liberal or radical university populations, other opposition areas have grown up, as in Seattle's Capital Hill, parts of Madison, Allston and Brighton in Boston, and in Boulder.

The black and Hispanic quarter seemingly occupies the central city of necessity, but the opposition areas do so both by choice and by the intention to steal a bit of the "soul" of the first two. Like them, they tend to hold out an argument of discrimination if they are denied fairly autonomous "governance" of their own turfs. Community "control and planning" are the watchwords of these areas, which argue that the rest of society cannot possibly understand their needs and problems. Thus all are strongly opposed to efforts to create metropolitan governments, and commonly argue for a return to the nineteenth-century ward organization, which tended to be removed in the political reforms of the 1930's and '40s. Given this craving for local autonomy, the morphological qualities of the trolley-housing areas are attractive. Because of deterioration and an assumed obsolescence, the acculturated moved out of these areas to the "nativist" sub-

Tenements on New York's Lower East Side.

[33]*See my chapter "Man and Super-city: The Origin and Nature of the Intricate Social Geography of the Bay Area," in M. E. Eliot Hurst,* I Came to the City: Essays and Comments on the Urban Scene, *Boston: Houghton Mifflin Company, 1975, pp. 17–30.*

urbs, leaving them subject to effective ethnic or life-style political control.

This situation has a rather ambivalent quality: physically and economically, and probably socially, the urge is strong to confront suburban discrimination head-on and gain entry to those more favored areas, but politically the act of integration can be very damaging indeed. Hispanic-Americans or blacks can dominate parts or all of some central cities. Even the groups in social, political, and economic opposition can on occasion dominate a central city, as they did in Berkeley and Madison in the early 1970's. But diluted in the suburbs by the great mass of population reasonably content with a "native culture" and not interested in political ethnicity, all these groups would lose political power. Thus, they face a dilemma between "equal opportunity" and political power.

The only way they might gain both is to follow in the footsteps of the American Jewish population, which has shown a strong tendency toward selective suburbanization, with out-movement from central cities taking place in only a fraction of the suburban towns. Jewish suburbs occur in most metropolitan areas, though oddly not in the Bay Area City. Strongly Jewish sectors may be found in New York and Chicago but also in the Los Angeles, St. Louis, and Boston metropolitan areas—in the West Los Angeles-Beverly Hills alignment, and the Brookline-Natick alignment west of Boston. Doubtless no conscious effort was made to combine "equal opportunity" to suburbanize with maintenance of ethnic political power, but the clustering necessitated by Jewish dietary laws, religious and social attitudes, and desires to "preserve a Jewish way of life" seems to have led to that result.

Within the "central city," the other main residential component is comprised of fairly *new high-rise apartments*, largely built since the Second World War. Technological improvements in construction and elevators combined with a change in family size and a great growth in single-person households tend to encourage a moderate "return" of the middle class from the suburbs. In Manhattan, Chicago's Near North Side, and San Francisco, many had never left, though in most other cities the development of individual transportation and of massive suburbs in the period 1920 to 1950 had drawn most of the middle class well away from the center. Strong efforts through urban redevelopment have been applied to the construction of such attractive central-area housing, in a sense subsidizing middle-income housing on the argument that a more broad income spectrum would be beneficial at the heart of the metropolis.

A few cities include *areas of architectural distinction*, usually those areas surviving from the late eighteenth or the first half of the nineteenth century, which either maintained their higher-class orientation, or were returned to it after a class decline. Beacon Hill in Boston is undoubtedly the classic example, having maintained itself throughout the years between its initial development at the turn of the nineteenth century and the present. Walter Firey in his classic study, *Land Use in Central Boston*, has shown how social esteem is created and maintained.[34] In Philadelphia that esteem had to be recreated for the central Society Hill area in the years after 1945. The Garden District in New Orleans shared with Beacon Hill a permanence of preference, but Boston's "South End," Washington's Georgetown, and Chicago's "Old Town" had essentially to be pulled back from imminent destruction under the wrecker's ball. In city after city, policy makers increasingly realize today that the most distinctive area architecturally, and often the most human in scale morphologically, is the local "old town," with its sturdy houses with good lines, pleasant planting in many cases, and narrow streets that disallow too heavy passage of traffic. The older the better, not so much from an antiquarian concern as for the usually smaller size of the oldest remaining residential units. If Federalist houses can be found, as in Society Hill, Beacon Hill, or Federal Hill in Providence, they are smaller in size than the Grant-to-McKinley Era houses, where much money and many servants or subdividing is a necessity.

In the sphere of *public housing*, the central city is the common locale. As already noted, those projects were viewed as serving as a reception area, or at least an institutionalized zone of assimilation, for the in-migrants to the city from outside the country or from the rural areas within it. Furthermore, efforts to spread public housing around the metropolis have met stiff opposition from suburban town councils and residents. No doubt equity demands the opening of the suburbs to the poor as well as the more prosperous. Efforts have been made to pass legislation, or to take the route of legislation-through-the-courts, to gain this end. In April, 1976, the U.S. Supreme Court took the latter course, decreeing for Chicago a possibly mandatory dispersal of public housing into the suburbs.

But is such an opening a rather Pyrrhic victory? Many of the facilities needed for bare survival of the poor family, particularly public transportation, may be missing in the suburbs. So we must examine this question with less foreclosed thinking and passion and more analysis and pragmatism than has often been applied. Shall we end with a single, integrated "na-

---

[34]*Walter Firey*, Land Use In Central Boston, *Cambridge: Harvard University Press, 1947 (Harvard Sociological Studies, Vol. IV).*

tive" society and culture or a number of parallel "ethnic" cultures?[35] But as of the present, public housing remains largely confined to the morphological part of the city initially developed in the nineteenth century and cleared of building constructed then for the creation of public housing projects in the 1930's, '40's, and '50's.

From this cataloging of the main elements in the housing structure of the central city, the "zone in transition" and the "zone of workingmen's homes" of Park and Burgess, or the trolley-era city as I have termed it, we see clearly that this area is today the place of residence of most of the social groups that do not "fit" in the highly generalized and economic-class divided suburbs. Some fail to fit through their own wish, as in the opposition areas, and the others, notably the blacks, fail through the persistence of housing discrimination. Significantly, within this residential heart of the city, no real agreement as to institutions, accepted culture, and material goals serves to unite the area as the suburbs are basically united in a generally accepted native culture.

In the central city, opposition, self-initiated or imposed from outside, accounts for the presence of several populations. But there is no agreement, and often considerable violent friction, among those groups. In many places, the central-city middle and upper classes are there to assert rebellion against the suburbs and the suburban "norms." The alternative-life-style communities are there in opposition to almost all external standards and norms. The Hispanics are there because of language skill and income. The blacks are there through no fault of their own, but because over many years they could not move out. Now each group may find virtue in its reason for being there, but they commonly find friction with the other central groups and disagreement as to what the central area should be in physical, economic, and social terms.

This *zone of narrow-community identity* and intercommunity conflict assembles such unlike groups that they are united only in their disagreement with or exclusion from the suburbs. In more than a few cases, the exclusion from the suburbs is self-inflicted, to the degree that having refused to accept an integrated culture, it is rationally difficult for one to argue exclusion by such an act. Only an integrated, melting-pot culture is practically open to all on equal terms. To the degree it is not, it practices discrimination and enforces segregation; to the degree the person outside refuses to accept the composite norm, he separates himself and establishes a self-imposed opposition.

[35]*For a detailed consideration of these difficult alternatives, see my introductory essay "The American City: Workshop for a National Culture," in Adams, op. cit.*

This "Commune" on Parker Street in Berkeley, California, shows the way in which a previously nativist neighborhood may be transformed into "an area of opposition."

The City of the Masses: The Suburbs

That the central-city poor form the "masses" in American life is one of today's prime misconceptions. Fortunately they make up a relatively small component of urban population and an even smaller proportion of the total population; the reason they form such an element of attention is the fact that they represent a basic social failure in a country that has always held the belief that all persons can live in basic comfort, liberty, and dignity. That failure is real and most unfortunate, but it is also partial; we are likely to misunderstand the structure of our cities to the extent that we exaggerate it.

The suburb is America's greatest success, in settlement terms. On the basis of "user satisfaction," little question remains that more families are basically satisfied with their lives in the suburbs than are those to be found either in the central city or the countryside. Obviously this statement arises partly because more persons live in the suburb in America than in either of the other settlement components. But it also reflects a general satisfaction with the social and physical attributes of that largest component of the American population. The very bad press that the suburb has had is accounted for more by the distaste felt toward that area by the planners and intellectuals, who have the most to say about such questions, than by any vast rumblings among the natives. No one should argue that the popular will inevitably is the best informed or the most thoughtful, but in a democracy it is hard to hold that it is simply invalid or unimportant.

Finally, the nature of their environment is a matter of great concern to all classes of people, and the planners or intellectuals cannot be allowed to determine for others what the acceptable and the chosen environment will be so long as the question is one of aesthetics and emotions rather than any demonstration of injustice to others. The plight of the central-city poor is not produced by the nature of the suburb but rather by their inability to go there and earn a living. And many loud voices notwithstanding, the encroachment of the suburbs on the country is neither so great in scale nor so indefensible as it is played up by the environmental radicals. The spread is the result of too fast a growth of urban population rather than any inner mechanism of suburbanization. Only population control and a relative rise in the appeal of the countryside can solve this situation, if it is a problem.

One of the most common attacks by social critics on the suburbs is on the nature of suburban culture and life. They argue that it is materialistic, self-satisfied, lacking in "color" and ethnic identity, and consumption oriented. When comparison is made with other components of settlement, and even with other lands, it is hard to see that these qualities in any way define the suburb as separate from western society as a whole. Suburbs were born in the high ideals of getting people out of the unhealthy environment of the late-nineteenth-century central city, and they have grown large in serving perhaps the most democratic society that has yet been created. The suburban society is created by the people who live there rather than decreed by a planning elite, as in Scandinavia and the radical socialist countries of eastern Europe, which have far fewer suburbs but vastly less individuality and freedom.

Morphologically, the suburbs are the residence of the masses in American life. Thus the greatest supply of workers—particularly the skilled workers increasingly in demand, the largest market for the sale of goods, and the greatest support for many cultural and recreational activities is to be found there. The impact on the economic activities of city life of the growth of the suburbs has been enormous. Industry now is most heavily developed in suburban or satellite areas of cities. Wholesaling is to a large degree located there, not so much because the largest market is to be found there —a true fact but not necessarily a controlling one in

this case—but rather because the suburbs now have the best overall transportation. And most of the growth in retailing experienced since 1945 has taken place in the suburbs.

Given the great size and population resident in the suburbs, as well as the speed with which this area grew into an urban existence, morphological analysis is rather tricky. Unlike the central-city areas, the suburb is not a historical component of most cities. Rather specialized suburban areas grew up around very large cities even in the Middle Ages. Note has already been taken of the Savoy district between London and Westminster, with its large houses for aristocrats even in the twelfth and thirteenth century. And similar *hôtels* of the wealthy and powerful could be found outside Paris.

England seems, oddly enough, to have invented the suburb; odd because she was and remains a society obsessed with the "countryside"—a minority and elitist environment—and fiercely critical of the suburbs, the home of today's masses. But in the Middle Ages only a relatively peaceful and safe land could have houses unprotected by walls. Wars in England were mostly civil, which meant that fighting was within cities as much as between them, so the walls lost their practical necessity and living beyond them exposed one to no more physical threat than living within them.

The main meaning of the wall then became legal rather than military. This distinction came on the Continent only at the end of the nineteenth century, when walls could no longer protect a city and came instead merely to define it. As early as the years just before the French Revolution (1784–1789), a customs barrier had been erected around Paris, continuing the medieval practice of the *octroi*, termed the *Enceinte des Fermiers Generaux*, for which a series of customs houses—the Barrières de La Violette, Enfer, Chartres, and the like that still survive—were constructed.[36] This practice of distinguishing legally between the city and its potential suburban areas carried over into the interwar years when the limits of the city of Paris remained pretty much along the line of the *Enceinte des Fermiers Generaux*, but vast growth took place in a ring of essentially industrial suburbs beyond "the gates." Because those gates assumed such legal and symbolic significance, new ones were built even between the wars, such as those at Porte St.-Cloud, Porte Dorée, and Porte de la Muette. In the case of Paris and other large cities with a Latin tradition, the upper classes seemed reluctant to leave the city, which meant that the suburbs became far more proletarian than in the northern

[36]*Pierre Couperie*, Paris Through the Ages, *New York: George Braziller, 1968. This reference is to section XII and the following one is to section XVII.*

countries of Europe. Perhaps this is why the Parisians still continued to build "gates" as late as the 1920's.

If the suburb is older than the Industrial Era, it still was a rather chance and unstructured thing before it. The *hôtels* of Paris, the "houses" around London, the cottages and villas around Regent's Park, and the family homesteads in Milton outside Boston were still few in number, and mainly characteristic of court cities where an aristocracy came for the "season," only to return to distant estates when it was over. Only when the size of cities began to increase rapidly, and when the need for large productive facilities further increased the pressure on land, was some structure more complex than the coherent and single-centered medieval-town-grown-large needed. In most countries, an organized rural settlement pattern was overtaken in its inner edges around the traditional city by the process of urbanization. Villages were transformed into industrial satellites of the city, or suburbs for the housing of its population. Around Paris, Brussels, and London these villages came to be incorporated into the city, forming what we now think of as suburbs. For example, even in the nineteenth century the village of Passy west of Paris was still a favorite residence for artists and writers because of its bucolic surroundings, despite the fact it had been considered urban enough to be the site of Benjamin Franklin's villa while he served as American commissioner to France during the Revolution. Today Passy is the pinnacle of Parisian social esteem because it is thought of as a discrete community, rather an urban village within the traditional walls.

In Europe, the general pattern is that the spread of the city is overrunning the surrounding villages, as well described in one of Georges Simenon's last novels, *Moving*. But in America, the morphological advance of the city is not so confined to a single pattern. In the older cities of the Northeast, particularly in New England and around Philadelphia, the growth of cities did come through the physical incorporation of previous villages, where they existed to be overrun. But in the Middle West and the West, cities were often the first places created, and their growth might well come sufficiently fast to spread outward into open farming country devoid of villages. As a result, we must in America distinguish between the *incorporation pattern* of the East, and the *simple expansion pattern* into little-structured areas found in the West.

Boston is a city of suburbs, themselves often subdivided into village centers that have existed for several hundred years, whereas most California cities represent a single center that spread into unorganized "county land" devoid of settlement structure above the level of the large farm with dispersed farmsteads. The contrast in the internal structure of the suburbs is con-

siderable, with the "placelessness" of the California tract quite absent in the East.[37] Thus we may hold that the first consideration in the analysis of suburban structure is the matter of preurban settlement form. In Europe and the American East, the earlier structure of villages is clearly reflected in the growth of suburbs, but in the American West the vastness and the sometimes criticized "shapelessness" of the suburbs comes in large measure from the absence of any very detailed preurban settlement form.

Once the city begins to grow, one must recall the differences among the various morphological processes. As was true of the central business district, also in the suburbs the obvious first process is that of *initiation of urban structure*—the act of changing the use of land from rural or waste to urban purposes. The relatively short history of suburban development has meant that in most areas within that band of urbanization the only widespread process is that of initiation. In fact, one of the economic pillars of this outlying housing development is that it uses basically unoccupied space, wherein the preparation costs are held down along with the imputed value of the land. Within the older parts of cities, new buildings on old sites encounter two costs that are often dampening to development: the first is the cost of clearing the site and preparing it for reuse; the second is the often inflated valuation of the land, based not upon its current utility value but rather on some higher value that it had attributed to it in the past. If urban *devaluation* were more common, urban blight might well be far less so.

The one value that a preused site may have that is missing on the development frontier is what planners delight in calling "infrastructure"—the necessary services and connections to make the site usable. With tract development, the practice has become to shift the cost of providing the infrastructures of sewers, water mains, electric and gas lines, streets, sidewalks, and the like onto the developer, who in turn passes it directly on to the original purchasers or renters. The result of inflation is such that the new provision of infrastructure is increasingly costly, while the reuse of existing infrastructure becomes increasingly attractive. But only recently has this been the case, so as yet only a modest return to the older areas of cities and the older sections of the suburbs is occurring. Without question, however, this reversion will become rapidly a dominant concern in the suburbs. Since it has not yet done so, we are still dealing with the notion that every-

[37]*For a discussion of this problem, see James E. Vance, Jr., "Areal Political Structure and Its Influence on Urban Patterns," in the* Yearbook of the Association of Pacific Coast Geographers, *1960, pp. 40–49.*

thing in the suburbs is a first-generation structure, and only a modest transformation of the original use.

The first-generation quality of suburban land-use is reflected in the uniformity of use within districts and the architectural similarity within the same areal units. Much of the social science and aesthetic condemnation of suburbs grows out of this absence of multiple stages. Fortunately the immediate future will change much of this pattern, so some of the chorus of abuse may be quieted. Until it is, we must endure it and look instead at the basis of first-generation structure.

That *first-generation structure* becomes strongly economic-class oriented because the initial purchase price of the housing in the suburbs determines most of the physical characteristics of an area. Much as prices have risen sharply, and in some areas the economic class of the present occupants may be higher than that of the original buyers, the physical form of a tract does not change appreciably. The form of the houses within a tract, however, may be greatly transformed. One of the great, often-overlooked virtues of single-family, detached housing in the suburbs is that it is expansible in a way no public or private high-rise, row, or apartmented housing is.

The rapid increase in desired family size between the 1930's and the 1950's, the general improvement in the standard of living among unionized labor, and the changing material expectations of working-class families all made *the transformation suburb* an essential of the elevating American urban life-style. Some post-war housing tracts have deteriorated, but, in general, suburbs have shown a far better resistance to obsolescence and "slumming" than have the apartmented areas built even as late as the 1920's and '30's. It is my strong belief that the wave of fashion for "condominiums" and "townhouses" will soon show that the residential dynamics of deterioration were not abolished with FHA, but rather they were dampened considerably by the turn to single-family detached housing that it made possible. A change in morphology toward apartmented housing stands likely to return us to the previous pattern of rapid obsolescence, with all the real costs in urban spread and social welfare that it implies.

Two fundamental factors clearly shape the morphology of the suburbs: the first is the tendency for cities to grow outward in more or less concentric bands of development, and the second is the tendency for subdivisions within those bands to be determined by differences in the cost of housing. The distinguished land economist Homer Hoyt was the first to formalize the dynamic background of those segments of bands when, in 1939, he prepared a report for the Federal Housing Administration, entitled *The Structure and*

Growth of Residential Neighborhoods in American Cities.[38] Hoyt argued the case for the existence of radiating sectors of land-use centering on the city core and divided from one another not merely by the contrast between economic and housing use, but as well by contrasts in the economic class of housing. He held a basic domination of the pattern by the high-cost housing areas preempted the most desirable vectors for expansion.

Normally these areas were outward extensions directly from the high-income residential area of the central city. In Boston, for example, Beacon Hill extended directly into the Back Bay, itself adjacent to Brookline, the first well-to-do suburb. The alignment was continued in successive stages of peripheral growth by Newton west of Brookline and Wellesley west of New-

Map of Camberwell.

[38]*Homer Hoyt*, The Structure and Growth of Residential Neighborhoods in American Cities, *Washington: U.S. Government Printing Office, 1939.*

ton. In San Francisco, a similar alignment began above the original downtown at Nob Hill, spread along the ridge of Russian Hill to Pacific Heights and finally through the Presidio Wall to Land's End, where North America gave out. In his analyses of a number of American cities, large and small, Hoyt found the repetition of the division of the land-use into radiating sectors so marked as to justify the advancement of a theory of growth so structured.

Hoyt's study also found three ways that a building could be added to a city. "It may (1) expand vertically in areas already settled through the replacement of single-family by multifamily structures, (2) fill the interstices in the existing settled area—*i.e.*, build on vacant lots in blocks already partially developed with structures, or, (3) extend the existing settled area on the periphery of the city by the erection of homes on newly subdivided land."[39] We have seen that second- or third-generation construction on a lot is not at all common in the suburbs, though it may soon become rather more so, so Hoyt's first manner of addition to the residential supply is mainly applicable to the central city. Even the second way, lot in-filling, has become fairly uncommon in suburban development for the reason that, since the advent of FHA, there has been a greatly increased tendency for increments to come in "tracts," that is sizable acreages of land added as a unitized development which is "built out" to completion.

Before FHA, the standard pattern in housing development was for real estate companies to buy parcels of land and subdivide into lots, which were sold to individuals who might then hold the space for speculative gain or for their own ultimate use when they saved enough money to build a house, or build immediately. In some cases small builders would buy a few lots in such a subdivision and develop them house after house, using the proceeds of one sale to finance the construction of the next house.

In a recent study of Stockton (California), Roger Barnett has shown that such subdivision of lots can easily oversupply the market: it took fifty years for the earliest platting of Stockton (by its original land-owners, the Webers) to be sold. And consistently up to the 1930's and the advent of FHA, Stockton had a large surplus of subdivided lots waiting for both sale and utilization for buildings. Seemingly, practice arose, not formalized but evolving within a complex market into a joint procedure, for a "reserve" of potentially plattable land area to exist just beyond the limit of actual subdivision. Owners in that reserve would resist selling in small parcels for immediate construction in

the hope for a later, larger major platting. Beyond the reserve belt, hopes were so distant in time that small in-lots would be sold if sought for immediate construction.[40]

The Bands of Suburban Development

The morphology of the suburban area was sharply changed when subdivision of lots with direct sale to small owners was replaced by tract development. In the older, *inner-band of suburban development*, street alignments were frequently discontinuous and normally badly lined up. Jogs and doglegs were the normal pattern. In addition plots could vary somewhat in size, but showed a tendency toward general meanness of extent. Because the subdivider made his money selling as many lots as possible in relation to the infrastructure he had to supply—and that was often short-lived, and even observable only in dry weather—he tended to favor very narrow street frontages, overly deep lots if people demanded more space, and rectangularity of block design so as to make surveying easy, to keep down the length of street front per lot, and to cut the maximum number of lots from the acreage he owned. The suburbs of many cities in the United States before 1934 showed no variation from the pattern of the railroad-town plat laid out when the first line came to the city in the mid-nineteenth century.

With the coming of FHA, mortgage bankers began to lend on houses as well as land, and in large blocks of mortgages. As a result they became much more concerned with the general character of the housing tract, finding curving streets a stronger sales feature than straight ones, and demanding lots large enough and well shaped enough so as not to hinder the sale of the house built on it. Generally, they showed more concern for the future than had the subdividers of earlier years, who might be out of the area with their profit in their pocket within a couple of years after the surveyor's stakes were first driven into the weedy field. In general,

---

[39]Ibid., p. 96.

[40]*Roger Barnett*, Suburban Subdivision: The Morphogenesis of Housing in Stockton, 1850–1950, *unpublished Ph.D. thesis, Department of Geography, University of California, Berkeley, 1973.*

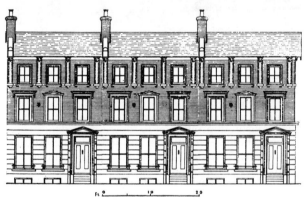

Terrace houses in Camberwell changed in architectural style during the second half of the nineteenth century, but their basic form remained the same.

the morphological distinction between pre-FHA housing areas and those built after its inception can be observed even when flying over a city because of this sharp change in the layout of streets away from rigid regularity toward curving streets.

Transportation Shapes Incremental Bands

The development of incremental bands around the city core commenced in earnest with the coming of the trolley car in the 1890's and the 1900's. To begin with, merely a larger *potential suburban area* had been created which might be subdivided into salable lots as the car-lines spread farther from the center, providing, in turn, the beginning of circumferential transit routes in the city. The tendency was to build *apartmented buildings* along the tracks—true "French flats," or merely tenement and rooming houses. Away from the main streets, *single-family houses* would have been more common, though initially they probably were reproductions of the older, densely packed and tall central-city houses rather than the more open suburban model that was to develop. The trolley tracks began the proruption of the edge of the city, with development extending considerably farther out along the car-lines than in the interstices, where pedestrial movement remained the only practical form of mobility.

That tendency toward linear extension found an even more extreme and earlier form in the pattern which developed along commuter railroads. There, the alignment became discontinuous with a string of *beads of settlement* extending along the railroad, with open land between the settlements that grew up around stations. The outer limit of the "suburbs" came where frequent service was no longer provided and where the cost of daily commuting became prohibitive. In general terms, the railroad pattern was one of large, closely-spaced beads near the city, and small, widely-separated ones at the edge.

The trolley came as the next stage in suburban transport, filling in the gaps between railroad clusters and making for a continuous carpet of residence outward from the older central city. Its outer limit resulted more from the time trolley travel took than cost; these vehicles were relatively slow, so commuting great distances on the electric cars was rather impractical. For that reason the trolley housing tended more toward the filling of gaps than the profligate flinging of beads of settlement at a great distance, as in Fairfield County, Connecticut, reached by a long train commute from New York. This contrast between the morphology of railroad suburbs and those of the trolley cars tended to reinforce the sector pattern that Homer Hoyt dis-

Camberwell, in South London, developed as a morphological band not far south of the Thames where row houses could be built in great numbers once the railroads came to tie the area to the working city along and north of the river.

cerned. Not merely a time differential existed between the two media, but a cost one as well. Commuters who used the train tended to come from the better-paid occupations, so the railroad suburbs were generally the ones with the more expensive housing.

The automobile twice left an effect on the suburbs. Early in this century, the wealthier suburbs began to be a home, probably the main home, for the car. The benefit enjoyed by private mechanical transport in a suburb is much higher than that found in the central city, with its wealth of taxi and public transport. But for a decade or more the car was used in the suburbs mainly for recreation and shopping journeys, and not for commuting. Only with the coming of good arterial roads, some of "super-highway" quality with grade separation and divided lanes as in the 1930's, was the second coming of the automobile felt. Then cars entered into use for commuting, allowing people to travel to other than central-city locations for work. Factories, warehouses, and ultimately shopping facilities and even offices could move to the suburbs, and still be reached by both a labor force and a management group.

Once the automobile was widely used in commuting, the form of the suburbs changed, and a new incremental band of distinctive pattern was shaped around cities. This change was contemporaneous with the institution of FHA financing, so it is hard to divide the responsibility for the change. What emerged was a *band of large-unit incrementation* in tracts, no longer necessarily within walking distance of either a suburban station or a trolley-line. In fact in the 1930's most of the suburban trolley-lines were torn up, as they proved disastrously unprofitable to operate. Instead Ford began to build "station wagons" to be used by suburban families in taking breadwinners to the commuting train. Soon those same workers found the station wagon could as easily take them to a suburban workplace where employee parking was provided. Late in the act, Chrysler brought out a "suburban" for this larger and less affluent lot. But the Ford term stuck, and the term "suburban" has gone out of our language except for use as a car-licensing term in several states around New York City. One can judge the peculiar role of suburbs in post-war British thinking by noting that when English car manufacturers followed American styles they insisted on calling these "estate cars." With the post-war institution of the greenbelt around London, the term gained a certain grim truth.

There remains considerable application of the Hoyt model to this automobile band of suburbs, such as sectors in most large metropolises that rank higher, or lower, in economic class of housing. But in general the basis of urban morphogenesis is no longer relative location with respect to, or distance from, the city center. Instead we have today a world of *urban realms*, each of

In 1940 California built the first urban "freeway" between Pasadena and downtown Los Angeles. This Arroyo Seco Freeway is shown soon after it opened when it was the only one in existence. In the following forty years thousands of miles of urban freeways in most western countries have followed the general pattern of the Arroyo Seco and have worked great changes in urban morphology.

economic, social, and political significance and each contributing the main force in shaping itself. In truth neither the Park and Burgess nor the Hoyt model is very appropriate today, with little causal relationship between what goes on in the suburbs and distance or vector from the city core. We now need a model of city form based on reality, which is that the suburb is the home of the masses as well as standing independent as a self-acting urban system, related to other self-acting systems such as the traditional one focussed on the early center of the metropolitan area, but not subservient to it. The major failure that has followed on the opening of the Bay Area Rapid Transit system (BART) in California, which was designed with this subservience of the suburbs to the core in mind, adds urgency to the search for such a new egalitarian model for a city of realms. BART has shown that a core-oriented rapid transit system defies modern urban geography and thus courts service and financial disaster.

A Model for a City of Realms

The city of realms came into existence when the areal extent of the metropolitan area increased to the point that the majority of persons living in an outlying section of the city no longer had constant direct ties to the central city. For such a situation to arise sufficient employment and shopping had to be available in the suburban band so that the trip "downtown" became exceptional. To set a precise date for the emergence of *realms* is difficult for all cities—or for any city, for that

matter—just as it was hard indeed to say just when towns beyond the city fringe changed into suburbs.[41] One of the aspects of human organization is that we realize that most conditions exist only after they have come fully into existence, but we neither anticipate fully nor understand them while they are underway. But we can say that by the mid- to late-1950's large metropolitan areas began to show clear evidence of the existence of such realms. In a monograph presenting the analysis of the physical form of the San Francisco Bay region—the Bay Area City—published in 1964, I proposed such a regionalization within the metropolis,[42] and the idea was subsequently adopted in constructing a major simulation model of the metropolitan economy, whose successful operation seemed to confirm the functional existence of realms. Earlier work in Boston[43] and subsequent work in a number of major metropolises has geographically confirmed the validity of the concept, and has suggested refinements.

The growth of suburbs led to the creation of realms through a *process of parturition and inheritance of functions.* As the city grew, it ultimately "gave birth" to offspring, and like biological offspring, those progeny obtained an initial strongly dependent status. Similarly, a strong biological inheritance from the parent

[41]*For a discussion of how an outlying town becomes a suburb, see James E. Vance, Jr., "Labor-shed, Employment Field, and Dynamic Analysis in Urban Geography,"* Economic Geography, *Vol. 36 (1960).*

[42]*James E. Vance, Jr.* Geography and Urban Evolution in the San Francisco Bay Area, *Berkeley: Institute for Governmental Studies, 1964.*

[43]*James E. Vance, Jr.,* The Growth of Suburbanism West of Boston: A Geographic Study of Transportation-Settlement Relationships, *unpublished Ph.D. thesis, Clark University, 1952.*

was observable in the realms born in the next generation. I have no wish to suggest a biological quality to the city, but I wish to emphasize that the outlying realms are closely related and initially highly dependent upon the central city, though with the passage of time the dependence declines, even as they begin in maturity to show striking resemblances to the parent central city. And, as with the passage of generations in families, a considerable material shift is made from the older parent city to the younger outlying realms. This transfer of land-use has raised many of the severe social and economic problems that now affect the no-longer-wealthy central city.

If, then, sometime in the 1950's a "city of realms" began to be evident, what were the determinants of its structure? To begin with, the process of parturition, as we have noted, changed outlying areas from the suspected functional potential for semi-independent existence—first felt when suburbs began to be large and separate enough so some activities found in the central city came to be replicated there—to actual semi-independence. Suburbs at the time of first creation would have some social institutions—churches, schools, and social organizations—as well as basic food-shopping facilities, though in the earliest stages these would be very limited. But as the suburb grew, the complexity and choice among these facilities would increase, encouraging less "return to the city" for obtaining the good or service.

Fundamental to the emergence of the suburban realms was the creation of outlying employment and outlying shopping. We have seen how manufacturing moved out of the city. We may assign the tipping point, when factories were likely to be more suburban than central, to the period surrounding the Second World War. But we must look more closely at the creation of outlying shopping facilities.

The Rise of Outlying Shopping

We shall first note a few aspects of the complex evolution of retail activity. Clearly persons in cities have always had to purchase goods and services, so there is no need here to "invent the wheel" in our explanation. With the Industrial Revolution, masses of people were forced into a money economy, but held at an extremely low level of ability to consume. Thus, the earliest of retailing establishments were rather general in nature,

having to depend upon the selling of *mass-appeal goods*. The urban proletariat could buy only basic foods, clothing, and little else, so a shopkeeper would tend to combine lines of trade if he sought to move into a working-class quarter and open a shop. Essentially he would need all the trade of the neighborhood if he were to survive. Both in cities and in farming villages we find that the commodity-combining shop, the general store, was the pioneer of trade.[44]

As populations increased and disposable income improved, *narrow-appeal goods* could be introduced to trade, but only again by combining their sale. At that juncture in the middle of the past century, the department store was created for the first time, making less-basic goods available to the lower-middle class and then later to the working class. But to gain access to these diversely stocked stores, those social groups had to go to the heart of the city, so that the establishment located there could hope for the greatest potential market for its now-widened choice of merchandise.

As population increased and disposable income enlarged, some specialization could occur in selling away from the general store toward a more numerous group divided from one another by product specialization. That specialization came either in price-class of goods or in lines carried. Expensive goods could be sold in specialty stores where mark-ups would be high; cheaper goods, secured in part by lower mark-ups, would require a high level of commodity combining to keep those prices down. Thus, the department store was evolved to make narrower-appeal goods lines available to a wider market, by keeping their unit prices within reasonable limits. To gain maximum access to markets for limited-appeal goods, a central location—the most central, in fact—was necessary. For this reason we find that department stores could not depart from the heart of the city, even from the parts of it best served by public transit. When subways came to Boston, their crossing was best developed at Summer and Winter and Washington streets, where the dominant department stores—Jordan's and Filene's—came to be located. In New York the creation of subway and rail lines even after 1900, to use Walter Firey's phrase, "contracted" the retail district to a peak point near Herald Square (and Pennsylvania Station) soon after 1910 and the opening of the Hudson and East River rail

[44]*This section represents a summation of a paper of mine, "Emerging Patterns of Commercial Structure in American Cities," in* Proceedings of the International Geographical Union Symposium in Urban Geography, *Lund, Sweden: Lund Studies in Geography, Series No. 24, 1960, pp. 485–518. Reprinted in Robert Putnam, Frank Taylor, and Philip Kettle,* A Geography of Urban Places, *Toronto: Methuen Publications, 1970, pp. 215–239.*

tunnels. Mass-selling specialty shops clustered around these two points of contraction and their department stores, whereas the high-price, narrow-market specialty shops came to be strung out along Fifth Avenue and then Fifty-seventh Street, with their more limited transit facilities.

At first as suburbs grew they had only very general commodity-combining shops—the general stores. A new source of mass-appeal goods at fairly modest prices was provided in the branch department stores that grew up in the suburbs after the Second World War. Specialty shops had no such widespread provision in the suburbs. A considerable aggregation of well-to-do people—as in Westchester County or on the San Francisco peninsula—might be served by a high-price shopping center, such as that at Stanford in Palo Alto. But in the absence of such an appreciable cluster, no high-price specialization would be found in the suburbs; recourse would have to continue to the central business district for those goods. This high-price specialty shopping in the suburbs was far more commonly handled, in fact, in the centers of older towns—such as Wellesley, Ardmore, Evanston, Beverly Hills, and San Mateo—than in newly-built integrated shopping centers.

Eventually such a body of population had become resident in the suburbs that it proved possible to subdivide the mass-selling into a number of middle-sized, directly intercompetitive, integrated shopping centers. Because these centers had of need to operate with goods of modest mark-up and to divide the metropolitan market into parcels of far smaller support than that which had backstayed the central business district before 1945, the range of goods and services in outlying areas could not match those in the center. Yet the city-center support was diminished sufficiently that such specialization there became more economically hazardous, causing many firms simply to give up business or amalgamate with other firms, reducing the overall level of specialization within the metropolitan area. This narrowing of the number and choice among outlets may have played a significant role in encouraging the merger, in turn, of producers. To remain in business, they would have had to gain large sales from the fewer retailers who survived, given the reduction in the number of independent firms within a metropolitan market and the ramification of branches of those few that survived.

The Nature of Urban Realms

What, then, determines the extent of a realm, its internal structure, and its character? The extent of realms depends upon (1) terrain and topographical barriers, (2) the overall size of the metropolis, (3) the amount and type of economic activity contained within it, and (4) the regional geography of transportation. Where there are striking contrasts in terrain and controlling water bodies, realms may be both clearly defined and relatively modest in size. Taking the Bay Area City as an example, we find five or six basic realms clearly delimited by terrain. To the west of San Francisco Bay is the realm comprised of San Francisco city, defined by the Bay, the Golden Gate, the Pacific Ocean, and a block of steep country (San Bruno Mountain) that separates the city from its suburbs in San Mateo County to the south.

Eastern San Mateo County is a distinctive realm of suburban residence, with fully-matured shopping centers and a considerable number of electronic and other high-technology industries that depend for their location upon the local amenities and the presence of the major airport in the region, rather than upon the traditional city of San Francisco.

This unit merges without precise borders into the Santa Clara Valley realm to the south, where the city of San Jose is a dominant feature, but not a separate central-city realm. In fact, though San Jose is the twenty-fifth American city in population, it is largely without a central business district. The normal functions of the city core are likely to be found spread anywhere within the Santa Clara Valley, so within this highly urbanized realm, obviously a very large one, we should not distinguish between the "suburban realm" and the "city realm." They are one.

North of the Golden Gate, eastern Marin County and adjacent parts of Sonoma County form a fourth Bay Area realm, more definitely residential in character but certainly affecting its own life-style and viewing itself as distinct from all others. This realm is high-income country, an area with a larger-than-normal proportion of single-person households, a place where "style" becomes a god and one's "image" is his most cherished, and burnished, possession. Marin is not only anti-urban, it is also anti-suburban, seeking to contain further growth, preserve the long-distance view as free of housing as possible, and maintain the notion that such an earthly paradise can be the possession of only a few, and those with "taste." The residents of this iso-

Many of the components of the more recent suburbanization in the band of large-unit incrementation are observable in this picture of the "county seat" of Marin County, California. In the middleground, the building shaped like the hands of a clock is Frank Lloyd Wright's last major structure, the Marin County Center, the administrative-judicial center of a growing and wealthy suburban county. In the foreground are large tracts of single-family houses and the Northgate Shopping Center with two branch department stores. To the left are more recent apartment clusters and a very large "mobile-home park" just being completed.

lated peninsula must normally work elsewhere, as their disdain of development leaves them, more than most suburban areas, an appendage of the central city. Their boundaries are clear, their self-conception as a distinct realm could hardly be more full-muscled; yet they would starve without San Francisco and the East Bay. But we could hardly deny them the independence that means so much to them.

In the East Bay part of this composite City are two basic realms. The first is the traditional industrial-transportation center of Oakland and its neighbors which grew into major population size with the coming of the railroad in 1869 and the industrialization and development of wholesaling that soon followed. This part of the Bay Area City is most like the rest of America, the section with a large blue-collar proletariat living in housing tracts that could be copied from those in the Middle West or the Northeast, and the area with the best views and the best climate. This is also the part of the Bay Area City where the ethnics live, having been redeveloped out of large sections of San Francisco. The delimitation of the East Bay realm is precise to the north as Carquinez Strait, to the east as the Berkeley Hills, and to the west as San Pablo and San Francisco bays. Only to the south is the line a zone, similar to the one separating San Mateo County from the Santa Clara Valley.

Finally, a realm is emerging east of the Berkeley Hills in a group of closely related valleys within the Inner Coast Ranges. There, around Walnut Creek, a realm similar in constitution, settlement, and social views to the realm of San Mateo County is emerging, comprised mainly of fairly prosperous white-collar workers who have found themselves a suburban home. But unlike Marin, this realm is not totally parasitic; factories, even refineries, and some working-class towns are hidden among the more shaded and archetypal California suburbs of the realm.

We could set about defining realms in other major metropolises. Boston, for example, clearly has the central cities—Boston, Cambridge, Somerville, and a couple of others whose structure cries out of the nineteenth century—and three major suburban realms, divided in this less-broken terrain by their vector from the city rather than by mountain and bay. New York certainly must be distinguished at least into central city, Long Island, New Jersey, and Westchester-Connecticut, and quite possibly subdivided within those obvious parts. I wish merely to suggest that any large city is no longer a single evolving system, as envisaged by either Park and Burgess or Homer Hoyt. Instead, we deal with parts that have their own character, attitudes, political organization, and functions. We must seek to understand how each realm can evolve without constant reference to the central city. Ties cannot be absolutely broken. Urban Northeast New Jersey clearly prospers or suffers in part by what goes on in New York City. But only in part. And major differences arise between the suburban development in "Jersey" and on "the Island." Even their respective distinctive folk speech differs, to the point that natives, and outsiders, can distinguish a Jerseyite from a Long Islander. We must in such circumstances attempt to discern the way in which these separate realms evolve and are structured.

The Shaping Processes of Urban Realms

In the shaping of realms, transportation is the foremost consideration. The internal coherence of these areas is furnished by the interaccessibility of the components. A realm is not necessarily isolated from other realms, but it is drawn together by the greater ease found in visiting economically important areas within itself rather than outside it. Shopping and working will be easiest for the residents if they remain within their own realm, though, as we have seen in the case of the Marin

Concord, Massachusetts, in 1976 is the epitome of the nativist suburb in an increasingly plural American society.

peninsula north of San Francisco, parasitic realms without major employment may be drawn together by other activities. The presence of terrain and water barriers is not essential to the delimitation of such regions, though these features tend to produce the clearest boundaries. The flow and focus of transportation routes can serve nearly as well to divide one realm from another. In the case of the Boston realms noted, lines radial from the city center tend to afford internal coherence to the suburbs through which they pass, which shapes those realms and separates them from each other.

The one transportation route leading outside the realm that has much significance to its character is that connecting to the central city. Where such lines are easy, swift, or pleasant, they tend to encourage the use, for residence, of the outlying realm by those employed in the metropolitan core. The greater ease of access from Westchester County and Connecticut to the office districts of midtown Manhattan has encouraged the use of that realm for housing the office workers there—those in the communications industries, those employed in large corporate offices which tend to cluster in midtown, and those in retail employment. Nearly as good transportation connects Long Island with that area, so it also is used as a housing realm for these central-city workers. Lower Manhattan, the financial district, is less well served from Westchester and Connecticut but better served from New Jersey, so it would gain workers from this more accessible residence.

This connection might seem to suggest that the outlying realms of the city are just as they were in the very beginning: residential areas tied firmly to the central area for most of their economic and institutional needs. Yet this is no longer the case. Recent studies, as yet unpublished, by Allan Pred have shown that with the emergence of large conglomerate corporations, whose headquarters are commonly in major metropolitan cores, a factory or other economic enterprise in an outlying realm may as likely have its corporate control exercised by a distant city as by the one it adjoins. I believe it is commonly overlooked that this tendency toward merger and conglomeration has a strong impact within cities as well as nationally. Economic activities there are now far more national in control than they were, and perhaps more national than local in some cities and some industries. As a result, a national company selects a site, or continues to use a particular site, in terms of a strategy of location that has little or nothing to do with ties to the core of that metropolis. We find that branches of department stores with headquarters in other cities often are located in the suburbs; Marshall Field has expanded to a Milwaukee shopping center, as Neiman-Marcus has to the Galleria Post Oak in Houston and to Northbrook in Chicago;

Bloomingdale's is in Chestnut Hill outside of Boston, and Ohrbach's in Los Angeles is nearly in Beverly Hills. Factories in the same way are sited where national firms find the conditions right, and that today is most infrequently in the central city.

Thus, the commuting tie from an outlying realm to the central city is more a survival of the past than a tie of the present. The reason behind this fact is found in the way realms are first shaped.

We have seen the strong tendency for the initiation and first delimitation of a realm to depend on these external routings from the central city. So long as little or no interconnection occurs among the sectors focussing on the central business district, save through that downtown nexus, what ties exist in the emerging realm will tend to be aligned radially from the city center. The early railroads began this alignment. Later competitors to those pioneers tended also to seek the same downtown terminus, adding to the linearity and radial alignment of these important transportation routes, which became the integrating mechanism of the realm as it grew. The whole history of metropolitan transportation has shown this radial tendency. Railroads merely followed the routing that had existed before they were invented and, in turn, the development of modern highways followed similar paths and identically radial courses.

The development of the trolley car began the detachment of realms from too great a dependence upon the city core. With the creation of streetcar lines, we witness the first circumferential routings to be developed in metropolitan areas. These assumed particular importance in shaping outlying shopping streets and districts, as Malcolm Proudfoot's work on Philadelphia and Chicago in the 1930's demonstrated. The ability to create these foci subsequent to the one first located in the central business district made the integrated suburban realm possible.[45] Similarly, the ability to use trolley lines to move about the suburbs made possible the creation of mass-employment factories in that area.[46] A final modification of the originally dominant radial quality of intrarealm transportation came with the creation right after the Second World War of circumferential arterial highways in most large metropolitan areas. These by-pass and circumferential highways tied radials together well outside the city core, further reducing the need to turn to the central realm in daily life.

Another transportation change that came largely

[45]Malcolm J. Proudfoot, "City Retail Structure," Economic Geography, Vol. 13 (1937), pp. 425–428.
[46]For a discussion of the worker commuting patterns within a suburban realm, see my "Labor-shed, Employment Field, and Dynamic Analysis in Urban Geography," already cited.

after the Second World War also played an important role in emancipating the outlying realms from central-city dominance. This change was the rapid rise in use and importance of air travel. By necessity, airports were outside the central city, unlike the train and bus stations they partially replaced. Not only did they encourage assemblies of employment in their environs, but also they weakened the need to turn to the center to gain access to distant transportation. In many metropolitan areas, as in the Bay Area City, the major airport is seemingly the nucleus of the second largest employment concentration after the downtown. And some cities—the Bay Area again, New York-Northeastern New Jersey, Chicago, Houston, and Los Angeles—have two or more major airports, so the replication of focus is not merely at a single site in the suburban realms.

The detachment of the outlying realm from the central city is then the result of a subsequent "integration" of transportation within that realm, to the extent that it need no longer turn to the central realm to gain access either to adjacent realms or to distant cities.

Is there, then, a structure within the outlying realm about which we can cite certain general characteristics? Again we must look at the question historically. The first suggestions of the emergence of a suburban realm came at two extremes of the social spectrum: the first residential clusters came in fairly high-income residential beads growing up along a railroad line, whereas the first working-class settlement came in mill villages or towns located in the countryside near the city. These two kinds of settlement furnish the existing particles around which the subsequent growth in the realm took place. Normally that accretive growth bore a similarity to the central particle—high-income housing, for example, was located next to, or at least in the same general alignment as, the initial area of that class of shelter. Hoyt's work demonstrates the near universality of that relationship. In the same way, the existence of a mill village or town tends to bring in the end a factory city—a satellite to begin with but, as the metropolitan area grows, ultimately merely an industrial city within the suburbs, such as Paterson (New Jersey).

A strong element of terrain influence is evident. High-class residence has commonly been located on the prettiest sites, or at least the more elevated. In the Bay Area we have evidence from as early as the late eighteenth century, when Capt. George Vancouver visited the Bay, that San Mateo and the areas to the south of it were an idyllic English park landscape. Not surprisingly, when the first wealthy suburbanization came outside San Francisco, it came in Vancouver's park. Similarly, William Penn looked upon what is now Bucks County as "the most beautiful of landscapes, far ahead of what can be found in England." Little wonder

that it became the resort not merely of wealthy Philadelphians but also of wealthy New Yorkers. Generally, high-income housing areas are likely to be the prettiest areas surrounding the city, or at least the prettiest areas that were reasonably approachable by rail transport in the second half of the nineteenth century.

Lesser landscapes and areas less costly of access tended to be developed in middle- and lower-middle-class housing. In a study of San Francisco transportation published in 1913, the renowned transit authority Bion J. Arnold clearly demonstrated a class distinction between the commuting to the San Mateo County suburbs, by rail, and that to the East Bay cities, by ferry.[47] Due to the lower cost of ferry travel, the fare to the East Bay, as distant as San Mateo County, was considerably less. In other cities, similar cost differentials also served to divide the class of housing, most notably between those suburbs reached by train and those by trolley. As a result of the historical staging in this movement, with the better-paid moving out of the city first and to the more attractive sites, the less pleasant and more mixed land-use areas fell to the lot of the later comers.

In these ways, three basic levels of suburban housing emerged: high-income suburban residence, middle-income suburban residence, and working-class residence associated with local employment in the outlying areas. The Park and Burgess model is neither historically correct nor geographically true. The bands of class they imagined existed only partially on the ground. Similarly, the Hoyt model loses much of its validity as the development in the outlying realm becomes self-generating and self-determined rather than tied to the center.

We have seen how very much the realms outside the city were shaped by transport in the past. We should appreciate that we are again entering a time of transportation change. Most observers seem convinced that the mass dependence on cars, particularly for daily commuting, must decline. Proposals have been made for elaborate transit systems for cities of the sort that were built just before the First World War. BART, such a heavy and costly system, has been completed, with mechanically disastrous results—it is simply over-engineered—but geographically as well, BART has been a severe disappointment. This system was constructed to the level necessary for a service similar to New York City, where 3.7 million people ride each day; but after three years of operation BART is carrying only around 120,000 people. Line length differs; New York

[47]*Bion J. Arnold,* Report on the Improvement and Development of the Transportation Facilities of San Francisco, *San Francisco, 1913. This report has recently been reprinted by the Arno Press.*

has about 250 miles while BART has 75 miles. But BART's pitiful showing can only be assigned to a most costly misunderstanding of the structure of the modern city, particularly one comprised of realms. BART was built for a city that no longer exists, at a cost of nearly two billion dollars. We can hardly afford a repetition now that the truth has been shown conclusively. Instead it should be appreciated that we do have such a city of realms, that the craving to reach the city core is modest indeed and concentrated mainly in that relatively small minority of suburban population that works in the central business district. For them something less than BART would do nicely, leaving money for other critically needed transportation development.

Recently there has been a remarkable reassertion of interest among planners in what is currently called "light rail." This system is the trolley car reborn with improvements in the car and attempts to create a separated right-of-way for the line, but *on the surface*. Currently, costs have been computed up to fifty million dollars a mile to build subways in cities, and very considerable sums even in less densely built-up sections, but light rail lines may be built for a more economical $4 to $8 million per mile.[48] Given the desire to shape public transit for a city of realms, such construction is the only economically and socially justified system of fixed-rail-guided transit. The distances are too great in the suburban realm to think about BART-type solutions, and the needs are much more for transportation internal to those realms than for that to the central city. Without doubt the pitiful showing of BART comes in part, large part I believe, from its total failure as a local transit system *within* realms and its obsession with interrealm transit, which is today the lesser of the two forms of movement in cities.

[48]The New York Times, *July 9, 1975.*

A City of Place, a City of Ethnicity and Life-style

We might, in conclusion, draw a sharp distinction between the central city and the outlying realms in terms of the critical structural feature of each, when it comes to social geography. Our discussion has shown that in the outlying realms of the metropolis, the overriding concern is with *place*, the particular suburb in which you live and the class of people and occupations found there. People associate themselves with Wellesley or River Forest or Walnut Creek, not with a particular ethnicity or even a distinctive life-style. In the general "nativist culture" in the outlying realms, social and economic mobility assume greater importance than maintaining the faith or the language or the culture of one's father. People seek to live as one should in the town they have chosen, as the novels of John Updike and Peter De Vries clearly demonstrate. These people are seeking a place with which to identify, and using that place as the structure for manageable identity in a vast metropolitan city. The long commuting journeys, the high costs of some suburban living, and the acceptance of a composite culture are all prices people pay, not to flee the city, as is often argued by ethnic rhetoreticians, but rather to gain a sustainable identity in the modern metropolitan world. Not all people have usable ethnic roots, and many wish to forget those that survive, not out of shame but because they realize that ethnic identification ultimately sets barriers to one's life. If ethnicity is to be dropped, then the "nativist" suburb is a necessary institution, and the congregation there of persons wishing not to divide themselves against other people is a social good. But because the suburban realms are unmanageable in social size, they have come to be subdivided internally into "places" which are the geographical unit with which the suburbanite associates.

The central city remains the place where *ethnicity* is still the determining factor in all-too-many cases. Some of this ethnicity is a great social evil forced unwillingly upon a group—can black people ever overcome it?—but some of it is consciously sought and maintained. To the extent that society should permit as much liberty as possible, this deliberate practice of ethnicity should be defended; but to the extent that it is negatively imposed from outside, it should be fought. In any event we should not assume that the ethnic division of urban populations is either the normal, the natural, or the desirable way.

Related to this matter of ethnicity is the adoption of the "alternative life-style," or that in opposition to the suburban majority. As we have seen, this style is the nonethnic's "ethnicity," a way in which to set oneself apart in the absence of any clear ethnic distinction. For this reason, the typical location for such opposition areas remains in the central-city realm.

Urban Structure beyond the Edge of the City

All of the forces at work reordering the structure of the city clearly can work beyond the edge of the physically integrated city. Improvements in transportation, increases in the leisure time and income of city people, and the search for an even different identity-with-place from that found in the suburban realm have led people to seek a form of urban residence beyond the edge of the city. This A. C. Spectorsky called "exurban," and we may usefully adopt that term. Actually the residential development in Bucks County, Pennsylvania, is considerably given over to exurban living. Around the Bay Area City are counties heavily influenced by an exurban population—Napa County, Sonoma County, and Santa Cruz County. An exurban belt probably adjoins most major cities. And within that belt, which is mainly given over to agriculture or forestry in occupation, will be particles or even small clusters of settlement which come outward from the city, maintaining important cultural, social, and economic ties backward toward the metropolis. As was the case with the early particles of suburban residential development, these germs, around which an *exurban structure* may form, are populated by the relatively well-to-do, are in the prettiest places in the exurban band, and normally are served by the best transportation available to such distant areas. Thus, we see that the dynamics of the model of realms can be applied as well to what is now, and may increase as, the new frontier of the city.

The City: A Mighty Maze! But Not Without a Plan

In search of a system for analysis of physical structure in the city, we have had to go back far enough in time to gain confidence that the germs of urban process would be found. At first, the beginning of medieval urbanization might seem to suffice—as the first epoch of city formation from which development has been unbroken to the present. But western culture preserved enough remnants of the classical city to make medieval urbanization a recommencement with some established notions rather than a true beginning. Even in the Classical Era, cities were not utterly new; the settlements of the Indus Valley and Mesopotamia are considerably more ancient. But certain significant characteristics of Archaic Greece seem to recommend starting our story then and there. The first is that cities began then to take on a new function—implementing and extending a network of economic trade in what we would today call "a system of cities." Not only were cities progressively more numerous, but also they began to be established along the lines of general principles repeated from one older place to its newer urban plantations. This establishment of standardized practices—essentially morphogenetic processes—came strongly from the second significant difference between these cities in the eastern Mediterranean and most of those that came before: the change from the earliest use of cities as religious and governmental places to those functions perhaps only subservient to the basic economic purpose of the settlement. Political and religious power may be difficult to share, leading to few and rather idiosyncratic cities, but economic power is not: trading has always needed partners even when the condition of that trade was not the equal treatment of all participants. A final virtue of beginning our story with Archaic Greece comes from the availability from that time of commentaries that allow us to judge not merely the physical form of the time but as well some of the reasons that lay behind the acts of city builders then at work.

At the edge of a spreading metropolis there is commonly an area of urban influence without a dominating suburban morphology. This picture of St. Helena in the Napa Valley shows not merely the most famous vineyard in the western hemisphere, with the most distinguished Louis Martini winery in the center foreground surrounded by neat vineyards, but as well the town of St. Helena which houses the vintners and their workers and some "city people" who have either retired to this enjoyable community or who go there for weekends, sometimes to try their hand at winemaking. The value of the land for vineyards is so high that housing-tract development has been largely forfended.

The story of urban morphogenesis since the earlier years of the first millennium before Christ has of necessity to deal with a vast array of cities and many shifting conditions. However, the threads that tie it all together are the processes that have evolved over time, but which have shown themselves equally amenable to a reasonably comprehensible analytical system. Experiments early in the history of an urban function have led to established practices. Unsorted and unspecialized land-assignments have gained those qualities they lacked through experimentation and the learning process which creates culturally established practices, the reason that we cannot so confidently begin our tale with the earlier years of the second millennium of our era as we would if our commencement were with the

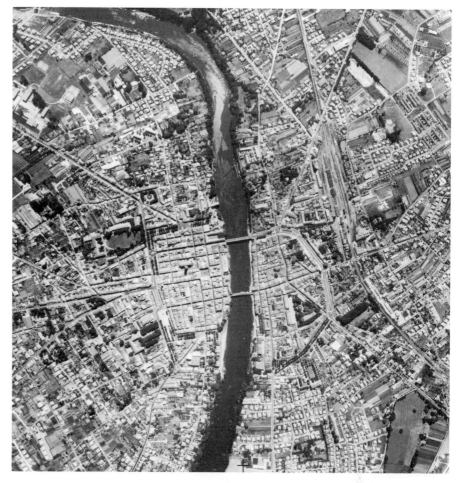

Villeneuve-sur-Lot began as a medieval bastide in 1253 and has witnessed many changes in urban morphogenesis over the years, not the least in the last half-century. This may be seen by comparing this 1976 air photo with that for the late 1920's shown on page 186. But still we can see that this scene of man is a mighty maze but not without a plan.

medieval city. We can see the impact of scalar increase in cities, not merely in the past hundred years with which this chapter deals, but in the nearly three thousand years with which this volume deals. Similarly, we are able to follow through over that longer period the role that transportation innovation has played in the structure of cities.

Significant breaks have occurred in this continuity of urban historical geography. The standardization of morphogenetic practice represented by the shift to the Milesian orthogonal grid, the creation of the system of cities as instruments of tribute more than economic development worked in the hands of the Roman conquerors, the rise of trade in the High Middle Ages, for whatever reason it returned, and the creation of the mercantile-capitalist economic system that spread cities across the seven seas and forced them to grow to giant size all stand as examples of new uses of the town. But they also stand in a history that can be seen as one

wherein the processes endure, though their motivation may change.

Today we find that even a seemingly changed world is being guided by these long-standing morphogenetic processes. The emergence of the city of realms within the metropolis and the system of cities within the major national region is merely an indication of the great continuity. Specialization follows on generalization and functional growth leads to morphological separation. In truth the answer to the question posed at the very beginning of this book as to the existence of urban morphogenetic processes can be made clearly in the affirmative. What changes are not the processes at work shaping the physical structure of the city, but rather the roles which man gives to the city. Clearly, I believe, "this scene of man" is ever-changing; yet, in physical terms, it is indeed "a mighty maze! but not without a plan."

INDEX

City-county relations (*cont.*)
    in industrial era, 347, **418**
City formation, 332
City halls, Amsterdam, 221
    Boston, 24, **25**, 372
    early modern, 373
    medieval, 130, 154
    modern, 134
    Toronto, 24
City planning, 16, **44**
    Greek, 42, **44**
City republics of Middle Ages, 35, 115,
    123, 141
City as innovators, 12, 112, 359
City-state, Greek, 28, 41, 51
    Roman, 73
    medieval, 132, 172
Civil administration, 84
Clark, Colin, 278
Clark, George, 210, 211
Class, assembly, 160, 161, 162
    conflict, 133
    districts, 309
    economic, 168, 231, 405
    stratification, 41, 161, 168, 182, 227,
        240, **391**, 396
    separation, 226
Claudius, 63
Cleveland, Ohio, 354, 362, 367, 369, 374
Clifton, Eng., **244**, 245
    view of in 18th cent., **200**
Climate as a control of cities, 206–207
Cloaca maxima, 56, 61
Clothiers, 282
Clovis, 98
Cluny and Cluniac, **115**, 117
Clustering, 371
Clwydmouth (Rhuddlan), Wales, 179
Coal, 272, 273, 287, 318, 328, 343, 344
Coalbrookdale, Eng., 272
Coast, Ostian, It., 66
Cockerill, William, 318, 320
Coeur, Jacques, 143, **144, 169,** 169–172,
    216
Colbert, Jean Baptiste, 211
Colchester, Eng., 112
Cole, G. D. H., and R. Postgate, 240
Coleman, R. V., 249
Collectivism, 79
Collegiality, 29, 118, 147, 151, 159, 174
Cologne, Ger., 83, 120, 379
Colonial city, Greek, 42, 52
    Roman, 42, 68, 205
    in Middle Ages, 176
    in America, 208, 246, 248
Colonization, American, 248
    Greek, 42, 52
    personal, 94
    Roman, 42, 68, 205
    French, in America, 247
    Medieval, 176

16th cent., 205
Spanish, 205
Colonne Vendôme, **99**
Colquhon, Patrick, 240
Colosseum (Amphitheatrum Flavium),
    58, 61
Combwork, 122
Commendation, 85, 108
Commerce, 62, 106, 116, 130, 137, 140,
    146, 148, 211, 239, 302
Commercial center, 49, 246
Commercial intelligence, 295
Commercial law, 251
Commercial Revolution, 141, 182, 217,
    356
Commodity-combining shops, 410
Common, town, 255, 257, **413**
Common man (people), 4, 49, 118, 135,
    137, 138, 144, 228
Commonwealth, abstract, 211
    in England, 109
Communes, 99, **99,** 113, 114, 133, 137,
    139, 141, 146, 171, 172, **402**
Communication, 353
Community, territorial, 150
Commuting, automobile, 367, 408
    class-distinction in, 415
    downtown, 353
    in regional city, 353
    steam-engine, 365
Competition, process of, 376
    dynastic, 179
Component, normative, evolved, 180
    Greek, 42
    planned, 180
Concord, Mass., **413**
Concretion (*see* Process of assemblage)
Conflagrations, 58, 65 (*see also* Great
    Fire of London)
Conglomeration, Corporate, 414
Congregation, general process, 27, 35,
    36, 230, 231, 239, 242, 295
    season (*see* West End, Charleston,
        and Savannah)
Connectivity of cities, 361 (*see also*
    System of cities)
Connecticut Valley, 255
Connection, process of, 27
Connectivity, in city, 26
Conscious design of environment, 224
Conservation of radial effort, 155
Conservation principle of growth, 57
Constantine, 54, 77
Constantinople (Istanbul), 69, 72, 73,
    82, 102, 110, 120, 170
Consul and consulate, 172, 190
Contado, 114, 121, 132, 140, 174
Continuous material flow, 386
Contraction, process of, 78
Contractualism (Firey), process of, 410
Contrat d'Hostices, 193, 194

Conurbation, 332
Conzen, M. R. G., 121, 125, 126, 129,
    183
Cooking, and diet, 145, 153, 155, 160
Copenhagen, Den., 66, 180
Coppock, J. T. and H. Prince, 235
Cordes, Fr., **185,** 198
Core of the city, evolution of, 379
Cornière, 190, 192, 195 (*see also*
    Arcades)
Corporation (*see also* Gilds):
    city, 100, 116, 142
    other, 138, 151, 174, 326
Cotswolds, Eng., 276, 281, 282
Cotterell, Geoffrey, 220
Cotton, 272, 289, 295
Council estates (Britain), 390, 395
Counter model, 175
Counter-reformation, 204
Counties Palatine of Eng., 250
Country houses, 300
County, 250, 279, **412**
    dominant, 251
Couperie, Pierre, 216
Cours-la-Reine (Paris), 216
The Court, 159, 213, 233, 235
Courts and courtyards, 128, 129, 142,
    304
Covent Garden (London), 234, 235, 383
Coxe, Tench, 326
Crimea, 63
Cromford, Eng., 284, **285,** 290, 300, 305
Crompton, Samuel, 284, 331
Cromwell, Oliver, 109, 249
Crowds, 229
Crusades, Albigensian, 29
    first, 72
    fourth, 70, 120
    general, 72, 102, 112, 121, 139, 171
    second, 73
    third, 73
Cuba, 9
Cult of the exterior, 228
Cultural pluralism, 394
Customer access districts, 383

Dale, David, 330
Dallas, Tex., 23, 353, 362, 369, 383
Danube, 119, 357
Darby, Abraham, 273
Dark Ages, 67, 71, 79, 82, 92, 100
Datini, Francesco di Marco, 137–141,
    276
Decline of cities, 77
Decumanus, 55, 57 (*see also* Cardo)
Deductive reasoning, 148
Defoe, Daniel, 280, 286, 287, 300
De Gaulle, Charles, 223
Democracy, 118, 172, 230
    as an aspect of high urbanization, 9
Demosthenes, 44

Denizen status, 108, 110, 150
Denver, Colo., 353, 362, 383
Department store, 371, **381**, 410
Departure and replacement, process
  of, 369
Derbyshire, Eng., 305
  map of, **285**
Determinism, physical, 2, 310
Detroit, Mich., 354, 362, 367, 369, 386,
  397
Devaluation of urban land, 404
De Vries, Peter, 416
Dialectical materialism, and role of
  countryside, 300
Dickens, Charles, 337
Dickinson, Robert E., 197
Dinant, Bel., 150, 318
Dinkelsbuhl, Ger., **90**
Diocletian, 77
Dioecism, process of, 65, 67, 69
Discard, process of, 371
  zone of, 374, 383
Disraeli, Benjamin, 298, 317
Dissenters, 178
Distretto, 140
Districts of comparison, 371
Division of land, practices, 43–44
Doller R., Fr., 322
Domesday survey, 278
Domestic industry (putting out), 141,
  274, 281, 297, **327**
Dominant cities, 210, 347, 354
  old, 354, 364–365
Domme, Fr., 188
Domus, 59
Drake, Daniel, 266–269
  his map, **268**
Drink, 160, 309
Dualism, 172, 178 (*see also* Patarenes
  and Cathari)
Dudley Castle, Eng., 278, **279**
Dunham, Arthur Louis, 290
Dürerhaus, Nürnberg, Ger., **151**
Durrett, Reuben T., 266
Düsseldorf, Ger., 362
Dutch, industrialization, 9
  in New York, 252
  possession of Luxembourg, 9
  other, 202
Dyeing, proc. of, 277
Dynasties, competition of, 179
  possessions of, 90
Dyos, H. J., 314–315

East, W. Gordon, 280
East Anglia, Eng., 282
Eastbourne, Eng., 262
East End of London, 312
East India companies, 204
Economics, medieval, 182

Economy, command, 357
  false, and rural beautification, 300
  natural, 250, 281
  orderly, 147, 153
  quantitative, 273–276
Edict of Nantes, effect of revocation on
  cities, 223
Edward I of Eng., 179
Eeles, Adrian, 214
Egalitarianism, 194, 195
Egypt, 63, 70, 72
Elements, plan, 121
Ellis, Hamilton, 312
Ely, Eng., 163
Emancipation of city in Middle Ages,
  102
Employment, factory, 342
Emporium, early modern, 203
  Roman, 64, 70, 157, 208
  World's, 239
Enclosure movement, 12, 276, 291
Engels, Friedrich, 35, 240, 298–305,
  365, 392
  diagram of Manchester slums, **304**
Engineering, factories, 340, 342
  Greek, 46
  Roman, 59
England, 31, 77, 92, 96, 136, 171, 176,
  180, 193, **198, 214, 215,** 223, **225,
  232, 240, 270,** 273, **275, 278, 279,
  285, 288, 292, 296, 301, 304, 307,
  314, 315, 352, 405, 408**
  canals, rivers, and roads in, **288**
English, 7, 110, 202, 203
English Nation in Antwerp, 204
English Renaissance model of cities,
  261–264, 266
  maps of, **263, 265**
Entail, law of, 234, 243
Entrepôts, 120, 162, 176, 222, 246
Environment, physical, 223
  quality of, 225
Essen, Ger., 373
Estates, landed, 168
  housing, 243
  map of London, **236**
Ethnicity, as a factor in
  morphogenesis, 168, 393, 416
  map of, **345**
Etruscan city, 28, **52,** 66, 208
Etruscan gateway of Perugia, **54**
Etruscans, 28, 52, **52**
Eunomic (*see* Land-assignment)
Europe, feudal parts of, **86**
  feudal-rural structure of, 346
Evans, Arthur, 41
Evans, Oliver, 278, 343
Evanston, Ill., 411
Evansville, Ind., 374
Evelyn, John, 238
Eviction of tenants, 299, 311

Evolution, urban, 26, 352
Evreux, Fr., 96
Exarchate, 141
Excise taxation, assizes, 106, 156
  commuting urban, 151
  on entry to trade, 90
  market tolls, 81
  murrage tolls, 81
  other excises, 100, 140, 150, 151
  other tolls, 222
Exclusion, process of, 374
Exeter, Eng., 244
Exhibition of 1851, 276, 326
Expansible city, 118, 233, 406
Expansibility of single-family house,
  405
Exploration and discovery, age of, 202
Express office, 383
Extension, process of, 376
Exterior space, impact of on design,
  228
Extraterritorial districts, 110, 158
Extraterritoriality, 81, 108, 110, 142,
  158, 163, 176
Exurbia, Hungarian, 358
  medieval, 161, 162
  19th cent., 315
  Roman, 83, 65
  20th cent., 357, 417, **418**

Facade houses, **131,** 220
Factors, people as, 142, 273, 275, 277
Factories, buildings of, **275,** 277, 310,
  330, 333, 336, 368
  emergence of in America, 328
  family, 325, 331
  first American cotton, 329
  first Mancunian cotton, 297
  first for luxuries in France, 272, 318
  headquarters of as a factor, 204, **275,**
  277
  integrated, 333
  location of, 277, 310, 330, 389
  pattern of, 310, 322
  railroad site of, 387
  river-front site of, 387
  size increasing, 387
  suburbanization of, 387
  truck-located, 388
Fairfield County, Conn., 407
Fairs, 108, **109,** 113, 120, 150, 155, 163
Fall River, Mass., 344
Family factory, 325, 331
Faneuil Hall (Boston), **24**
Fashionable neighborhoods, 216, 224
Faubourgs, **92,** 99, 120, 126, 149, 155,
  159, 174, 319, 368 (*see also*
  Bourgs)
Faubourg Ste. Honoré (Paris), 379
Fécamp, Fr., 96
Fecht R., Fr., 322

Central London Rly., 379
London Underground, 379
Paris, Budapest, Berlin, 379
Succession, process of, 312, 369
Sugar, colonies, 202
houses, 226
Suger, abbot of St. Denis, 187
Sullivan, R. J., 225
Sully, duc de, 211
Summerson, John, 230, 231, 235, 241
Super-blocks, 260
Supervisory-service cities, 362
Support of cities, 77
Suppression of church lands, 235
Swabia, Ger., 100
Swidden, 322
Switzerland, 113
Switzerland, high level of urbanization
in, 9
La Sylvestrie, *manoire* near
Villeneuve-sur-Lot, Fr., **95**
Sympolis, 324
Synoecism, 9, 50, 55, 56, 65, 67, 106,
148
Synthesis, 19
Syracusa, It., 94, 130
Syria, 70, 183
System of cities, bastidal, 176–177,
194, 199
Greek, 45
medieval, 101, 117, 119, 138, 140
modern, 352, 361
Roman, 73, 77, 88
space within creates regional cities,
354
Systemic function of cities, 174

Tacitus, 80
Tait, James, 292
Taiwan, 295
Taranto, It., 124
Taste as a social measure, 238, 242
Taunton, Mass., 342
Tax, 44, 174
murrage, 174
property, 377
rates, 386
single, 399
Taylor, W. Cooke, 317
Temin, Peter, 325
Temples, Greek, 40, **41**
Roman, 208
Tenements, 258, **327, 400**
Ternary division of land
(Hippodamian), **44,** 45–47
in bastide, 193
Testut, Lucien, 195
Textile manufacture, **323**
cotton, 289, **292,** 329

early factories, **279,** 326, 329, **330,
333**
fine textiles need machines, 322
Slater-type mills, 334
stages in the evolution of, 287
steam mills, 343
woolen mills, 138, 139, **159,** 174, 276,
282, **283,** 286–287, 319, 326
Textiles, as a medium of exchange, 327
Thames R., Eng., 159
Thann R., Fr., 322
Thea and theater, 40, 48
Three-decker, in Gardner, Mass., **397**
Threshold, 89 (*see also* Central-place
theory)
von Thünen, J., 67, 296
Thur R., Fr., 322
Tiber R., It., 63
Timgad, Alg., 62
Tivoli, It., 66, **66**
Todd, R. E., and F. B. Sanborn, 338
Toledo, Ohio, 374
Tons (wine), 197
Tories, 297
Toulouse and Toulousain, Fr., 97, 113,
115, 140, 178, 183, 198
Toulouse, counts of, 178
Tournai, Bel., 318
Les Tournelles Palace (Paris), 216
Tournon, Fr., **166**
Tours, Fr., 83, 95
Tout, T. F., 178
Tower-house, 131–135, **134,** 215
Town, New England, 253
Town-meetings, New England, 249,
250
Towns commercial, 159
of control, 247
of emulation, 262
essential to mercantilism, 253
founding of, 40, 373
hierarchy of, 89, 106, 108
Law of the Indies, **206–207,** 210
overlord, 203
planted, 176, 204
speculator's, 266, 268
as symbol of domination, 203
Tract rather than lot development,
406
Trade, American, 246, 248
Baltic, 222
bastidal, 193–194
Byzantine, 70
colonial, 42, 324
conditions of, 356
cotton, 295
early modern, 230
empire, 281
Greek, 42
Industrial Revolution, 272

long-distance, 112, 171, 180, 194,
195, 235, 368, 373
luxury items in, 81
manufacturing behind, 138
medieval, 88, 107, 108, 109, 110, 114,
117, 123, 138–139, 146, 149, 157,
162, 169, 173, 222
mercantilist, 169, 204, 210
Muslim, 202
non-retributive, 115
Ostian, 71
Roman, 62, 63
trade-originating in Europe, map of,
111
world-wide, 328
Traders, **71,** 108, 147
Traders, foreign, 106
Trading companies, 211, 233
Trading frontiers, 213, 241, 246
Training ground, 208
Trains, cheap and workingmen's, 311,
312
Trajan's, column, 3
port, 64
Transfer payments from city to
countryside, 299
Transformation of housing to trade,
242
Transportation, 303
cycle of urban, 367
differentiation in, 365
elevated, **367, 375**
light-rail, 366, 416
mechanical, 353
public, 400
urban creates realms, 414
Trebizond, Turkey, 70
The Tremont House (Boston), 381
Trevithick, Richard, 279
Tribal quarters in Roman cities, 65
Tributary area, 107, 114
Tribute, 42, 78, 84, 107, 117, 139
Trier, Ger., 77, 83, **88,** 100, 119, **119,**
146
Trois Rivières, Québec, 247
Trolleys, electric, 366, 400, 407
Trolleys in cities, 400
Trucking, motor, 385
heavy use in Britain, 390
Truck system during industrialization,
135, 308
Tryon, Rolla Milton, 325
Tuileries palace (Paris), 216
Tunis, 139
Tuns (*see* Tons)
Turbines, 278
Turin, It., **5,** 120
Turks, 70, 85, 170
Turnerian thesis, 182, 194
Turnpikes, 281, 289

White Mts., N.H., 363
Wholesaling, 213, 224, **384**
  American, 342, 347
  Dark Ages, 81
  industrial era, 289, 295, 303, 332
  location of, 382, 385
  medieval, 107, 110, 135, 138, 155,
    156, 170
  modern, 353, 355, 374, 382–385, 403
  railroad station district, 383, **384**
  Roman, 62, 64, 81
Willenhall, Eng., 298
William the Conqueror (the Bastard),
  96, 97, 250
Williams, D. M., 295
Williamsburg, Va., 262, 264

Winchester, Eng., 109, 155
Wind, 207
Windows, Dutch 17th cent., 220
  Georgian, 243
  medieval, 153
  Roman, 61, 62
Wine and wine trade, 160, 180, 181,
  194–199, 222, 226, **418**
Winnipeg, Can., 383
Worcester, Mass., 255
Worcestershire, Eng., 279
Work-day, 226
Workshop district in the countryside,
  274
Wren, Christopher, 238
Wright, Carroll D., 329

Wright, Frank Lloyd, 23, 412, **412**
Wurster, William W., 24
Würzburg, Ger., 224

Yarn, sale of, 326
Yerba Buena Cove (San Francisco), 387
Yerkes, Charles Tyson, 314
York, Eng., 127
Yorkshire, Eng., map of, **283**
Ypres, Bel., 135, 150, **159**, 318, 321

Zelinski, Wilbur, 357
Zollverein, 93
"Zone of narrow community identity,"
  402
Zumthor, Paul, 219

77 78 79 80 9 8 7 6 5 4 3 2 1